The front matter for our print textbooks will be ready soon.

Scan the QR code below to register for updates when it's available.

© 2024 Mathspace Pty Ltd

Copyright Notice

This Work is copyright. All rights are reserved. No part of this Work may be reproduced, stored in a retrieval system, or transmitted in any form or by any means without prior written permission of the Publisher.

For permission to use material from this text or product, please email hello@mathspace.co

Mathspace Inc.
228 Park Ave S #15992
New York NY 10003-1502

For our full digital offering, visit mathspace.co

Mathspace Virginia: Algebra 1 Volume 2 for 2023 SOLs - Print Teacher Edition

ISBN: 978-1-963022-12-4

Contents

6 Polynomials & Factoring — 670

- 6.01 Add and subtract polynomials (A.EO.2) — 674
- 6.02 Multiply polynomials (A.EO.2) — 693
- 6.03 Divide polynomials by a monomial (A.EO.2) — 721
- 6.04 Factor GCF (A.EO.2) — 732
- 6.05 Factor by grouping (A.EO.2) — 749
- 6.06 Factor trinomials (A.EO.2) — 763
- 6.07 Factor using appropriate methods (A.EO.2) — 777
- 6.08 Divide polynomials (A.EO.2) — 796

7 Quadratic Functions — 812

- 7.01 Characteristics of quadratic functions (A.F.2) — 817
- 7.02 Quadratic functions in factored form (A.F.2) — 845
- 7.03 Quadratic functions in vertex form (A.F.2) — 874
- 7.04 Quadratic functions in standard form (A.F.2) — 909
- 7.05 Compare linear, quadratic, and exponential functions (A.F.1, A.F.2) — 936

8 Quadratic Equations — 962

- 8.01 Solve quadratics using graphs and tables (A.EI.3, A.F.2) — 966
- 8.02 Solve quadratics by factoring (A.EI.3, A.F.2) — 989
- 8.03 Solve quadratics using square roots (A.EI.3) — 1006
- 8.04 Solve quadratics using the quadratic formula (A.EI.3) — 1030
- 8.05 Solve quadratics using appropriate methods (A.EI.3) — 1059

9 Data Analysis — 1076

- 9.01 Data and sampling (A.ST.1) — 1080
- 9.02 Scatterplots (A.ST.1) — 1109
- 9.03 Linear regression (A.ST.1) — 1139
- 9.04 Quadratic regression (A.ST.1) — 1170
- 9.05 Analyze bivariate data (A.ST.1) — 1196

mathspace.co

6 Polynomials & Factoring

Big ideas
- The properties of real numbers can be applied to many types of expressions.
- A standard algorithm can be applied to rewrite many different kinds of expressions.

Chapter outline

6.01	Add and subtract polynomials	674
6.02	Multiply polynomials	693
6.03	Divide polynomials by a monomial	721
6.04	Factor GCF	732
6.05	Factor by grouping	749
6.06	Factor trinomials	763
6.07	Factor using appropriate methods	777
6.08	Divide polynomials	796

Bees use hexagonal patterns in their honeycombs, which can be modeled using polynomials!

6. Polynomials & Factoring

Topic overview

Foundational knowledge

 Evaluating standards proficiency

The skills book contains questions matched to individual standards. It can be used to measure proficiency for each.

Students should be proficient in these standards.

8.PFA.1 — The student will represent, simplify, and generate equivalent algebraic expressions in one variable.

A.EO.1 — The student will represent verbal quantitative situations algebraically and evaluate these expressions for given replacement values of the variables.

Big ideas and essential understanding

The properties of real numbers can be applied to many types of expressions.
6.01, 6.02 — Operations can be applied to polynomials in much the same way that they can be applied to real numbers.

6.03, 6.08 — Polynomials can be divided using steps similar to those used when dividing real numbers.

A standard algorithm can be applied to rewrite many different kinds of expressions.
6.04 — Factoring out the greatest common factor provides the foundation for all other techniques for factoring quadratic expressions.

6.05 — Factoring by grouping is an application of factoring out the greatest common factor. It is a standard algorithm that can be applied to factoring any factorable quadratic expression.

6.06 — The same standard algorithm can be applied to rewrite any factorable quadratic expression, though other methods may prove more efficient.

6.07 — The structure of an expression can provide information on the most efficient way to rewrite it.

Standards

A.EO.2 — The student will perform operations on and factor polynomial expressions in one variable.

A.EO.2a — Determine sums and differences of polynomial expressions in one variable, using a variety of strategies, including concrete objects and their related pictorial and symbolic models.
6.01 Add and subtract polynomials

A.EO.2b — Determine the product of polynomial expressions in one variable, using a variety of strategies, including concrete objects and their related pictorial and symbolic models, the application of the distributive property, and the use of area models. The factors should be limited to five or fewer terms (e.g., $(4x + 2)(3x + 5)$ represents four terms and $(x + 1)(2x^2 + x + 3)$ represents five terms).
6.02 Multiply polynomials

A.EO.2c — Factor completely first- and second-degree polynomials in one variable with integral coefficients. After factoring out the greatest common factor (GCF), leading coefficients should have no more than four factors.
6.04 Factor GCF
6.05 Factor by grouping
6.06 Factor trinomials
6.07 Factor using appropriate methods

A.EO.2d — Determine the quotient of polynomials, using a monomial or binomial divisor, or a completely factored divisor.
6.03 Divide polynomials by a monomial
6.08 Divide polynomials

A.EO.2e — Represent and demonstrate equality of quadratic expressions in different forms (e.g., concrete, verbal, symbolic, and graphical).
6.06 Factor trinomials
6.07 Factor using appropriate methods

Future connections

A2.EO.3 — The student will perform operations on polynomial expressions in two or more variables and factor polynomial expressions in one and two variables.

Continuous Assessment

Measure standards proficiency with check-ins

Before starting a new topic, it's a great time to go online and have students complete a Skills Check-in to measure their readiness for the topic.

6.01 Add and subtract polynomials

Subtopic overview

Lesson narrative

In this lesson, students will build on their knowledge of the properties of operations with integers and apply it to a new context of polynomials. Students will use structure to identify the best approach for applying operations to polynomials in order to combine like terms when adding and subtracting polynomials. Students will use precise vocabulary when identifying types of polynomials. By the end of the lesson, students will be able to create and rewrite polynomial expressions to represent quantities for contextual situations involving combining like terms.

Learning objectives

Students: Page 316

After this lesson, you will be able to...
- add and subtract polynomials.
- represent sums and differences of polynomials using pictorial models, including algebra tiles.
- explain why addition and subtraction of polynomials produce another polynomial.

Key vocabulary

- binomial
- leading term
- standard form (of a polynomial)
- degree (of a polynomial)
- monomial
- trinomial
- leading coefficient
- polynomial

Essential understanding

Operations can be applied to polynomials in much the same way that they can be applied to real numbers.

Standards

This subtopic addresses the following Virginia 2023 Mathematics Standards of Learning standards.

Mathematical process goals

MPG1 — Mathematical Problem Solving

Teachers can incorporate this goal into their instruction by giving students real-life situations that can be modeled using polynomial expressions. For instance, they can present problems related to calculating the area of a complex shape or modeling the growth of a population and guide students on how to apply the concepts of adding and subtracting polynomials to solve these problems.

MPG5 — Mathematical Representations

Teachers can use concrete manipulatives or pictorial representations (such as algebra tiles) to model the addition and subtraction of polynomials. They can then encourage students to create their own symbolic representations of these problems. Additionally, teachers can show how different representations of the same mathematical concept (like visual models and algebraic expressions) convey the same information.

Content standards

A.EO.2 — The student will perform operations on and factor polynomial expressions in one variable.

A.EO.2a — Determine sums and differences of polynomial expressions in one variable, using a variety of strategies, including concrete objects and their related pictorial and symbolic models.

Prior connections

8.PFA.1 — The student will represent, simplify, and generate equivalent algebraic expressions in one variable.

A.EO.1 — The student will represent verbal quantitative situations algebraically and evaluate these expressions for given replacement values of the variables.

Future connections

A2.EO.3 — The student will perform operations on polynomial expressions in two or more variables and factor polynomial expressions in one and two variables.

Lesson Preparation

Suggested review

Depending on your students' level of prior knowledge, consider revisiting the following lessons:

- **Grade 7** — 3.05 Equivalent algebraic expressions
- **Grade 8** — 2.01 Represent algebraic expressions
- **Grade 8** — 2.02 Simplify expressions and distributive property
- **Algebra 1** — 1.01 Algebraic expressions

Tools

You may find these tools helpful:
- Scientific calculator
- Highlighter
- Algebra tiles

Student lesson & teacher guide

Add and subtract polynomials

Students are introduced to definitions that will help them classify polynomials before moving on to an exploration that relates adding and subtracting multi-digit integers to adding and subtracting polynomials.

Students: Pages 316

6.01 Add and subtract polynomials

After this lesson, you will be able to...
- add and subtract polynomials.
- represent sums and differences of polynomials using pictorial models, including algebra tiles.
- explain why addition and subtraction of polynomials produce another polynomial.

Add and subtract polynomials

Polynomial expressions can be added and subtracted much like real numbers.

> **Polynomial**
> The sum or difference of terms which have variables raised to non-negative integer powers and which have coefficients that are constant

Identifying like terms and combining horizontally or vertically
Targeted instructional strategies

Students should be given a list of terms such as

$$3x^2,\ 8x,\ 3x^3,\ -x,\ 3,\ 8x^2,\ -1$$

and be asked to group any terms together that they believe have features in common, and describe why any terms that did not get grouped are isolated. Once students feel comfortable identifying like terms, present students with a problem including the terms they grouped, such as:

$$(3x^2 - x + 3) + (3x^3 + 8x - 1 + 8x^2)$$

Ask students to discuss the difference between the original grouping task and the problem shown, making sure to point out the + in between the polynomials.

Show students that to combine like terms, the polynomials can be arranged horizontally or vertically with like terms grouped:

$$3x^3 + (3x^2 + 8x^2) + (-x + 8x) + (3 - 1)$$

can also be written as

$$\begin{aligned}&3x^2\ -x + 3\\ &+(3x^3 + 8x^2 + 8x - 1)\end{aligned}$$

Ask students to try both strategies and discuss advantages and disadvantages to each. Then ask students what would be different in the solving of

$$(3x^2 - x + 3) - (3x^3 + 8x - 1 + 8x^2)$$

Compare and connect
English language learner support

Present students with two polynomials to add and subtract, like $(3x^2 + 2x + 1)$ and $(x^2 - 4x + 3)$.

Have students both add and subtract the polynomials using different methods, such as:
- Vertical: Aligning like terms vertically.
- Horizontal: Combining like terms in a single horizontal expression.

Ask students to identify similarities in the process, such as combining like terms. They should also identify any differences in the approaches, such as ease of visualization or steps involved. They should then connect each method to different scenarios where each could be preferable, including whether the same method is easier for both addition and subtraction.

Color coding like terms
Student with disabilities support

Students have already learned how to add and subtract algebraic terms by combining any like terms. Adding and subtracting polynomials can be done in the same way.

If a student has difficulty differentiating terms like x and x^2, help students to recognize that they are not like terms.

This can be done by highlighting or otherwise indicating the different types of terms in the polynomials to indicate that they should be combined independently of each other:

$$(5x^2 + 2x + 12) - (3x^2 - 9x - 8)$$

When written in this way, it should be more obvious that we want to add the coefficients of x^2 and the coefficients of x independently.

Misaligning terms when adding or subtracting vertically
Address student misconceptions

When using the vertical algorithm to add or subtract polynomials, an easy mistake to make is misaligning the terms, or having two different types of terms in the same column. This is more likely to happen when one or both of the polynomials have absent terms (equivalent to those terms having a coefficient of 0).

For example, the sum

$$(2x^3 + x^2 - 12) + (-3x^2 + 11x - 6)$$

may be misaligned in the vertical algorithm as

$$\begin{array}{r} 2x^3 +x^2 -12 \\ + -3x^2 +11x -6 \\ \hline \end{array}$$

which can easily lead to an error.

6.01 Add and subtract polynomials

Exploration

Students: Page 316

> ### Exploration
>
> Compare
>
> $$\begin{array}{r} 2x^3 +4x^2 +0x +5 \\ +0x^3 +3x^2 +2x +3 \\ \hline 2x^3 +7x^2 +2x +8 \end{array}$$
>
> to
>
> $$\begin{array}{r} 2405 \\ +323 \\ \hline 2728 \end{array}$$
>
> 1. Create an addition problem like the example provided where the sum of the coefficients is greater than 9. What happens?
> 2. Create and solve a subtraction problem using the vertical algorithm. Do polynomials behave the same as numbers when subtracting?

Suggested student grouping: In pairs

Students compare a visual of vertical addition of polynomials to adding multi-digit numbers. Students should discover that terms in polynomials are like the place value in multi-digit numbers, but that we don't carry tens to the next term like we do with place value.

Ideal student responses

These ideal responses may differ from other correct student responses. Less formal responses can be connected with the more precise mathematical language presented here.

1. **Create an addition problem like the example provided where the sum of the coefficients is greater than 9. What happens?**

   The coefficients of the terms that have a sum greater than 9 will just be the sum, and we do not carry the tens place to the next term.

2. **Create and solve a subtraction problem using the vertical algorithm. Do polynomials behave the same as numbers when subtracting?**

   When adding polynomials, the solution is a polynomial. When subtracting polynomials, the solution is a polynomial. However, when subtracting polynomials where the term being subtracted has a larger coefficient, we will write the term's difference as a negative number and we will not borrow from the next term like we do with multi-digit subtraction.

Purposeful questions

- What do you notice about the variable term in the solution when each term in the polynomials is added?
- Why can we write $2x^3 + 4x^2 + 0x + 5$ as $2x^3 + 4x^2 + 5$?
- What are the similarities between 'carrying over' in addition and 'borrowing' in subtraction for integers? Do these apply to polynomials?

Possible misunderstandings

- Students may 'carry over' or 'borrow' when adding or subtracting polynomials, in the same way that they would with multi-digit numbers. Let students know these strategies are not necessary because polynomials are a collection of algebraic terms each with their own coefficient, so the place values in one term do not affect any other terms.
- Students may add $4x^2$ with $3x^2$ by writing $7x^4$, so remind students that combining like terms such as $4x$ and $3x$ will not change the variable's exponent, only the coefficient. This is a good time to review that $4x$ is equivalent to $4x^1$, but we do not write singular variables with an exponent.

After the exploration, a visual explanation using algebra tiles of adding and subtracting polynomials in terms of combining like terms is stated. Then, students learn more definitions for classifying polynomials and their parts.

Students: Pages 316–318

We can use algebra tiles to model sums and differences of polynomials.

The difference $(6x^2 + 4x - 5) - (4x^2 - 2x + 3)$ can be modeled with algebra tiles. Lining up like terms, vertically, we can write:

$$\begin{array}{r} 6x^2 + 4x - 5 \\ -4x^2 - 2x + 3 \end{array}$$

The subtraction can be viewed as the expression:

$$(6x^2 + 4x - 5) + (-1)(4x^2 - 2x + 3)$$

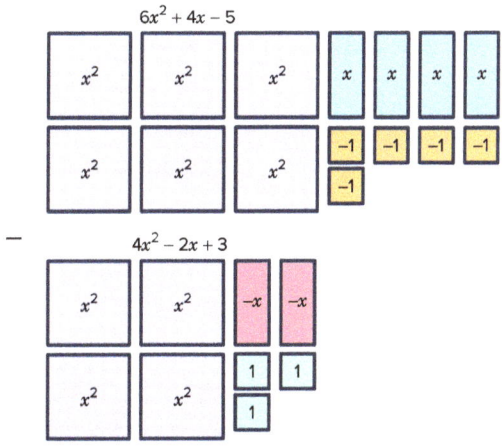

Using the opposites of the expression $4x^2 - 2x + 3$ with the algebra tiles, we get the expression:

$$(6x^2 + 4x - 5) + (-4x^2 + 2x - 3)$$

Equivalently, distributing the –1:

$$\begin{array}{r} 6x^2 + 4x - 5 \\ +-4x^2 - 2x - 3 \\ \hline 2x^2 + 6x - 8 \end{array}$$

Creating zero pairs and combining like terms with the algebra tiles, we are left with the expression:

$$2x^2 + 6x - 8$$

Therefore, the difference between the revenue from the gaming computers can be modeled by $2x^2 + 6x - 8$.

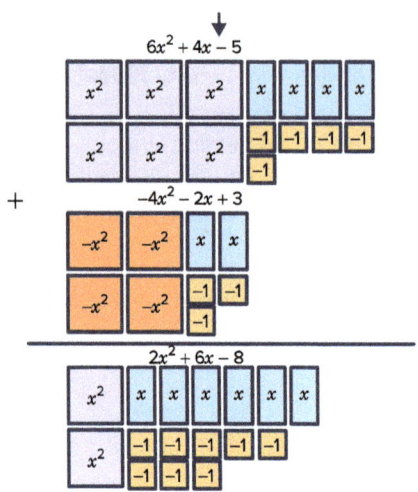

Adding and subtracting polynomials creates more polynomials. The following vocabulary is helpful to know when working with polynomials:

Standard form (of a polynomial)
A way of writing a polynomial expression; $a_n x^n + a_{n-1} x^{n-1} + ... + a_1 x + a_0$, where n is a non-negative integer and each a_i is a coefficient.

Degree of a polynomial
The value of the highest exponent on a variable in the polynomial

Leading term
The term in a polynomial with the highest exponent of the variable

Leading coefficient
The coefficient of the leading term

Monomial
A polynomial with one term

Binomial
A polynomial with two terms

Trinomial
A polynomial with three terms

Examples

Students: Page 318

Example 1

Consider the polynomial
$$3x - 6 + x^2$$

a   Rewrite the expression in standard form.

Create a strategy
Recall that the standard form of a polynomial is written with the terms in order from the term with the highest variable exponent to the lowest. We can use the commutative property to change the order of the polynomials.

Apply the idea
$$x^2 + 3x - 6$$

Purpose
Show students how to order the terms to write a polynomial in standard form.

Expected mistakes
Students may not keep the sign of the term with the correct term. Color coding terms or underlining terms to include their sign will remind students which terms are positive and which terms are negative.

Reflecting with students
Ask students how they could represent the constant term as a term involving x. What would the coefficient be? What would the exponent on the variable be?

Students: Page 318

b State the degree of the polynomial.

Apply the idea
$x^2 + 3x - 6$ is a polynomial of degree 2.

Reflect and check
Since the polynomial has 3 terms, it may be called a trinomial.

Purpose
Show students that the highest exponent or the exponent of the leading term is the degree of the polynomial.

Expected mistakes
Students may add the exponents of the terms and incorrectly state that the degree of the polynomial is 3.

Reflecting with students
Ask students to consider whether the order of the terms will ever impact the type of polynomial represented.

Students: Page 318

c Identify the quadratic term, the linear term, and the constant term of the polynomial.

Apply the idea
- Quadratic term: x^2
- Linear term: $3x$
- Constant term: –6

Reflect and check
Polynomials of degree 2 are called quadratic polynomials.

Purpose
Show students how each term in the polynomial is classified. A term with a variable exponent of 2 is quadratic, a term with a variable exponent of 1 is linear, and a term with a variable exponent of 0 is constant.

Expected mistakes
Students may incorrectly classify terms. For the constant term, it might help to note for students that the word constant means that something remains the same. Without a variable which can change in value, the number –6 remains the same.

Reflecting with students
Ask students to build their own trinomial using a quadratic, linear, and constant term. Mix up asking for various terms and ask students to build other types of polynomials.

Students: Page 319

Example 2

Consider the polynomials $x^3 - 6x + 2$ and $x^2 + 9x + 7$.

a Find the sum of the two polynomials.

Create a strategy

Since we want to find the sum of the two polynomials, combine the like terms.

Apply the idea

$\text{Sum} = (x^3 - 6x + 2) + (x^2 + 9x + 7)$ Add the polynomials together
$= x^3 - 6x + 2 + x^2 + 9x + 7$ Remove the parentheses (Associative Property)
$= x^3 + x^2 + 3x + 9$ Combine the like terms

Reflect and check

If we want to use the vertical algorithm method, we need to make sure we correctly align the like terms.

$$\begin{array}{r} x^3 \quad\quad -6x \quad +2 \\ +\quad\quad x^2 \quad +9x \quad +7 \\ \hline x^3 \quad +x^2 \quad +3x \quad +9 \end{array}$$

Purpose

Show students how to add two polynomials together.

Expected mistakes

Students may add the leading terms even though they are not like terms.

Reflecting with students

Ask students to explain why the sum of the polynomials has four terms when the given polynomials had three.

Students: Page 319

b Explain why the sum of two polynomials is also a polynomial.

Apply the idea

By definition, a polynomial is the sum or difference of terms which have variables raised to non-negative integer powers and which have coefficients that may be real or complex.

Adding one polynomial to the other is the same as adding more terms to one polynomial. This doesn't change the fact that it is a polynomial, so the sum of two polynomials will always be a polynomial.

Reflect and check

We can use the same explanation for why the difference between two polynomials is also a polynomial, and we can extend this explanation to include the sum or difference of any number of polynomials.

Purpose

Show students that polynomials are closed under addition.

Expected mistakes

Students may have difficulty articulating why this is true. Relate the addition of polynomials back to the addition of integers from the exploration. Review that integers are closed under addition because the sum of two integers is an integer.

Polynomials are closed under addition because a polynomial is the sum of algebraic terms with non-negative integer coefficients, and the sum of two polynomials will simply be the sum of the algebraic terms from both polynomials.

Reflecting with students
Ask advanced learners whether they think it is impossible to find two polynomials whose sum is not a polynomial. Explain to students that we can sometimes disprove mathematical statements by providing a counterexample to a claim. However, it is not possible for the sum of two polynomials to not be a polynomial so no such counterexample will exist in this case.

Include terms with zero coefficients
Targeted instructional strategies *use with Example 2*

When adding or subtracting polynomials that do not have all matching terms, we can include these terms with zero as the coefficient to better match up the terms. This can be especially useful when using the vertical algorithm to add or subtract.

Consider that

$$2x^3 + x^2 - 12 = 2x^3 + x^2 + 0x - 12$$

and

$$-3x^2 + 11x - 6 = 0x^3 - 3x^2 + 11x - 6$$

so we can easily align our terms in a vertical algorithm:

$$\begin{array}{rrrrr} & 2x^3 & +x^2 & +0x & -12 \\ - & (0x^3 & -3x^2 & +11x & -6) \\ \hline & 2x^3 & +4x^2 & -11x & -6 \end{array}$$

Students: Pages 319–320

Example 3

Simplify the expression:

$$(3x^2 - 5x + 1) - (x^2 + 7x - 10)$$

Apply the idea

$(3x^2 - 5x + 1) - (x^2 + 7x - 10) = 3x^2 - 5x + 1 - x^2 - 7x + 10$ Distribute the subtraction
$\qquad\qquad\qquad\qquad\qquad\quad = (3x^2 - x^2) + (-5x - 7x) + (1 + 10)$ Group the like terms together
$\qquad\qquad\qquad\qquad\qquad\quad = 2x^2 - 12x + 11$ Simplify

Reflect and check

A color-coded visualization helps confirm that our distribution is correct.

$(3x^2 - 5x + 1) - (x^2 + 7x - 10) = 3x^2 - 5x + 1 - x^2 - 7x + 10$ Distribute the subtraction
$\qquad\qquad\qquad\qquad\qquad\quad = (3x^2 - x^2) + (-5x - 7x) + (1 + 10)$ Group the like terms together
$\qquad\qquad\qquad\qquad\qquad\quad = 2x^2 - 12x + 11$ Simplify

Purpose
Show students how to subtract polynomials.

Expected mistakes
Students may assume that if a term has no coefficient, nothing is actually subtracted. Remind students that the coefficient of a term without one shown is always 1.

Reflecting with students
Ask students to find the difference of the polynomials using the vertical algorithm and explain which method they prefer.

Distributing the subtraction
Address student misconceptions

use with Example 3

When finding the difference between two polynomials, students may only apply the subtraction to the first term of the subtracted polynomial instead of the whole expression.

Remind students to use parentheses around the polynomials when they add or subtract them, as this will remind them to distribute the subtraction instead of only applying it to a single term.

This is also an easy mistake to make when using the vertical algorithm to subtract two polynomials.

Students: Page 320

Example 4

Write at least two equivalent expressions for the length of a fence around a rectangular yard with a length of $2x^3 + 5$ feet and a width of $x^2 + 6$ feet.

Create a strategy
Draw a diagram of the yard and label its length and width.
Use the length and width to write the perimeter.

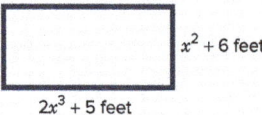

Apply the idea
The perimeter of the yard is the sum of the sides. One expression for the length of the fence would be

$$(2x^3 + 5) + (x^2 + 6) + (2x^3 + 5) + (x^2 + 6) \text{ ft}$$

By finding the sum of the binomials representing the length and width of the yard, another expression would be

$$2x^2 + 22 + 4x^3 \text{ ft}$$

The expression written in standard form begins with the term with the highest degree and ends with the term with the lowest degree, shown below:

$$4x^3 + 2x^2 + 22 \text{ ft}$$

Purpose
Show students various equivalent forms of the same expression.

Expected mistakes
Students may not understand how to write equivalent forms of the same expression when they are accustomed to writing an expression in its most simplified form. While the initial expression for the perimeter is not simplified, we can verify that it is equivalent to another expression that represents the perimeter of the yard.

Reflecting with students
Ask students to write at least two more equivalent expressions for the length of the fence. This might include an expression with required distribution.

Students: Pages 320–321

Example 5

Model and simplify $(8x^2 + 4) + (12x^2 + 6x + 6)$.

Create a strategy

Represent each term with tiles and combine the similar terms.

Apply the idea

The expression $8x^2 + 4$ is the same as having eight x^2 tiles and four unit (or 1) tiles.

The expression $12x^2 + 6x + 6$ is the same as having twelve x^2 tiles, six x tiles, and 6 unit (or 1) tiles.

The expression $(8x^2 + 4) + (12x^2 + 6x + 6)$ can be represented as:

6.01 Add and subtract polynomials

mathspace.co

Combine the like terms and count each type of tile.

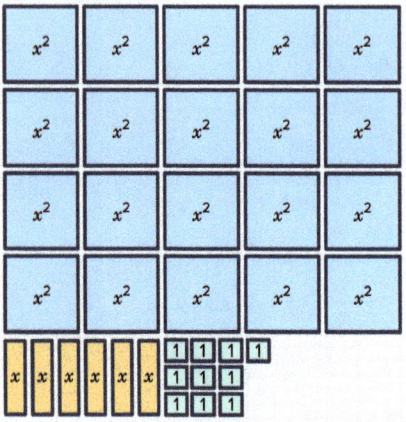

So, there are twenty x^2, six x, and ten unit tiles.
The result is $20x^2 + 6x + 10$.

Purpose
Show students how to add polynomials using algebra tiles.

Expected mistakes
Students may forget to combine like terms, resulting in a polynomial with unnecessary terms. Remind students to look for and combine terms that have the same variable to the same power.

Students: Page 321

> **Idea summary**
> We add polynomials by combining like terms. We subtract polynomials by adding the negative terms.

Practice

Students: Pages 322–325

What do you remember?

1 Choose the best word from this set:

   term, coefficient, variable, constant

   to describe:

   a   The number 3 in the term $3x$
   b   The letter x in the term $6x$
   c $4x$ in the expression $4x + 7$
   d   The number 7 in the expression $5x + 7$
   e   The number -5 in $4 - 5x$
   f   The letter u in the term $-12u$
   g   The number 8 in $6z + 8$
   h $-3y$ in $2 - 3y + 4z$

2. Describe each pair of terms as *like* or *unlike*.
   a 10p and 5p
   b 3 and y
   c $5n^2$ and 8n
   d 5p and 5
   e 10a and −9a
   f 2ab and 6ba
   g 15p and 15q
   h 8 and 8z
   i $7m^2$ and 7m
   j 8z and −8z
   k 12b and −21b
   l 13xy and 14yx

3. Donna earns $15 per hour of work and is paid double for every hour worked on the weekend. At the end of a week, Donna calculates her pay for that week to be 15x + 30y dollars.
   a What variable represents the number of hours Donna worked during the weekdays?
   b What variable represents the number of hours Donna worked during the weekends?

4. In the expression $3x^2 + 5x + 7x^2 - 2x$, which terms are like terms? Explain your answer.

5. Write a simplified expression for each set of algebra tiles.
   a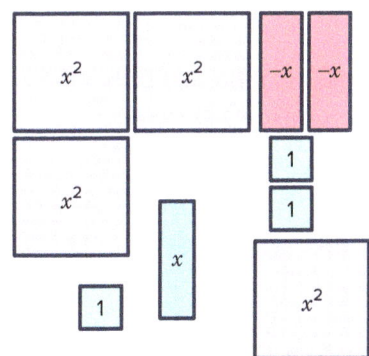
   b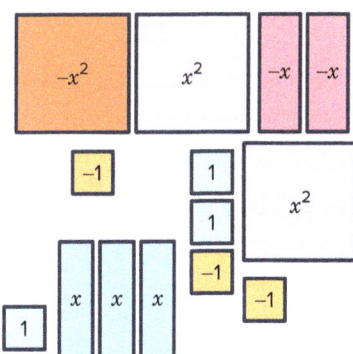

6. Compare and contrast adding two-digit integers and adding binomials.

Let's practice

7. Simplify:
   a 2a + 5a
   b 10x + 6x
   c 4b + 3b
   d 12y − 3y
   e 3c + 4c + 7c
   f 15x − 6x − 2x
   g 19b − 12b − 6b
   h −3n + 6n + 3n
   i 8x − 3x + 7x
   j x + 9 + 7
   k 9x + 4x
   l 12p − 9p
   m $2u^2 + 9u^2$
   n 4m − 4m

8. State whether each expression is equal to 11y.
   a 9 + y + 10y − 9
   b 6y − 5y
   c 5y + 6y
   d 11 + y
   e 9y + 3y − 1
   f 10y + 1

9. State whether each expression is equal to 8r + 9?
   a 9 + 8r
   b 9r + 8
   c 17r
   d 72r
   e 9r + 8 − r + 1
   f 10r + 2 − 2r + 7

10 Complete each step by writing the expression modeled by the algebra tiles.

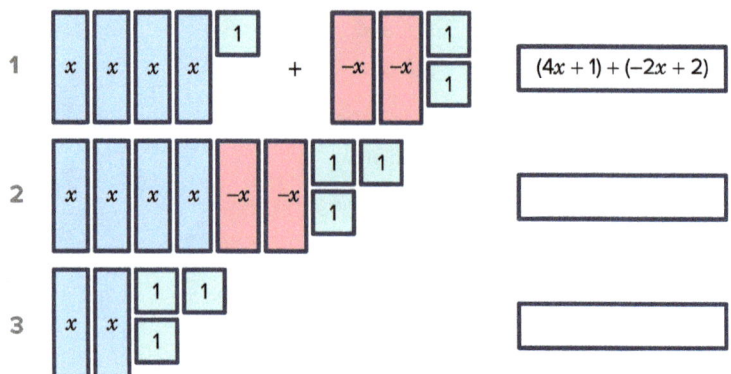

11 Consider the expression $(2x^2 - 4x + 7) - (5x^2 + 3x - 2)$. Explain how to represent both polynomials with algebra tiles, perform the subtraction, and represent the resulting polynomial using the tiles.

12 Simplify:
  a $(5x + 1) + (2x - 3)$
  b $(x + 1) - (2x - 1)$
  c $(-6x^3 - 2) - (4x^3 - 3x^2)$
  d $(-2x^2 - x - 5) + (6x^2 - 9x - 8)$
  e $\left(-\frac{1}{2}x^2 - 1\right) + \left(\frac{3}{8}x^2 + \frac{1}{4}x\right)$
  f $\left(\frac{3}{2}x^3 - \frac{5}{2}x^2 - 1\right) + \left(\frac{1}{2}x^3 - \frac{1}{2}x^2 + x\right)$
  g $(2x^2 - 3x - 9) - (-6x^2 + 6x - 2)$
  h $(9x^3 - 3x + 2) - (-6x^3 - 5x^2 - 5x)$
  i $(2x^2 + 1) + (x^2 + 3x) + (4x - 5)$
  j $(-2x + 7) - (7x^2 + 8x - 5) + 7x$

13 Simplify:
  a $\left(\frac{11}{5}x^2 + 7x - 2\right) - (x + 7) + \left(\frac{9}{5}x^2 + 2x\right)$
  b $(-0.2 - 9.5x - 1.4x^2) + (2.6 - 7.8x + 7.7x^2)$
  c $(7.6x^2 - 0.5x + 7.3) - (1.4x^2 - 3.4x - 9.6)$
  d $(-8x^6 + 9x^4 - 11x^3 - 13) + (10x^6 + 5x^5 - 3x^3 - 2x^2)$

14 Fill in the blanks to make each equation true.
  a $(x^3 - x + 7) + (\square x^3 + \square x + 3) = 10$
  b $(\square x^2 - 5x - 5) - (\square x + 3) = 4x^2 - 2x - 8$
  c $(\square x^\square) + (2x^3 - 3x + 1) = 2x^3 + x + 1$
  d $(4x + 1) - (\square x^\square + \square) = 0$

15 If $A(x) = -2x^2 - 3$, $B(x) = -6x + 3$ and $C(x) = 6x^2 + 2x$, form a simplified expression for $A(x) + B(x) + C(x)$.

16 If $A(x) = 5x^2 + 2$, $B(x) = -3x + 3$ and $C(x) = -2x^2 + 7x$, form a simplified expression for $A(x) - B(x) - C(x)$.

17 If $A(x) = -6x^2 - 6$, $B(x) = 4x - 7$ and $C(x) = x^2 - 5x$, form a simplified expression for $B(x) - A(x)$.

18 A rectangle with the given dimensions is to have a right triangle cut out from one corner. Write and simplify a polynomial sum or difference to model each of the following:
  a An expression for the length represented by y.
  b An expression for the perimeter of the rectangle before the triangle has been removed.
  c If the area of the rectangle is $5x^2 + 16x + 3$ and the area of the triangle is $x^2 + 3x$, determine the area leftover once the triangle has been removed.

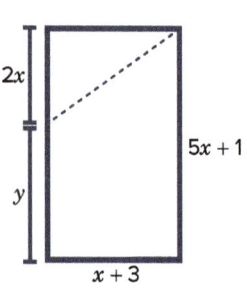

19 A polynomial of degree m and a polynomial of degree n, with $m \geq n$, are added together. Find the highest possible degree of the result.

20 The revenue generated by Leticia's seafood restaurant is modeled by $R(m) = -3.2m^2 + 10.9m + 990$, and the profit of her restaurant is modeled by $P(m) = 2.3m^2 - 29.3m + 830$, where m is the number of meals produced.

Find the polynomial that models the costs of Leticia's restaurant.

21 Joanita's hat manufacturing business sells its hats exclusively through two retailers. The profit generated through selling at Just Stuff is modeled by $A(q) = -0.5q^2 + 22.5q + 510$, and the profit generated through selling at Glorious Gifts is modeled by $B(q) = 2.9q^2 + 36.5q + 70$, where q is the number of hats sold.

Form an expression for the polynomial that models Joanita's total profit.

22 Find a polynomial that represents the perimeter of a square with side length $\frac{1}{4}x^2 + 6x$.

23 A rectangle has a length of $l = 3x + 5$ and a perimeter of $P = 12x$. Find the width of the rectangle.

24 A piece of paper with dimensions 8.5 inches by 11 inches will have a square with length x cut out from each corner to form a box.

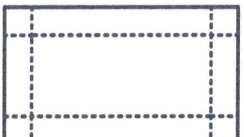

Write and simplify a polynomial sum that can be used to represent the perimeter of the shape formed once the corners have been removed.

25 Maureen's paddock has dimensions as shown in the diagram. All dimensions are in meters.

  a Write a fully simplified expression for the perimeter of the paddock.

  b On Mondays, Maureen runs the entire perimeter of the paddock twice. Write a fully simplified expression for the distance she runs each Monday.

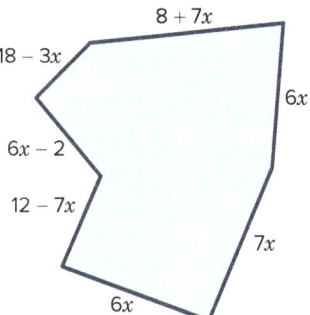

  c On Saturdays, Maureen goes for a much shorter run. The route is shown in the diagram by the thick, dark line. She runs from the Start to the End once.

  Determine how much further she runs on Mondays than on Saturdays.

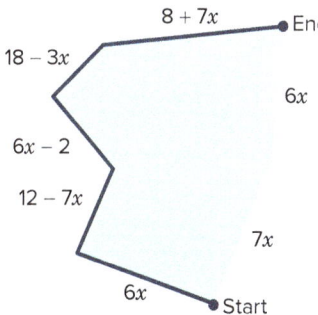

Let's extend our thinking

26 Simplify:

  a $8x + 6y - 2y - 4x$

  b $-4\frac{1}{2}m + 9n + 5m + 10n$

  c $\frac{x}{2} - 9y - \frac{7x}{4} + 11y$

  d $11m + 8n + 14m$

  e $9xy + 12yx$

  f $6p + 8q - 6p$

  g $2.5x + 9y - 5x + 10y$

  h $7a + 11a - 9b + b$

  i $8x - 7y - 6z + 10z$

  j $\frac{1}{9}a - 8b + 4c + \frac{1}{3}a + b$

  k $13m - 2.2n - 8m + 1.5n$

  l $-3s + 4t - 6t + 9s$

27 Simplify:

a $(8a^2b^2 - 7a^2b + 8ab - 11) + (-3a^2b^2 + 6a^2b + 5ab)$

b $(4x^2y - 9xy^2 + 4) + (-7x^2y + 4xy^2 + 8)$

c $(3x^2y^2 - 2xy^2 + 4y^2) + (-9x^2y^2 + 3xy^2 - 8y^2)$

28 Tom simplified the expression $7x + 6p - 4x + 2$ and found it to be $3x + 6p + 2$. Xanthe simplified the same expression and found it to be $11x + 6p + 2$. Explain who is correct and why.

29 Show that the expression $12ab + 7c - 8ab - 9c$ is equivalent to the expression $-6c + 2ab + 4c + 6ab - 4ba$.

30 Determine whether each statement is always, sometimes, or never true. Explain your reasoning with examples.

a Two polynomials added together will result in a polynomial.

b A linear function is a polynomial.

c A polynomial added to a non-polynomial will result in a polynomial.

d A non-polynomial added to a non-polynomial will result in a polynomial.

31 Is it ever possible that $8m + 5n = 13mn$?

32 Explain how two trinomials can be added together to produce a binomial.

33 Given that $(ax + 5) + (4x^2 - 4x + 4) + (3x + 2) = 4x^2 + 4x + 11$ for all values of x, solve for a.

34 Consider $[ax^2 + (b - 5)x - 1] + [x^2 - 5x + 2] = 2x^2 + 2x + 1$.

a Find the value of a.

b Find the value of b.

35 Consider the following work:

$$(-3x^3 + 7x^2 - x - 4) - (-2x^3 + ax^2 + bx + 6) = cx^3 + 6x^2 + 4x - 10$$
$$(-3 - 2)x^3 + (7 - a)x^2 + -(1 + b)x + (-4 - 6) = cx^3 + 6x^2 + 4x - 10$$
$$-5x^3 + (7 - a)x^2 + -(1 + b)x + (-10) = cx^3 + 6x^2 + 4x - 10$$

$7 - a = 6$ $\qquad\qquad$ $-(1 + b) = 4$

$a = 1$ $\qquad\qquad\qquad$ $-1 - b = 4$

$\qquad\qquad\qquad\qquad\qquad$ $b = -3$

Therefore, $a = 1$, $b = -3$, and $c = -5$.

a Identify and explain any mistakes.

b Give the correct values for a, b, and c.

Answers

6.01 Add and subtract polynomials

What do you remember?

1. a Coefficient   b Variable
   c Term   d Constant
   e Coefficient   f Variable
   g Constant   h Term

2. a Like   b Unlike   c Unlike   d Unlike
   e Like   f Like   g Unlike   h Unlike
   i Unlike   j Like   k Like   l Like

3. a x b y

4. In the expression $3x^2 + 5x + 7x^2 - 2x$, the terms $3x^2$ and $7x^2$ are like terms because they both have the variable x raised to the power of 2. The terms $5x$ and $-2x$ are also like terms because they both have the variable x raised to the power of 1.

5. a $4x^2 - x + 3$ b $x^2 + x$

6. Answers will vary.
   Similarities:
   When adding polynomials we combine like terms (terms with the same power of the variables). When adding whole numbers we combine digits with the same place-value (same power of ten). Also, a two-digit number has two place values to add and a binomial has two terms to add.
   Differences:
   When adding whole numbers we carry over excess from the sum if it goes into the next power of ten. When adding polynomial terms, there is never excess that goes into the next term. Also, when adding two-digit numbers, they always have the same place values (units and tens). But when adding binomials, they don't necessarily have like terms (e.g. $x^3 + 2$ and $x^2 + 4x$).

Let's practice

7. a $7a$ b $16x$ c $7b$ d $9y$
   e $14c$ f $7x$ g b h $6n$
   i $12x$ j $x + 16$ k $13x$ l $3p$
   m $11u^2$ n 0

8. a Yes   b No   c Yes   d No
   e No   f No

9. a Yes   b No   c No   d No
   f Yes   e Yes

10.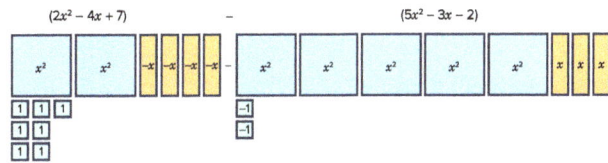

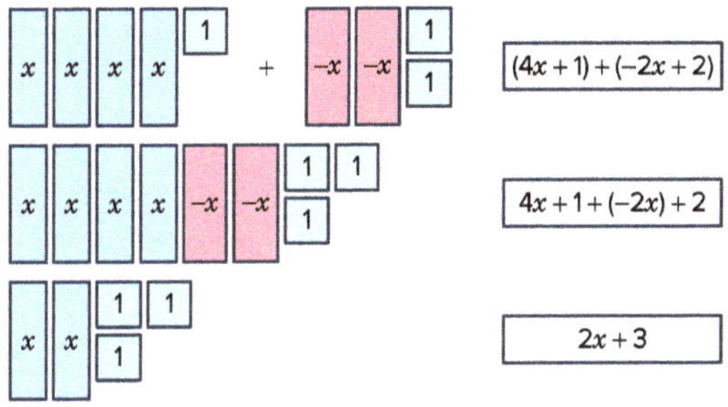

11. 1. Represent the polynomials with algebra tiles:

    2. Distribute the negative sign to the second polynomial.

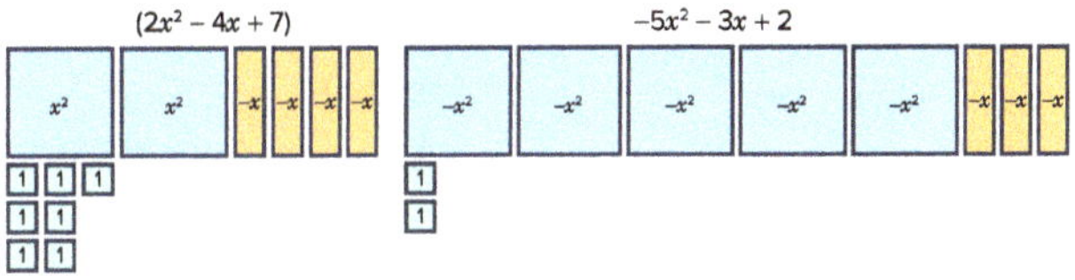

    3. Remove two x^2 tiles from each set since $x^2 - x^2 = 0$.

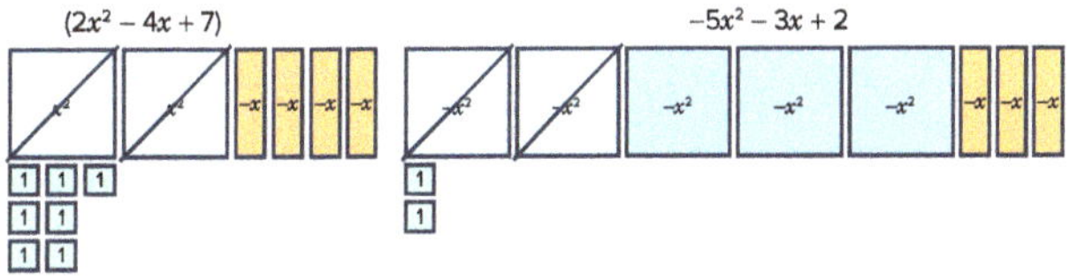

    4. Combine the like terms and count.
       $-3x^2 - 7x + 9$

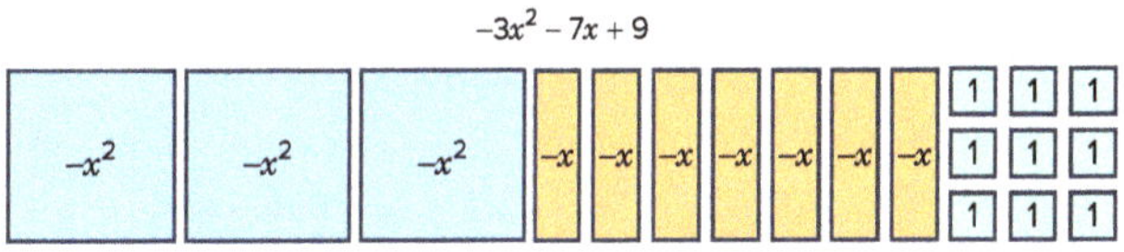

12. a $7x - 2$ b $-x + 2$
    c $-10x^3 + 3x^2 - 2$ d $4x^2 - 10x - 13$
    e $-\dfrac{x^2}{8} + \dfrac{x}{4} - 1$ f $2x^3 - 3x^2 + x - 1$
    g $8x^2 - 9x - 7$ h $15x^3 + 5x^2 + 2x + 2$
    i $3x^2 + 7x - 4$ j $-7x^2 - 3x + 12$

13. a $4x^2 + 8x - 9$
    b $6.3x^2 - 17.3x + 2.4$
    c $6.2x^2 + 2.9x + 16.9$
    d $2x^6 + 5x^5 + 9x^4 - 14x^3 - 2x^2 - 13$

14. a -1 and 1 b 4 and -3 c 4 and 1 d $4, 1$ and 1

15. $4x^2 - 4x$

16. $7x^2 - 4x - 1$

17. $6x^2 + 4x - 1$

18. a $(5x + 1) - (2x) = 3x + 1$
    b $(5x + 1) + (5x + 1) + (x + 3) + (x + 3) = 12x + 8$
    c $(5x^2 + 16x + 3) - (x^2 + 3x) = 4x^2 + 13x + 3$

19 m

20 $-5.5m^2 + 40.2m + 160$

21 $2.4q^2 + 59q + 580$

22 $x^2 + 24x$ units

23 $w = 3x - 5$

24 $(8.5 - 2x) + x + x + (8.5 - 2x) + x + x + (11 - 2x) + x + x + (11 - 2x) + x + x = 39$

25 a $(22x + 36)$ m b $(44x + 72)$ m
    c $(35x + 36)$ m

Let's extend our thinking

26 a $4x + 4y$ b $\frac{1}{2}m + 19n$
    c $\frac{-5x}{4} + 2y$ d $25m + 8n$
    e $21xy$ f $8q$
    g $-2.5x + 19y$ h $18a - 8b$
    i $8x - 7y + 4z$ j $\frac{4}{9}a - 7b + 4c$
    k $5m - 0.7n$ l $6s - 2t$

27 a $5a^2b^2 - a^2b + 13ab - 11$
    b $-5xy^2 - 3x^2y + 12$
    c $-6x^2y^2 + xy^2 - 4y^2$

28 Tom is correct as the sign on the left of the coefficient tells us whether to add or subtract. $-4x$ means we subtract $4x$ from $7x$, not add.

29 $12ab + 7c - 8ab - 9c = 4ab - 2c$
    $-6c + 2ab + 4c + 6ab - 4ba = 4ab - 2c$
    Therefore
    $12ab + 7c - 8ab - 9c = -6c + 2ab + 4c + 6ab - 4ba$

30 a Always true. A polynomial is a collection of terms in the form mx^n where m is a real number and n is a non-negative integer. When adding polynomials together, terms are either combined if they have the same value of n or left alone if not. That means all terms in the resulting polynomial will also be a collection of terms in the form mx^n and will also be a polynomial.
    b Always true. A linear function can only have a linear term in the form mx and/or a constant term in the form b, both of which are terms in a polynomial.
    c Never true. At least one term in the non-polynomial will not combine with any of the terms in the polynomial and such terms will be left in the resulting sum unchanged, which makes the resulting sum a non-polynomial.
    For example:
    $\left(x^2 + \frac{1}{x}\right) + (3x - 5) = x^2 + 3x - 5 + \frac{1}{x}$

    d Sometimes true. If the terms that don't fit the polynomial definition are equal, but with opposite signs, they will eliminate each other and the result will be a polynomial.
    For example: $\left(x^2 + \frac{1}{x}\right) + \left(3x - \frac{1}{x}\right) = x^2 + 3x$

31 Yes, if $m = 1$ and $n = 1$ the expression is true.

32 If the three terms in each trinomial have the same exponents, so that there are three pairs of like terms, and one of the pairs of like terms have the same coefficient but with opposite signs, then those two terms will eliminate each other when added.
    For example, $x^2 + 2x + 1$ and $x^2 - 2x + 4$ would add together to give $2x^2 + 5$.

33 $a = 5$

34 a $a = 1$ b $b = 12$

35 a When collecting coefficients for the x^3 term, they forgot to subtract -2. When solving for b, they subtracted 1 instead of adding 1 to both sides.
    b $a = 1$, $b = -5$, and $c = -1$

6.02 Multiply polynomials

Subtopic overview

Lesson narrative

In this lesson, students will build on their prior knowledge of the distributive property as well as area models to multiply two or more polynomials. Students will justify why polynomials are closed under multiplication using precise mathematical language and definitions. For binomials, students will use the structure of the expressions to recognize patterns and create generalizable formulas and help them evaluate products more efficiently. By the end of the lesson, students will be able to create and rewrite polynomial expressions to represent quantities for contextual situations involving multiplying polynomials. This skill will also prepare students for factoring quadratic trinomials in the next topic.

Learning objectives

Students: Page 326

After this lesson, you will be able to...
- multiply a monomial and a polynomial.
- multiply polynomials.
- represent polynomial multiplication using an area model.
- explain why multiplication of polynomials produces another polynomial.

Key vocabulary

- difference of two squares
- polynomial identity

Essential understanding

Operations can be applied to polynomials in much the same way that they can be applied to real numbers.

Standards

This subtopic addresses the following Virginia 2023 Mathematics Standards of Learning standards.

Mathematical process goals

MPG3 — Mathematical Reasoning

Teachers can foster mathematical reasoning by asking students to justify their steps when multiplying monomials and polynomials. They can challenge students to analyze and evaluate different methods of multiplication, including the use of area models, to determine the most efficient approach.

MPG4 — Mathematical Connections

Teachers can help students make mathematical connections by relating the multiplication of polynomials to real-life situations, such as calculating the volume of complex shapes or predicting population growth. They can also link current lessons to prior knowledge of algebraic expressions, showing how these concepts build upon each other.

MPG5 — Mathematical Representations

Teachers can incorporate this goal by using concrete manipulatives (like algebra tiles) and pictorial representations (like area models) to demonstrate the multiplication of polynomials. They can also encourage students to use these different representations themselves, showing them how to visualize the process of polynomial multiplication and understand the relationships between the coefficients and exponents.

Content standards

A.EO.2 — The student will perform operations on and factor polynomial expressions in one variable.

A.EO.2b — Determine the product of polynomial expressions in one variable, using a variety of strategies, including concrete objects and their related pictorial and symbolic models, the application of the distributive property, and the use of area models.

The factors should be limited to five or fewer terms (e.g., $(4x + 2)(3x + 5)$ represents four terms and $(x + 1)(2x^2 + x + 3)$ represents five terms).

Prior connections

8.PFA.1 — The student will represent, simplify, and generate equivalent algebraic expressions in one variable.

A.EO.1 — The student will represent verbal quantitative situations algebraically and evaluate these expressions for given replacement values of the variables.

Future connections

A2.EO.3 — The student will perform operations on polynomial expressions in two or more variables and factor polynomial expressions in one and two variables.

Lesson Preparation

Suggested review

Depending on your students' level of prior knowledge, consider revisiting the following lessons:

- **Grade 8** — 2.02 Simplify expressions and distributive property
- **Algebra 1** — 6.01 Add and subtract polynomials

Tools

You may find these tools helpful:
- Scientific calculator
- Graph paper
- Highlighter

Student lesson & teacher guide

Multiplying polynomials

Students start with an exploration. In the exploration, students relate calculating the area of rectangles to calculating the area of rectangles using monomials and binomials in an effort to extend their prior knowledge of these properties to monomials and binomials.

Connecting the distributive property to polynomial multiplication
Targeted instructional strategies

To connect the distributive property to multiplying polynomials, display the following problems and have students distribute independently:

$$3x(x - 2)$$
$$-5(x - 2)$$

Write the two resulting expressions side-by-side and show adding and combining like terms.

$$(3x^2 - 6x) + (-5x + 10)$$
$$3x^2 + (-6x - 5x) + 10$$
$$3x^2 - 11x + 10$$

Students should then predict how to simplify

$$(3x - 5)(x - 2)$$

using the two original distribution problems.

Adjustable pre-drawn box method template
Student with disabilities support

To support students using the box method to multiply polynomials, provide students with an adjustable grid layout. Ideally, the template can be done on grid paper and extra space can be given around the template so students can add lines or draw their own boxes on the grid paper.
A sample box method template is shown:

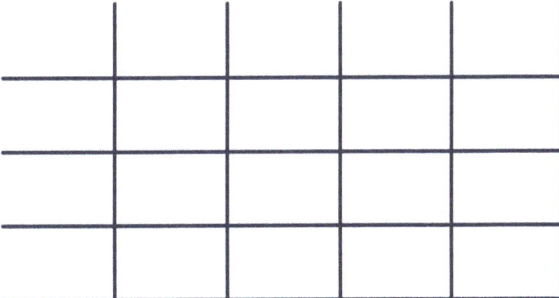

6.02 Multiply polynomials   695
mathspace.co

Students may also benefit from having a highlighted version of the template with outlines colored for the terms of the problem and a different color used for the results of the multiplication.

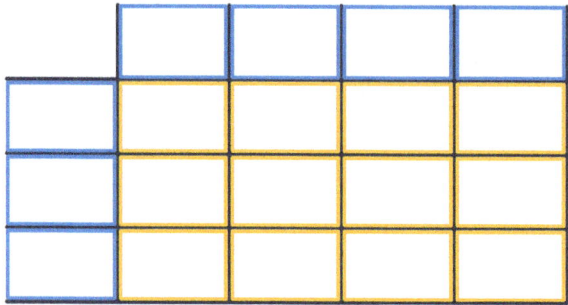

Avoid missing terms with color coding or area models
Address student misconceptions

When multiplying polynomials where one factor has two or more terms and the other has three or more terms, students may miss terms. Consider encouraging students to write extra steps, use an area model, or annotate the question with different colors to help ensure no terms are missed.

$$(3x^2 + 4x - 5)(2x - 7)$$

$$= 3x^2(2x) + 4x(2x) - 5(2x) + 3x^2(-7) + 4x(-7) - 5 - (7)$$

Like terms

$$= 6x^3 + 8x^2 - 10x - 21x^2 - 28x + 35$$

Like terms

$$= 6x^3 - 13x^2 - 38x + 35$$

	$3x^2$	$4x$	-5
$2x$	$6x^3$	$8x^2$	$-10x$
-7	$-21x^2$	$-28x$	35

It is very common to see students simplify $(a + b)^2$ to $a^2 + b^2$ and $(a - b)^2$ to $a^2 - b^2$, which is incorrect. Challenge this misconception by having students show the work of applying the distributive property or giving an example like $(10 - 4)^2 = 6^2 = 36$, but $10^2 - 4^2 = 100 - 16 = 84$ to show it numerically.

Exploration

Students: Page 326

6.02 Multiply polynomials

After this lesson, you will be able to...
- multiply a monomial and a polynomial.
- multiply polynomials.
- represent polynomial multiplication using an area model.
- explain why multiplication of polynomials produces another polynomial.

Multiply polynomials

Exploration

Complete the area models for multiplication shown:

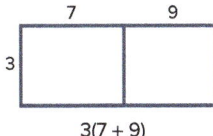

Complete the new area models for multiplication:

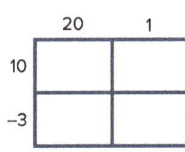

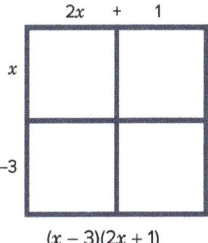

1. What do the area models have in common?
2. What's different about the area models?
3. Make a conjecture about how multiplying polynomials relates to multiplying integers.

Suggested student grouping: In pairs
Students use area models to apply the distributive property and the product property for exponents. Students make connections between multiplying integers and polynomials.

Ideal student responses
These ideal responses may differ from other correct student responses. Less formal responses can be connected with the more precise mathematical language presented here.

1. **What do the area models have in common?**
   The side lengths of the area models each have labels. The number of terms is the same as the number of side lengths.

6.02 Multiply polynomials 697

mathspace.co

2. **What's different about the area models?**
   The first set of area models uses distribution that looks familiar and could be solved without the models. However, more multiplication is required with the second set of area models, so it's harder to distribute in a familiar way.

3. **Make a conjecture about how multiplying polynomials relates to multiplying integers.**
   Multiplying polynomials is similar to multiplying integers, because the integer coefficient of each term is multiplied the same way an integer is multiplied. The difference between multiplying polynomials and integers is that the polynomials now have variables, which require properties of exponents.

Purposeful questions
- Can you find the product without using the area model at all? How does the model help us?
- How can we find the area of one specific box in the model?
- How would you multiply one term with another term?
- Are the second set of area models more challenging or easier to you? Why is that?

Possible misunderstandings
- Students might perform the distributive property without the model and then get confused when they are presented with binomial × binomial. It is important to use the model with the distributive property so that students see why a model is useful for any multiplication of polynomials.

After the exploration, students learn that area models can be used with polynomials that have a variety of number of terms. Area models are connected to algebra tiles and are used with contextual problems with visuals. Students note that polynomials are closed under multiplication, similar to integers, and what to expect with the product of polynomials.

Students: Pages 326–327

Consider the garden plot:

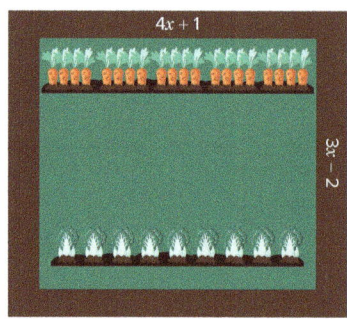

The length of a rectangular garden plot is $4x + 1$ feet. The width of the plot is $3x - 2$ feet. The area can be represented as the product $(4x + 1)(3x - 2)$. We can use models to simplify the product as a polynomial.

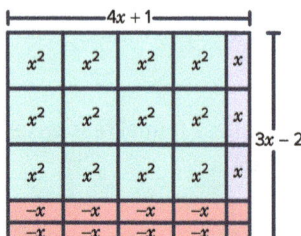

An algebra tiles model

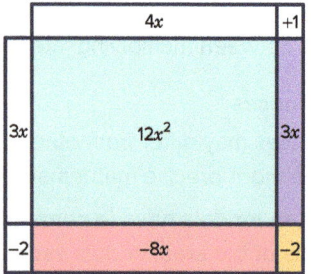

A box/area model

Notice the algebra tiles model shows each individual tile, but the box model combines some like terms together. Both models show the product of $(4x + 1)(3x - 2) = 12x^2 + 3x - 8x - 2$. Which we can simplify by combining like terms to $12x^2 - 5x - 2$.

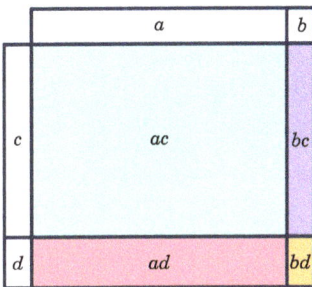

The distributive property can be used to multiply two polynomials:

$$(a + b)(c + d) = ac + ad + bc + bd$$

Area models help us visualize the different terms from the distributive property. They can help us organize the multiplication of polynomials, so we don't miss any terms. Then, we can combine like terms to get the simplest polynomial.

The product of two polynomials will always result in a new polynomial where
- The degree of the new polynomial will be the sum of the degrees of the multiplied polynomials.
- The number of terms may vary from the original polynomials depending on how like terms are combined.

Examples

Students: Page 327

Example 1

Multiply $3x(2x^2 - 5x + 4)$.

Apply the idea

We can use the distributive property to get the product of the monomial $3x$ and the trinomial $2x^2 - 5x + 4$.

$$3x(2x^2 - 5x + 4) = 3x(2x^2) + 3x(-5x) + 3x(4)$$
$$= 6x^3 - 15x^2 + 12x$$

Since there are no more like terms and the expression is already in standard form, the final answer is $6x^3 - 15x^2 + 12x$.

Reflect and check

$6x^3 - 15x^2 + 12x$ is considered a polynomial of degree 3, since 3 is the value of the highest exponent on a variable in the polynomial.

Purpose
Show students how to multiply a monomial and a polynomial.

Expected mistakes
Students may multiply the coefficients only. Remind students of the product property of exponents.

Reflecting with students
Ask students how they would explain aloud how to multiply the monomial and polynomial to a classmate.

Break down the distribution process use with Example 1
Targeted instructional strategies

Demonstrate and explain steps as they are applied. Some students may benefit from seeing it in more steps with connections to prior learning. For example,

$$-2x^2(4x^3 - 2x + 3) = (-2x^2)(4x^3) - (-2x^2)(2x) + (-2x^2)(3)$$ Distribute $-2x^2$
$$= -2 \cdot 4x^{2+3} + 2 \cdot 2x^{2+1} - 2 \cdot 3x^2$$ Multiply coefficients and add exponents
$$= -8x^5 + 4x^3 - 6x^2$$ Simplify operations

Students: Page 328

Example 2

Consider the polynomials $7y + 2$ and $4y - 5$.

a Find the product of the two polynomials.

Create a strategy

Multiply the polynomials using distribution.

Apply the idea

We can create an area model to multiply the two polynomials:

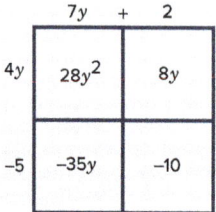

Combining each of the terms, we get:

$$28y^2 - 35y + 8y - 10 = 28y^2 - 27y - 10$$

Reflect and check

We can also use the distributive property to get the product of $7y + 2$ and $4y - 5$.

$(7y + 2)(4y - 5) = 4y(7y + 2) - 5(7y + 2)$ Distributive property
$ = 4y(7y) + 4y(2) - 5(7y) - 5(2)$ Distributive property
$ = 28y^2 + 8y - 35y - 10$ Distributive property
$ = 28y^2 - 27y - 10$ Combine like terms

Since the expression is already in standard form, the final answer is $28y^2 - 27y - 10$.

Purpose

Show students how to multiply two binomials.

Reflecting with students

Ask students how they know what size area model to draw for multiplying two binomials.

Students: Page 328

b Explain why the product of two polynomials is also a polynomial.

Apply the idea
A polynomial is a collection of terms in the form mx^n where m is a real number and n is a non-negative integer.

We know that the product of two algebraic terms with non-negative integer exponents is an algebraic term with non-negative integer exponents. Since multiplying polynomials together results in a sum of such products, by definition the result is a polynomial expression.

Reflect and check
We can use this explanation to think about what happens when we perform multiple operations on polynomials. What happens if we add two polynomials and multiply this result by another polynomial? What if we multiply three polynomials? Is our result still a polynomial?

Purpose
Show students that polynomials are closed under multiplication.

Expected mistakes
Students might not be able to articulate why the statement is true. Refer to the exploration with the integer multiplication with area models. We know that the product of two integers is an integer, and that it is similar for the product of two polynomials.

Reflecting with students
Introduce advanced learners to the term "closure" of polynomials. We say that polynomials are closed under addition, subtraction, and multiplication because the sum, difference, or product of polynomials will also be a polynomial.
Similarly, rational numbers are closed under addition, multiplication, and addition because the sum, difference, or product of rational numbers will also be a rational number.

Students: Page 329

Example 3

Inhar is designing a cubic storage container with odd-numbered side lengths. They decide to let $2x + 1$ yards represent the length of each side.

a Confirm that the side length will always be odd.

Create a strategy
Analyze the given side length.

Apply the idea
Since $2x + 1$ represents the side lengths of the container, we can note that twice any number is always an even product. If we add an odd number like 1 to that, the side length $2x + 1$ will always be odd.

Purpose
Show students why $2x + 1$ must always be an odd number.

Expected mistakes
Students may have difficulty articulating why the statement is true. Reviewing why $2x + 1$ will always be odd using examples of x is sufficient.

Reflecting with students
Ask advanced learners whether $2x - 1$, where x is a whole number, could represent odd side lengths. (No, because when $x = 0$, the side length would be negative.) What types of numbers could we use instead of whole numbers so that this expression would be a valid side length? (Natural numbers)

Extend the problem further by asking what expression could represent even-numbered side lengths, making sure to define the variable well (for example, $2n$, where n is a natural number).

Students: Page 329

b Write an expression for the surface area of the storage container.

Create a strategy
Draw and label a diagram of the storage container first, then use it to calculate the surface area.

Apply the idea

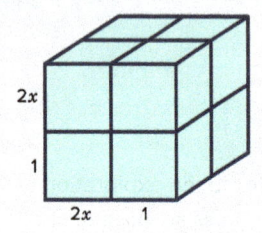

We can calculate the area of one face on the storage container, then multiply the polynomial expression by 6 faces on the cube-shaped container.

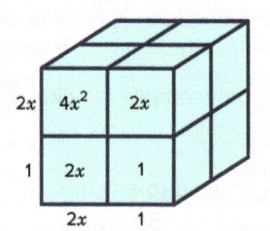

Area of one face: $4x^2 + 2x + 2x + 1 = 4x^2 + 4x + 1$ square yards

Surface area of container:
$6(4x^2 + 4x + 1) = 24x^2 + 24x + 6$ square yards

Purpose
Show students how to write the expression for the surface area of the cubic container.

Expected mistakes
Students may find the area of one face of the container and assume that is the surface area. Students may attempt to calculate the volume of the storage container by multiplying the length, width, and height.

Reflecting with students
Ask students to determine the surface area of the storage container given a specific value of x.

Students: Pages 329–330

c Write an expression for the volume of the storage container.

Create a strategy
Use the formula for the volume of a cube to calculate the volume of the storage container.

Apply the idea
Since the formula for the volume of a cube is $V = l \cdot w \cdot h$, we can calculate the volume of the storage container as shown:

$V = (2x + 1)(2x + 1)(2x + 1)$	Substitute expressions for l, w, and h
$= (2x + 1)[(4x^2 + 2x + 2x + 1)]$	Distributive property
$= (2x + 1)(4x^2 + 4x + 1)$	Combine like terms
$= (8x^3 + 8x^2 + 2x) + (4x^2 + 4x + 1)$	Distributive property
$= 8x^3 + 12x^2 + 6x + 1$ cubic yards	Combine like terms

Reflect and check

A labeled diagram of the storage container can help us conceptualize the problem.

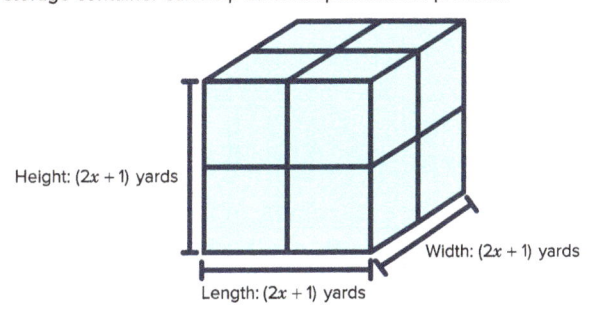

Height: $(2x + 1)$ yards
Width: $(2x + 1)$ yards
Length: $(2x + 1)$ yards

Purpose
Show students how to multiply more than one polynomial.

Expected mistakes
Students may have difficulty starting the multiplication problem when seeing three polynomials. Show students that we start by multiplying two polynomials, then take the product and multiply it by the last polynomial.

Reflecting with students
Ask students to explain why the volume of the storage container is in cubic yards and the surface area of the storage container is in square yards.

Students: Page 330

Example 4

Consider the diagram of the product of the expression $(x - 1)(x - 4)$.

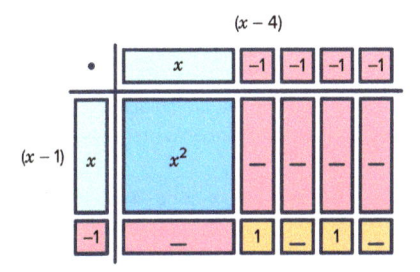

a   Find the missing values on the diagram to complete the visual representation of multiplying $(x - 1)(x - 4)$.

Create a strategy
Use the algebra tiles on the left side and the algebra tiles on the top row to find the area of the tiles with missing values.

Apply the idea

The diagram that shows the visual representation of multiplying $(x - 1)(x - 4)$ is given by:

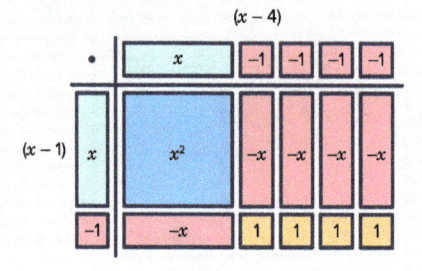

Purpose

Check students can use algebra tiles to multiply two binomials.

Expected mistakes

Students may mistake the negative algebra tiles for positive ones, leading to an incorrect diagram. Discuss with students the importance of keeping track of negative values when multiplying algebraic expressions using algebra tiles.

Students: Page 331

b   Write the product of $(x - 1)(x - 4)$.

Create a strategy

Add all like terms of the algebra tiles from part (a).

Apply the idea

$(x - 1)(x - 4) = x^2 - x - x - x - x - x + 1 + 1 + 1 + 1$ Add all the algebra tiles
$= x^2 - 5x + 4$ Evaluate

Reflect and check

You may encounter some products of polynomials that require combining exponents with a degree greater than 1. Recall the expanded form of the product property for exponents that says $ax^m \cdot bx^n = abx^{m+n}$.

So, we have:

$5x^3 \cdot 4x^2 = 5 \cdot x \cdot x \cdot x \cdot 4 \cdot x \cdot x$
$= 5 \cdot 4 \cdot x \cdot x \cdot x \cdot x \cdot x$
$= 20x^5$

Purpose

Ensure students can write an expression from an algebraic diagram.

Expected mistakes

Students may write their x term with a positive coefficient since they may count the number of tiles without thinking of their value, resulting in a wrong simplified expression. Having students write out $(-1 -1 -1 -1 -1) x$ after writing out the algebra tiles will help clarify the operations needed.

Concrete-Representational-Abstract (CRA) Approach
Targeted instructional strategies

use with Example 4

Concrete: Begin by engaging students with algebra tiles to physically model the multiplication of polynomials. Provide tiles that represent variables and constants: large squares for x^2, rectangles for x, and small squares for constants. Have students arrange one polynomial along the top of an area grid and the other along the side. For example, to multiply $(x + 2)$ by $x + 3$, they place tiles for x and +2 along the top and tiles for x and +3 along the side. Students then fill in the grid by multiplying the corresponding tiles, creating a physical area model. This hands-on activity helps them see how each term combines to form the product.

Representational: Transition to drawing area models on paper to represent the multiplication visually. Instruct students to sketch a rectangle divided into sections based on the terms of the polynomials. Label the top of the rectangle with x and +2 and the side with x and +3. Inside each section, have them write the product of the corresponding terms (e.g., $x \times x = x^2$, $x \times 3 = 3x$). Encourage them to shade or color-code different sections to highlight like terms. This visual representation connects the physical tiles to abstract algebraic concepts, reinforcing their understanding of how the terms multiply.

Abstract: Move on to multiplying polynomials using algebraic notation and symbols. Guide students through the distributive property without the aid of visuals: $(x + 2)(x + 3) = x(x + 3) + 2(x + 3)$. Simplify the expression step by step to get $x^2 + 3x + 2x + 6$, and then combine like terms to obtain $x^2 + 5x + 6$. Emphasize the patterns they observed in the concrete and representational stages. Practice additional problems to reinforce this process, helping students become comfortable with abstract manipulation of polynomials.

Connecting the stages: Help students make connections between the concrete tiles, the drawings, and the abstract equations. Discuss how the area model with tiles corresponds to their sketches and how both relate to the algebraic steps. Encourage students to explain how each term in the final expression comes from the multiplication of specific terms in the polynomials. Use side-by-side comparisons to illustrate these connections. By linking all three stages, students deepen their understanding and see how operations on polynomials mirror those on real numbers, preparing them for more advanced concepts like factoring.

Students: Page 331

> **Idea summary**
> Polynomials can be multiplied using the distributive property. Using an area model for multiplying polynomials helps keep track of terms.

Special products of binomials

Students are informed that patterns may be relevant when multiplying polynomials, leading to special products. An exploration with special products of binomials follows.

Critique, correct, and clarify
English language learner support

Provide students with special products of binomials incorrectly expanded, both with and without using the identity rules. Examples could include:

$(x + 3)^2 = x^2 + 3^2$ Distribute exponent
$\quad\quad\quad = x^2 + 9$ Simplify

$(x + 4)(x - 4) = x^2 - 4x + 4x + 16$ Distribute each term in the first set of ( )
$\quad\quad\quad\quad\quad = x^2 + 16$ Simplify

$(4x - 1)^2 = (4x)^2 + 2(4x)(1) + (1)^2$ Square of a binomial (sum)
$\quad\quad\quad\quad = 16x^2 + 8x + 1$ Simplify

Students should work in pairs or small groups to identify the errors in mathematical reasoning or applying polynomial identities. Once the errors have been identified, students should expand the products correctly, adjusting the explanation steps as needed. Students should discuss with their partner or group and write a brief explanation of why the original steps were incorrect and how their corrected steps lead to the correct solution.

Exploration

Students: Page 331

Special products of binomials

For some products of binomials, we can look for patterns to help us simplify more efficiently.

Exploration

Consider the expansions of the following binomials of the form $(a + b)(a + b) = (a + b)^2$:

- $(x + 3)(x + 3) = x^2 + 6x + 9$
- $(x + 5)(x + 5) = x^2 + 10x + 25$
- $(5s - 3)^2 = 25s^2 - 30s + 9$
- $(x + 6)^2 = x^2 + 12x + 36$
- $(2r + 3s)^2 = 4r^2 + 12rs + 9s^2$

1. What do you notice about the linear coefficient of the product?
2. What do you notice about the constant of the product?
3. Is there a general rule for this type of product?

Consider the expansions of the following binomials of the form $(a + b)(a - b)$:

- $(x + 3)(x - 3) = x^2 - 9$
- $(x - 5)(x + 5) = x^2 - 25$
- $(x + 6)(x - 6) = x^2 - 36$
- $(2r + 3s)(2r - 3s) = 4r^2 - 9s^2$
- $(5s - 3)(5s + 3) = 25s^2 - 9$

1. What do you notice about the linear coefficient of the product?
2. What do you notice about the constant of the product?
3. Is there a general rule for this type of product?

Suggested student grouping: Small groups

Students are given two lists of expanded forms of special product examples: $(a + b)(a + b) = (a + b)^2$ and $(a + b)(a - b)$. The goal is to look at patterns that appear with the given examples.

Ideal student responses

These ideal responses may differ from other correct student responses. Less formal responses can be connected with the more precise mathematical language presented here.

1. **What do you notice about the linear coefficient of the product?**

   For $(a + b)(a + b) = (a + b)^2$, the linear coefficient of the product is twice the product of a and b. For $(a + b)(a - b)$, the linear coefficient of the product is zero.

2. **What do you notice about the constant of the product?**

   For $(a + b)(a + b) = (a + b)^2$, the constant of the product is b multiplied by itself. Note that the sign of the constant is positive, since the signs of b are the same in the original product. For $(a + b)(a - b)$, the constant of the product is the b-term multiplied by itself. Note that the sign of the constant is negative, since the signs of b are positive and negative in the original product.

3. **Is there a general rule for this type of product?**

   In general, the multiplication pattern for each is
   $$(a + b)^2 = (a + b)(a + b) = a^2 + 2ab + b^2$$
   $$(a + b)(a - b) = a^2 - b^2$$

Purposeful questions

- Let's look at the linear coefficient of each product. What pattern do you see between the numbers in the binomial and the linear coefficient?
- Let's look at the constant of each product. What pattern do you see between the numbers in the binomial and the linear coefficient?
- Is your pattern true every time you multiply the binomials?

Possible misunderstandings

- For the first set of products, students might assume that the linear coefficient of the product $(a + b)(a + b)$ is b multiplied by itself, but the examples $(2r + 3s)^2 = 4r^2 + 12rs + 9s^2$ and $(5s - 3)^2 = 25s^2 - 30s + 9$ prove otherwise.

Following the exploration, students are shown a visual representation of special products and are given the general rules for special binomial products and definitions for the square of a binomial and the product of a sum and difference. Some other common misconceptions are noted.

Students: Page 332

Some products of binomials follow special patterns.

For example, consider the product of a binomial squared, $(a + b)^2$:

	a	b
a	a^2	ab
b	ab	b^2

We can expand $(a + b)^2$ to $(a + b)(a + b)$ and represent them with an area model. Evaluating with this model and combining like terms, we get the product $a^2 + 2ab + b^2$.

So, we have:

$$(a + b)^2 = (a + b)(a + b) = a^2 + 2ab + b^2$$

Now consider the product of a sum and a difference, $(a + b)(a - b)$:

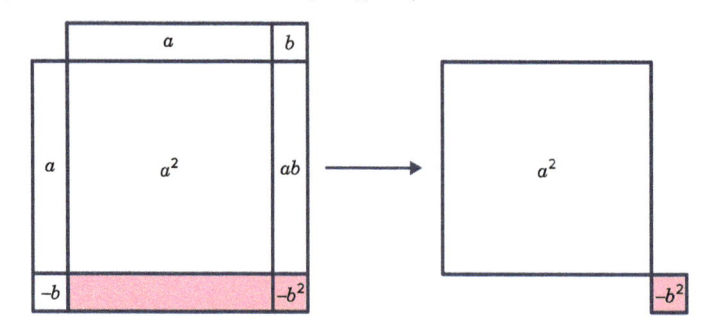

	a	b
a	a^2	ab
$-b$	$-ab$	$-b^2$

→

a^2	
	$-b^2$

Notice that the term ab and $-ab$ are opposites and combine to make zero. We call this a zero pair. So, $(a + b)(a - b) = a^2 - b^2$.

A binomial of the form $a^2 - b^2$ is called a **difference of two squares**.

If we remember the patterns for these special products, we can multiply two polynomials without using the distributive property.

For binomials, we have the following special binomial products, which are called **identities**:

Square of a Sum
$(a + b)^2 = a^2 + 2ab + b^2$

Square of a Difference
$(a - b)^2 = a^2 - 2ab + b^2$

Product of a sum and difference
$(a + b)(a - b) = a^2 - b^2$

Note: $(a + b)^2 \neq a^2 + b^2$ and $(a - b)^2 \neq a^2 - b^2$.

Examples

Students: Pages 332–333

Example 5

Multiply and simplify the following binomials.

a $(x - 4)^2$

Create a strategy

We check first whether $(x - 4)^2$ is a special binomial product and identify its form.

Apply the idea

Since $(x-4)^2$ is a square of a binomial in the form $(a-b)^2$, we use the formula and simplify the expression:

$$(a-b)^2 = a^2 - 2ab + b^2 \qquad \text{Identity for the square of a binomial}$$
$$(x-4)^2 = x^2 - 2(x)(4) + 4^2 \qquad \text{Substitute } a = x \text{ and } b = 4$$
$$= x^2 - 8x + 16 \qquad \text{Evaluate the multiplication and exponent}$$

Reflect and check

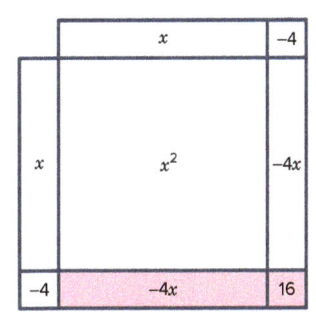

	x	-4
x	x^2	$-4x$
-4	$-4x$	16

We can also use an area model to find the product.

Combining like terms, we get:

$(x-4)^2 = x^2 + 16$

Purpose

Show students how to use the special product pattern for the square of a binomial (difference) to substitute and solve a multiplication problem.

Expected mistakes

Students may forget about the special product pattern and apply the exponent incorrectly to each term within the parentheses, leading to $x^2 - 16$.

Reflecting with students

Ask students if they have any way that they recall the pattern without memorizing the entire $a^2 - 2ab + b^2$. Students might notice that when $a = x$, the linear term is twice the value of b in this specific example and the constant term is b multiplied by itself, noting the sign of b.

Students: Page 333

b $(x+4)(x-4)$

Create a strategy

We check first whether $(x+4)(x-4)$ is a special binomial product and identify its form.

Apply the idea

Since $(x+4)(x-4)$ is a product of a sum and difference, we use the formula and simplify the expression:

$$(a+b)(a-b) = a^2 - b^2 \qquad \text{Identity for the product of a sum and difference}$$
$$(x+4)(x-4) = x^2 - 4^2 \qquad \text{Substitute } a = x \text{ and } b = 4$$
$$= x^2 - 16 \qquad \text{Evaluate the exponent}$$

Reflect and check

Using an area model, we see $(x + 4)(x - 4) = x^2 - 16$.

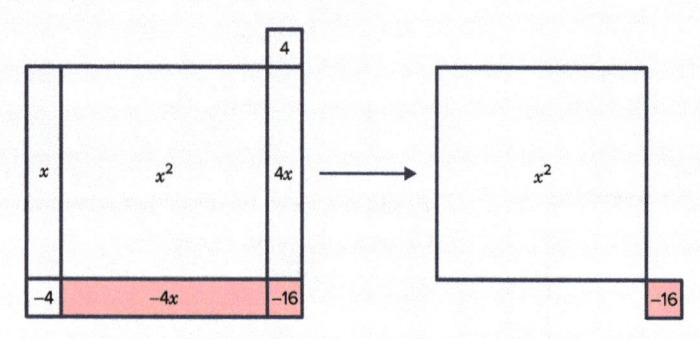

Purpose
Show students how to use the special product pattern for the product of a sum and a difference.

Expected mistakes
Students might forget that the linear term combines to zero if they choose to use distribution as opposed to the pattern to solve.

Reflecting with students
Ask students to provide their own examples of the product of a sum and a difference.

Students: Page 334

c $(2x + 5)(2x - 5)$

Create a strategy

We check first whether $(2x + 5)(2x - 5)$ is a special binomial product and identify its form.

Apply the idea

Since $(2x + 5)(2x - 5)$ is a product of a sum and difference, we use the formula and simplify the expression:

$(a + b)(a - b) = a^2 - b^2$ Identity for the product of a sum and difference
$(2x + 5)(2x - 5) = (2x)^2 - 5^2$ Substitute $a = 2x$ and $b = 5$
$ = 4x^2 - 25$ Evaluate the exponents

Purpose
Show students the special product pattern for thte product of a sum and difference when the a-term has a coefficient other than one.

Expected mistakes
Students may forget to square the coefficient of the a-term. Use distribution to show why we must also square the coefficients.

Reflecting with students
Ask students how this problem may be more challenging than the problem in part (b). This is a good time for students to identify expected mistakes on their own, such as forgetting to square the coefficient of the a-term.

Students: Page 334

d Multiply and simplify: $3(2x + 5y)^2$

Create a strategy

We check first whether $3(2x + 5y)^2$ involves a special binomial product and identify its form.

Apply the idea

Since $(2x + 5y)^2$ is a square of a binomial in the form $(a + b)^2$, we use the formula and simplify the expression:

$(a + b)^2 = a^2 + 2ab + b^2$ Identity for the square of a binomial
$3(2x + 5y)^2 = 3[(2x)^2 + 2(2x)(5y) + (5y)^2]$ Substitute $a = 2x$ and $b = 5y$ and multiply by 3
$= 3[4x^2 + 20xy + 25y^2]$ Evaluate the exponents and multiplication
$= 12x^2 + 60xy + 75y^2$ Distributive property

Purpose

Show students how to combine the square of a sum with distribution.

Expected mistakes

Students may incorrectly square the term that is being multiplied by the quantity. Show students that it is not squared with the quantity.

Reflecting with students

Give students example values of x and y to substitute into the expressions and confirm that the initial problem is equivalent to its solution.

When and when not to square a number
Address student misconceptions

use with Example 5

When squaring a term with a coefficient, many students forget that the exponent also applies to the coefficient. This misconception would result in the following work:

$(2x + 5)(2x - 5) = (2x)^2 - 5^2$ Substitute the given values
$= 2x^2 - 25$ Simplify

In this case, encourage students to go back and distribute the multiplication without using the pattern to check their answer. Note that $(2x)^2 = (2x)(2x) = 4x^2$, not $2x^2$.

Students may try to distribute in the 3 before squaring the binomial in part (d), resulting in $(6x + 10y)^2 = 36x^2 + 120xy + 100y^2$ instead of $12x^2 + 60xy + 75y^2$.

Encourage students to notice that the square is not being applied to the 3, so if they distribute first, they are actually squaring it which is incorrect. To further explain why this violates the order of operations, consider the expression $3(2x + 5y)(2x + 5y)$ and that we would only distribute the 3 into one of the parentheses.

Students: Page 334

Idea summary

Recognizing the patterns in special binomial factors may be helpful in multiplication problems and upcoming lessons. Remember the patterns:

- Square of a Sum: $(a + b)^2 = a^2 + 2ab + b^2$
- Square of a Difference: $(a - b)^2 = a^2 - 2ab + b^2$
- Product of a sum and difference: $(a + b)(a - b) = a^2 - b^2$

Practice

Students: Pages 334–339

What do you remember?

1 Complete:

The distributive property states $a(b + c) = a \cdot \square + a \cdot \square$

2   a   Evaluate $5(12 - 6)$ b   Evaluate $5 \cdot 12 - 5 \cdot 6$
  c   Complete $5(12 - 6) = 5 \cdot \square - 5 \cdot \square$

3 Distribute:

  a $-m(m + 1)$
  b $y(y - 9)$
  c $7wy(y + w)$
  d $y(y - 4) + 10$
  e $2a\left(\dfrac{a^2}{2} + \dfrac{a}{2} + 1\right)$
  f $\dfrac{2}{5}n\left(\dfrac{5}{10}n - \dfrac{1}{2}\right)$

4 The area of the whole rectangle is $16 \cdot 20 = 320$ units^2.

  a   Find the area of the shaded rectangle.
  b   Find the area of the unshaded rectangle.
  c   Find the sum of the two areas.
  d   Does $16(18 + 2) = 16 \cdot 18 + 16 \cdot 2$?

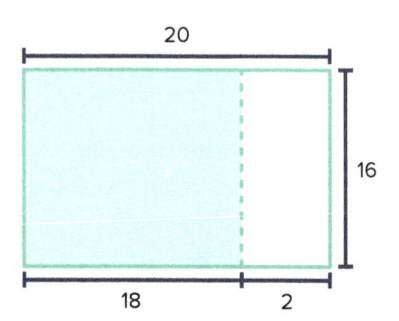

5 The area of this figure is represented by the expression $(y + 3)(y + 6)$.

  a   Find the area of:
    i   Rectangle A
    ii Rectangle B
    iii Rectangle C
    iv Rectangle D

  b   Write an equivalent, simplified expression for the area of the figure.

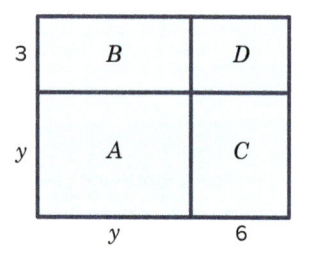

6 Match each product with an area model.

C

	x	3
x	$9x^2$	$3x$
-3	$-3x$	-9

D

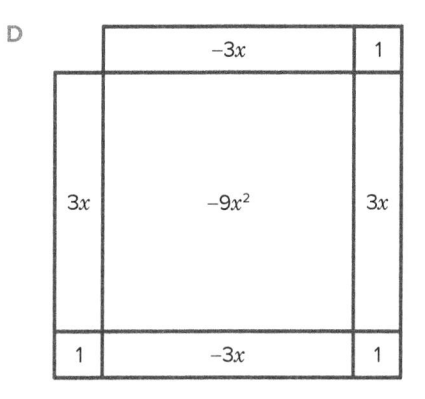

	$-3x$	1
$3x$	$-9x^2$	$3x$
1	$-3x$	1

  i $(3x + 1)(3x - 1)$ ii $(-3x + 1)(3x + 1)$ iii $(x + 3)(x - 3)$ iv $(x + 3)(x + 3)$

Let's practice

7 Simplify each product:
  - a $(7y - 6)(6y + 6)$
  - b $9(y + 8)(y + 2)$
  - c $(v + 5)(5v^2 - 3v - 5)$
  - d $4x(5x(x - 3) + 2x)$
  - e $\left(\frac{3}{5}m - 5\right)\left(\frac{1}{3}m - 3 + m^2\right)$
  - f $\frac{3}{4}y - \frac{1}{4}y(y - 2) + 6y^2$

8 Multiply and simplify:
  - a $(x^2 + 3)^2$
  - b $3x(7x - 5y)^2$
  - c $(3x - 8)(3x + 8)$
  - d $(-7y - 8)(-7y + 8)$
  - e $6(8x - 9y)(8x + 9y)$
  - f $(11 - a)(11 + a) - 10$
  - g $\left(x + \frac{1}{2}\right)^2$
  - h $\left(m + \frac{3}{4}\right)\left(m - \frac{3}{4}\right)$
  - i $\left(\frac{1}{8}y + \frac{1}{2}\right)\left(\frac{1}{8}y - \frac{1}{2}\right)$
  - j $9\left(\frac{1}{3}x + \frac{2}{3}y\right)^2$

9 Complete the expansion of the following perfect squares:
  - a $(x - 3)^2 = x^2 - \square x + \square$
  - b $(x + \square)^2 = x^2 + \square x + 36$

10 Simplify:
  - a $4(x + 8) - 2$
  - b $7 + 5(3x + 4)$
  - c $5 + 3(x + 4)$
  - d $8(3x + 4) - 6x$
  - e $34 + 9(4x - 5)$
  - f $5x - 8(2x - 3)$
  - g $9x - 5(2x + 3)$
  - h $-8(5x - 7) - 9$
  - i $4y + 5 + 6(y - 9)$
  - j $4(5(x - 3) + 2)$

11 Use the diagram and areas of rectangles to demonstrate that $4(x + 6) = 4x + 24$

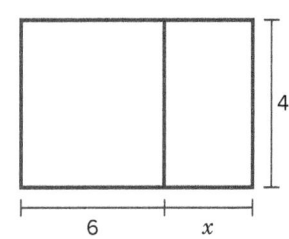

Rectangle with height 4, split into two parts of width 6 and x.

12 This rectangle has width $x + 2$ and length $x + 6$.

Use the diagram and areas of rectangles to find a simplified expression for $(x + 2)(x + 6)$.

Area I	Area II
Area III	Area IV

13 Multiply the following binomials using the algebra tiles.

  i Find the missing values to complete the visual representation of multiplying the binomials.
  ii Find the simplified expression for the binomials.

  a i The diagram shows the visual representation to simplify $(x + 2)(x - 3)$.

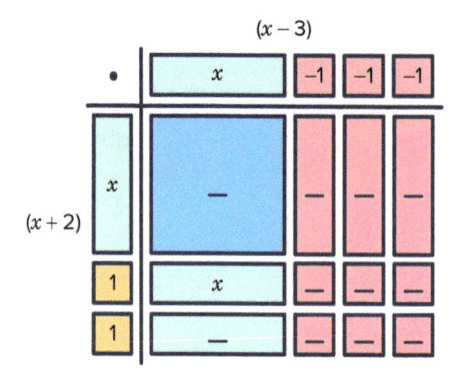

  ii $(x + 2)(x - 3) = \Box$

  b i The diagram shows the visual representation to simplify $(x - 4)(x - 3)$.

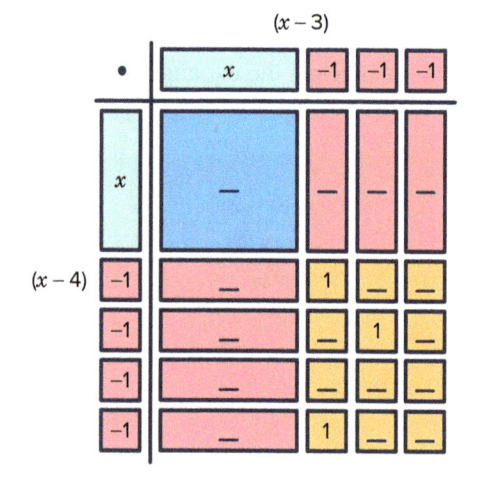

  ii $(x - 4)(x - 3) = \Box$

  c i The diagram shows the visual representation to simplify $(x + 2)(x + 5)$.

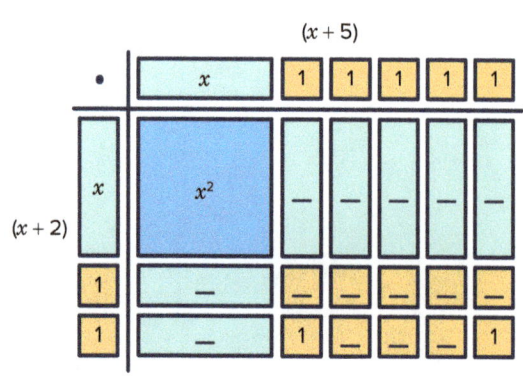

  ii $(x + 2)(x + 5) = \Box$

d i The diagram shows the visual representation to simplify $(x + 2)(2x - 1)$.

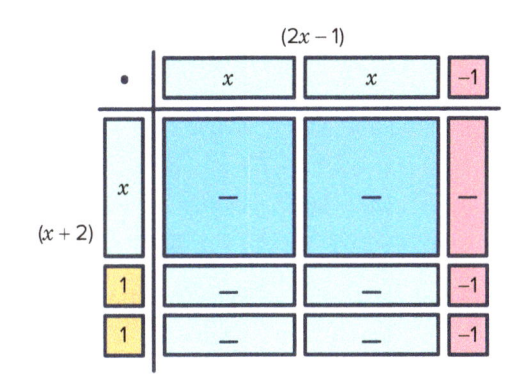

   ii $(x + 2)(2x - 1) = \square$

14 Anette decides to use the area model to complete a polynomial multiplication question, $(10x + 2)(10x + 3)$. To warm-up, she decides to try a simple integer example:

$12(13) =$

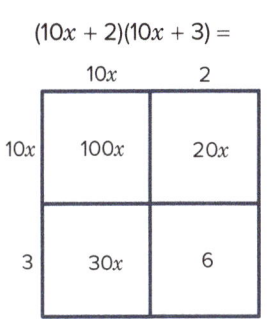

$100 + 20 + 30 + 6 = 156$

$(10x + 2)(10x + 3) =$

$100x + 20x + 30x + 6 = 150x + 6$

a State the error in Anette's polynomial product. Correct her work and solution.
b Show how you would set up the area model to find the product $(10x + 3)(x^2 + 10x + 2)$. Find the product using any method.

15 If Mackenzie creates a polynomial with degree 4 and Edgardo creates a polynomial with degree 3, state what we know about the product of their polynomials.

16 Sonya wants to extend the width and length of their vegetable patch by x ft. Their vegetable patch currently has a width of 5 ft and a length of 7 ft. For each of the following:
   i   Write a simplified expression in terms of x.
   ii State the unit of the answer to the expression from (i). Explain why you chose this unit.

   a The new length of the vegetable patch.
   b The area of the new vegetable patch.
   c The perimeter of the new vegetable patch.

17 The diagram shows a square with side length x.
   a What is the area of a square with side length x?
   b Write an expression for Area I.
   c Write an expression for Area II.
   d Show that $x(x - 4) + 4x = x^2$

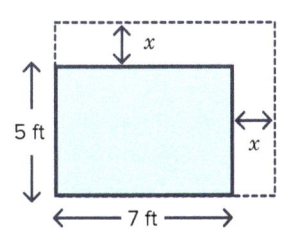

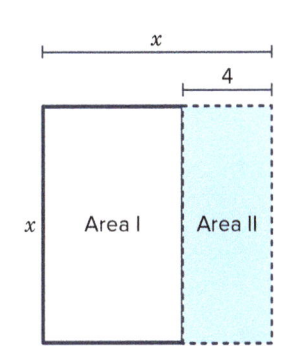

18 A square with side lengths measuring $x - 1$ centimeters has each side enlarged by a factor of 2. Write a simplified expression for the area of the new square.

6.02 Multiply polynomials   715

Let's extend our thinking

19. Find the missing values that make each equation true.
    a. $(x + \square)(x - 7) = x^2 - 3x + \square$
    b. $(2x - 1)(\square x - 5) = 2x^2 + \square x + 5$
    c. $(\square x + 3)(\square x + 6) = 12x^2 + 30x + \square$

20. Show the following results about special products are valid:
    a. $(a + b)^2 = a^2 + 2ab + b^2$
    b. $(a - b)^2 = a^2 - 2ab + b^2$
    c. $(a + b)(a - b) = a^2 - b^2$

21. Show how you can use one of the special products $(a \pm b)^2$ to find each perfect square without a calculator.
    a. 21^2
    b. 19^2
    c. 33^2
    d. 47^2

22. Write a simplified expression for the product of three consecutive integers, where the middle integer is m.

23. Consider the rectangle shown:

    Write a simplified expression for the area of the rectangle.

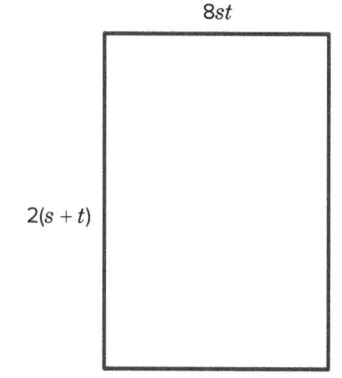

    $8st$

    $2(s + t)$

24. A rectangular garden has a length that is one foot less than twice the width.
    a. Write and simplify an expression for the area of the rectangle.
    b. A 2 foot border is to be placed all around the garden. Write and simplify an expression for the area of the border.
    c. The landscaper designing the garden has 100 square feet of pavers to use for the border. Determine the largest garden the landscaper can border before running out of pavers. Assume the landscaper will only use positive-integer dimensions.

25. A flat rate large box from USPS has dimensions of 1 ft × 1 ft × 5.5 in. If Jerome decides to put a layer of insulation in his box x inches thick, write a simplified polynomial expression that models
    a. The dimensions of the open volume left in the box in inches.
    b. The volume he has left in his box to fill.

26. Consider the following problem: "Find two binomials whose product results in a polynomial with 5 terms".
    a. Yao was given the problem, but they think it's impossible. State whether you agree or disagree. Explain.
    b. Create two different products of two polynomials that results in an answer with exactly 5 terms.

27. Determine whether each statement is always, sometimes, or never true. Explain your reasoning with examples.
    a. Two polynomials multiplied together will result in a polynomial
    b. A term with a negative exponent is a polynomial
    c. A polynomial multiplied by a non-polynomial will result in a polynomial

28. Explain how the area of a square given a binomial side length will always be a special product.

29. Polynomial multiplication can be used to find the total area of a rectangle that has a border, where the length and width each represent a factor in the product.
    a. Write an algebraic model that can be used to find the total area of a square with an unknown side length and a border with an unknown border width.
    b. Use your model to find the total area of a square with a side length of $2m + 1$ and a border width of 3.

30. Determine whether the conjectures are true or false. Create algebraic expressions to justify your response.
    a. The product of any two consecutive even numbers is one more than a perfect square.
    b. The product of any two consecutive odd numbers is one less than a perfect square.

Answers

6.02 Multiply polynomials

What do you remember?

1. a $a(b+c) = a \cdot b + a \cdot c$

2. a 30
   b 30
   c $5(12-6) = 5 \cdot 12 - 5 \cdot 6$

3. a $-m^2 - m$
   b $y^2 - 9y$
   c $7wy^2 + 7w^2y$
   d $y^2 - 4y + 10$
   e $a^3 + a^2 + 2a$
   f $\dfrac{n^2}{5} - \dfrac{n}{5}$

4. a 288 units^2
   b 32 units^2
   c 320 units^2
   d Yes

5. a i $A = y^2$
      ii $B = 3y$
      iii $C = 6y$
      iv $D = 18$
   b $y^2 + 9y + 18$

6. i A   ii D   iii C   iv B

Let's practice

7. a $42y^2 + 6y - 36$
   b $9y^2 + 90y + 144$
   c $5v^3 + 22v^2 - 20v - 25$
   d $20x^3 - 52x^2$
   f $\dfrac{3}{5}m^3 - \dfrac{24}{5}m^2 - \dfrac{52}{15}m + 15$
   g $\dfrac{5}{4}y + \dfrac{23}{4}y^2$

8. a $x^4 + 6x^2 + 9$
   b $147x^3 - 210x^2y + 75xy^2$
   c $9x^2 - 64$
   d $49y^2 - 64$
   e $384x^2 - 486y^2$
   f $111 - a^2$
   g $x^2 + x + \dfrac{1}{4}$
   h $m^2 - \dfrac{9}{16}$
   i $\dfrac{y^2}{64} - \dfrac{1}{4}$
   j $x^2 + 4xy + 4y^2$

9. a $(x-3)^2 = x^2 - 6x + 9$
   b $(x+6)^2 = x^2 + 12x + 36$

10. a $4x + 30$
    b $15x + 27$
    c $3x + 17$
    d $18x + 32$
    e $36x - 11$
    f $-11x + 24$
    g $-x - 15$
    h $-40x + 47$
    i $10y - 49$
    j $20x - 52$

11. Total area = $4(6 + x)$
    Area small rectangle = $4x$
    Area large rectangle = 24
    Total area equals Area small rectangle plus Area large rectangle
    Therefore $4(x + 6) = 4x + 24$.

12. $(x+2)(x+6) = x^2 + 8x + 12$

13. a i [algebra tiles diagram showing $(x+2)(x-3)$]
       ii $(x+2)(x-3) = x^2 - x - 6$
    b i [algebra tiles diagram showing $(x-4)(x-3)$]
       ii $(x-4)(x-3) = x^2 - 7x + 12$
    c i [algebra tiles diagram showing $(x+2)(x+5)$]
       ii $(x+2)(x+5) = x^2 + 7x + 10$
    d i [algebra tiles diagram showing $(x+2)(2x-1)$]
       ii $(x+2)(2x-1) = 2x^2 + 3x - 2$

14 a $(10x)(10x) = 100x^2$, but Anette put $100x$ instead. Her final answer should have been $100x^2 + 20x + 30x + 6 = 100x^2 + 50x + 6$.

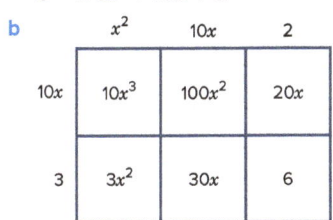

  b

	x^2	$10x$	2
$10x$	$10x^3$	$100x^2$	$20x$
3	$3x^2$	$30x$	6

  $10x^3 + 100x^2 + 20x + 3x^2 + 30x + 6 =$
  $10x^3 + 103x^2 + 50x + 6$

15 The result will be a polynomial with degree 7.

16 a i $7 + x$

  ii The units will be ft, since we don't need to change the units as we are only adding x ft to each side of the vegetable patch which is already measured in feet.

  b i $x^2 + 12x + 35$

  ii The units will be ft^2, as we are finding the product of two lengths.

  c i $4x + 24$

  ii The units will be ft, as we are adding two lengths.

17 a $A = x^2$ **b** $x(x - 4)$ **c** $4x$

  d Area I plus Area II equals Area of Square. Therefore $x(x - 4) + 4x = x^2$

18 $4x^2 - 8x + 4$ cm^2

Let's extend our thinking

19 a 4 and −28 **b** 1 and −11

  c Answers may vary. 2, 6, and 18 is one possibility. 3, 4, and 18 is another.

20 a $(a + b)^2 = (a + b)(a + b)$
  $= a(a + b) + b(a + b)$
  $= a^2 + ab + ab + b^2$
  $= a^2 + 2ab + b^2$

  b $(a - b)^2 = (a - b)(a - b)$
  $= a(a - b) - b(a - b)$
  $= a^2 - ab - ba + b^2$
  $= a^2 - 2ab + b^2$

  c $(a + b)(a - b) = a(a - b) + b(a - b)$
  $= a^2 - ab + ba - b^2$
  $= a^2 - b^2$

21 a $(20 + 1)^2 = (20^2 + 2(20) + 1) = 441$

  b $(20 - 1)^2 = (20^2 - 2(20) + 1) = 361$

  c $(30 + 3)^2 = (30^2 + 2(90) + 9) = 1089$

  d $(50 - 3)^2 = (50^2 - 2(150) + 9) = 2209$

22 $m^3 - m$

23 $(16s^2t + 16st^2)$ units^2

24 a If x feet represents the width of the garden, then the area will be $x(2x - 1) = 2x^2 - x$ square feet.

  b $(x + 4)(2x + 3) - x(2x - 1) = 12x + 12$

  c A garden with a width of 7′ and a length of 13′ will need 96 square feet of pavers to create a 2′ border.

25 a The new dimensions in inches are $(12 - 2x)$, $(12 - 2x)$, and $(5.5 - 2x)$.

  b Jerome will have a volume of $(-8x^3 + 118x^2 - 552x + 792)$ in^3 left to fill.

26 a Agree. The maximum number of terms that can be produced by multiplying two binomials is $2 \cdot 2 = 4$ if no terms combine.

  b Answers will vary. A monomial multiplied by a five term polynomial will always results in a five term polynomial. Another possible solution is a binomial multiplied by a trinomial that results in a 4th degree polynomial with exactly one pair of terms combining.
  For example,
  $(x^2 + 3)(x^2 - 2x + 1) = x^4 - 2x^3 + 2x^2 - 6x + 3$

27 a Always true. A polynomial is a collection of terms in the form mx^n where m is a real number and n is a non-negative integer. When multiplying polynomials together, terms are multiplied, and if they are the same variable, their exponents are added together, so the exponents will still be non-negative integers. That means all terms in the resulting polynomial will also be a collection of terms in the form mx^n and will also be a polynomial.

  b Never true. A polynomial can never have terms with negative exponents, as a polynomial is a collection of terms in the form mx^n where m is a real number and n is a non-negative integer.

  c Sometimes true. Consider the example $(4x^3 + x) \cdot x^{-1} = 4x^2 + 1$. If a polynomial is multiplied by a non-polynomial of the form ax^{-b}, where a is a real number, and b is a positive integer whose magnitude is less than or equal to the magnitude of the exponent of the term with the lowest degree in the polynomial, the result will be a polynomial.

28 The area of a square is $A = s^2$ where s is the side length of the square. If s is a binomial such as $(a + b)$ then the area of the square is the special product $(a + b)^2$.

29 a Variable choices will vary.
  Let x represent the side length of the square and let y represent the width of the border. Then the area of the square will always be $(x + y)^2 = x^2 + 2xy + y^2$.

  b Let $x = (2m + 1)$ and let $y = 3$ so that $(x + y)^2$ becomes $(2x + 1 + 3)^2 = (2x + 4)^2$. Then the total area is $4x^2 + 16x + 16$.

30 **a** False: $(2x)(2x+2) = 4x^2 + 4x$. Although $4x^2$ is a perfect square since both 4 and x^2 are perfect squares, $4x$ will not be a perfect square if x is not and there is no constant value that would imply +1.

Alternatively, note that $4x^2 + 4x + 1 = (2x+1)^2$. So the product is actually one less than a perfect square.

b True. $(2x-1)(2x+1) = 4x^2 - 1 = (2x)^2 - 1$

6.03 Divide polynomials by a monomial

Subtopic overview

Lesson narrative

When dividing a polynomial by a monomial, each term of the polynomial is divided by the monomial, after which each individual fraction left over is simplified using the rules of exponents. By the end of this lesson, students will be able to divide a polynomial by a monomial.

Learning objective

Students: Page 340

After this lesson, you will be able to...
- divide a polynomial by a monomial.

Key vocabulary

- common factor
- dividend
- divisor

Essential understanding

Polynomials can be divided using steps similar to those used when dividing real numbers.

Standards

This subtopic addresses the following Virginia 2023 Mathematics Standards of Learning standards.

Mathematical process goals

MPG4 — Mathematical Reasoning

Teachers can integrate this goal into their instruction by showing students the connection between factoring and dividing in the context of polynomials. They can guide students to see that factoring a polynomial is essentially the reverse process of multiplying, which is connected to division. This understanding can be reinforced by highlighting how the factored form of a polynomial can be used to simplify division problems. By relating these different mathematical procedures, students can start to see the interconnectedness of various mathematical concepts and techniques.

MPG5 — Mathematical Representations

Teachers can integrate this goal by using a variety of methods to represent mathematical ideas. For example, demonstrating the division of polynomials by a monomial using concrete manipulatives and pictorial representations. They should also encourage students to make connections between these different representations, such as between the symbolic notation and the concrete model.

Content standards

A.EO.2 — The student will perform operations on and factor polynomial expressions in one variable.

A.EO.2d — Determine the quotient of polynomials, using a monomial or binomial divisor, or a completely factored divisor.

Prior connections

8.PFA.1 — The student will represent, simplify, and generate equivalent algebraic expressions in one variable.

A.EO.1 — The student will represent verbal quantitative situations algebraically and evaluate these expressions for given replacement values of the variables.

Future connections

A2.EO.3 — The student will perform operations on polynomial expressions in two or more variables and factor polynomial expressions in one and two variables.

Lesson Preparation

Suggested review

Depending on your students' level of prior knowledge, consider revisiting the following lessons:

- **Algebra 1** — 5.03 Quotient of powers

Tools

You may find these tools helpful:
- Scientific calculator

Student lesson & teacher guide

Divide by a monomial

Students are introduced to the method of dividing a polynomial by a monomial by dividing each term of the polynomial by the monomial separately. Area models with algebra tiles and written steps are then used to demonstrate a visual way of dividing a polynomial by a monomial.

Students: Page 340

6.03 Divide polynomials by a monomial

After this lesson, you will be able to...
- divide a polynomial by a monomial.

Divide by a monomial

To divide a polynomial by a monomial, divide each term of the polynomial by the monomial. To do this, use the quotient rule and divide coefficients and subtract exponents with the same base.

> **Dividing a polynomial by a monomial**
> $$\frac{a+b}{c} = \frac{a}{c} + \frac{b}{c}$$

Polynomial division can be modeled with algebra tiles.

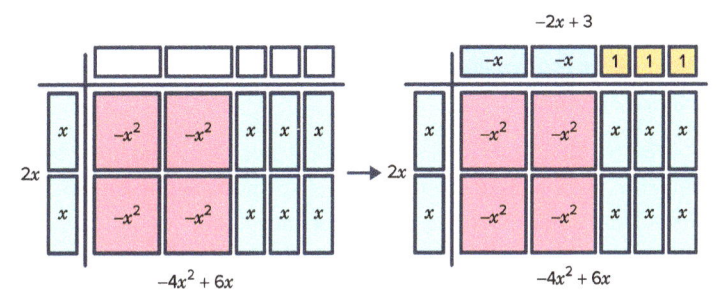

Create an area model where:
1. The tiles on the inside add up to the dividend (numerator).
2. The tiles on one side add up to the divisor (denominator).
3. The sum of the tiles along the other side must be the quotient (the result of the division).

Note: Final answers are usually written without any negative exponents.

Reviewing division of exponent rules and connections to polynomials
Targeted instructional strategies

In previous section, students practiced dividing monomial expressions by dividing or reducing coefficients, and subtracting exponents. Students should begin this section by practicing dividing monomial expressions, and a helpful exercise is to provide several monomial terms, and ask students to divide them by the same monomial. For example:

Divide each of the following by $2y$:

$$-14y^5 \quad 2y^3 \quad -6y^3 \quad 4y$$

Ask students to then consider the following problem:

$$\frac{-14y^5 + 2y^3 - 6y^3 + 4y}{2y}$$

Ask students to connect their answers to the previous exercise to the new problem, joining their answers together with addition or subtraction.

6.03 Divide polynomials by a monomial 723

mathspace.co

Stronger and clearer each time
English language learner support

Students should respond to the following prompt:

What steps do we take to divide a polynomial by a monomial?

$$\frac{12x^4 + 6x^3 - 9x^2 + 3x}{3x}$$

Students begin by individually solving the problem and writing a description of their steps either after or next to the steps.

In the first meeting, pair students to discuss their initial explanations. Encourage students to ask each other questions for clarity, such as:
- What happens to each term of the polynomial?
- How do you handle each part of the division?

Students revise their explanations based on the discussion. Students should rotate pairs and follow the same editing structure for 2 – 3 rotations. Students should push for more precision, ensuring their step-by-step instructions are clear and concise.

Have students write a final, detailed explanation of the process, incorporating feedback from their discussions.

Polynomial division by a monomial using color coding
Student with disabilities support

Students can visually follow the division process and recognize patterns using color coding. Ask students to highlight each term of a polynomial division problem in different colors. Guide them to divide each colored term by the monomial and use the same color to highlight the simplified terms.

An example of this method is shown:

$$\frac{8y^4 + 16y^3 + 24y^2}{4y} = \frac{8y^4}{4y} + \frac{16y^3}{4y} + \frac{24y^2}{4y}$$
$$= 2y^3 + 4y^2 + 6y$$

Having students mark their answer space with their colors ahead of time will also help students remember all terms as they simplify and write their final answer.

Disappearing Constants
Address student misconceptions

When simplifying, many students have trouble remembering when a value of 1 does not need to be written in the simplified polynomial expression.

For example, many students will believe that the following the are same terms.

$$\frac{15x^5 - 6x^3 + 3x^2}{3x^2} = \frac{15x^5 - 6x^3 + \cancel{3x^2}}{\cancel{3x^2}}$$

This will give a final polynomial answer of $5x^3 - 2x$, when the final answer should be $5x^3 - 2x + 1$.

Encourage students to write out each term being divided separately, such as $\frac{15x^5}{3x^2} - \frac{6x^3}{3x^2} + \frac{3x^2}{3x^2}$.

724 Mathspace Virginia SOL Algebra 1 Teacher Edition
mathspace.co

Examples

Students: Page 340

Example 1

Simplify the following: $\dfrac{3x^5 + 4x^2}{x}$

Create a strategy

Apply the rule $\dfrac{a+b}{c} = \dfrac{a}{c} + \dfrac{b}{c}$.

Apply the idea

$\dfrac{3x^5 + 4x^2}{x} = \dfrac{3x^5}{x} + \dfrac{4x^2}{x}$ Divide each term by x

$= 3x^4 + 4x$ Simplify

Since there are no negative exponents and the expression is already in standard form, the final answer is $3x^4 + 4x$.

Purpose
Divide a polynomial by a monomial with a coefficient and power of 1.

Expected mistakes
Students may add an x to each term rather than take one away. Encourage students to write out the variables with the operations performed on the exponents.

Reflecting with students
Dividing by a monomial of x is similar to taking an x out of each term. Discuss with students how expanded form can be used to divide variables as a visual exercise.

Advanced learners: Closure of polynomials
Targeted instructional strategies   use with Example 1

Introduce advanced learners to the term "closure" of polynomials if it was not introduced in the previous lessons. We say that polynomials are closed under addition, subtraction, and multiplication because the sum, difference, or product of polynomials will also be a polynomial.

Then, ask students whether they think polynomials are closed under division. Remind them of the definition of a polynomial: The sum or difference of terms which have variables raised to non-negative integer powers and which have coefficients that are constant.

If students only consider the examples in the lesson, they might incorrectly conclude that polynomials are closed under division. Provide them with an example like the one shown:

$$\dfrac{5x^5 - x^4 + 2x^2 + 1}{x}$$

Then, ask questions such as:
- Is the dividend a polynomial? How do you know?
- Is the divisor a polynomial?
- Is the quotient a polynomial? Why or why not?

Students should use the negative exponent rule to show that the last term of the quotient has a negative exponent on the variable, so it is not a polynomial. Thus, a polynomial divided by another polynomial is not always a polynomial, so polynomials are not closed under division.

Students: Page 341

Example 2

Simplify the following: $\dfrac{6y^3 - 15y^2 + 24y}{3y}$

Create a strategy

Apply the rule $\dfrac{a+b}{c} = \dfrac{a}{c} + \dfrac{b}{c}$.

Apply the idea

$\dfrac{6y^3 - 15y^2 + 24y}{3y} = \dfrac{6y^3}{3y} - \dfrac{15y^2}{3y} + \dfrac{24y}{3y}$ Divide each term by $3y$

$= 2y^2 - 5y + 8$ Simplify

Since there are no negative exponents and the expression is already in standard form, the final answer is $2y^2 - 5y + 8$.

Reflect and check

We can check the answer by multiplying it with the monomial in the denominator. The product should be the numerator in the original expression.

$3y(2y^2 - 5y + 8) = 6y^3 - 15y^2 + 24y$ Check

Purpose

Divide a polynomial by a monomial.

Expected mistakes

Students may not take out the y from the $24y$ term when dividing by $3y$. Encourage students to cross out variables where possible as a visual reminder when a term no longer needs a variable.

Reflecting with students

In many cases, dividing by a monomial can be similar to taking out a greatest common factor. Give students a preview of factoring by expanding the polynomial's terms into a product of primes and expanded variables, and demonstrate how dividing cancels out similar factors.

Expand and cancel to divide a polynomial by a monomial use with Example 2
Targeted instructional strategies

As an additional method of solution, show students expanding each term in the polynomial and cancel terms to find a solution. For example, walk students though each step of the problem shown:

$\dfrac{16h^3 - 18h^4}{2h^2} = \dfrac{16h^3}{2h^2} - \dfrac{18h^6}{2h^2}$ Write as separate quotients

$= \dfrac{2 \cdot 2 \cdot 2 \cdot 2 \cdot h \cdot h \cdot h}{2 \cdot h \cdot h} - \dfrac{2 \cdot 3 \cdot 3 \cdot h \cdot h \cdot h \cdot h \cdot h \cdot h}{2 \cdot h \cdot h}$ Expand terms

$= \dfrac{\cancel{2} \cdot 2 \cdot 2 \cdot 2 \cdot \cancel{h} \cdot \cancel{h} \cdot h}{\cancel{2} \cdot \cancel{h} \cdot \cancel{h}} - \dfrac{\cancel{2} \cdot 3 \cdot 3 \cdot \cancel{h} \cdot \cancel{h} \cdot h \cdot h \cdot h \cdot h}{\cancel{2} \cdot \cancel{h} \cdot \cancel{h}}$ Cancel matching factors in the numerator and denominator

$= 2 \cdot 2 \cdot 2 \cdot h - 3 \cdot 3 \cdot h \cdot h \cdot h \cdot h$ Rewrite with remaining factors

$= 8h - 9h^4$ Simplify products

Students: Page 341

> **Example 3**

The triangle shown has an area of $13n^3 + 11n^2 + 29n$.
Find a simplified polynomial expression for its height.

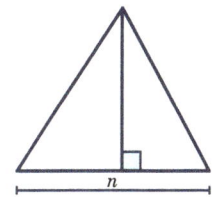

Create a strategy

Substitute the expressions into the area of triangle formula $A = \frac{1}{2}bh$.

Apply the idea

$A = \frac{1}{2}bh$	Write the area of triangle formula
$13n^3 + 11n^2 + 29n = \frac{1}{2} \cdot n \cdot h$	Substitute $A = 13n^3 + 11n^2 + 29n$ and $b = n$
$(13n^3 + 11n^2 + 29n) \times 2 = \left(\frac{1}{2} \cdot n \cdot h\right) \cdot 2$	Multiply both sides by 2
$26n^3 + 22n^2 + 58n = nh$	Evaluate the multiplication
$\frac{26n^3 + 22n^2 + 58n}{n} = \frac{nh}{n}$	Divide both sides by n
$26n^2 + 22n + 58 = h$	Evaluate the division
$h = 26n^2 + 22n + 58$ units	Symmetric property of equality

Purpose

Use the formula for area of a triangle and expressions to represent area and the base in order to solve for height.

Reflecting with students

Discuss with students how the process could be applied for the area of different polygons, such as a rectangle.

Students: Page 341

> **💡 Idea summary**
>
> When dividing a polynomial by a monomial, we divide each term of the polynomial by the monomial then simplify each individual fraction using the rules of exponents.

Practice

Students: Pages 342–344

What do you remember?

1 Determine whether each statement regarding the division of polynomials by monomials is true or false. Justify your conclusion.

    a When dividing a polynomial by a monomial, it is possible to reduce the number of terms.

    b The degree of the polynomial will always decrease after dividing by a monomial

    c The result of dividing a polynomial by a monomial will have a constant term if the degree of the monomial matches the degree of any term in the polynomial.

    d The result of dividing a polynomial by a monomial will be another polynomial.

2 Explain the difference between the two expressions:

$$\frac{5x^2 + 10x + 5}{5} \text{ and } 5x^2 + 10x + \frac{5}{5}$$

3 Simplify the following:

    a $\dfrac{70v}{710}$ **b** $\dfrac{49x}{35}$

    c $\dfrac{16z}{80}$ **d** $\dfrac{25k}{80}$

4 Simplify the following:

    a $\dfrac{15k}{20k}$ **b** $\dfrac{28d}{35d}$

    c $\dfrac{9l}{15l}$ **d** $\dfrac{7p^8}{14p^5}$

    e $\dfrac{42y}{18y}$ **f** $\dfrac{18p^7}{9p^3}$

    g $\dfrac{8k}{12k}$ **h** $\dfrac{20r^2}{-25r}$

    i $-\dfrac{9x^3y^3}{12x^2y}$ **j** $\dfrac{4q^6}{8q^4}$

    k $\dfrac{27n^3m^{11}}{-54nm^2}$ **l** $-\dfrac{15x^4y}{25x^2y^2}$

5 Use algebra tiles to model the equation $\dfrac{6x^2 - 8x}{2x} = 3x - 4$.

Let's Practice

6 Find the missing length which represents the quotient in each area model.

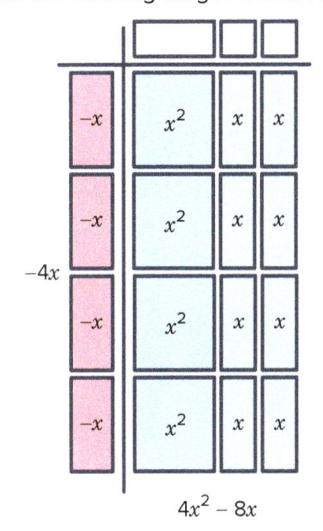

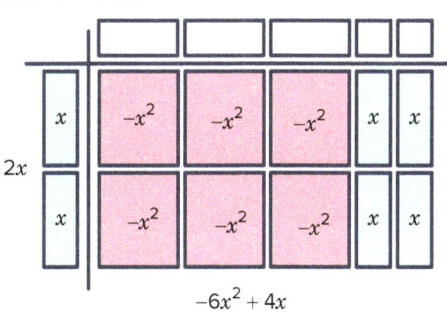

a

$4x^2 - 8x$

b

$-6x^2 + 4x$

7 Simplify the following:

a $\dfrac{15k}{20k}$

b $\dfrac{70v}{710}$

c $\dfrac{3}{4}xy \div \dfrac{1}{4}y$

d $\dfrac{18p^7}{9p^3}$

e $\dfrac{30mn^2}{9m^2n}$

f $\left(\dfrac{1}{3}x^3 + \dfrac{2}{3}x^5\right) \div x$

g $\dfrac{18x^3 - 12x^2 + 24}{3}$

h $\dfrac{80z^2 + 10z}{10z}$

i $(30j^2) \div (35j)$

j $\left(\dfrac{1}{2}m\right) \div \left(\dfrac{5}{4}m\right)$

k $(b^3 - 4b^2 + 2b) \div (4b)$

l $(9w^3v^2 + 45w^2v^2 + 18wv) \div (9wv)$

m $\dfrac{z+8}{8}$

n $\dfrac{3x^3 + 4x^2}{x}$

o $\dfrac{48t^2 - 16t}{96t^3}$

p $\dfrac{18x^3 - 12x^2 + 24}{3}$

q $\dfrac{12m^2 + 6m}{18m}$

r $\dfrac{20x^4 - 35x^3 + 15x^2 + 30x}{5x}$

8 Fill in the blanks:

a $\dfrac{\Box x^6 - \Box x^7}{3x^\Box} = 5x^3 - 3x^4$

b $\dfrac{\Box x^4 - \Box x^5}{3x^\Box} = 4x^2 - 3x^3$

9 Consider the following statement $y^5 \div y = y^4$ for all nonzero real numbers y.
  a Determine whether the statement is true or false.
  b Is the statement still true when y is zero?

6.03 Divide polynomials by a monomial

10 Consider the area of the following rectangles:

Find a polynomial expression for its length.

a Area = $(4x^4 - 8x)$ square units

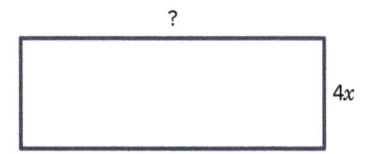

b Area = $(6x^3 + 4x^2 + 10x + 14)$ square units

11 The triangle shown has an area of $12n^3 + 18n^2 + 5n$. Find a polynomial expression for its height.

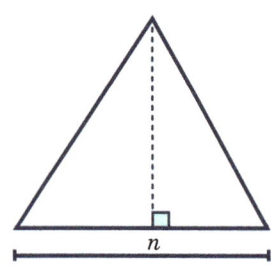

Let's extend our thinking

12 Fill in the blanks to make a true algebraic statement.

a $\dfrac{\square}{5ab} = 6bc$

b $\dfrac{2x^3 - 10x^2 + 8x}{\square} = x^2 - 5x + 4$

c $\dfrac{\square + 20m^2n^2 + 21m^3n}{14\square} = n^2 + \dfrac{10}{7}mn + \square$

13 Consider the following statement: $x^9 \div x^3 = x^3$ for all nonzero real numbers x.

a What is $x^9 \div x^3$ actually equal to?

b Identify a nonzero real number for which the original statement is *true*.

14 Consider the problem $\dfrac{24x^6}{6x^2}$.

Identify and correct the error in each of the following student's work.

Lawrence:

$\dfrac{24x^6}{6x^2} = 18x^4$

Marika:

$\dfrac{24x^6}{6x^2} = 4x^3$

15 Create an example and describe the result when a polynomial is divided by a monomial that:

a Has a coefficient larger than the coefficients of the terms in the polynomial.

b Has a variable with a larger degree than the terms in the polynomial.

Answers

6.03 Divide polynomials by a monomial

What do you remember?

1. a False. We can't create a coefficient of zero when dividing a single term of a polynomial by a monomial so no terms will eliminate.
   b False. If you divide by a constant monomial the degree will not change.
   c True. Suppose the monomial has degree n and the term has degree n. Then $\frac{ax^n}{bx^n} = \frac{a}{b}$ will be a constant.
   d False. If the degree of the monomial is larger than the degree of any of the terms in the polynomial the result will not be a polynomial.

2. In the first expression we are dividing all terms in the numerator by 5. In the second expression only the constant term at the end is being divided by 5.

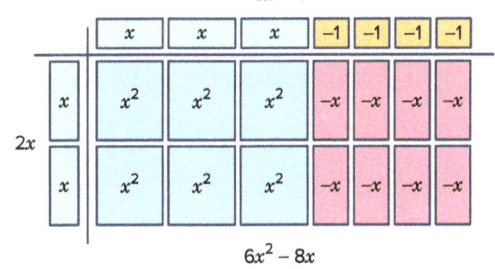

3. a $\frac{7v}{71}$ b $\frac{7x}{5}$ c $\frac{z}{5}$ d $\frac{5k}{16}$

4. a $\frac{3}{4}$ b $\frac{4}{5}$ c $\frac{3}{5}$ d $\frac{p^3}{2}$
   e $\frac{7}{3}$ f $2p^4$ g $\frac{2}{3}$ h $-\frac{4r}{5}$
   i $-\frac{3xy^2}{4}$ j $\frac{q^2}{2}$ k $-\frac{n^2m^9}{2}$ l $-\frac{3x^2}{5y}$

5. [algebra tiles diagram showing $\frac{6x^2 - 8x}{2x} = 3x - 4$]

Let's practice

6. a $-x + 2$ b $-3x + 2$

7. a $\frac{3}{4}$ b $\frac{7v}{71}$
   c $3x$ d $2p^4$
   e $\frac{10n}{3m}$ f $\frac{x^2}{3} + \frac{2}{3}x^4$
   g $6x^3 - 4x^2 + 8$ h $8z + 1$
   i $\frac{6j}{7}$ j $\frac{2}{5}$

   k $\frac{1}{4}b^2 - b + \frac{1}{2}$ l $w^2v + 5wv + 2$
   m $\frac{z}{8} + 1$ n $3x^2 + 4x$
   o $\frac{3t-1}{6t^2}$ p $6x^3 - 4x^2 + 8$
   q $\frac{2m+1}{3}$ r $4x^3 - 7x^2 + 3x + 6$

8. a $\frac{15x^6 - 9x^7}{3x^3} = 5x^3 - 3x^4$ b $\frac{12x^4 - 9x^5}{3x^2} = 4x^2 - 3x^3$

9. a True b No

10. a $(x^3 - 2)$ units b $(3x^3 + 2x^2 + 5x + 7)$ units

11. $24n^2 + 36n - 10$ units

Let's extend our thinking

12. a $\frac{30ab^2c}{5ab} = 6bc$
    b $\frac{2x^3 - 10x^2 + 8x}{2x} = x^2 - 5x + 4$
    c $\frac{14mn^3 + 20m^2n^2 + 21m^3n}{14mn} = n^2 + \frac{10}{7}mn + \frac{3}{2}m^2$

13. a x^6 b 1

14. Lawrence subtracted both the coefficients and the exponents of the variable. However, when dividing by a monomial the coefficients should be divided and the exponents should be subtracted. Marika, on the other hand, divided both the coefficients and the exponents when she should have divided the coefficients and subtracted the exponents.

15. a Each term of the resulting polynomial will have a fractional coefficient.
    $$\frac{x^2 + 2}{4} = \frac{1}{4}x^2 + \frac{1}{2}$$
    b The terms will have negative exponents and the expression will no longer be a polynomial.
    $$\frac{x^2 + 2}{x^3} = x^{-1} + 2x^{-3} = \frac{1}{x} + \frac{2}{x^3}$$

6.04 Factor GCF

Subtopic overview

Lesson narrative

In this lesson, students will learn about make generalizations about dividing polynomials by a monomial through the modeling of contextual situations involving dividing polynomial expressions by common factors and structures of polynomials. In the lesson, students will make mathematical connections to greatest common factors of integers and the distributive property to rewrite polynomial expressions in factored form. Students will be able to justify the equivalence of polynomial expressions and engage in error analysis. By the end of the lesson, students will be able to create polynomial expressions to represent quantities for contextual situations and work flexibly between standard and factored forms of polynomial expressions, as needed.

Learning objective

Students: Page 345

After this lesson, you will be able to...
- factor out the GCF from a polynomial expression.

Key vocabulary

- common factor
- factor
- greatest common factor (GCF)

Essential understanding

Factoring out the greatest common factor provides the foundation for all other techniques for factoring quadratic expressions.

Standards

This subtopic addresses the following Virginia 2023 Mathematics Standards of Learning standards.

Mathematical process goals

MPG1 — Mathematical Problem Solving

Teachers can incorporate problem-solving into their lessons by presenting real-life scenarios that require factoring polynomials to solve. For example, propose a problem where students must use their knowledge of polynomials and factoring to determine the dimensions of a rectangular garden given its area and length. Encourage students to apply their skills to solve these problems and discuss the strategies they used.

MPG3 — Mathematical Reasoning

Teachers can incorporate mathematical reasoning into their lessons by asking students to validate the steps they took to factor a polynomial. For example, after factoring out the GCF, students could be asked to use the distributive property to confirm the correctness of their factoring. This encourages them to think critically and make logical connections between mathematical procedures.

MPG4 — Mathematical Connections

Teachers can help students make connections by relating the process of factoring polynomials to prior knowledge of algebraic expressions and operations on polynomials. Additionally, teachers could highlight how factoring polynomials can be applied to other areas of math and real-world situations, such as calculating the area or volume of shapes.

Content standards

A.EO.2 — The student will perform operations on and factor polynomial expressions in one variable.

A.EO.2c — Factor completely first- and second-degree polynomials in one variable with integral coefficients.

After factoring out the greatest common factor (GCF), leading coefficients should have no more than four factors.

Prior connections

8.PFA.1 — The student will represent, simplify, and generate equivalent algebraic expressions in one variable.

A.EO.1 — The student will represent verbal quantitative situations algebraically and evaluate these expressions for given replacement values of the variables.

Future connections

A2.EO.3 — The student will perform operations on polynomial expressions in two or more variables and factor polynomial expressions in one and two variables.

Engage Activity

Food hall trays   60 mins

Students will design various rectangular food trays with a specific area and find the length and width of each one.

Understanding and skills

Will use
- Dividing rational numbers.
- Adding, subtracting, and multiplying polynomials.

Will develop
- Dividing a polynomial expression by a monomial with integer coefficients.

Preparation and materials
- Open and complete the student preview, anticipating classroom responses.
- **Materials:** Paper, pencil (recommended)

> **Support students with disabilities**
> **Support conceptual processing - understand mathematical relationships and make connections**
>
> To support students in making connections between visualizing how to find the side lengths of a rectangle, remind students of the area model used for multiplying polynomials. This will help students check if their side lengths have the desired area as well as begin to generalize reasoning for how to divide polynomials by a monomial.

> **Support for English language learners**
> **Critique, correct, and clarify**

Before students share their responses, display the following incorrect calculation and reasoning:

A food tray with side lengths $10xy$ and $10x^2y + 6x$ has an area of $20x^3y + 60xy^2$.

Ask students to identify the errors, critique the reasoning, and write a short explanation of how the students' reasoning could be improved.

Classroom guide

Hook

Notice and wonder • 5 mins

Students write observations about an equation where the left hand side is in factored form and the right hand side is in expanded form. There is a unknown factor on the left hand side of the equation.

What do you notice? What do you wonder?

$(x + 3)(?) = x^3 + 3x^2$

Slide 1 from Student Engage Activity

Implementation details

Students may notice that the left side of the equation is in factored form, and the right side is in expanded form. They may wonder what the value of ? is, or wonder what values of x make the equation true.

Encourage students to think about what the unkown value represented by the question mark would be. Highlight responses that explain why $? = x^2$.

Launch

5 mins

Amuse-me amusement parks plans to design rectangular food trays for the park's food hall. They want to create multiple types of rectangular food trays with the same area. Each food tray will consist of two sections, which will vary in dimensions.

Slide 2 from Student Engage Activity

Give students time to read the information individually before forming groups.

Important mathematical concepts: Length, width, area, dimensions

Important contextual information: Food trays

Suggested grouping: Form groups of 3 or 4 and assign numbers

> **Continue when**
> Students have read the Launch and understand the context of the problem.

Explore

Numbered heads together • 35 mins

Anticipated strategies

Students who have successfully completed the activity will have three different food trays with an area of $20x^3y + 60xy^2$ and have determined the length and width of each food tray. Students will also have chosen one food tray and justified why they would use it at the amusement park.

The greatest common factor of $20x^3y + 60xy^2$ is $20xy$. The common factor is composite so there are multiple food trays that could be created, such as with a width of $4xy$ and a length of $5x^2 + 15y$.

There is no correct answer for which food tray to choose and encourage students to justify their reasoning. While x and y are unknown values, some students may plug in values for x and y and justify their choice by how narrow or wide the tray is. Students may justify their answer by choosing trays that are closer to a square in their proportions, or justify not selecting a tray because it is too long and narrow to reasonably use for putting food and drinks on it.

Finding dimensions using an area model

Students may use the rectangle shape with two sections from the launch to find the dimensions of the different food trays, which is similar to using an area model to find missing terms in a polynomial expression.

Algebraically finding dimensions

Students may notice common factors in the two terms and algebraically guess and check or multiply terms to determine dimensions that when multiplied produce the same area.

Misconceptions

Using dimensions that do not produce equivalent areas

What is the area of your food tray? How do you know? How can you check that the dimensions of the tray produce the correct area? What is the area formula for a rectangle?

Purposeful questions

- What are the dimensions of your food trays? How do you know that they have equal area?
- Which food tray would you pick to use? Why?
- Can you justify that your food trays have the same area in another way?
- What if you knew a side length and the area, how could you find the missing side length?

> **Continue when**
> Students have determined the dimensions of each tray and showed that the area is correct for their length and width. Students have also picked one food tray for the amusement park and justified why they picked it.

Discuss

15 mins

Have a group discussion where groups can share their tray designs, as well as justify the area is correct for their chosen dimensions. Consider making connections from the discussion to dividing polynomials by monomials in general.

Discussion guide

Choose several groups to share their food tray of choice, the dimensions of the food tray, and their process for how they found the dimensions of the tray. Write the dimensions of the food trays and summary of reasoning on the board as students share. Encourage students that worked more visually and more algebraically to share and compare methods.

If students have chosen some of the food trays with the same dimensions, ask students to share any other food tray possible dimensions that have not been shared and any methods that have not yet been shared to determine the dimensions of the food tray.

Next, ask the class:

Can you determine the side length of a rectangle if you know the area and one of the sides?

And allow students time to respond and share their thoughts with the class.

Lesson Preparation

Suggested review

Depending on your students' level of prior knowledge, consider revisiting the following lessons:

- **Grade 8** — 2.02 Simplify expressions and distributive property
- **Algebra 1** — 6.02 Multiply polynomials

Tools

You may find these tools helpful:
- Scientific calculator

Student lesson & teacher guide

Factor GCF

Students begin the lesson with a review of what a greatest common factor (GCF) is, and learn about what part of variable expressions are part of a GCF. They then engage in an exploration determining the greatest common factor of two expanded variable expressions.

Students: Page 345

6.04 Factor GCF

After this lesson, you will be able to...
- factor out the GCF from a polynomial expression.

Engage activity
Ask your teacher to get started
Food hall trays
Students will design various rectangular food trays with a specific area and find the length and width of each one.

Factor GCF

There can be many steps when factoring a polynomial expression. To begin with, we first want to identify the **greatest common factor** (GCF) of the terms in the expression.

> **Greatest common factor (GCF)**
> The largest whole number or algebraic expression that evenly divides the given expression.

The GCF of two or more terms includes the largest numeric factor of the coefficients of each term and the lowest power of any variable that appears in every term. (If a variable does not appear in a term, it can be thought of as if it had an exponent of 0.)

Concrete-Representational-Abstract (CRA) Approach
Targeted instructional strategies

Concrete: Begin by engaging students with physical manipulatives to explore factoring polynomials. Use algebra tiles or colored counters to represent the terms in a polynomial expression. For example, to represent the polynomial $6x + 12$, provide six x tiles and twelve unit tiles. Have students physically group the tiles to find common factors. Encourage them to arrange the tiles into equal groups or rectangles, showing how the terms can be divided by the greatest common factor (GCF). This hands-on activity helps students see how common factors are shared among terms in a polynomial.

Representational: Transition to the representational stage by having students draw pictures of the manipulative arrangements. Ask them to sketch the grouped tiles or rectangles they created. For instance, they can draw a rectangle divided into sections that represent the factors of the polynomial. Label the sides of the rectangle with the factors (e.g., one side labeled 6, the other side labeled $(x + 2)$ for $6(x + 2)$. These drawings help students connect the physical grouping to a visual model, reinforcing the concept of factoring out the GCF.

Abstract: Move on to the abstract stage by introducing the symbolic method of factoring polynomials. Teach students how to identify the GCF of the coefficients and variables in the terms. Using the example $(6x + 12)$, guide them to see that the GCF is 6. Show them how to factor out the GCF: $6x + 12 = 6(x + 2)$. Provide practice with various polynomial expressions, having students factor out the GCF using algebraic notation. Emphasize how this symbolic process relates to the concrete and representational stages they've worked through.

Connecting the stages: Help students make connections between all three stages by referring back to the manipulatives and drawings when working abstractly.

Ask guiding questions like:
- "How does factoring out the GCF here relate to the groups you made with the tiles?"
- "Can you picture the rectangle you drew when you see this factored expression?"

Encourage students to use the representation that makes the most sense to them. By linking the concrete materials, visual drawings, and abstract symbols, students can better understand and monitor their thinking about factoring polynomials.

Compare and connect
English language learner support

To support students in comparing and connecting different methods of finding the Greatest Common Factor (GCF) and applying it to various polynomial expressions, begin by introducing the two primary methods: prime factorization and listing factors.

Students will compare and connect methods of factoring out a GCF using a common polynomial as an example, For example,

$$12x^3 - 18x^2$$

Split students into two groups, where one group finds the greatest common factor by prime factorization, and the other finds the greatest common factor by listing factors. Both groups should factor out the greatest common factor. Each group should create a display of their process that includes:
- Steps for finding the GCF with the given method, both mathematically and in words.
- Show the GCF being divided out of the polynomial expression.
- Write the final factored polynomial expression.
- Show how the GCF outside the parentheses can be distributed to recreate the original polynomial.

Students should go on a gallery walk to compare the different methods, discussing the advantages and disadvantages of each. Next, guide students should test the comparisons of these methods by applying them to various polynomial expressions with different numbers of terms, variables, and exponents.

Encourage students to discuss in groups the challenges and efficiencies of each method, noting which method they preferred for different types of polynomials. Have groups present their findings, fostering a classroom dialogue on why certain methods may be more effective in different scenarios. Students should reflect on these comparisons using sentence frames like:
- I found the method of prime factorization useful because …
- When dealing with polynomials with subtraction, I noticed …

Finally, consolidate these discussions into a reference chart created collaboratively with student input, ensuring it evolves as a resource throughout the unit. This approach deepens students' understanding of factoring out the GCF and helps them connect various methods to different polynomial formats.

Use area models to visualize factoring a GCF
Student with disabilities support

Using an area model to divide a polynomial by its GCF may be helpful in organizing a student's thinking. For example, when factoring $2x$ out of $8x^3 + 20x^2 - 14x$, the division

$$\frac{8x^3 + 20x^2 - 14x}{2x} = \frac{8x^3}{2x} + \frac{20x^2}{2x} - \frac{14x}{2x}$$

becomes the example shown, where the first term has been completed for you.

	$4x^2$	?	?
$2x$	$8x^3$	$20x^2$	$-14x$

Show students how the size of the model can be adjusted for the number of terms, and how to ensure that terms are connected to the correct operations of + or −.

Taking out a factor smaller than the greatest common factor
Address student misconceptions

Students might only factor out a common factor, rather than the greatest common factor. Encourage students to check all terms in the parentheses to ensure there are no remaining common factors. If there are any remaining common factors, they can be factored out in another step. For example:

1. $8x^2y^3 + 12x^3y^5 = 2xy(4xy^2 + 6x^2y^4)$ Factor out the common factor of $2xy$
2. $= 2xy \cdot 2xy^2(2 + 3xy^2)$ Factor out $2xy^2$ from the parentheses
3. $= 4x^2y^3(2 + 3xy^2)$ Simplify to notice the GCF was $4x^2y^3$

Notice after step 1 that there is a still a common factor of $2xy^2$, so we can factor that out in another step and then simplify.

Exploration

Students: Page 345

> ## Exploration
>
> The expanded form for $5x^3y^4z$ is $5 \cdot x \cdot x \cdot x \cdot y \cdot y \cdot y \cdot y \cdot z$
>
> The expanded form for $2y^3z^5$ is $2 \cdot y \cdot y \cdot y \cdot z \cdot z \cdot z \cdot z \cdot z$
>
> 1. How many y's are common in both expressions?
> 2. How many z's are common in both expressions?
> 3. What is the GCF of the two expressions?

Suggested student grouping: In pairs

In this exploration, students will be working on understanding the concept of expanding algebraic expressions and determining the greatest common factor (GCF). They will compare two expanded expressions to identify the common terms and calculate the GCF.

Ideal student responses

These ideal responses may differ from other correct student responses. Less formal responses can be connected with the more precise mathematical language presented here.

1. **How many y's are common in both expressions?**
   There are three y's common in both expressions.
2. **How many z's are common in both expressions?**
   There is one z common in both expressions.
3. **What is the GCF of the two expressions?**
   The GCF of the two expressions is y^3z.

Purposeful questions
- How can exponents be used to represent the number of each type of variable common to both expressions?
- How does the exponent of the variable greatest common factor connect to the exponents of the original two terms?

Possible misunderstandings
- Students may assume a greatest common factor must include a number other than 1 as a coefficient and include 5 and 2 in their GCF. They may also include the x^3 since it will have the same exponent as the y^3 in the GCF.

Students are reminded of multiplying a monomial and a polynomial so that they can relate this to factoring a monomial out of a polynomial. This is described as the opposite of distribution. Students are then provided the steps for factoring out a GCF from a polynomial expression.

Students: Page 345

Once an expression has been factored, we can verify the factored form by multiplying. The product should be the original expression.

When multiplying polynomials, we apply the distributive property:
$$a(b + c) = ab + ac$$
We can also apply this in reverse, known as **factoring** an expression:
$$xy + xz = x(y + z)$$
Given a polynomial expression, we can factor out a GCF. The process is the opposite of distribution and will reverse polynomial multiplication.

Follow these steps for factoring out a GCF:

1. Identify the GCF
2. Rewrite each term as a product of the GCF and the remaining factors
3. Rewrite the whole expression as a product of the GCF and the remaining factors in parentheses

Examples

Students: Page 346

Example 1

Find the greatest common factor of the given terms.

a 60 and 24.

Create a strategy

List the prime factorization of 60 and 24, then determine the common factors that comprise the GCF.

Apply the idea

The prime factorization of 60 is $2 \cdot 2 \cdot 3 \cdot 5$
The prime factorization of 24 is $2 \cdot 2 \cdot 2 \cdot 3$.
The GCF is the product of the common factors: $2 \cdot 2 \cdot 3 = 12$.
Therefore, the GCF of 60 and 24 is 12.

Reflect and check

We can also create factor trees for 60 and 24, then identify the common factors.

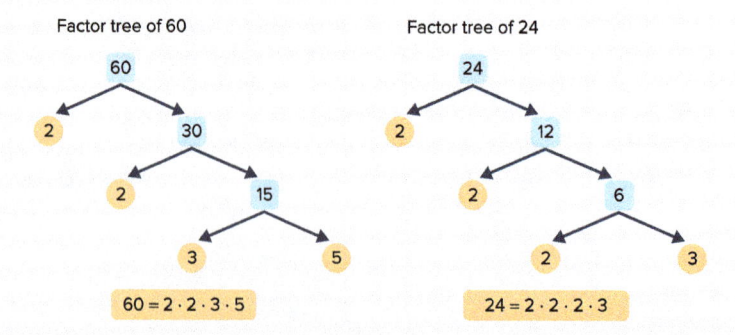

Factor tree of 60

$60 = 2 \cdot 2 \cdot 3 \cdot 5$

Factor tree of 24

$24 = 2 \cdot 2 \cdot 2 \cdot 3$

The GCF is the product of the common factors: $2 \cdot 2 \cdot 3 = 12$.
Therefore, the GCF of 60 and 24 is 12.

Purpose
Show students how to find the GCF of the integers.

Expected mistakes
Students may state that a common factor is the GCF because it is a common factor of the two integers, as opposed to the actual GCF. If you work through the prime factorization of the integers, show students that the common factors of the integers must be multiplied together in order to get the GCF.

Reflecting with students
Ask students to divide the original two numbers by the greatest common factor and then break down the results into their prime factorizations. Ask students to notice whether there are any remaining common factors in the two factorizations.

Students: Page 346

b $60x^3y^2$ and $24xy^4$.

Create a strategy
List the whole number factors of the coefficients of $60x^3y^2$ and $24xy^4$ and find the expression with the lowest power of each of the variables.

Apply the idea
We know that the largest whole number that 60 and 24 are divisible by is 12. The expression with the lowest power of each of the variables is xy^2.

Putting this together, the greatest common factor is $12xy^2$.

Reflect and check
We can also expand both expressions to find the common factors:

$60x^3y^2 = 2 \cdot 2 \cdot 3 \cdot 5 \cdot x \cdot x \cdot x \cdot y \cdot y$

$24xy^4 = 2 \cdot 2 \cdot 2 \cdot 3 \cdot x \cdot y \cdot y \cdot y \cdot y$

So, the GCF is $2 \cdot 2 \cdot 3 \cdot x \cdot y \cdot y = 12xy^2$.

Purpose
Show students the GCF of the terms by focusing on the coefficients and then focusing on the variables.

Expected mistakes
Students might assume that they need to multiply all of the variable terms in the expressions. Instead, expanding each of the variable terms and determining the common terms between each expression, similarly to finding a GCF of integers with prime factorization, will work.

Reflecting with students
Ask students why the lowest power of each of the variables would lead to the GCF of the variable terms. Use the expected mistake to show students why expanding and then multiplying the common variables between the expressions leads to the lowest power of each of the variables as the GCF.

🎓 Finding greatest common factors with variables
Targeted instructional strategies

While students have experience finding the greatest common factor (GCF) of numbers, students would benefit from practice finding the GCF of terms with numbers and variables.

To connect the process of finding the greatest common factor of numbers and variables, provide a pair of terms and show the prime factorization method. For example, $24y^3$ and $56y^5$:

$$24y^3 = 2 \cdot 2 \cdot 2 \cdot 3 \cdot y \cdot y \cdot y$$
$$56y^5 = 2 \cdot 2 \cdot 2 \cdot 7 \cdot y \cdot y \cdot y \cdot y \cdot y$$
Expand into prime factorization

$$24y^3 = 2 \cdot 2 \cdot 2 \cdot \cancel{3} \cdot y \cdot y \cdot y$$
Identify matching pairs of factors and cancel non-matching factors

$$56y^5 = 2 \cdot 2 \cdot 2 \cdot \cancel{7} \cdot y \cdot y \cdot y \cdot \cancel{y} \cdot \cancel{y}$$
$$= 2 \cdot 2 \cdot 2 \cdot y \cdot y \cdot y$$
Write out product of matching factors

GCF of $24y^3$ and $56y^5 = 8y^3$
Simplify

Point out that the greatest common factor of terms with the same variables is the variable with the lower exponent.

Students: Page 347

Example 2

Factor the expression $8x^2 + 4x$.

Create a strategy

Find the GCF and divide it out of each term.

Apply the idea

The GCF of $8x^2$ and $4x$ is $4x$.
Dividing out the GCF, we get:
$$8x^2 \div 4x = 2x$$
$$4x \div 4x = 1$$

So we have:
$$8x^2 + 4x = 4x(2x) + 4x(1)$$
$$= 4x(2x + 1)$$

Reflect and check

Although the term $4x$ is in the original expression when it is factored out the second term does not become zero. Otherwise, when we check the answer by distributing the multiplication, $4x$ will be lost altogether.

We can check our factorization using the distributive property:
$$4x(2x + 1) = 4x(2x) + 4x(1) = 8x^2 + 4x$$

Purpose
Show students how to identify the GCF and then factor it.

Expected mistakes
Students may only factor part of the GCF, such as $2x$, and think they have finished factoring the expression. Remind students to always check if there are any remaining common factors required to factor. They can do this by checking for any common variables in all the terms, and any common factors in the coefficients of all the terms.

Reflecting with students
Encourage advanced learners or all students to create their own polynomial expressions and show how to factor out the greatest common factor (GCF). Allow them to choose different coefficients or variables and

challenge them to use a polynomial that is longer than a binomial. Ask them to explain why the GCF is what it is in each case and how factoring simplifies the expression.

Misapplying exponent rules and disappearing terms
Address student misconceptions

use with Example 2

Students may attempt to apply the laws of exponents to the coefficents as well as the exponents, which may lead to a constant being eliminated from a final answer. This could result in a solution like:

$$\frac{12x^5}{7x^3} + \frac{7x^3}{7x^3} = (12-7)x^{5-3} + (7-7)x^{3-3}$$
$$= 5x^2 + 0x^0$$
$$= 5x^2$$

Challenge this misconception by having students write the numerator and denominator in expanded form to refresh their memories as to why we subtract the exponents when dividing.

Students: Page 347

Example 3

Factor the expression $3x(x - 4) + 7(x - 4)$.

Create a strategy
This time, the expressions are already factored. We can use this to help identify the GCF.

Apply the idea
In particular, notice that both terms $3x(x - 4)$ and $7(x - 4)$ have a factor of $(x - 4)$.

The remaining parts of each expression, $3x$ and 7, have no factors in common. So the GCF is $(x - 4)$, which we can use to factor the expression:

$$3x(x-4) + 7(x-4) = (x-4)\left(\frac{3x(x-4) + 7(x-4)}{x-4}\right)$$
$$= (x-4)\left(3x \cdot \frac{\cancel{x-4}}{\cancel{x-4}} + 7 \cdot \frac{\cancel{x-4}}{\cancel{x-4}}\right)$$
$$= (x-4)(3x+7)$$

Purpose
Show students an idea of what factoring by grouping, which will appear in a future lesson, will look like when factoring a GCF.

Expected mistakes
Students may see that $(x - 4)$ is common, but not necessarily see the expression as a factor. Remind students that a factor is a number or quantity that is multiplied, and we read $(x - 4)$ as "the quantity of x minus 4."

Reflecting with students
Ask students to verify that the given expression is equivalent to its factored form by performing the multiplication for both.

Abstract binomial GCF by drawing boxes
Student with disabilities support

use with Example 3

Encourage students to abstract problems that appear complex. For example, for binomial common factors, show them that they can be written as a box or single variable and then substituted back in.

Make the explicit connection to the situation where the GCF is a monomial such as $3ax + 7a$ and have students factor to get $a(3x + 7)$. We can also draw a box around the binomial so students consider it as a single term giving $3x\square + 7\square = \square(3x + 7)$, eventually leading to $3x(x - 4) + 7(x - 4) = (x - 4)(3x + 7)$.

Students: Page 347

> **Idea summary**
> Follow these steps for factoring out a GCF:
> 1. Identify the GCF
> 2. Rewrite each term as a product of the GCF and the remaining factors
> 3. Rewrite the whole expression as a product of the GCF and the remaining factors in parentheses

Practice

Students: Pages 348–350

What do you remember?

1 For each of these numbers:
  i List the factors.
  ii State the greatest common factor.

  a 6 and 12
  b 9 and 24
  c 14 and 32
  d 28 and 42

2 For these prime factorizations:

$$180 = 2 \cdot 2 \cdot 3 \cdot 3 \cdot 5$$
$$600 = 2 \cdot 2 \cdot 2 \cdot 3 \cdot 5 \cdot$$

Find the greatest common factor of 180 and 600.

3 For each of these algebraic expressions:
  i List the factors.
  ii State the greatest common factor.

  a $3x^2$ and $2x$
  b $12xy^4$ and $24xy$
  c 14 and $7abc$
  d x^2y^3 and x^2y^2

4 Identify the greatest common factor between the following sets of terms:
  a $8a$ and $9a$
  b $3x$ and $6x^2$
  c $4b$ and b^2
  d $4y^2$ and $6y^2$
  e $5p^2, 3p^2$ and p
  f $45n, 55n^2$ and $20n^2$
  g $4m^2, -7m, 8m$ and $-14m^2$
  h $-42k, -21k^2, -7k^2$ and $-28k^3$

5 Simplify the following expressions:

a $\dfrac{42a}{60a}$ b $\dfrac{12v}{120}$ c $\dfrac{16p^5}{2p^2}$ d $\left(\dfrac{1}{3}x^3 + \dfrac{2}{3}x^5\right) \div x$

e $\dfrac{16x^3 + 20x^2 - 28}{4}$ f $\dfrac{80z^2 + 10z}{10z}$ g $(30j^2) \div (35j)$ h $\left(\dfrac{1}{2}m\right) \div \left(\dfrac{5}{4}m\right)$

i $(b^3 - 4b^2 + 2b) \div (4b)$ j $\dfrac{30n^5}{9n^2}$

6 Fill in the blanks to make a true algebraic statement.

a $\dfrac{\square}{4a} = 4a^2$ b $\dfrac{2x^3 - 10x^2 + 8x}{\square} = x^2 - 5x + 4$

c $\dfrac{\square + 20m^2 + 22}{2m} = 7m^2 + \square + \dfrac{11}{m}$

7 Determine which of the following represent a factored form of the expression $-12x + 20x^2$:

a $-4 \cdot 3x + 5$ b $-2(6x - 10)$ c $4x(5 - 3x)$ d $x(-12 + 20x)$

Let's practice

8 Complete each factorization:

a $y^2 + 5y = y(\square + \square)$ b $2t^2 + 2t = 2t(\square + \square)$ c $3y^2 + 6y = \square(y + 2)$

d $-m^2 + 19m = \square(m - 19)$ e $-y^2 - 2y = \square(y + 2)$ f $8v - v^2 = v(\square - \square)$

9 Factor the following expressions:

a $6v + 30$ b $-2s - 10$ c $-12s + 10$ d $y^2 + 4y$

e $2u^2 - 8u$ f $4t + 2t^2$ g $42x - x^2$ h $9z^2 - 18z$

i $r^3 + r^2 + 6r$ j $w(w - 2) - (w - 2)$ k $9(3x + 4) + 4(3x + 4)$ l $8t(t - 3) + 9(t - 3)$

10 Completely factor each of the following polynomials.

a $-6y^4 + 14y^3 - 10y^2$ b $14h^4 + 28h^6 + 56h^3$

c $18x^2 - 24x + 36 - 72x^4$ d $-3a^3 - 9a^2 - 15a^4$

e $18m^7 - 15m^3 + 14m + 35m^6$ f $-d^{12} + d^8 - d^{15}$

g $\dfrac{3}{2}x^8 + \dfrac{1}{2}x^4 - \dfrac{5}{2}x^5$ h $0.1h + 0.2h^3 - 0.4h^5$

11 Xander was asked to factor the expression $35x^2y + 10xy^2 - 5xy$. Identify his error.

Xander:

The greatest common factor is $5xy$ so the factored form of the expression is $5xy(7x + 2y)$.

12 Alex and Beth are both asked to factor $-5x + 10y$. Alex wrote down $-5(x - 2y)$ and Beth wrote down $5(2y - x)$. Who is correct? Explain.

13 A farmer wants to create a set of adjacent fields which all have the same width. He plans to create the smallest field in the shape of a square, with the largest field 9 times the size of the smallest field, and the middle field to have a length that is 5 units more than the smallest field.

a Write expressions for the area of each field.

b Use factoring to determine the dimensions of the entire field.

Let's extend our thinking

14 Identify the common factor of any two terms.

15 Identify the greatest common factor between the following sets of terms:
- a $45n$, $55n^2$ and $20n^2$
- b $4m^2$, $-7m$, $8m$ and $-14m^2$
- c $-42k$, $-21k^2$, $-7k^2$ and $-28k^3$
- d $45n$, $55n^2y$ and $40mn^3$
- e $3a^2mn$, $2ya^4x$ and $5xma^3$
- f $3a^2bx$, $4na^4m$ and $12mba^3$

16 Fully factor each expression:
- a $44uv - 8u^2v$
- b $-8w^2 + 3w^2y$
- c $5k^2t + 40k^2t^2$
- d $49p^2q - 28pq^2$
- e $-16a^2 - 18a^2b$
- f $-30w^2 - 25w^2y$
- g $-10u^2v + 9uv^2$
- h $4x + 12 + 16yx$
- i $3x + 9 + 12yx$
- j $2x + 10x^2y + 8yx$
- k $4x^2y + 8xy^2 + 12xz^2$
- l $5ab^2c + 25bc^3 + 100abc$
- m $30b^2c + 10abc + 20c^2$
- n $5a^2b^2 + 2ab - 3a^2b^2 - 4ab$
- o $5x^2y^2 + 15yz^2 + 25y^2 + 60y$

17 Create an expression with at least three factorizations. Then, write out each factorization including the fully factored form.

18 Explain how dividing monomials relates to factoring the greatest common factor.

19 Explain why the greatest common factor of the variables in any expression has the *least* possible exponent of any of the terms.

20 The rectangle shown has an area of $4x^2 - 16x$ square units.
What expression describes the length of the rectangle?

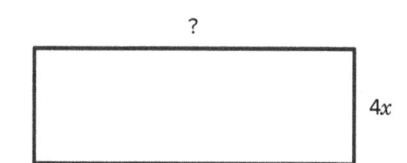

21 A property management company has a rectangular plot of land available for parking. The area of this plot is represented by the expression $20n + 5n^2$.
- a Determine the dimensions of the block of land.
- b Given the the length is longer than the width for all $n > 1$, which expression is the length and which is the width?
- c The length is further divided into 5 equal sections, and one of these sections is fenced off for storage. What is the length of fencing needed?

22 You are to design a photo collage made of two large square photos with a side length of x and four smaller rectangular photos that have a height of x and a width of 4 inches.
- a Find an algebraic expression for the area of the rectangle formed if the photos are all placed in a single row. Draw an example of what this arrangement would look like.
- b Fully factor your answer from part (a) and then draw a photo arrangement that would match these dimensions.

Answers

6.04 Factor GCF

What do you remember?

1. a i 1, 2, 3, 6   1, 2, 3, 4, 6, 12
   ii 6
   b i 1, 3, 9   1, 2, 3, 4, 6, 8, 12, 24
   ii 3
   c i 1, 2, 7, 14   1, 2, 4, 8, 16, 32
   ii 2
   d i 1, 2, 4, 7, 14, 28   1, 2, 3, 6, 7, 14, 21, 42
   ii 14

2. 60

3. a x b $12xy$ c 7 d x^2y^2

4. a a b $3x$ c b d $2y^2$
   e p f $5n$ g m h $-7k$

5. a $\frac{7}{10}$ b $\frac{v}{10}$
   c $8p^3$ d $\frac{x^2(1+2x^2)}{3}$
   e $4x^3 + 5x^2 - 7$ f $8z + 1$
   g $\frac{6j}{7}$ h $\frac{2}{5}$
   i $\frac{1}{4}b^2 - b + \frac{1}{2}$ j $\frac{10n^3}{3}$

6. a $16a^3$ b $2x$ c $14m^3$ and $10m$

7. a No   b No   c No   d Yes

Let's practice

8. a $y(y + 5)$ b $2t(t + 1)$
   c $3y(y + 2)$ d $-m(m - 19)$
   e $-y(y + 2)$ f $v(8 - v)$

9. a $6(v + 5)$ b $-2(s + 5)$ c $-2(6s - 5)$
   d $y(y + 4)$ e $2u(u - 4)$ f $2t(2 + t)$
   g $x(42 - x)$ h $9z(z - 2)$ i $r(r^2 + r + 6)$
   j $(w - 2)(w - 1)$ k $13(3x + 4)$ l $(t - 3)(8t + 9)$

10. a $-2y^2(3y^2 - 7y + 5)$
    b $14h^3(h + 2h^3 + 4)$
    c $6(3x^2 - 4x + 6 - 12x^4)$
    d $-3a^2(a + 3 + 5a^2)$
    e $m(18m^6 - 15m^2 + 14 + 35m^5)$
    f $-d^8(d^4 - 1 + d^7)$
    g $\frac{1}{2}x^4(3x^4 + 1 - 5x)$
    h $0.1h(1 + 2h^2 - 4h^4)$

11. When factoring $5xy$ out of the term $-5xy$ you get $\frac{-5xy}{5xy} = -1$ but Xander eliminated the term instead.

12. They are both correct. If you expand the answer each gave you will see that they both produce $-5x + 10y$.

13. a Let the width of the smallest field be x so that its area is x^2. The largest field has an area of $9x^2$ and the middle field has an area of $x(x + 5)$.
    b The area of the entire field is the sum of each smaller field: $x^2 + 9x^2 + x(x + 5)$. The factored form of this expression is $x(11x + 5)$ so the width of the field is x and the length is $11x + 5$.

Let's extend our thinking

14. 1

15. a $5n$ b m c $-7k$ d $5n$
    e a^2 f a^2

16. a $4uv(11 - 2u)$ b $w^2(3y - 8)$
    c $5k^2t(1 + 8t)$ d $7pq(7p - 4q)$
    e $-2a^2(8 + 9b)$ f $-5w^2(6 + 5y)$
    g $uv(-10u + 9v)$ h $4(x + 3 + 4xy)$
    i $3(x + 3 + 4yx)$ j $2x(1 + 5xy + 4y)$
    k $4x(xy + 2y^2 + 3z^2)$ l $5bc(ab + 5c^2 + 20a)$
    m $10c(3b^2 + ab + 2c)$ n $2ab(ab - 1)$
    o $5y(x^2y + 3z^2 + 5y + 12)$

17. Answers will vary. For example: $2x^2 + 4x$ has three factorizations: $2(x^2 + 2x)$, $x(2x + 4)$, and the fully factored form which is $2x(x + 2)$.

18. When the greatest common factor is a monomial, we can use monomial division to determine what expression is left after the factoring is complete.

19. The greatest common factor represents the largest value that can be divided evenly from each term. If the greatest common factor of a variable had an exponent larger than any of the original terms, then dividing it out would leave a negative exponent.
    For example, consider the expression $x^2 + x^3$. If we divide both terms by x^2 (the smaller exponent) then we are left with $1 + x$. If instead we try to divide both terms by x^3 (the larger exponent) then we would be left with $x^{-1} + 1$.

20. $x - 4$

21. a $5n(4 + n)$, so the dimensions are $5n$ and $4 + n$
    b Length = $5n$, Width = $4 + n$
    c Each section is now $n \cdot (4 + n)$ and to fence this the perimeter is $8 + 4n$ units of fencing.

22 a $x(2x+16)$

b $2x(x+8)$

6.05 Factor by grouping

Subtopic overview

Lesson narrative

In this lesson, students will learn how to factor a polynomial expression using a method of grouping. They will be reminded of their previous skills of factoring out the greatest common factor in order to prepare them for the grouping method. In addition to learning the process of factoring by grouping, students will learn to identify the structures that allow for factoring by grouping and justify the equivalency of polynomial expressions.

Learning objective

Students: Page 351

After this lesson, you will be able to...
- factor polynomials by grouping.

Key vocabulary

- factor by grouping

Essential understanding

Factoring by grouping is an application of factoring out the greatest common factor. It is a standard algorithm that can be applied to factoring any factorable quadratic expression.

Standards

This subtopic addresses the following Virginia 2023 Mathematics Standards of Learning standards.

Mathematical process goals

MPG3 — Mathematical Reasoning

Teachers can incorporate this goal into their lessons by encouraging students to justify their steps when factoring by grouping. Students should be guided to use logical reasoning to explain why they arranged the terms in a certain way, why they grouped the terms as they did, and why they factored out the common binomial.

MPG5 — Mathematical Representations

Teachers can incorporate this goal by encouraging students to use a variety of methods to represent their factoring by grouping process. This could include diagrams, flowcharts, or symbolic notation. Students could also be asked to translate between different representations, such as interpreting a written description of the factoring process in mathematical notation.

Content standards

A.EO.2 — The student will perform operations on and factor polynomial expressions in one variable.

A.EO.2c — Factor completely first- and second-degree polynomials in one variable with integral coefficients.

After factoring out the greatest common factor (GCF), leading coefficients should have no more than four factors.

Prior connections

8.PFA.1 — The student will represent, simplify, and generate equivalent algebraic expressions in one variable.

A.EO.1 — The student will represent verbal quantitative situations algebraically and evaluate these expressions for given replacement values of the variables.

Future connections

A2.EO.3 — The student will perform operations on polynomial expressions in two or more variables and factor polynomial expressions in one and two variables.

Engage Activity

Treasure floor
60 mins

Students will create a tiled floor design for an amusement park game and determine the area and dimensions of the rectangular shape created in multiple ways.

Understanding and skills

Will use	Will develop
Factoring greatest common factor (GCF).	Rewriting polynomials with four terms as the product of two linear factors.

Preparation and materials
- Open and complete the student preview, anticipating classroom responses.
- **Materials:** Pencil, paper
- Download and print copies of the students graphic organizer from the student Launch slide.

Support students with disabilities
Support visual-spatial - create and interpret visual representations

Provide printed copies of the downloadable asset to students containing multiple tiles and the dimensions of each tile. This will help students visualize the design they are creating as well as support their algebraic justification.

Support for English language learners
Collect and display

As pairs are working, listen for and collect vocabulary, phrases, and methods students use for designing their tiled floor as well as finding the area and dimensions of their design and other rectangular space. Continue to update collected student language throughout the entire activity. Remind students to borrow language from the display as needed.

Some terms and phrases may include: factoring, greatest common factor, grouping, multiply, divide

Classroom guide

Hook
Co-craft questions • 5 mins

Students create questions about a design made up of rectangular pieces that fit together.

What mathematical questions could we ask about this image?

Implementation details

Students may produce questions such as:
- What are the dimensions of the overall rectangle?
- What is the area of the overall rectangle?
- What are the dimensions of the individual rectangles?
- What is the area of each individual rectangle?

Highlight student questions regarding the dimensions of the rectangle, area, and quantity of each piece.

Slide 1 from Student Engage Activity

Launch
5 mins

Amuse-me amusement park is creating a new attraction where patrons will search for treasure in an Egyptian tomb. One part of the attraction that has not been designed yet is the tiled floor.

As part of the attraction, patrons must step on the correct tiles to avoid setting off a trap and losing the treasure.

The four tiles that are to be used in the design are rectangular and have the following dimensions:

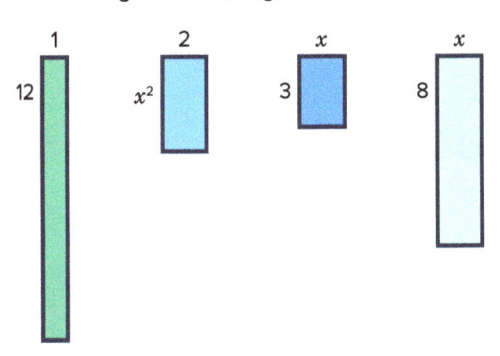

Tile 1: 12×1; Tile 2: x^2 with dimensions $x \times 2$; Tile 3: $3 \times x$; Tile 4: $8 \times x$

Slide 2 from Student Engage Activity

Provide students with the downloadable asset which has each tile on it. You may wish to have students cut out rectangles to use while creating their design in the Explore.

Suggested grouping: Form pairs

Explore

Think-pair-share • 25 mins

Anticipated strategies

Use the manipulatives to design the tiled floor

Students may use the manipulatives to create the floor design and find the area.

Work algebraically from the start:

Students may find the area of a rectangular design algebraically and then sketch the design.

Misconceptions

Creating a non-rectangular design

What would be the dimensions of your larger rectangular design? Can you show me visually and algebraically?

Purposeful questions

- What is your design so far? Is it rectangular? How do you know?
- What is the area of the rectangular shape created by using one of each type of tile? Can you show me visually and algebraically?
- Can you write the area in any other way?
- What is the area and dimensions of your own design? How do you know?
- If you only knew the area of the design, could you find the dimensions of the rectangles?

> **Continue when**
> Students have created a design, labeled the dimensions, and calculated the area.

Discuss

25 mins

Discussion guide

Have students share their tile floor designs as well as the area and dimensions of the larger rectangular shape. Ask students how they determined the area and dimensions. Encourage groups that found the dimensions visually to share and then ask groups that focused on the algebraic justification.

As an extension you may provide the following prompts:
- Rewrite the area of your design in as many equivalent ways as possible
- What is the area of the design made by using each tile exactly once?

After using the extension prompts you may have a discussion about how you can verify several forms of an expression are equivalent.

Lesson Preparation

Suggested review

Depending on your students' level of prior knowledge, consider revisiting the following lessons:

Algebra 1 — 6.04 Factor GCF

Tools

You may find these tools helpful:
- Scientific calculator
- Highlighter

Student lesson & teacher guide

Factor by grouping

Students begin with an exploration that involves factoring a GCF. Students are asked the possible factorization of an unfamiliar polynomial expression that involves factoring a GCF.

Connecting greatest common factors and factoring by grouping
Targeted instructional strategies

To connect factoring out the greatest common factor and factoring by grouping, display the following binomials and have students factor out the greatest common factor of each:

$$6x^2 + 9x \text{ and } -4x - 12$$

Once students factor each binomial, display the factored forms and ask what the two binomials have in common.

$$6x^2 + 9x = 3x(2x + 3)$$
$$-8x - 12 = -4(2x + 3)$$

Show students that polynomials with four terms can be separated into smaller polynomials to factor separately. Ask students to predict what steps factored $6x^2 + 9x - 8x - 12$ into $(3x - 4)(2x + 3)$.

Critique, correct, clarify
English language learner support

Ask students to factor the expression $-2a^3 + 2 + 2a^2 - 2a$.

Before students share their responses, display the following three worked solutions or share actual student responses anonymously.

Solution A:

$$-2a^3 + 2a^2 - 2a + 2 = -2(a^3 - a^2 + a - 1)$$
$$= -2(a^2(a - 1) + 1(a - 1))$$
$$= -2(a - 1)(a^2 + 1)$$

Factor out −2 from all terms
Factor out the GCF (a^2 and 1)
Factor out the common binomial factor

Solution B:

$$-2a^3 + 2a^2 - 2a + 2 = -2(a^3 - a^2 + a - 1)$$
$$= -2(a^2(a - 1) + (a - 1))$$
$$= -2(a - 1)(a^2)$$

Factor out −2 from all terms
Factor out the GCFs
Factor out the common binomial factor

Solution C:

$$-2a^3 + 2a^2 - 2a + 2 = (-2a^3 + 2a^2) + (-2a + 2)$$
$$= -2a^2(a - 1) + 2(-a + 1)$$
$$-2a^3 + 2a^2 - 2a + 2 = -2a^3 + 2a^2 - 2a + 2$$

Split based on common factors
Factor out the GCF ($-2a^2$ and 2)
Cannot be factored by grouping as the binomials are not the same

Invite students to identify the errors, critique the reasoning, and write a correct explanation. Invite one or two students to share their critiques and corrected explanations with the class.

Listen for and amplify the language students use around the order of the steps and how to identify equivalent expressions. This will help students understand how to factor by grouping.

Note that Solution A is a valid strategy that can help make the numbers smaller to work with at the beginning, but could introduce complications with the need for double parentheses, Solution B has an error on the last step as it does not recognize that 1 is the remaining factor, and Solution C should have factored out −2, not 2 from the second pair of terms to make the binomials the same. Emphasize that the binomials must be the same, but before saying it cannot be factored by grouping we should try to rearrange the order or check for a different common factor.

Decomposition of factoring by grouping problem for students
Student with disabilities support

Provide a model of a detailed solution, highlighting and annotating the steps. Use Computational Thinking to decompose the problem into smaller, more manageable parts. Then Algorithmic thinking can be used to go through the factoring process.

For example, the question $x^2 + 5x + 8x + 40$ could be broken up into:

1. Factor the first pair: $x^2 + 5x$.
2. Factor the second pair: $8x + 40$.
3. Check that there is a common binomial factor. If not, go back and rearrange.
4. Make connections between the two parts and substitute your answers from parts (1) and (2) into $x^2 + 5x + 8x + 40$.
4. Fully factor the expression from part (4).

A greatest common factor of 1
Address student misconceptions

Consider the example:

Factor the expression $3a^3 - 4a^2 + 3a - 4$.

Solution:

$$3a^3 - 4a^2 + 3a - 4 = (3a^3 - 4a^2) + (3a - 4) \quad \text{Split based on common factors}$$
$$= a^2(3a - 4) + 1(3a - 4) \quad \text{Factor out the GCF } (a^2 \text{ and } 1)$$
$$= (3a - 4)(a^2 + 1) \quad \text{Factor out the common binomial factor}$$

Since $(3a - 4)(a^2 + 1)$ cannot be factored further, it is the final answer.

Some students may struggle with going from step 1 to step 2 as they are not sure what to factor out of $3a - 4$ as there is not common factor other than 1. Encourage students to consider the reverse operation what we would need to multiply by to get back $3a$ and -4 if we were distributing the multiplication, to provide further scaffolding, next ask what the Multiplicative identity property says or have students fill in the blank in $3a = \square \cdot 3a$.

Exploration

Students: Page 351

6.05 Factor by grouping

After this lesson, you will be able to...
- factor polynomials by grouping.

Engage activity
Ask your teacher to get started
Treasure floor
Students will create a tiled floor design for an amusement park game and determine the area and dimensions of the rectangular shape created in multiple ways.

Factor by grouping

Exploration

Consider the polynomial expression $x^4 + 7x^3 + 6x + 42$.
Factor out the greatest common factor for each of the following:
- $x^4 + 7x^3$
- $6x + 42$

1. Based on your answers above, what do you think the factored form of $x^4 + 7x^3 + 6x + 42$ could be?

Suggested student grouping: In pairs
Students are presented with a polynomial containing four terms, and are asked to factor the GCF from the first two terms, followed by factoring the GCF from the second two terms. Students may notice that the remaining binomials are also the same, and could factor the four-term polynomial using this information.

Ideal student responses
These ideal responses may differ from other correct student responses. Less formal responses can be connected with the more precise mathematical language presented here.

1. **Based on your answers above, what do you think the factored form of $x^4 + 7x^3 + 6x + 42$ could be?**
   Since both sets of terms has a common factor of $(x + 7)$, the factored form of $x^4 + 7x^3 + 6x + 42$ could be $(x + 7)(x^3 + 6)$.

Purposeful questions
- What is the GCF of the first set and the second set? How can we use this to write a factored form of the given polynomial?
- Could you somehow combine your solutions for each set of factored terms?

Possible misunderstandings
- Students may not recognise the common binomial factor or how this can lead to the full factorization. Encourage students to rewrite the original expression in terms of the sets of factored terms and then look for what the two sets have in common. Temporarily replacing the binomial factor with a letter or symbol may help students identify the factorization. For example, replacing $(x + 7)$ with A, we obtain $Ax^3 + 6A$.

6.05 Factor by grouping   755

mathspace.co

Students learn a general form and procedure for factoring by grouping. Then, students are presented with an example to follow the method of factoring by grouping.

Students: Pages 351–352

When a polynomial with four terms does not have a GCF, sometimes we can group pairs of terms and factor their GCFs to factor the polynomial.

Recall the expansion of the following expression:

$$(a + b)(x + y) = a(x + y) + b(x + y) = ax + ay + bx + by$$

We can reverse these steps with expressions that contain four terms by factoring in pairs. This is called **factoring by grouping**.

> **Factoring by grouping**
> A method for factoring an expression containing at least four terms, by grouping the terms in pairs and taking out common factors

Follow the steps shown with the example to factor by grouping:

$6x^3 - 16 + 4x - 24x^2 = 2(3x^3 - 8 + 2x - 12x^2)$ 1. Factor out a GCF, if possible

$= 2[(3x^3 - 12x^2) + (-8 + 2x)]$ 2. Rearrange the terms so that the first pair and the second pair each have a common factor, if possible

$= 2[(3x^2(x - 4) + 2(-4 + x)]$ 3. Factor out a GCF from the binomial expressions

$= 2(x - 4)(3x^2 + 2)$ 4. Factor out the common binomial expression

$= 2(x - 4)(3x^2 + 2)$ ✓ 5. Verify that the final expression cannot be factored further, otherwise continue factoring

Examples

Students: Page 352

Example 1

Factor the expression $10x^2 + 4x + 15x + 6$.

Create a strategy

We arrange the terms first, grouping those with common factors. We factor out the GCF on each pair and the common binomial factor afterward.

Apply the idea

$10x^2 + 4x + 15y + 6 = (10x^2 + 4x) + (15x + 6)$ Group based on common factors
$ = 2x(5x + 2) + 3(5x + 2)$ Factor out each GCF ($2x$ and 3)
$ = (5x + 2)(2x + 3)$ Factor out the common binomial factor

Since $(5x + 2)(2x + 3)$ cannot be factored further, it is the final answer.

---

756 Mathspace Virginia SOL Algebra 1 Teacher Edition
mathspace.co

Reflect and check

We can perform a midway check that we are factoring by grouping appropriately when we factor out the GCF from each set of binomials in the step $2x(5x + 2) + 3(5x + 2)$.

If we factor out the GCF at this step and the binomial factors are not equivalent, then we will want to check that we factored out the GCF correctly. If the factoring is correct, we may need to try a different approach. There may be a better way to arrange the terms from the polynomial.

Not every polynomial expression will be factorable, but we can try a few different approaches, checking our work along the way.

Purpose

Show students how to factor a polynomial expression that contains more than one variable by grouping.

Reflecting with students

Challenge students to group the terms a different way and factor the expression by grouping. Students could rewrite the terms as $10x^2 + 15x + 4x + 6$.

$$10x^2 + 4x + 15x + 6 = (10x^2 + 15x) + (4x + 6) \quad \text{Group based on common factors}$$
$$= 5x(2x + 3) + 2(2x + 3) \quad \text{Factor out each GCF ($5x$ and 2)}$$
$$= (2x + 3)(5x + 2) \quad \text{Factor out the common binomial factor}$$

The commutative property tells us that for a product, we can write the factors in either order, so this is also correct.

Encourage critical thinking about grouping
Targeted instructional strategies

use with Example 1

Encourage students to consider why we sometimes reorder the terms to factor by grouping and sometimes we do not need to. Provide the following four orderings for the terms in equivalent expressions:

- $6x^3 + 10x^2 - 27x - 45$
- $6x^3 - 27x + 10x^2 - 45$
- $6x^3 - 45 - 27x + 10x^2$
- $6x^3 - 27x - 45 + 10x^2$

Ask the students:

1. Which can be factored by grouping as they are, and which will need to be rearranged?
2. Which ones were possible as they were, but took more steps?
3. Is there anything else you notice or wonder?

Encourage students to generalize this idea and apply it to other questions. Ideally, students would develop and be able to explain the conditions for applying different strategies.

Students: Page 353

Example 2

Show at least two different ways we can arrange and group the polynomial $4a^2 - 10b + 5ab - 8a$ and factor it.

Create a strategy

Determine if the polynomial has common factors between the first and second pair of terms, then factor it and rearrange the polynomial so that the first or second set of terms has a common factor, then factor it again.

Apply the idea

Write the expression as $4a^2 + 5ab - 8a - 10b$ and factor it.

$4a^2 - 10b + 5ab - 8a = 4a^2 + 5ab - 8a - 10b$	Rearrange the terms
$4a^2 + 5ab - 8a - 10b = (4a^2 + 5ab) + (-8a - 10b)$	Group based on common factors
$= a(4a + 5b) - 2(4a + 5b)$	Factor out the GCF (a and -2)
$= (4a + 5b)(a - 2)$	Factor out the common binomial factor

Since $(4a + 5b)(a - 2)$ cannot be factored further, it is the final answer.

Write the expression as $4a^2 - 8a - 10b + 5ab$ and factor it.

$4a^2 - 10b + 5ab - 8a = 4a^2 - 8a - 10b + 5ab$	Rearrange the terms
$4a^2 - 8a - 10b + 5ab = (4a^2 - 8a) + (-10b + 5ab)$	Group based on common factors
$= 4a(a - 2) + 5b(-2 + a)$	Factor out the GCF ($4a$ and $5b$)
$= (a - 2)(4a + 5b)$	Factor out the common binomial factor

Since $(a - 2)(4a + 5b)$ cannot be factored further, it is the final answer.

Reflect and check

Alternatively, we can group $4a^2$ and $-8a$ and $5ab$ and $-10b$ together and get the same answer.

$4a^2 + 5ab - 8a - 10b = (4a^2 - 8a) + (5ab - 10b)$	Group based on common factors
$= 4a(a - 2) + 5b(a - 2)$	Factor out the GCF ($4a$ and $5b$)
$= (a - 2)(4a + 5b)$	Factor out the common binomial factor

We can check the answer by multiplying the factored form $(4a + 5b)(a - 2)$.

$(4a + 5b)(a - 2) = a(4a + 5b) - 2(4a + 5b)$	Distributive property
$= 4a^2 + 5ab - 8a - 10b$	Distributive property

Purpose
Show students how to factor the same polynomial expression by grouping in more than one way.

Expected mistakes
Students may factor a GCF of 2 from the second set of terms in the first example, instead of −2. This would lead to different binomial factors, $(4a + 5b)$ and $(-4a - 5b)$. Emphasize that the binomials must be the same, and to be aware of the signs of terms when factoring.

Reflecting with students
Ask students why the solutions for the factorization for both rearranged expressions are correct. The order of the binomials does not matter because of the commutative property of multiplication.

Concrete-Representational-Abstract (CRA) Approach
Targeted instructional strategies

use with Example 2

Concrete: Begin by engaging students with algebra tiles to represent each term in the polynomial $4a^2 - 10b + 5ab - 8a$. Assign different shapes or colors to represent each term: use large squares for a^2, rectangles for ab, small squares for a, and circles for b. Include negative tiles or flip the tiles over to represent negative coefficients. Have students physically arrange the tiles to model the polynomial. Encourage them to experiment with grouping the tiles in different ways to find common factors, exploring at least two different arrangements.

Representational: Transition to the representational stage by asking students to draw diagrams of the tile arrangements they created. They can sketch the shapes used for each term and label them appropriately. Guide them to clearly show the groupings by circling or boxing the grouped terms in their drawings. Encourage them to rearrange the terms in their drawings to reflect the different groupings they discovered with the tiles. This helps students visualize the factoring process on paper.

Abstract: Move to the abstract stage by demonstrating how to write the polynomial and factor it using algebraic notation. Show how the physical groupings correspond to rearranging the terms in the expression. Write out the steps to factor by grouping, such as rearranging the polynomial to $4a^2 + 5ab - 8a - 10b$, grouping terms, factoring out the greatest common factors, and then factoring out the common binomial factor. Encourage students to connect each algebraic step back to their drawings and manipulations with the tiles. This helps them understand how the abstract symbols represent the concrete and visual actions they performed earlier.

Connecting the stages: Help students make connections between all three stages by discussing how each one builds on the previous.

Ask guiding questions like:
- "How did the way you grouped the tiles help you decide how to group the terms in your drawing?"
- "Can you see how the factors you pulled out in the equations match the groups you made with the tiles?"

Highlight how the concrete manipulation of tiles led to the representational drawings, which in turn made the abstract algebraic factoring clearer. This reinforces their understanding and shows them how to apply these strategies to other problems

Students: Page 353

Idea summary

Follow these steps when factoring by grouping:

1. Factor out the GCF from the expression, if possible
2. Arrange the terms so that the first two have a common factor and the last two have a common factor, if possible
3. Factor out the GCF for each pair of terms
4. Factor out the common binomial expression
5. Confirm that the binomial factors cannot be factored further, otherwise continue factoring

Practice

Students: Pages 354–355

What do you remember?

1 For the expression $3(x + 7) + x(x + 7)$, what is the common factor?

2 Determine which expression need to be rearranged in order to factor by grouping. Do not factor.
  a $a^2 - 4a - 3a + 12$
  b $6x^2 - 20 + 8x - 15x$
  c $1 + 100x^2 - 10x - 10x$
  d $7 + x - 28x - 4x^2$

3 Write an algebraic expression that can be factored to $(x + 3)(2x - 1)$.

4 Factor the following expressions:
  a $a(a + 6) + 2(a + 6)$
  b $2b(b - 3) - 5(b - 3)$
  c $5x(x + 2) - (x + 2)$
  d $2x(x - 7) + 3(7 - x)$
  e $5d(d + 3) + 20(d + 3)$
  f $8y(y - 4) + 10(4 - y)$
  g $y(y + 5) + 7(y + 5)$
  h $a(a - 4) - 3(a - 4)$
  i $p(p - 3) + 6(p - 3)$
  j $5(q + 4) - q(q + 4)$
  k $5(r - 3) - r(r - 3)$
  l $6r(2r - s) - rs(2r - s)$
  m $7t(t + u) + 2u(t + u)$
  n $x(y - z) - w(y - z)$
  o $5y(4w + 3x) - z(4w + 3x)$
  p $8y(y - 4) + 3(4 - y)$

Let's practice

5 Factor the following expressions:
  a $x^2 + 5x + 8x + 40$
  b $x^2 - 5x + 10x - 50$
  c $z^2 - 7z + 2z - 14$
  d $2k^2 + 12k + k + 6$
  e $2b^2 + 6b + b + 3$
  f $3x^2 - 10x + 3x - 20$
  g $-4y^2 + 30y - 5y - 36$
  h $x^2 - 3x + 8x - 24$
  i $x^2 + 2x + 5x + 10$
  j $20a^2 - 12a + 5a - 3$
  k $3y^2 + 6y + 4y + 8$
  l $9t^2 + 6t + 12t + 8$
  m $8x + xz - 16y - 2yz$
  n $24 + 3y + 8x + xy$
  o $7xy + wx + 7yz + wz$
  p $2mp + 6 + 3p + 4m$
  q $5mp + 6 + 2p + 15m$
  r $2x + 18yz + 12xy + 3z$

6 Factor the following expressions:
  a $(y + 4)(y + 7) + x(y + 7)$
  b $2f(g + h) + (g + h)^2$

7 Identify and explain the error:
$$6x - 21x^3 + 14x - 4 = 3x(2 - 7x) + 2(7z - 2)$$
$$= (3x + 2)(2 - 7x)$$

8 Complete the factoring process below and explain each step::
$$7x + 7 + x + x^2 = \square(x + 1) + x(1 + \square)$$
$$= \square(x + 1) + x(\square + 1)$$
$$= (x + 1)(\square + x)$$

9 The expression for the area of the rectangle shown is $3x^2 + 18x + x + 6$.
Write the expression of the area in factored form.

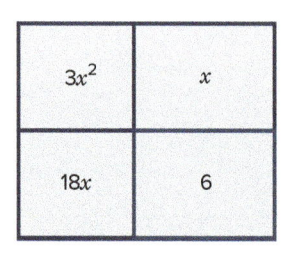

$3x^2$	x
$18x$	6

10 One expression for the area of the rectangle shown is $m^2 + 14m + 45$.
The rectangle is made up of four smaller rectangles.

Use the diagram to express the area of the large rectangle in factored form.

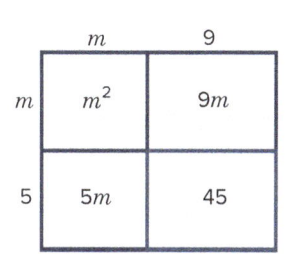

	m	9
m	m^2	$9m$
5	$5m$	45

11 Find an expression for the total area of the following rectangles in factored form:

a

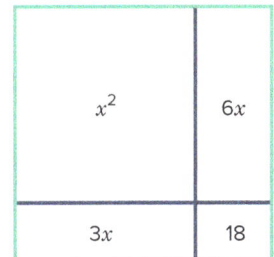

x^2	$6x$
$3x$	18

b

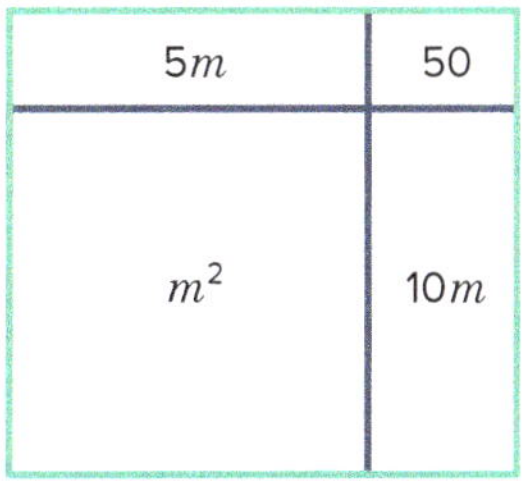

$5m$	50
m^2	$10m$

Let's extend our thinking

12 Factor the following expressions:
  a $3y^3 + 6y^2 - 15y - 30$
  b $3x^3 - x^2 + 27x - 9$
  c $17x^3 + 5x^2 + 17x + 5$
  c $a^3 + 5a^2 + a + 5$

13 Factor the following expressions:
  a $8x(2y + 3w) - z(2y + 3w)$
  b $8z(5x^2 + 4y) - (5x^2 + 4y)$
  c $2x + xz - 40y - 20yz$
  d $50 + 5y + 10x + xy$
  e $12xy + wx + 12yz + wz$
  f $6y - yw + w^2 - 6w$
  g $8xy + 4x^2 - 6xy^2 - 3x^2y$
  h $16ab + 6b^2 - 32ac - 12bc$

14 The polynomial expression $x^2 + 9x + 18$ is factored by grouping and one of its factors is $(x + 6)$. Rewrite the polynomial in the form $x^2 + \square x + \square x + 18$ and factor the expression.

15 For each polynomial:
  i Find three pairs of values that make the polynomial factorable.
  ii Determine what the pairs from part (i) have in common.

  a $x^3 - 3x^2 + \square x + \square$
  b $x^3 + \square x^2 + x + \square$

16 By rewriting $4x^2 + 17x + 4$ as an expression having four terms and factoring in pairs, factor the expression completely.

Answers

6.05 Factor by grouping

What do you remember?

1. $x + 7$

2. a Factorable as is b Rearrange first
   c Rearrange first d Factorable as is

3. $2x^2 - x + 6x - 3$

4. a $(a+6)(a+2)$ b $(b-3)(2b-5)$
   c $(5x-1)(x+2)$ d $(x-7)(2x-3)$
   e $5(d+4)(d+3)$ f $2(y-4)(4y-5)$
   g $(y+5)(y+7)$ h $(a-4)(a-3)$
   i $(p-3)(p+6)$ j $(q+4)(5-q)$
   k $(r-3)(5-r)$ l $(2r-s)(6r-rs)$
   m $(t+u)(7t+2u)$ n $(y-z)(x-w)$
   o $(4w+3x)(5y-z)$ p $(y-4)(8y-3)$

Let's practice

5. a $(x+5)(x+8)$ b $(x-5)(x+10)$
   c $(z+2)(z-7)$ d $(2k+1)(k+6)$
   e $(2b+1)(b+3)$ f $(3x+5)(x-4)$
   g $-(4y-9)(y-4)$ h $(x-3)(x+8)$
   i $(x+2)(x+5)$ j $(4a+1)(5a-3)$
   k $(3y+4)(y+2)$ l $(3t+2)(3t+4)$
   m $(x-2y)(8+z)$ n $(3+x)(8+y)$
   o $(x+z)(7y+w)$ p $(p+2)(2m+3)$
   q $(p+3)(5m+2)$ r $(2x+3z)(1+6y)$

6. a $(y+7)(y+4+x)$ b $(g+h)(2f+g+h)$

7. $(2-7x) \neq (7x-2)$ so either a factor of $-3x$ needs to be taken out of the first group or a factor of -2 needs to be taken out of the second group.

8. $7x + 7 + x + x^2 = 7(x+1) + x(1+x)$ Factor out the GCF from each pair
   $= 7(x+1) + x(x+1)$ Commutative property
   $= (x+1)(7+x)$ Factor out the binomial GCF from each group

9. $(3x+1)(x+6)$

10. $(m+5)(m+9)$

11. a $(x+6)(x+3)$ b $(m+5)(m+10)$

Let's extend our thinking

12. a $3(y+2)(y^2-5)$ b $(3x-1)(x^2+9)$
    c $(x^2+1)(17x+5)$ d $(a+5)(a^2+1)$

13. a $(2y+3w)(8x-z)$ b $(5x^2+4y)(8z-1)$
    c $(x-20y)(2+z)$ d $(5+x)(10+y)$
    e $(12y+w)(x+z)$ f $(6-w)(y-w)$
    g $x(2y+x)(4-3y)$ h $2(8a+3b)(b-2c)$

14. $x^2 + 6x + 3x + 18 = (x+3)(x+6)$

15. a i Answers will vary.
           1 and -3
           2 and -6
           3 and -9
       ii The second number is always the first number multiplied by -3.
    b i Answers will vary.
           1 and 1
           2 and 2
           3 and 3
       ii They have to be the same number.

16. $(x+4)(4x+1)$

6.06 Factor trinomials

Subtopic overview

Lesson narrative

In this lesson, students will use the patterns and structures they have seen when factoring by grouping and multiplying two binomials in the context of factoring trinomials. Students will learn to recognize the role of the leading coefficient in choosing a factoring strategy. By the end of this lesson, students will be able to apply factoring by grouping to trinomials and be able to describe a factoring strategy for a polynomial based on the structure of the expression.

Learning objective

Students: Page 356

After this lesson, you will be able to...
- factor trinomials completely.

Key vocabulary

- trinomial
- zero pair

Essential understanding

The same standard algorithm can be applied to rewrite any factorable quadratic expression, though other methods may prove more efficient.

Standards

This subtopic addresses the following Virginia 2023 Mathematics Standards of Learning standards.

Mathematical process goals

MPG3 — Mathematical Reasoning

Teachers can incorporate this goal into their lessons by encouraging students to justify their steps when factoring by grouping. Students should be guided to use logical reasoning to explain why they arranged the terms in a certain way, why they grouped the terms as they did, and why they factored out the common binomial.

Content standards

A.EO.2 — The student will perform operations on and factor polynomial expressions in one variable.

A.EO.2c — Factor completely first- and second-degree polynomials in one variable with integral coefficients. After factoring out the greatest common factor (GCF), leading coefficients should have no more than four factors.

A.EO.2e — Represent and demonstrate equality of quadratic expressions in different forms (e.g., concrete, verbal, symbolic, and graphical).

Prior connections

8.PFA.1 — The student will represent, simplify, and generate equivalent algebraic expressions in one variable.

A.EO.1 — The student will represent verbal quantitative situations algebraically and evaluate these expressions for given replacement values of the variables.

Future connections

A2.EO.3 — The student will perform operations on polynomial expressions in two or more variables and factor polynomial expressions in one and two variables.

Lesson Preparation

Suggested review

Depending on your students' level of prior knowledge, consider revisiting the following lessons:

Algebra 1 — 6.05 Factor by grouping

Tools

You may find these tools helpful:
- Scientific calculator
- Highlighter

Student lesson & teacher guide

Factoring trinomials

Students begin with an exploration into factoring trinomials by grouping.

Connecting the box model to factoring by grouping
Targeted instructional strategies

Many methods exist for factoring a trinomial into two binomials, but students may benefit from seeing the process of working backwards from a completed box model to the factored binomials.

Display the polynomial $x^2 + 10x - 24$, and tell students that the middle term can be rewritten as two x terms that multiply to be -24. Finding these two factors rewrites the trinomial as $x^2 + 12x - 2x - 24$.

These four terms can be written in a box model that students saw previously for multiplication.

x^2	$+12x$
$-2x$	-24

Taking the greatest common factor of each row and column gives us the terms inside the binomials that would multiply to be the polynomial written in the model.

GCF x	x^2	$+12x$
GCF -2	$-2x$	-24

	GCF x	GCF 2
	x^2	$+12x$
	$-2x$	-24

The greatest common factors of each row and column can be grouped to make the factored form of $x^2 + 10x - 24$, $(x - 2)(x + 12)$.

	\multicolumn{2}{c}{$x + 12$}
x	x^2	$+12x$
-2	$-2x$	-24

This connect factoring trinomials to the familiar process of multiplying polynomials.

Stronger and clearer each time
English language learner support

To support English Language Learners in understanding the lesson on factoring trinomials using the grouping method, start by having each student write out their steps for factoring a given trinomial, such as $3x^2 + 2x - 8$, and explain their reasoning behind each step. Emphasize moving away from trial and error by asking them to focus on why they chose specific pairs of factors.

Next, have students pair up and exchange their written steps. Each student explains their process to their partner, who will then ask clarifying questions such as
- Why did you choose these factors?
- Can you explain the step where you grouped the terms?

The goal is to encourage detailed explanations that avoid trial and error, focusing instead on the mathematical reasoning behind choosing factor pairs. Students should take note of any suggestions or new terms they learn during this exchange.

After the first pairing, have students switch to new partners and repeat the process. This time, press for even more details, ensuring the explanation includes clear reasoning for each step. Questions might include
- How do these factors multiply to the constant term?
- How did you check your work?

This helps solidify their understanding and ability to articulate the factoring process. Finally, students revise their initial written steps using the feedback from both partner discussions. The revised writing should clearly state how they identified pairs of factors, explain the grouping process in detail, use precise mathematical vocabulary, and ensure that the steps logically follow one another.

For example, an initial attempt might simply say, "I guessed the factors of 3 and −8 and tried them out." A refined explanation would be, "First, I multiplied 3 and −8 to get −24, then looked for factor pairs that multiplied to −24 and added to 2. I chose 6 and −4, then rewrote the trinomial as $3x^2 + 6x - 4x - 8$. Factoring the first two terms and the last two terms gives $3x(x + 2) - 4(x + 2)$. Grouping the terms makes the final factored form $(3x - 4)(x + 2)$."

This iterative process helps students develop a clear, well-structured explanation of how to factor trinomials using the grouping method, emphasizing a systematic approach over trial and error.

Provide different factoring methods
Student with disabilities support

Students may have difficulties remembering the identities for the special products. Help them make connections to their previous work with factoring trinomials by encouraging them to connect to their prior knowledge of factoring by grouping or factoring by inspection.

Have students write a difference of two squares, like $a^2 - 25$, as a trinomial $a^2 + 0a - 25$. Now they simply need to identify the two numbers whose product is −25 and whose sum is 0. Then they can rewrite the expression as $a^2 + 5a - 5a - 25$ and proceed to factor using their preferred method.

Many students will quickly become comfortable with the identities and will appreciate how much more efficient they are but others will prefer to use a method they are more familiar with. Any strategy that works should be acknowledged.

Multiplying factored polynomials to check steps
Address student misconceptions

Students may lose track of or make errors with signs. For example, factoring $x^2 + 5x - 6$ as $(x + 2)(x + 3)$ or $(x + 1)(x - 6)$. Challenge these misconceptions by having students find the product of their answer to ensure the original question is returned. Encourage students to seek support from peers if they cannot identify the error.

When c is negative in the standard form $ax^2 + bx + c$ students often mix up the signs of the two terms we decompose the middle term into, as they have opposite signs. Before beginning to factor by grouping encourage students to do a quick check that the polynomial they get after breaking up the middle term is indeed equal to the original polynomial. They could identify the error at the end by checking the product of the two binomials, but it is better to identify the error at the point of misconception.

Exploration

Students: Page 356

6.06 Factor trinomials

After this lesson, you will be able to...
- factor trinomials completely.

Factor trinomials

Trinomials can be rewritten as polynomials with four terms and factored by grouping.

Exploration

Consider the polynomial expressions factored by grouping below:

$3x^2 + 7x + 2$ $2x^2 + 11x + 12$ $x^2 + 5x + 6$

$3x^2 + 6x + 1x + 2$ $2x^2 + 8x + 3x + 12$ $x^2 + 3x + 2x + 6$

$3x(x + 2) + 1(x + 2)$ $2x(x + 4) + 3(x + 4)$ $x(x + 3) + 2(x + 3)$

$(x + 2)(3x + 1)$ $(x + 4)(2x + 3)$ $(x + 3)(x + 2)$

1. What patterns do you notice between the original expression and the terms used to rewrite the linear term?
2. Choose one of the linear terms and rewrite the term in a different way than shown, then determine whether the polynomial can still be factored by grouping.

Suggested student grouping: In pairs
Students are presented with three trinomials that are rewritten as polynomials with four terms, and then shown how the expressions are factored by grouping. Students discover a pattern for rewriting trinomial expressions in order to factor by grouping. A suggestion for implementation is to have students explore individually for a couple minutes before discussing with a partner.

Ideal student responses

These ideal responses may differ from other correct student responses. Less formal responses can be connected with the more precise mathematical language presented here.

1. **What patterns do you notice between the original expression and the terms used to rewrite the linear term?**
   The linear term is rewritten as the sum of two linear terms in order to make the trinomial into a polynomial with four terms. The product of the coefficients of the new linear terms is also equivalent to the products of the coefficient of the trinomial's quadratic term and the trinomial's constant.

2. **Choose one of the linear terms and rewrite the term in a different way than shown, then determine whether the polynomial can still be factored by grouping.**
   As long as the linear term is rewritten as two terms whose coefficients multiply to the same product as the product of the coefficient of the trinomial's quadratic term and the trinomial's constant, it is possible to factor the polynomial by grouping.

Purposeful questions
- What relationship do you think there is between the color-coded terms?
- What is the coefficient of the term x^2?

Possible misunderstandings
- Students may not make a connection between the coefficients of the new linear terms having a product equivalent to the product of the coefficient of the trinomial's quadratic term and the trinomial's constant. This may need to be made explicit to students in order to determine how to resolve question 2.

Students are introduced to a general procedure used for factoring by grouping given a trinomial. They are then shown how factoring polynomials can be represented by algebra tiles. They learn that a zero pair is formed when two terms cancel each other out.

Students: Pages 356–357

When using the grouping method to factor a trinomial, the coefficients of the terms used to rewrite the linear term have a sum equivalent to the linear coefficient from the original polynomial and a product equivalent to the product of the trinomial's leading coefficient and constant.

Steps in factoring a quadratic trinomial of the form $ax^2 + bx + c$:

1. Factor out any GCF.
   (If a is negative, we can also divide out a factor of –1 before continuing.)
2. Find two numbers, r and s, that multiply to ac and add to b.
3. Rewrite the trinomial with four terms in the form $ax^2 + rx + sx + c$.
4. Factor by grouping.
5. Check whether the answer will not factor further and verify the factored form by multiplication.

Remember to include any common factors divided out at the start, so each step results in an equivalent expression.

Algebra tiles can also be useful in factoring. Consider the expression $3x^2 + 7x - 6$ as the area of a rectangle. If we can find the lengths of this rectangle, then we will have two expressions that multiply to $3x^2 + 7x - 6$ because the area of a rectangle is $A = l \cdot w$.

We don't yet know the side lengths of the rectangle, but we will take 3 of the x^2 tiles, 7 of the $+x$ tiles, and 6 of the -1 tiles and arrange them as closely into a rectangle as we can.

We will start by lining up all of the x^2 tiles, then put the x tiles underneath to match the equal lengths. Finally, put the –1 tiles next to the x tiles to match the equal lengths.

Notice we have some empty spaces that need to be filled in.

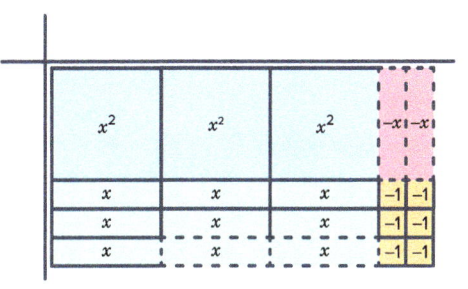

Notice that x tiles will fit perfectly into the empty spaces. However, we don't want to change the value of the expression so we need to make sure to add zero pairs.

A **zero pair** is two values that add to 0. x and $-x$ is a zero pair.

Since there are 4 empty spaces for x tiles, we can fill 2 spaces with (positive) x tiles and 2 spaces with $-x$ tiles. Technically this represents the expression $3x^2 + 9x - 2x - 6$ which is equivalent to $3x^2 + 7x - 6$ by combining like terms.

Now we can use the lengths of the sides of the rectangle to determine the expressions that can be multiplied together to create the original expression $3x^2 + 7x - 6$.

The x^2 tile has side lengths of x and x. The x tiles have a shorter side length of 1 and a longer side length of x. The $-x$ tiles have a shorter side length of -1 and a longer side length of x.

The shorter side length of the rectangle is $x + 3$ units and the longer side length is $3x - 2$ units.

This shows us:
$$3x^2 + 7x - 6 = 3x^2 + 9x - 2x + 6 = (x + 3)(3x - 2).$$

Examples

Students: Pages 357–358

Example 1

Factor $x^2 + 10x - 24$.

Create a strategy

Since there are no common factors for all three terms, we proceed with finding the value of two integers that multiply to $ac = (1)(-24) = -24$ and add up to $b = 10$. After finding these integers, we use them to rewrite the middle term $10x$ as a sum of two terms and then factor the trinomial by grouping.

Apply the idea

The factors of -24 are 1 and -24, -1 and 24, 2 and -12, -2 and 12, 3 and -8, -3 and 8, 4 and -6, -4 and 6. Among these factors, -2 and 12 are the pair that add up to 10.

We can use this to rewrite the trinomial and factor by grouping as follows:

$$\begin{aligned} x^2 + 10x - 24 &= x^2 + 12x - 2x - 24 &&\text{Rewrite polynomial with four terms} \\ &= x(x + 12) - 2(x + 12) &&\text{Factor each pair} \\ &= (x + 12)(x - 2) &&\text{Divide out common factor of } (x + 12) \end{aligned}$$

There are no more common factors to be divided out, so the fully factored form of the polynomial is $(x + 12)(x - 2)$.

Reflect and check

We can perform a midway check that we are factoring by grouping appropriately when we factor out a GCF from each set of binomials in the step $x(x + 12) - 2(x + 12)$.

If we factor out a GCF at this step and the binomial factors are not equivalent, we may have split the linear term from $x^2 + 10x - 24$ incorrectly or factored out a GCF incorrectly. This is an important place to stop and check that we are factoring appropriately.

Also note that we could have also rewritten the polynomial as $x^2 - 2x + 12x - 24$. This would have resulted in a different middle step in factoring by grouping but the same end result.

Purpose
Show students how to factor a trinomial by grouping.

Expected mistakes
Students may choose any factor pair and ignore that their sum must also be equal to 10. Remind students of the pattern in the exploration.

Reflecting with students
Challenge students to attempt to rewrite the trinomial expression using any of the factors and ignoring that their sum must be equivalent to 10. For instance, students might atttempt to rewrite the expression as $x^2 - 24x + 1x - 24$ and factor it by grouping. Help students determine why we cannot use this approach for factoring by grouping. The new expression will not be equivalent to the given expression.

Show students how to check their own work
Targeted instructional strategies
use with Example 1

Encourage students to self-evaluate and check their answer using the skill of multiplying polynomials.

$$\begin{aligned} (x + 12)(x - 2) &= (x)(x - 2) + (12)(x - 2) &&\text{Distribute } x - 2 \\ &= x^2 - 2x + 12x - 24 &&\text{Distribute } x \text{ and } 12 \\ &= x^2 + 10x - 24 &&\text{Combine like terms} \end{aligned}$$

Students: Pages 358–359

Example 2

Factor $3x^2 - 27$.

Create a strategy

We can factor a GCF of 3 out of the polynomial and write the polynomial as $3(x^2 - 9)$. Since the linear term is missing from the polynomial, we can write the polynomial as $3(x^2 + 0x - 9)$. There are no common factors. We will find the value of two integers that multiply to $ac = (1)(-9) = -9$ and add up to $b = 0$. After finding these integers, we use them to rewrite the middle term $0x$ as a sum of two terms. Then factor the trinomial by grouping.

Apply the idea

The factors of −9 are 1 and −9, −1 and 9, 3 and −3. Among these factors, 3 and −3 are the pair that add up to 0.

We can use this to rewrite the trinomial and factor by grouping as follows:

$3(x^2 + 0x - 9) = 3(x^2 + 3x - 3x - 9)$ Rewrite polynomial with four terms

$\qquad\qquad\qquad = 3[x(x + 3) - 3(x + 3)]$ Factor each pair

$\qquad\qquad\qquad = 3(x + 3)(x - 3)$ Divide out common factor of $(x + 3)$

There are no more common factors to be divided out, so the fully factored form of the polynomial is $3(x + 3)(x - 3)$.

Reflect and check

Recall that the special product of a difference of squares $(a + b)(a - b) = a^2 - b^2$. Notice that the factored form of the binomial $x^2 - 9 = (x + 3)(x - 3)$.

This can also be verified using algebra tiles:

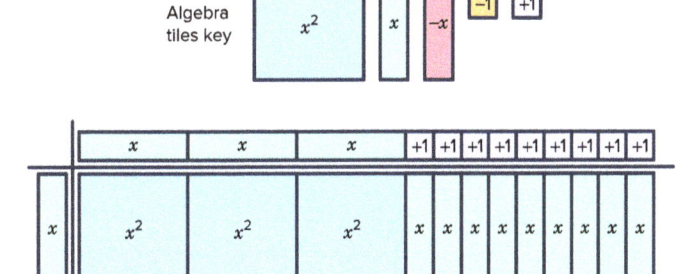

Notice the x terms form a total of 0. So, we know:

$$3x^2 - 27 = (3x + 9)(x - 3) = 3(x + 3)(x - 3)$$

Purpose
Show students how to factor a polynomial expression that is not a trinomial, but can be rewritten as a trinomial and factored by grouping.

Expected mistakes
Students may assume that they cannot factor the expression by grouping and state that the polynomial cannot be factored. Remind students that we have tools for factoring that we can use to help us factor, and that we should try to exhaust those options before giving up.

Reflecting with students
Ask students how they could refine this solution to be more efficient. For example, students could use the special product of a sum and difference to help them factor the expression after factoring a GCF.

> **Compare and connect**
> **English language learner support**
> use with Example 2
>
> Ask students to identify similarities and differences between being asked to find the product of $(a - b)(a + b)$ and being asked to factor $a^2 - b^2$ (or any of the patterns). Consider using the following sentence stems as an added support:
> - "Factoring a difference of squares, $a^2 - b^2$, and multiplying the product of a sum and a difference, $(a - b)(a + b)$, are similar because…"
> - "Factoring a difference of squares, $a^2 - b^2$, and multiplying the product of a sum and a difference, $(a - b)(a + b)$, are different because…"
> - "One thing that is the same between the two questions is…"
> - "One thing that is the different between the two questions is…"
> - "Factoring a difference of squares, $a^2 - b^2$, and multiplying the product of a sum and a difference, $(a - b)(a + b)$, are related because…"

Students: Pages 359–360

Example 3

Factor $5x^2 - 18x + 9$.

Create a strategy

Since there are no common factors for all three terms, we proceed with finding the value of two integers that multiply to $ac = 5 \cdot 9 = 45$ and add up to $b = -18$. After finding these integers, we use them to rewrite the middle term $-18x$ as a sum of two terms and then factor the trinomial by grouping.

Apply the idea

The factor pairs of 45 are 1 and 45, –1 and –45, 3 and 15, –3 and –15, 5 and 9, –5 and –9. Note that since the middle term of the trinomial is negative, we need to consider negative and positive factors. Of these factors, –15 and –3 are the pair that adds up to –18.

We can use this to rewrite the trinomial and factor by grouping as follows:

$5x^2 - 18x + 9 = 5x^2 - 15x - 3x + 9$ Rewrite polynomial with four terms
$ = 5x(x - 3) - 3(x - 3)$ Factor each pair to leave behind a common binomial
$ = (x - 3)(5x - 3)$ Divide out the common factor of $(x - 3)$

There are no more factors to be taken out, so the fully factored form of the polynomial is $(x - 3)(5x - 3)$.

Reflect and check

We can check the answer by multiplying the factored form $(5x - 3)(x - 3)$.

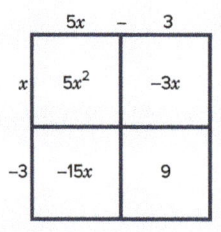

	$5x$	-3
x	$5x^2$	$-3x$
-3	$-15x$	9

The polynomial $5x^2 - 3x - 15x + 9$ simplifies to $5x^2 - 18x + 9$.

Purpose

Show students how to factor a trinomial when the leading coefficient is not 1.

Expected mistakes
Students may incorrectly factor by missing positive or negative signs. Remind students to check that their common binomials are in fact common before moving on to completing their factorization.

Reflecting with students
Prompt advanced learners to brainstorm and discuss situations where the factored form is more beneficial than the expanded form of the polynomial. For example, it is difficult to tell whether the polynomial is prime or composite, but the factored form shows that it is obviously not prime.

Invite students to consider real-world problems where one form may provide more insights than the other. The simplest example is the area of a rectangle. The original expression is best for determining the area, but the factored expression is best for finding the side lengths.

Students: Page 360

> ### Idea summary
> Steps in factoring a quadratic trinomial:
> 1. Factor out any GCF.
>   (If a is negative, we can also divide out a factor of –1 before continuing.)
> 2. Find two numbers, r and s, that multiply to ac and add to b.
> 3. Rewrite the trinomial with four terms, in the form $ax^2 + rx + sx + c$.
> 4. Factor by grouping.
> 5. Check whether the answer will not factor further and verify the factored form by multiplication.
>
> Remember to include any common factors divided out at the start, so each step results in an equivalent expression.

Practice

Students: Pages 360–362

What do you remember?

1. Complete this statement: To factor $x^2 + 9x + 18$, we need to find two numbers whose product is ⬚ and whose sum is ⬚.

2. Given that $a < b$, find the values of a and b in each pair of equations:

    a. $a + b = 19$
       $ab = 90$

    b. $a + b = -2$
       $ab = -63$

    c. $a + b = -10$
       $ab = 24$

3. Use the diagram and your knowledge of areas of rectangles to write the factored form of $x^2 + 6x + 4x + 24$

	x	+	6
x	x^2		$6x$
+			
4	$4x$		24

4 Factor each quadratic expression completely:
  a $x^2 + 2x + 3x + 6$
  b $3x^2 - x + 12x - 4$

5 For each of the following quadratic equations:
  i List all factors of the constant term.
  ii Factor the expression completely.
  a $x^2 + 11x + 18$
  b $x^2 + 16x + 64$
  c $x^2 + 17x + 72$

SOL 6 Which is a factor of $3m^2 - 4m - 15$?
  A $3m - 5$
  B $3m + 5$
  C $m - 5$
  D $m + 5$

Let's practice

7 Use the algebra tile model to factor the expression $x^2 - 2x - 8$.

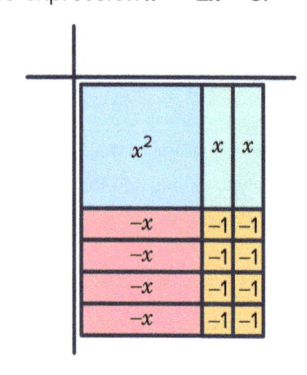

8 Factor the following quadratic expressions completely:
  a $x^2 - 8x + 15$
  b $x^2 + 11x + 24$
  c $x^2 + x - 90$
  d $x^2 + 22x + 120$
  e $x^2 - 34x - 72$
  f $x^2 + x - 56$
  g $3x^2 - 27x - 30$
  h $35m^2 + 140m + 105$
  i $2x^2 + 28x + 96$
  j $x^2 + 10x + 25$
  k $x^2 + 14x + 49$
  l $x^2 - 16x + 64$
  m $81 + 18x + x^2$
  n $36 - 12x + x^2$
  o $4x^2 + 40x + 100$
  p $-3x^2 + 12x - 12$

9 Brandon claims that the polynomial $3x^2 + 15x - 42$ will follow the factoring form of trinomials with a leading coefficient $a \neq 1$.

Explain Brandon's error, then fully factor the expression.

10 Draw a set of algebra tiles that shows that $(2x + 1)(2x - 1) = 4x^2 - 1$.

11 Rewrite the following quadratic expression in factored form (as a product of two linear factors):
  a $4x^2 - 32x + 15$
  b $5x^2 - 47x + 18$
  c $2x^2 - 19x + 45$
  d $10x^2 - 77x - 24$
  e $24x^2 + 22x - 35$
  f $6x^2 - 19x + 15$
  g $-6x^2 + 13x - 5$
  h $-35x^2 + 97x - 66$
  i $81x^2 + 36x + 4$
  j $49x^2 - 28x + 4$

12 Fully factor each expression:
  a $60x^2 - 70x - 100$
  b $2x^4 - 25x^3 + 42x^2$
  c $9x^2 + 12x + 3$
  d $27 - 123x - 60x^2$

13 A square has an area of $x^2 + 12x + 36$. Determine the length of the sides of this square.

14 A cube has a surface area of $6x^2 + 36x + 54$. Find an expression for the length of one side of the cube.

15 Fully factor each expression:

a $27x^2 - 48$
b $x^3 + 10x^2 + 25x$
c $x^4 - 16$
d $2x^4 - 1250$

Let's extend our thinking

16 Consider the following polynomials:
$$2x^2 + x + 1,\ 3x^2 - 2x - 4,\ 6x^2 + 10x - 5,\ 12x^2 - 12x + 1$$
a What do the polynomials have in common?
b How do you determine if a polynomial where $a \neq 1$ is not factorable?

17 Using the digits 1 to 9 with no repeats, fill in the blanks to create a factorable trinomial and provide the factored form:
$$4x^2 + \square\square x + \square$$

18 Using the digits 1 to 9 with no repeats, fill in the blanks to create a perfect square trinomial:
$$\square x^2 + \square\square x + \square\square$$

19 The expression $16x^2 - 24x + \square$ is a perfect square trinomial. Determine the missing value.

20 A photographer wants to put a border around her photo.
a Why might the photographer use x units to represent the width of the border?
b Use factoring to find expressions for the dimensions of the photograph with its border if the total area is $4x^2 + 24x + 35$ square units.
c What is the area of the photograph? Explain how you reached your solution.

21 Factor the quadratic expression:
$$6ab^2 - 36ab - 162a$$

22 Rewrite the quadratic expression in factored form:
$$3x^2 - 24xy + 48y^2$$

23 Consider the factorable polynomial $12x^2 + bx - 6$, where b is a positive integer.
a Find the largest possible value for b and list the factors.
b Find the smallest possible value for b and list the factors.

24 Sheldon and Gabriella each factored $16x^2 + 48x + 36$.
Whose work is incorrect? Identify and explain the error.

Sheldon:
$16x^2 + 48x + 36 = 16x^2 + 24x + 24x + 36$
$ = 8x(2x + 3) + 12(2x + 3)$
$ = (8x + 12)(2x + 3)$
$ = 4(2x + 3)(2x + 3)$

Gabriella:
$16x^2 + 48x + 36 = (4x + 6)(4x + 6)$
$ = 2(2x + 3)(2x + 3)$

25 A shape is formed from a square with side lengths of $3x$ that has a smaller square, with side lengths of 4, cut out from the center.
a Write a simplified expression for the area of this shape.
b A rectangle is created to have the same area found in part (a). Determine the dimensions for the rectangle.

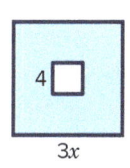

Answers

6.06 Factor trinomials

What do you remember?

1. 18, 9

2. a $a = 9, b = 10$ b $a = -9, b = 7$
   c $a = -6, b = -4$

3. $(x + 6)(x + 4)$

4. a $(x + 2)(x + 3)$ b $(3x - 1)(x + 4)$

5. a i 1, 2, 3, 6, 9, 18
      ii $(x + 2)(x + 9)$
   b i 1, 2, 4, 8, 16, 32, 64
      ii $(x + 8)(x + 8)$
   c i 1, 2, 3, 4, 6, 8, 9, 12, 18, 24, 36, 72
      ii $(x + 8)(x + 9)$

6. B

Let's practice

7. The algebra tiles total an area of $x^2 - 2x - 8$ and the product of the width and length is $(x - 4)(x + 2)$.

8. a $(x - 5)(x - 3)$ b $(x + 3)(x + 8)$
   c $(x - 9)(x + 10)$ d $(x + 10)(x + 12)$
   e $(x + 2)(x - 36)$ f $(x + 8)(x - 7)$
   g $3(x - 10)(x + 1)$ h $35(m + 1)(m + 3)$
   i $2(x + 6)(x + 8)$ j $(x + 5)^2$
   k $(x + 7)^2$ l $(x - 8)^2$
   m $(9 + x)^2$ n $(6 - x)^2$
   o $4(x + 5)^2$ p $-3(x - 2)^2$

9. Although this expression appears to have a leading coefficient of 3.3 is a common factor that can be factored out of the expression which leaves a trinomial where $a = 1$. The fully factored form is $3(x^2 + 5x - 14) = 3(x + 7)(x - 2)$.

10.

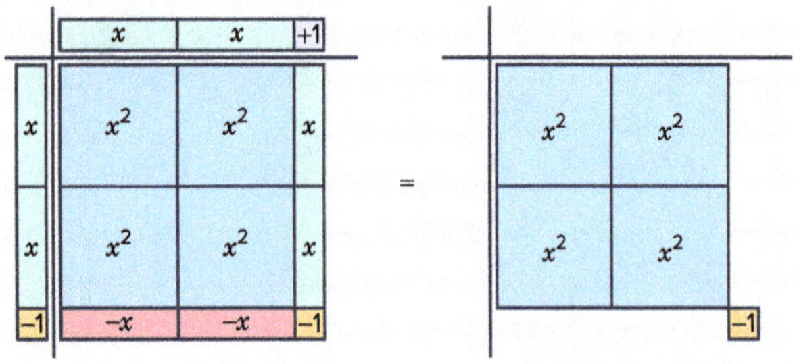

11. a $(2x - 1)(2x - 15)$ b $(5x - 2)(x - 9)$
    c $(2x - 9)(x - 5)$ d $(10x + 3)(x - 8)$
    e $(4x + 7)(6x - 5)$ f $(3x - 5)(2x - 3)$
    g $(5 - 3x)(2x - 1)$ h $(7x - 11)(6 - 5x)$
    i $(9x + 2)^2$ j $(7x - 2)^2$

12. a $10(6x + 5)(x - 2)$ b $x^2(2x - 21)(x - 2)$
    c $3(3x + 1)(x + 1)$ d $-3(4x + 9)(5x - 1)$

13. $x + 6$

14. $x + 3$

15. a $3(3x + 4)(3x - 4)$ b $x(x + 5)^2$
    c $(x^2 + 4)(x + 2)(x - 2)$ d $2(x^2 + 25)(x + 5)(x - 5)$

Let's extend our thinking

16. a Each polynomial has a leading coefficient $a \neq 1$ and none of the polynomials can be factored.
    b Find the product $a \cdot c$, then look for factors of ac that can add or subtract to be equal to the value of b. If no such factors exist, the polynomial is not factorable.

17. $4x^2 + 12x + 5 = (2x + 1)(2x + 5)$ is one possible answer.

18. Answers may vary.
    $9x^2 + 54x + 81$ and $4x^2 + 36x + 81$ are two possibilities.

19. 9

20. a She would use x units to represent the width of her border if she did not know yet what size border she wanted.
    b The expression for area factors as $(2x + 5)(2x + 7)$ square units, so, the dimensions of the photograph are $2x + 5$ units and $2x + 7$ units.
    c If the border is a width of x units, you would subtract $2x$ from each dimension since there is a border on both sides. That leaves the dimensions as 5 units and 7 units, so, the area of the photograph is 35 square units.

21. $6a(b - 9)(b + 3)$

22. $3(x - 4y)^2$

23. a The largest possible value for b is 71 and the factors are $(12x - 1)(x + 6)$
    b The smallest possible value for b is 1 and the factors are $(4x + 3)(3x - 2)$.

24. Gabriella did not pull out the common factor correctly. Since there is a factor of 2 in *both* factors of her expression, she needs to factor out a greatest common factor of 4.

25. a $9x^2 - 16$
    b $3x + 4$ and $3x - 4$

6.07 Factor using appropriate methods

Subtopic overview

Lesson narrative

In this lesson, students will explore structures of certain types of polynomials and their factored forms to make generalizations. Students will determine the best method for factoring polynomials and justify the use of that method. By the end of the lesson, students will be able to create polynomial expressions to represent quantities for contextual situations and work flexibly between various forms of polynomial expressions as needed.

Learning objectives

Students: Page 363

After this lesson, you will be able to...
- identify patterns to factor polynomials efficiently.
- use the structure of a polynomial to rewrite it in factored form.

Key vocabulary

- difference of two squares
- perfect square trinomial

Essential understanding

The structure of an expression can provide information on the most efficient way to rewrite it.

Standards

This subtopic addresses the following Virginia 2023 Mathematics Standards of Learning standards.

Mathematical process goals

MPG5 — Mathematical Reasoning

Teachers can incorporate this goal by encouraging students to use a variety of methods to represent their factoring by grouping process. This could include diagrams, flowcharts, or symbolic notation. Students could also be asked to translate between different representations, such as interpreting a written description of the factoring process in mathematical notation.

Content standards

A.EO.2 — The student will perform operations on and factor polynomial expressions in one variable.

A.EO.2c — Factor completely first-and second-degree polynomials in one variable with integral coefficients. After factoring out the greatest common factor (GCF), leading coefficients should have no more than four factors.

A.EO.2e — Represent and demonstrate equality of quadratic expressions in different forms (e.g., concrete, verbal, symbolic, and graphical).

Prior connections

8.PFA.1 — The student will represent, simplify, and generate equivalent algebraic expressions in one variable.

A.EO.1 — The student will represent verbal quantitative situations algebraically and evaluate these expressions for given replacement values of the variables.

Future connections

A2.EO.3 — The student will perform operations on polynomial expressions in two or more variables and factor polynomial expressions in one and two variables.

Engage Activity

Special factoring   60 mins

Students will be writing their own factoring rules and applying them to perfect square trinomials and the difference of two squares.

Understanding and skills

> **Will use**
> Factoring trinomials.

> **Will develop**
> Recognizing special factoring patterns found in factoring perfect square.

> **Could extend**
> Applying special factoring patterns found in factoring perfect square trinomials and the difference of two squares.

Preparation and materials
- Open and complete the student preview, anticipating classroom responses.
- **Materials:** None.

Support students with disabilities
Support memory - use previously taught skills and concepts

Provide the formula(s) for expanding a quadratic in factored form:
$$(x - a)(x - b) = x^2 - (a + b)x + ab$$

Where:
- a and b are real numbers.

Support for English language learners
Critique, correct, and clarify

While students are discussing the calculations for factoring quadratic functions, display the following incorrect calculation and reasoning:

The quadratic expression $x^2 + 8x + 12$ has the factors $(x - 3)$ and $(x - 4)$.

Ask students to identify the error, critique the reasoning, and write a short explanation of how the students' reasoning could be improved.

Classroom guide

Hook
Which one doesn't belong • 5 mins

Students choose one of four binomial products.

Implementation details

Highlight student responses that recognize differences in the structure of the expressions such as identical binomials, opposite signs, or similar values. Some students may choose to expand the binomial product or look for differences in the expanded forms.

Which one doesn't belong?
Select one option.

| $(x + 1)(x + 1)$ | A | $(x + 1)(x - 1)$ | B |
| $(2x + 1)(2x - 1)$ | C | $(x - 1)(x - 2)$ | D |

Slide 1 from Student Engage Activity

Launch
5 mins

Remind students of what it means to factor a trinomial expression.

Important mathematical concepts: Factoring, trinomials, quadratic expressions

Suggested grouping: Form pairs.

> **Continue when**
> Students have read the Launch and understand the context of the problem.

Explore

Think-pair-share • 15 mins

Anticipated strategies

Find patterns

Students may notice patterns in the terms that are listed in each of their selected expressions, and use those patterns to generalize rules about factoring.

What are the relationships between unfactored form and factored form of the polynomials?

Factor three of the following expressions:

$x^2 - 64$	A	$x^2 - 12x + 36$	B
$x^2 - 16x + 64$	C	$x^2 - 25$	D

Slide 4 from Student Engage Activity

Create area models

Students may use area models to try and determine how to factor each of their chosen polynomials. Then, they can look for patterns in the dimensions of each area model and summarize their findings.

Factor polynomials

Students will factor three of the four polynomials. The polynomials and their corresponding factored forms are as follows:

- $x^2 - 64 = (x + 8)(x - 8)$
- $x^2 - 12x + 36 = (x - 6)^2$
- $x^2 - 16x + 64 = (x - 8)^2$
- $x^2 - 25 = (x + 5)(x - 5)$

Students will also come up with their own factoring rules for the two types of polynomials, namely perfect square trinomials and the difference of two squares. Students will be apply their rules to determine what types of numbers make up the special polynomials that they've been working with.

Misconceptions

Creating only one rule for both forms

Do you notice anything different about your three polynomials? What about in their factored form? How would you describe each type of polynomial? Do you think we can define our factoring rule with just one rule? Or more?

Purposeful questions

Use the following questions to check for understanding and encourage critical thinking:
- Can you draw a picture or make a model to show that?
- How could you prove that?
- Is that true for all cases?
- What would happen if..? What if not?
- Do you see a pattern here? Can you make another trinomial that fits the pattern?

> **Continue when**
> All students have factored three polynomials and described rules for factoring.

Discuss

35 mins

Begin with small group discssions, then share out to the whole class to formalize and iterate on their self-written factoring rules. Make connections to generalized factoring rules wherever possible.

Discussion guide

The discussion should be used as a time for students to share their factoring rules, compare their results with their classmates', and then iterate on their rules.

Start the discussion by having each pair join with another pair to share their factoring rule(s) and the types of numbers that they need to have in order to create the required factors. Give groups time to adjust or update their rules after sharing and comparing.

Next, invite each group to share their rules and patterns for which these rule apply. Group and display these examples with a visual divide between the two forms.

For each rule type (perfect square trinomials and difference of two squares) ask students to produce example expression that the class can then try factoring according the directions in each rule described. If time permits, you may want to ask students to consider an expression like $x^2 + bc + (2c)^2$ and ask what we might be able to determine about the possible values for a if the factored form of the expression is known to be $(x + a)^2$ (it can be shown that a and b must be even numbers). This will allow students to deepen their understanding of the generalized rules they produced.

Lesson Preparation

Suggested review

Depending on your students' level of prior knowledge, consider revisiting the following lessons:

Algebra 1 — 6.02 Multiply polynomials
Algebra 1 — 6.04 Factor GCF
Algebra 1 — 6.05 Factor by grouping
Algebra 1 — 6.06 Factor trinomials

Tools

You may find these tools helpful:
- Scientific calculator

Student lesson & teacher guide

Factor using appropriate methods

Students review special products that will help them with factoring. An exploration that requires analyzing patterns follows.

Students: Pages 363

6.07 Factor using appropriate methods

After this lesson, you will be able to...
- identify patterns to factor polynomials efficiently.
- use the structure of a polynomial to rewrite it in factored form.

Engage activity
Ask your teacher to get started
Special factoring
Students will be writing their own factoring rules and applying them to perfect square trinomials and the difference of two squares.

Factor using appropriate methods

When factoring, there are a few special products that, if we learn to recognize them, can help us factor polynomials more quickly. Recall these special products:

Perfect square trinomials	**Difference of two squares**
A trinomial that is made by multiplying a binomial by itself	Two perfect square expressions being subtracted from each other
$a^2 + 2ab + b^2 = (a+b)^2$ or $a^2 - 2ab + b^2 = (a-b)^2$	$a^2 - b^2 = (a+b)(a-b)$

Note: The sum of squares, $a^2 + b^2$, is called prime (non-factorable).

Similar to a prime number, a prime polynomial has no factors other than 1 and itself. In other words, it has no factors with a degree less than the degree of the original polynomial.

Connecting perfect squares to special products
Targeted instructional strategies

In previous grades, students learned that perfect squares are numbers that can be modeled as a square. Remind students of the pattern of perfect squares with a visual like the one shown.

1^2	2^2	3^2	4^2	5^2
●	●● ●●	●●● ●●● ●●●	●●●● ●●●● ●●●● ●●●●	●●●●● ●●●●● ●●●●● ●●●●● ●●●●●
1	4	9	16	25

782   Mathspace   Virginia SOL Algebra 1 Teacher Edition
mathspace.co

Show students examples of models of special products using algebra tiles that form a square with their corresponding polynomials written underneath. Ask students to identify what shape each model has in common, and what they notice about the numerical values in the polynomials underneath.

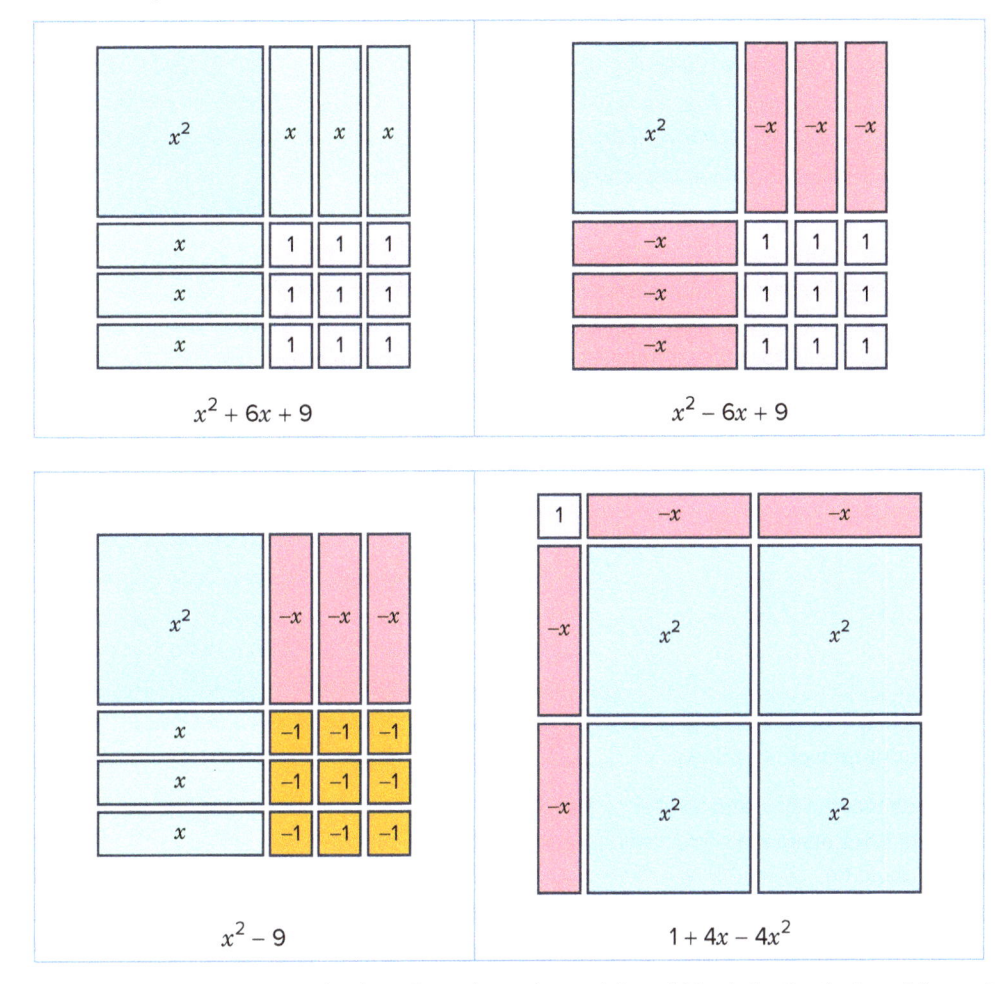

$x^2 + 6x + 9$

$x^2 - 6x + 9$

$x^2 - 9$

$1 + 4x - 4x^2$

Students should predict how numerical values from the polynomial could look for the factored form given the patterns from the perfect square patterns and algebra tile models.

Compare and connect
English language learner support

Ask students to identify similarities and differences between being asked to find the product of $(a - b)(a + b)$ and being asked to factor $a^2 - b^2$ (or any of the patterns). Consider using the following sentence stems as an added support:
- "Factoring a difference of squares, $a^2 - b^2$, and multiplying the product of a sum and a difference, $(a - b)(a + b)$, are similar because…"
- "Factoring a difference of squares, $a^2 - b^2$, and multiplying the product of a sum and a difference, $(a - b)(a + b)$, are different because…"
- "One thing that is the same between the two questions is…"
- "One thing that is the different between the two questions is…"
- "Factoring a difference of squares, $a^2 - b^2$, and multiplying the product of a sum and a difference, $(a - b)(a + b)$, are related because…"

Decompose the problem into smaller chunks and use an algorithm
Student with disabilities support

Encourage students to use Computational Thinking by decomposing the problem into smaller chunks and providing an annotated example. For example, when factoring the polynomial shown:
$$81x^2 - 72x + 16$$

1. Fill in the box : $81x^2 = \Box^2$, call the value in the box a.
2. Fill in the box: $16 = \Box^2$, call the value in the box b.
3. Check that $72x$ can be written as $2ab$
4. Fill in the pattern: $a^2 - 2ab + b^2 = (a - b)^2$ with the values of a and b from steps 1 and 2.

While this template is helpful for checking if a polynomial fits certain identities, students can also factor using the strategies previously used for other trinomials.

While trinomials can be factored as is, when factoring difference of squares, a linear term with a coefficient of 0 can be added between the two terms. For example:

$a^2 - 25 = a^2 + 0a - 25$ Rewrite with $+0a$
$ = a^2 + 5a - 5a - 25$ Find pair to rewrite for factoring by grouping
$ = a(a + 5) - 5(a + 5)$ Factor out the GCF
$ = (a - 5)(a + 5)$ Write as product

Avoid mistakes by checking that an expression is equivalent to a special product
Address student misconceptions

Students may notice that the first and last terms are perfect squares and skip the step of checking whether or not the middle term does make it a perfect square trinomial. For example, when asked to factor $4x^2 + 13x + 9$ an incorrect solution could be:

1. $4x^2 + 13x + 9 = (2x)^2 + 13x + 3^2$ Rewrite as a perfect square trinomial
2. $ = (2x + 3)^2$ Use the pattern

While the correction solution is $4x^2 + 13x + 9 = (4x + 9)(x + 1)$.

Exploration

Students: Page 363

Exploration

Consider the factored form of each polynomial expression:

$(x + 7)(x - 7)$ $(x - 6)(x - 6)$ $(2x + 5)(2x + 5)$ $(x + 4)(x + 4)$

$x^2 - 49$ $x^2 - 12x + 36$ $4x^2 + 20x + 25$ $x^2 + 8x + 16$

1. What do you notice about the factored form of the given polynomials?

Suggested student grouping: Small groups

Students are presented with factored polynomials and their original polynomial form. Students should notice special products and patterns that arise between polynomials and their factored form.

Ideal student responses

These ideal responses may differ from other correct student responses. Less formal responses can be connected with the more precise mathematical language presented here.

1. **What do you notice about the factored form of the given polynomials?**

   The form of the factored polynomials can be generalized as $(a \pm b)(a \pm b)$. There is a pattern in the quadratic term, the linear term, and the constant of each polynomial depending on its factored form. The quadratic term for each polynomial is a^2. The linear term for each polynomial is the product $\pm 2ab$. The constant term for each polynomial is the product $\pm b^2$. These are a mixture of special products but they each follow a similar pattern between the two terms of the binomials that are multiplied together.

Purposeful questions

- What examples of factored binomials and their polynomials can you come up with based on the patterns you see here?
- Do you prefer to memorize the algorithm for the special products or look for another pattern?

Possible misunderstandings

- Students may struggle to see patterns with few examples. Provide examples of other difference of two squares and perfect square trinomials to help students identify patterns.

Advanced learners: Analyzing structure to inform factoring methods
Targeted instructional strategies

Encourage advanced students or all students to analyze the structure of the polynomial expressions they are factoring to discover patterns within different types of polynomials. While working through the following examples, ask them to describe structures or identify patterns in the polynomial expressions. Ask questions like, "What similarities do you notice among these polynomials, and how do those similarities help in factoring them efficiently?"

This will prompt students to derive generalizations and efficiently factor a polynomial based on the structures they observe. Additionally, this exercise helps students assess and articulate their problem-solving strategies.

Students are provided with a procedure for factoring using appropriate methods. They are also shown how models with algebra tiles connect to special products and their factored form.

Students: Pages 363–364

> When polynomials are special products, the factored form has a pattern. Knowing how the terms of the binomials relate to the terms of the expanded polynomial can help us find the factored form of these special polynomials more quickly.
>
> When factoring polynomials, recall that the first step is to look for and factor out the greatest common factor of all terms. We can then factor by grouping, or identify a more efficient method if we recognize the patterns of special products.

For example, consider the product of a binomial squared, $(a+b)^2$:

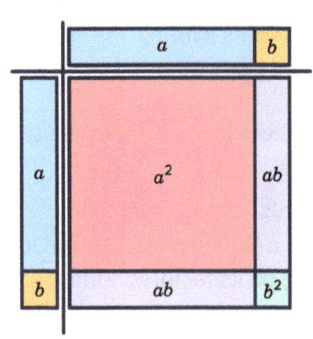

We can expand $(a+b)^2$ to $(a+b)(a+b)$ and represent them with an area model. Evaluating with this model and combining like terms, we get the product $a^2 + 2ab + b^2$.

So, we have:
$$(a+b)^2 = (a+b)(a+b) = a^2 + 2ab + b^2$$

Follow these steps for determining if a trinomial is a **perfect square trinomial** and factoring:

1. Factor out the GCF
2. Determine a from the leading term and b from the constant term
3. Verify whether the linear term is equal to $2ab$
4. If yes, use the structure of perfect square trinomials to write the factors

Now consider the product of a sum and a difference, $(a+b)(a-b)$:

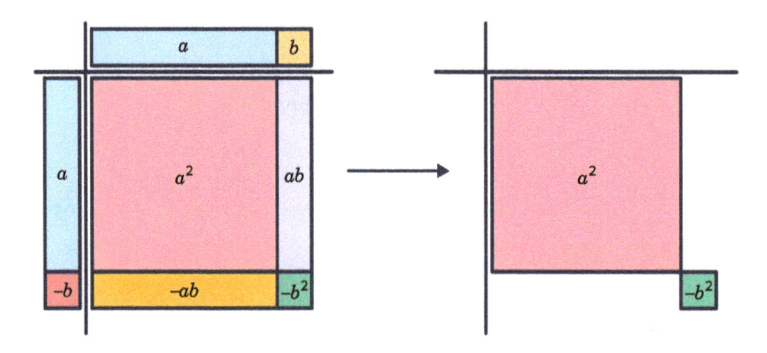

Notice that the term ab and $-ab$ are opposites and combine to make zero. We call this a zero pair. So, $(a+b)(a-b) = a^2 - b^2$.

Follow these steps for determining if a binomial is a **difference of two squares** and factoring:

1. Factor out the GCF
2. Determine a from the leading term and b from the constant term
3. Verify whether a and b are perfect squares by identifying their square roots
4. If yes, use the structure of a difference of squares to write the factors

Examples

Students: Page 365

Example 1

Factor $3p^2 + 12p + 12$

Create a strategy

We can factor a GCF of 3 out of the polynomial and write the polynomial as $3(p^2 + 4p + 4)$. Determine if the polynomial expression is a perfect square trinomial.

Since $a = p$ and $b = 2$ and the linear term is $2ab = 2(p)(2) = 4p$, we can verify that this is a perfect square trinomial and we can use special products to factor.

Apply the idea

Since $p^2 + 4p + 4$ is a perfect square trinomial, we use the identity in factoring:

$$a^2 + 2ab + b^2 = (a + b)^2 \quad \text{Identity for a perfect square trinomial}$$
$$= (p + 2)^2 \quad \text{Substitute } a = p \text{ and } b = 2$$

There are no more common factors to be divided out, so the fully factored form of the polynomial is $3(p + 2)^2$.

Reflect and check

If we instead were to factor by grouping, we will find the value of two integers that multiply to $ac = (1)(4) = 4$ and add up to $b = 4$. After finding these integers, we use them to rewrite the middle term $4p$ as a sum of two terms and then factor the trinomial by grouping.

The factors of 4 are 1 and 4, 2 and 2. Among these factors, 2 and 2 are the pair that adds up to 4. We can use this to rewrite the trinomial and factor by grouping as follows:

$$3(p^2 + 4p + 4) = 3(p^2 + 2p + 2p + 4) \quad \text{Rewrite polynomial with four terms}$$
$$= 3[p(p + 2) + 2(p + 2)] \quad \text{Factor each pair}$$
$$= 3(p + 2)(p + 2) \quad \text{Divide out the common factor of } (p + 2)$$

There are no more common factors to be divided out, so the fully factored form of the polynomial is $3(p + 2)^2$.

Purpose

Show students how to factor a GCF and a perfect square trinomial with a sum.

Expected mistakes

Students may forget the general form of a perfect square trinomial. Keeping the general forms of the special products nearby may help students recall the patterns.

Reflecting with students

Challenge students to factor the expression by grouping. Then, ask students which method they prefer for factoring.

Students: Pages 365–366

Example 2

Fully factor $9x^2 - 24x + 16$.

Create a strategy

We check first whether $9x^2 - 24x + 16$ is a special product and identify its type.

Since $a = 3x$ and $b = 4$ and the linear coefficient is $-2ab = 2(3x)(4) = -24x$, we can verify that this is a perfect square trinomial and we can use special products to factor.

Apply the idea

Since $9x^2 - 24x + 16$ is a perfect square trinomial, we can use the identity in factoring:

$$a^2 - 2ab + b^2 = (a - b)^2 \quad \text{Identity for a perfect square trinomial}$$
$$= (3x - 4)^2 \quad \text{Substitute } a = 3x \text{ and } b = 4$$

Reflect and check

We can check the answer by multiplying the factored form $(3x - 4)^2$.

$$(3x - 4)^2 = 9x^2 - 24x + 16 \quad \text{Identity for square of a binomial}$$

Purpose
Show students how to factor a perfect square trinomial with a difference.

Expected mistakes
Students may ignore the negative symbol attached to $24x$. Remind students to consider how the factoring changes with the signs of the terms.

Reflecting with students
Ask students how they can check that the factored form they wrote is correct. Students can multiply the binomials to confirm that the product is the original polynomial.

> **Combining patterns for perfect square trinomials**   use with Example 2
> **Student with disabilities support**

Some students will benefit from seeing $a^2 - 2ab + b^2 = (a - b)^2$ and $a^2 + 2ab + b^2 = (a + b)^2$ as a separate patterns, but students who find notation and manipulating symbols challenging may find it easier to consider that the second term in the parentheses can be positive or negative and that dictates the sign of the middle term. Some students will appreciated seeing the pattern in words instead of variables.

$$\text{First}^2 + 2 \cdot \text{First} \cdot \text{Second} + \text{Second}^2 = (\text{First} + \text{Second})^2$$

In this case, First = $9x$ and Second = -4, so we can write it as:

$$81x^2 - 72x + 16 = (9x)^2 + 2(9x)(-4) + (-4)^2 \quad \text{Notice that First} = 9x \text{ and Second} = -4$$
$$= (9x - 4)^2 \quad \text{Substitute}$$

Students: Page 366

Example 3

Factor $1 - x^2$.

Create a strategy
We check first whether $1 - x^2$ is a special product and identify its type.
Since it can be rewritten as $(1)^2 - (x)^2$ the polynomial is a difference of squares and we can use special products to factor.

Apply the idea
Since $1 - x^2$ is a difference of two squares, we use the identity in factoring:

$$a^2 - b^2 = (a + b)(a - b) \quad \text{Identity for a difference of two squares}$$
$$= (1 + x)(1 - x) \quad \text{Substitute } a = 1 \text{ and } b = x$$

Reflect and check

We can check the answer by multiplying the factored form $(1+x)(1-x)$.

$$(1+x)(1-x) = 1-x^2 \qquad \text{Identity for product of a sum and difference}$$

We can also check our answer using algebra tiles:

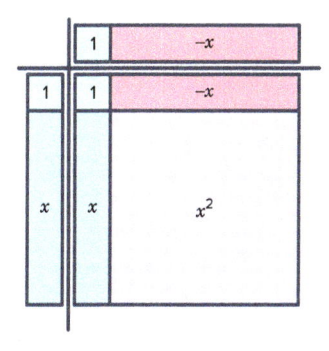

So, $(1-x)(1+x)$ is equivalent to $1-x+x-x^2 = 1-x^2$.

Purpose
Show students how to factor a difference of two squares.

Expected mistakes
Students may write the solution as $(x+1)(x-1)$ because they are accustomed to writing the variable first in the binomials. Remind students that factored the pattern follows the root of the first square term followed by the root of the second square term.

Reflecting with students
Ask students what the factored form of $1+x^2$ would be. Remind students that the sum of two squares is a prime polynomial that is not factorable.

1 is a perfect square
Address student misconceptions

use with Example 3

Some students may not recognize 1 as a perfect square because it is its own square and square root. Supporting students with the step of going from $1-x^2 \rightarrow 1^2 - x^2$ may be required.

Also, it is important to have examples where the constant is first as some students may not recognize this as a difference of squares as quickly.

Students: Page 367

> ### Example 4
>
> Factor $4m^2 + 40m + 36$.
>
> **Create a strategy**
>
> We can factor a GCF of 4 out of the polynomial and write the polynomial as $4(m^2 + 10m + 9)$. Determine if the polynomial expression is a perfect square trinomial.
>
> Since $a = m$ and $b = 3$ and the linear term should be $2ab = 2(m)(3) = 6m$ and $6m \neq 10m$, we can verify that this trinomial is *not* a perfect square trinomial and instead factor by grouping.
>
> **Apply the idea**
>
> The factors of 9 are 1 and 9, 3 and 3. Among these factors, 1 and 9 are the factor pair that adds up to 10.
>
> We can use this to rewrite the trinomial and factor by grouping as follows:
>
> | | |
> |---|---|
> | $4(m^2 + 10m + 9) = 4(m^2 + m + 9m + 9)$ | Rewrite polynomial with four terms |
> | $= 4[m(m + 1) + 9(m + 1)]$ | Factor each pair |
> | $= 4(m + 1)(m + 9)$ | Divide out the common factor of $(m + 1)$ |
>
> There are no more common factors to be divided out, so the fully factored form of the polynomial is $4(m + 1)(m + 9)$.
>
> **Reflect and check**
>
> If the polynomial could not be rewritten as four terms and factored by grouping, we would determine that the polynomial is not factorable.

Purpose
Show students how to factor a GCF followed by factoring by grouping.

Reflecting with students
Ask students why factoring a GCF first may be important. Factoring a GCF first allows us to work with smaller numbers.

Students: Page 367

> ### 💡 Idea summary
> By recognizing the patterns of factoring using special products, we can factor more efficiently:
> - Perfect square trinomials: $a^2 + 2ab + b^2 = (a + b)^2$ or $a^2 - 2ab + b^2 = (a - b)^2$
> - Difference of two squares: $a^2 - b^2 = (a + b)(a - b)$

Practice

Students: Pages 367–370

What do you remember?

1. For each trinomial in the form $ax^2 + bx + c$:
   i. Find two integer values that have a sum of b and a product of c.
   ii. Write the quadratic in factored form.

   a. $x^2 + 2x - 24$
   b. $x^2 - 4x - 77$
   c. $x^2 - 17x + 66$
   d. $x^2 + 10x + 24$

2. Consider each quadratic expression. The factored form of the expression is $(Ax + C)(Bx + D)$. Determine the following:
   i. the product of A and B
   ii. the signs for A and B: opposite or the same
   iii. the product of C and D
   iv. the signs for C and D: opposite or the same

   a. $15x^2 + 14x - 16$
   b. $-45x^2 + 29x - 4$

3. Fully factor the quadratic expressions:
   a. $n^2 - 36$
   b. $4 - u^2$
   c. $121m^2 - 64$
   d. $4 - 49y^2$
   e. $3t^2 - 12$
   f. $5x^2 - 320$
   g. $121x^2 - 49y^2$
   h. $x^2 - 16x + 64$
   i. $81 + 18x + x^2$
   j. $36 - 12x + x^2$
   k. $4x^2 + 40x + 100$
   l. $49x^2 - 28x + 4$

4. Describe the similarities and differences between factoring a polynomial in the form $ax^2 + bx + c$ where $a = 1$ or where $a \neq 1$.

Let's practice

5. For each of the following expressions:
   i. State an appropriate strategy or combination of strategies for factoring. Explain your choice.
   ii. Factor the expression fully.

   a. $x^2 + 17x + 72$
   b. $3x^2 + 3x - 60$
   c. $x^2 + 2x + 1$
   d. $3n^2 - 363$
   e. $2x^2 - 6x + 5x - 15$
   f. $9x^2 - 12x + 4$
   g. $(x + 16)^2 - x^2$
   h. $8p(p^2 - 9) - 5(p^2 - 9)$

6. Factor the following expressions fully using appropriate techniques:
   a. $y^2 - 13y + 12$
   b. $3x^2 + 24x + 48$
   c. $12x - 3x^2 - 20 + 5x$
   d. $9a^2 - 100$
   e. $-2x^2 - 5x + 3$
   h. $6x^2 - 36x + 48$
   g. $4x^2 - 64$
   h. $x^2 - 6x + (x + 1)(x - 6)$

7. A square carpet with side length x is modified by shortening one side by 6 inches and lengthening the other by 7 inches.
   a. Find the area of the carpet. Write your answer in factored form.
   b. Find the area of the modified carpet in the form $x^2 + bx + c$.
   c. Describe the relationship between the values 7, 6, 1 and −42.

8 A square table of side length x has one of its dimensions decreased by 4. This can be expressed visually by the area model shown.

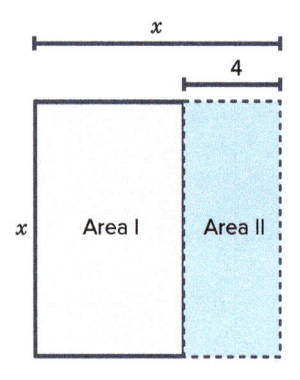

Determine if the following expressions are equivalent to the area $x(x-4)$:

a   Area I + Area II
b x^2 – Area II
c   Area I
d x^2 – Area I

9 A square rug originally had a side length of $2x$ inches. One of its dimensions is extended by 3 inches. We can model the area of the rug as a collection of rectangles, as shown in the diagram. The square on the left of the diagram has a side length of $2x$ inches and the short side of each rectangle is 1 inch.

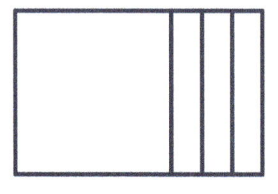

a   Write a factored expression that represents the area of the rug.
b   Find the areas of each section from the rug.
c   Find the total area of the rug in terms of x. Give your answer in the standard form $ax^2 + bx + c$.

10 The area of a quilt can be expressed as $x^2 + 6x + 4x + 24$.

a   Label the area model so that it represents the area of the quilt.

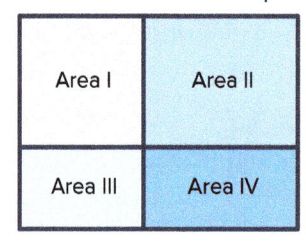

b   Express the area of the quilt in factored form.

11 Suppose we want to write the trinomial $x^2 + bx + c$ in the form $(x+p)(x+q)$. Read each condition and explain what must be true regarding the signs of p and q.

a c is negative.
b c and b are both positive.
c c is positive and b is negative.

Let's extend our thinking

12 Determine whether each of the following polynomials can be factored:

a $x^2 + 12x + 15$
b $-x^2 + 17x - 70$
c $x^2 + x - 42$
d $x^2 + 19x - 90$
e $x^2 + 25$
f $x^2 + 9x + 5$
g $6x^2 - 13x - 5$
h $4x^2 - 20x - 25$

13. Find two digits (1 to 9) to fill in the blanks and create a trinomial in the form $ax^2 + bx + c$ that
    a. Maximizes the value of b.
       $(x + \square)(x + \square)$
    b. Minimizes the value of c.
       $(x + \square)(x + \square)$
    c. Minimizes the value of b.
       $(x + \square)(x - \square)$

14. A quadratic polynomial is of the form $ax^2 + bx + c$, where a is non-zero, and has a special factored form.
    a. If $b = 0$, identify the form that the quadratic could be. State what must be true about the sign of c.
    b. If $b < 0$, identify the form that the quadratic could be. State what must be true about the sign of c.

15. Factor the following expressions fully using appropriate techniques:
    a. $4b^2 - 81c^2$
    b. $x^2y^2 - 36x^2$
    c. $9a^2 + 24ab + 16b^2$
    d. $-2x^4 + 2x^3 + 24x^2$
    e. $x^2 - x^2y + xy - x$
    f. $80x^4 + 92x^3 + 24x^2$
    g. $15x^2y + 50xy - 40y$
    h. $xy^2 + 4x$
    i. $81 - n^4$
    j. $4x^3 + 16x^2 - x - 4$

16. Rewrite the expression $(a^2 - b^2)(c^2 - d^2)$ as a difference of two squares.

17. Maribel is crafting a large blanket to give to her parents for their anniversary. Her plan is to combine a patchwork of family photographs with the flags from her parents' home countries. She hasn't determined the exact size of the blanket yet, and instead has expressions for the possible dimensions of each piece of fabric.

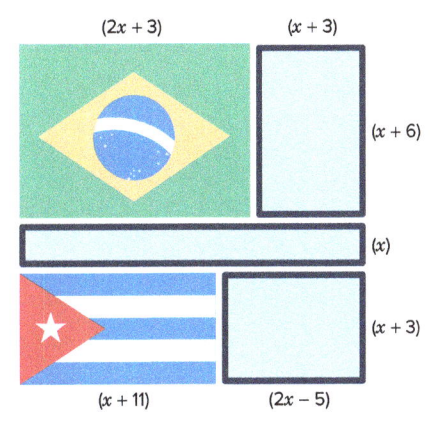

    (2x + 3)
    (x + 3)
    (x + 6)
    (x)
    (x + 3)
    (x + 11)
    (2x − 5)

    a. Write an expression for the total area of the blanket. Show at least three possible factorizations for the area.
    b. Find a value for x that creates a blanket with reasonable dimensions. Be sure to include units.

Answers

6.07 Factor using appropriate methods

What do you remember?

1. a i −4, 6
      ii $(x − 4)(x + 6)$
   b i 7, −11
      ii $(x + 7)(x − 11)$
   c i −6, −11
      ii $(x − 6)(x − 11)$
   d i 6, 4
      ii $(x + 6)(x + 4)$

2. a i 15
      ii The same
      iii −16
      iv Opposite
   b i −45
      ii Opposite
      iii −4
      iv Opposite

3. a $(n − 6)(n + 6)$
   b $(2 − u)(2 + u)$
   c $(11m + 8)(11m − 8)$
   d $(2 + 7y)(2 − 7y)$
   e $3(t + 2)(t − 2)$
   f $5(x − 8)(x + 8)$
   g $(11x + 7y)(11x − 7y)$
   h $(x − 8)^2$
   i $(9 + x)^2$
   j $(6 − x)^2$
   k $4(x + 5)^2$
   l $(7x − 2)^2$

4. In both cases, we are looking for a pair of binomials where the leading coefficients of the factors will multiply to be a and the constant terms will multiply to be c. The difference is that in a polynomial where $a \neq 1$ the factors of the constant c won't add up to the coefficient of the linear term, b.

Let's practice

5. a i Finding two numbers that have a sum of 17 and a product of 72
      ii $(x + 9)(x + 8)$
   b i Common factor then find two numbers that have a sum of 1 and a product of −20
      ii $3(x − 4)(x + 5)$
   c i Perfect square trinomial
      ii $(x + 1)^2$
   d i Common factor then difference of squares
      ii $3(n + 11)(n − 11)$
   e i Factoring by grouping
      ii $(2x + 5)(x − 3)$
   f i Perfect square trinomial
      ii $(3x − 2y)^2$
   g i Difference of squares
      ii $32(x + 8)$
   h i Binomial common factor, then difference of squares
      ii $(8p − 5)(p − 3)(p + 3)$

6. a $(y − 1)(y − 12)$
   b $3(x + 4)^2$
   c $(3x − 5)(4 − x)$
   d $(3a − 10)(3a + 10)$
   e $−(2x − 1)(x + 3)$
   f $6(x − 2)(x − 4)$
   g $4(x + 4)(x − 4)$
   h $(x − 6)(2x + 1)$

7. a $(x − 6)(x + 7)$
   b $x^2 + x − 42$
   c The sum of 7 and −6 is 1. The product of 7 and −6 is −42.

8. a No   b Yes   c Yes   d No

9. a $2x(2x + 3)$
   b Area of square rug is $4x^2$ in^2
      Area of each rectangle is $2x$ in^2
   c $4x^2 + 6x$ in^2

10. a

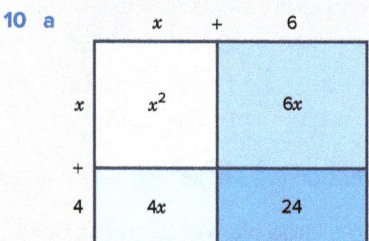

	x	+	6
x	x^2		$6x$
+			
4	$4x$		24

   b $(x + 6)(x + 4)$

11. a Exactly one of p or q must be negative.
    b Both p and q must be positive.
    c Both p and q must be negative.

Let's extend our thinking

12. a No   b Yes   c Yes   d No
    e No   f No   g Yes   h No

13. a $(x + 9)(x + 8) = x^2 + 17x + 72$
    b $(x + 2)(x + 1) = x^2 + 3x + 2$
    c $(x + 1)(x − 9) = x^2 − 8x − 9$

14. a If $b = 0$, the quadratic might be able to be factored as a difference of two squares. For this to be the case, we must also have $c < 0$.
    b If $b < 0$, the quadratic might be able to be factored as a perfect square. For this to be the case, we must also have $c > 0$.

15. a $(2b + 9c)(2b − 9c)$
    b $x^2(y + 6)(y − 6)$
    c $(3a + 4b)^2$
    d $−2x^2(x − 4)(x + 3)$
    e $x(x − 1)(1 − y)$ or $−x(x − 1)(y − 1)$
    f $4x^2(5x + 2)(4x + 3)$
    g $5y(3x − 2)(x + 4)$
    h $x(y^2 + 4)$
    i $(9 + n^2)(3 + n)(3 − n)$
    j $(x + 4)(2x + 1)(2x − 1)$

16 $(a^2 - b^2)(c^2 - d^2) = a^2c^2 - a^2d^2 - b^2c^2 + b^2d^2$
$= a^2c^2 + b^2d^2 - a^2d^2 - b^2c^2$
$= a^2c^2 + 2abcd + b^2d^2 - a^2d^2 - 2abcd - b^2c^2$
$= a^2c^2 + 2abcd + b^2d^2 - (a^2d^2 + 2abcd + b^2c^2)$
$= (ac + bd)^2 - (ad + bc)^2$

17 a The total area of the blanket is $9x^2 + 45x + 54$. Many factorizations exist. Three possible answers are: $(3x + 6)(3x + 9)$, $9(x + 2)(x + 3)$, or $9(x^2 + 5x + 6)$

b Answers will vary. Since dimensions can't be zero or negative, all answers must have $x > 2.5$.

For example, if $x = 10$ inches, the overall dimensions for the blanket would be 36 inches by 39 inches and each piece would have dimensions of 21 inches, 15 inches, 23 inches, 13 inches, 16 inches and 10 inches which will all reasonably display a photograph.

6.08 Divide polynomials

Subtopic overview

Lesson narrative

In this lesson, students will learn how to divide two polynomials using the process of factoring and dividing out the common factors. Students will review and use a variety of types of factoring in order to simplify the polynomial expression, including factoring out negatives and the greatest common factor.

Learning objective

Students: Page 371

> **After this lesson, you will be able to...**
> - divide a polynomial by a binomial or factored divisor.

Key vocabulary

- dividend
- divisor

Essential understanding

Polynomials can be divided using steps similar to those used when dividing real numbers.

Standards

This subtopic addresses the following Virginia 2023 Mathematics Standards of Learning standards.

Mathematical process goals

MPG2 — Mathematical Communication

Teachers can integrate this goal by asking students to write out their thought process when solving problems, using the correct mathematical notation and vocabulary. They should encourage students to explain their reasoning when dividing out common factors and simplifying the resulting expression. This can involve group discussions or presentations to the class.

MPG4 — Mathematical Connections

Teachers can integrate this goal by relating the concept of dividing polynomials to concepts previously learned, such as adding, subtracting, multiplying, and factoring polynomials. They can also show how this concept is related to other disciplines, such as physics or economics, which often use polynomial functions to model real-world scenarios.

MPG5 — Mathematical Representations

Teachers can integrate this goal by encouraging students to use different representations to understand and solve problems involving polynomial division. This could include using physical manipulatives, drawing diagrams, or using symbolic notation. For example, teachers could ask students to use algebra tiles to physically represent the process of dividing polynomials.

Content standards

A.EO.2 — The student will perform operations on and factor polynomial expressions in one variable.

A.EO.2d — Determine the quotient of polynomials, using a monomial or binomial divisor, or a completely factored divisor.

Prior connections

8.PFA.1 — The student will represent, simplify, and generate equivalent algebraic expressions in one variable.

A.EO.1 — The student will represent verbal quantitative situations algebraically and evaluate these expressions for given replacement values of the variables.

Future connections

A2.EO.3 — The student will perform operations on polynomial expressions in two or more variables and factor polynomial expressions in one and two variables.

Lesson Preparation

Suggested review

Depending on your students' level of prior knowledge, consider revisiting the following lessons:

- **Algebra 1** — 6.04 Factor GCF
- **Algebra 1** — 6.05 Factor by grouping
- **Algebra 1** — 6.06 Factor trinomials
- **Algebra 1** — 6.07 Factor using appropriate methods

Tools

You may find these tools helpful:
- Scientific calculator

Student lesson & teacher guide

Divide polynomials

Students are presented vocabulary for dividing and a step-by-step process for dividing a polynomial by another polynomial using algebraic tiles. Steps for dividing algebraically are also provided.

Students: Page 371

6.08 Divide polynomials

After this lesson, you will be able to...
- divide a polynomial by a binomial or factored divisor.

Divide polynomials

Dividing polynomials involves a process known as algebraic manipulation. We can view our **dividend** as the numerator of a fraction and our **divisor** as the denominator.

Consider the expression: $\frac{3x^2+7x-6}{3x-2}$. The dividend is $3x^2 + 7x - 6$ and the divisor is $3x - 2$. We can use algebra tiles to model the division. We will create a rectangle to represent the dividend, and the side lengths of the rectangle will represent its factors.

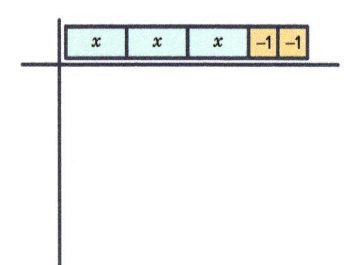

We already know one of the factors is the divisor so we can make one of the side lengths $3x - 2$.

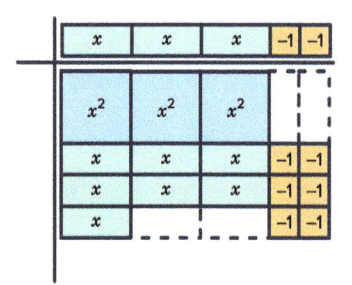

Next we fill in the rectangle with 3 of the x^2 tiles, 7 of the positive x tiles, and 6 of the –1 tiles to represent the dividend $3x^2 + 7x - 6$, making sure to line up tiles with equal lengths.

Notice that there are some empty spaces that we need to fill in with zero pairs.

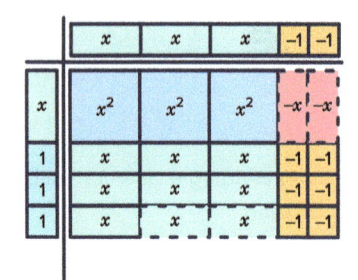

The empty spaces are the right size for x tiles. Since we need to add zero pairs so that we don't change the value of the expression we will fill 2 of the spaces with positive x tiles and the other 2 spaces with $-x$ tiles.

Now we can see that the length of the left side of the rectangle is $x + 3$. This means that $\frac{3x^2+7x-6}{3x-2} = x+3$.

Students: Page 372

We can approach this algebraically by following these steps:
1. Completely factor both the numerator and denominator.
2. Identify all common factors that are present in both the numerator and the denominator. These could be monomial or binomial factors.
3. Divide out all common factors from the numerator and denominator.
4. Simplify the resulting expression.

Expanding terms to demonstrate division
Targeted instructional strategies

The process of division can be demonstrated as canceling out matching factors in the numerator and denominator after expanding terms into their prime factors.
Begin by demonstrating an example with a monomial, such as

$$\frac{56x^5}{4x^2} = \frac{2 \cdot 2 \cdot 2 \cdot 2 \cdot 7 \cdot \cancel{x} \cdot \cancel{x} \cdot x \cdot x \cdot x}{2 \cdot 2 \cdot \cancel{x} \cdot \cancel{x}} \qquad \text{Expand and divide out common factors}$$
$$= 2 \cdot 7 \cdot x \cdot x \cdot x \qquad \text{Write out remaining factors}$$
$$= 14x^3 \qquad \text{Simplify}$$

Connect this process to different representations of factors without expanding, such as a term outside of parentheses.

$$\frac{2y(y+5)}{2y} = \frac{\cancel{2y}(y+5)}{\cancel{2y}} \qquad \text{Divide out common factors}$$
$$= y + 5 \qquad \text{Simplify}$$

Finally, demonstrate this with factored forms of trinomials from previous sections.

$$\frac{3(x+2)(x-1)}{x+2} = \frac{3\cancel{(x+2)}(x-1)}{\cancel{x+2}} \qquad \text{Divide out common factors}$$
$$= 3(x-1) \qquad \text{Write out remaining factors}$$

This can be used as an introduction to division problems showing a factorable trinomial in the numerator and a binomial in the denominator.

Information gap
English language learner support

Pair students and give each a card with a different factorable trinomial with the same binomial factor in the denominator. For example, one student receives $\frac{2x^2+7x+3}{x+3}$, while the other gets $\frac{3x^2+10x+3}{x+3}$. Students should not show each other their cards at any point. Students should be told that the goal is to find the sum of their binomials after dividing.

Each student factors their numerator independently, such as $(2x + 1)(x + 3)$ and $(3x + 1)(x + 3)$ from the original example, respectively. They must then communicate to identify the common binomial factor and simplify their expressions. Once they divide, they can work together to combine like terms and find the sum of their binomials.

This collaboration ensures mutual understanding and enhances their mathematical communication skills. Afterward, pairs present their solutions, explaining their factoring process and simplification, fostering engagement and deeper comprehension.

6.08 Divide polynomials   799
mathspace.co

Provide a table of important vocabulary and connect with examples
Student with disabilities support

Create a table with key vocabulary terms about quotients of polynomials. Provide an example that exhibits all key terms and help students write definitions of each with corresponding parts from the displayed example. Encourage students to use these terms in their mathematical discussions and written work.

$$\frac{3x^2+4x-15}{3x-5} = \frac{(3x-5)(x+3)}{3x-5}$$

Term	Definition	Example
Numerator		$3x^2 + 4x - 15$ and $(3x - 5)(x + 3)$
Denominator		$3x - 5$
Dividend		$3x^2 + 4x - 15$ and $(3x - 5)(x + 3)$
Divisor		$3x - 5$
Factor		$3x - 5$ and $x + 3$
Polynomial		$3x^2 + 4x - 15$

Misunderstanding 'dividing out common terms'
Address student misconceptions

A frequent misconception is that students often think of dividing out common terms as "canceling" them, which implies those terms become zero.

$$\frac{x^2+5x+4}{x+4} \neq \frac{x^2+5\cancel{x}+4}{\cancel{x}+4} \neq x^2+5$$

It's crucial to emphasize that when we divide out identical terms from the numerator and denominator, we are not making them disappear or turn into zero. Instead, they simplify to 1, as anything divided by itself is 1.

Examples

Students: Page 372

Example 1

Factor and simplify: $\dfrac{2x^2 + 10x - 100}{2x + 20}$

Create a strategy

We need to factor both the numerator and denominator by first factoring the greatest common factor of the terms in each expression.

Apply the idea

$\dfrac{2x^2 + 10x - 100}{2x + 20} = \dfrac{2(x+10)(x-5)}{2(x+10)}$ Factor the numerator and denominator

$= \dfrac{\cancel{2}\cancel{(x+10)}(x-5)}{\cancel{2}\cancel{(x+10)}}$ Divide out the common factors

$= x - 5$ Simplify common factors to 1

Reflect and check

When we have multiple common factors, it is as simple as dividing out each factor separately.

Purpose

Check students can simplify rational expressions by factoring and dividing out common factors in the numerator and denominator.

Expected mistakes

A student might not factor the expressions completely before dividing out common factors.
For example, after identifying the greatest common factor (GCF) of the numerator as 2, they might factor out the 2 but neglect to further factor the quadratic expression. This could lead them to represent the numerator as $2(x^2 + 5x - 50)$ instead of $2(x + 10)(x - 5)$.

🎓 Advanced learners: Thinking about restrictions to variables
Targeted instructional strategies

In upper level mathematics, students will be expected to state restrictions on variables before performing any type of division of polynomials. Introduce this concept to advanced learners while working through the examples, and encourage them to list the restrictions to the variables.

For this example, ask students to consider what would happen if we substituted $x = -10$ into the original expression. Because we cannot divide by 0, the expression would be undefined. In addition, if $x = -10$, $\dfrac{x+10}{x+10} = \dfrac{0}{0} \neq 1$, so we wouldn't be able to divide $\dfrac{x+10}{x+10}$.

By first stating that $x \neq -10$, the expression $\dfrac{x+10}{x+10} = 1$, so we can simplify the expression. This is why restricting the variables is an important part of the simplification process.

Students: Page 372

Example 2

Factor and simplify: $\dfrac{a^2-81}{9-a}$

Create a strategy

We can use the formula for factoring a difference of two squares: $A^2 - B^2 = (A+B)(A-B)$

Apply the idea

$\dfrac{a^2-81}{9-a} = \dfrac{(a+9)(a-9)}{-(a-9)}$ Factor the numerator and denominator

$= \dfrac{(a+9)\cancel{(a-9)}}{-\cancel{(a-9)}}$ Divide out the common factors and simplify to 1

$= -(a+9)$ Simplify common factors to 1

Purpose

Show students how to divide polynomials when factoring using an appropriate method, such as factoring a difference of squares.

Reflecting with students

Ask students to consider if there's a difference between "simplifying" and "canceling out" terms. This can serve as a segue to address common misconceptions.

Displaying list of common special factors and factoring methods   use with Example 2
Targeted instructional strategies

Having a list of these special factors and methods displayed prominently in the classroom or students' study area can serve as a handy reference and reinforcement of these key concepts.

The list can include patterns like the difference of squares: $a^2 - b^2 = (a-b)(a+b)$, perfect square trinomials: $a^2 + 2ab + b^2 = (a+b)^2$ and $a^2 - 2ab + b^2 = (a-b)^2$, and methods such as factoring a GCF and factoring by grouping.

Encourage students to refer to this list when working on problems, and to practice recognizing these patterns in different problems. This will help them develop a strong understanding of factoring methods and improve their problem-solving efficiency.

Students: Page 373

> **Example 3**

Factor and simplify: $\dfrac{8x^2 - 36x - 20}{(2x+1)(2x-1)}$

Create a strategy
Start by factoring the numerator. Then, we can divide out common factors.

Apply the idea

$\dfrac{8x^2 - 36x - 20}{(2x+1)(2x-1)} = \dfrac{4(x-5)(2x+1)}{(2x+1)(2x-1)}$ Factor numerator

$= \dfrac{4(x-5)\cancel{(2x+1)}}{\cancel{(2x+1)}(2x-1)}$ Divide out common factors

$= \dfrac{4(x-5)}{2x-1}$ Simplify common factors to 1

Purpose
Check students can simplify rational expressions by factoring and dividing out common factors in the numerator and denominator.

Reflecting with students
Students may not factor out a greatest common factor from the polynomial, which may keep students from identifying the matching factor. Students may get $\dfrac{(8x+4)(x-5)}{(2x+1)(2x-1)}$ and think there is no factor that divides out of the problem. Students should check their binomials in the numerator to see if any additional common factors can be taken out.

Develop an algorithm for dividing polynomials
Targeted instructional strategies

Incorporate Algorithmic Thinking by guiding students to develop a procedure for dividing polynomials. Begin by going through a few examples in with whole group instruction and then have students examine the solutions and develop a set of steps. Encourage them to apply this algorithm to various examples, refining their understanding with each iteration. For example:

1. Factor the numerator polynomial completely.
2. Factor the denominator polynomial completely.
3. Identify any common factors shared by the numerator and denominator.
4. Divide out (cancel) the common factors from both the numerator and denominator
5. Simplify the resulting expression to obtain the final simplified quotient.

Students: Page 373

> 💡 **Idea summary**
>
> To divide polynomials:
> 1. Completely factor the numerator and denominator
> 2. Divide out all common factors between the numerator and denominator
> 3. Simplify the resulting expression (if necessary)

Practice

Students: Pages 373–375

What do you remember?

1 Choose all of the following that are correct steps in dividing a polynomials.
  a Divide out all common factors from the numerator and denominator.
  b Identify all common factors that are present in both the numerator and the denominator.
  c Completely factor both the numerator and denominator.
  d Subtract the common factors from the numerator and denominator.
  e Simplify the resulting expression.

2 State whether each of the following factors could be divided out of:

$$\frac{2(3x+1)(x-1)(x^2-2)}{(3x+1)(x^2+2)(x-1)}$$

  a 2 b $3x+1$ c $x-1$ d x^2-2

3 State whether each of the following factors could be divided out of:

$$\frac{(n+1)(n+2)(n^2-1)}{(n+1)(n-1)}$$

  a $n+1$ b $n+2$ c $n-1$ d n^2-1

4 Assume all variables are non-zero:
  i What is the greatest common factor of the numerator and denominator?
  ii Write the numerator and denominator as a product of the greatest common factor and the remainder.
  iii Simplify fully.

  a $\dfrac{4(a-5)}{20a}$ b $\dfrac{(b-3)(b+4)}{8b(b+4)}$

5 Fill in the blanks:

  a $\dfrac{25x-40}{55} = \dfrac{5(\square)}{5(\square)} = \dfrac{\square}{\square}$ b $\dfrac{9m^2+24m}{18m^2} = \dfrac{3m(\square)}{3m(\square)} = \dfrac{\square}{\square}$

Let's Practice

6 Simplify:

a) $\dfrac{(x+3)(x-2)}{x+3}$ b) $\dfrac{(2x-5)(x+4)}{x+4}$ c) $\dfrac{x-7}{2(x-7)(x+4)}$ d) $\dfrac{(x+6)(x+8)}{(x+6)(x-9)}$

7 Which polynomial expression is equivalent to this expression if $s \neq -1$?

$$\dfrac{5+s-4s^2}{1+s}$$

A) $3s - 5$ B) $5 - 4s$ C) $5 - 4s^2$ D) $6 - 4s^2$

8 Simplify:

a) $\dfrac{x^2 - 8x + 16}{x - 4}$ b) $\dfrac{x^2 + 7x + 12}{x + 4}$ c) $\dfrac{m^2 - 16}{m - 4}$ d) $\dfrac{m^2 - 64}{8 + m}$

e) $\dfrac{a^2 - 121}{11 - a}$ f) $\dfrac{h^2 + 4h + 4}{(h + 2)}$ g) $\dfrac{t^2 + 6t + 9}{5(t + 3)}$ h) $\dfrac{u^2 - 8u + 16}{u - 4}$

i) $\dfrac{x^2 + 7x + 12}{x + 4}$ j) $\dfrac{a^2 + 8a + 15}{a + 5}$ k) $\dfrac{m^2 - 16}{m - 4}$ l) $\dfrac{m^2 - 64}{8 + m}$

m) $\dfrac{u - 2}{2 - u}$ n) $\dfrac{5y - 30}{6 - y}$ o) $\dfrac{a^2 - 121}{11 - a}$ p) $\dfrac{h^2 + 4h + 4}{(h + 2)}$

q) $\dfrac{t^2 + 6t + 9}{5(t + 3)}$ r) $\dfrac{10q^2 + 20q - 990}{5(q - 9)}$ s) $\dfrac{3x^2 - 18x - 216}{4(x + 6)}$ t) $\dfrac{b^2 - 4b + 4}{7(b - 2)}$

9 Factor and simplify:

a) $\dfrac{d^2 + 9d + 20}{(d + 5)(d + 1)}$ b) $\dfrac{v^2 - 3v - 18}{(v - 6)(v + 2)}$ c) $\dfrac{2p^2 + 5p - 3}{(p - 3)(2p - 1)}$ d) $\dfrac{6f^2 + 11f + 4}{(f + 1)(3f + 4)}$

e) $\dfrac{5e^2 + 2e - 3}{(e + 1)(2e + 7)}$ f) $\dfrac{x^2 + 9x + 20}{(x + 5)(x + 1)}$ g) $\dfrac{x^2 - 3x - 18}{(x - 6)(x + 2)}$ h) $\dfrac{2x^2 + 5x - 3}{(x - 3)(2x - 1)}$

10 Simplify:

a) $\dfrac{2x^2 + 8x}{x^2 + 4x}$ b) $\dfrac{x - 10}{x^2 - 100}$ c) $\dfrac{m^2 - 1}{2m^2 - 2}$ d) $\dfrac{2z^2 + 10z - 100}{2z + 20}$

e) $\dfrac{x - 10}{x^2 - 100}$ f) $\dfrac{3y + 6}{y^2 - 4}$ g) $\dfrac{m^2 - 16}{5m + 20}$ h) $\dfrac{h^2 + 6h + 9}{h^2 - 9}$

i) $\dfrac{k^2 - 3k - 10}{k^2 - 5k}$ j) $\dfrac{4z^2 + 8z - 192}{2z + 16}$ k) $\dfrac{8(p - r)^2}{8p^2 - 8r^2}$ l) $\dfrac{3y + 6}{y^2 - 4}$

11 Consider the problem $\dfrac{4n^2(n^2 - 1)}{4(n + 1)}$.

Identify and correct the error in each of the following student's work.

Andre: $\dfrac{4n^2(n^2 - 1)}{4(n + 1)} = \dfrac{n^2(n^2 - 1)}{n + 1}$

Liz: $\dfrac{4n^2(n^2 - 1)}{4(n + 1)} = (n - 1)$

12 Find the quotient of the following expressions:

a) $\dfrac{5x - 3 + 2x^2}{x + 3}$ b) $\dfrac{8x^2 - 12 - 4x}{6x - 9}$

c) $\dfrac{1 + 10x^2 + 7x}{(2x + 1)(x - 2)}$ d) $\dfrac{18m + 27m^2 - 9}{9m^2 - 1}$

e) $\dfrac{-6 + 13q + 15q^2}{6q + 5q^2}$ f) $\dfrac{8z^2 - 1 - 7z}{4z^2 - 4}$

13 Ralph rode his bike for a distance of $(4d^2 - 6d)$ km over a time of $(3d^2 + 2d)$ hours. What is the simplified expression for the speed he traveled?

Let's extend our thinking

14 Explain why $\dfrac{x+5}{x+1}$ does not equal $\dfrac{5}{1}$. Illustrate your answer with an example.

15 Fill in the blanks to make a true algebraic statement.

   a $\dfrac{\square}{5(a+1)} = (a-2)$

   b $\dfrac{(2y)(3y-1)(2y^2+1)}{\square} = 2y$

16 What would be the result of dividing $2g^2 - 10g + 12$ by $g^2 - 5g + 6$?

17 Mark divided a polynomial using the following steps. Do you agree with his solution? Why or why not?

   Factor and Simplify: $\dfrac{3m^2 - 6m - 45}{m^2 - 2m - 15}$

   $\dfrac{3m^2 - 6m - 45}{m^2 - 2m - 15} = \dfrac{(3m+9)(m-5)}{(m+3)(m-5)}$ Completely factor the numerator and denominator

   $= \dfrac{(3m+9)\cancel{(m-5)}}{(m+3)\cancel{(m-5)}}$ Divide out the common factors

   $= \dfrac{(3m+9)}{(m+3)}$ Rewrite in simplest form

18 Find the quotient of the following expressions:

   a $\dfrac{3x(x-2) + 14x - 3}{x+3}$

   b $\dfrac{x^2 - 2x - 3 + 2(x+1)}{2x - 2}$

19 At a landfill site, a hole in the shape of a rectangular prism is to be dug out. The length of the rectangular cross-section measures $2x$ meters and the width is $(x + 1)$ meters. If they need the volume of the landfill to be $2x(x^2 - 4x - 5)$ cubic meters, find the expression for the depth of the hole.

20 Create and solve an example of polynomial division where the degree of the denominator is greater than that of the numerator.

Answers

6.08 Divide polynomials

What do you remember?

1. a This is a step in dividing polynomials
   b This is a step in dividing polynomials
   c This is a step in dividing polynomials
   d This is not a step in dividing polynomials. Factors have to do with how many times a term will go into another term using multiplication, not subtraction.
   e This is a step in dividing polynomials

2. a No. This is not a common factor because it is not a factor of the denominator.
   b Yes. This is a common factor because it is a factor of the numerator and the denominator.
   c Yes. This is a common factor because it is a factor of the numerator and the denominator.
   d No. This is not a common factor because it is not a factor of the denominator.

3. a Yes. This is a common factor because it is a factor of the numerator and the denominator.
   b No. This is not a common factor because it is not a factor of the denominator.
   c Yes. This is a common factor because it is a factor of the numerator and the denominator. You first have to completely factor the numerator.
   d No. This is not a common factor because it is not a factor of the denominator.

4. a i 4   ii $\dfrac{4(a-5)}{4(5a)}$ iii $\dfrac{a-5}{5a}$
   b i $b+4$ ii $\dfrac{(b-3)(b+4)}{8b(b+4)}$ iii $\dfrac{b-3}{8b}$

5. a $\dfrac{25x-40}{55} = \dfrac{5(5x-8)}{5(11)} = \dfrac{5x-8}{11}$
   b $\dfrac{9m^2+24m}{18m^2} = \dfrac{3m(3m+8)}{3m(6m)} = \dfrac{3m+8}{6m}$

Let's practice

6. a $x-2$ b $2x-5$ c $\dfrac{1}{2(x+4)}$ d $\dfrac{x+8}{x-9}$

7. B

8. a $x-4$ b $x+3$ c $m+4$ d $m-8$
   e $-(a+11)$ f $(h+2)$ g $\dfrac{t+3}{5}$ h $u-4$
   i $x+3$ j $a+3$ k $m+4$ l $m-8$
   m -1 n -5 o $-(a+11)$ p $(h+2)$
   q $\dfrac{t+3}{5}$ r $2(q+11)$ s $\dfrac{3(x-12)}{4}$ t $\dfrac{b-2}{7}$

9. a $\dfrac{d+4}{d+1}$ b $\dfrac{v+3}{v+2}$ c $\dfrac{p+3}{p-3}$ d $\dfrac{2f+1}{f+1}$
   e $\dfrac{5e-3}{2e+7}$ f $\dfrac{x+4}{x+1}$ g $\dfrac{x+3}{x+2}$ h $\dfrac{x+3}{x-3}$

10. a 2   b $\dfrac{1}{x+10}$ c $\dfrac{1}{2}$ d $z-5$
    e $\dfrac{1}{x+10}$ f $\dfrac{3}{y-2}$ g $\dfrac{m-4}{5}$ h $\dfrac{h+3}{h-3}$
    i $\dfrac{k+2}{k}$ j $2(z-6)$ k $\dfrac{p-r}{p+r}$ l $\dfrac{3}{y-2}$

11. Andre forgot to factor $n^2 - 1$. This mean his answer still has a common factor of $n+1$ left in both the numerator and denominator. Liz incorrectly divided out $4n^2$ from the numerator and only 4 from the denominator.

12. a $2x-1$ b $\dfrac{4(x+1)}{3}$ c $\dfrac{5x+1}{x-2}$ d $\dfrac{9(x+1)}{3x+1}$
    e $\dfrac{3x-1}{x}$ f $\dfrac{8x+1}{4(x+1)}$

13. $\dfrac{4d-6}{3d+2}$ km/hr

Let's extend our thinking

14. The expression $\dfrac{x+5}{x+1}$ does not equal $\dfrac{5}{1}$ because they represent different mathematical relationships and values for different inputs of x. Let's consider an example where $x=2$. For $\dfrac{x+5}{x+1}$, when we substitute $x=2$, we get $\dfrac{2+5}{2+1} = \dfrac{7}{3}$. However, for $\dfrac{5}{1}$, regardless of the value of x, the fraction remains constant at $\dfrac{5}{1} = 5$. So, in this example, $\dfrac{2+5}{2+1} = \dfrac{7}{3}$ while $\dfrac{5}{1} = 5$, which clearly shows that they are not equal.

15. a $5a^2 - 5a - 10$ b $(3y-1)(2y^2+1)$

16. 2

17. Mark is not correct. While he has the right steps, he did not complete factor the numerator and $x+3$ is still left as a common factor

18. a $3x-1$ b $\dfrac{x+1}{2}$

19. $x-5$

20. Example: $\dfrac{(x+1)(x+2)}{(x+1)(x-1)(x+2)}$

    In general, the degree of the denominator must always remain greater than the degree of the numerator, by the same amount as the original problem.

Topic 6 Assessment: Polynomials and Factoring

1 Simplify each expression.

a $(3x^3 + 2x - 8) + (9x^5 - 5x^3 + 2x + 3)$

b $\left(\dfrac{3}{2}x^2 - 5\right) - \left(\dfrac{1}{2}x^2 - 3x + \dfrac{2}{3}\right)$

c $(x^2 - 4x + 6)(6x - 5)$

d $\dfrac{6x^3 - 4x^2 - 10x}{2x}$

2 Revenue is the profit minus the cost. The revenue generated by Leticia's seafood restaurant is modelled by $R(m) = -3.2m^2 + 10.9m + 990$, and the profit of her restaurant is modelled by $P(m) = 2.3m^2 - 29.3m + 830$, where m is the number of meals produced.

Find the polynomial that models the cost of Leticia's restaurant.

3 Simplify each product:

a $12a(3a^3 - 7)$

b $4x\left(\dfrac{x^2}{4} - \dfrac{x}{8} + 5\right)$

c $(9 - 8r)^2$

d $\left(\dfrac{2}{7}p - 11\right)\left(\dfrac{2}{7}p + 11\right)$

4 Find an expression for the total area of the following rectangles in factored form:

a

a^2	$15a$
$7a$	105

b

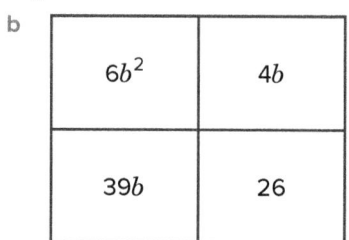

$6b^2$	$4b$
$39b$	26

5 Factor each polynomial completely:

a $\dfrac{8}{7}x^2 - \dfrac{2}{7}x$

b $q^3 - 7q^2 + q - 7$

c $y^2 - y - 132$

d $6t - 27$

e $x^2 + 18x + 81$

f $2x^3 + 16x^2 + 30x$

6 A cube has a surface area of $6x^2 + 48x + 96$.

Find an expression for the length of one side of the cube.

7 The volume of the box that a telescope comes in can be represented by the expression $21m^2 + 14m - 56$.

Find possible dimensions of the box.

8 Simplify each expression.

a $\dfrac{(x+3)(x+4)}{x+3}$

b $\dfrac{4x^2 - 9}{2x - 3}$

c $\dfrac{2x^2 + 2x - 12}{(x-2)(x+1)}$

9 What is the quotient of $(16x^2 + 10x - 44)$ and $(2x + 4)$? Assume the denominator does not equal zero.

A $32x^3 + 84x^2 - 48x - 176$

B $16x^2 + 12x - 40$

C $8x - 11$

D $8x + 11$

10 The rectangle shown below has an area of $36x^4 - 24x^2$ square units. Find a polynomial expression for its length.

? | $6x$

11 The volume V of the rectangular prism is given by $V = x^3 + 5x^2 - 9x - 45$. Find an expression for the missing dimension.

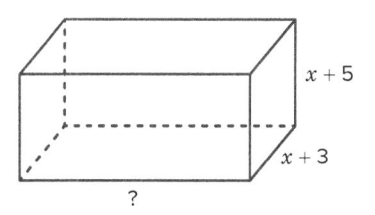

12 When factored completely, identify the factors of this polynomial:
$$6x^2 + 5x - 6$$

2	$3x - 2$	$x - 2$	$2x + 3$
3	$3x + 2$	$x + 2$	$x + 3$

13 Which of the following binomials is factor of $x^2 + 3x - 18$?

    A $x - 3$ B $x - 6$ C $x + 3$ D $x + 6$

Performance task

14 The form of an expression can help you to identify and interpret its parts in order to solve real-world problems. For each of the following, choose the form of the expression that is best for solving the problem, explain why it is useful, and then use it to find the solution.

    i   Wallace needs to find the volume of a shipping box so he can know how many cookies he can fit inside to send to his grandmother. He also needs to make sure each of the dimensions of the box is less than 12 in so it can fit in her post office box. The height, h, of the box is 6 in.

         A $h^3 + 4h^2 - 5h$ B $h(h + 5)(h - 1)$ C $-5h + h^2(h + 4)$

    ii   Orli wants to buy two nice outdoor rugs to cover her patio and needs to know the area they should each be. Let $x = 3$ ft.

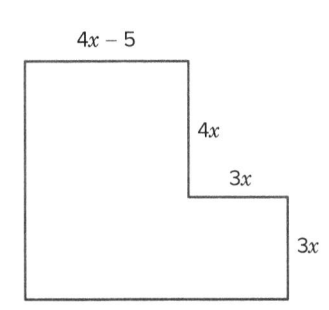

         A $(4x - 5)(4x) + (3x)(7x - 5)$
         B $(4x - 5)(7x) + (3x)(3x)$
         C $x(37x + 35)$

Answers

Topic 6 Assessment: Polynomials and Factoring

1. a $9x^5 - 2x^3 + 4x - 5$
   b $x^2 - \frac{17}{3} + 3x$
   c $6x^3 - 29x^2 + 56x - 30$
   d $3x^2 - 2x - 5$
   A.EO.2a, A.EO.2b, A.EO.2d

2. $-5.5m^2 + 40.2m + 160$
   A.EO.2a

3. a $36a^4 - 84a$
   b $x^3 - \frac{x^2}{2} + 20x$
   c $81 - 144r + 64r^2$
   d $\frac{4p^2}{49} - 121$
   A.EO.2b

4. a $(a + 15)(a + 7)$
   b $(3b + 2)(2b + 13)$
   A.EO.2b, A.EO.2e

5. a $\frac{2}{7}x(4x - 1)$
   b $(q - 7)(q^2 + 1)$
   c $(y - 12)(y + 11)$
   d $3(2t - 9)$
   e $(x + 9)^2$
   f $2x(x + 5)(x + 3)$
   A.EO.2c

6. $x + 4$
   A.EO.2c

7. 7, $3m - 4$ and $m + 2$
   A.EO.2c

8. a $x + 4$ b $2x + 3$ c $\frac{2(x + 3)}{x + 1}$
   A.EO.2d

9. C
   A.EO.2d

10. $6x^3 - 4x$
    A.EO.2d, A.EO.2e

11. $x - 3$
    A.EO.2d, A.EO.2e

12. $3x + 2$ and $2x + 3$
    A.EO.2c

13. A, D
    A.EO.2c

Performance task

14. i **B**, the factored form clearly shows all 3 dimensions of the box which will allow Wallace to easily check that none of them exceeds 12 in. He will then be able to quickly multiply the dimensions to find the volume. The dimensions are 6 in, 11 in, and 5 in so the box can be mailed to his grandmother. The volume is 330 in^3.

    ii **A** or **B** because there are two ways she could lay the rugs. These two expressions show the dimensions of each individual rug. The third expression shows the dimensions of a rectangular patio that has the same area as Orli's but a rug with those dimensions would not be appropriate. For expression **A** the area of the rugs is 84 ft^2 and 144 ft^2. For expression **B** the area of the rugs is 147 ft^2 and 81 ft^2.

    A.EO.2a, A.EO.2b, A.EO.2c A.EO.2d, A.EO.2e, MP1, MP5

7 Quadratic Functions

> **Big ideas**
> - A family of functions is defined by a unique set of characteristics shared by all functions that belong to that family. These characteristics give insight into the types of real-world situations that a function models.
> - There are many ways to represent a function (equation, table, graph, written description, etc.). The way a function is represented can affect what conclusions can be made.
> - Functions provide a representation for how related quantities vary. This makes functions a good way to represent many real world situations.

Chapter outline

7.01	Characteristics of quadratic functions (A.F.2)	817
7.02	Quadratic functions in factored form (A.F.2)	845
7.03	Quadratic functions in vertex form (A.F.2)	874
7.04	Quadratic functions in standard form (A.F.2)	909
7.05	Compare linear, quadratic, and exponential functions (A.F.1, A.F.2)	936

The word "quadratic" comes from "quad", meaning square, due to the squared term in the equation!

7. Quadratic Functions

Topic Overview

Foundational knowledge

Evaluating standards proficiency

The skills book contains questions matched to individual standards. It can be used to measure proficiency for each.

Students should be proficient in these standards.

8.PFA.3 — The student will represent and solve problems, including those in context, by using linear functions and analyzing their key characteristics (the value of the y-intercept (b) and the coordinates of the ordered pairs in graphs will be limited to integers).

Big ideas and essential understanding

A family of functions is defined by a unique set of characteristics shared by all functions that belong to that family. These characteristics give insight into the types of real-world situations that a function models.

7.01 — Quadratic functions have a linear rate of change. The features of a quadratic function can give insight into the real-world scenario the function represents; particularly the intercepts and vertex.

7.03 — Different representations of a function may highlight or hide different characteristics but they do not change the function itself. The vertex form of a quadratic function highlights the coordinates of the vertex and as a result the axis of symmetry.

7.04 — Different representations of a function may highlight or hide different characteristics but they do not change the function itself. The standard form of a quadratic function highlights the y-intercept.

7.05 — All of the functions in a given family share certain characteristics that can be identified from their equations, graphs, or input/output pairs.

There are many ways to represent a function (equation, table, graph, written description, etc.). The way a function is represented can affect what conclusions can be made.

7.02 — Different representations of a function may highlight or hide different characteristics but they do not change the function itself. The factored form of a function highlights the x-intercepts.

Functions provide a representation for how related quantities vary. This makes functions a good way to represent many real world situations.

7.05 — Linear and exponential functions can be distinguished by their rate of change.

Standards

A.F.1 — The student will investigate, analyze, and compare linear functions algebraically and graphically, and model linear relationships.

A.F.1a — Determine and identify the domain, range, zeros, slope, and intercepts of a linear function, presented algebraically or graphically, including the interpretation of these characteristics in contextual situations.
7.05 Compare linear, quadratic, and exponential functions

A.F.1f — Graph a linear function in two variables, with and without the use of technology, including those that can represent contextual situations.
7.05 Compare linear, quadratic, and exponential functions

A.F.1g — For any value, x, in the domain of f, determine $f(x)$, and determine x given any value $f(x)$ in the range of f, given an algebraic or graphical representation of a linear function.

7.05 Compare linear, quadratic, and exponential functions

A.F.2 — The student will investigate, analyze, and compare characteristics of functions, including quadratic and exponential functions, and model quadratic and exponential relationships.

A.F.2b — Given an equation or graph, determine key characteristics of a quadratic function including x-intercepts (zeros), y-intercept, vertex (maximum or minimum), and domain and range (including when restricted by context); interpret key characteristics as related to contextual situations, where applicable.
7.01 Characteristics of quadratic functions
7.02 Quadratic functions in factored form
7.03 Quadratic functions in vertex form
7.04 Quadratic functions in standard form
7.05 Compare linear, quadratic, and exponential functions

A.F.2c — Graph a quadratic function, $f(x)$, in two variables using a variety of strategies, including transformations $f(x) + k$ and $kf(x)$, where k is limited to rational values.
7.01 Characteristics of quadratic functions
7.02 Quadratic functions in factored form
7.03 Quadratic functions in vertex form
7.04 Quadratic functions in standard form
7.05 Compare linear, quadratic, and exponential functions

A.F.2d — Make connections between the algebraic (standard and factored forms) and graphical representation of a quadratic function.
7.02 Quadratic functions in factored form
7.04 Quadratic functions in standard form

A.F.2e — Given an equation or graph of an exponential function in the form $y = ab^x$ (where b is limited to a natural number), interpret key characteristics, including y-intercepts and domain and range; interpret key characteristics as related to contextual situations, where applicable.
7.05 Compare linear, quadratic, and exponential functions

A.F.2f — Graph an exponential function, $f(x)$, in two variables using a variety of strategies, including transformations $f(x) + k$ and $kf(x)$, where k is limited to rational values.
7.05 Compare linear, quadratic, and exponential functions

A.F.2g — For any value, x, in the domain of f, determine $f(x)$ of a quadratic or exponential function. Determine x given any value $f(x)$ in the range of f of a quadratic function. Explain the meaning of x and $f(x)$ in context.
7.02 Quadratic functions in factored form
7.03 Quadratic functions in vertex form
7.04 Quadratic functions in standard form
7.05 Compare linear, quadratic, and exponential functions

A.F.2h — Compare and contrast the key characteristics of linear functions ($f(x) = x$), quadratic functions ($f(x) = x^2$), and exponential functions ($f(x) = b^x$) using tables and graphs.
7.05 Compare linear, quadratic, and exponential functions

Future connections

A.EI.2 — The student will represent, solve, explain, and interpret the solution to a system of two linear equations, a linear inequality in two variables, or a system of two linear inequalities in two variables.

A.ST.1 — The student will apply the data cycle (formulate questions; collect or acquire data; organize and represent data; and analyze data and communicate results) with a focus on representing bivariate data in scatterplots and determining the curve of best fit using linear and quadratic functions.

A2.EI.6 — The student will represent, solve, and interpret the solution to a polynomial equation.

A2.F.1 — The student will investigate, analyze, and compare square root, cube root, rational, exponential, and logarithmic function families, algebraically and graphically, using transformations.

A2.F.2 — The student will investigate and analyze characteristics of square root, cube root, rational, polynomial, exponential, logarithmic, and piecewise-defined functions algebraically and graphically.

Continuous Assessment

🚩 Measure standards proficiency with check-ins

Before starting a new topic, it's a great time to go online and have students complete a Skills Check-in to measure their readiness for the topic.

7.01 Characteristics of quadratic functions

Subtopic overview

Lesson narrative

In the lesson, students will examine graphs, equations, and contextual situations of quadratic functions to identify key characteristics, including the domain and average rate of change intervals. By the end of the lesson, students will be able to make sense of problems and analyze context to interpret key features of quadratic graphs and tables and reason abstractly and quantitatively to find solutions by connecting key features to the quantities they represent.

Learning objectives

Students: Page 378

After this lesson, you will be able to...
- identify and interpret key features of quadratic functions given a real-world context.
- identify and interpret characteristics of quadratic functions including domain, x-intercepts, range, y-intercepts, and values of quadratic functions.

Key vocabulary

- axis of symmetry
- parabola
- quadratic function
- vertex

Essential understanding

Quadratic functions have a linear rate of change. The features of a quadratic function can give insight into the real-world scenario the function represents; particularly the intercepts and vertex.

Standards

This subtopic addresses the following Virginia 2023 Mathematics Standards of Learning standards.

Mathematical process goals

MPG3 — Mathematical Reasoning

Teachers can enhance students' mathematical reasoning skills by asking them to justify their solutions to problems or explain why certain characteristics are true for quadratic functions. For example, they could ask why the graph of a quadratic function is a parabola or why the domain of a quadratic function is always all real numbers.

MPG5 — Mathematical Representations

Teachers can encourage students to use a variety of representations by having them graph quadratic functions or represent them symbolically. They can also use technology, such as graphing calculators or online graphing tools, to help students explore and visualize quadratic functions and their key characteristics. For instance, they can encourage students to use these tools to observe how changes in the values of a, b and c affect the shape and position of the parabola. Additionally, they can have students represent real-world situations, like the trajectory of a thrown ball, using quadratic equations and graphs.

Content standards

A.F.2 — The student will investigate, analyze, and compare characteristics of functions, including quadratic and exponential functions, and model quadratic and exponential relationships.

A.F.2b — Given an equation or graph, determine key characteristics of a quadratic function including x-intercepts (zeros), y-intercept, vertex (maximum or minimum), and domain and range (including when restricted by context); interpret key characteristics as related to contextual situations, where applicable.

A.F.2c — Graph a quadratic function, $f(x)$, in two variables using a variety of strategies, including transformations $f(x) + k$ and $kf(x)$, where k is limited to rational values.

Prior connections

A.F.1 — The student will investigate, analyze, and compare linear functions algebraically and graphically, and model linear relationships.

Future connections

A2.F.2 — The student will investigate and analyze characteristics of square root, cube root, rational, polynomial, exponential, logarithmic, and piecewise-defined functions algebraically and graphically.

Engage Activity

Social networks   60 mins

Students will determine the number of social connections in a social network based on the number of users.

Understanding and skills

> **Will develop**
>
> Identifying the pattern for a quadratic function represented visually or in a table.
>
> Finding missing outputs to complete a table representing a quadratic function.

Preparation and materials
- Open and complete the student preview, anticipating classroom responses.
- **Materials:** Paper, pencil, graphing calculator (recommended)

Support students with disabilities
Support language - write explanations of mathematical thinking

To help students be able to explain their graphs, equations, or tables, use sentence starters such as:
- "The number of friends one person can have is ▢."
- "If each friend is connected with everyone else, then adding one more person will ▢."

Support for English language learners
Three reads

Have students read the task aloud. On the first read, ask students to describe the situation.

Prompt: Students read the problem.

Students think/write: Answer the question "What is the problem about?"

Answers may look like:
- How many connections can you have between x people?
- How to display the same information in different ways.
- What is the total number of possible connections on a social network?

Share: Students are called upon to discuss their answers with the class.

On the second read, ask students to interpret the question.

Prompt: Students read the problem.

Students think/write: Answer the question "What does an answer look like?"

Answers may look like:
- An equation.
- A graph.
- A table.

On the third read, have students identify important information.

Prompt: Students read the problem.

Students think/write: Answer the question "What are the important pieces of information given in the question?"

Answers may look like:
- There are 10, 30, 100, 1000 users.
- Connections are two way. If they are friends with you, you are friends with them.

Classroom guide

Hook

Notice and wonder • 5 mins

Students write observations about two different sets of social network connections.

Implementation details

Encourage students to describe the different possible connections in a social network, like the ones shown in the image. Highlight responses that relate to the total possible connections in the network based on the number of users shown as the activity focuses on students exploring the number of connections ("I follow you, you follow me" type connections) based on the number of users in the social network.

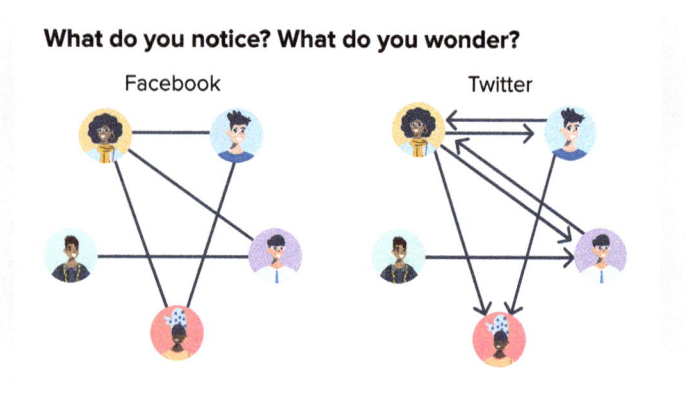

What do you notice? What do you wonder?

Facebook   Twitter

Slide 1 from Student Engage Activity

Launch

5 mins

Have you ever wondered 'What is the total number of possible connections in a social network?' You will work with your group to investigate this question. You can assume that the social network consists of friends such that, "I follow you, you follow me", are the only possible connection types.

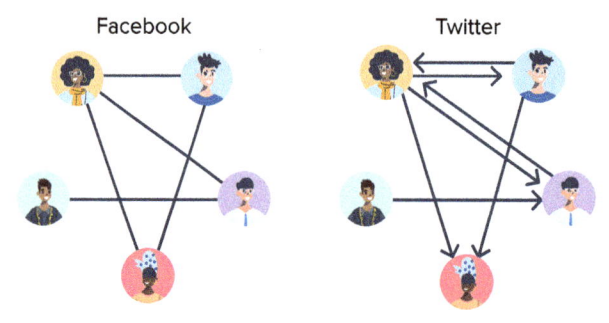

Facebook   Twitter

Slide 2 from Student Engage Activity

Provide time for students to read the instructions and prompt them to consider think the number of connections in a social network with 1, 2, or 3 people. Before forming groups, ask a few students to share the number of connections possible. Invite students to display for the class how they modeled their solution and encourage multiple representations in recording the number of connections, such as in a table or visual representation.

Important mathematical concepts: Quadratic functions.

Important contextual information: Social networks, users, and "I follow you, you follow me" connections.

Suggested grouping: Form groups of 3 or 4 and assign roles

> **Continue when**
> Students have read the Launch and understand the context of the problem.

Explore

Group roles • 35 mins

In your groups, create a presentation showing how to determine the total possible connections in social networks with different numbers of users.

Make sure to include the following in your group's work:
- Number of total possible connections for 10, 30, 100, and 1000 users.
- At least two different representations that show how the number of connections changes based on the number of users.

Slide 4 from Student Engage Activity

Students will be creating diagrams, tables, graphs, or evaluating a function or rule in order to find out how many connections various amounts of social network users can have.

Anticipated strategies

Create a visual representation

Create a diagram or model

Students may create a diagram or visual model, similar to the images shown in the Hook, to show different connections based on the number of users. Encourage students to generalize their findings as it will become increasingly difficult with more users.

Create a table

Students may create a table to record the number of possible connections.

Users in social network	Total connections
1	0
2	2
3	6
4	12
5	20
10	90
30	870
100	9900
1000	999 000

Create a graph

Students may create a graph that shows the number of possible connections in terms of the number of users in the social network.

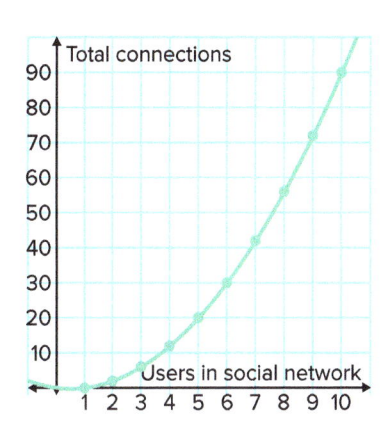

Create a rule

Students may determine a rule to find the number of possible connections in a social network.

$$\text{Rule: } n(n-1) = n^2 - n$$

Misconceptions

Misunderstanding connection type and working with a nonquadratic relationship.

What are possible connections in this problem? How many connections would there be on the social network if there were 1 person, 2 people, or 3 people as users? Why? How do you know?

Purposeful questions

Use the following questions to check for understanding and encourage critical thinking:
- How many connections are there when there are 10, 30, or 100, 1000 users? How do you know?
- Is there another way you can represent the number of connections in the social network based on the number of users?
- Can you explain in words how you see the number of connections changing based on the number of users?

> **Continue when**
>
> Students have determined the number of total possible connections for 10, 30, 100, and 1000 users and used at least two different representations that show how the number of connections changes based on the number of users.

Discuss

15 mins

Have a class discussion in order to determine how many connections different amount of social network users can have. Consider sequencing the strategies presented by the methods used for determining connections, starting with diagrams, then tables, graphs, and finally, rules.

Discussion guide

Invite students to share their methods for determining the number of connections based on the different number of users in a social network. Encourage groups to share different representations, such as a visual representation, table, graph, or rule.

If the class did not use one of the representations as justification, ask the class if there are any other representations that could have been used and provide groups time to generate or discuss the missing representation. Note that students are not expected to write equations or a rule on their own, but it is a good extension question that students may have explored on their own or to have them think about for the first time in the discussion. Ask the class about how many connections would be in a social network with n users to encourage this generalization.

Next, ask groups how the relationship they have observed compares to relationships they have learned before (linear and exponential). Ask students to describe in words how they see the number of connections changing based on the number of users. Quadratic relationships will be introduced formally in the next lesson, but students may describe that the change in increase for the number of connections increases by a constant value for each consistent change in number of users.

Extension:
- Research a social network that you or someone you know uses. Find the number of users and calculate the possible number of total connections. Is the number of total possible connections close to the number of actual connections for an average user? Why or why not?
- Draw at least three models that show different possible connection types (such as "I follow you, but you don't follow me back" and "We both follow each other"). For each model, record the total connections and the number of users. How are these models similar or different to one another?

Lesson Preparation

Suggested review

Depending on your students' level of prior knowledge, consider revisiting the following lessons:

Algebra 1 — 2.04 Characteristics of functions

Tools

You may find these tools helpful:
- Graphing calculator
- Graph paper

Lesson supports

The following supports may be useful for this lesson. More specific supports may appear throughout the lesson:

Elaborate on the axis of symmetry
Targeted instructional strategies

Students may benefit from further discussion about the axis of symmetry. Relate the axis of symmetry to lines of symmetry from previous grades.

Remind students about the definition of symmetry, and encourage them to check that if a parabola is symmetric, they can fold one side over and it overlaps the other side. The overlapping points will have the same y-value and are the same x-distance from the line of symmetry.

Teachers can make more connections by relating the equation of the axis of symmetry to equations of vertical lines from Topic 3.

Always, sometimes, or never
English language learner support

Have students consider whether the following statements are always, sometimes, or never true to check their understanding of the vocabulary present in this topic.
- A zero occurs when a function intercepts the x-axis (answer: always)
- A quadratic function has a single y-intercept (answer: always)
- The vertex is a maximum point on the graph (answer: sometimes - it may instead be the minimum point on the graph)
- The domain of a quadratic function is limited by the position of the vertex (answer: never)
- The vertex is on the axis of symmetry (answer: always)
- A quadratic function has two zeroes (answer: sometimes - it depends on the location of the vertex and the direction the parabola opens)

Label key features on a quadratic graph
Student with disabilities support

Provide students with example graphs of quadratic functions to draw, highlight, and label key features including domain, range, maximum, minimum, intercept, and vertex. These features can be color-coded and annotated for reference for future problems.

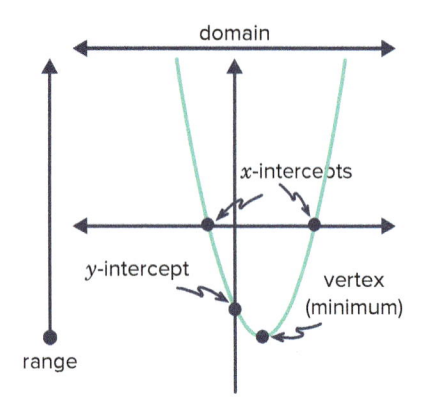

Positive leading coefficient

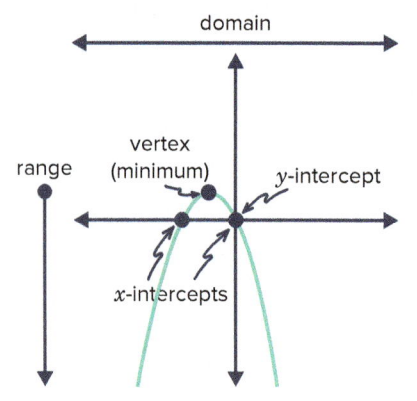

Negative leading coefficient

Quadratic functions are symmetric about the vertex
Address student misconceptions

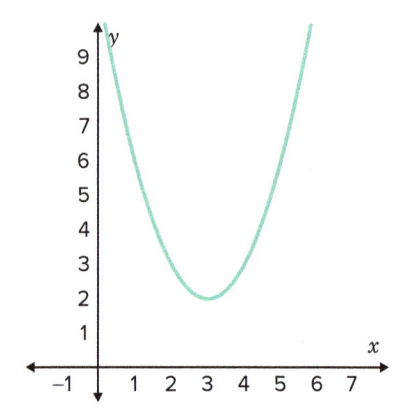

When writing the range of a function such as $f(x) = (x - 3)^2 + 2$ from a graph or an equation, a common error a student may make is to say the range is less than or equal to 3, the x-coordinate of the vertex.

This shows the student has a misconception in associating domain and range with the independent and dependent variables, respectively.

For students with this misconception, have them practice with discrete points in identifying the domain and range and then continue practicing with continuous graphs.

Student lesson & teacher guide

Characteristics of quadratic functions

Students learn new characteristics that are attributed to quadratic functions. Key features such as the axis of symmetry, vertex, domain and range, and number of x-intercepts are described and accompanied by a graph illustrating the feature.

Students: Pages 378–379

7.01 Characteristics of quadratic functions

After this lesson, you will be able to...
- identify and interpret key features of quadratic functions given a real-world context.
- identify and interpret characteristics of quadratic functions including domain, x-intercepts, range, y-intercepts, and values of quadratic functions.

Engage activity
Ask your teacher to get started
Social networks
Students will determine the number of social connections in a social network based on the number of users.

Characteristics of quadratic functions

A **quadratic function** is a polynomial function of degree 2. A quadratic function can be written in the form $f(x) = ax^2 + bx + c$ where a, b, and c are real numbers.

From the graph of a quadratic function, called a **parabola**, we can identify key features including domain and range, x- and y-intercepts, and if it has a maximum or a minimum. The parabola also has the following two features that help us identify it, and that we can use when drawing the graph:

Axis of symmetry
A line that divides a figure into two parts, such that the reflection of either part across the line maps precisely onto the other part. For a parabola, the axis of symmetry is a vertical line passing through the vertex.

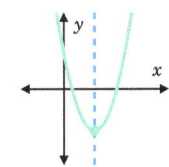

Vertex
The point where the parabola crosses the axis of symmetry. The vertex is either a maximum or minimum on the parabola.

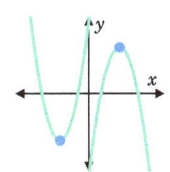

7.01 Characteristics of quadratic functions 825

mathspace.co

We can determine the key features of a quadratic function from its graph:

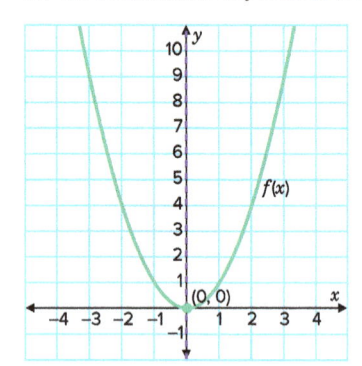

This is a graph of the quadratic parent function: $f(x) = x^2$
- Axis of symmetry: $x = 0$
- Vertex: (0, 0)
- y-intercept at (0, 0)
- x-intercept at (0, 0)
- Domain: $\{x \mid -\infty < x < \infty\}$
- Range: $\{y \mid y \geq 0\}$

We can identify the x-intercepts of some quadratic equations by drawing the graph of the corresponding function.

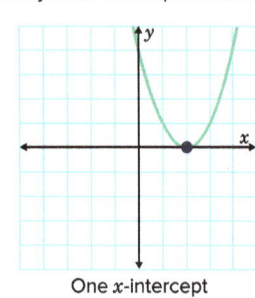

One x-intercept 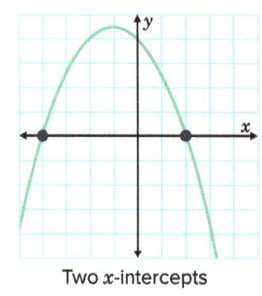   Two x-intercepts 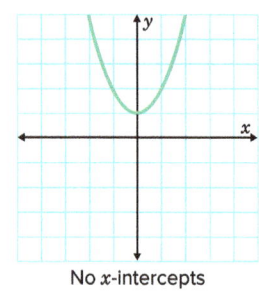   No x-intercepts

The x-intercepts of a quadratic function can also be seen in a table of values, provided the right values of x are chosen and the equation has at least one real x-intercept.

Concrete-Representational-Abstract (CRA) Approach
Targeted instructional strategies

Concrete: Engage students with a hands-on activity to model quadratic functions in a real-world context. Use a rolled piece of paper or a ball to demonstrate the path of an object thrown into the air. Have students measure and record the height of the object at different time intervals using a tape measure and stopwatch. They can place markers or sticky notes at each measured point to visualize the path. This physical movement helps students experience the shape of a quadratic function through the object's motion.

Representational: Transition from the hands-on activity to visual representations of the data collected. Guide students to plot the recorded points on graph paper, creating a coordinate plane. Have them draw the curve that connects the points, forming a parabola. Encourage students to identify and label key features on their graphs, such as the vertex, x-intercepts, and y-intercepts.

Abstract: Move to the symbolic representation by introducing the quadratic equation that models the object's motion. Teach students how to write the equation in the form $y = ax^2 + bx + c$ using the data from their graphs. Work with them to calculate the values of a, b, and c based on the points they've plotted. Discuss how to find the domain and range from the equation and interpret these in the context of the real-world scenario. Solve problems using algebraic methods, reinforcing how the equation relates back to the physical activity and the graph.

Connecting the stages: Help students make connections between the concrete activity, their graphs, and the equation. Encourage them to reflect on how the motion of the object (concrete) corresponds to the shape of the graph (representational) and how both are described by the quadratic equation (abstract).

Ask guiding questions like:
- "How does the highest point of the ball relate to the vertex of the parabola?"
- "What do the x-intercepts tell us about the object's motion?"

This integration reinforces their understanding and allows them to choose the most helpful representation when solving problems.

Examples

Students: Pages 379–380

Example 1

Consider the quadratic function: $f(x) = x^2 - 2x + 1$

a Graph the function.

Create a strategy

We can create a table of values that satisfy $f(x)$ and use it to help graph the function. It can be useful to choose values for x that are positive and negative, as well as $x = 0$:

x	-2	-1	0	1	2	3	4
$f(x)$							

To complete the table, evaluate the function for each x-value.

Here is how we can obtain $f(-2)$:

$$f(-2) = (-2)^2 - 2(-2) + 1$$
$$f(-2) = 4 + 4 + 1$$
$$f(-2) = 9$$

Repeat this process for each x-value in the table.

x	-2	-1	0	1	2	3	4
$f(x)$	9	4	1	0	1	4	9

Now we can use these points to graph the quadratic function $f(x)$

Apply the idea

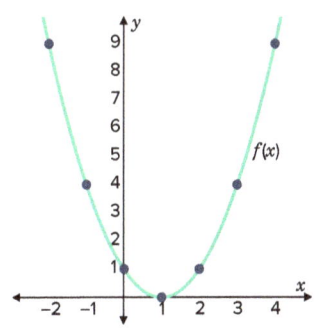

Reflect and check

Having the vertex in your table is useful, since it tells you where the parabola has a minimum or maximum. Sometimes the table values you select will not include the vertex of the function, depending on the quadratic function being graphed. If you plot your initial table values and find you are unsure where the parabola changes direction, you can add additional values to your table until you can identify the vertex.

Note that the quadratic function has one x-intercept, at $x = 1$.

Purpose

Show students how to graph a quadratic function by constructing a table of values.

Expected mistakes

Students may assume that they should know how to graph a quadratic function by reading its equation like the way they graphed linear functions. However, when learning to graph linear functions, a basic approach is by creating a table of values.

Students: Page 380

b State the axis of symmetry.

Create a strategy

The axis of symmetry is a vertical line that passes through the vertex.

Apply the idea

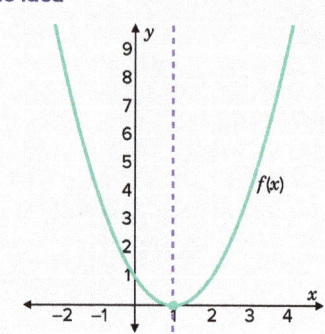

The axis of symmetry is $x = 1$.

Purpose

Show students how to determine the axis of symmetry from a graph.

Expected mistakes

Students may state the axis of symmetry as the x-value of the vertex, and not an equation. Remind students that the axis of symmetry is a line, so it is always an equation.

Reflecting with students

After students have drawn a number of graphs of quadratic functions from given equations, ask them to reflect on any patterns or shortcuts they found to drawing the correct graph.

Encourage students to look for corresponding similarities in questions and answers. For example, students may connect the constant term of the equation to the y-intercept, or connect the sign of the leading coefficient to whether the vertex is a maximum or minimum.

Advanced learners: Exploratory analysis of quadratic graphs use with Example 1
Targeted instructional strategies

After students have graphed the quadratic function using a table of values, encourage advanced learners to analyze the patterns and symmetry of the graph more deeply. Pose open-ended questions like, "What patterns do you notice in the y-values of the points?" and "How do the points relate to the axis of symmetry?" or "How can these patterns help you predict other points?"

Students should recognize that the axis of symmetry can be used to find mirror points. Additionally, they may notice that the y-values on either side of the axis of symmetry increase by odd numbers. Make students aware that this is only true for some quadratics (ones where the leading coefficient is 1), which they will explore more when they learn about quadratic equations.

Students: Pages 380–381

Example 2

Consider the graph of the quadratic function $g(x)$:

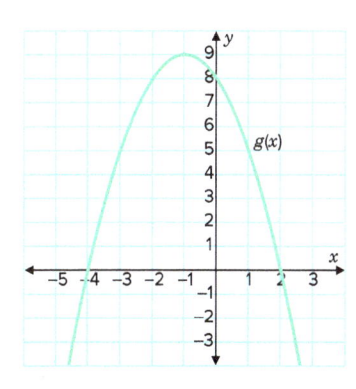

a   Find the x-intercepts and y-intercept.

Create a strategy

To find the x-intercepts, locate the places where the parabola crosses the x-axis.

To find the y-intercept, locate the place where the parabola crosses the y-axis.

Apply the idea

We can identify the intercepts on the graph:

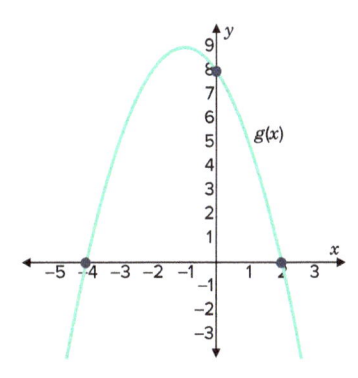

From the graph we can see the there are two x-intercepts at (–4, 0) and (2, 0), and there is one y-intercept at (0, 8).

Purpose

Show students how to identify the x- and y-intercepts of a quadratic function from its graph.

Expected mistakes

Students may write the coordinates of the intercepts backwards, such as the y-intercept as (8, 0). Review the coordinates of the points along each axis.

Students: Page 381

b   Determine the domain and range.

Create a strategy

To find the domain of $g(x)$, we want to find all possible x-values for which $g(x)$ could be graphed.

To find the range, we want to find all possible values of $g(x)$. The vertex of a parabola affects the range of the function, as it will be the maximum or minimum value of $g(x)$.

7.01 Characteristics of quadratic functions   **829**

mathspace.co

Apply the idea
We can see that for a parabola, there are no restrictions on which x-values can be graphed as each side of the parabola continues infinitely in either x direction.

Domain: $\{x \mid -\infty < x < \infty\}$

This parabola opens down, so the y-value of the vertex is the maximum value of the function. The parabola continues infinitely in the negative y direction.

Range: $\{y \mid y \leq 9\}$

Reflect and check
For the domain, we may also see it written as "all real values of x" or in interval notation as "$(-\infty, \infty)$" instead of using inequality or set notation.

Purpose
Show students how to determine the domain and range of a quadratic function from its graph.

Expected mistakes
Some students may incorrectly exclude the vertex from the range. Clarify for students that the vertex should be included in the range.

Students may state the maximum value of the range as 8, which is the location of the y-intercept. Point out to students that the graph continues to the vertex, which has a maximum y-value of 9.

Students: Page 382

c Describe what happens to the graph as x gets very large and positive.

Create a strategy
We can look at the graph and see what is happening for larger and larger values of x. We may need imagine the graph extending beyond what is shown.

Apply the idea
As x gets very large, the graph continues down and the function values are negative with a very large size. It is decreasing faster and faster.

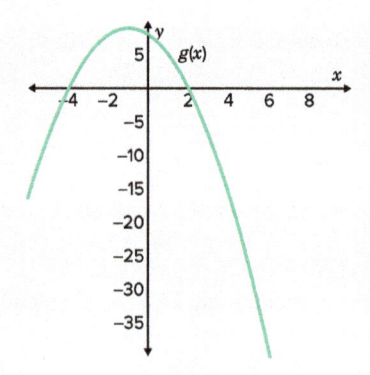

Reflect and check
The function values for $g(x)$ also become large and negative as x becomes large and negative.

Purpose
To build confidence with describing the shape of a parabola.

Reflecting with students

Consider reflecting with students by using technology that allows students to zoom out so they can "see" more of the parabola, especially for "very large x-values" as suggested in the problem.

Students: Pages 382–383

Example 3

The graph shows the height, y (in feet), of a softball above ground x seconds after it was thrown in the air.

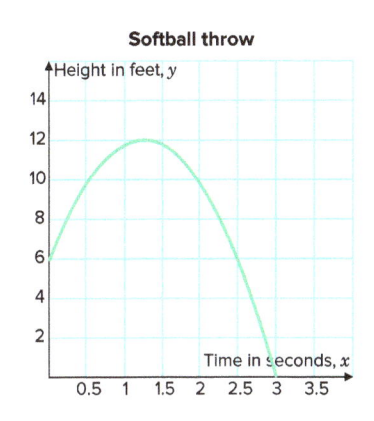

Softball throw

a Find the y-intercept and describe what it means in context.

Create a strategy

We want to find the place where the parabola crosses the y-axis.

Once we find the y-intercept, we want to connect this to the context of the softball. Since the y-axis represents the height of the softball in feet above the ground, we can use it to identify the height of the softball at 0 seconds.

Apply the idea

We can identify the y-intercept on the graph:

Softball throw

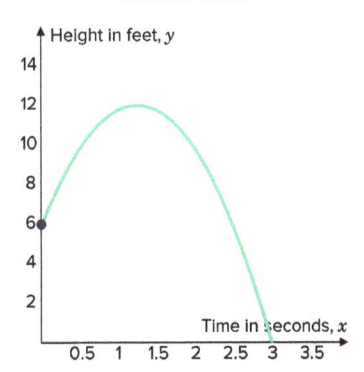

The y-intercept is (0, 6).

The y-intercept tells us that the softball was thrown from a height of 6 feet above the ground.

Purpose

Show students how to interpret the y-intercept of a quadratic function in context.

Expected mistakes
Students may state that the ball was 6 feet above the ground zero seconds after the ball was thrown. While this is technically a correct description, we should consider what is actually happening in the context. The ball was thrown from that height initially.

Students: Page 383

> **b** Find the value of the x-intercept and describe what it means in context.
>
> **Create a strategy**
>
> We want to find the place where the parabola crosses the x-axis.
>
> Once we find the x-intercept, we want to connect this to the context of the softball. Since the x-axis represents the time in seconds after being thrown, we can use it to identify how many seconds the softball hits the ground.
>
> **Apply the idea**
>
> We can identify the x-intercept on the graph:
>
> **Softball throw**
>
> [Graph showing a parabola with Height in feet, y on vertical axis (0 to 14) and Time in seconds, x on horizontal axis (0.5 to 3.5). The parabola starts at (0, 6), peaks near 12, and crosses the x-axis at (3, 0).]
>
> The x-intercept is (3, 0).
>
> The x-intercept tells us that the softball hits the ground 3 seconds after it was thrown in the air.

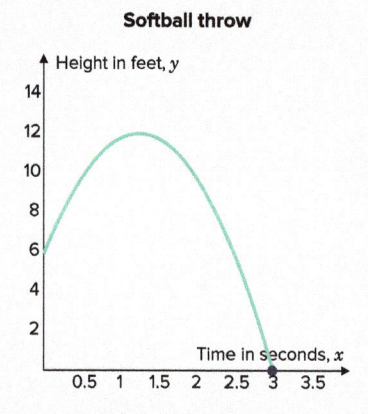

Purpose
Show students how to interpret the x-intercept of a quadratic function in context.

Reflecting with students
Ask students to identify the other x-intercept which they can do using the axis of symmetry. Then, explain why it is not discussed in the problem. The other x-intercept is not shown because it occurs during a negative time period. Time can be negative in different contexts, but, here, it doesn't make sense as this is before the ball was in motion.

Students: Page 384

c Find the value of the vertex and describe what it means in context.

Create a strategy

In order to find the vertex, we want to find the maximum point of the parabola.

Once we find the vertex, we want to connect this to the context of the softball. We know that the x-value of the vertex represents time in seconds after the softball is thrown and the y-value of the vertex represents the height of the softball above ground in feet.

Apply the idea

We can identify the vertex on the graph:

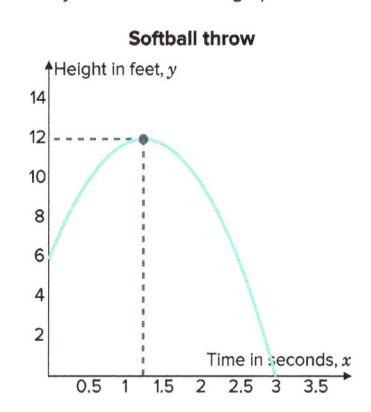

Softball throw

The vertex is (1.25, 12).

After 1.25 seconds, the softball reaches a maximum height of 12 feet above the ground.

Purpose

Show students how to interpret the vertex of a quadratic function in context.

Expected mistakes

Students may have trouble finding the value halfway between 1 and 1.5. Encourage students to discuss the scaling of the graph and what each of the lines represents. Remind students half of 0.5 is 0.25.

Students: Page 384

d State the domain and describe what it means in context.

Create a strategy

The domain of the context should be reasonable. We can use the graph of the function to determine the domain and explain its meaning in context.

Apply the idea

Domain: $0 \leq x \leq 3$

The domain of the function starts at $x = 0$ seconds when the softball was recorded from where it was initially thrown. The domain of the function ends at $x = 3$ seconds when the softball lands on the ground.

Purpose

Show students how to interpret the domain of a quadratic function in context.

Expected mistakes

Students may assume that the domain of the function is $-\infty < x < \infty$. Point out to students that for this context, we should be intentional about what the domain is. Negative x-values are not valid here as the ball was not set in motion until $x = 0$. The ball cannot continue traveling downward after hitting the ground, so x-values after $x = 3$ do not make sense either.

Students: Page 384

> **💡 Idea summary**
>
> From the graph of a quadratic function, we can identify key features including:
> - Domain and range
> - x- and y-intercepts
> - Maximum or minimum function value
> - Vertex
> - Axis of symmetry

Practice

Students: Pages 381–388

What do you remember?

1 Which table of values best represents the rule shown?

> The square of the sum of x and 3 is equal to y.

A
x	y
4	13
5	14

B
x	y
4	25
5	34

C
x	y
4	19
5	28

D
x	y
4	49
5	64

2 Choose the graph that has each set of characteristics:

a
- Axis of symmetry at $x = -1$
- x-intercepts: $(-7, 0)$, $(5, 0)$

Select the graph that represents the function.

834 Mathspace Virginia SOL Algebra 1 Teacher Edition
mathspace.co

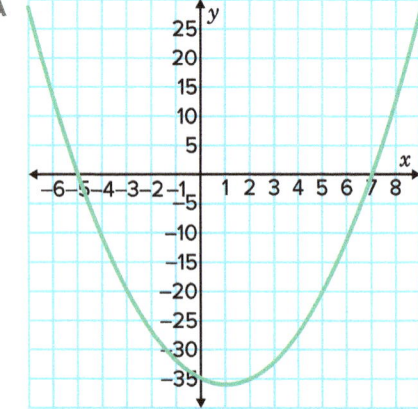

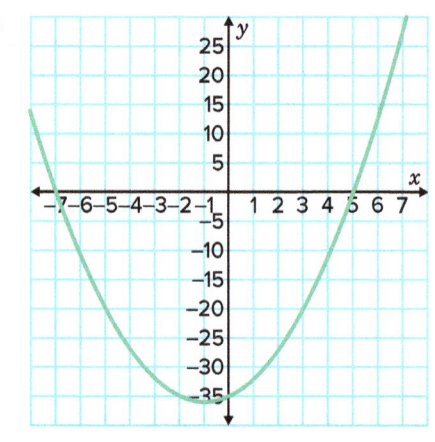

C

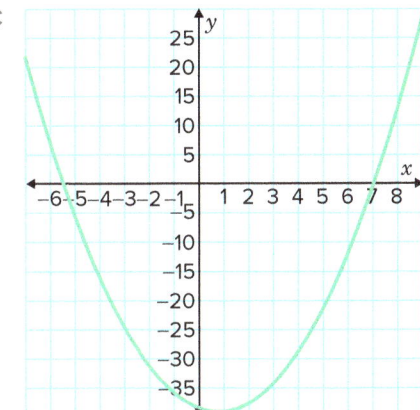

D

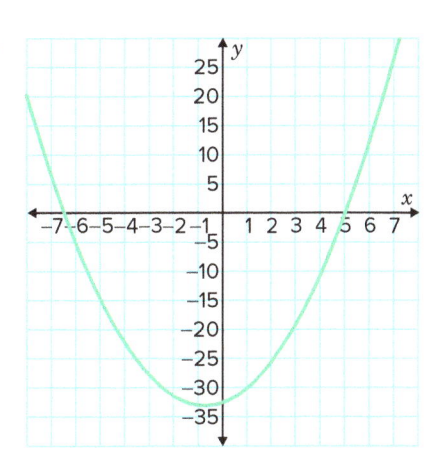

b
- Vertex is a maximum
- x-intercept: (6, 0)
- y-intercept: (0, −36)

Select the graph that represents the function.

A

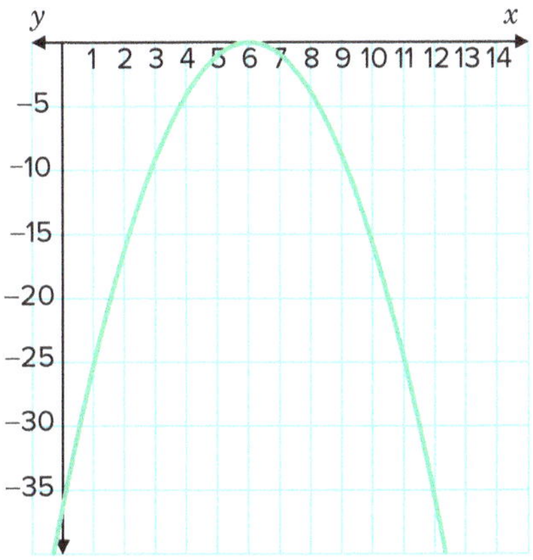

B

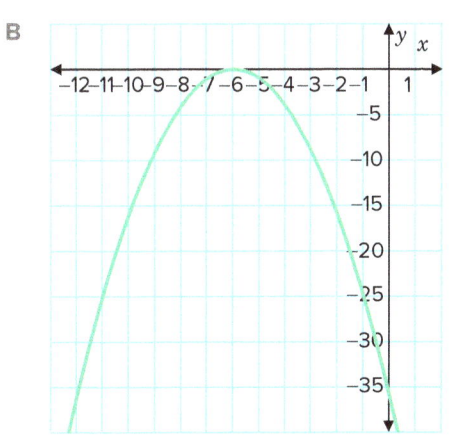

C

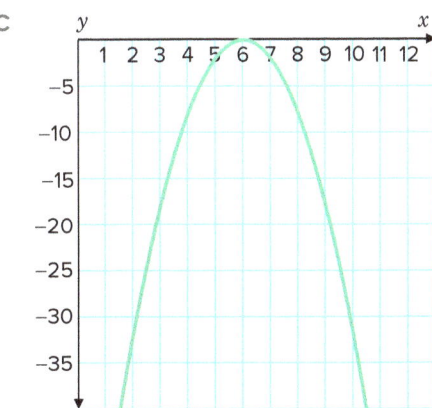

D

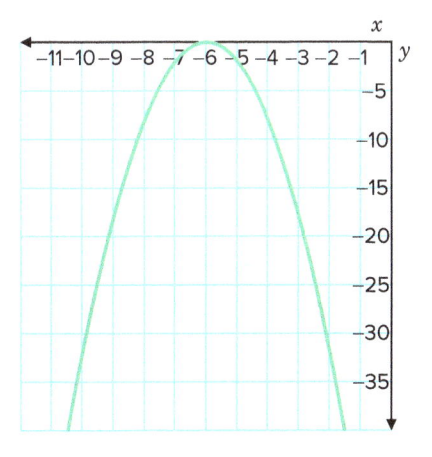

c
- No x-intercept
- Axis of symmetry: $x = 10$
- Range: $y \leq -6$

7.01 Characteristics of quadratic functions

Select the graph that represents the function.

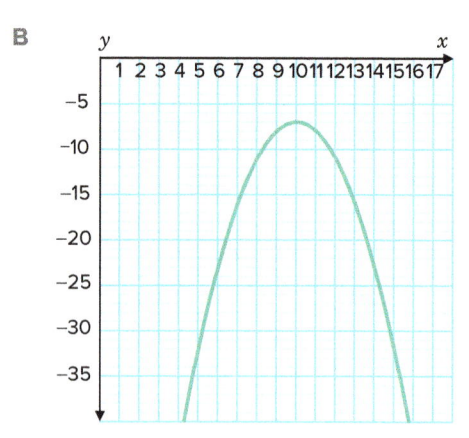

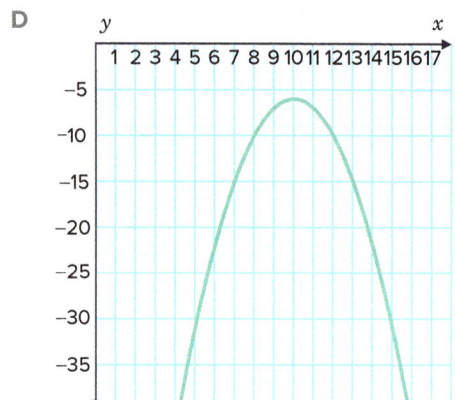

A, **B**, **C**, **D**

---

3 Consider the graph of the quadratic function.

State the number of x-intercept(s) the quadratic function has based on the graph.

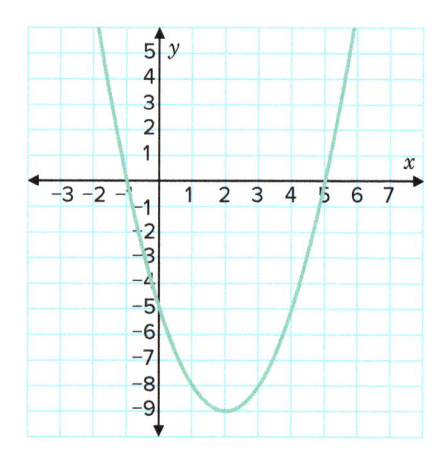

4 For each table, complete the following:

i   Graph the quadratic function shown in the following tables.
ii Find the coordinates of the vertex.
iii Determine whether the vertex is a maximum or minimum point.
iv Determine the axis of symmetry.
v   State the number of x-intercept(s).

a

x	0	1	2	3	4	5	6
y	−7	−2	1	2	1	−2	−7

b

x	−7	−6	−5	−4	−3	−2	−1
y	11	6	3	2	3	6	11

5 Determine how many x-intercept(s) the equation $x^2 + 64 = 0$ has.

836 **Mathspace** Virginia SOL Algebra 1 Teacher Edition
mathspace.co

Let's practice

6 Consider the graph of the function $y = f(x)$.

   a State the number of x-intercept(s) of the function.

   b Determine the domain of the function.

   c Determine the range of the function.

   d Describe the behavior of the function for large values of x.

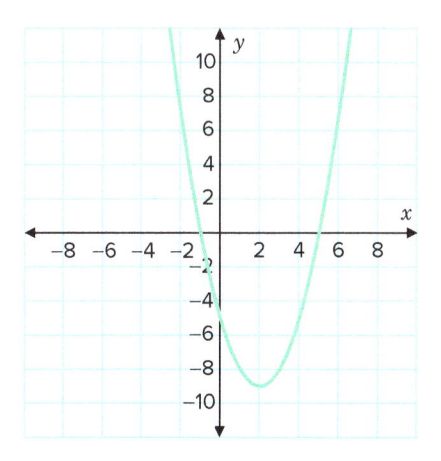

7 Consider the function $g(x) = -(x + 5)(x + 1)$.

   a Copy and complete the table.

x	−6	−5	−4	−3	−2	−1	0
$g(x)$							

   b Determine the equation of the axis of symmetry.

   c Determine if the graph will have a maximum or a minimum.

   d Graph the function.

   e Determine the number of x-intercept(s) based on the graph.

8 Consider the function $h(x) = x^2 - 4x + 4$.

   a Copy and complete the table:

x	−1	0	1	2	3	4	5
$h(x)$							

   b Find the coordinates of the x- and y-intercepts.

   c Find the coordinates of the vertex.

   d Determine the domain and range.

   e Determine the equation of the axis of symmetry.

   f Determine if the graph will have a maximum or minimum.

   g Graph the function.

9 Zahra jumps off a diving platform and the path of her dive is modeled by the function $f(x) = -x^2 + 2x + 8$, where $f(x)$ is her height in meters above the pool, and x is the horizontal distance in meters from the edge of the diving platform.

   a Select the graph of the function:

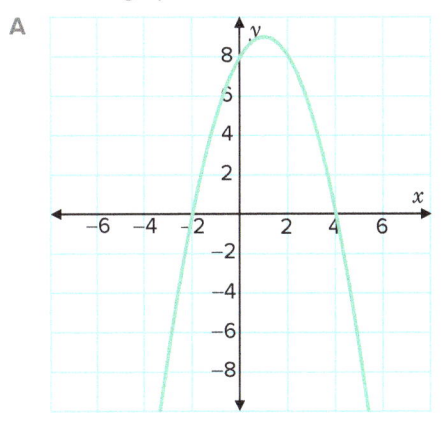

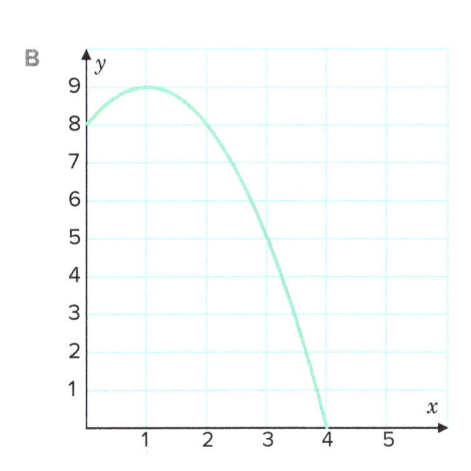

      A   B

C

D

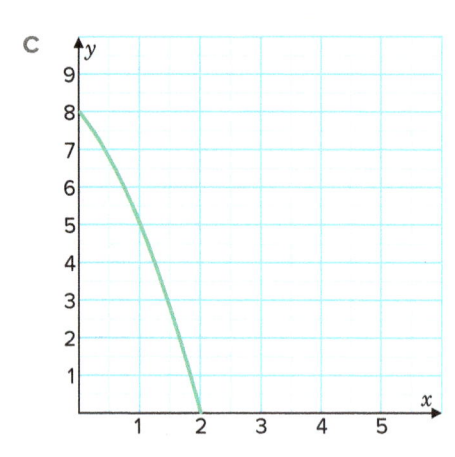

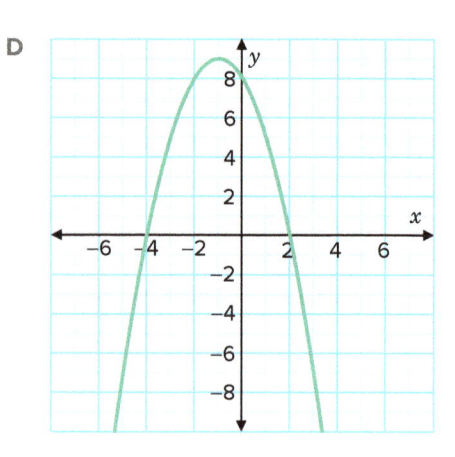

b Find the height of the diving platform.
c Find the maximum height of Zahra's dive.
d Determine and interpret the domain and range of the function.

10 A frisbee is thrown upward and away from the top of a cliff. The height, y meters, of the frisbee at time, x seconds, is given by the equation $y = -20(x - 6)(x + 2)$.

a Select the graph of the function:

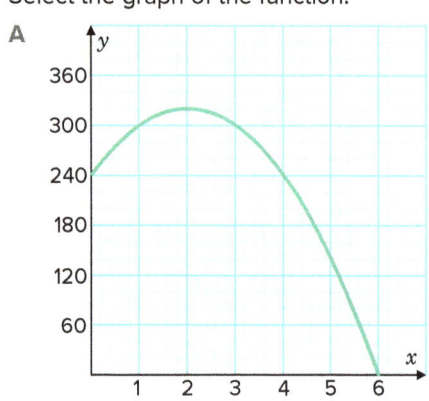

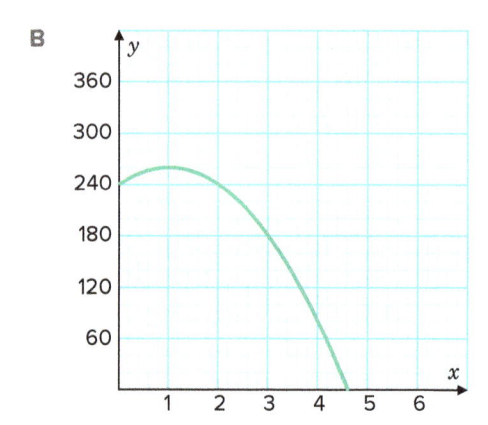

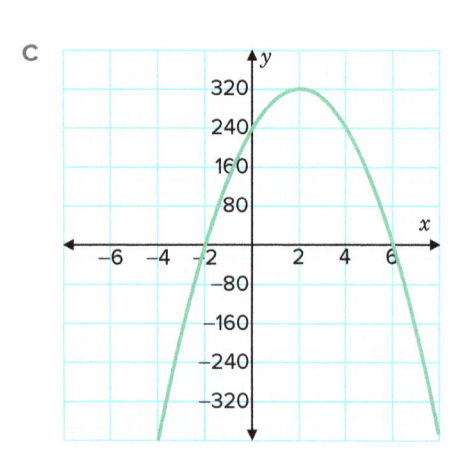

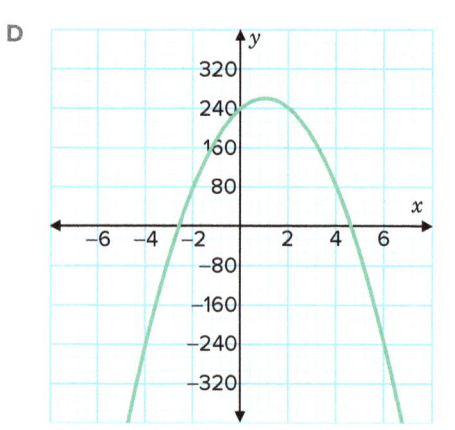

A

B

C

D

b Determine the height at which the frisbee is thrown.
c Find the maximum height the frisbee reached.
d Determine the domain and range of the function.

11 For each of the following quadratic functions, find the:
   i x-intercept(s) ii y-intercept iii vertex

   a $y = x^2 - 4x + 4$
   b $y = (x + 4)(x - 2)$
   c $y = x^2 - 2x - 3$
   d $y = -x^2 - 2$

12 For each of the following quadratic functions, find the:

i Domain
ii Range

a $y = x^2 + 2x + 1$
b $y = -(x-5)(x+1)$
c $y = (x-3)^2$
d $y = -x^2 - 2x - 1$

13 Find the range when the domain is {−6, −1, 0, 5, 7} for each of the following quadratic functions:

a $y = x^2 - 2x + 3$
b $y = -x^2 + 3x - 1$
c $y = -2(x+1)(x-4)$
d $y = 3(x-2)^2 + 1$

14 Use the graph of $f(x)$ to evaluate for the following values.

a $x = -5$
b $x = -2$
c $f(x) = -9$
d $f(x) = 0$

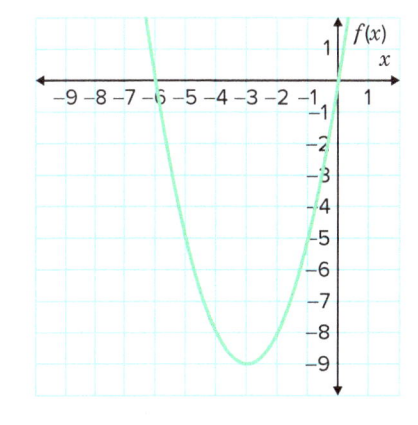

15 The graph shows the height of a soccer ball above ground, in feet, after it is kicked in terms of x seconds.

a Find the y-intercept.
b Describe what the y-intercept means in context.
c Find the x-intercept.
d Describe what the x-intercept means in context.
e Find the coordinates of the vertex.
f Describe what the vertex means in context.

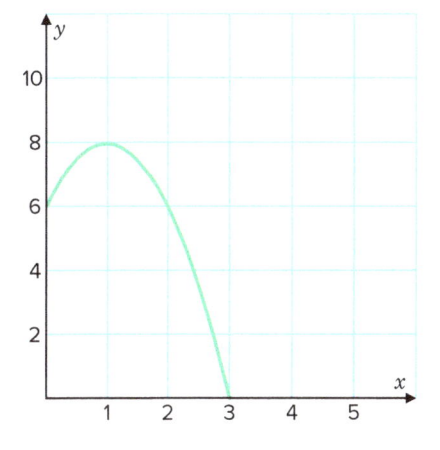

16 A clothing company is designing a new jacket and wants to determine how to maximize their profit once the jacket is ready to be sold. The graph represents the total profit, P, the shop will make at each price point, x, the jacket could sell for.

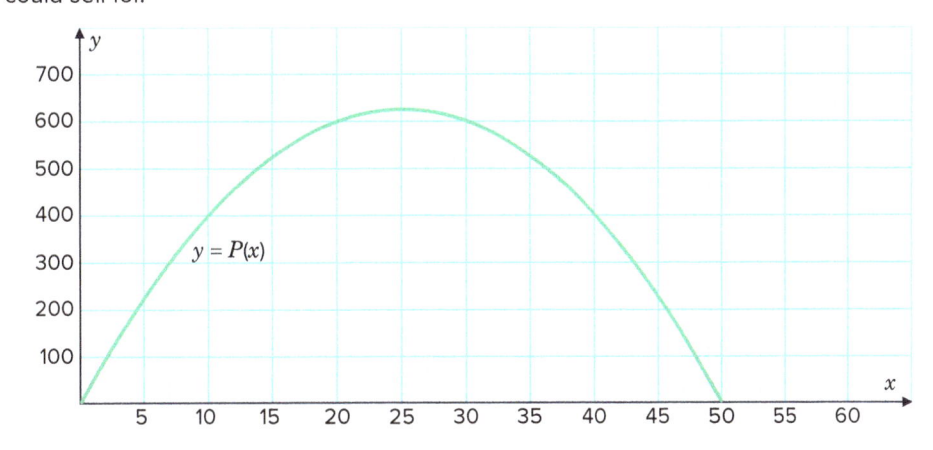

a Find the value of the vertex and describe what the vertex means in context.
b Determine the domain that results in a profit for the clothing company.
c Determine the corresponding range of profit.
d The manager believes that selling a jacket at a higher price will always result in a larger profit. Explain how increasing the price of the jacket affects the profit.

7.01 Characteristics of quadratic functions   839

mathspace.co

Let's extend our thinking

17 Sketch the graph of quadratic equations with the following key features:

a
- Axis of symmetry at $x = 1$
- Vertex is a minimum
- x-intercepts: (−2, 0), (4, 0)

b
- Has a maximum function value
- x-intercept: (5, 0)
- y-intercept: (0, −25)

c
- No x-intercept
- Axis of symmetry: $x = 8$
- Range: $y \leq -9$

18 Elise is the owner of a restaurant. Elise wants to install new wooden floors in several rooms. The rooms in the restaurant are square. The wood costs $6.25 per square foot. The cost of the flooring in terms of its side length is shown by the quadratic function $C(x) = 6.25x^2$.

a Determine how much Elise should expect to spend on flooring if the room has side lengths of 12 ft.
b Determine how much the price would change if the side lengths decreased by 3 ft.
c Graph the given quadratic model, $C(x) = 6.25x^2$. Make sure to choose appropriate labels and scale.
d Describe what changes and what stays the same about the graph of the quadratic model if the cost per square foot decreases.

19 Graham, Habib, and Joel throw or kick footballs around the same time. The vertical height of Graham's football is shown in the graph. The function $G(t)$ represents the vertical distance of the football above the ground, in feet, and t represents time, in seconds.

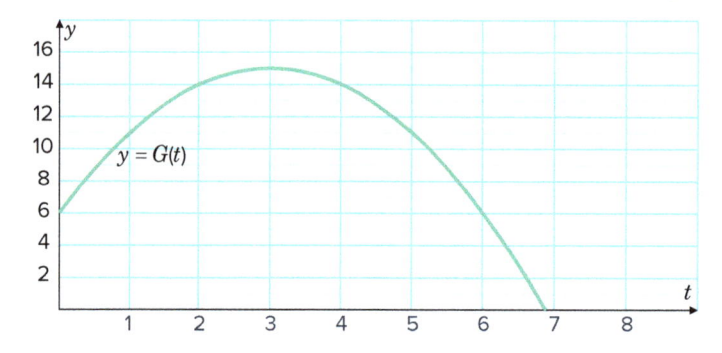

The vertical height of Habib's football is shown in the table. $H(t)$ represents the vertical distance of the football above the ground, in feet, and t represents time, in seconds.

t	0.172	2	3	4	5	5.828
$H(t)$	0	14	16	14	8	0

The height of Joel's football can also be modeled with a quadratic function that has the following key features. Let $J(t)$ represent the vertical distance of the football above the ground, in feet, and t represent time, in seconds.

- y-intercept: (0, 5)
- Vertex at (1, 5.5)
- t-intercept: (4.317, 0)

Use the above information to complete the following:

a Graph the three quadratic functions on the same coordinate plane.
b Determine whose football reached the ground the quickest after being kicked or thrown. Explain your answer.
c Determine whose football reached the greatest height. Explain your answer.
d Describe what $G(0)$ and $H(0)$ mean in context.
e Habib claims that his football reaches the maximum height the quickest. Determine whether or not Habib is correct. Explain your answer.

20 Rafael is trying to explain the design for a painting to his friend, over the phone. Describe how Rafael could use key features of quadratic functions to share his idea.

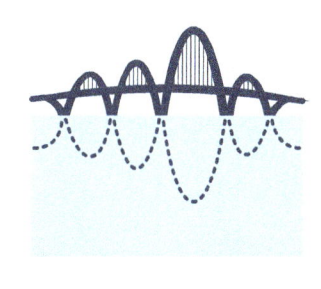

21 Write the equation of a quadratic function that has the following key features and sketch a graph of the function:
   a Two x-intercepts that have the same absolute value but opposite signs
   b One x-intercept that is a fraction and the other is a prime number
   c One unique x-intercept that is less than 1 but greater than 0
   d x-intercepts at (7, 0) and (−2, 0), and has a y-intercept at (0, 14)
   e x-intercepts at (−1, 0) and (−10, 0), and has a y-intercept at (0, 30)

22 Determine how many unique quadratic equations exist for each of the following key features:
   a x-intercepts at (−7, 0) and (10, 0)
   b One unique x-intercept at (−4, 0) and y-intercept at (0, −20)
   c Vertex at the origin and passes through (2, 14)
   d x-intercepts at (15, 0) and (−7, 0), and is symmetric about the y-axis

23 Ori models his golf shot using the quadratic equation:
$$y = -x^2 + 10x - 16$$
where y is the height of the ball (in yards) and x is the time after placing the ball on the ground (in seconds). Use graphing technology to explore this function.

Describe and justify a real-world problem involving this equation which has:
   a One viable x-intercept
   b Two viable x-intercepts
   c No viable x-intercept

Answers

7.01 Characteristics of quadratic functions

What do you remember?

1. a D

2. a B   b A   c D

3. Two

4. a i [graph]
      ii (3, 2)   iii Maximum   iv $x = 3$ v Two
   b i [graph]
      ii (−4, 2)   iii Minimum   iv $x = −4$ v Zero

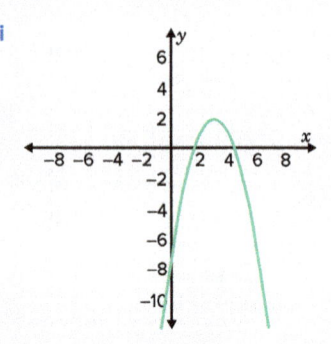

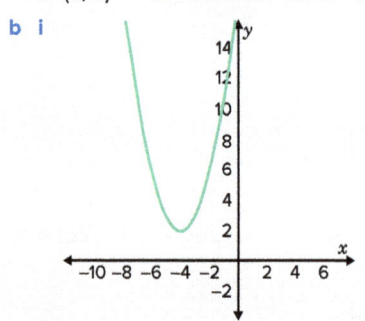

5. None

Let's practice

6. a Two
   b $\{x \mid -\infty < x < \infty\}$
   c $\{y \mid y \geq -9\}$
   d As x gets large the function increases more and more quickly. The function values will get extremely large and positive.

7. a
x	−6	−5	−4	−3	−2	−1	0
$g(x)$	−5	0	3	4	3	0	−5

   b $x = -3$ c Maximum

   d [graph]
   e Two

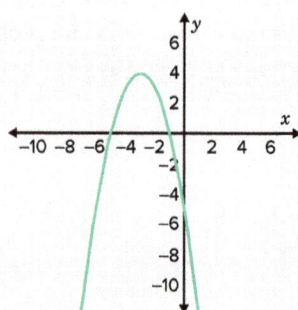

8. a
x	−1	0	1	2	3	4	5
$h(x)$	9	4	1	0	1	4	9

   b (2, 0), (0, 4)
   c (2, 0)
   d Domain: $-\infty < x < \infty$, Range: $y \geq 0$
   e $x = 2$
   f Minimum
   g [graph]

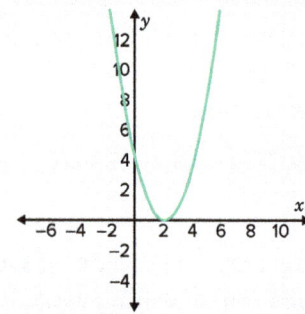

9. a B
   b 8 m
   c 9 m
   d Domain: $\{x \mid 0 \leq x \leq 4\}$, this means that during the dive she traveled 4 meters horizontally.
      Range: $\{y \mid 0 \leq y \leq 9\}$, this means that during the dive her maximum height was 9 meters above the pool and that her dive ended when she entered the pool.

10. a A   b 240 m
    c 320 m   d Domain: [0, 6], Range: [0, 320]

11. a i (2, 0)   ii (0, 4)
       iii (2, 0)
    b i (−4, 0) and (2, 0)
       ii (0, −8)   iii (−1, −9)
    c i (−1, 0) and (3, 0)   ii (0, −3)
       iii (1, −4)
    d i None   ii (0, −2)
       iii (0, −2)

12. a i All real numbers   ii $y \geq 0$
    b i All real numbers   ii $y \leq 9$
    c i All real numbers   ii $y \geq 0$
    d i All real numbers   ii $y \leq 0$

13 a {3, 6, 18, 38, 51}   b {−55, −29, −11, −5, −1}
    c {−100, −48, −12, 0, 8}   d {13, 28, 76, 193}

14 a $f(-5) = -5$ b $f(-2) = -8$
    c $x = -3$ d $x = -6$ and 0

15 a (0, 6)
    b The y-intercept represents the height from which the soccer ball is kicked.
    c (3, 0)
    d The x-intercept represents the time at which the soccer ball hits the ground.
    e (1, 8)
    f After 1 second, the soccer ball reached the maximum height of 8 feet above the ground.

16 a (25, 625). If the price per jacket is $25, then the maximum profit of $625 is reached.
    b $0 < x < 50$
    c $0 < y \leq 625$
    d The profit is increasing over the interval of the domain: $0 < x < 25$. The profit is decreasing over the interval of the domain: $25 < x < 50$. A higher priced jacket does not necessarily mean a greater profit for the company. The profit is at its maximum when the jacket costs $25. The profit model is a quadratic function, so the profit will only decrease after it reaches the maximum.

Let's extend our thinking

17 a Any graph that has the key features

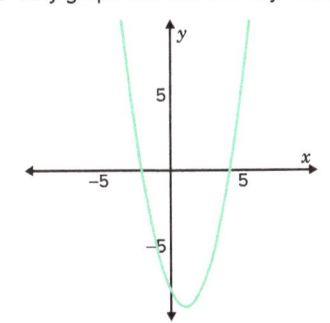

    b

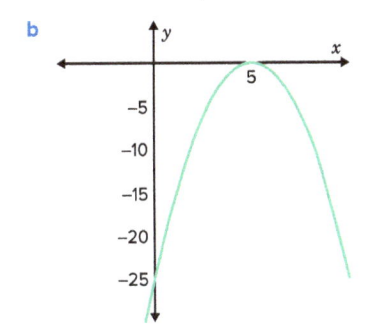

c Any graph that has the key features

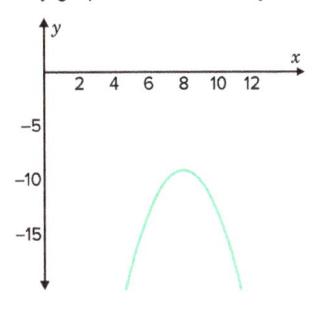

18 a Elise should expect to pay $900
    b The price would decrease by $393.75
    c 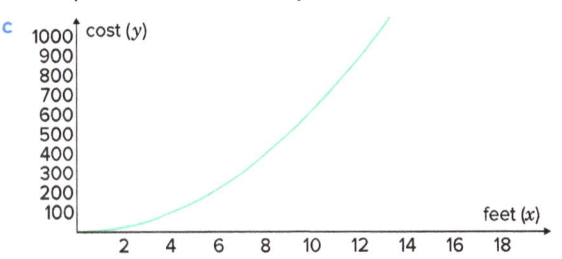
    d The decrease in in price per square foot makes the parabola wider. The x and y-intercept, domain and range, vertex, axis of symmetry, end behavior, and intervals of the domain for where the function is positive/negative and increasing/decreasing stay the same.

19 a 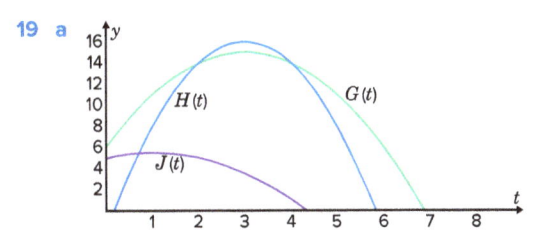
    b Joel's football reached the ground the quickest as the football hit the ground in 4.317 seconds. It took Habib's football 5.828 seconds to reach the ground and it took Graham's football just under 7 seconds to hit the ground.
    c Habib's football reaches the greatest height of 16 ft. Graham's football reaches a maximum height of 15 ft and Joe's football reaches a maximum height of 5.5 ft.
    d $G(0)$ and $H(0)$ represent the initial heights at which Graham and Habib throw the football, in this case 6 ft and 5 ft, respectively.
    e Habib is incorrect. Joel's football reaches the maximum height after 1 second, while Habib's football takes 2.828 seconds to reach the maximum height and Graham's football takes 3 seconds to reach the maximum height.

20. Rafael could have his friend draw a coordinate plane with the x-axis being the water and the y-axis being the left side of his drawing. Rafael could tell his friend how to scale the x and y-axis. Once this is complete, Rafael can describe the vertices for the 8 major parabolas, each being its own quadratic function. Describing key features, such as the domain, range, if it has a maximum or minimum, and vertex location would allow Rafael to share his design idea.

21. a $(x-3)(x+3) = y$

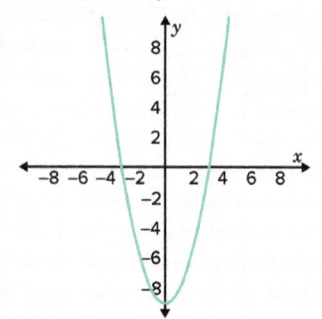

   b $(3x+5)(x-1) = y$

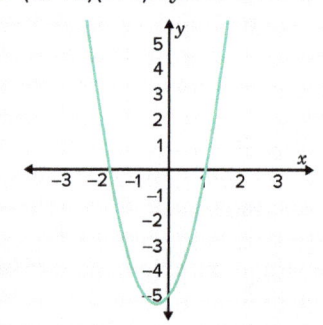

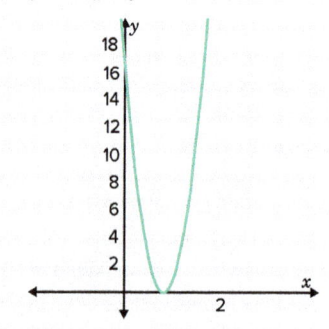

   c $(5x-4)^2 = y$

   d $-(x+2)(x-7) = y$

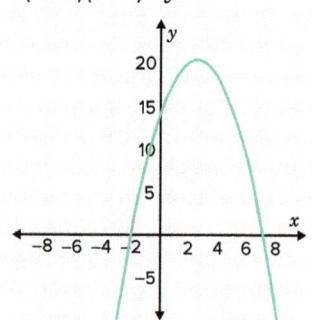

   e $3(x+10)(x+1) = y$

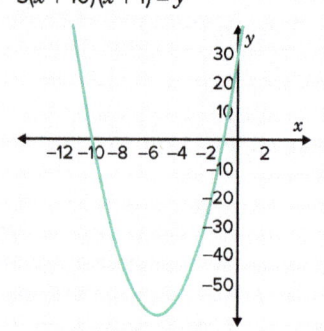

22. a An infinite number of quadratic equations
    b One quadratic equation
    c One quadratic equation
    d No quadratic equation exists

23. Answers may vary.
    a Determine the time that the ball will hit the ground.
       This problem has only one viable x-intercept because we know that the golf ball hits the ground after being in the air, so a non-viable x-intercept is at (2, 0) and a viable x-intercept at (8, 0).
    b Determine the times when the ball is on the ground.
       This problem has two viable x-intercepts at (2, 0) and (8, 0) and there is no restriction on when this happens.
    c Determine the times when the ball is on the ground a minute after the ball is hit.
       This problem has no x-intercept because at (2, 0) and (8, 0), they are both outside of the time period that we are interested in.

7.02 Quadratic functions in factored form

Subtopic overview

Lesson narrative

In this lesson, students will learn how the factored form of a quadratic function relates to some of its key characteristics. Students will examine the structures of factored equations, compared to the graphs and use repeated reasoning to make generalizations between the general factored form of a graph and the x-intercepts. Students will make sense of problems by analyzing context to interpret key features and then reason abstractly and quantitatively to create quadratic models using a choice of tools and methods, such as graphs, tables, and diagrams. Students will use precision when labeling and creating scales for graphs. By the end of the lesson, students will be able to represent quadratic contextual situations with graphs, tables, and equations in factored form, as well as justify and interpret their models.

Learning objectives

Students: Page 393

After this lesson, you will be able to...
- compare and connect representations of quadratic functions.
- graph quadratic functions using different strategies, including transformations.
- identify key characteristics of a quadratic function written in factored form.
- use the factored form of a quadratic to make predictions and draw conclusions in a contextual situation.

Key vocabulary

- factored form
- solution (to an equation)
- factor
- x-intercept
- root
- zero (of a function)

Essential understanding

Different representations of a function may highlight or hide different characteristics but they do not change the function itself. The factored form of a function highlights the x-intercepts.

Standards

This subtopic addresses the following Virginia 2023 Mathematics Standards of Learning standards.

Mathematical process goals

MPG1 — Mathematical Problem Solving

Teachers can integrate this goal into their instruction by providing students with practice problems that challenge them to apply the concept of factoring polynomials and the factored form of a quadratic function to solve complex problems. For example, they could provide a real-world problem that involves the area of a rectangular plot with a fixed perimeter, which can be represented by a quadratic function, and ask students to factor the function to find the dimensions of the rectangle that maximize the area.

MPG4 — Mathematical Connections

Teachers can incorporate this goal by highlighting the connections between the concepts they are teaching and previous lessons. For instance, they could draw attention to the similarities and differences between factoring polynomials and factoring quadratic functions, and between the graphical representation of linear and quadratic functions. They can also show how mathematical concepts can be applied in different subjects and real-world contexts, like the relationship between quadratic functions and areas of rectangular plots in physical scenarios.

MPG5 — Mathematical Representations

Teachers can integrate this goal by instructing students to represent quadratic functions in factored form both algebraically and graphically. They can also encourage the use of various methods and tools to visualize these representations, such as graphing calculators or online graphing tools. Teachers can further emphasize the importance of understanding the relationships between different representations, such as the link between the factored form of a quadratic function and its graph.

Content standards

A.F.2 — The student will investigate, analyze, and compare characteristics of functions, including quadratic and exponential functions, and model quadratic and exponential relationships.

A.F.2b — Given an equation or graph, determine key characteristics of a quadratic function including x-intercepts (zeros), y-intercept, vertex (maximum or minimum), and domain and range (including when restricted by context); interpret key characteristics as related to contextual situations, where applicable.

A.F.2c — Graph a quadratic function, $f(x)$, in two variables using a variety of strategies, including transformations $f(x) + k$ and $kf(x)$, where k is limited to rational values.

A.F.2d — Make connections between the algebraic (standard and factored forms) and graphical representation of a quadratic function.

A.F.2g — For any value, x, in the domain of f, determine $f(x)$ of a quadratic or exponential function. Determine x given any value $f(x)$ in the range of f of a quadratic function. Explain the meaning of x and $f(x)$ in context.

Prior connections

A.F.1 — The student will investigate, analyze, and compare linear functions algebraically and graphically, and model linear relationships.

Future connections

A2.EI.6 — The student will represent, solve, and interpret the solution to a polynomial equation.

A2.F.2 — The student will investigate and analyze characteristics of square root, cube root, rational, polynomial, exponential, logarithmic, and piecewise-defined functions algebraically and graphically.

Engage Activity

Creating a business plan   60 mins

Students will create a business plan based on a factored, quadratic function.

Understanding and skills

> **Will use**
>
> Graphing linear functions.
>
> Finding and interpreting key features of quadratics.

> **Will develop**
>
> Graphing a quadratic function given in factored form.
>
> Determining and interpreting key features of a quadratic function.

Preparation and materials
- Open and complete the student preview, anticipating classroom responses.
- **Materials:** Graph paper and pencil

Support students with disabilities
Support conceptual processing - self monitor understanding and ask clarifying questions

Have students reflect on their own learning using questions from KWL strategy:
"What do I Know? What do I Want to learn? What have I Learned?"

Answers may look like:

Know
- I know that a negative x^2 value will give a downwards facing curve.
- I know that P is the profit and x is the amount spent.
- I know the function is quadratic.

Want to learn
- I want to learn why the function was given in factored form.
- I want to learn how to graph the function.
- I want to learn what materials were used to make the piñatas.

Learned
- I learned that when a factor is equal to zero the function equals zero.
- I learned when the function equals zero it goes through the x-axis.

Support for English language learners
Collect and display

As pairs are working, listen for and collect vocabulary, phrases, and methods students use for creating a business plan for Rosaria. Consider grouping language for each part of the process (calculating material cost and profit, graphing the equation, and interpreting the information to give advice). Continue to update collected student language throughout the entire activity. Remind students to borrow language from the display as needed.

Some terms and phrases may include: cost, profit, quadratic, function, key points, minimum, maximum, intercepts, points, and coordinate plane.

Classroom guide

Hook

Notice and wonder • 5 mins

Students write observations about two quadratic graphs showing cost and profits.

Implementation details

Students might notice that as costs increase, there is a maximum profit which is achieved, followed by a decline back to none or negative profit. Students may also notice more general observations, such as the fact that there is a relationship between profits and costs, and they may wonder what specific situation is being represented by the function.

Key observations that students might make:
- The profit begins and ends after a certain amount of money is spent.
- The maximum amount of profit is between two x-intercepts.
- Why does the profit go back down when more money is spent?
- Is there a way to increase the profit?

What mathematical questions could we ask about these graphs?

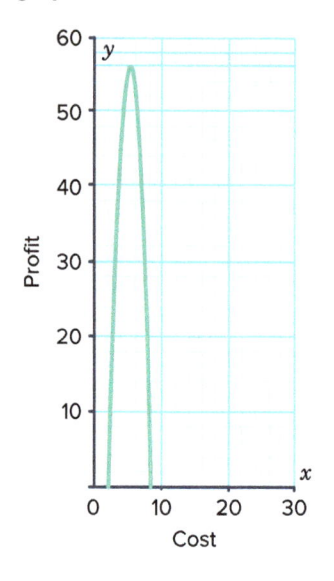

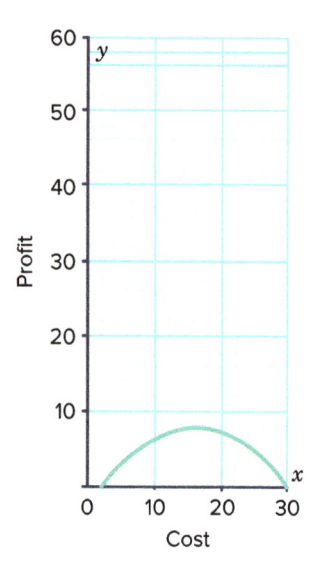

Slide 1 from Student Engage Activity

Launch

5 mins

Rosaria is starting a piñatas business with her two sisters, Valentina and Paola, to sell at the local swap meet.

She wants to make sure that the business will be profitable before sinking too much time and energy into the project. With some help from their math teacher, Rosaria has represented the cost versus profits with the following quadratic equation:

$$P = -0.06(x - 105)(x - 230)$$

where P is profit and x is money spent on materials.

Slide 2 from Student Engage Activity

Ask students to share whether they have ever started a business, even something as informal as a lemonade stand, tutoring, or babysitting. Call upon students' experiences to ask what kind of plans they made before starting the business. Discuss that businesses usually put together plans to predict the costs and profits they can expect under various situations. If time allows, have students brainstorm what concrete components they would want to be part of a business plan. This will make it easier for groups to determine what their finished product will look like

Important mathematical concepts: Quadratic equation, x-intercepts, points, key points, maximum, minimum

Important contextual information: Profit, costs, piñata, materials, business plan

Suggested grouping: Form pairs

> **Continue when**
> Students have read the Launch and understand the context of the problem.

Explore

Think-pair-share • 35 mins

Students will graph the quadratic equation, identify the maximum profits, and provide business advice.

Anticipated strategies

Graph a function

Graph a factored quadratic

Students will graph a quadratic function given an equation in factored form.

The graph looks like the following:

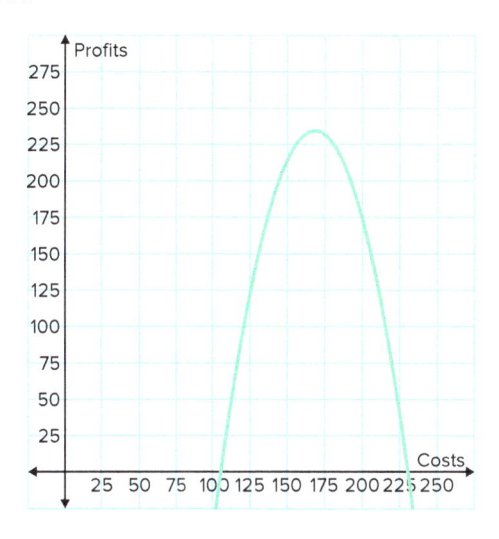

Identify key points on a graph

Students will identify key points on their graphs in order to answer contextual questions.

The x-intercepts are at 105 and 230 and the maximum is at (167.5, 234.375).

Interpret the graph and equation

Come up with business advice

As for the business advice, students can draw certain information from their graph, including but not limited to:
- What is the maximum profit that Rosaria can earn based on this model? $234.38 in profit according to this model.
- How much money does Rosaria need to spend on her business before she begins to make a profit? $110.
- How much money does Rosaria need to spend on her business to make the maximum profit? $167.50.
- How much money does Rosaria need to spend before she stops making a profit? $230.

Misconceptions

Graphing the quadratic.

What technology do we have available to graph functions? How much is reasonable for Rosaria to spend when starting her business and how can we choose input values to help us graph the function? What should this graph look like when we are done?

Choosing a scale.

What are the key features of a quadratic? Are these key features visible on your graph? Should they be? Which key features have meaning in this context?

Purposeful questions

Use the following questions to check for understanding and encourage critical thinking:
- Does it make sense for profits to increase as the costs increase? Why does that work?
- Why do the profits decrease?
- What do all the key points on the graph represent?

- Why is the quadratic equation presented in factored form?
- Can you create connections between the equation and the key points?
- Did we need to graph the function to create a business plan?

> **Continue when**
> All students have graphed the function and interpreted 2-3 key points on the graph as they relate to Rosaria's business.

Discuss
15 mins

Use a gallery walk for students to share their work with the class leading to a whole class discussion. Consider making connections from the discussion to the factored form of quadratic equations in general.

Discussion guide

The discussion should be two-fold: Firstly about the interpretation of the profit versus cost graph, and secondly, about the formalization of the relationship between the factored quadratic formula and the x-intercepts.

Begin the discussion with a gallery walk so that students can see other partners' business plans. Have partners explain how they plotted their graphs and what their graphs mean. You can ask students to identify key points, like x-intercepts and maximums, and use that information to talk about the profits versus costs of Rosaria's business. Some students may have noticed a relationship between the x-intercepts and the factored form of the quadratic, and some students may have been able to concretely identify and name a relationship. If any partners have done this, be sure to emphasize the connection once they have presented to the class.

As you wrap up the discussion around Rosaria's business plan, you can ask students to take a step back from the scenario and notice connections between the key features of the graph and the factored quadratic equations. Students may be able to recognize that the x-intercepts of the graph are easily found by looking at the equation and seeing that the values are the two zeros on the graph of the function.

Lesson Preparation

Suggested review

Depending on your students' level of prior knowledge, consider revisiting the following lessons:

Algebra 1 — 6.06 Factor trinomials
Algebra 1 — 7.01 Characteristics of quadratic functions

Tools

You may find these tools helpful:
- Graphing calculator
- Graph paper

Student lesson & teacher guide

Quadratic functions in factored form

Students begin with an exploration of a graph that represents the vertical height of an object over time.

Students: Pages 393–394

7.02 Quadratic functions in factored form

After this lesson, you will be able to...
- compare and connect representations of quadratic functions.
- graph quadratic functions using different strategies, including transformations.
- identify key characteristics of a quadratic function written in factored form.
- use the factored form of a quadratic to make predictions and draw conclusions in a contextual situation.

Engage activity
Ask your teacher to get started
Creating a business plan
Students will create a business plan based on a factored, quadratic function.

Quadratic functions in factored form

One way to represent quadratic functions is using the **factored form**. This form allows us to identify the x-intercepts, the direction of opening, and scale factor of the quadratic function.

$$y = a(x - x_1)(x - x_2)$$

x_1, x_2 x-values of the x-intercepts
a scale factor

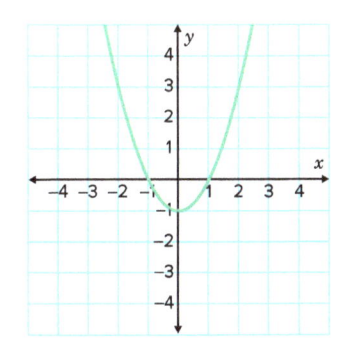

If $a > 0$, then the quadratic function opens upwards and has a minimum value.

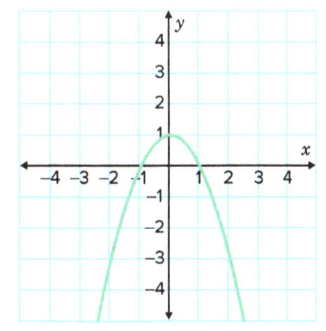

If $a < 0$ then the quadratic function opens downwards and has a maximum value.

The x-intercepts are the points where $f(x) = 0$, so we refer to x_1 and x_2 as the **zeros** of the function.

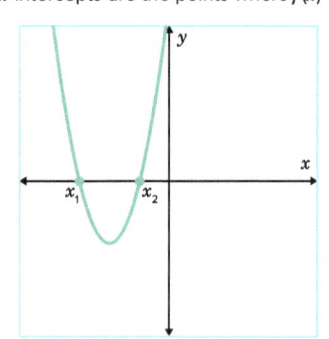

- $(x_1, 0)$ and $(x_2, 0)$ are the **x-intercepts** of the function $y = f(x)$
- x_1 and x_2 are **zeros** of the function
- $(x - x_1)$ and $(x - x_2)$ are **factors** of the function $y = f(x)$
- x_1 and x_2 are **solutions** or **roots** of the equation $f(x) = 0$

To draw the graph of a quadratic function, we generally want to find three different points on the graph, such as the x- and y-intercepts.

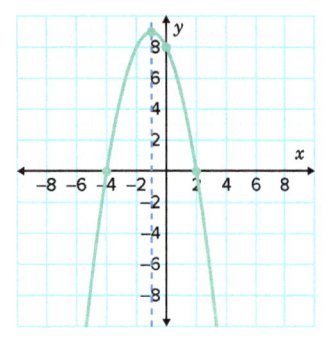

Since the graph of a quadratic function has a line of symmetry passing through the vertex, we know the vertex lies halfway between the two x-intercepts.

We can also determine the direction in which the graph opens by identifying if the scale factor, a, is positive or negative.

Finding the vertex from factored form
Targeted instructional strategies

Students may be unsure of how to determine the coordinates of the vertex from just the intercepts. Ask students where they think the axis of symmetry would be with respect to the x-intercepts.

Point out to students that the x-intercepts have the same y-value, so they must be symmetric about the vertex. This means that the average of their x-values will give us the axis of symmetry. In other words, the axis of symmetry is halfway between the x-intercepts.

Compare and connect
English language learner support

Encourage students to connect previously learned concepts, such as x-intercepts, direction of parabola opening, axis of symmetry and vertex, to the values in the factored form for quadratic functions. This can be done by asking them to connect features of the equation to its corresponding graph.

For example, the equation $y = \dfrac{1}{2}(x-1)(x+3)$ has the graph:

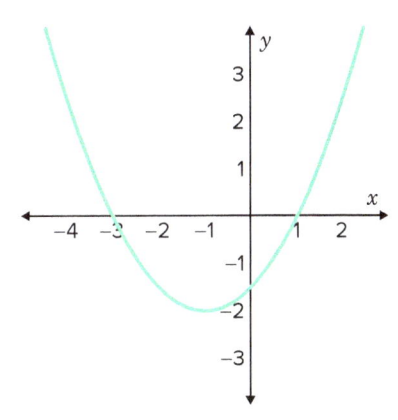

Students may make connections such as:
- The values of 1 and 3 in the equation match the magnitudes of the x-intercepts on the graph.
- The signs of the 1 and 3 in the equation are opposite from the signs of their matching intercepts on the graph.

Providing students with multiple examples to compare and connect can help students familiarize themselves with the key features of the factored form for quadratic function equations.

Incorrectly identifying the sign of the x-intercepts
Address student misconceptions

Students may incorrectly identify the sign of the x-intercepts from an equation in factored form. This is particularly common for equations with negative roots, like $y = (x + 2)(x + 3)$.

Ask students what values of x would result in the equation giving $y = 0$ and guide them to the conclusion that $x = -2$ and $x = -3$ are the correct values for the x-values of the x-intercepts.

Help students make connections between the intercepts and the zeros, reminding students that if either factor is equal to zero, then y will also be equal to zero. In this example, $x = -2$ and $x = -3$ are the values that will make the equation equal to zero.

Exploration

Students: Page 393

> ## Exploration
>
> Consider the graph below, which shows the vertical position, y in feet, of a water balloon thrown by a child from the low diving board of a pool over time, x in seconds:
>
> The function representing the projectile motion of the water balloon is $y = -3x^2 + 3x + 6$.
>
> 1. Shorena says that the function $y = -3(x + 1)(x - 2)$ is equivalent to the given function. How can we determine if she is correct?
> 2. How do the characteristics of the graph relate to the context?
> 3. How might the function $y = -3(x + 1)(x - 2)$ relate to the graph?

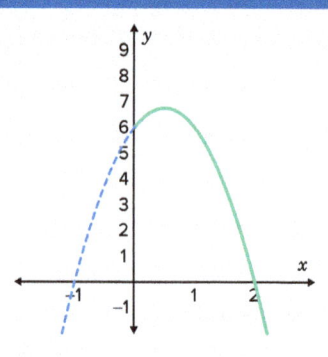

Suggested student grouping: Small groups

Students are given the context of a graph of a water balloon's vertical height over time and the equation of the function in standard form, $y = ax^2 + bx + c$. Students relate the given function to the factored form of the function and should discover that the factored form highlights the x-intercepts of the function.

Ideal student responses

These ideal responses may differ from other correct student responses. Less formal responses can be connected with the more precise mathematical language presented here.

1. **Shorena says that the function $y = -3(x + 1)(x - 2)$ is equivalent to the given function. How can we determine if she is correct?**
   We can multiply the factors in the equation and determine if the equation is equivalent to the given function.

2. **How do the key features of the graph relate to the context?**
   Graphically, we see that the water balloon has been thrown from 6 feet above the water. This is the y-intercept. We also see that the x-intercepts are at $(-1, 0)$ and $(2, 0)$. In the context of the problem, the water balloon hits the pool after 2 seconds. The vertex on the graph is at approximately $(0.5, 6.7)$, meaning the water balloon's maximum height is about 6.7 feet after half of a second.

3. **How might the function $y = -3(x + 1)(x - 2)$ relate to the graph?**
   The x-intercepts on the graph are at $(-1, 0)$ and $(2, 0)$. We can see the opposite of these numbers in the equation. The -3 in the equation indicates that the graph will open downward.

Purposeful questions

- What are the key features of the graph? Can you find each of these from the given equations?
- Why do you think that part of the graph has a dashed curve while the other part of the graph has as solid curve?
- Which x-intercept is irrelevant to the context of the problem? How do you know?

Possible misunderstandings
- Students may assume that since the functions are in different forms that the functions themselves are different and so there is no way to show they both represent the same graph. Remind students that we learned about multiplying polynomials in the previous chapter and can apply those skills here to Shorena's polynomial function.

Students are introduced to the factored form of a quadratic function and how it relates to its graph. An approach to graphing a quadratic function given in factored form is presented.

Examples
Students: Page 395

Example 1

Consider the graph of a quadratic function:

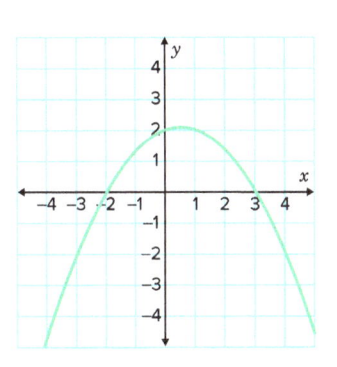

a   Identify the coordinates of the x- and y-intercepts of the function.

Create a strategy

The x-intercepts occur when $y = 0$ and the y-intercept occurs when $x = 0$.

Apply the idea

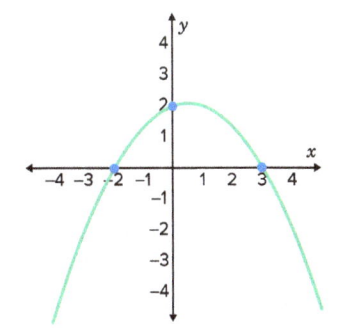

The x-intercepts are $(-2, 0)$ and $(3, 0)$.
The y-intercept is $(0, 2)$.

Purpose

Show students how to identify the x- and y-intercepts of a graphed quadratic function.

Reflecting with students

Ask students what features they may already know about the equation of the graphed function. Students may be able to point out that the scale factor of the quadratic function will be negative because the graph opens downward. Some students may attempt to use the intercepts to build the factored form of the equation.

Students: Pages 395–396

b Find the equation of the quadratic function in factored form.

Create a strategy
Substitute the x-intercepts for x_1 and x_2 in the equation $y = a(x - x_1)(x - x_2)$, then use any other point on the graph to substitute for x and y and solve for a.

Apply the idea
Since the x-values of the x-intercepts are –2 and 3, we know that the factored form will be:
$$y = a(x + 2)(x - 3)$$
for some value of a. We can find a by substituting in the coordinates of the y-intercept into the function.

To find a:

$y = a(x + 2)(x - 3)$	Factored form
$2 = a(0 + 2)(0 - 3)$	Substitute (0, 2)
$2 = a(2)(-3)$	Evaluate the addition and subtraction
$2 = -6a$	Evaluate the multiplication
$-\dfrac{1}{3} = a$	Divide both sides by –6

The equation of the quadratic function in factored form:
$$y = -\frac{1}{3}(x + 2)(x - 3)$$

Purpose
Show students how to write the equation of a quadratic function in factored form given its graph.

Expected mistakes
Students may initially write the factored form of the quadratic as $y = a(x - 2)(x + 3)$, since the x-intercepts are (–2, 0) and (3, 0), and ignore the signs of the general form, which subtracts the x-values of the x-intercepts.

Reflecting with students
Ask students if substituting the y-intercept (0, 2) into the factored form to find the scale factor was the only approach to calculating the scale factor. Point out to students that any point on the graph could be substituted into the equation to find the value of the scale factor, a.

Students: Page 396

> **Example 2**
>
> Consider the quadratic function:
> $$y = 2x^2 + 4x - 48$$
>
> a State the coordinates of the x-intercepts.
>
> **Create a strategy**
>
> In the factored form $y = a(x - x_1)(x - x_2)$, the values of x_1 and x_2 are the x-values of the x-intercepts. The y-value of the x-intercepts is $y = 0$. Factor the quadratic, then determine its x-intercepts.
>
> We can factor out a GCF of 2, so that the equation becomes $y = 2(x^2 + 2x - 24)$.
>
> Since there are no common factors for the remaining three terms and the trinomial is not a perfect square trinomial, we proceed to factor by grouping by finding the value of two integers that multiply to $ac = (1)(-24) = -24$ and add up to $b = 2$. After finding these integers, we use them to rewrite the middle term $2x$ as a sum of two terms.
>
> **Apply the idea**
>
> The factor pair whose sum is 2 is -4 and 6.
>
> We can use this to rewrite the trinomial and factor by grouping as follows:
>
> | | |
> |---|---|
> | $2(x^2 + 2x - 24) = 2(x^2 - 4x + 6x - 24)$ | Rewrite polynomial with four terms |
> | $= 2[x(x - 4) + 6(x - 4)]$ | Factor each pair |
> | $= 2(x - 4)(x + 6)$ | Divide out common factor of $(x - 4)$ |
>
> There are no more common factors to be divided out, so the fully factored form of the quadratic function is $y = 2(x - 4)(x + 6)$.
>
> The x-intercepts are $(4, 0)$ and $(-6, 0)$.
>
> **Reflect and check**
>
> Notice that $x + 6$ is the same as $x - (-6)$.

Purpose

Show students how to factor a quadratic function in order to identify its x-intercepts.

Expected mistakes

Students may incorrectly factor $x^2 + 2x - 24$. Remind students that we can check that our factoring is correct by multiplying the factored form and confirming that it is equivalent to the original polynomial.

Reflecting with students

Ask students what other resources they can use to check that their solution is correct. Students may graph the given function and graph the function they wrote in factored form using technology to confirm that the graphs are the same.

Students: Page 397

b Determine the coordinates of the y-intercept.

Create a strategy
The y-value of the y-intercept is the result when $x = 0$. We can substitute $x = 0$ into the factored form to find this value.

Apply the idea
To find the y-value of the y-intercept:

$y = 2(x - 4)(x + 6)$	Given quadratic function
$y = 2(0 - 4)(0 + 6)$	Substitute $x = 0$
$y = 2(-4)(6)$	Evaluate the subtraction and addition
$y = -48$	Evaluate the multiplication

The y-intercept is $(0, -48)$.

Reflect and check
The original function shows the y-intercept, which we can identify without making any calculations.

Purpose
Show students how to algebraically find the y-intercept from a quadratic function in factored form.

Students: Page 397

c Determine the coordinates of the vertex.

Create a strategy
The vertex lies on the axis of symmetry, so the x-coordinate of the vertex will be exactly in the middle between the two x-intercepts. We can find the middle value by taking the average of 4 and −6. We can then substitute this x-coordinate value into the function to find the y-coordinate.

Apply the idea
To find the x-coordinate:
The average of 4 and −6 is half way between them. We can calculate that $\frac{4+(-6)}{2} = -1$, so the x-coordinate of the vertex and the axis of symmetry is $x = -1$.

To find the y-coordinate:

$y = 2(x - 4)(x + 6)$	Given quadratic function
$y = 2(-1 - 4)(-1 + 6)$	Substitute $x = -1$
$y = 2(-5)(5)$	Evaluate the subtraction and addition
$y = -50$	Evaluate the multiplication

The vertex is $(-1, -50)$.

Purpose
Show students how to find the vertex of a quadratic function from factored form.

Expected mistakes
Students may expect that the vertex should somehow be highlighted in the given form or the factored form of the quadratic function. Remind students that while we can identify some key features of quadratic functions from factored forms, the vertex is not one of them.

Reflecting with students

Challenge students to visualize what the graph of the function looks like now that they've calculated the intercepts and the vertex. Point out that making connections between the form of the quadratic function and its graph is a skill that is useful when verifying that our math is correct.

Students: Pages 397–398

d Draw the graph of the function.

Create a strategy

The scale factor is 2 which is positive, so the graph will open up. We can draw the graph through any three points that we know are on it.

Apply the idea

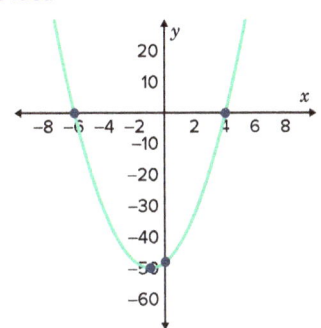

Reflect and check

Any three points is enough to draw the graph, but knowing where the vertex is can make it easier since the vertex is on the axis of symmetry.

Purpose

Show students how to use key features of a quadratic function to graph it.

Reflecting with students

Challenge students to consider how they would write the factored form equation from the graph if they were initially given the graph as opposed to the equation.

Students: Page 398

Example 3

Identify the characteristics of $h(x) = \frac{1}{6}(3x + 2)(x - 7)$.

a Identify the factors of the function.

Create a strategy

The function is given in factored form $y = a(x - x_1)(x - x_2)$ where a, $(x - x_1)$ and $(x - x_2)$ are the factors.

Apply the idea

The factors of $h(x)$ are $\frac{1}{6}$, $(3x + 2)$ and $(x - 7)$.

Reflect and check

$\frac{1}{6}$ is the greatest common factor (GCF) of $a(x - x_1)(x - x_2)$ but is still a factor of the function.

Purpose

Demonstrate to students how to identify the factors of a function given in the form $y = a(x - x_1)(x - x_2)$.

Students: Pages 398–399

b Identify the roots of the function.

Create a strategy
The roots of the function are the x values, x_1 and x_2, where $h(x) = 0$.

Apply the idea
To solve for the roots algebraically, set each of the variable factors equal to zero.

$$3x + 2 = 0 \text{ and } x - 7 = 0$$

Rearrange each equation to isolate the term with the variable.

$$3x = -2 \text{ and } x = 7$$

Isolate the variable by dividing by the coefficient of x.

$$x = -\frac{2}{3} \text{ and } x = 7$$

The roots of $h(x)$ are $x = -\frac{2}{3}, 7$

Reflect and check
Notice in part (a) we also identified the factor of $\frac{1}{6}$ but we did not use it to find roots. That is because a factor without a variable will not result in a root because $\frac{1}{6} \neq 0$.

We can substitute these values back into the equation to check our answers. If we substitute $x = -\frac{2}{3}$ and $x = 7$ and get $h(x) = 0$, then we know our roots are correct.

Let's start with the root $x = -\frac{2}{3}$.

$$h(x) = \frac{1}{6}\left(3\left(-\frac{2}{3}\right) + 2\right)\left(-\frac{2}{3} - 7\right) \quad \text{Substitute } x = -\frac{2}{3}$$

$$= \frac{1}{6}(-2 + 2)\left(\frac{2}{3} - 7\right) \quad \text{Evaluate the multiplication}$$

$$= \frac{1}{6}(0)\left(-\frac{23}{3}\right) \quad \text{Evaluate inside the parentheses}$$

$$= 0 \quad \text{Zero product property}$$

Next, let's try the root $x = 7$.

$$h(x) = \frac{1}{6}(3 \cdot 7 + 2)(7 - 7) \quad \text{Substitute } x = 7$$

$$= \frac{1}{6}(21 + 2)(7 - 7) \quad \text{Evaluate the multiplication}$$

$$= \frac{1}{6}(23)(0) \quad \text{Evaluate inside the parentheses}$$

$$= 0 \quad \text{Zero product property}$$

Evaluating for each root gave an output of 0 confirming that both are in fact roots of the function.

Purpose
Show students how to find the roots of a function given in factored form.

Students: Page 399

c Identify the zeros of the function.

Create a strategy

The zeros of a function are the same as its roots.

Apply the idea

In part (b) we solved for the roots, x_1 and x_2, and got $x = -\frac{2}{3}, 7$. These are also the zeros of the function.

Purpose

Show students that the zeros of a function are the same as its roots.

Students: Page 399

d State the x-intercepts of the function.

Create a strategy

The points $(x_1, 0)$ and $(x_2, 0)$ are the x-intercepts for $h(x)$.

Apply the idea

The zeros or roots of $h(x)$ are $-\frac{2}{3}$ and 7.

These are the x-values of the x-intercepts. The y-value of any y-intercept is 0 because the x-axis is at $x = 0$.

The x-intercepts of the function are at $\left(-\frac{2}{3}, 0\right)$ and $(7, 0)$.

Reflect and check

We can check our x-intercepts by graphing $h(x)$.

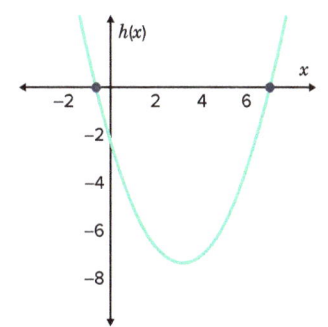

There are two points where the parabola crosses the x-axis, at $x = -\frac{2}{3}$ and $x = 7$.

Purpose

Help students understand how to find the x-intercepts of a function.

7.02 Quadratic functions in factored form   861
mathspace.co

Students: Page 400

Example 4

The graph of a quadratic function has x-intercepts at $(-2, 0)$ and $(1, 0)$ and passes through the point $(-3, -2)$. Write an equation in factored form that models this quadratic.

Create a strategy

To write the equation for this quadratic in factored form we need to first identify the roots or zeros of the equation. We can then substitute these values for x_1 and x_2.

The x-intercepts of the function are at $(-2, 0)$ and $(1, 0)$, so we know the equation has roots/zeros of $x = -2$ and $x = 1$.

Apply the idea

Since the zeros are $x = -2$ and $x = 1$, we can identify the factors by rearranging those equations so they are equal to 0:

By adding 2 to both sides of $x = -2$ and subtracting 1 from both sides of $x = 1$ we get:

$$x + 2 = 0 \text{ and } x - 1 = 0$$

We can put these in the factored form as the factors:

$$y = a(x + 2)(x - 1)$$

We can find a by substituting the coordinates of the additional point, $(-3, -2)$, into the function. To find a:

$y = a(x + 2)(x - 1)$	Factored form
$-2 = a(-3 + 2)(-3 - 1)$	Substitute $x = -3$ and $y = -2$
$-2 = a(-1)(-4)$	Evaluate the addition
$-2 = 4a$	Evaluate the multiplication
$-\dfrac{1}{2} = a$	Divide both sides by 4

Substituting the value we found for a, the equation of the quadratic function in factored form is:

$$y = -\frac{1}{2}(x + 2)(x - 1)$$

Reflect and check

Checking the graph of the equation, we can see that it satisfies the given information.

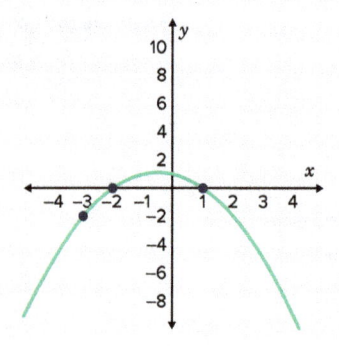

Purpose

Show students how to write a quadratic equation in factored form given the x-intercepts and a point on the graph.

Students: Page 401

> **Example 5**

Find the equation that models the graph shown.

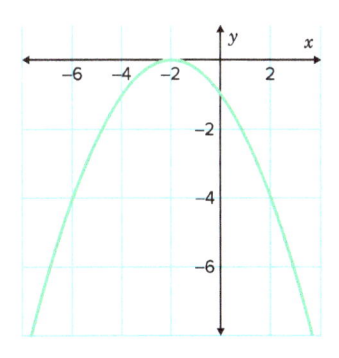

Create a strategy

This quadratic function only has 1 x-intercept, which is also the vertex. When this happens, the function is in the form $f(x) = a(x - x_1)^2$. Remember, we need an additional point, like the y-intercept, to find the exact equation to this function.

Apply the idea

Since the x-intercept is at $(-2, 0)$, the function takes the form $f(x) = a(x + 2)^2$.

Next, we can use the y-intercept of $(0, -1)$ to find the value of the leading coefficient.

$f(x) = a(x + 2)^2$	Given equation
$-1 = a(0 + 2)^2$	Substitute $x = 0$ and $y = -1$
$-1 = a(2)^2$	Evaluate the addition
$-1 = 4a$	Evaluate the exponent
$-\dfrac{1}{4} = a$	Divide both sides by 4

The equation of the graph is $f(x) = -\dfrac{1}{4}(x + 2)^2$.

Reflect and check

We could have used any point on the parabola to solve for the scale factor, a. There is another point at $(-6, -4)$. We would substitute $x = -6$ and $y = -4$, then the equation would take the form $-4 = a(-6 + 2)^2$.

$$-4 = a(-6 + 2)^2$$
$$-4 = a(-4)^2$$
$$-4 = 16a$$
$$-\dfrac{1}{4} = a$$

Notice that this is the same thing we got earlier because no matter which points we substitute in we will get the same function because they are all points on the same parabola.

Purpose

Show students how to find the equation of a quadratic function given its graph.

🎓 Advanced learners: Engaging in natural extensions to deepen understanding
Targeted instructional strategies
use with Example 5

Extend the problem for advanced learners by adding additional constraints or posing new questions. For example, prompt them to find another quadratic function that shares the same vertex and has the same shape but opens upward instead of downward.

Then, encourage students to explore how altering the parameters in a quadratic equation impacts its graph. Ideally, students should notice that the new graph is simply a reflection of the original across the x-axis,, so the only thing that change in the equation is the sign of the leading coefficient, a.

Engaging in these natural extensions deepens their understanding of the relationship between algebraic expressions and their graphical representations.

Students: Page 402

Example 6

A cannonball is fired from the edge of a cliff which is 15 meters above sea level. The peak of the cannonball's arc is 20 meters above sea level and 10 meters horizontally from the cliff edge. The cannonball lands in the sea 30 meters away from the base of the cliff.

The path of the cannonball is shown on the following graph, but the axes have not been labeled.

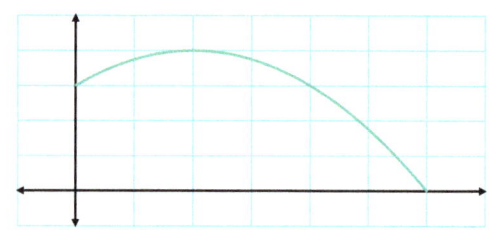

a Label the axes of the graph to match the information provided.

Create a strategy

To make the graph match the information, we want to make sure that the axes labels and scales accurately represent the path of the cannonball and make sense for the context. Both axes will have meters as their units.

Apply the idea

We can see that the path on the graph starts at a point on the vertical axis and ends at a point on the horizontal axis. So, we can make the vertical axis represent the height, with $y = 0$ being sea level, and the horizontal axis represent distance, with $x = 0$ being the edge of the cliff.

We can then add values onto the axes to show that the cannonball starts at the edge of the cliff at (0, 15), reaches its peak at (10, 20), and then falls into the sea at (30, 0).

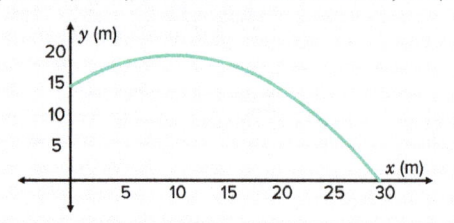

Reflect and check

Another way to show the scale of the axes is to label some key points. For example:

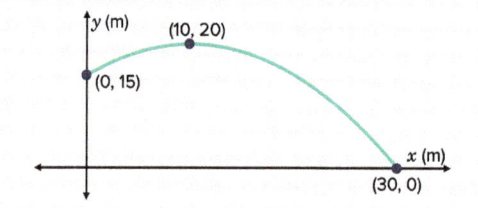

Purpose

Show students how to use context to appropriately label a graph and its scale.

Students: Pages 402–403

b Determine the factored equation which models the path of the cannonball.

Create a strategy

To match the graph in part (a), we can let x represent the horizontal distance from the cliff, and let y represent the height above sea level.

To find the factored equation that models the cannonball, we need to know both x-intercepts and the scale factor.

We know that one of the x-intercepts is at $x = 30$, and that the vertex is at $x = 10$. Remember that the vertex lies on the axis of symmetry of a quadratic function, so we can use this to find the other x-intercept.

We can find the scale factor by substituting any point into the equation (that isn't an x-intercept) and solving for the scale factor that makes the equation true.

Apply the idea

Since both x-intercepts have the same y-value, they will be mirrored across the axis of symmetry. Since $x = 30$ is 20 more units than $x = 10$, the other x-intercept will be at 20 less units than $x = 10$. So, the other x-intercept is at $x = -10$.

If we let the scale factor of the equation be a, then our equation will be:

$$y = a(x + 10)(x - 30)$$

We can find the scale factor by substituting in a point on the graph (let's use the y-intercept) and solving for a.

$y = a(x + 10)(x - 30)$	Model equation
$15 = a(0 + 10)(0 - 30)$	Substitute (0, 15)
$15 = a(10)(-30)$	Evaluate the addition and subtraction
$15 = -300a$	Evaluate the multiplication
$-\dfrac{1}{20} = a$	Divide both sides by -300

So, the equation which models the path of the cannonball is:

$$y = -\frac{1}{20}(x + 10)(x - 30)$$

Purpose

Show students how to write the factored form of a quadratic function from its graph, even if both x-intercepts are not shown.

Expected mistakes

Students may struggle to identify the other x-intercept without seeing it on the graph. Remind students that quadratic functions are symmetrical and we can use that information to determine other points on a graph that aren't shown.

Students may also forget to include the scale factor in their factored form and incorrectly conclude that equation is $y = (x + 10)(x - 30)$. Remind students to check their equation by substituting any known points, that are not x-intercepts, into the equation.

Reflecting with students

Ask students to notice the sign of a. Is this what they would expect, based on the graph? Why? Students should be able to point out that a negative value means the graph opens downward.

Students: Page 403

c A second cannonball is fired, and this one can be modeled by the equation:
$$y = -\frac{1}{15}(x+12)(x-27)$$

Use this model to predict where the cannonball landed.

Create a strategy

We can use what we know about the general factored form of the equation to provide information about the cannonball's path.

Apply the idea

Since the a value is negative, we know this function will open downward. This makes sense for a cannonball, as it will arc upwards to a maximum vertical height before falling back down, due to gravity. The x-intercepts will be at −12 and 27. Since the cannonball is being fired away from the cliff in the positive x-direction, we know that $x = -12$ is a non-viable solution. So, the second cannonball lands in the sea 27 meters from the base of the cliff.

Purpose

Show students how to use a quadratic equation in factored form to solve a problem in context about an x-intercept.

Reflecting with students

Ask students to examine the factored equation. Why does substituting −12 in for x cause the y-value to be 0? Why does substituting 27 in for x cause the y-value to be zero? Students have not yet been introduced to the zero-product property, but should be able to informally explain what happens when any one term in a product is zero.

Use key features to indicate a scale
Student with disabilities support

use with Example 6

If students find it difficult or laborious to add the scale of the axes to their graph, instead recommend that they label some key points which can be used to indicate scale.

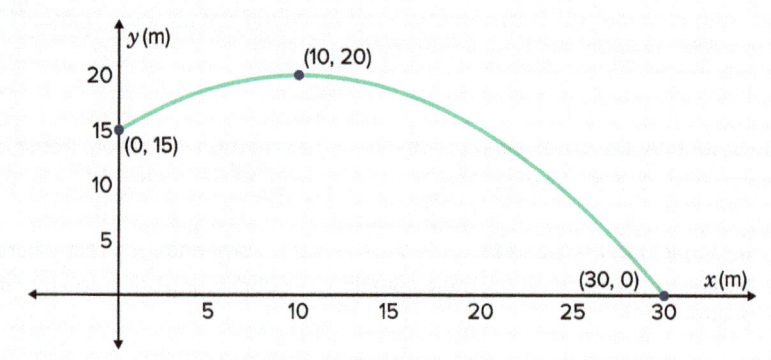

Students: Page 403

> **Idea summary**
>
> To write the equation of the graph of a quadratic function in factored form, substitute the x-intercepts for x_1 and x_2 in the equation $y = a(x - x_1)(x - x_2)$, then use any other point on the graph to substitute for x and y and solve for a, the scale factor.

Practice

Students: Pages 404–408

What do you remember?

1 State the factored form for a quadratic equation and describe its graphical features.

2 Describe the axis of symmetry of a quadratic function.

3 For each of the following quadratic equations, state the roots:
    a $y = (x - 1)(x - 4)$
    b $y = (x - 3)(x + 7)$
    c $y = x(x - 4)$
    d $y = 2(x - 1)(x + 5)$

4 For each of the following quadratic functions, determine the y-value of the y-intercept:
    a $y = 3(x - 1)(x - 8)$
    b $y = x(x + 9)$

5 Consider the following graph of a function.

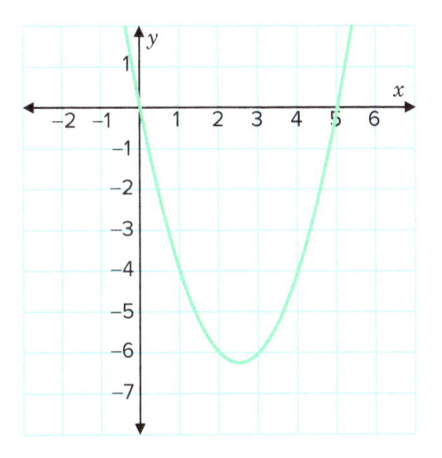

Select the equation that represents the function:
    A $y = x(x + 5)$
    B $y = x(5 - x)$
    C $y = -x(x - 5)$
    D $y = x(x - 5)$

6 Consider the following graph of a function.

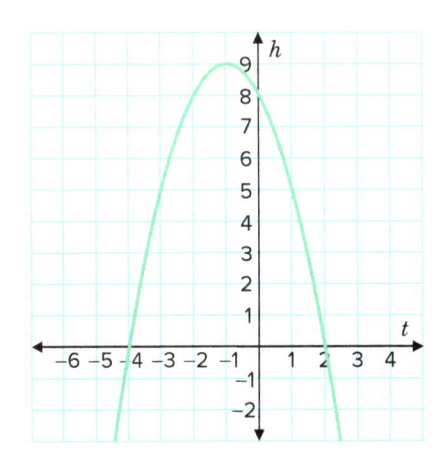

Select the equation that represents the function:
    A $h = (2 - t)(t - 4)$
    B $h = -(2 - t)(t - 4)$
    C $h = (t + 2)(t - 4)$
    D $h = -(t - 2)(t + 4)$

7 Use the table of values to graph the function.

x	0	2	4	6	8
y	12	0	−4	0	12

8 Consider the function $y = -\frac{1}{3}(x-6)(x+2)$.

Select the graph that represents the function:

A

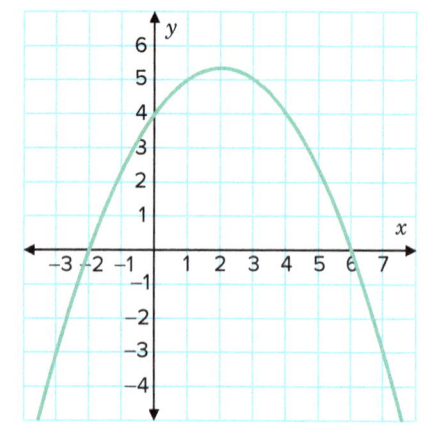

B

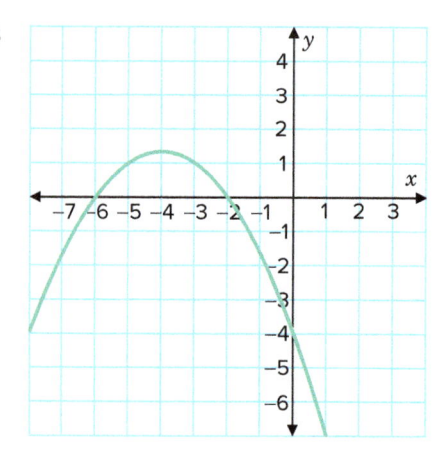

C

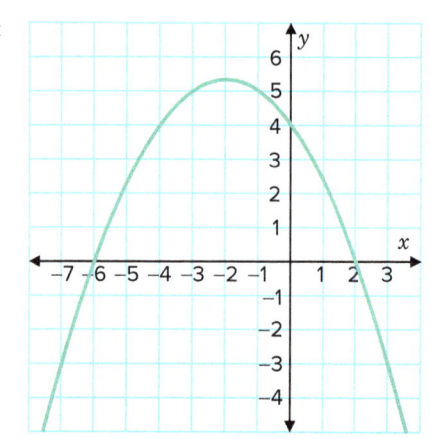

D

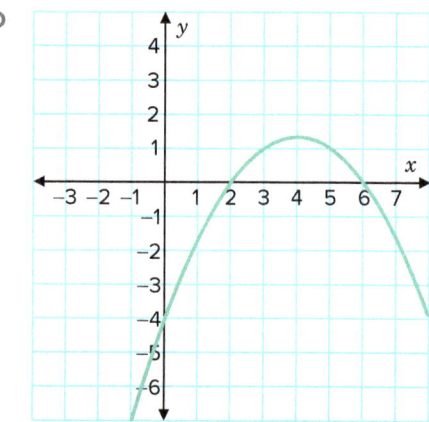

9 Graph a quadratic function with x-intercepts of (5, 0) and (–3, 0), a y-intercept of (0, 60), and its vertex is a maximum.

Let's practice

10 For each quadratic function:
  i   State the coordinates of the x-intercepts.
  ii Determine the axis of symmetry.
  iii Determine the coordinates of the vertex.
  iv Graph the function.

  a $y = (x-2)(x+4)$
  b $y = -2(x-1)(x-5)$

11 For each graph:
   i   State the zeros.
   ii State the y-value of the y-intercept.
   iii Write the equation of the quadratic function in factored form.

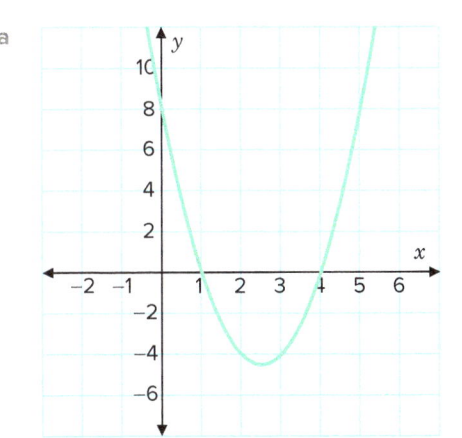

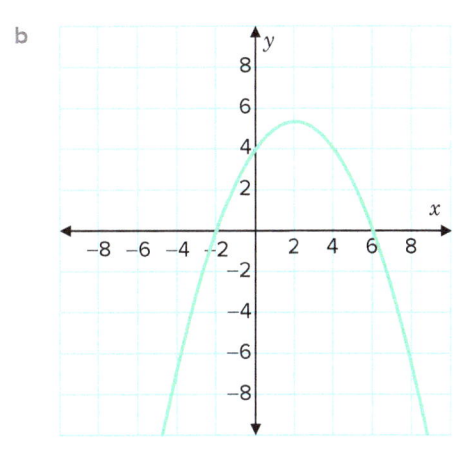

   a
   b

12 For each of the following quadratic functions, find the:
   i   Solutions   ii y-intercept   iii vertex

   a $y = (x - 3)(x + 1)$
   b $y = (x + 2)(x - 5)$
   c $y = (x - 4)(x + 6)$
   d $y = -(x - 1)(x + 2)$

13 For each of the following quadratic functions, find the:
   i   Domain   ii Range

   a $y = (x - 1)(x - 2)$
   b $y = -(x + 3)(x - 4)$
   c $y = (x - 2)(x - 2)$
   d $y = -(x + 1)(x + 1)$

14 Find the range when the domain is $\{-6, -1, 0, 5, 7\}$ for each of the following quadratic functions:
   a $y = (x + 4)(x - 1)$
   b $y = -(x - 3)(x + 2)$
   c $y = -2(x - 2)(x + 3)$
   d $y = 3(x + 1)(x - 2)$

15 Use the function $f(x) = -2(x + 4)(x - 1)$ to evaluate for the following values:
   a $x = -5$
   b $x = -2$
   c $x = \frac{1}{2}$
   d $f(x) = 0$

16 A quadratic function has x-intercepts of (5, 0) and (−3, 0), and a y-intercept of (0, 60).
    Write the equation of the function in factored form.

17 A quadratic function passes through the points (−2, 0), (9, 0) and (0, −6).
    Write the equation of the function in factored form.

18 The zeros of a quadratic function are $x = -4$ and $x = -7$. The graph of the function passes through the point (−3, 12).
    Write the equation of the function in factored form.

19 Satellite dishes follow the shape of a parabola to optimally receive signals. Winston models the cross section of a satellite dish with the points (–2, 0) and (2, 0) being the edges of the satellite and the x-axis representing the top opening of the satellite dish. The satellite dish is $\frac{1}{2}$-foot deep.

  a Select the graph that represents the problem:

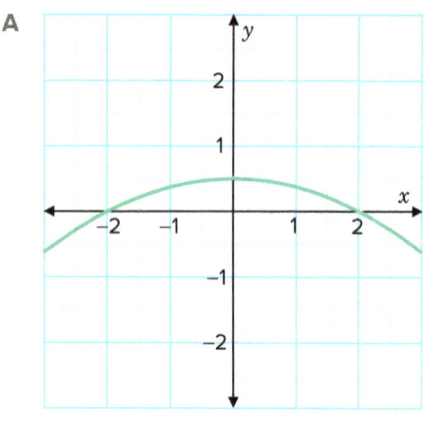

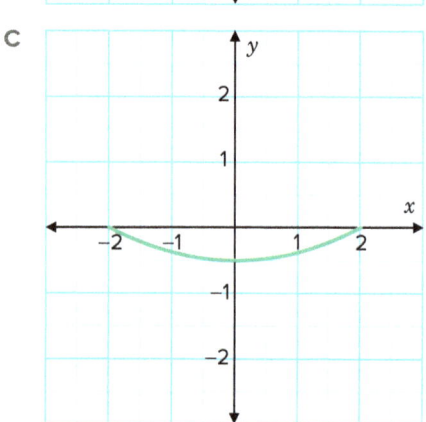

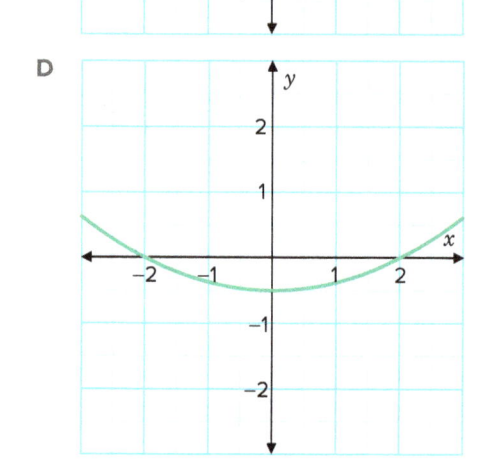

  A

  B

  C

  D

  b Find the vertex of the satellite dish.

20 Xia notices that the Sunshine State Arch is in the shape of a quadratic function. They know that the arch has a height of 110 ft and the feet of the arch are 100 ft apart. Xia chooses to let the x-intercepts of the arch be the origin and (100, 0).

  a Determine the coordinates of the vertex of the arch.
  b Write the equation of the quadratic function for Xia's representation of the Sunshine State Arch in factored form.
  c Find the domain and range of the Sunshine State Arch.

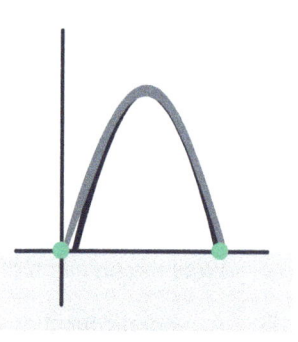

Let's extend our thinking

21 Create a quadratic function in the form $f(x) = (x - \square)(x - \square)$ that meets the given condition.
  a Two positive x-intercepts.
  b Two negative x-intercepts.
  c One positive and one negative x-intercept.
  d One positive x-intercept.
  e One x-intercept at (0, 0).

22 Rewrite the quadratic functions from the previous question in the form $f(x) = ax^2 + bx + c$ and determine the similarities and differences between the values of a, b, and c depending on the type of solution the quadratic has.

23 Ami throws a javelin forward in a parabolic arc from the ground. Using photos that her friend Maryellen is taking from the stands, she determines that 10 yards horizontally from where she threw the javelin, it reaches a maximum height 5 yards above the ground.

Ami models her throw with the origin of a coordinate plane being the point 20 yards behind her.

   a For Ami's model, state the roots.

   b Write the equation for the quadratic function modeling the path of Ami's throw in factored form.

24 Burnell jumps up and off a 4 meter high springboard into the diving pool below.

Burnell's jump can be represented by the equation

$$y = -2(x - 2)(x + 1)$$

where y is Burnell's height above the water and x is the horizontal distance from the springboard towards the pool (both in meters).

   a Graph the equation modeling Burnell's jump. Label any x- and y-intercepts.

   b Use the model to predict where Burnell will enter the water. Explain your answer.

25 Wilson tosses an eraser into the air and counts how long it takes for the eraser to return to his hand. He estimates that it takes 2 seconds and that he is tossing the eraser 6 ft into the air.

Wilson models the height of the eraser above his hand in feet as a function h of time t in seconds, letting $t = 0$ be when he tosses the eraser and $h = 0$ be the height of his hand.

   a Explain how to find the intercepts of the function and state them.

   b Assuming that the path of the eraser is symmetric going up and coming down, state the coordinates of the vertex of the function.

   c Graph the function. Choose appropriate labels and scales.

   d Write the equation of the function in factored form.

26 A quadratic function has the factored form equation $y = k(x - x_0)(x - 12)$.

If the function has a vertex at the point (8, 15), determine the values of x_0 and k. Justify your answers.

Answers

7.02 Quadratic functions in factored form

What do you remember?

1. $y = a(x - x_1)(x - x_2)$

   The values of x_1 and x_2 are the x-values of the x-intercepts of the quadratic function. The scale factor of the function is represented by a.

2. The axis of symmetry of a quadratic is the vertical line that can be drawn so each side of the quadratic function mirrors the other. This line passes through the vertex of the quadratic function.

3. a $x = 1, 4$ b $x = 3, -7$
   c $x = 0, 4$ d $x = 1, -5$

4. a $y = 24$ b $y = 0$

5. D

6. D

7. [graph]

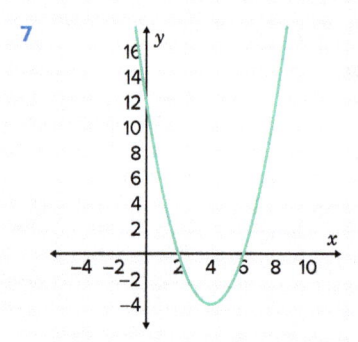

8. A

9. Answers may vary

   [graph]

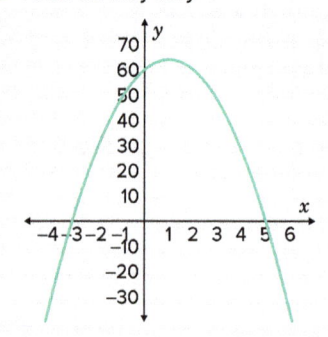

Let's practice

10. a i (2, 0) and (−4, 0) ii $x = -1$
    iii (−1, −9)
    iv [graph]

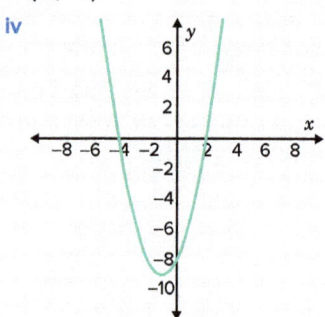

    b i (1, 0) and (5, 0) ii $x = 3$
    iii (3, 8)
    iv [graph]

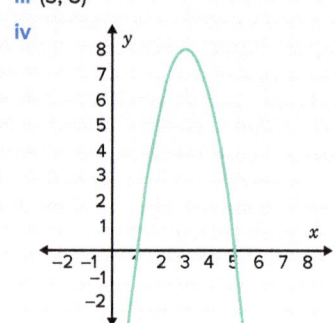

11. a i $x = 1, 4$ ii $y = 8$
    iii $y = 2(x - 1)(x - 4)$
    b i $x = -2, 6$ ii $y = 4$
    iii $y = -\frac{1}{3}(x - 6)(x + 2)$

12. a i $x = 3, -1$ ii (0, −3) iii (1, −4)
    b i $x = -2, 5$ ii (0, −10) iii (1.5, −12.25)
    c i $x = 4, -6$ ii (0, −24) iii (−1, −25)
    d i $x = 1, -2$ ii (0, 2) iii (−0.5, 2.25)

13. a i All real numbers ii $y \geq -\frac{1}{4}$
    b i All real numbers ii $y \leq 12.25$
    c i All real numbers ii $y \geq 0$
    d i All real numbers ii $y \leq 0$

14. a {−6, −4, 14, 36, 66} b {−36, −14, 4, 6}
    c {−100, −48, 12} d {−6, 0, 54, 120}

15. a $f(-5) = -12$ b $f(-2) = 12$
    c $f\left(\frac{1}{2}\right) = \frac{9}{2}$ d $x = -4$ and $x = 1$

16. $y = -4(x - 5)(x + 3)$

17. $y = \frac{1}{3}(x + 2)(x - 9)$

18. $y = 3(x + 4)(x + 7)$

19. a C b $\left(0, -\frac{1}{2}\right)$

20 a (50, 110)   b $y = -\dfrac{11}{250}x(x-100)$

   c Domain: $0 \leq x \leq 100$
   Range: $0 \leq y \leq 110$

Let's extend our thinking

21 a Answers should be in the form of $f(x) = (x-a)(x-b)$ where a and b are positive real numbers.
   For example, $f(x) = (x-5)(x-3)$ has positive x-intercepts

   b Answers should be in the form of $f(x) = (x+a)(x+b)$ where a and b are positive real numbers.
   For example, $f(x) = (x+1)(x+2)$ has negative x-intercepts

   c Answers should be in the form of $f(x) = (x+a)(x-b)$ where a and b are positive real numbers.
   For example, $f(x) = (x-4)(x+1)$ has one negative and one positive x-intercept

   d Answers should be in the form of $f(x) = (x-a)(x-a)$ or $f(x) = (x-a)^2$ where a is a positive real number.
   For example, $f(x) = (x-6)^2$ has one positive x-intercept

   e Answers should be in the form of $f(x) = x(x-b)$ where b is any real number.
   For example, $f(x) = x(x+1)$ has one x-intercept at $(x, 0)$

22 The functions will be dependent on the values chosen in the previous question.

The signs of b and c will be different depending on the signs of the x-intercepts. Specifically: when both x-intercepts have the same sign c is positive. When the x-intercepts have different signs c is negative. b is positive when both x-intercepts are positive and b is negative when both x-intercepts are negative. When the x-intercepts are positive and negative, b will be either positive or negative depending on which x-intercept is larger. The coefficient a is not influenced by the values of the x-intercepts in this form.

23 a $x = 20, 40$ b $y = -\dfrac{1}{20}(x-20)(x-40)$

24 a

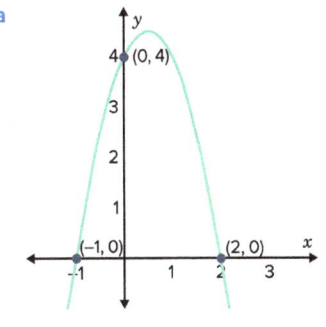

b Since y represents Burnell's height above the water, he will enter the water when $y = 0$. In other words, the x-intercepts of the model represent where Burnell might enter the water. This will be at either $(-1, 0)$ or $(2, 0)$.

We also know that x represents Burnell's horizontal distance from the springboard towards the pool. Since Burnell is jumping into the pool, the x-value when he enters the water must be positive.

This means that Burnell will enter the water at the coordinates $(2, 0)$, which is 2 meters horizontally from the springboard. The other x-intercept, $(-1, 0)$ is a non-viable solution because it has a negative x-value.

25 a The horizontal intercepts represent the times when the eraser is 0 ft above Wilson's hand. This will be exactly when Wilson tosses the eraser and when it returns to his hand. Since Wilson tosses the eraser at $t = 0$ and it takes 2 seconds for it to return to his hand, the horizontal intercepts are $(0, 0)$ and $(2, 0)$. Since one of the horizontal intercepts is at the origin, we have the vertical intercept is also $(0, 0)$.

   b $(1, 6)$

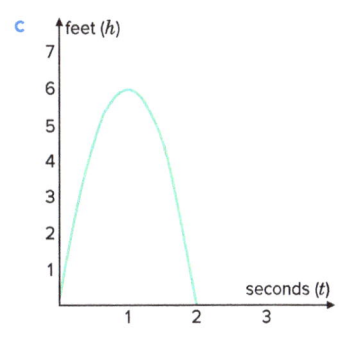

   c

   d $y = -6x(x-2)$

26 Since the vertex lies on the axis of symmetry, we know that 8 is the average of 12 and x_0. So then, we must have $x_0 = 4$. If we substitute the coordinates of the vertex into the function, we get:
$$15 = k(8-4)(8-12)$$
If we solve this equation we get $k = -\dfrac{15}{16}$.

7.03 Quadratic functions in vertex form

Subtopic overview

Lesson narrative

In this lesson, students will use technology and coordinate grids and repeated reasoning to make generalizations about the relationship of quadratic equations in vertex forms and the graphs key characteristics. Students will also explore an interactive visual model to represent the process of completing the square. By the end of the lesson, students will be able to examine equations in vertex form to identify and explain the transformations of the parent quadratic function and work flexibly between quadratic equations in vertex form and their graphs to answer questions about contextual situations.

Learning objectives

Students: Page 409

> **After this lesson, you will be able to...**
> - write the equation for a quadratic function in vertex form.
> - identify the key features of a quadratic function in vertex form.
> - use transformations to graph a quadratic function in vertex form.

Key vocabulary

- completing the square
- perfect square trinomial
- vertical translation
- dilation
- reflection
- horizontal translation
- vertex form

Essential understanding

Different representations of a function may highlight or hide different characteristics but they do not change the function itself. The vertex form of a quadratic function highlights the coordinates of the vertex and as a result the axis of symmetry.

Standards

This subtopic addresses the following Virginia 2023 Mathematics Standards of Learning standards.

Mathematical process goals

MPG2 — Mathematical Communication

The goal can be integrated by encouraging students to express their reasoning and solutions clearly using mathematical language. This could involve explaining their thought process in determining the vertex, x-intercepts, and y-intercept of a quadratic function in vertex form, or discussing how they graphed the function.

MPG3 — Mathematical Reasoning

This goal can be integrated into instruction by prompting students to justify their steps in converting a quadratic function from standard form to vertex form, or in determining the key characteristics of a quadratic function given its vertex form. They should use logical reasoning to analyze their own and others' arguments and to determine whether conclusions are valid.

MPG4 — Mathematical Connections

Teachers can help students make connections between different areas of mathematics and between mathematics and other disciplines by relating the concept of a vertex and the form of a quadratic function to real-world situations. They should also connect the different forms of quadratic functions (standard, vertex, and factored forms) and how they can be used interchangeably to analyze and interpret key characteristics of the function.

Content standards

A.F.2 — The student will investigate, analyze, and compare characteristics of functions, including quadratic and exponential functions, and model quadratic and exponential relationships.

A.F.2b — Given an equation or graph, determine key characteristics of a quadratic function including x-intercepts (zeros), y-intercept, vertex (maximum or minimum), and domain and range (including when restricted by context); interpret key characteristics as related to contextual situations, where applicable.

A.F.2c — Graph a quadratic function, $f(x)$, in two variables using a variety of strategies, including transformations $f(x) + k$ and $kf(x)$, where k is limited to rational values.

A.F.2g — For any value, x, in the domain of f, determine $f(x)$ of a quadratic or exponential function. Determine x given any value $f(x)$ in the range of f of a quadratic function. Explain the meaning of x and $f(x)$ in context.

Prior connections

A.F.1 — The student will investigate, analyze, and compare linear functions algebraically and graphically, and model linear relationships.

Future connections

A2.F.2 — The student will investigate and analyze characteristics of square root, cube root, rational, polynomial, exponential, logarithmic, and piecewise-defined functions algebraically and graphically.

Engage Activity

Kicks for Charity   60 mins

Students will use an applet to play a soccer game and try to determine the quadratic function that guarantees the soccer ball passes through a given vertex.

Understanding and skills

Will use

Identifying key features of graphs.

Will develop

Writing the equation of a quadratic functions in vertex form when given a graph, table, or written description.

Identifying the effect of a given transformation on a quadratic function in vertex form.

Preparation and materials
- Open and complete the student preview, anticipating classroom responses.
- **Materials:** None

Support students with disabilities
Support organization - collect and record data

Provide students with the following table:

Point 1	Point 2	Equation that goes through points

This will help students make observations regarding trigonometric ratios and angles.

Support for English language learners
Compare and connect with discussion supports

Ask students to reflect on the differences between the easier and harder versions of the applet. Consider sharing the following sentence prompts:
- The difference between the levels is ...
- I can get a star on the easy version because ...
- I could use equations to solve for the star because ...

876   Mathspace   Virginia SOL Algebra 1 Teacher Edition
mathspace.co

Classroom guide

Hook
Notice and wonder • 5 mins

Students write observations about an applet with three, adjustable quadratic functions.

What do you notice? What do you wonder? Explore the applet.

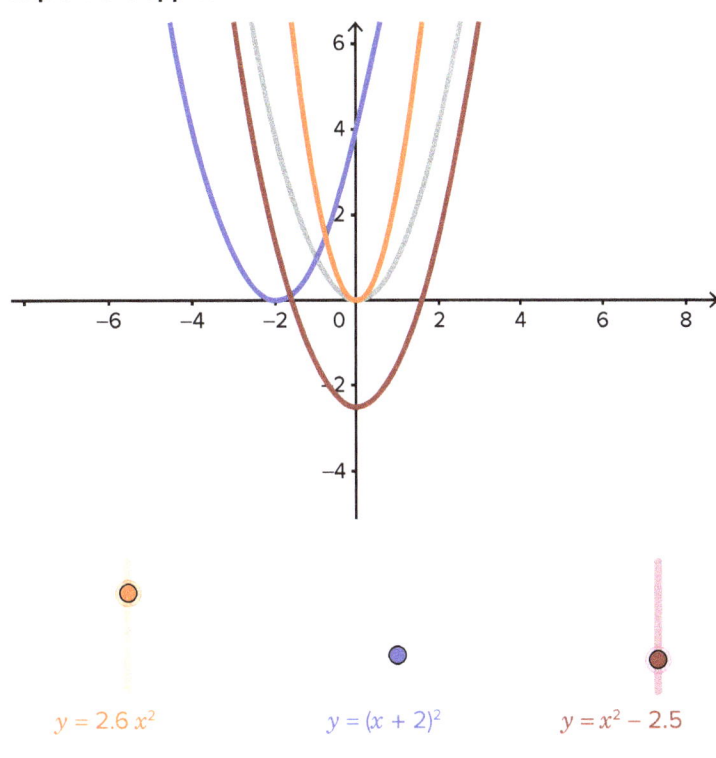

Implementation details

Encourage students to explore the applet and highlight student responses about how the parameters a, h, and k affect each parabola. Use the hook as an opportunity to review key features of graphs of quadratic functions, such as vertical and horizontal shifts, stretching and compressing of the parent function, and the graph's concavity.

$y = 2.6\,x^2$ $y = (x + 2)^2$ $y = x^2 - 2.5$

Slide 1 from Student Engage Activity

Launch
5 mins

Explore the applet.

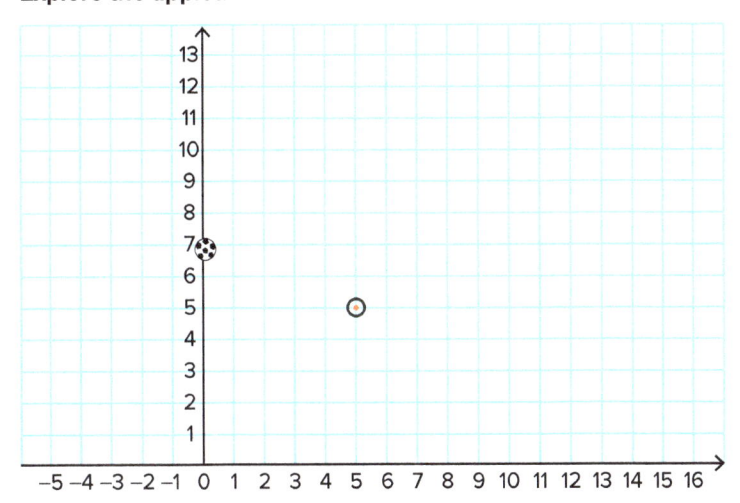

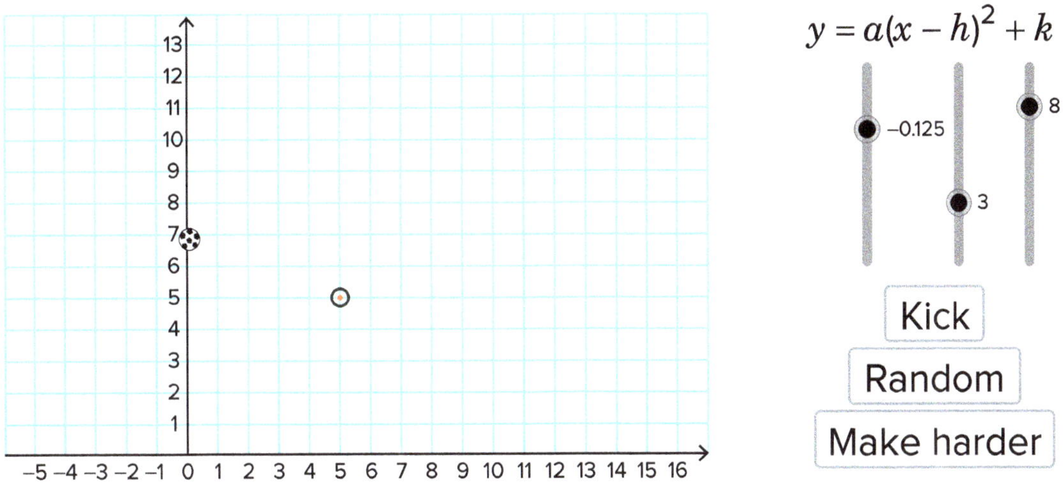

$$y = a(x - h)^2 + k$$

−0.125   3   8

Kick

Random

Make harder

Slide 2 from Student Engage Activity

7.03 Quadratic functions in vertex form
mathspace.co

Ask the class if anyone plays soccer or follows the Miami FC team or other soccer teams, calling upon student knowledge and interest in soccer will increase engagement in the task. Allow students time to explore the soccer challenge applet and to read the instructions of the game. Note: It may increase student buy-in if you encourage excitement around the charity and $10, 000 aspect of the task.

Students may want to choose a charity they would contribute to, and you can create a chart on the board for students to record each time they are able to 'earn' $10, 000 by correctly finding the quadratic equation to model the kick of the soccer ball.

Important mathematical concepts: Quadratic equation, parameters, vertical and horizontal shifts, stretching and compressing of functions, concavity, and transformations.

Important contextual information: Miami FC soccer team and charity.

Suggested grouping: Form pairs

> **Continue when**
> Students have read the Launch and understand the context of the problem.

Explore   Think-pair-share • 35 mins

Students will come up with at least three equations to represent a soccer ball going through different points.

Anticipated strategies

Connect transformations to quadratics

Students may remember how to transform other functions, and connect how a, h, and k affect the parent quadratic function $y = x^2$.

Trial, error, and improvement

Students may explore the applet and notice that (h, k) is the vertex of the parabola and that a affects the vertical stretch and compression through testing various kicking attempts. With this information, students can create equations.

Algebraic testing

Students may test whether the vertex (h, k) satisfies the equation algebraically.

Some students may notice that (h, k) is the vertex and that a vertically stretches or compresses the function. Other students may find (h, k) and then plug in another point on the function to solve for a so that the function passes through the vertex and the other desired point. Encourage students to use multiple strategies and record their observations.

Misconceptions

Not generalizing how a, h, and k affect the quadratic function.

Have you tried changing one parameter at a time? What would the equation and graph be for each case? Can you record this somewhere? What do you notice?

Purposeful questions

Use the following questions to check for understanding and encourage critical thinking:
- What is the goal of this kicking challenge?
- What is your plan to adjust the equation so that the kick hits the goal or is closer to hitting the goal? What makes you say that?
- What observations do you notice about the graph and equation?
- How do the parameters affect the graph?

> **Continue when**
> Students have completed three kicking challenges, recorded the equation for each, and generalized the process of finding the function that should model the path of the soccer ball.

Discuss   15 mins

Have a group discussion where some partners' can share their equations and can be tested in front of the class. Consider sequencing the strategies presented from transformations, to trial and error, to algebraic testing.

Discussion guide

Invite students to share their generalizations of the process for finding the function that should model the path of the soccer ball. Write student responses on the board and ask the class to generalize the class observations as needed, such as how a, h and k affect the function.

Test out some of the equations that students share to ensure that they do hit the target. If you are keeping track of the scores, mark down the winnings of partners' at this time.

Choose one generalization for the class to test out. Display the explanation and ask groups to try and follow the directions to find the equation for another simulation of the kicking challenge.

As an extension you may wish to give students the following prompt:

Compare the following functions and how the parameters affect the functions:

$$y = ax^2 \qquad\qquad y = (bx)^2$$

Lesson Preparation

Suggested review

Depending on your students' level of prior knowledge, consider revisiting the following lessons:

- **Algebra 1 —** 6.07 Factor using appropriate methods
- **Algebra 1 —** 7.01 Characteristics of quadratic functions
- **Algebra 1 —** 7.02 Quadratic functions in factored form

Tools

You may find these tools helpful:
- Graphing calculator
- Clear plastic sheets
- Tracing paper
- Blank coordinate grid

Student lesson & teacher guide

Vertex form

The following supports may be useful for this section. More specific supports may appear throughout the lesson:

Students: Pages 409–411

7.03 Quadratic functions in vertex form

After this lesson, you will be able to...
- write the equation for a quadratic function in vertex form.
- identify the key features of a quadratic function in vertex form.
- use transformations to graph a quadratic function in vertex form.

Engage activity
Ask your teacher to get started

Kicks for Charity
Students will use an applet to play a soccer game and try to determine the quadratic function that guarantees the soccer ball passes through a given vertex.

Vertex form

One way to represent quadratic functions is using **vertex form**. This form allows us to identify the coordinates of the vertex of the parabola, as well as the direction of opening and scale factor that compresses or stretches the graph of the function.

$$f(x) = a(x - h)^2 + k$$

(h, k) coordinates of the vertex

a scale factor

When given the graph of the function, we can write the equation in vertex form using transformations.

A parabola can be **vertically translated** by increasing or decreasing the y-values by a constant number. A translation of $y = x^2$ up by k units gives the equation $y = x^2 + k$.

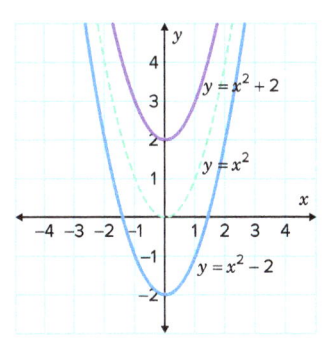

This graph shows $y = x^2$ translated vertically up by 2 to get $y = x^2 + 2$, and down by 2 to get $y = x^2 - 2$.

Similarly, a parabola can be **horizontally translated** by increasing or decreasing the x-values by a constant number. However, the x-value together with the translation must be squared together. That is, to translate $y = x^2$ to the left by h units we get $y = (x + h)^2$.

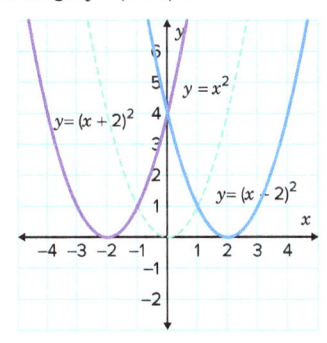

This graph shows $y = x^2$ translated horizontally left by 2 to get $y = (x + 2)^2$ and right by 2 to get $y = (x - 2)^2$.

A parabola can be **dilated** by multiplying every y-value by a constant number greater than 1. So to expand the parabola $y = x^2$ by a scale factor of a we get $y = ax^2$. We can compress a parabola by using a scale factor between 0 and 1.

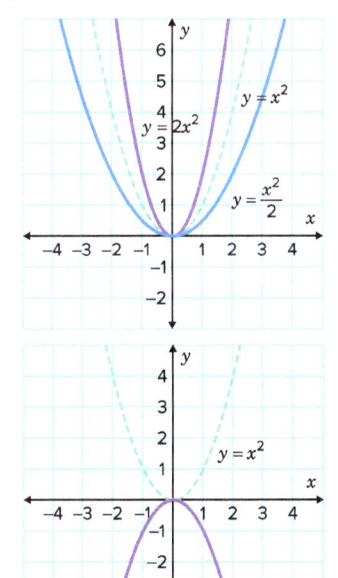

This graph shows $y = x^2$ vertically expanded by a scale factor of 2 to get $y = 2x^2$ and compressed by a scale factor of 2 to get $y = \dfrac{x^2}{2}$.

Finally, we can **reflect** a parabola across the x-axis by multiplying by -1. So to reflect $y = x^2$ across the x-axis we get $y = -x^2$. Notice that reflecting will change the parabola from opening up to opening down.

7.03 Quadratic functions in vertex form   881

mathspace.co

The x-value of the vertex, h, represents the horizontal translation; the y-value, k, represents the vertical translation; and the leading coefficient, a, represents the shape of the parabola and the direction it opens. The parent function of a quadratic is $f(x) = x^2$, so writing these translations in function notation becomes $af(x - h) + k = a(x - h)^2 + k$.

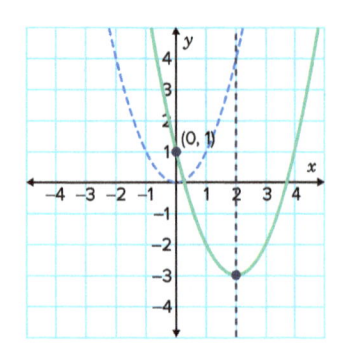

As an example, consider the graph of $y = (x - 2)^2 - 3$
- Translation of the parent function 3 units down and 2 units right with a vertex at (2, −3)
- Axis of symmetry $x = 2$
- y-intercept at (0, 1) can be calculated by substituting $x = 0$ into the function

When writing a quadratic function from its graph, we can begin by identifying the vertex and substituting these values into the function for h and k. Then, we can use another point on the parabola, like the y-intercept, to help us find the value of a.

Relate the transformations in vertex form back to the parent quadratic function
Targeted instructional strategies

Relate the different constants and coefficients in the vertex form of a quadratic function to the transformations of $y = x^2$, explaining why these transformations should follow a particular order (or otherwise be taken into account).

Consider the general vertex form $y = a(x - h)^2 + k$. To get this function from $y = x^2$, we apply the following transformations:

1. If a is negative, then we reflect across the x-axis
2. Vertical stretch or compression by a factor of the magnitude of a
3. Horizontal translation by h units, left or right depending on the sign of h
4. Vertical translation by k units, up or down depending on the sign of k

Let students experiment with performing these steps in different orders. Explain that steps 1, 2 and 3 can be done interchangeably, but steps 1 and 2 should come before step 4. This is because vertical translation moves the vertex off the x-axis, which changes how the other transformations affect the graph.

Compare and connect
English language learner support

Encourage students to connect previously learned concepts, such as x-intercepts, direction of parabola opening, axis of symmetry and vertex, to the values in the vertex form for quadratic functions. This can be done by asking them to connect features of the equation to its corresponding graph.

For example, the equation $y = \frac{1}{2}(x-3)^2 + 1$ has the graph:

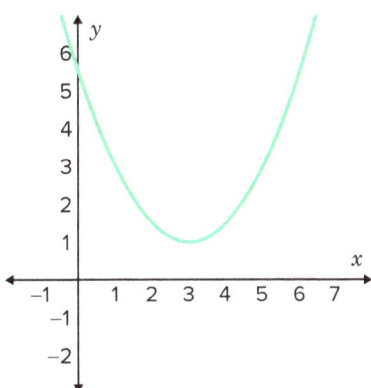

Students may make connections such as:
- The values of 1 and 3 in the equation match the magnitudes of the coordinates of the vertex on the graph.
- The $\frac{1}{2}$ in the equation matches the scale factor in the graph compared to $y = x^2$.
- The y-value of the y-intercept, 5.5, is not one of the coefficients or constants in the equation.

Providing students with multiple examples to compare and connect can help students familiarize themselves with the key features of the factored form for quadratic function equations.

Break down vertex form
Student with disabilities support

To incorporate decomposition, guide students to break down vertex form into its individual components: a, h, and k. Examine how each parameter affects the graph by focusing on one at a time. For instance, keep h and k constant and vary a to explore changes in the graph's width and direction. The applet from the exploration can be used to emphasize the impact of each parameter.

Clarify left and right translations
Address student misconceptions

Students may suggest that $f(x) = (x + 5)^2$ is a horizontal translation of 5 units to the right. Challenge this misconception using a graphing tool to show that $f(x) = (x + 5)^2$ has a vertex at $(-5, 0)$, and so has been translated to the left from the parent function $f(x) = x^2$. Alternatively, use a table of values to see what happens to the vertex and other key features.

Exploration

Students: Page 409

> **Interactive exploration**
> Explore online to answer the questions
>
> 🌐 mathspace.co

Use the interactive exploration in 7.03 to answer these questions.

1. What happens to the orange graph as the slider moves from a positive to a negative number?
2. What happens to the blue graph as the slider moves from a positive to a negative number?
3. What happens to the red graph as the slider moves from a positive to a negative number?

Suggested student grouping: Small groups

Students explore on a GeoGebra applet which shows how changing a, h, and k in the vertex form of a quadratic equation will change its graph. Students are not formally introduced to vertex form $y = a(x - h)^2 + k$, but will draw conclusions about the vertical stretches and compressions that a changes on the graph of the function, the horizontal translations of h, and the vertical translations of k.

Ideal student responses

These ideal responses may differ from other correct student responses. Less formal responses can be connected with the more precise mathematical language presented here

1. **What happens to the orange graph as the slider moves from a positive to a negative number?**
   As the orange slider which changes the coefficient of x^2 moves, we can see that positive coefficients will keep the graph of the function opening upward, while negative coefficients change the function to a downward-opening graph. In addition, $|a| > 1$ stretches and $0 < |a| < 1$ compresses the graph vertically.

2. **What happens to the blue graph as the slider moves from a positive to a negative number?**
   As the blue slider changes, we can see that positive numbers in the slider are subtracted, and the graph has a horizontal shift to the right. Negative numbers are represented with an addition sign in the equation, and the graph has a horizontal translation to the left when the numbers on the slider are negative.

3. **What happens to the red graph as the slider moves from a positive to a negative number?**
   As the red slider moves, we can see that the graph vertically translates above the x-axis when the slider moves to positive numbers, and vertically translates the y-intercept below the x-axis when the slider moves to negative numbers.

Purposeful questions

- Does the slider change the location of the vertex? If yes, how are they connected?
- Does the slider change the shape of the parabola?
- Can you describe the effect of each slider in terms of translations, dilations or reflections?

Possible misunderstandings

- Since the vertex form of a quadratic function shows the value in parentheses being subtracted, students may be confused as they try to describe how the graph changes as the blue graph's slider moves from a positive number to a negative number. Point out to students that when they move the slider physically up, the number for the equation is positive, even though it's being subtracted. When we move the slider physically down, the number for the equation is negative, even though we are seeing addition in the equation itself. The sliders in the applet will all move to positive numbers at the top and negative numbers as we slide them down.

Help visualize transformations with physical tools
Student with disabilities support

For students who have difficulty visualizing the transformations of the parent function x^2, prepare physical manipulatives that can replicate these transformations.

For example, graph different dilations of x^2, such as $2x^2$ and $\frac{1}{3}x^2$, onto sheets of clear plastic grid paper or tracing paper. Provide a coordinate plane with the same size grid squares over which students can lay these sheets and move them around to visualize transformations.

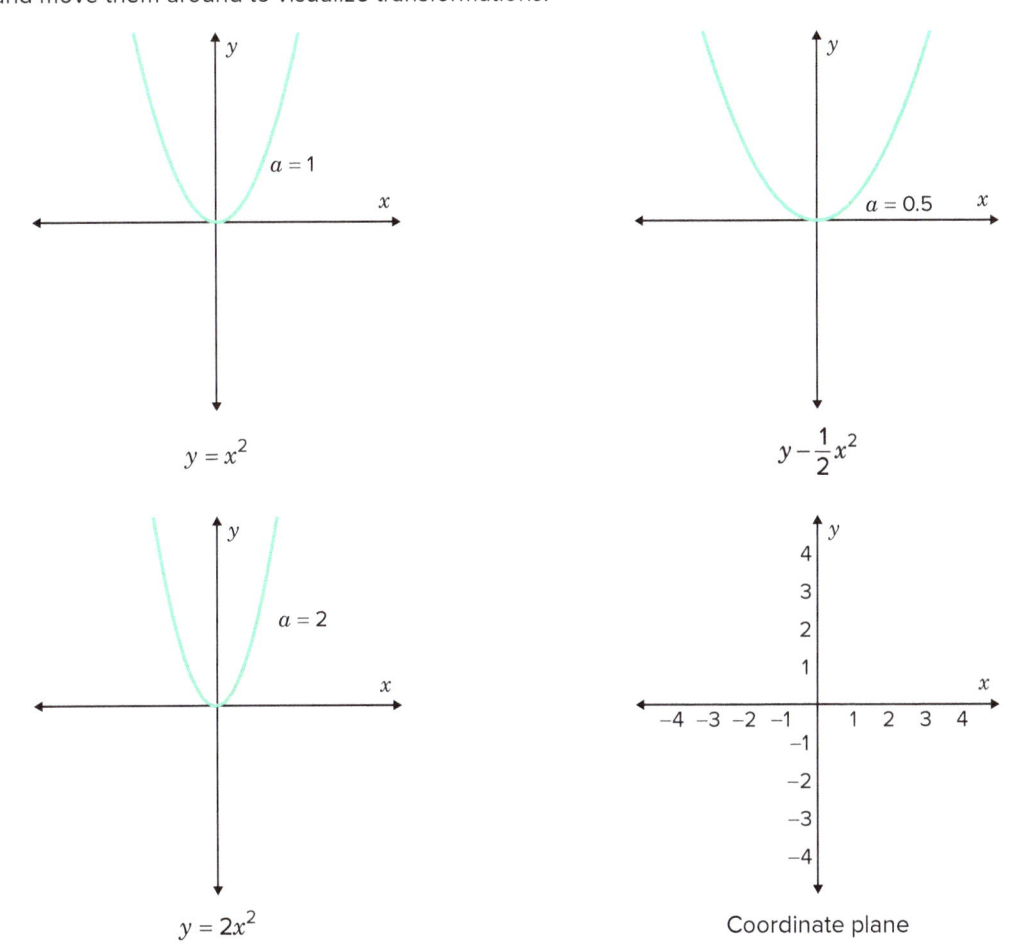

$y = x^2$, $a = 1$

$y = \frac{1}{2}x^2$, $a = 0.5$

$y = 2x^2$, $a = 2$

Coordinate plane

Explain how the manipulatives can represent different transformations:
- Horizontal and vertical translation can be represented by moving the sheet up, down, left or right on the coordinate plane.
- Reflection across an axis can be represented by physically flipping the sheet across that axis.
- Vertical stretch and compression can be represented by swapping out the current sheet for one with the correct scale factor without changing the position of the vertex.

Additionally or alternatively, students can use a GeoGebra applet with sliders for a, h and k to visualize what aspect of the graph each variable affects.

https://www.geogebra.org/m/Cav9fa27

🔍 Mislabeling the signs of h and k in the vertex
Address student misconceptions

Students may incorrectly identify the sign of the coordinates of the vertex from an equation in vertex form

$$y = a(x - h)^2 + k$$

as either $(-h, k)$ or $(h, -k)$.

This is likely to happen if students are expecting the two variables of h and k to have the same sign, as with x_1 and x_2 in the factored form.

Ask students to check if the vertex they have found is a point on the curve by substituting the coordinates back into the equation.

Students are introduced to the vertex form of a quadratic function and review how the graph of a quadratic function in vertex form relates to its graph.

Examples

Students: Page 411

Example 1

Consider the following function:

$$m(x) = -\frac{1}{2}(x - 2)^2 + 8$$

a Find the vertex.

Create a strategy

The function is given in vertex form $y = a(x - h)^2 + k$ where the vertex is the point (h, k).

Apply the idea

In the equation $m(x) = -\frac{1}{2}(x - 2)^2 + 8$ the x-coordinate of vertex is $h = 2$ and the y-coordinate of vertex is $k = 8$.

With $h = 2$ and $k = 8$, the ordered pair of the vertex is at $(2, 8)$.

Purpose

See if students can identify the x and y coordinates of the vertex from an equation.

Expected mistakes

Students may say the vertex is $(-2, 8)$. Help students make connections back to the function's translations to understand the that $(x - 2)^2$ moves the function to the right, meaning the x-value of the vertex will be positive.

Students: Page 411

b State the domain.

Create a strategy

To find the domain of $m(x)$, we want to find all possible x-values for which $m(x)$ could be graphed.

Apply the idea

We know that for a parabola, there are no restrictions on which x-values can be graphed as each side of the parabola continues infinitely in either x direction.

Domain: $\{x \mid -\infty < x < \infty\}$

Purpose
See students' understanding of the domain of a quadratic function.

Students: Page 411

c State the range.

Create a strategy
To find the range, we want to find all possible values of $m(x)$. The vertex of a parabola affects the range of the function, as it will be the maximum or minimum value of $m(x)$.

Apply the idea
This parabola opens down, so the y-value of the vertex is the maximum value of the function. The parabola continues infinitely in the negative y direction.
Range: $\{y | y \leq 8\}$

Purpose
Check if students are able to identify the range given an equation.

Reflecting with students
Students may not consider the sign of the leading coefficient and assume the vertex is a minimum, leading them to reverse the direction of the inequality. Remind them at when the leading coefficient, or the a a-value is negative, the parabola is reflected across the x-axis.

Students: Pages 412–413

d Draw the graph of the function.

Create a strategy
The scale factor is $-\frac{1}{2}$ which is negative, so the graph will open down. We can draw the graph through any three points that we know are on it.

Apply the idea

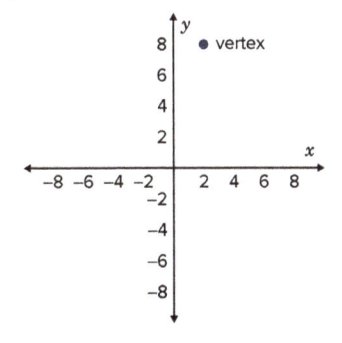

Start by plotting the vertex, found in part (a), on the graph.

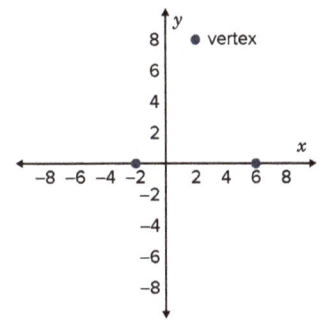

We can solve for the x-intercepts by substituting $m(x) = 0$ and solving for x.

$$0 = -\frac{1}{2}(x-2)^2 + 8$$

$$-8 = -\frac{1}{2}(x-2)^2$$

$$16 = (x-2)^2$$

$$\pm 4 = x - 2$$

$x = 2 + 4$ and $x = 2 - 4$

$x = 6$ and $x = -2$

7.03 Quadratic functions in vertex form

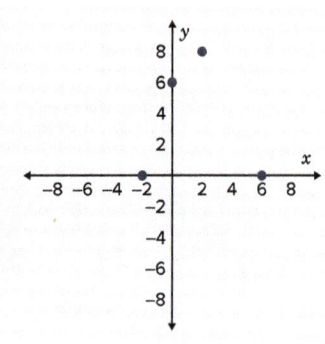

We can solve for the y-intercept by substituting $x = 0$ and solving for $m(x)$.

$$m(x) = -\frac{1}{2}(0-2)^2 + 8$$

$$m(x) = -\frac{1}{2}(-2)^2 + 8$$

$$m(x) = -\frac{1}{2}(4) + 8$$

$$m(x) = -2 + 8$$

$$m(x) = 6$$

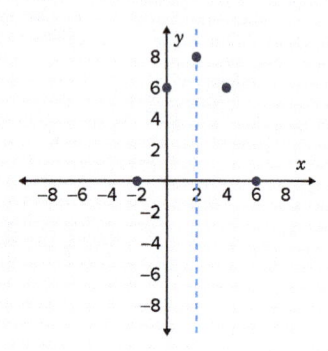

Then, we can get an additional point by reflecting the y-intercept across the axis of symmetry.

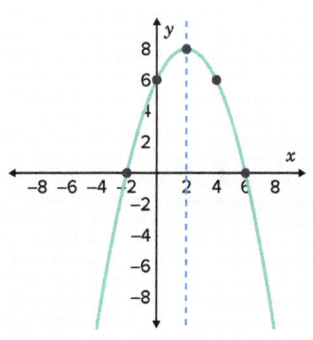

To finish the drawing of the graph of the function, connect the points plotted to draw the parabola.

Reflect and check
Technically we only need 3 points to graph a parabola, but finding more points can make our graph more precise.

Purpose
Check if students can draw the graph of a function from its equation.

Expected mistakes
Students may make the mistake of thinking the y-intercept is at (0, 8). Have students substitute $x = 0$ into the equation to verify the y-intercept. Point out that $y = 8$ is the y-value of the vertex, not the y-intercept.

Reflecting with students
To graph a function, it may be easier for students to find a few points that lie on the graph. They could do this with the intercepts or by substituting any value of x into the equation.

Students: Page 413

Example 2

The table of values represents a quadratic function.

x	−4	−3	−2	−1	0	1	2
$p(x)$	−5	0	3	4	3	0	−5

a   Write the function $p(x)$ in vertex form.

Create a strategy

We can use the fact that a quadratic function has symmetry about its vertex to identify the location of the vertex from the table.

Apply the idea

Looking at the values of $p(x)$, we can see that it has a maximum value of 4 and falls off symmetrically on either side. So, we know that the vertex is the point (−1, 4), so we can use that to set up the equation

$$p(x) = a(x + 1)^2 + 4$$

We can now find the value of a by substituting any other pair of values from the table, such as (0, 3). Doing so, we get

$$3 = a(0 + 1)^2 + 4$$

which we can solve to get $a = -1$.

So the quadratic function shown in the table of values is

$$p(x) = -(x + 1)^2 + 4$$

Purpose

Show students how to use a table of values to write the equation of a quadratic function in vertex form.

Expected mistakes

Students may write the equation $f(x) = (x + 1)^2 + 4$ without considering the leading coefficient. Ask them to describe how the y-values change as x increasing. This should help them realize that the parabola opens downward.

Reflecting with students

Ask students if using a table is enough information for them to write the equation of the function in vertex form or if they prefer to also have a graph of the function. Allowing students to be resourceful in their problem solving will give them confidence to find solutions using their preferred methods.

Students: Page 414

b   Determine the value of $p(x)$ when $x = 6$.

Create a strategy

We can substitute $x = 6$ into the equation that was created in part (a) in order to predict what $p(x)$ will be equal to.

Apply the idea

The equation found in part (a) is

$p(x) = -(x + 1)^2 + 4$ Original equation
$p(6) = -(6 + 1)^2 + 4$ Substitute $x = 6$
$= -(7)^2 + 4$ Evaluate the addition
$= -49 + 4$ Evaluate the exponent
$= -45$ Evaluate the addition

This means that when $x = 6$, $p(x)$ is equal to −45.

7.03 Quadratic functions in vertex form   889

mathspace.co

Purpose
Show students how to find the value of a function in vertex form at a given value of x.

Reflecting with students
Ask students how to find the value of $p(x)$ when $x = 6$ if they were only using the table of values. Students should be able to follow a pattern in order to find the unknown value of the function without the equation.

x	−4	−3	−2	−1	0	1	2	3	4	5	6
$p(x)$	−5	0	3	4	3	0	−5	−12	−21	−32	−45

−1   −3   −5   −7   −9   −11   −13

Students should be able to see that each value subtracts the next odd integer to find the value.

Students: Page 414

c   Determine the x- and y-intercepts of the function.

Create a strategy
Use the table of values to identify the x-intercepts when $y = 0$ and the y-intercept when $x = 0$.

Apply the idea
The x-intercepts occur at (−3, 0) and (1, 0).
The y-intercept occurs at (0, 3).

Purpose
Show students how to determine the intercepts of a function given in table form.

Reflecting with students
Ask students to explain how to find the intercepts from the graph or equation. We know that from the graph or equation, the y-intercept is the point where $x = 0$, and the x-intercept is the point where $y = 0$. The equation would require some algebraic working, while a graph would require some analyzation.

> **Plot the points from the table to help visualize key features** use with Example 2
> **Student with disabilities support**
>
> Students may have difficulty determining the shape of the relationship from a table of values, as this requires the awareness of a lot of different numeric values at once. Support students by advising them to plot the points on a coordinate plane to see the shape of the relationship and help identify key features of the relationship.

Students: Page 414

> **Example 3**

The quadratic function $f(x) = 2x^2$ has been transformed to produce a new quadratic function $g(x)$, as shown in the graph:

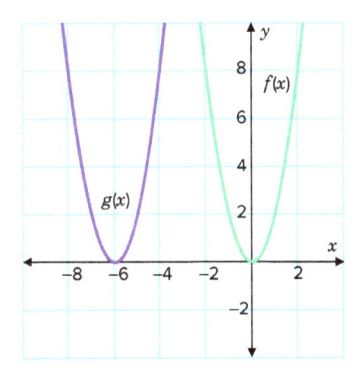

a Describe the transformation from $f(x)$ to $g(x)$.

Apply the idea

The function $g(x)$ has the same shape and size as $f(x)$, but has been shifted to the left. Comparing the vertices of the two parabolas, we can see that this is a translation of 6 units to the left.

Reflect and check

We could confirm that $g(x)$ is a horizontal shift left by evaluating $f(x + 6) = 2(x + 6)^2$:

$g(-8) = 8$ and $f(-8 + 6) = 2(-8 + 6)^2 = 2(-2)^2 = 2(4) = 8$

$g(-6) = 0$ and $f(-6 + 6) = 2(-6 + 6)^2 = 2(0)^2 = 2(0) = 0$

$g(-4) = 8$ and $f(-4 + 6) = 2(-4 + 6)^2 = 2(2)^2 = 2(4) = 8$

Purpose
Show students how to describe a transformation of a quadratic function given its graph.

Reflecting with students
Ask students how they can explain that the graph has not had a stretch or compression. Remind students that just eyeballing and explaining that they do not see a stretch or compression is not enough evidence. Students may argue that other points on the original graph have direct translations to the translated graph.

Students: Page 415

b Write the equation of the function $g(x)$ in vertex form.

Create a strategy
Remember that vertex form for a quadratic is $g(x) = a(x - h)^2 + k$, where the vertex is at the point (h, k).

Apply the idea
$f(x) = 2x^2$ has been translated 6 units to the left to produce $g(x)$, and we can see that its vertex is at $(-6, 0)$. So $g(x)$ has can be written as $g(x) = 2(x + 6)^2$.

Purpose
Show students how to write the equation of a function in vertex form given an equation and its translation.

Expected mistakes
Students may incorrectly write the function as $g(x) = (2x + 6)^2$, placing the scale factor that shows the vertical stretch from the parent function inside of the parentheses. Point out to students that the scale factor should be placed outside of the set of parentheses when the quadratic function is written in vertex form.

Students: Page 415

c Describe the transformations of the graph of $f(x)$ resulting in the function $h(x) = -2(x + 6)^2 + 3$.

Create a strategy
Since $f(x)$ opens upward and has a vertex at $(0, 0)$, the vertex form of $h(x)$ gives information about its vertex and direction of its opening.

Apply the idea
The function $h(x)$ will open downward and be a reflection of $f(x)$ across the x-axis, since the value of a became negative.

The vertex of $h(x)$ is $(-6, 3)$. The vertex became a maximum value and shifted the graph up 3 units and to the left 6 units.

Purpose
Show students how to describe the transformation of a function given its transformed function written in vertex form.

Expected mistakes
Students may forget that changing the sign of the scale factor of a function written in vertex form will reflect the function vertically. Remind students that the scale factor works in the same way it works for quadratic functions written in factored form.

Students: Page 415

d Sketch the graph of $h(x)$

Create a strategy
Use the description of the transformations of $g(x)$ from part (c) and graph of $g(x)$ to sketch $h(x)$.

Apply the idea
Start by reflecting $g(x)$ across the x-axis using points from its graph.

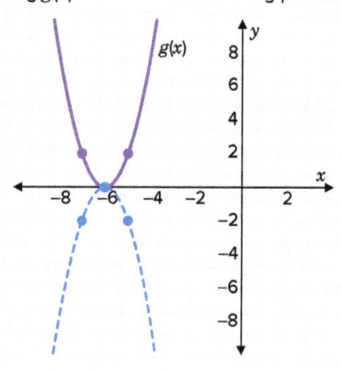

Perform a vertical shift 3 units up.

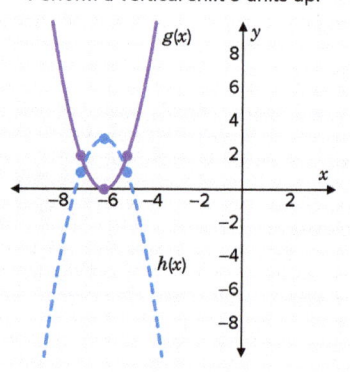

The graph of $h(x)$ follows:

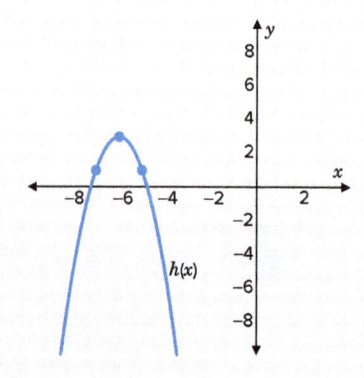

Purpose
Show students how to graph a transformation of a function written in vertex form. Develop decomposition skills by performing one transformation at a time.

Expected mistakes
Students may sketch graphs that are inaccurate by attempting to eyeball the reflection and translation. Encourage students to mark at least three points on the graph of $h(x)$ that they can transform and keep the shape of the graph. The more points they can follow, the more accurate their graph will be when it gets to its final location on the coordinate plane.

Reflecting with students
Make students aware that the order of transformations matters. If we translate and then reflect, we would get a different graph.

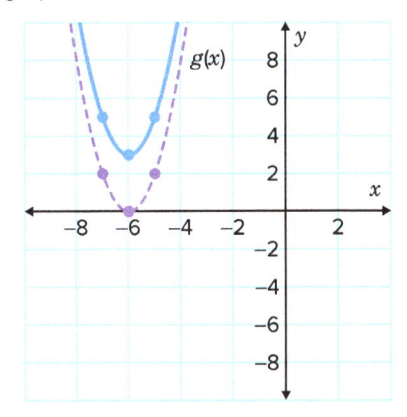

First, perform shift 3 units up.

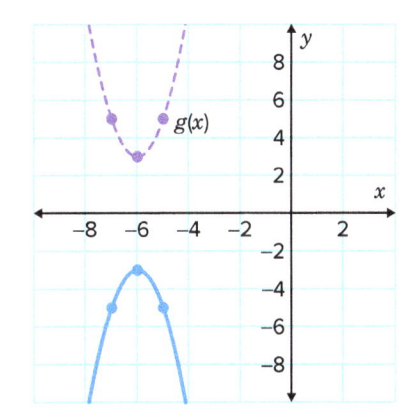

Then, reflect across the x-axis.

Notice this is not the same graph from the original order of transformations.

Students: Page 416

Example 4

Meri throws a rock into Crescent Lake. The height of the rock above ground is a quadratic function of time. The rock is thrown from 4.4 ft above ground. After 1.5 seconds, the rock reaches its maximum height of 24 ft. Write the quadratic equation in vertex form.

Create a strategy
The maximum height of the rock at 24 feet indicates that this is where the vertex of the function is located. This occurs at 1.5 seconds. Substitute the vertex of the graph and the y-intercept into the vertex form of a quadratic function to determine the equation.

Apply the idea
The vertex is located at (1.5, 24), so we can substitute $h = 1.5$ and $k = 24$.

The rock is thrown from 4.4 feet, so the y-intercept is located at (0, 4.4) and we can substitute $x = 0$ and $y = 4.4$.

$y = a(x - h)^2 + k$ Vertex form of a quadratic function
$4.4 = a(0 - 1.5)^2 + 24$ Substitute $x = 0$, $y = 4.4$, $h = 1.5$, and $k = 24$
$-19.6 = a(-1.5)^2$ Subtract 24 from both sides
$-19.6 = a(2.25)$ Evaluate the exponent
$-8.7 = a$ Divide by 2.25 on both sides

The quadratic equation in vertex form that models the rock's height above the ground as a function of time is $y = -8.7(x - 1.5)^2 + 24$.

7.03 Quadratic functions in vertex form

Purpose

Show students how to write a quadratic function in vertex form based on a contextual situation.

Expected mistakes

Students may not know how to substitute the values of the given context into an equation without visualizing the graph. Allow students to sketch the path of the rock on a coordinate grid and label its key features before attempting to write its equation.

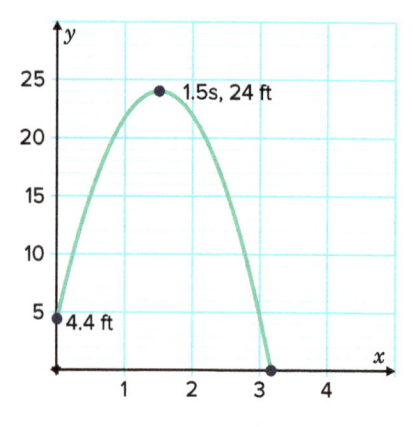

Students: Page 416

> 💡 **Idea summary**
>
> The vertex form of a quadratic function is:
>
> $$f(x) = a(x - h)^2 + k$$
>
> (h, k) coordinates of the vertex
> a scale factor
>
> Changing the values of a, h, and k will transform the graph in different ways:
> - a: vertical stretch or compression
> - h: horizontal translation
> - k: vertical translation

Completing the square

Students: Pages 416–417

Completing the square

Completing the square is a method we use to rewrite a standard quadratic expression in vertex form.

Completing the square allows us to rewrite our equation so that it contains a **perfect square trinomial**. A perfect square trinomial takes on the form $A^2 + 2AB + B^2 = (A + B)^2$, which is the same format we need to have an equation in vertex form.

For quadratic equations where $a = 1$, we can write them in perfect square form by following these steps:

1. $y = x^2 + bx + c$
2. $y = x^2 + 2\left(\dfrac{b}{2}\right)x + c$ Rewrite the x term
3. $y = x^2 + 2\left(\dfrac{b}{2}\right)x + \left(\dfrac{b}{2}\right)^2 + c - \left(\dfrac{b}{2}\right)^2$ Add and subtract $\left(\dfrac{b}{2}\right)^2$ to keep the equation balanced
4. $y = \left(x + \dfrac{b}{2}\right)^2 + c - \left(\dfrac{b}{2}\right)^2$ Factor the perfect square trinomial
5. $y = (x - h)^2 + k$ Match the completed square to vertex form

If $a \neq 1$, we can first divide through by a to factor it out.

The quadratic equation, when rewritten by completing the square, becomes the vertex form of a quadratic equation.

Exploration

Students: Page 416

> **Interactive exploration**
> Explore online to answer the question
> mathspace.co

Use the interactive exploration in 7.03 to answer the question.

1. What patterns do you notice when working through the process of completing the square?

Suggested student grouping: Individual

Students explore an applet where they create an incomplete square, and then use a perfect square trinomial to 'complete' the square. After creating several incomplete squares and analyzing the process by which the GeoGebra completes the square, students should notice that by creating a perfect square trinomial and adding or subtracting the missing number of pieces from the square, they can write a polynomial in vertex form that represents the incomplete square.

Ideal student responses

These ideal responses may differ from other correct student responses. Less formal responses can be connected with the more precise mathematical language presented here.

1. **What patterns do you notice when working through the process of completing the square?**
   The number added or subtracted to the factored form of the perfect square trinomial is equivalent to the number of pieces of the square in surplus or missing. Each time we complete the square, the constant of the perfect square trinomial is both added and subtracted from the polynomial.

Purposeful questions

- How many squares would complete the red square? How many more or less squares are needed to complete the red square?
- Where does the quadratic term on the left side of the equation come from? Where does the linear term on the left side of the equation come from? Where does the constant term on the left side of the equation come from?
- What is happening when we check the box to complete the square?

Possible misunderstandings

- Students may not see any pattern in completing the square with the applet. Walking through an example with the entire class, and annotating the applet and the polynomials will help students see where the visual model fits with the algebraic representation. Students may be able to predict how to come up with the perfect square trinomial and added or subtracted constant themselves after engaging with the applet and following a pattern a few times with the class or one-on-one.

Students learn the process of completing the square in order to rewrite a quadratic function in vertex form.

Students: Page 417

> **Example 5**

Consider the following equation:
$$y = x^2 - 4x + 6$$

a Rewrite the equation in vertex form by completing the square.

Create a strategy

We'll follow the standard complete the square method and stop working once our equation is in vertex form, $y = a(x - h)^2 + k$.

Apply the idea

$y = x^2 - 4x + 6$	Original equation
$y = x^2 - 4x + \left(\dfrac{-4}{2}\right)^2 + 6 - \left(\dfrac{-4}{2}\right)^2$	Add and subtract $\left(\dfrac{b}{2}\right)^2$
$y = x^2 - 4x + 4 + 6 - 4$	Evaluate the exponents
$y = (x - 2)^2 + 6 - 4$	Factor $x^2 - 4x + 4$
$y = (x - 2)^2 + 2$	Evaluate the subtraction

We've completed the square and the equation is now in vertex form.

Reflect and check

We must add and subtract $\left(\dfrac{b}{2}\right)^2$ to the right side of the equation so that the value of the equation does not change.

Purpose

Show students how to complete the square in order to rewrite a quadratic function given in standard form as vertex form.

Expected mistakes

Students may add the value of $\left(\dfrac{b}{2}\right)^2$ to one side of the equation, but forget to subtract it as well.

Reflecting with students

Challenge advanced learners to rewrite the equation $y = 2x^2 - 4x + 6$ in vertex form by completing the square. They will need to factor the leading coefficient out first, which gives $y = 2(x^2 - 2x + 3)$. When they complete the square, they will need to multiply the constant term by 2 when moving it outside of the parentheses. They should end up with the equation $y = 2(x - 1)^2 + 4$.

Students: Page 418

b Determine the vertex of the quadratic function and if it is a minimum or maximum.

Create a strategy

Use the vertex form of the quadratic function from part (a) to determine its vertex and whether it is a minimum or maximum value.

Apply the idea

The quadratic function in vertex form is $y = (x - 2)^2 + 2$, meaning the vertex is located at the point (2, 2).

Since the value of a is 1, we know that the graph opens upward and the vertex is a minimum value.

Purpose

Show students how to identify the vertex in vertex form and determine the direction in which the graph opens.

Expected mistakes
Students may forget how to determine if the vertex is a minimum or maximum value. Emphasize how the leading coefficient highlights this key feature of the graph.

Students: Page 418

c Sketch the graph of the parabola.

Create a strategy

We can find key points of our parabola to sketch it. In part (a) we found the x-value of the vertex, and in part (b) we found the vertex form of our equation which shows us the y-value of our vertex. We can also use the vertex form to consider the x- and y-intercepts.

Apply the idea

The y-value of the vertex is 2 since the vertex form of the equation is $y = (x − 2)^2 + 2$. This means that the vertex is located at (2, 2). We know the scale factor a is 1, so the parabola opens upward. Since the vertex is above the x-axis and opens up, the graph will not cross the x-axis and there are no x-intercepts.

Find the y-intercept:

$y = (x − 2)^2 + 2$ Vertex form of the equation
$y = (0 − 2)^2 + 2$ Substitute $x = 0$
$y = 6$ Evaluate

Therefore, the y-intercept is (0, 6).

We can use the vertex and y-intercept to sketch the parabola, remembering there is an axis of symmetry at the vertex.

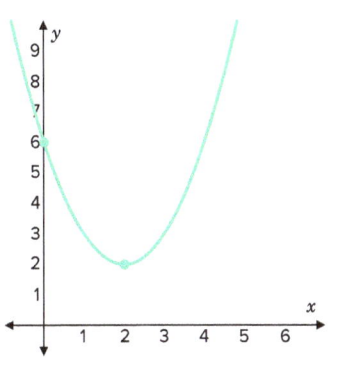

Purpose
Show students how to graph a quadratic function from vertex form.

Expected mistakes
Students may attempt to use only the vertex to sketch a parabolic graph. Remind students that we can find other key features of the function and plot them. For this example, having two points was enough but since we know that parabolas are symmetric, we can identify that the point (4, 6) is a third point that we can use to help us sketch the function.

Reflecting with students
Ask students if we can tell from the equation that there are no x-intercepts and therefore no need to substitute $y = 0$ and attempt to solve. Since the equation indicates that the graph opens upwards and has been translated vertically upwards there will be no x-intercepts.

> **The value of k is not always the y-coordinate of the y-intercept**   use with Example 5
> **Address student misconceptions**

Students may identify +2 as a constant term in the equation and incorrectly equate this with being the y-value of the y-intercept. Remind students that the y-value of the y-intercept can be found by substituting $x = 0$ into the equation.

Point out to students that in the vertex form of a quadratic function, there is another constant term inside the parentheses which we need to take into account.

Students: Page 418

> **Idea summary**
>
> A quadratic function in standard form can be converted to vertex form by completing the square:
>
> 1. $y = x^2 + bx + c$
> 2. $y = x^2 + 2\left(\dfrac{b}{2}\right)x + c$ Rewrite the x term
> 3. $y = x^2 + 2\left(\dfrac{b}{2}\right)x + \left(\dfrac{b}{2}\right)^2 + c - \left(\dfrac{b}{2}\right)^2$ Add and subtract $\left(\dfrac{b}{2}\right)^2$ to keep the equation balanced
> 4. $y = \left(x + \dfrac{b}{2}\right)^2 + c - \left(\dfrac{b}{2}\right)^2$ Factor the perfect square trinomial
> 5. $y = (x - h)^2 + k$ Match the completed square to vertex form
>
> If $a \neq 1$, we can first divide through by a to factor it out.

Practice

Students: Pages 419–424

What do you remember?

1. Determine the axis of symmetry of this quadratic function.

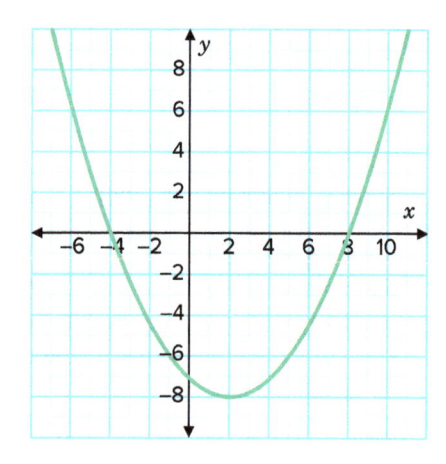

2 Write an equation for each quadratic function in vertex form.

a

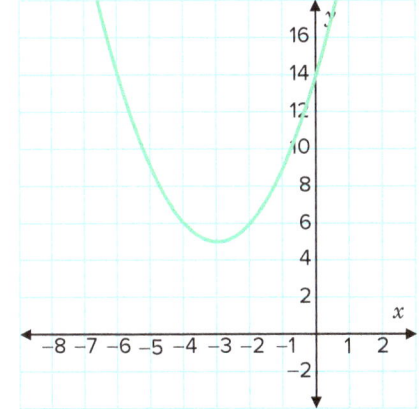

b

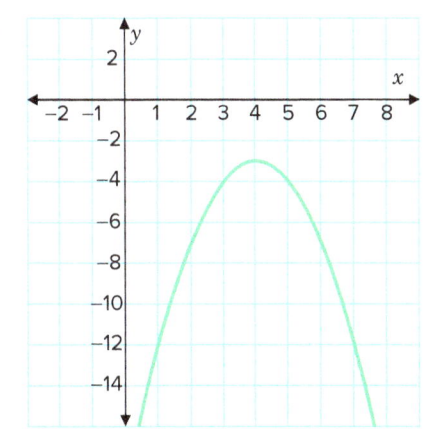

c

x	$h(x)$
0	−6
1	−1
2	2
3	3
4	2
5	−1
6	−6

d

x	$j(x)$
−6	11
−5	6
−4	3
−3	2
−2	3
−1	6
0	11

3 For the following quadratic equations:
  i   Rewrite the equation in vertex form by completing the square.
  ii Identify the coordinates of the vertex.

  a $y = x^2 - 4x + 3$
  b $y = -x^2 + 6x - 2$
  c $y = -x^2 - 5x - 4$
  d $y = -2x^2 + 8x - 7$

4 Write the equation of the transformed graph in vertex form.
  a $y = x^2$ is horizontally translated 10 units to the right and vertically translated 2 units up
  b $y = x^2$ is horizontally translated 9 units to the left and is vertically stretched by a factor of 9 units
  c $y = x^2$ is reflected across the x-axis and vertically translated 8 units down

5 For each of the following, state whether the transformation from the parent function $f(x) = x^2$ to the function $g(x)$ is a translation up, down, left, or right:
  a $g(x) = (x - 8)^2$
  b $g(x) = x^2 - 5$
  c $g(x) = (x + 9)^2$
  d $g(x) = x^2 + 0.75$

6 Consider the following graph of a function.
  Select the equation that represents the function:
  A $y = -(x + 5)^2 + 25$
  B $y = (x - 5)^2 + 25$
  C $y = (x + 5)^2 - 25$
  D $y = -(x + 5)^2 - 25$

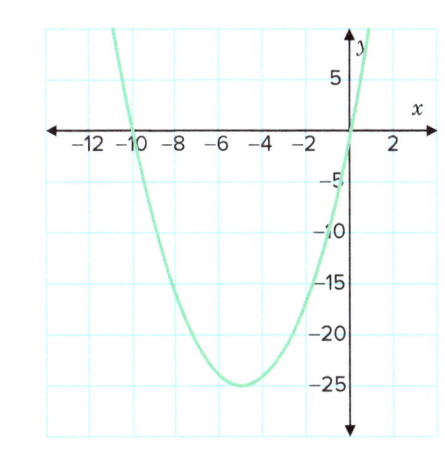

7.03 Quadratic functions in vertex form

7 Consider the table of values of a function.

x	1	2	3	4	5
y	−6	0	2	0	−6

Sketch a graph of the function labeling any points of interest.

8 Consider the function $y = \frac{1}{4}(x+4)^2 + 5$.

Sketch a graph of the function labeling any points of interest.

Let's practice

9 For each of the graphs:
  i Describe the transformation from $y = x^2$.
  ii Write the equation.

a

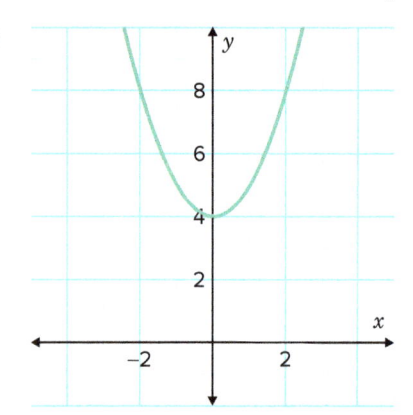

b

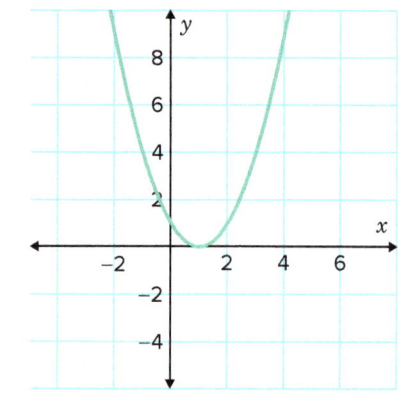

c

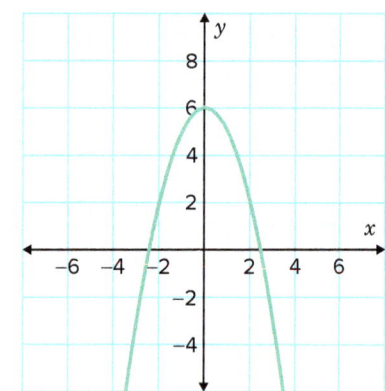

d

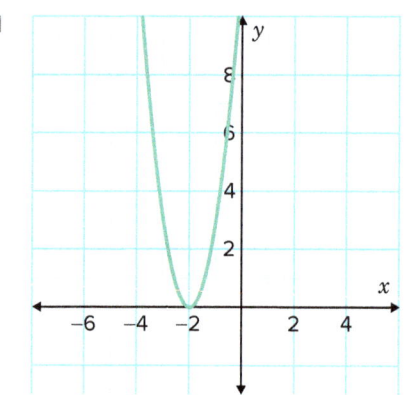

e

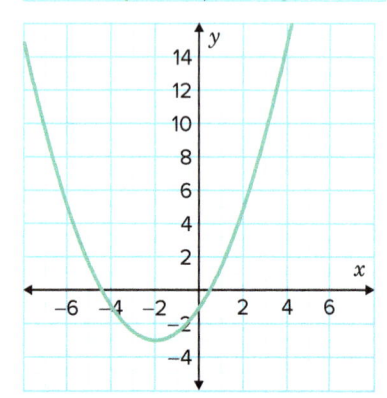

f

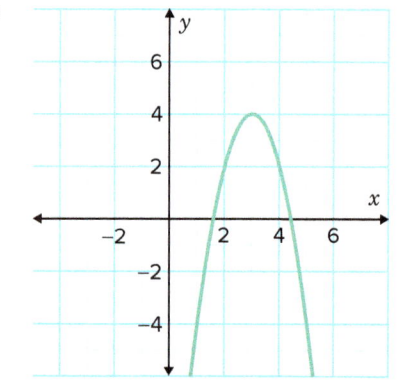

10 For each equation:
  i Describe the transformations from $y = x^2$.
  ii Sketch the graph of the parabola.

  a $y = (x - 3)^2 - 4$
  b $y = -(x + 3)^2 - 6$
  c $y = 3(x + 1)^2 + 4$
  d $y = -0.5(x - 6)^2 + 1$

11 Each of the following describes the transformations of a function from the parent function $f(x) = x^2$. Write the equation of each transformed function in vertex form.

  a Vertical stretch by a scale factor 2 and translated right 1 unit and down 3 units.
  b Reflection over the x-axis, vertically compressed by a scale factor of 3, and translated right 2 units and up 2 units.
  c Reflection over the x-axis, vertically stretched by a scale factor of 3, and translated left 5 units and down 4 units.
  d Vertically stretched by a scale factor of 3, translated left 1 unit, and translated up 2 units.

12 Sketch the graph of each parabola.

  a $y = (x + 3)^2 - 9$
  b $y = -(x - 2)^2 + 1$
  c $y = -(x + 4)^2 - 2$
  d $y = \left(x + \dfrac{1}{2}\right)^2 + \dfrac{11}{4}$

13 Write the vertex form equation that represents each of the following graphs:

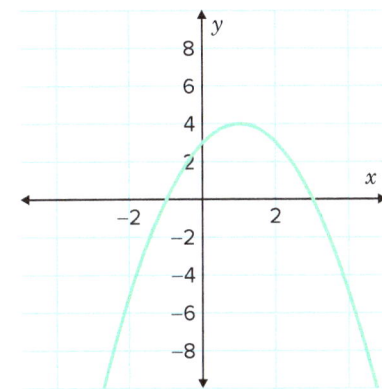

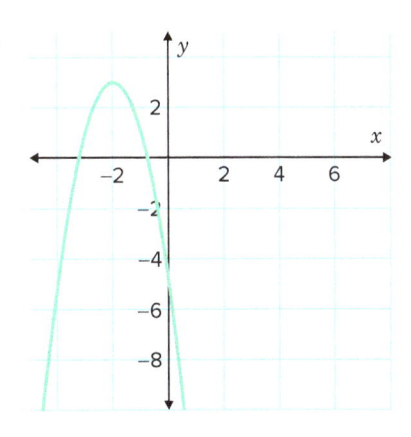

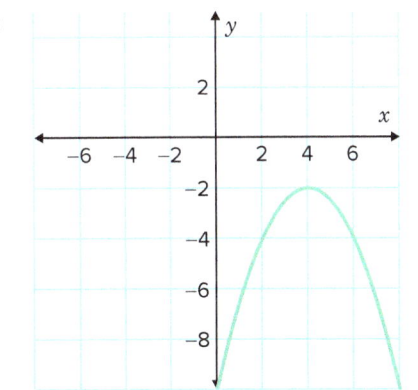

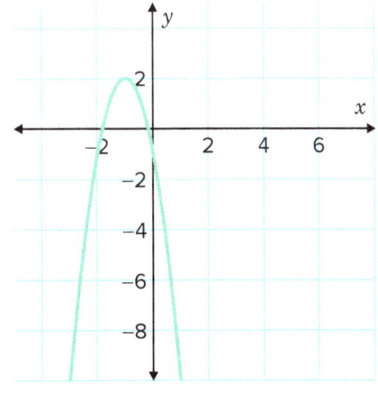

14 For each of the following:
  i Rewrite the equation in vertex form.
  ii Sketch the graph of the parabola.

  a $y = x^2 - 4x + 2$
  b $y = x^2 + 10x$
  c $y = x^2 + 4x - 4$
  d $y = x^2 + 5x + 3$

15 Explain how the maximum or minimum value of a quadratic function can be found by completing the square.

16 For each of the following quadratic functions:
   i   State whether the transformation from $f(x)$ to $g(x)$ is a horizontal translation, vertical translation, vertical stretch, or vertical compression by k units.
   ii State the value of k.

a

b

c

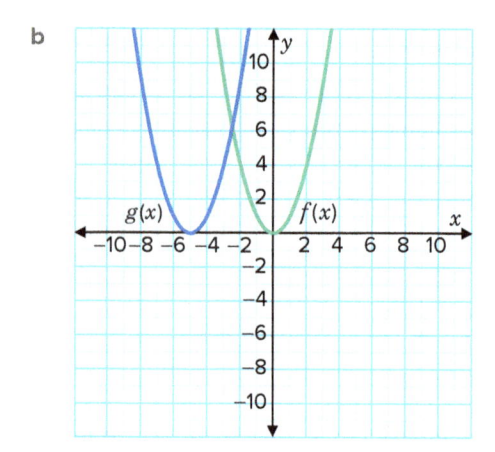

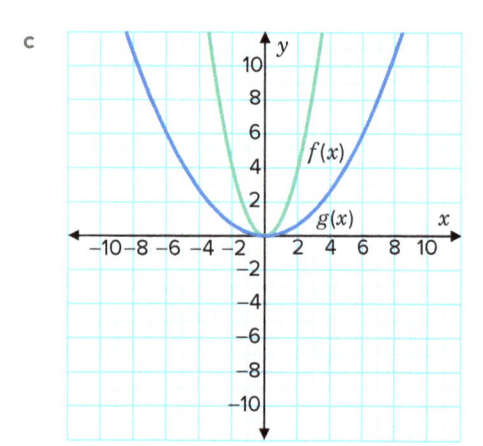

17 For each quadratic function:
   i   Determine the coordinates of the vertex.
   ii   Determine the x-intercept.
   iii Determine the y-intercept.
   iv   Draw a graph of the quadratic function.

   a $m(x) = (x - 3)^2$
   b $n(x) = (x + 4)^2 - 1$
   c $p(x) = -(x - 1)^2 - 7$
   d $r(x) = 3(x + 5)^2$

18 For each of the following quadratic functions, find the:
   i x-intercept(s)
   ii y-intercept
   iii vertex

   a $y = (x - 1)^2 - 4$
   b $y = (x + 2)^2 - 1$
   c $y = (x - 3)^2 + 5$
   d $y = -2(x - 2)^2 + 3$

19 For each of the following quadratic functions, find the:
   i   Domain
   ii Range

   a $y = 2(x - 3)^2 + 4$
   b $y = -3(x + 1)^2 + 5$
   c $y = (x - 4)^2 - 2$
   d $y = -0.5(x + 2)^2 + 1$

20 Find the range when the domain is $\{-6, -1, 0, 5, 7\}$ for each of the following quadratic functions:
   a $y = 3(x + 1)^2 - 2$
   b $y = -2(x - 3)^2 + 4$
   c $y = 4(x + 2)^2 + 1$
   d $y = -3(x - 4)^2 - 5$

21. Rodney observed that the water stream of a fountain is in the shape of a parabola. This water stream lands on an underwater spotlight. He models the path of the water stream with the maximum height of 8 feet, represented by the vertex (4, 8) and the underwater spotlight, represented by the point (8, 0).

    a Select the graph that represents the problem:

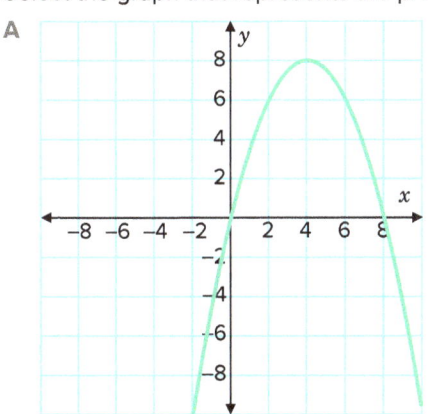

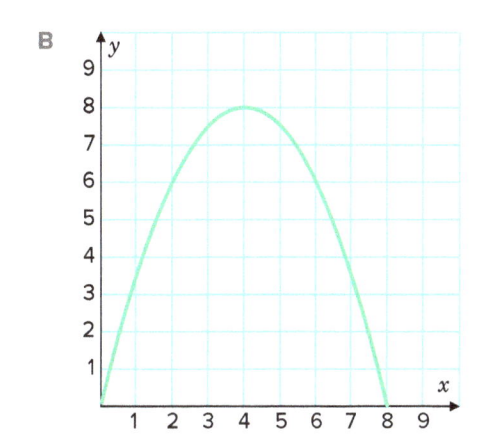

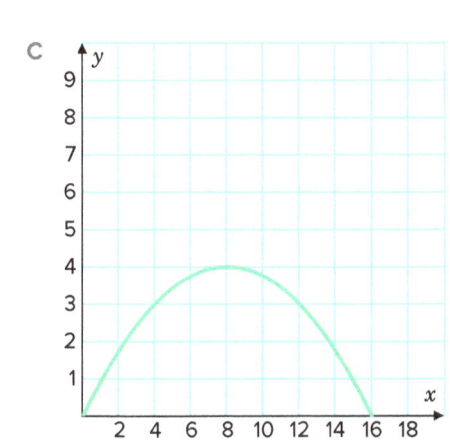

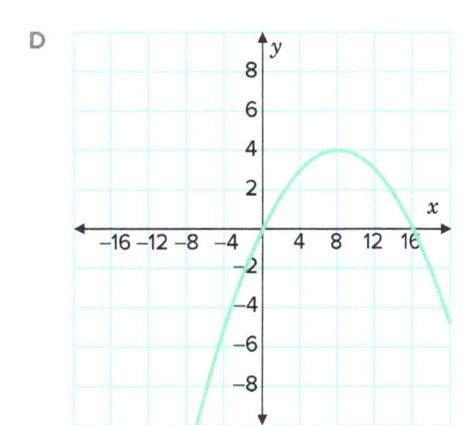

    A   B   C   D

    b Determine appropriate labels and units for the axes.
    c Determine the domain and range of the function.

22. For each quadratic equation:
    i   Determine the coordinates of the vertex.
    ii   Determine the equation of the axis of symmetry.
    iii Determine if it has a maximum or minimum.
    iv   Determine the domain and range.
    v   Draw a graph of the quadratic function.

    a $y = -\frac{1}{2}(x-4)^2 + 1$

    b $y = 5\left(x - \frac{1}{4}\right)^2 - 20$

23. Ashtyn throws a rock into Crescent Lake. The height of the rock above ground is a quadratic function of time. The rock is thrown from 4.4 ft above ground. After 1.5 seconds, the rock reaches its maximum height of 24 ft. Write the quadratic equation in vertex form.

24. A roller coaster has a part that is modeled by a quadratic function. Hau loves roller coasters and wants to be able to build a small model with his 3D Printer. Assume that the roller coaster passes through points (0, 0) and (57, 0) and reaches a maximum height of 90 ft. Help Hau build a model of the roller coaster by writing an equation for the parabola in vertex form.

25 Karima and Riley are playing soccer. Karima just kicked a soccer ball and Riley is playing goalie 2 ft in front of the goal post. The following diagram shows the situation on a coordinate plane. The soccer ball is kicked at (1, 0.6) and the goal post is 13 ft away from Karima's back foot. The maximum height of the soccer ball is 5.5 ft and this occurs when it is 8 ft away from Karima.

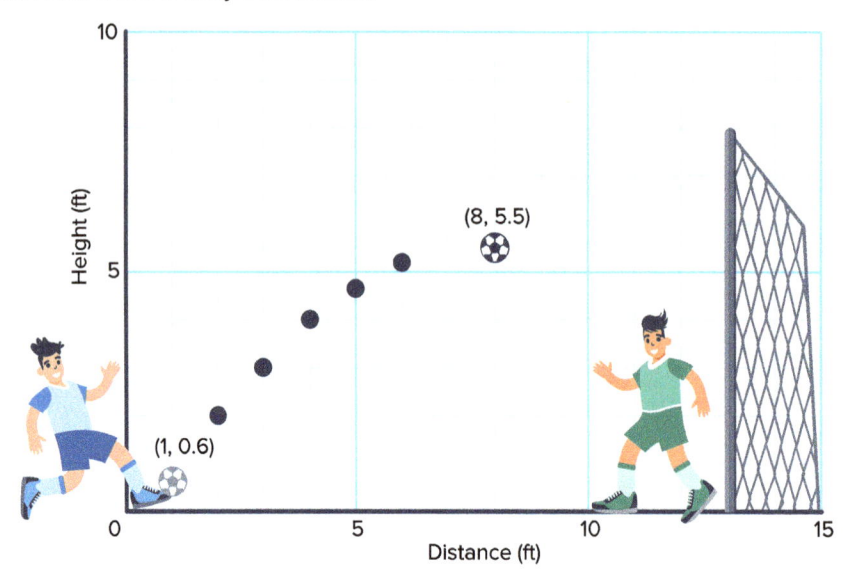

    a Write a quadratic function that models the height of the soccer ball in feet in terms of the horizontal distance from Karima's starting position.

    b Riley jumps to try to block the soccer ball and will block soccer balls that are between 4 ft and 8 ft high. State whether Riley will be able to block Karima's kick. Explain your answer.

Let's extend our thinking

26 Determine how many quadratic equations could share a common vertex.

27 Consider the following diagram:

    a Describe a situation that could be modeled by the following three quadratic functions. For each part, make sure to identify the vertex and another possible point on the function.

    b Write equations for the quadratic functions from your above description.

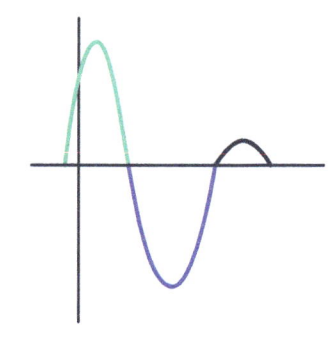

28 Consider the family of quadratic equations of the form $y = \Box(x - \Box)^2 - \Box$ where the boxes contain the integers 2, 3, and 5.

    a Write a quadratic equation with the lowest possible minimum value.

    b Describe the similarities and differences between members of the family.

29 Compare and contrast the following functions, given that a is a positive real number:

$$f(x) = -3a(x - h)^2 + k \text{ and } g(x) = a(x - h)^2 - k$$

Answers

7.03 Quadratic functions in vertex form

What do you remember?

1. $x = 2$

2. a $f(x) = (x + 3)^2 + 5$ b $g(x) = -(x - 4)^2 - 3$
   c $h(x) = -(x - 3)^2 + 3$ d $j(x) = (x + 3)^2 + 2$

3. a i $y = (x - 2)^2 - 1$ ii $(2, -1)$
   b i $y = -(x - 3)^2 + 7$ ii $(3, 7)$
   c i $y = -(x + 2.5)^2 + 2.25$ ii $(-2.5, 2.25)$
   d i $y = -2(x - 2)^2 + 1$ ii $(2, 1)$

4. a $y = (x - 10)^2 + 2$ b $y = 9(x + 9)^2$
   c $y = -x^2 - 8$

5. a Right   b Down   c Left   d Up

6. C

7. [graph]

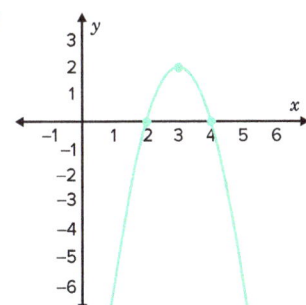

8. [graph]

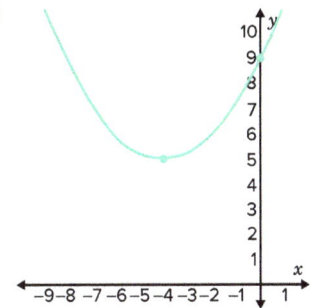

Let's practice

9. a i Vertical translation up 4 units.
      ii $y = x^2 + 4$
   b i Horizontal translation right 1 unit.
      ii $y = (x - 1)^2$
   c i Reflection over the x-axis and a vertical translation up 6 units.
      ii $y = -x^2 + 6$
   d i Vertical stretch by a scale factor 3 and a horizontal translation left 2 units.
      ii $y = 3(x + 2)^2$

   e i Vertical compression by a scale factor 2, a horizontal translation left 2 units, and a vertical translation down 3 units.
      ii $y = 0.5(x + 2)^2 - 3$
   f i Reflection over the x-axis, vertical stretch by a scale factor 2, a horizontal translation right 3 units, and a vertical translation up 4 units.
      ii $y = -2(x - 3)^2 + 4$

10. a i Horizontal shift 3 units to the right and vertical shift 4 units down
    ii [graph]

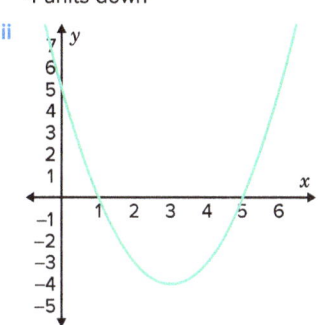

    b i Reflection about the x-axis, horizontal shift 3 units to the left and vertical shift 6 units down
    ii [graph]

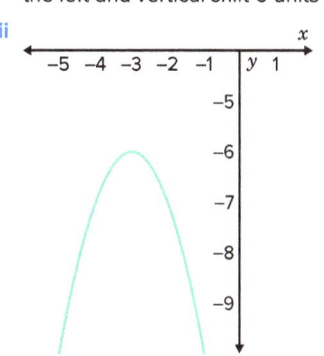

    c i Horizontal shift 1 unit to the left, vertical shift 4 units up and dilated (compressed) by a factor of 3.
    ii [graph]

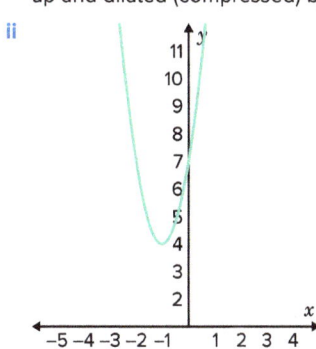

d i Horizontal shift 6 units to the right, vertical shift 1 unit up and dilated (compressed) by a factor of 0.5.

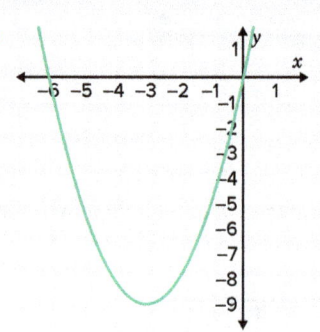

ii

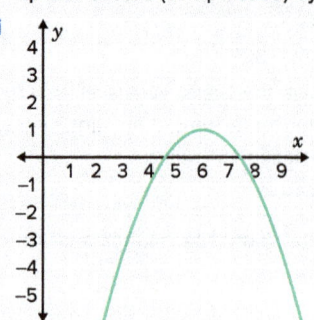

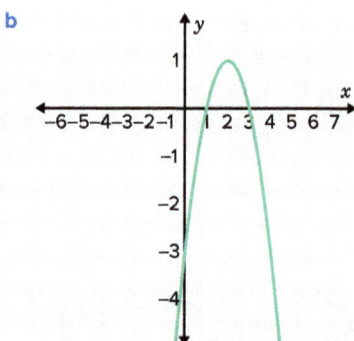

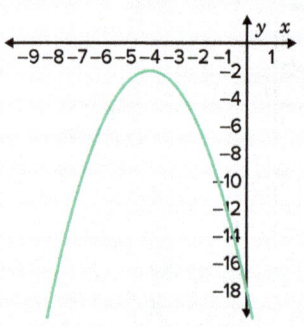

d

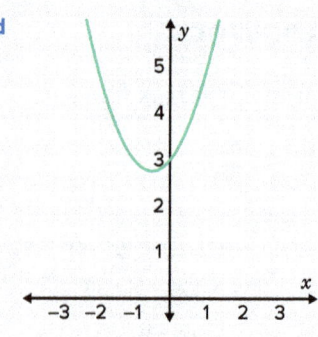

13 a $y = -1(x-1)^2 + 4$ **b** $y = -2(x+2)^2 + 3$
c $y = -0.5(x-4)^2 - 2$ **d** $y = -3(x+1)^2 + 2$

11 a $g(x) = 2(x-1)^2 - 3$ **b** $g(x) = -\dfrac{1}{3}(x-2)^2 + 2$
c $g(x) = -3(x+5)^2 - 4$ **d** $g(x) = 3(x+1)^2 + 2$

14 a i $y = (x-2)^2 - 2$

ii

12 a

b

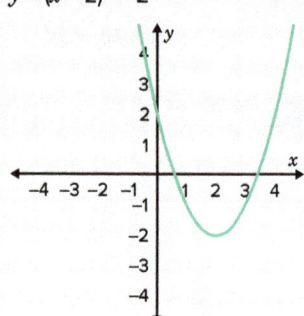

b i $y = (x+5)^2 - 25$

ii

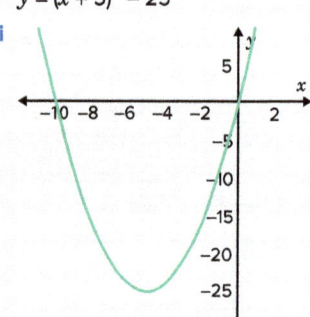

c i $y = (x+2)^2 - 8$

ii

c

906   Mathspace   Virginia SOL Algebra 1 Teacher Edition
mathspace.co

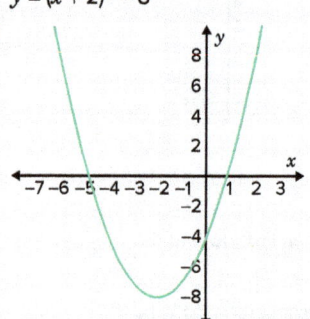

d i $y = \left(x + \frac{5}{2}\right)^2 - \frac{13}{4}$

ii

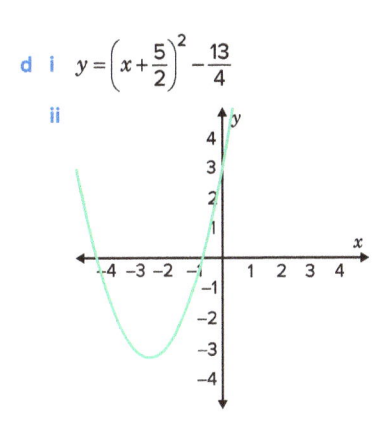

15 When completing the square, a quadratic is converted to vertex form. In vertex form, $a(x - h)^2 + k$, the value (h, k) is the vertex of the graph.

16 a i Vertical translation up ii $k = 3$
 b i Horizontal translation left ii $k = 5$
 c i Vertical compression ii $k = \frac{1}{6}$

17 a i (3, 0) ii (3, 0) iii (0, 9)
 iv

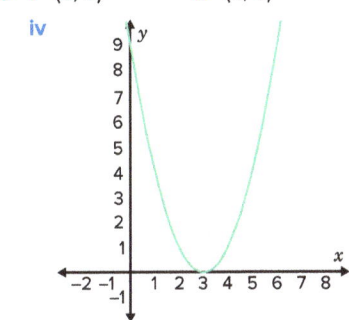

 b i (−4, −1) ii (−5, 0), (−3, 0) iii (0, 15)
 iv

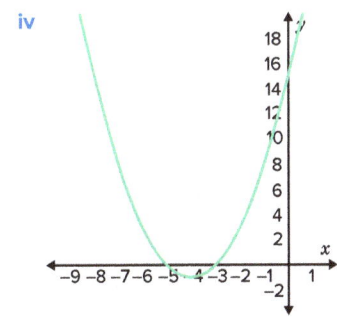

 c i (1, −7) ii None iii (0, −8)
 iv

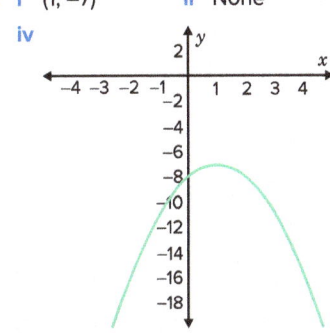

d i (−5, 0) ii (−5, 0) iii (0, 75)
 iv

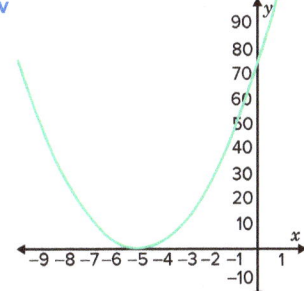

18 a i (1, 0) and (−1, 0) ii (0, −3) iii (1, −4)
 b i (−2, 0) ii (0, 3) iii (−2, −1)
 c i (3, 0) ii (0, −4) iii (3, 5)
 d i (2, 0) ii (0, 1) iii (2, 3)

19 a i All real numbers ii $y \geq 4$
 b i All real numbers ii $y \leq 5$
 c i All real numbers ii $y \geq -2$
 d i All real numbers ii $y \leq 1$

20 a {82, 1, −2, 73, 142} b {−62, −14, 4, −42, −92}
 c {65, 13, 1, 105, 169} d {−107, −29, −5, −80, −158}

21 a B
 b x-axis: Height (in feet), y-axis: Distance (in feet).
 c Domain: $0 \leq x \leq 8$
   Range: $0 \leq y \leq 8$

22 a i (4, 1) ii $x = 4$
   iii Maximum
   iv Domain: $-\infty < x < \infty$
      Range: $y \leq 1$
   v

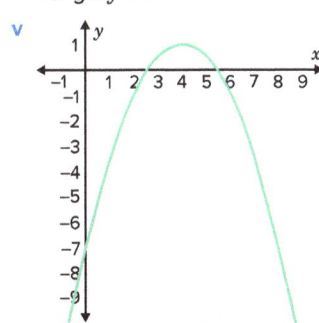

 b i $\left(\frac{1}{4}, -20\right)$ ii $x = \frac{1}{4}$ iii Minimum
   iv Domain: $-\infty < x < \infty$
      Range: $y \geq -20$

v

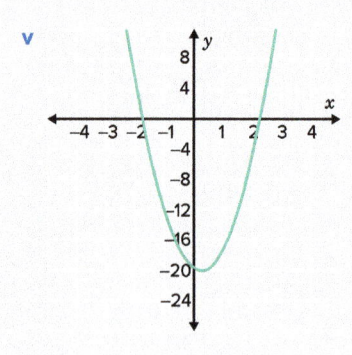

[Graph showing a parabola opening upward with vertex near (2, -24), x-axis from -4 to 4, y-axis from -24 to 8]

23   $y = -\frac{392}{45}(x - 1.5)^2 + 24$

24   $y = -\frac{40}{361}(x - 28.5)^2 + 90$

25   a $h(x) = -0.1(x - 8)^2 + 5.5$

   b   Yes, Riley is standing at 11 ft, so $h(11) = 4.6$ ft. Riley will be able to block the kick because the soccer ball is above 4 ft and less than 8 ft.

Let's extend our thinking

26   An infinite amount of quadratic equations share a common vertex because there are an infinite amount of values for the leading coefficient, a.

27   a   Any situation that has three vertices and three points described to fit the provided diagram.

   The height of a fish above water in feet in terms of the horizontal distance from a kayak is shown. The height of fish starts to be tracked at (–1, 0), when the fish is 1 ft to the left of the kayak. The fish jumps over the kayak and the maximum height of 7 ft occurs 2 ft away from the kayak.

The fish hits the water 5 ft to the right of the kayak. The fish then goes 9 ft below water when the fish is 9.5 ft to the right of the kayak.

The fish jumps back out of the water 14 ft to the right of the kayak. The maximum height of the shorter jump is 1.5 ft when 15.25 ft to the right of the kayak.

   b $y = \frac{-7}{9}(x - 2)^2 + 7$

   $y = \frac{4}{9}(x - 9.5)^2 - 9$

   $y = -\frac{24}{25}(x - 15.25)^2 + 1.5$

28   a $y = 2(x - 3)^2 - 5$ or $y = 3(x - 2)^2 - 5$

   b   Similarities between all equations: The parabolas open up, vertical stretch by a factor greater than 1, vertex is in quadrant 4

   Differences: The coordinates of the vertex and vertical stretch factor change based on the equation.
   Examples:
   $y = 2(x - 3)^2 - 5$, vertex at (3, –5), vertical stretch by a factor of 2
   $y = 3(x - 2)^2 - 5$, vertex at (2, –5), vertical stretch by a factor of 3
   $y = 5(x - 2)^2 - 3$, vertex at (2, –3), vertical stretch by a factor of 5

29   Both $f(x)$ and $g(x)$ are quadratic functions. Both functions have an axis of symmetry at $x = h$. $f(x)$ has a maximum value of $y = k$ and $g(x)$ has a minimum value of $y = -k$. $f(x)$ is reflected over the x-axis and opens down while $g(x)$ opens up. $f(x)$ has a vertical stretch by a factor of $3a$ and $g(x)$ has a vertical stretch by a factor of a.

7.04 Quadratic functions in standard form

Subtopic overview

Lesson narrative

In this lesson, students will use technology and coordinate grids to make generalizations about the relationship of quadratic equations in standard forms and the graph's key characteristics. Students will use values in the standard form of a quadratic to determine the axis of symmetry, vertex, and draw the graph. By the end of the lesson, students will use the symmetry of quadratic functions to work flexibly between quadratic equations in standard form and their graphs to answer questions about contextual situations.

Learning objectives

Students: Page 425

After this lesson, you will be able to...
- compare and connect representations of quadratic functions.
- identify key characteristics of a quadratic function written in standard form.
- graph a quadratic equation written in standard form.

Key vocabulary

- axis of symmetry
- vertex
- standard form (of a quadratic equation)

Essential understanding

Different representations of a function may highlight or hide different characteristics but they do not change the function itself. The standard form of a quadratic function highlights the y-intercept.

Standards

This subtopic addresses the following Virginia 2023 Mathematics Standards of Learning standards.

Mathematical process goals

MPG4 — Mathematical Connections

To integrate mathematical connections into their instruction, teachers can have students relate what they are learning about quadratic functions to other topics in mathematics or other disciplines. For example, they can discuss how quadratic functions are used in physics to model the motion of objects under the force of gravity. Teachers can also encourage students to make connections between the different forms of quadratic functions and their graph representations.

MPG5 — Mathematical Representations

Teachers can incorporate mathematical representations into their instruction by having students graph quadratic functions in standard form and analyze the effects of changing the values of a, b, and c. They can also have students use technology, such as graphing calculators or online graphing tools, to explore and visualize the relationship between the equation and the graph of the quadratic function. Additionally, they can ask students to explain the relationship between the standard form of a quadratic function and its key characteristics, such as vertex, x-intercepts, (zeros), y-intercepts, maximum or minimum value, and domain and range.

Content standards

A.F.2 — The student will investigate, analyze, and compare characteristics of functions, including quadratic and exponential functions, and model quadratic and exponential relationships.

A.F.2b — Given an equation or graph, determine key characteristics of a quadratic function including x-intercepts (zeros), y-intercept, vertex (maximum or minimum), and domain and range (including when restricted by context); interpret key characteristics as related to contextual situations, where applicable.

A.F.2c — Graph a quadratic function, $f(x)$, in two variables using a variety of strategies, including transformations $f(x) + k$ and $kf(x)$, where k is limited to rational values.

A.F.2d — Make connections between the algebraic (standard and factored forms) and graphical representation of a quadratic function.

A.F.2g — For any value, x, in the domain of f, determine $f(x)$ of a quadratic or exponential function. Determine x given any value $f(x)$ in the range of f of a quadratic function. Explain the meaning of x and $f(x)$ in context.

Prior connections

A.F.1 — The student will investigate, analyze, and compare linear functions algebraically and graphically, and model linear relationships.

Future connections

A2.F.2 — The student will investigate and analyze characteristics of square root, cube root, rational, polynomial, exponential, logarithmic, and piecewise-defined functions algebraically and graphically.

Engage Activity

Planetary trebuchets   60 mins

Students will investigate an applet modeling projectiles launched with different parameters for gravity, initial velocity, and initial height.

Understanding and skills

> **Will use**
>
> Knowing key features of a quadratic.

> **Will develop**
>
> Understanding that the initial height, or y-intercept, of a quadratic function is equal to the constant value in its standard form equation.
>
> Understanding that the initial velocity and gravity both influence the coefficient of the linear term in the standard form equation of a quadratic.
>
> Understanding that the force of gravity is directly related to the coefficient of the quadratic term in a standard form equation.

Preparation and materials
- Open and complete the student preview, anticipating classroom responses.
- **Materials:** None.

Support students with disabilities
Support language - write explanations of mathematical thinking

Use sentence starters such as:
- The projectile behaves differently …
- The velocity of the projectile affects …
- The x-intercept of the function denotes …

to help students to test their ideas.

Support for English language learners
Critique, correct, and clarify

Have students consider which of the following statements are always, sometimes, or never true to check their understanding of the vocabulary:
- The coefficient of the x^2 term represents the gravity of the planet. (answer: sometimes)
- The coefficient of the x term represents the velocity. (answer: sometimes)
- The vertex is the maximum or minimum of the function. (answer: always)

Classroom guide

Hook
Which one doesn't belong • 5 mins

Students choose one of four quadratic equations in standard form with varying values of the coefficients and number of terms in each equation.

Implementation details

Encourage students to connect the values of each term with what it might mean for the graph of the quadratic.

Ask students what they notice about the coefficients and constants in each equation. Ask how these values affect the graph of the equation as well as its solutions.

Which one doesn't belong?
Select one option.

$y = x^2 + 6x + 8$ **A** $y = x^2 - 8$ **B**

$y = x^2 + 8x - 16$ **C** $y = 2x^2 + 6x - 8$ **D**

Slide 1 from Student Engage Activity

Launch
5 mins

Allow students time to explore how the applet works. If needed, discuss the vocabulary terms used to describe quadratic functions.

Important mathematical concepts: Quadratic functions, x and y-intercepts, constant, standard form, coefficient, maximum, minimum, concavity, vertex, axis of symmetry, parameters

Important contextual information: Trebuchets, catapult, projectile, initial height, velocity, gravity

Suggested grouping: Form pairs

Consider the following applet.

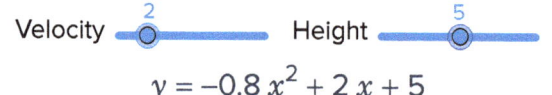

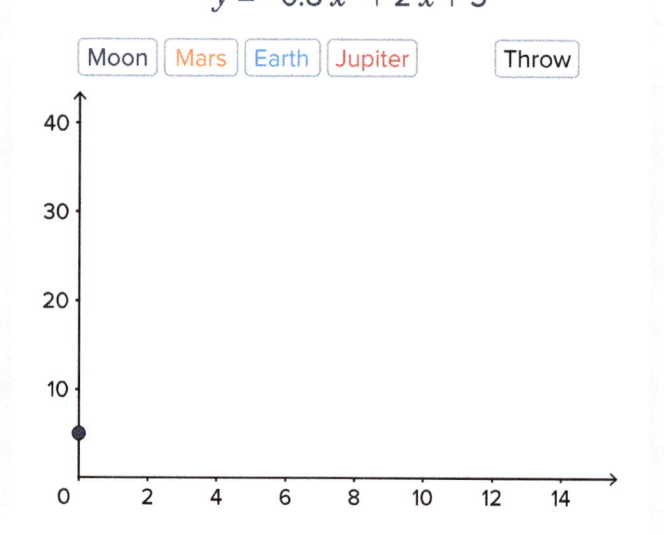

Velocity: 2   Height: 5

$y = -0.8\, x^2 + 2\, x + 5$

Moon | Mars | Earth | Jupiter   Throw

Slide 2 from Student Engage Activity

Continue when

Students have explored the applet and understand how the applet functions.

Explore
Think-pair-share • 35 mins

Students will explore the applet and determine how the key features of the quadratic are connected to the features of the projectile, as well as come up with an equation modeling its flight path.

Anticipated strategies

Isolate applet parameters
Velocity, height, and planets

Students may isolate applet parameters. They can start by moving the velocity slider and making note of how both the equation, each feature of the parabola, and the flight path are related. Then they can repeat the observations with the height slider and the planet selection.

Isolate each feature
x and y-intercepts, vertex, axis of symmetry, and so forth

Students can focus on one feature at a time, such as the y-intercept, and move each projectile parameter while observing if and how that feature changes before moving onto the next feature.

Some key findings that students may derive with either strategy are as follows:
- The constant value of the standard form equation is the y-intercept of its graph influences the height of the vertex and the location of the x-intercept.
- The initial velocity of the function is the coefficient of the linear term and directly changes the location of the axis of symmetry, vertex, and x-intercepts.
- The coefficient of the quadratic term is related to the planet the projectile is on and changes the location of the axis of symmetry, vertex, and x-intercepts.

Misconceptions

Misattributing features

What did you observe that led you to this conclusion? What other factors may have influenced this behavior?

Purposeful questions

Use the following questions to check for understanding and encourage critical thinking:
- What features were all influenced by the planet choice? What do they have in common?
- What features were not influenced by the planet choice? What do they have in common?
- Are there any patterns to how the features of the quadratic changed as the slider changed?

Continue when

Students have listed connections between the key features of the quadratic and its standard form equation.

Discuss   15 mins

Have a class discussion where pairs present their findings and compare with other groups. Consider making connections from the discussion to standard form equation components.

Discussion guide

Invite pairs to share their ideas and observations and survey how many pairs reached similar conclusions. Begin by inviting pairs to answer the following:
- How did each of the sliders and buttons on the applet change the equation?
- What do you think each of these represented?

Then, begin a discussion on what information is provided by the standard form of a quadratic equation:
- If given an equation like this, what about the quadratic would you know?
- What features of the quadratic may be harder to determine from this equation?
- If you wanted to graph this equation without technology, what strategies would you try?

As an extension you may wish to give students the following prompt:
- How could we find the key features of the quadratic if we were only given its standard form equation?

Lesson Preparation

Suggested review

Depending on your students' level of prior knowledge, consider revisiting the following lessons:

- **Algebra 1 —** 4.02 Substitution method
- **Algebra 1 —** 7.02 Quadratic functions in factored form
- **Algebra 1 —** 7.03 Quadratic functions in vertex form

Tools

You may find these tools helpful:
- Graphing calculator
- Graph paper

Student lesson & teacher guide

Quadratic functions in standard form

Students learn about the standard form of a quadratic function and how to identify some key features when given a quadratic function in standard form, including how to calculate the axis of symmetry and vertex.

Students: Pages 425–426

7.04 Quadratic functions in standard form

After this lesson, you will be able to...
- compare and connect representations of quadratic functions.
- identify key characteristics of a quadratic function written in standard form.
- graph a quadratic equation written in standard form.

Engage activity
Ask your teacher to get started
Planetary trebuchets
Students will investigate an applet modeling projectiles launched with different parameters for gravity, initial velocity, and initial height.

The standard form of a quadratic equation, where a, b, and c are real numbers is:

$$y = ax^2 + bx + c$$

a	scale factor
b	linear coefficient
c	y-value of the y-intercept

The **standard form of a quadratic equation** allows us to quickly identify the y-intercept and whether the parabola opens up or down.

The coordinates of the **vertex** are:

$$\left(-\frac{b}{2a}, f\left(-\frac{b}{2a}\right)\right)$$

We can substitute the x-coordinate of the vertex into the original equation in order to find the y-coordinate of the vertex.

For example, if we have the function $g(x) = 3x^2 + 12x - 15$ where $a = 3$, $b = 12$, and $c = -15$ we can start by finding the x-coordinate:

$x = -\dfrac{b}{2a}$	Equation for the x-coordinate of the vertex
$= -\dfrac{12}{2(3)}$	Substitute $a = 3$ and $b = 12$
$= -\dfrac{12}{6}$	Evaluate the multiplication
$x = -2$	Evaluate the division

We can substitute the x-coordinate of the vertex into the original equation in order to find the y-coordinate of the vertex.

$g(x) = 3x^2 + 12x - 15$	Original function
$= 3(-2)^2 + 12(-2) - 15$	Substitute $x = -2$
$= 3(4) + 12(-2) - 15$	Evaluate the exponent
$= 12 - 24 - 15$	Evaluate the multiplication
$= -27$	Evaluate the subtraction

The coordinates of the vertex of $g(x)$ are $(-2, -27)$. We can confirm this by looking at the graph:

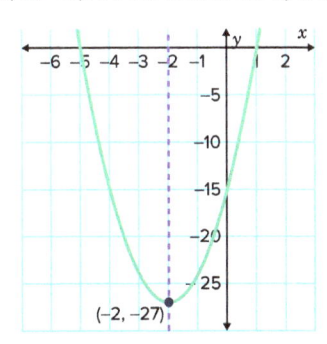

We can also see here that the **axis of symmetry** is the line:

$$x = -\frac{b}{2a}$$

The axis of symmetry always passes through the vertex.

🎓 Relate the equation for the axis of symmetry back to vertex form
Targeted instructional strategies

Students may find the formula for the axis of symmetry to be unintuitive and thus have difficulty remembering it. It may help to show students how the formula is derived. This would also be a good extension activity for advanced learners.

The formula for the axis of symmetry can be derived by rearranging the standard form into the vertex form by completing the square.

$$y = ax^2 + bx + c$$
$$= a\left(x^2 + \frac{b}{a}x + \frac{c}{a}\right)$$
$$= a\left(x^2 + \frac{b}{a}x + \frac{b^2}{4a^2} + \frac{c}{a} - \frac{b^2}{4a^2}\right)$$
$$= a\left(\left(x + \frac{b}{2a}\right)^2 + \frac{c}{a} - \frac{b^2}{4a^2}\right)$$
$$= a\left(x + \frac{b}{2a}\right)^2 + \frac{4ac - b^2}{4a}$$

We can see from the vertex form that the axis of symmetry is at $x = -\frac{b}{2a}$.

Let students know that they do not have to learn this proof, just that the first step can be sufficient for noticing that the x-coordinate of the vertex should have a negative sign when in terms of a and b.

🔊 Compare and connect
English language learner support

Create displays of the three following methods to graph a quadratic function. Alternatively, students could each create their own display and a teacher can choose a few that highlight different characteristics.

Consider the equation $f(x) = -x^2 + 2x + 3$:

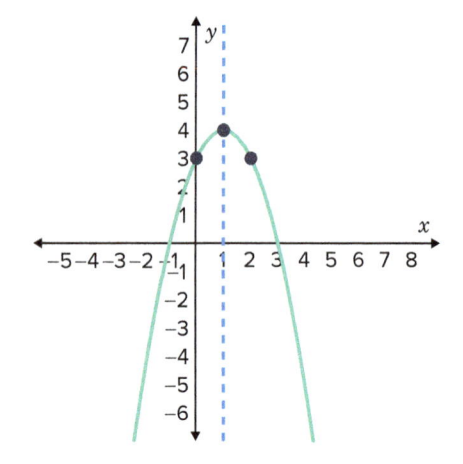

1. Find the axis of symmetry using the formula $x = -\frac{b}{2a}$
2. Find the vertex
3. Find the y-intercept
4. Find a third point using the axis of symmetry
5. Sketch the graph, labeling the key features

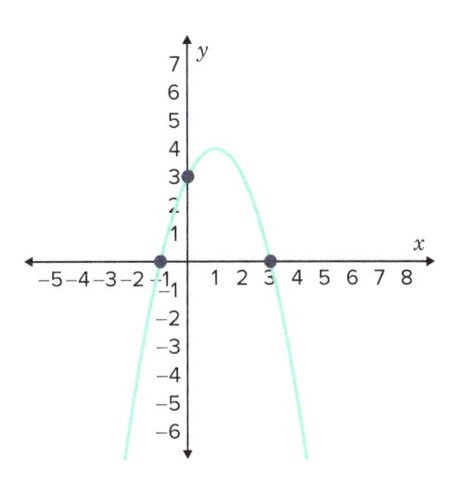

1. Identify the y-intercept
2. Write the equation in factored form: $f(x) = -(x + 1)(x - 3)$
3. Identify the x-intercepts
4. Sketch the graph, labeling the key features

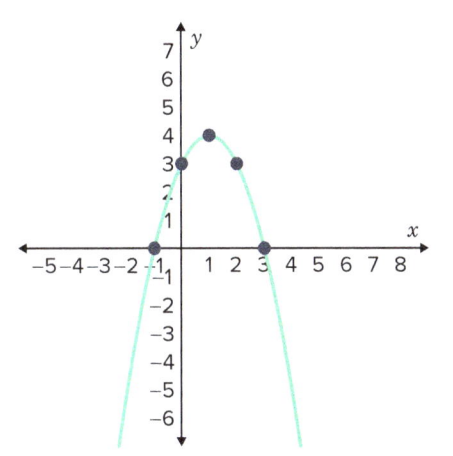

1. Create a table of values

x	−1	0	1	2	3
y	0	3	4	3	0

2. Sketch the graph

Pair up students to discuss which method they preferred and why, as well as any similarities or differences in the two methods.

For further investigation, present students with a quadratic equation that does not have any real roots and ask students to discuss why one method works while the other cannot.

Use GeoGebra to visualize how coefficients affect the graph
Student with disabilities support

Students may struggle to understand how each value in the standard form equation affects the graph of the equation. Provide students with some sort of visual support which demonstrates how the change in each value affects the graph. This can be achieved through a variety of examples or with an interactive manipulative such as a GeoGebra applet.
- a is the scale factor, so it affects the direction of the opening and vertical dilation
- b affects the position of the axis of symmetry (together with a)
- c is the constant term, so it affects the vertical position of the graph

Remind students of the equation for the vertex
Address student misconceptions

When using the formula for the axis of symmetry, students may forget $x = -\dfrac{b}{2a}$ finds the x-value of the vertex, not the actual vertex. Students often forget they can find the y-value by substituting the x-value back into the original equation.

Exploration

Students: Page 425

> **Interactive exploration**
> Explore online to answer the questions
> 🌐 mathspace.co

Use the interactive exploration in 7.04 to answer these questions.

1. What happens to the graph as the value of a changes?
2. What happens to the graph as the value of b changes?
3. What happens to the graph as the value of c changes?

Suggested student grouping: In pairs

Students explore an applet that allows them to change a, b, and c of a quadratic equation in standard form using sliders. Students should notice how the different values transform the parent function and be able to identify some of the key features that the standard form of a quadratic function highlights.

Ideal student responses

These ideal responses may differ from other correct student responses. Less formal responses can be connected with the more precise mathematical language presented here.

1. **What happens to the graph as the value of a changes?**
   As a becomes larger, the function experiences a vertical stretch. There is a vertical compression when $0 < |a| < 1$. Then, the graph reflects across the x-axis when $a < 0$.

2. **What happens to the graph as the value of b changes?**
   Changing b affects the location of the vertex with respect to the y-axis. When $b = 0$, the vertex of the parabola lies on the y-axis. When $a > 0$, b shifts the graph down and to the left for $b > 0$ and down and to the right for $b < 0$. When $a < 0$, b shifts the graph up and to the right for $b > 0$ and up and to the left for $b < 0$. Changing b does not affect the shape of the parabola.

3. **What happens to the graph as the value of c changes?**
   As the value of c changes, the graph experiences a vertical translation. For positive values of c, the graph is translated up c units. For negative values of c, the graph is translated down c units. The value of c is the y-coordinate of the y-intercept.

Purposeful questions

- Do any of the sliders have a similar effect as any of the parameters of factored form or vertex form?
- Does the slider change the location of the vertex?
- Does the slider change the shape of the parabola?
- Can you describe the effect of each slider in terms of translations, dilations or reflections?"

Possible misunderstandings

- Students may not try a variety of values of the parameters in combination with the one they are changing and over generalize the observed effect. For example, if the value of b is set to zero while altering the parameter c, a student may come to the incorrect conclusion that c gives the y-coordinate of the vertex in all cases.

Examples

Students: Page 426

Example 1

For the quadratic function $y = 3x^2 - 6x + 8$:

a Identify the axis of symmetry.

Create a strategy

We will use the formula $x = -\dfrac{b}{2a}$, so we need to identify the values of a and b from the equation.

$a = 3, b = -6$

Apply the idea

$x = -\dfrac{b}{2a}$	Equation for axis of symmetry
$x = -\dfrac{-6}{2(3)}$	Substitute $b = -6$ and $a = 3$
$x = -\dfrac{-6}{6}$	Evaluate the multiplication
$x = -(-1)$	Evaluate the division
$x = 1$	Evaluate the multiplication

The axis of symmetry is $x = 1$.

Purpose

Show students how to calculate the axis of symmetry of a quadratic function when given the function in standard form.

Students: Page 427

b State the coordinates of the vertex.

Create a strategy

Once we have the x-coordinate of the vertex from the axis of symmetry, we can substitute it into $y = 3x^2 - 6x + 8$ and evaluate to get y.

From part (a), we know that the axis of symmetry is $x = 1$ so the x-coordinate of the vertex is $x = 1$.

Apply the idea

$y = 3x^2 - 6x + 8$	Given equation
$y = 3(1)^2 - 6(1) + 8$	Substitute $x = 1$
$y = 3(1) - 6(1) + 8$	Evaluate the exponent
$y = 3 - 6 + 8$	Evaluate the multiplication
$y = 5$	Evaluate the subtraction and addition

The vertex is (1, 5).

Purpose

Show students how to use the axis of symmetry to calculate the vertex of a quadratic function in standard form.

Expected mistakes

Students may struggle to begin finding the vertex. Remind students that the x-coordinate of the vertex is the value of x for the axis of symmetry, which we have already calculated.

Reflecting with students

Challenge students to complete the square and convert the equation in standard form to vertex form: $y = 3(x - 1)^2 + 5$.

Students: Page 427

c   State the coordinates of the y-intercept.

Create a strategy

Since the y-intercept occurs when $x = 0$, substitute $x = 0$ into the equation and evaluate y.

When we are given an equation in standard form, the y-value of the y-intercept will be $y = c$.

Apply the idea

In this case, the value of c in the equation is 8.

So we have that the coordinates of the y-intercept are (0, 8).

Purpose
Show students how to identify the y-intercept of a quadratic function in standard form.

Expected mistakes
Students may mistake the y-coordinate of the vertex for the y-intercept. Point out to students that while this may sometimes be true, it is not always true for the vertex of a function and its y-intercept.

Students: Page 427

d   Draw a graph of the corresponding parabola.

Create a strategy

We have all the key features we need to create a graph. For more accuracy, we can use the axis of symmetry and y-intercept to find another point. This point will be a reflection of the y-intercept across the axis of symmetry.

We know that the parabola will open upwards because $a > 0$.

Apply the idea

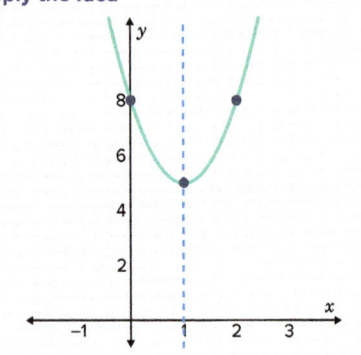

Axis of symmetry: $x = 1$

Vertex: (1, 5)

y-intercept: (0, 8)

Another point: (2, 8)

Reflect and check

From the graph we can identify that the vertex form of the equation would be:

$$y = 3(x - 1)^2 + 5$$

Purpose
Show students how to use at least three points on the graph of the function given in standard form to graph the quadratic function.

Reflecting with students
Ask students to explain why (2, 8) is a good third point to include on the graph. Since a quadratic is symmetrical about the axis of symmetry, we can see that the point (2, 8) is mirrored with the y-intercept.

Develop processes for graphing from standard form *use with Example 1*
Targeted instructional strategies

Encourage students to develop an algorithm for graphing quadratic functions in standard form. Begin by going through several examples as a group and then encourage them to write a set of steps that could be used for other examples. By following this sequential process, students will apply algorithmic thinking to connect the equation with its graph. For example:

1. Identify the coefficients a, b, and c in the quadratic equation $y = ax^2 + bx + c$.
2. Use a to determine the direction of opening
3. Calculate the axis of symmetry using $x = -\frac{b}{2a}$.
4. Find the vertex by substituting the axis of symmetry as the x-value into the original equation to find the corresponding y-value. The vertex is at (x, y).
5. Determine the y-intercept by evaluating the equation when $x = 0$ or noting it is $(0, c)$.
6. Select additional x-values on either side of the axis of symmetry and compute their y-values.
7. Plot the axis of symmetry, the vertex, the y-intercept, and any other points.
8. Draw the parabola that passes through all the plotted points.

Offer a technology alternative for graphing *use with Example 1*
Student with disabilities support

Let students know that they do not need to draw perfect graphs. Set a minimum requirement for graphing, such as only labeling the vertex, y-intercept, and drawing a roughly parabolic shape.

For graphs of standard form quadratic equations, students only need to label the vertex and one other point on the curve to define the parabola. This other point will usually be the y-intercept as it is easy to find.

For students with difficulty drawing graphs, allow the use of graphing technology such as Desmos or GeoGebra, or pair up students with one describing the graph and the other drawing.

Students: Page 428

Example 2

Naomi is playing a game of Kapucha Toli, where to start a play, a ball is thrown into the air. Naomi throws a ball into the air from a height of 6 feet, and the maximum height the ball reaches is 12.25 feet after 1.25 seconds.

a Sketch a graph to model the height of the ball over time.

Create a strategy

To sketch a graph, we'll use key points found by using the given information. We'll also use the units which are given, being feet and seconds.

We will let x represent the time since the ball was tossed in seconds.

We will let y represent the height of the ball in feet.

Apply the idea

It's given that the ball is thrown from a height of 6 feet. This means that at 0 seconds, the height of the ball is 6 feet. So our y-intercept is (0, 6).

We're told the maximum height of the ball is at 12.25 feet after 1.25 seconds. The maximum height will occur at the vertex of the graph, so the vertex is (1.25, 12.25). This also means that our axis of symmetry is $x = 1.25$.

We can use the axis of symmetry to determine a second point on the graph, the point across the axis of symmetry from the y-intercept. The point is (2.5, 6).

We can sketch our graph by plotting the y-intercept, the vertex, and the point found with our axis of symmetry.

Now we need to identify an appropriate scale.

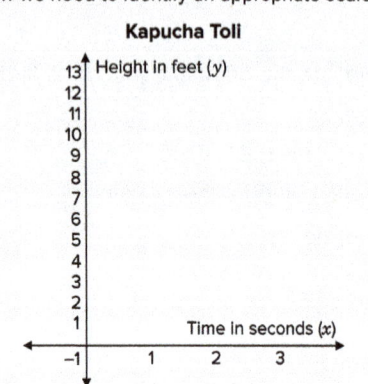

Kapucha Toli

We know that our graph will not go above $y = 12.25$ feet and that any part of the graph that goes below the x-axis will not be viable, so graphing $-1 \leq y \leq 13$ going up by 1 will show the full picture.

We know that time starts at $x = 0$ and the ball is on the way back down at $x = 2.5$, so graphing $0 \leq x \leq 4$ going up by 1 or 0.5 should be sufficient.

This is an appropriate way to label the axes.

Now we can graph the height of the ball over time.

Kapucha Toli

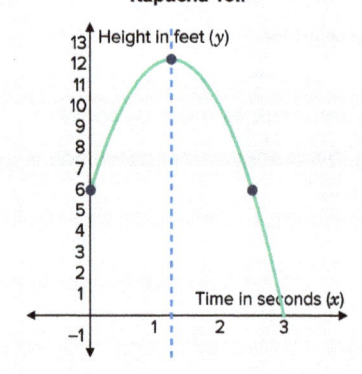

Purpose

Show students how to sketch the graph of a quadratic function given in context.

Expected mistakes

Students may leave out units on the axes. Remind students that labeling a graph for a problem in context will give the audience an idea of what is happening in the problem.

Reflecting with students

Ask students to identify the domain of the function for the context. The domain is $0 \leq x \leq 3$, since negative time does not make sense in the context of the problem.

Students: Page 429

b Predict when the ball will be 3 feet above the ground.

Create a strategy

We can use the sketch of our graph to predict when the ball will be at 3 feet.

Apply the idea

We can draw a horizontal line from $y = 3$ across until we reach the graph. After that, we can draw vertical line until we reach the x-axis to determine after how many seconds the ball is at 3 feet.

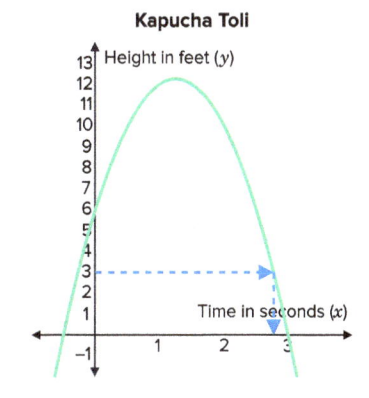

Kapucha Toli

We hit the x-axis around $x = 2.7$. Therefore, the ball is 3 ft above the ground after about 2.7 seconds.

Reflect and check

When reading from a graph, we often have to estimate. Any prediction between 2.6 and 2.9 would be reasonable in this case.

Purpose

Show students how to make a prediction using a graph.

Reflecting with students

Challenge students to give another way to determine when the ball is 3 feet above the ground. Students could find the equation of the function and substitute $y = 3$ in order to solve for x.

Students: Pages 429–430

c Write a quadratic equation in standard form to model the situation.

Create a strategy

To write the equation, we can use the key points and the graph we've sketched in previous parts.

Apply the idea

Since we know 3 points, we can use the standard form and substitution in order to solve for a, b, and c for our standard form quadratic equation which is of the form $y = ax^2 + bx + c$.

We know that c represents the y-value of the y-intercept which is (0, 6):

$$y = ax^2 + bx + 6$$

Now we can substitute our other two points to solve for a and b.

Next, we can substitute in (1.25, 12.25).

$y = ax^2 + bx + 6$	Standard form of a quadratic with $c = 6$
$12.25 = a(1.25)^2 + b(1.25) + 6$	Substitute (1.25, 12.25)
$12.25 = 1.5625a + 1.25b + 6$	Evaluate the exponent
$6.25 = 1.5625a + 1.25b$	Subtract 6 from both sides

Since we have two unknowns, we'll have to use our final point to create a second equation.

We'll now substitute in (2.5, 6).

$y = ax^2 + bx + 6$	Standard form of a quadratic with $c = 6$
$6 = a(2.5)^2 + b(2.5) + 6$	Substitute (2.5, 6)
$6 = 6.25a + 2.5b + 6$	Evaluate the exponent
$0 = 6.25a + 2.5b$	Subtract 6 from both sides

Now we have two equations with two unknowns. We can solve this system using the substitution method. Let's first isolate b in our second equation.

$0 = 6.25a + 2.5b$	Second equation
$-6.25a = 2.5b$	Subtract $6.25a$ from both sides
$\dfrac{-6.25a}{2.5} = b$	Divide by 2.5 on both sides
$-2.5a = b$	Evaluate the division

Now we can use the this in our first equation, letting $b = -2.5a$.

$6.25 = 1.5625a + 1.25b$	First equation
$6.25 = 1.5625a + 1.25(-2.5a)$	Substitute $b = -2.5a$
$6.25 = 1.5625a - 3.125a$	Evaluate the multiplication
$6.25 = -1.5625a$	Combine like terms
$-4 = a$	Divide both sides by -1.5625

Therefore $a = -4$. Finally, we can use $b = -2.5a$ to solve for b.

$b = -2.5a$	
$b = -2.5(-4)$	Substitute $a = -4$
$b = 10$	Evaluate the multiplication

Therefore $b = 10$. Now it's time to piece it all together. Since $a = -4$, $b = 10$, and $c = 6$, we know that our equation in standard form is:

$$y = -4x^2 + 10x + 6$$

Reflect and check

An alternative and simpler solution is to use the vertex to write it in vertex form and then using the intercept to solve for a.

Vertex form is $y = a(x - h)^2 + k$. The vertex is (1.25, 12.25), this gives us:

$$y = a(x - 1.25)^2 + 12.25$$

We can then substitute in the point (0, 6) and solve for a.

$y = a(x - 1.25)^2 + 12.25$	Vertex form of a quadratic with vertex (1.25, 12.25)
$6 = a(0 - 1.25)^2 + 12.25$	Substitute in (0, 6)
$6 = 1.5625a + 12.25$	Evaluate the parentheses
$-6.25 = 1.5625a$	Subtract 12.25 from both sides
$\dfrac{-6.25}{1.5625} = a$	Divide by 1.5625 on both sides
$-4 = a$	Evaluate the division

So now we have the equation:

$$y = -4(x - 1.25)^2 + 12.25$$

Now we need to convert to standard form:

$y = -4(x - 1.25)^2 + 12.25$	Equation in vertex form
$y = -4(x^2 - 2.5x + 1.5625) + 12.25$	Expand the binomial
$y = -4x^2 + 10x - 6.25 + 12.25$	Distributive property
$y = -4x^2 + 10x + 6$	Combine like terms

We get the same answer of: $y = -4x^2 + 10x + 6$.

Purpose

Show students how to write an equation of a quadratic function in standard form from its graph's key features.

Expected mistakes

Students may struggle to finish solving for a and b when they have an equation with two unknown variables. Remind students that solving systems of equations is how we approach solving for two unknowns, because it is possible to solve when we have two equations with two unknowns.

> **Three reads**
> **English language learner support**
>
> use with Example 2

Advise students to read through the instructions a few times, focusing on gathering different information each time in order to build up understanding of what the question is asking.

On the first read, students should aim to identify the scenario presented in the question. Ask students, "What do you think is happening in this question?" or "Can you explain what this question is about?"

On the second read, students should aim to interpret the problem by anwering questions like, "What is the question asking you to find?" and "What information should be included in the answer?"

On the third read, students should look for important information in the instructions. In this question, the important information includes:
- The ball was thrown initially from a height of 6 feet.
- The maximum height the ball reaches is 12.25 feet.
- The ball reaches its maximum height after 1.25 seconds.

Students can be prompted by framing these as questions like "What might be the variables in this situation?" or "Which pieces of information can you use to draw a graph?"

Students: Pages 431–432

Example 3

Write the standard form equation of the function shown on the graph.

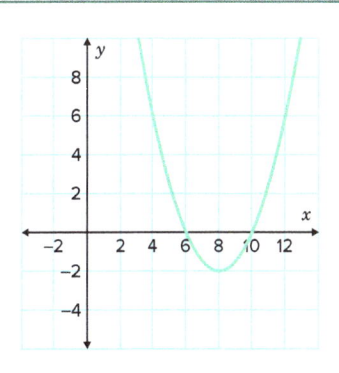

Create a strategy

Use the vertex to first write the equation in vertex form, then use another point on the parabola to solve for a, and finally convert to standard form.

Apply the idea

Vertex form is $y = a(x - h)^2 + k$. The vertex is $(8, -2)$, this gives us:

$$y = a(x - 8)^2 + (-2)$$

or

$$y = a(x - 8)^2 - 2$$

We can then substitute in the point $(4, 6)$ and solve for a.

$y = a(x-8)^2 - 2$	Vertex form equation
$6 = a(4-8)^2 - 2$	Substitute in $x = 4$ and $y = 6$
$6 = a(-4)^2 - 2$	Evaluate the subtraction
$6 = 16a - 2$	Evaluate the exponent
$8 = 16a$	Add 2 to both sides
$\frac{8}{16} = a$	Divide by 16 on both sides
$\frac{1}{2} = a$	Simplify the fraction

7.04 Quadratic functions in standard form 925
mathspace.co

Substituting $a = \frac{1}{2}$ we get the equation:
$$y = \frac{1}{2}(x-8)^2 - 2$$

Now we need to convert to standard form:

$y = \frac{1}{2}(x-8)^2 - 2$	Equation in vertex form
$y = \frac{1}{2}(x^2 - 16x + 64) - 2$	Expand the binomial
$y = \frac{1}{2}x^2 - 8x + 32 - 2$	Distributive property
$y = \frac{1}{2}x^2 - 8x + 30$	Combine like terms

$y = \frac{1}{2}x^2 - 8x + 30$ is the standard form equation of the function on the graph.

Reflect and check

Alternatively, we could have used the zeros and factored form.

Using the zeros of 6 and 10, we can write the equation in factored form $y = (x - x_1)(x - x_2)$. This gives us:
$$y = a(x - 6)(x - 10)$$

We can then substitute in the point (4, 6) and solve for a.

$y = a(x-6)(x-10)$	Factored form equation
$6 = a(4-6)(4-10)$	Substitute $x = 4$ and $y = 6$
$6 = a(-2)(-6)$	Evaluate the subtraction
$6 = 12a$	Evaluate the multiplication
$\frac{6}{12} = a$	Divide by 12 on both sides
$\frac{1}{2} = a$	Simplify the fraction

So now we have the equation:
$$y = \frac{1}{2}(x-6)(x-10)$$

Now we need to convert to standard form:

$y = \frac{1}{2}(x-6)(x-10)$	Equation in factored form
$y = \frac{1}{2}(x^2 - 10x - 6x + 60)$	Multiply the binomials
$y = \frac{1}{2}(x^2 - 16x + 60)$	Combine like terms
$y = \frac{1}{2}x^2 - 8x + 32$	Distributive property

Purpose

Show students how to write the standard form equation of a function using the vertex and another point on the function.

Students: Pages 432–433

Example 4

The whale jumps out the water at 3 seconds and reenters the water after 6.5 seconds. The whale reaches a maximum height of 49 feet after 4.75 seconds. Determine the equation in standard form that models the whale's jump.

Create a strategy

If we think of the water level as the x-axis, then the moments where the whale exits and reenters the water would represent the x-intercepts. The maximum height is the vertex of the parabola formed by the whale's jump path.

Apply the idea

Using the x-intercepts of 3 and 6.5, we can create the following equation, where x represents the time in seconds and y represents the height of the jump in feet:

$$y = a(x - 3)(x - 6.5)$$

Next, we can substitute the values of the maximum point, which occurs at (4.75, 49), to find the value of a.

$y = a(x - 3)(x - 6.5)$	Equation for whale's path
$49 = a(4.75 - 3)(4.75 - 6.5)$	Substitute $y = 49$ and $x = 4.75$
$49 = a(1.75)(-1.75)$	Evaluate the subtraction
$49 = -3.0625a$	Evaluate the multiplication
$-16 = a$	Division property of equality

Now, we know the factored form of the equation that models the whale's jump:

$$y = -16(x - 3)(x - 6.5)$$

The last step is to get it into standard form. We can do this by multiplying all the factors together.

$y = -16(x - 3)(x - 6.5)$	Equation for whale's path
$y = -16(x^2 - 6.5x - 3x + 19.5)$	Distributive property
$= -16x^2 + 104x + 48x - 312$	Distributive property
$= -16x^2 + 152x - 312$	Combine like terms

The equation in standard form that models the whale's jump is $y = -16x^2 + 152x - 312$.

Reflect and check

Notice that the parabola formed by the whale opens downward. If we did not have another point to help us find the value of a, our parabola would have been facing upward. Using the vertex helped us find a negative value for a which is what made the parabola face downward.

Purpose

Show students how to model a real-life situation using a quadratic function in standard form.

Expected mistakes

Students might write the factors incorrectly, using addition instead of subtraction. Remind students that if $x = 3$ is a zero, then we must rewrite this equation in terms of zero to find its factor.

Zero	$x = 3$
Equation in terms of zero	$x - 3 = 0$
Corresponding factor	$(x - 3)$

7.04 Quadratic functions in standard form

Reflecting with students

Before examining the solution strategy, ask students to brainstorm how the context might relate to a quadratic equation. What would the variables be? How does the initial information given in the problem relate to the graph of a quadratic function? Invite students to sketch a quick graph of the whale's jump to help them understand the problem. Then ask them to outline a strategy to find the solution.

Students: Page 433

> ### Idea summary
>
> The **standard form of a quadratic equation** highlights the y-intercept of a quadratic function.
>
> $$y = ax^2 + bx + c$$
>
> - a scale factor
> - b linear coefficient
> - c y-value of the y-intercept
>
> The **axis of symmetry** is the line:
>
> $$x = -\frac{b}{2a}$$
>
> The axis of symmetry is also the x-coordinate of the vertex. To find the y-coordinate, you substitute the x-coordinate back into the original function. Therefore, the coordinates of the vertex are:
>
> $$\left(-\frac{b}{2a}, f\left(-\frac{b}{2a}\right)\right)$$

Practice

Students: Pages 434–438

What do you remember?

1
  a   Describe the basic shape of a parabola.
  b   Given that the standard form of a quadratic is $y = ax^2 + bx + c$:
     i   What does the sign of a tell us?   **ii**   What does changing the value of c do?

2   For each quadratic function:
    i   Determine the axis of symmetry.   **ii**   State the coordinates of the vertex.
    iii   State the coordinates of the y-intercept.

    a $y = x^2 - 4x + 8$ **b** $y = -x^2 - 4x - 9$

3   Rewrite each equation in standard form.
    a $y = (3x - 1)(2x + 1)$ **b** $y = 2(x - 4)^2 + 1$ **c** $y = (x - 6)(x + 6)$ **d** $y = 5(x - 1)^2 - 5$

4   For each equation:
    i   Find $f(3)$.   **ii**   Find $f(-5)$.   **iii**   Find $f\left(\frac{3}{4}\right)$.

    a $f(x) = 2x^2 + 3x - 4$ **b** $f(x) = -x^2 + 2x + 10$ **c** $f(x) = -3x^2 - 5$ **d** $f(x) = 4x^2 - x + 1$

5 Consider the table of values of a function.

x	−6	−5	−4	−3	−2	−1
y	−8	−9	−8	−5	0	7

Select the graph that could represent the function:

A

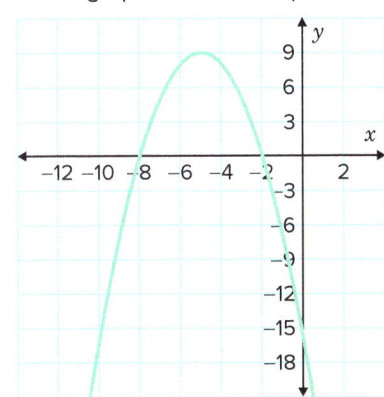

B

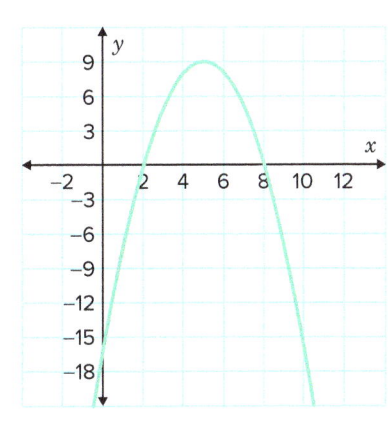

C

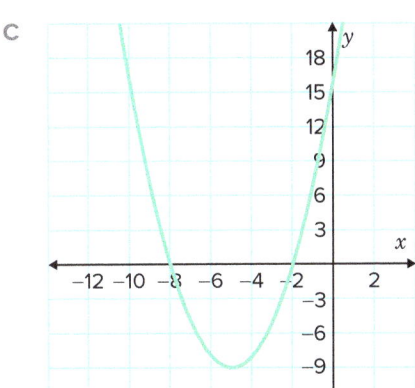

D

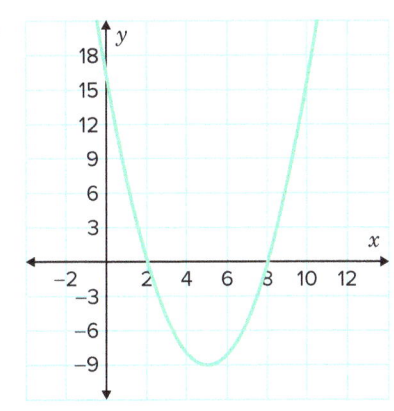

Let's practice

6 Consider the following graph of a function.

Select the equation that represents the function:

A $y = x^2 - 6x + 4$
B $y = x^2 + 6x - 4$
C $y = x^2 - 6x - 4$
D $y = x^2 + 6x + 4$

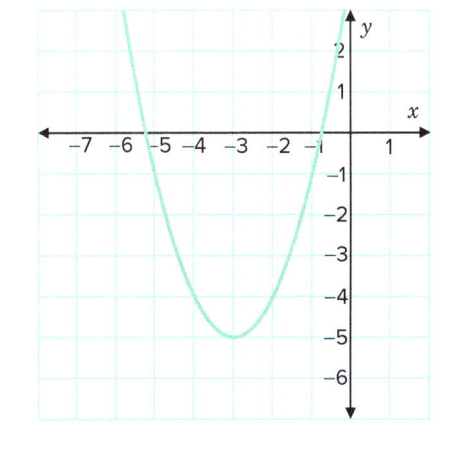

7 For each quadratic function:
  i   Determine the axis of symmetry.
  ii State the coordinates of the vertex.
  iii State the coordinates of the y-intercept.
  iv Draw a graph of the corresponding parabola.

  a $y = x^2 - 2x + 5$
  b $y = 2x^2 + 24x + 75$
  c $y = -x^2 + 6x - 8$
  d $y = 4x^2 - 64$
  e $y = 2x^2 + 2x + 9$
  f $y = -\frac{1}{4}x^2 + \frac{3}{2}x$

8 For each quadratic function:
  i State the coordinates of the y-intercept.
  ii Determine the coordinates of the x-intercept(s).
  iii Draw a graph of the corresponding parabola.

  a $y = x^2 - 3x - 10$
  b $y = x^2 - 9$
  c $y = 4 - 3x - x^2$
  d $y = 2x^2 + 12x + 18$
  e $y = 4x^2 + 8x - 5$
  f $y = -6x^2 + 10x + 4$

9 Consider the function
$$y = -2x^2 + 10x - 3$$
where x represents time in minutes and y represents the height of a ball from the ground in feet.
  a Draw a graph of the corresponding parabola. Make sure to label the axes.
  b Using your graph, predict when the ball will be 3 ft above the ground.

10 Write an equation in standard form to represent the following parabola.

  a 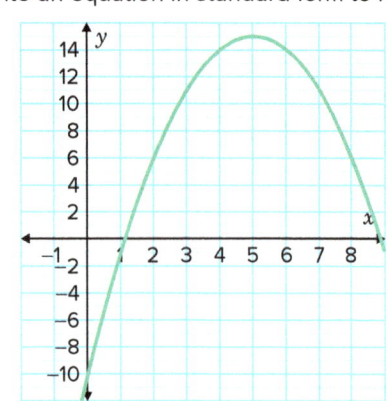
  b 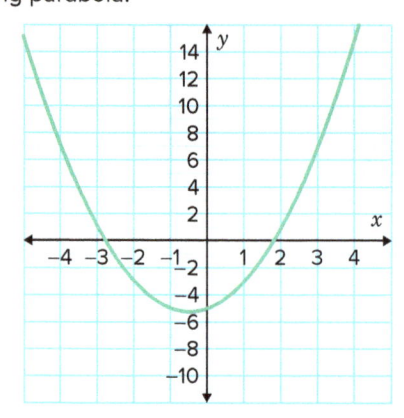
  c 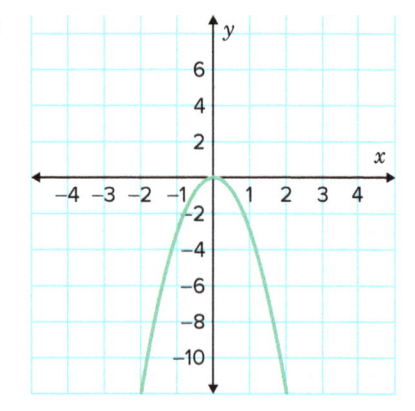
  d

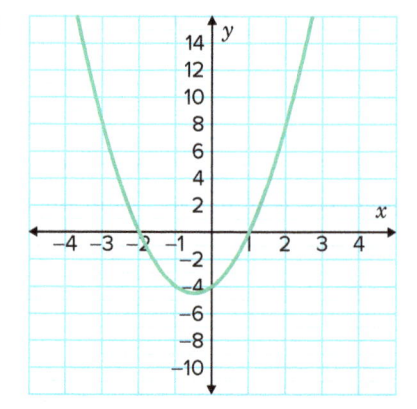

11 Darnell throws a bag of cookies to his friend, Ike, from a height of 3.25 ft. The cookies reach a maximum height of 19.25 ft, 1 second after being thrown.
  a Determine the equation in standard form that represents the situation.
  b Graph the corresponding parabola. Make sure to label the axes.
  c If Ike caught the cookies after 2 seconds, determine the height of the catch.

12 Carliss is starting a summer car wash business. Her profit function relates the total profit to the rate she charges for each car wash. The rate and profit are in dollars.
$$P(x) = -x^2 + 50x - 95$$
  a Carliss wants to make at least $525 this summer. Determine if she could make enough money based on her quadratic profit model. Explain your reasoning.
  b Draw a graph of $P(x)$.

13 The table shows points on a quadratic function.

x	–3	–2	–1	0	2
$A(x)$	–5	–8	–9	–8	0

Another quadratic function has the equation $B(x) = x^2 - 2x - 8$.

Determine what the quadratic functions have in common and what is different.

14 Orland and Delfino are comparing the vertex of the following graph and equation of quadratic functions:

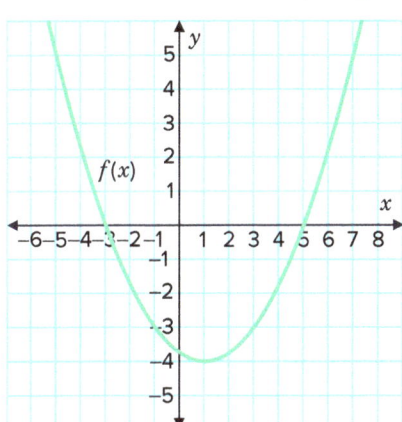

$$g(x) = -0.5x^2 + x + 7.5$$

Identify and explain their error(s):

Orland's work:

1. $x = \dfrac{-1}{2(0.5)}$ Finding axis of symmetry for $g(x)$
2. $x = -1$
3. $g(-1) = -0.5(-1)^2 + (-1) + 7.5$ Finding y-value of vertex
4. $g(-1) = -0.5 - 1 + 7.5$
5. $g(-1) = 6$

Vertex of $g(x)$ is (–1, 6) and vertex of $f(x)$ is (1, –4)

Delfino's work:

1. $x = \dfrac{-1}{-0.5}$ Finding axis of symmetry for $g(x)$
2. $x = 2$
3. $g(2) = -0.5(2)^2 + (2) + 7.5$ Finding y-value of vertex
4. $g(2) = -2 + 2 + 7.5$
5. $g(2) = 7.5$

Vertex of $g(x)$ is (2, 7.5) and vertex of $f(x)$ is (1, –5)

Let's extend our thinking

15 Kinsey wants to understand how vertex form and standard form of a quadratic function are related. Consider the vertex form of the function.

$$y = a(x - h)^2 + k$$

a Expand $a(x - h)^2 + k$ and write the equivalent equation in standard form.
b State the value of b in the equation from part (a).
c State the value of c in the equation from part (a).
d Explain how the equations are related.

7.04 Quadratic functions in standard form

16 Beau is competing at his high school swim meet and dives off a springboard that is 3 ft above the pool surface. He reaches a maximum height of 8 feet after 1 second.

    a Determine the equation in standard form that represents Beau's diving path.

    b Determine after how many seconds Beau will be at the same height as the springboard again.

    c If the pool is 12 feet deep, determine how many seconds after jumping it will take Beau to reach the bottom of the pool. Explain your reasoning.

17 Fill in the boxes to create a quadratic equation with the lowest possible minimum value. Use the digits 1 to 5 at most once.

$$y = \square x^2 + \square x + \square$$

18 A Happy Birthday banner is modeled by the quadratic function $h(x) = 0.2x^2 - x + 1.25$ where x is the distance from the left side of the banner and h, is the height above the ground. Both x and h are in feet. Currently, the lowest part of the banner touches the ground.

Immanuel is trying to create a virtual card and needs to know how to affect the look of the banner by changing parts of the quadratic function.

    a Determine a domain and range for the quadratic function that models the initial Birthday banner. Explain your reasoning.

    b Describe to Immanuel how changes to the quadratic function affect the shape of the Birthday banner.

Answers

7.04 Quadratic functions in standard form

What do you remember?

1. a A parabola is a ∪-shaped curve that opens either upward or downward.
   b i If the coefficient a is positive, the curve is ∪-shaped opening upward. If $a < 0$, then the curve is ∩-shaped, opening downwards.
   ii Changing the constant term c in a quadratic equation shifts the entire graph vertically. If c is positive, the graph moves upward, and if c is negative, the graph moves downward. The magnitude of the shift depends on the value of c.

2. a i $x = 2$ ii $(2, 4)$ iii $(0, 8)$
   b i $x = -2$ ii $(-2, -5)$ iii $(0, -9)$

3. a $6x^2 + x - 1$ b $2x^2 - 16x + 33$
   c $x^2 - 36$ d $5x^2 - 10x$

4. a i $f(3) = 23$ ii $f(-5) = 31$ iii $f\left(\frac{3}{4}\right) = -0.625$
   b i $f(3) = 7$ ii $f(-5) = -25$ iii $f\left(\frac{3}{4}\right) = 10.9375$
   c i $f(3) = -32$ ii $f(-5) = -80$ iii $f\left(\frac{3}{4}\right) = -6.6875$
   d i $f(3) = 34$ ii $f(-5) = 106$ iii $f\left(\frac{3}{4}\right) = 2.5$

5. C

Let's practice

6. D

7. a i $x = 1$ ii $(1, 4)$ iii $(0, 5)$
   iv

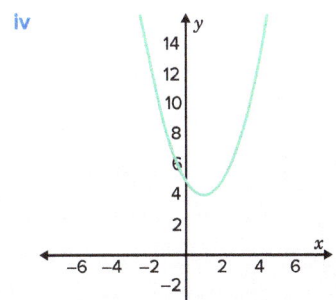

   b i $x = -6$ ii $(-6, 3)$ iii $(0, 75)$
   iv

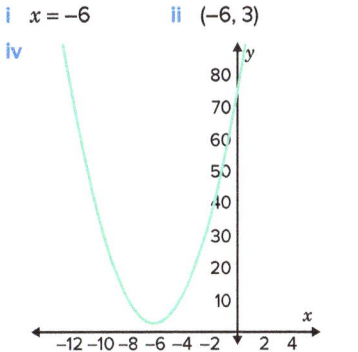

   c i $x = 3$ ii $(3, 1)$ iii $(0, -8)$
   iv

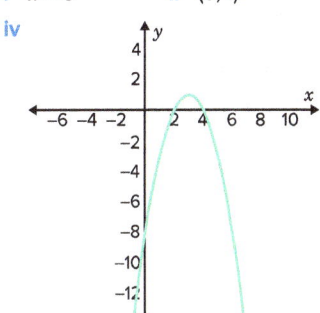

   d i $x = 0$ ii $(0, -64)$ iii $(0, -64)$
   iv

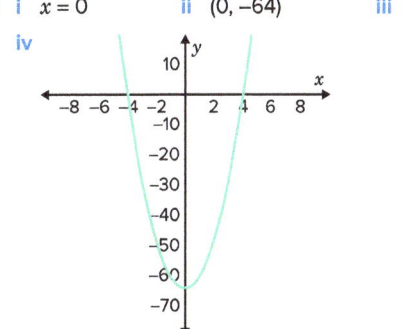

   e i $x = -0.5$ ii $(-0.5, 8.5)$ iii $(0, 9)$
   iv

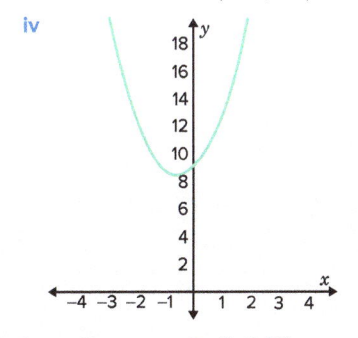

   f i $x = 3$ ii $(3, 2.25)$ iii $(0, 0)$
   iv

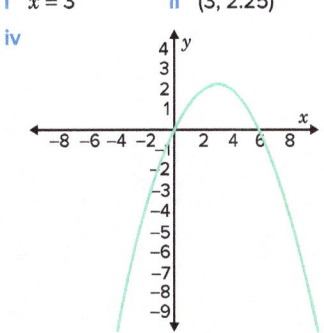

7.04 Quadratic functions in standard form 933

mathspace.co

8 a i (0, −10)   ii (−2, 0) and (5, 0)
    iii

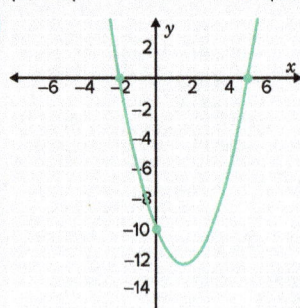

  b i (0, −9)   ii (−3, 0) and (3, 0)
    iii

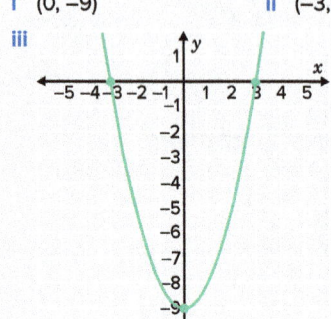

  c i (0, 4)   ii (−4, 0) and (1, 0)
    iii

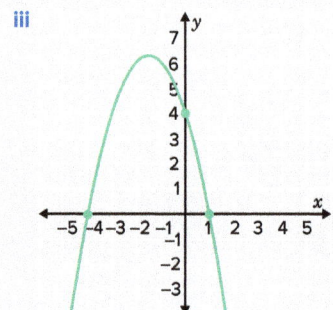

  d i (0, 18)   ii (−3, 0)
    iii

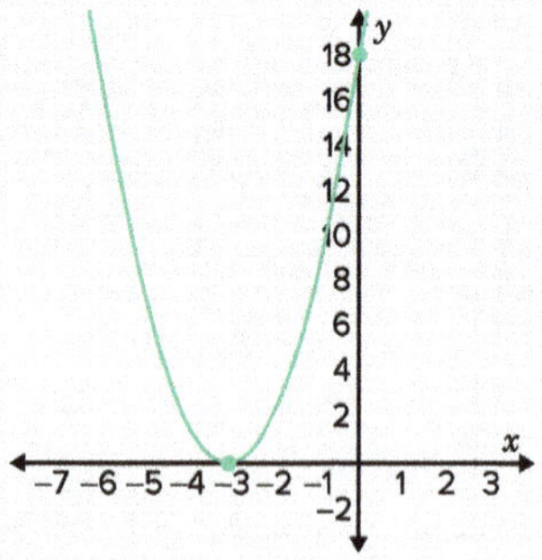

  e i (0, −5)   ii (−2.5, 0) and (0.5, 0)
    iii

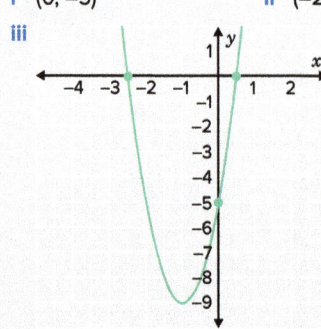

  f i (0, 4)   ii $\left(-\frac{1}{3}, 0\right)$ and (2, 0)
    iii

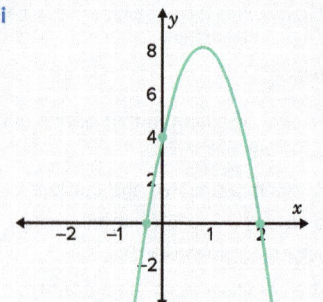

9 a

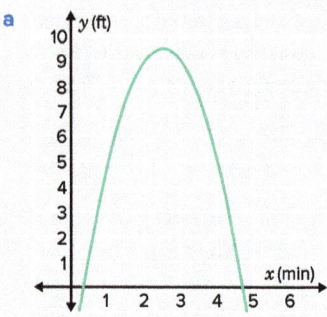

  b Because the y-axis represents height in feet, we can look at when our graph has a y-value of 3. This occurs twice, when x is around 0.7 and 4.3. Because x is in terms of minutes, we can say that the ball will be 3 ft above the ground around 0.7 and 4.3 minutes.

10 a $y = -x^2 + 10x - 10$ b $y = x^2 + x - 5$
   c $y = -3x^2$ d $y = 2x^2 + 2x - 4$

11 a $y = -16x^2 + 32x + 3.25$
   b

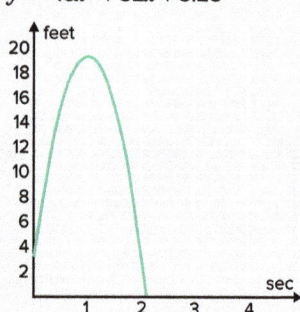

   c 3.25 ft

12 a Carliss could make $525 because the maximum profit is $530 if each car wash costs $25.
   b

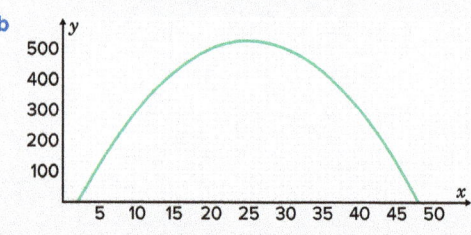

13. Both quadratic functions have a minimum value −9, opens upwards, and have the same y-intercept at (0, −8). $A(x)$ has an axis of symmetry of $x = -1$ and $B(x)$ has an axis of symmetry of $x = 1$.

14. Orland incorrectly used 0.5, when the a value of the quadratic function is −0.5. This error creates an incorrect axis of symmetry and y-value for the vertex.

    Delfino used an incorrect equation to find the axis of symmetry, as the equation is $x = \frac{-b}{2a}$. Delfino forgot the 2 in the denominator. This error creates an incorrect axis of symmetry and y-value for the vertex. Delfino labeled the vertex of $f(x)$ incorrectly as the vertex is (1, −4).

    The vertex of $g(x)$ is (1, 8) and the vertex of $f(x)$ is (1, −4).

Let's extend our thinking

15. a $y = ax^2 - 2ahx + ah^2 + k$
    b $y = ax^2 + (-2ah)x + (ah^2 + k)$ so $b = -2ah$
    c $y = ax^2 + (-2ah)x + (ah^2 + k)$ so $c = ah^2 + k$
    d Vertex form and standard form are equivalent quadratic equations in different forms. The equations give us different information more efficiently. We can find the vertex, (h, k), efficiently using vertex form. We can find the y-intercept, c, efficiently by substituting in 0 for x and evaluating the corresponding output using standard form. We can also find the axis of symmetry, $x = \frac{-b}{2a}$, in standard form and use it to find the y-value of the vertex.

    In both forms, the leading coefficient, a, is the vertical stretch/compression factor and tells us if the parabola will open up or down.

16. a $y = -5x^2 + 10x + 3$ b 2 seconds
    c After 3 seconds. Because Beau starts at 3 ft above the pool surface, we know that the pool surface is at a height of 0 feet. Therefore 12 feet deep would be the same thing as $y = -12$. We can plug this into our equation and see that $x = 3$, meaning that this will happen 3 feet after jumping.

17. $y = x^2 + 5x + 2$

18. a Domain: $0 \leq x \leq 5$. This is because the y-intercept is (0, 1.25) and the vertex is (2.5, 0). Parabolas are symmetric about the axis of symmetry and since the shape of the sign is symmetric, the sign must be 5 ft wide.

    Range: $0 \leq y \leq 1.25$

    This is because the leading coefficient is positive, so the minimum value occurs at the vertex. The maximum height of the banner would be at the end points of the banner and the left end point occurs at the y-intercept.

    b Changing the constant, c, will translate the quadratic function vertically up or down. Changing the linear coefficient, b, will move the vertex. Changing the leading coefficient, a will widen or narrow the parabola and change the vertex.

    Students are encouraged to create graphs of several cases to make generalizations.

7.05 Compare linear, quadratic, and exponential functions

Subtopic overview

Lesson narrative

In this lesson, students will compare key characteristics that linear, quadratic, and exponential functions have in common, such as intercepts, domain, and range. Students will examine the similarities and differences in rates of change for linear and exponential functions. Students will examine tables of values and explore graphs to compare the key characteristics of these functions. By the end of the lesson, students will know the characteristics of a linear, quadratic, and exponential functions and identify their differences.

Learning objective

Students: Page 439

After this lesson, you will be able to...
compare key characteristics of linear, quadratic, and exponential functions using graphs and tables.

Key vocabulary

- characteristic (of a function)

Essential understanding

All of the functions in a given family share certain characteristics that can be identified from their equations, graphs, or input/output pairs. Linear and exponential functions can be distinguished by their rate of change.

Standards

This subtopic addresses the following Virginia 2023 Mathematics Standards of Learning standards.

Mathematical process goals

MPG1 — Mathematical Problem Solving

Teachers can integrate this goal by posing complex, open-ended problems related to linear, quadratic, and exponential functions. For example, they might ask students to model a real-world situation using each type of function, then compare the models to determine which is most appropriate. They could also prompt students to use their knowledge of these functions to create their own problems and then solve them.

MPG3 — Mathematical Reasoning

This goal can be integrated by asking students to reason about the properties of linear, quadratic, and exponential functions, and how these properties influence the shape of the graph and the behavior of the function. Teachers could also challenge students to use logical reasoning to predict the effect of certain transformations on each type of function.

MPG4 — Mathematical Connections

To achieve this goal, teachers could highlight the connections between different types of functions, such as how the rate of change in a linear function relates to the slope of the line, or how the vertex of a quadratic function relates to its maximum or minimum value. Teachers could also emphasize the connections between mathematical concepts and real-world applications, such as how exponential functions can model population growth or compound interest.

Content standards

A.F.1 — The student will investigate, analyze, and compare linear functions algebraically and graphically, and model linear relationships.

A.F.2 — The student will investigate, analyze, and compare characteristics of functions, including quadratic and exponential functions, and model quadratic and exponential relationships.

A.F.1a — Determine and identify the domain, range, zeros, slope, and intercepts of a linear function, presented algebraically or graphically, including the interpretation of these characteristics in contextual situations.

A.F.1f — Graph a linear function in two variables, with and without the use of technology, including those that can represent contextual situations.

A.F.1g — For any value, x, in the domain of f, determine $f(x)$, and determine x given any value $f(x)$ in the range of f, given an algebraic or graphical representation of a linear function.

A.F.2b — Given an equation or graph, determine key characteristics of a quadratic function including x-intercepts (zeros), y-intercept, vertex (maximum or minimum), and domain and range (including when restricted by context); interpret key characteristics as related to contextual situations, where applicable.

A.F.2c — Graph a quadratic function, $f(x)$, in two variables using a variety of strategies, including transformations $f(x) + k$ and $kf(x)$, where k is limited to rational values.

A.F.2e — Given an equation or graph of an exponential function in the form $y = ab^x$ (where b is limited to a natural number), interpret key characteristics, including y-intercepts and domain and range; interpret key characteristics as related to contextual situations, where applicable.

A.F.2f — Graph an exponential function, $f(x)$, in two variables using a variety of strategies, including transformations $f(x) + k$ and $kf(x)$, where k is limited to rational values.

A.F.2g — For any value, x, in the domain of f, determine $f(x)$ of a quadratic or exponential function. Determine x given any value $f(x)$ in the range of f of a quadratic function. Explain the meaning of x and $f(x)$ in context.

A.F.2h — Compare and contrast the key characteristics of linear functions ($f(x) = x$), quadratic functions ($f(x) = x^2$), and exponential functions ($f(x) = b^x$) using tables and graphs.

Prior connections

8.PFA.3 — The student will represent and solve problems, including those in context, by using linear functions and analyzing their key characteristics (the value of the y-intercept (b) and the coordinates of the ordered pairs in graphs will be limited to integers).

Future connections

A.EI.2 — The student will represent, solve, explain, and interpret the solution to a system of two linear equations, a linear inequality in two variables, or a system of two linear inequalities in two variables.

A2.F.1 — The student will investigate, analyze, and compare square root, cube root, rational, exponential, and logarithmic function families, algebraically and graphically, using transformations.

A2.F.2 — The student will investigate and analyze characteristics of square root, cube root, rational, polynomial, exponential, logarithmic, and piecewise-defined functions algebraically and graphically.

A.ST.1 — The student will apply the data cycle (formulate questions; collect or acquire data; organize and represent data; and analyze data and communicate results) with a focus on representing bivariate data in scatterplots and determining the curve of best fit using linear and quadratic functions.

Lesson Preparation

Suggested review

Depending on your students' level of prior knowledge, consider revisiting the following lessons:

Algebra 1 — 2.04 Characteristics of functions
Algebra 1 — 3.03 Slope-intercept form
Algebra 1 — 5.08 Characteristics of exponential functions
Algebra 1 — 7.01 Characteristics of quadratic functions

Tools

You may find these tools helpful:
- Graphing calculator
- Highlighters
- Spreadsheet application

Lesson supports

The following supports may be useful for this lesson. More specific supports may appear throughout the lesson:

Concrete-Representational-Abstract (CRA) Approach
Targeted instructional strategies

Concrete: Engage students with hands-on activities to explore linear, quadratic, and exponential functions. Use physical objects like stacking blocks, rubber bands, and paper folding. For linear functions, have students create a staircase with blocks, adding one block at each step to show constant growth. For quadratic functions, use rubber bands stretched between pegs on a pegboard to form parabolic shapes. For exponential functions, demonstrate layering paper folds to show how quickly the number of layers grows. These activities help students physically experience how each function behaves differently.

Representational: Transition to visual representations by having students draw what they observed. For the linear function, they can draw a straight line showing constant growth. For the quadratic function, guide them to sketch a parabola based on the shape created with rubber bands. For the exponential function, have them plot the number of paper layers against the number of folds to create an exponential curve. Encourage students to label key features like intercepts, slope, and curvature.

Abstract: Move to working with equations and tables of values. Teach students the general forms: $y = mx + b$ for linear, $y = ax^2 + bx + c$ for quadratic, and $y = a \cdot b^x$ for exponential functions. Have them create tables of values by choosing x-values and calculating y-values using the equations. Discuss how the rate of change differs: constant for linear, changing for quadratic, and increasing rapidly for exponential functions. Solve problems that require identifying the domain, range, and intercepts from the equations.

Connecting the stages: Help students make connections between the physical activities, their drawings, and the equations.

Ask guiding questions like:
- "How does the staircase model relate to the straight line graph and the linear equation?"
- "What does the rapid increase in paper folds tell us about exponential growth?"

Encourage them to see how each stage represents the same concept in different ways. This will help them understand the characteristics of each function type and how to distinguish between them when using graphs and tables.

Student lesson & teacher guide

Comparing functions

Students begin with an exploration that involves comparing the patterns of different types of relationships.

Exploration

Students: Page 439

7.05 Compare linear, quadratic, and exponential functions

After this lesson, you will be able to...
compare key characteristics of linear, quadratic, and exponential functions using graphs and tables.

Comparing functions

In this lesson, we will use our prior knowledge of linear, quadratic, and exponential functions to identify key features and compare various functions represented in different ways.

Exploration

Consider the table:

x	$y = 3x$	$y = 3x^2$	$y = 3^x$
1	3	3	3
2	6	12	9
3	9	27	27
5	15	125	243

1. Compare the three functions and how they change as x increases.

Suggested student grouping: Small groups

Students are given a table of values and the equations for three different types of patterns: a linear, a quadratic, and an exponential. Students will compare how the values change based on the functions in the table, which aligns with how we saw their growth patterns in previous chapters.

Ideal student responses

These ideal responses may differ from other correct student responses. Less formal responses can be connected with the more precise mathematical language presented here.

1. **Compare the three functions and how they change as x increases.**

   For $y = 3x$, the values are increasing at a constant rate. For $y = 3x^2$ and $y = 3^x$, the values will increase at an increasing rate, with the exponential function increasing faster than the quadratic function.

Purposeful questions

- Do you notice a pattern for the function as x increases?
- Would a graph of each function help you to compare the functions and how they change as x increases?

Possible misunderstandings

- Students may not compare how the patterns change and instead state that the functions all increase. Point out to students that the functions have different growth patterns and encourage them to identify which pattern is linear, quadratic, and exponential.

Students are reminded of the growth patterns of linear, quadratic, and exponential functions. A list of the key features of functions is presented as review.

Students: Page 439

The way a function is represented can affect the characteristics we are able to identify for the function. Different representations can highlight or hide certain characteristics. Remember that **key features** of functions include:

- domain and range
- x- and y-intercepts
- maximum or minimum value(s)
- how the function increases or decreases
- vertex

One way to compare functions is to look at growth rates as the x-values increase over regular intervals. In order to compare the growth rates of quadratics with those of exponential or linear functions, we will look only at the half of the quadratic that is increasing.

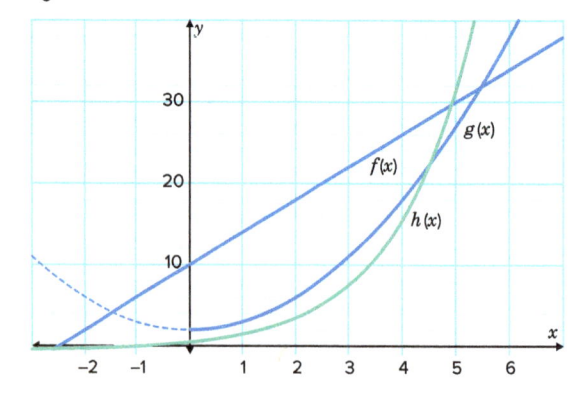

Notice starting at $x = 0$, $g(x)$ is greater than $h(x)$ and is increasing at a greater rate. But, as x continues to increase, the quadratic function $g(x)$ is increasing at a slower rate than the exponential function, and eventually the exponential function will overtake the quadratic function.

Notice that no matter what the intercepts are, an exponential growth function will always exceed a linear or quadratic growth function as values of x become larger.

List key features of functions and review which are easiest to identify
Targeted instructional strategies

Provide students with a list of key features they can be asked to compare for different functions. In pairs, have them identify strategies for determining a chosen key feature from a table of values, equation, or graph. Encourage students to consider if their approach would be different for linear, exponential or quadratic functions.

It can also be helpful to examine which key features are easiest to identify from each of the different representations. Use a group discussion to have students consider each key feature.
- domain and range
- x- and y-intercepts
- maximum or minimum value(s)
- how the function increases or decreases
- vertex

Some possible answers could be:

The domain of linear, quadratic, and exponential functions is "all real values of x," unless otherwise specified or determined by a constraint. It is easiest to see this with the graph. In a table of values, we can assume the pattern continues unless otherwise stated.

To identify the y-intercept, it is easiest from equations in the form $y = mx + b$, $y = ax^2 + bx + c$, or $y = ab^x$, as we can read the y-intercept directly from these forms. We can also see it fairly easily from the table if it is one of the given values, but otherwise we first have to find the equation or extrapolate from the table. From the graph, we need to look where the function crosses the y-axis. All of these functions will have exactly one y-intercept.

Collect and display
English language learner support

Use the "Collect and Display" routine to help students connect their own words to precise mathematical vocabulary when comparing linear, quadratic, and exponential functions. During discussions, listen for phrases students might use, such as "going up in a straight line," "making a U-shaped curve," "getting steeper quickly," or "leveling off eventually."

Record these phrases on a chart or board under headings like "Students' Descriptions." Next to each student's phrase, write the corresponding mathematical term—like "linear function," "parabola," "exponential growth," or "asymptote"—under a heading like "Mathematical Vocabulary." Include simple sketches or diagrams to illustrate each concept.

Encourage students to refer to this visual display when analyzing graphs and tables, and prompt them to use the precise vocabulary in their explanations. This approach supports English language learners by bridging their informal language to academic terms, enhancing their understanding of both mathematical concepts and the language used to describe them.

Use graphic organizers to highlight key features of functions
Student with disabilities support

Remind students of the key characteristics of functions that will be addressed in this subtopic. Provide a resource sheet or graphic organizer to help them draw connections and complete examples.

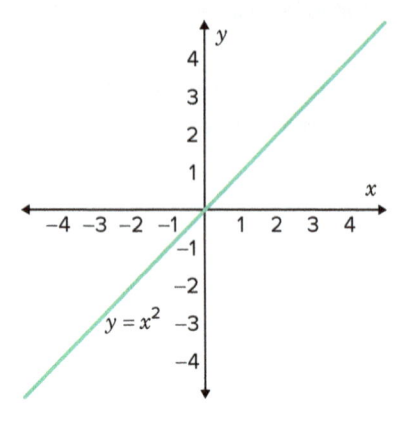

- Domain: $(-\infty, \infty)$
- Range: $(-\infty, \infty)$
- x-intercept: $(0, 0)$
- y-intercept: $(0, 0)$
- Increasing: $m > 0$
- Decreasing: $m < 0$
- Constant rate of change

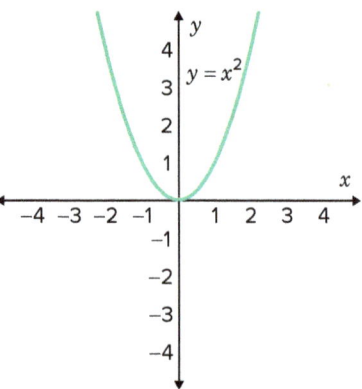

- Domain: $(-\infty, \infty)$
- Range: $[0, \infty)$
- x-intercept: $(0, 0)$
- y-intercept: $(0, 0)$
- Decreases at a decreasing rate when $x < 0$
- Increases at increasing rate when $x > 0$

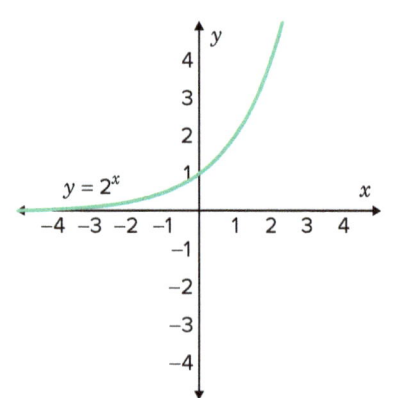

- Domain: $(-\infty, \infty)$
- Range: $(0, \infty)$
- x-intercept: None
- y-intercept: $(0, 1)$
- Increases at increasing rate
- Asymptote at $y = 0$

942 Mathspace Virginia SOL Algebra 1 Teacher Edition
mathspace.co

Key features not appearing on the graph
Address student misconceptions

Students may think that they cannot compare a key feature if it is not present in the graph. For example, that they cannot compare the number of x-intercepts for the two graphs:

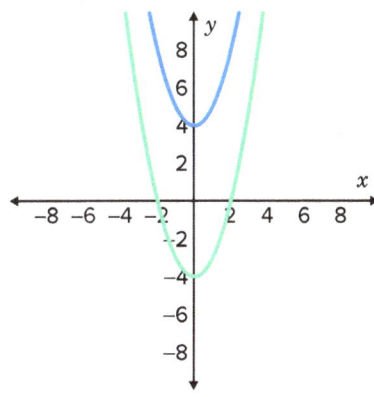

Challenge this misconception by asking students how they would answer the question "identify the ... for $f(x)$" to remind them that "none" or "zero" or "never" are valid answers.

Examples

Students: Page 440

Example 1

Which of the following functions increases the fastest for very large values of x?
- $y = 9 \cdot x$
- $y = 3^x$
- $y = 2x^2$
- $y = 4^x$

Create a strategy

Remember that exponential functions ($b > 1$) will always have a greater rate of change when compared to linear and quadratic functions as x increases toward infinity. Then, we must compare the constant factor b in the equation $y = a \cdot b^x$.

Apply the idea

As x increases toward infinity, we know that our greatest rate of change is from one of the exponential functions, $y = 3^x$ or $y = 4^x$. Remembering our lesson on characteristics of exponential functions, a greater constant factor, b, will result in a greater rate of change as x continues to increase. Therefore, $y = 4^x$ increases the fastest for very large values of x.

Reflect and check

How would you approach this problem if exponential equations had 2 different leading coefficients? For example, would $y = 2 \cdot 4^x$ or $y = 4 \cdot 2^x$ have a greater rate of change as x increases toward infinity?

Purpose
Check student understanding of different types of functions algebraically and their rates of change.

Reflecting with students
Challenge advanced learners to further articulate why exponential functions with larger bases grow faster than those with smaller bases, and why exponential functions eventually surpass linear and quadratic functions, regardless of the coefficients. An example student response is shown:
Exponential functions with larger bases grow faster because their outputs multiply by the base each time x increases. For example, in $y = 3^x$, the output triples with each increase in x, while in $y = 4^x$, it quadruples.

7.05 Compare linear, quadratic, and exponential functions 943
mathspace.co

Multiplying by 4 grows faster than multiplying by 3. Exponential functions eventually outgrow linear functions because linear functions grow by adding a constant amount, and multiplying grows faster than adding. Quadratics grow by an amount proportional to x^2, but exponential functions double, triple, etc., with each unit increase in x.

Students: Page 440

Example 2

Consider the functions shown. Assume that the domain of f is all real numbers.

- Function 1:

x	−1	0	1	2	3	4	5
$f(x)$	−3.75	−2	−0.25	1.5	3.25	5	6.75

- Function 2:

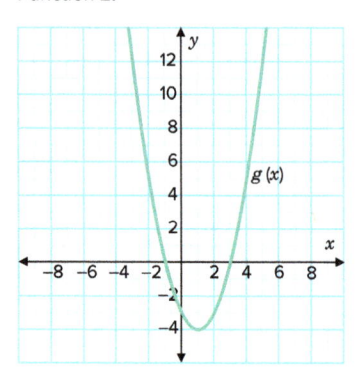

a Determine which function has a higher y-intercept.

Create a strategy

Remember that the y-intercept of a function occurs when $x = 0$. We can use this to evaluate the y-intercept of f and identify the y-intercept of g.

Apply the idea

For f, we can see from the table that $f(0) = -2$.

For g, we can see from the graph that $g(0) = -3$.

So the y-intercept of f is the point $(0, -2)$ and the y-intercept of g is the point $(0, -3)$, and therefore f has a higher y-intercept.

Purpose

Show students how to find the y-intercept for types of functions.

Reflecting with students

Ask students to explain what the y-intercept represents in a function, and how it can be identified from a graph and a table of values.

Students: Page 441

b Determine which function will be greater as x gets very large.

Create a strategy

We can consider how quickly each function changes to get an idea of how it will behave for very large values of x.

Apply the idea

We can see that $f(x)$ has a constant rate of change (slope) of 1.75. This is a linear function. From the graph, we can see that $g(x)$ increases at an increasing rate as x increases. So, we can see that Function 2 will eventually surpass Function 1 as x gets very large.

Purpose

Check that students can identify function types and understand an increasing quadratic function will always surpass a linear function.

Reflecting with students

Discuss with students the concept of rate of change and how it affects the growth of a function. Highlight the difference between a constant rate of change in a linear function and an increasing rate of change in a quadratic function.

Students: Page 441

Example 3

Consider functions representing three options to earn money one of the following ways:

Option 1
You are given $2 each day

Option 2

Days	Total Amount
1	$1
2	$4
3	$9
4	$16
5	$25
6	$36

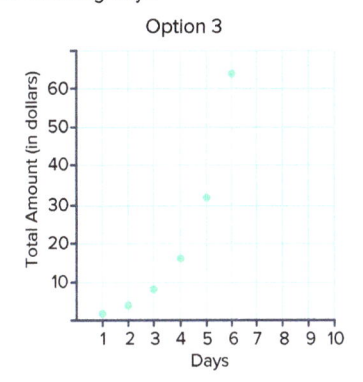

Option 3

Note: Option 3 starts with $2 on day one and doubles each day after this.

a Find the equation that represents each option, where x is the number of days that have passed.

Create a strategy

For each option, we can consider how the total amount of money changes as the days progress and derive an equation to represent the relationship.

Apply the idea

We can see that Option 1 has a constant rate of change regardless of the interval we considered. So, Option 1 can be represented by the linear function, $f(x) = 2x$.

Now, observing the table of values for Option 2, we can see that the total amount is just the square of the number of days passed. So, Option 2 can be represented by the function $f(x) = x^2$.

Finally, the relationship for Option 3 is represented in the graph, but also described to us. Since we are told that the function starts at $2 and is doubled each day, we can see that Option 3 is just represented by the function $f(x) = 2^x$.

Reflect and check

If the relationship between the days passed and the total amount weren't directly obvious in Option 2, we could have tested the data provided in the table to rule out a linear or exponential relationship.

For a linear relationship, the rate of change between any two points must be equal. We can check that this wasn't true for Option 2. So, we could have then tested if it represented an exponential relationship.

For an exponential relationship, the ratio of between two points, a unit apart, must be equal. We can see that for Option 2, $\frac{4}{1} \neq \frac{9}{4}$.

Therefore, we could see that Option 2 represented neither a linear or exponential relationship.

Purpose

Show students how to derive equations from different types of growth patterns, including linear, quadratic, and exponential.

Reflecting with students

Have students consider how they could write a formula for each function in a spreadsheet to quickly make a table of values.

As an extension for advanced students, encourage them to define each relationship both explicitly in terms of n and recursively. For example:

- Explicit form:

	A	B	C	D	E
1	Day	Option 1	Option 2	Option 3	
2	1	2	1	2	
3	$= A2 + 1$	$= 2*A3$	$= A3^2$	$= 2^{A3}$	
4	$= A3 + 1$	$= 2*A4$	$= A4^2$	$= 2^{A4}$	
5	⋮	⋮	⋮	⋮	

- Recursively:

	A	B	C	D	E
1	Day	Option 1	Option 2	Option 3	
2	1	2	1	2	
3	$= A2 + 1$	$= B2 + 2$	$= C2 + 2*A3 - 1$	$= D2*2$	
4	$= A3 + 1$	$= B3 + 2$	$= C3 + 2*A4 - 1$	$= D3*2$	
5	⋮	⋮	⋮	⋮	

Students: Page 442

b Find the value of each option at 8 days, 12 days, and 14 days.

Create a strategy

Construct a table of values with the amounts of money gained with each option.

Apply the idea

Days	Option 1 Total	Option 2 Total	Option 3 Total
1	$2	$1	$2
2	$4	$4	$4
3	$6	$9	$8
4	$8	$16	$16
5	$10	$25	$32
6	$12	$36	$64
7	$14	$49	$128
8	$16	$64	$256
9	$18	$81	$512
10	$20	$100	$1024
11	$22	$121	$2048
12	$24	$144	$4096
13	$26	$169	$8192
14	$28	$196	$16 384

At 8 days, Option 1 will make $16, Option 2 will make $64, and Option 3 will make $256.
At 12 days, Option 1 will make $24, Option 2 will make $144, and Option 3 will make $4096.
At 14 days, Option 1 will make $28, Option 2 will make $196, and Option 3 will make $16 384.

Reflect and check

We could calculate the total amount of money on days 8, 12 and 14 using the functions found in part (a), instead of constructing a table.

Purpose

Show students how to determine the value of each option on specific days using different representations: numerical, tabular, and graphical.

Reflecting with students

Ask students: "If you could choose one of these options to earn money for 30 days, which one would you choose and why?"

Students: Page 442

c Determine which option will be greater for larger and larger values of x.

Create a strategy

Use the table comparison from part (b) to determine which option will be greater for larger and larger values of x.

Apply the idea

As x gets larger and larger, we can see that Option 3, the exponential option, will be far greater than Options 1 or 2.

Reflect and check

An exponential function will always exceed a linear or quadratic function as values of x become larger.

Purpose

Students demonstrate their understanding of exponential growth compared to linear and quadratic growth.

Reflecting with students

Ask students to describe the differences in the growth patterns among the three options. Why does the exponential function grow faster?

Visual supports for understanding functions
Student with disabilities support

use with Example 3

Use graphs to represent the functions for each option to earn money. The students can observe how the total amount of money changes with the number of days for each option and compare the graphs to understand which option will be greater for larger and larger values of x.

Students can also use color-coding to differentiate between the three options. For example, they can use one color to represent Option 1, another color for Option 2, and a third color for Option 3. This can help them visually distinguish between the different options and their rates of change.

Students: Page 443

> **Idea summary**
>
> It is important to be able to compare the key features of functions whether they are represented in similar or different ways:
>
> - domain and range
> - x- and y-intercepts
> - maximum or minimum value(s)
> - how the function increases or decreases
> - vertex

Practice

Students: Pages 443–447

What do you remember?

1 For each pair of functions, determine which function y is changing more rapidly:

   a • Function 1:

x	0	1	2	3
y	3	10	17	24

      • Function 2:

x	−1	0	1	2
y	−1	3	7	11

   b • Function 3:

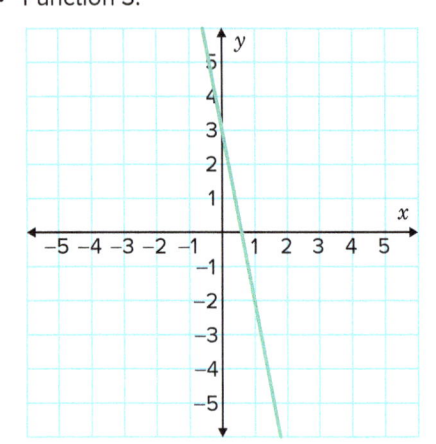

      • Function 4:

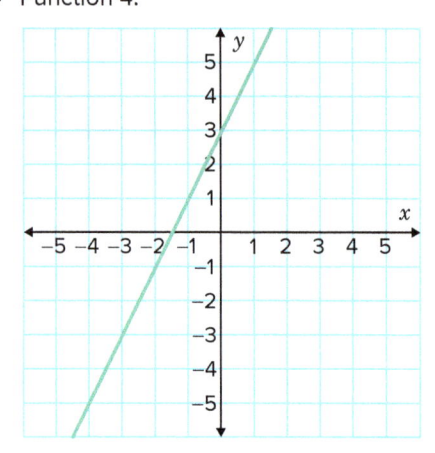

2 For each pair of table and its graph, determine whether a linear or quadratic function could represent it:

   a

x	−3	−2	−1	0	1
y	3	6	7	6	3

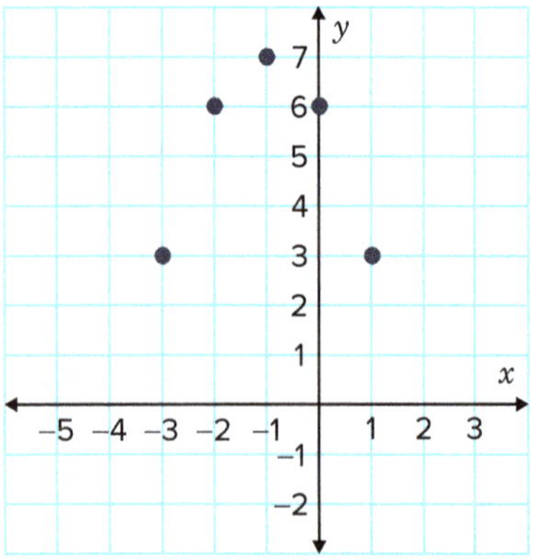

   b

x	−2	−1	0	1	2
y	0	$\frac{1}{2}$	1	$\frac{3}{2}$	2

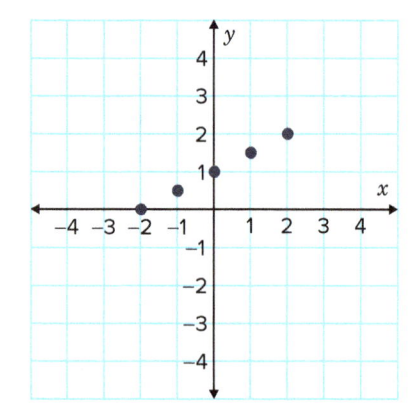

3 For large values of x, does the function $f(x) = 3x - 1$ or $g(x) = 3x^2 - 1$ increase at a faster rate?

4 The graphs of $f(x)$, $g(x)$ and $h(x)$ are shown. Use the graphs to complete the following:

  a Identify the graphs as exponential, linear, or quadratic.
  b Evaluate each function for $x = 2$.
  c Which function do you think will have the largest value at $x = 100$? Explain
  d Approximate the value of x for each function when the function value is 12.

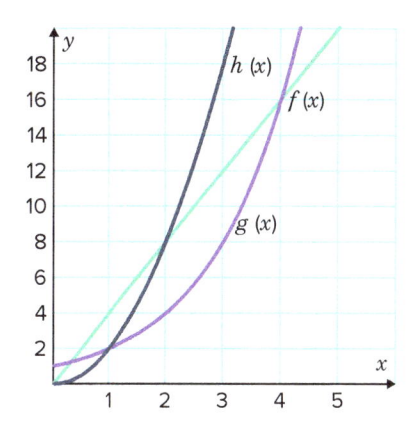

5 The population of two different bacteria, labeled J and K, are given by the shown table of values:

Bacteria J:

t (Time in days)	0	1	2	3	4
P (Population)	1	120	480	1080	1920

Bacteria K:

t (Time in days)	0	1	2	3	4
Q (Population)	1	50	2500	1.25×10^5	6.25×10^6

  a The population P of bacteria J at time t can be modeled using the general equation $P(t) = at^2$, where $a \geq 0$. By using the table of values, graph $P(t)$ for $t > 0$.
  b The population Q of bacteria K at time t can be modeled using the general equation $Q(t) = b^t$, where $b > 1$. By using the table of values, graph $Q(t)$ for $t > 0$.
  c Determine which population of bacteria is growing faster.

Let's practice

6 For each pair of functions, determine which has the greater y-intercept:

  a
  - Function 1: $y = 4x^2 + 6x + 3$
  - Function 2: $y = 4x + 6$

  b
  - Function 3: 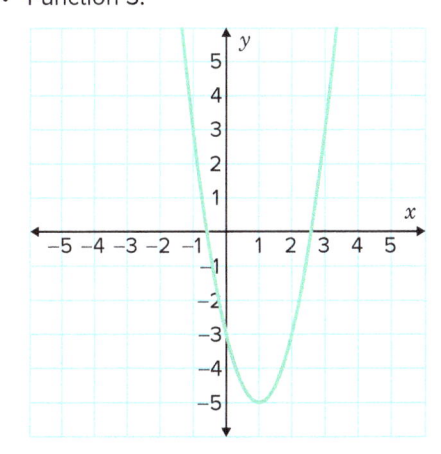
  - Function 4:

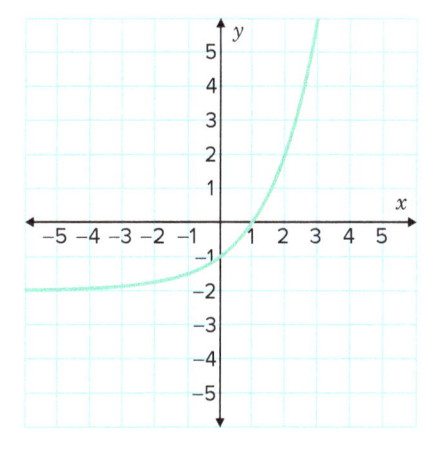

  c
  - Function 1: The line with a slope of 4 that crosses the y-axis at $(0, 6)$.
  - Function 2: The parabola given by the equation $y = x^2 + 4$.

d
- Function 3:

x	2	4	6
y	2	-2	-6

- Function 4:

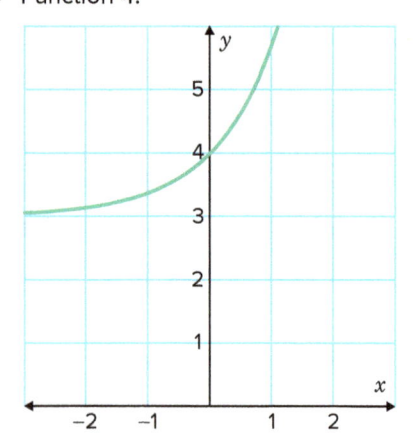

e
- Function 5:

x	2	4	6
y	19	35	51

- Function 6:
  $y = 4^x + 6$

7 Consider each pair of functions:
- Function A:
  $y = -4^x + 3$
- Function B:

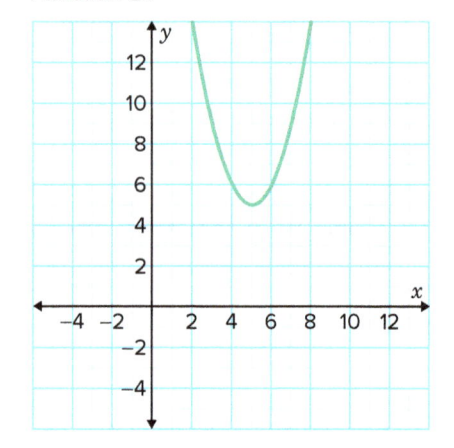

a Determine how many x-intercept(s) function A has.
b Determine how many x-intercept(s) function B has.
c Which function has a smaller value for $f(4)$?

8 The parabola C is given by $y = \dfrac{(x-3)^2}{9} + 7$ and the exponential function D is given by $y = -8^x + 1$.
a Graph the functions on the same coordinate plane.
b Determine which function has the lower y-intercept.

9 The parabola E is given by $y = 12(x - 1)^2 - 4$ and the exponential function F is given by $y = 3^x + 4$.
a Graph the functions on the same coordinate plane.
b State which function increases at a faster rate for very large values of x.

10 The parabola J is given by $y = -9x^2 + 20$.

The table shows the function values for exponential function K:

x	-2	-1	1	2	3
y	$\frac{5}{9}$	$\frac{5}{3}$	15	45	135

a Determine if the exponential function K is increasing or decreasing.
b Graph the functions J and K on the same coordinate plane.
c Determine what transformation we can apply to the function $y = 3^x$ to produce function K.
d Which function has a larger value of y when $x = 6$? What is the that y-value?

11 The line P is given by $y = -4 + \frac{4x}{3}$ and the parabola Q is given by $y = -(x-1)(x-4)$.

a Graph the line P and the parabola Q on the same coordinate plane.
b Identify how many times P and Q intersect.
c Identify which function has the higher function value at $x = 0$.

12 The table of values for the function P and for the function Q are provided.

Function P:

x	-2	-1	0	1	2
y	9	6	3	0	-3

Function Q:

x	0	1	2	3	4
y	6	3	2	3	6

a Determine what type of functions Function P and Function Q are.
b Graph the functions on the same coordinate plane.
c As x gets very large, determine which function will have the greater value.

Let's extend our thinking

13 Some friends decide to go camping for the weekend. They cannot all fit in one car so some of them catch a bus to the campground, which is 450 km from home. Those in the car started driving at 8:00 AM and arrived at the campground at 3:30 PM, driving at a constant speed. The bus also drives at a constant speed and takes the same route as the car. Its distance in kilometers (y) from home x hours after leaving is given by the equation $y = 71x$.

a Determine the speed of the car, in kilometers per hour.
b Determine the speed of the bus, in kilometers per hour.
c Determine which vehicle was traveling faster.

14 Consider the functions $f(x) = 2x$, $g(x) = 2x^2$ and $h(x) = 2^x$ for $x \geq 0$.

a Describe the pattern of how each of the functions increases. Explain how you identified the patterns.
b Compare how the three functions increase as x gets very large.

15 Two companies Crest Corporation and Mint Corporation are operating mines. Crest Corporation's operations are such that the total amount mined by the nth week is given by the equation $C = 10n^2$. The total amount mined by Mint Corporation over time is shown in the graph.

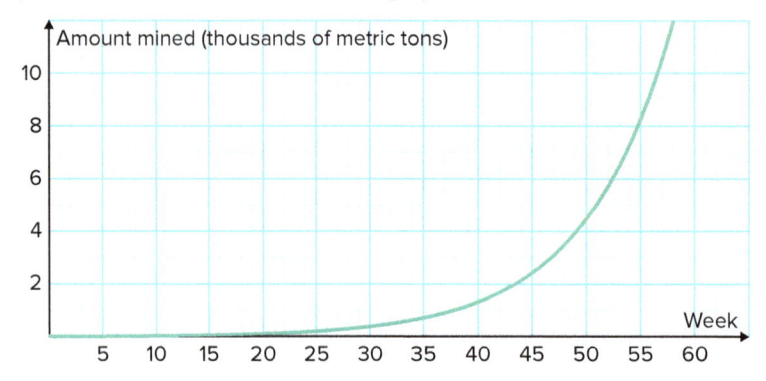

a If mining operations for both companies were to only last at most a year, determine which company will have mined the most minerals in that time.

b Determine if the two corporations will ever mine the same amount at the same time after the first week.

c At the point of intersection, the total quantity of minerals remaining in both mines is equal. If both mining companies continue to operate in the same way indefinitely, determine which company will exhaust their mine first. Explain your reasoning.

16 During a sudden viral outbreak, scientists must decide between two antivirals to try and control the situation. In a laboratory, they apply Adravil and Felicium to two samples of the virus, each containing 200 microbes.

They keep track of the number of microbes in each sample, and notice that the number of microbes using Adravil is increasing by a constant amount of 12 each hour. The table shows the results for Felicium.

Number of hours (t)	0	3	6	9
Number of microbes using Felicium	200	600	1800	5400

a Determine which antiviral will better control the number of microbes. Explain your choice.

b The new antiviral, Tretonin, shows the preliminary results:

Number of hours (t)	0	3	6	9
Number of microbes using Tretonin	200	202	208	218

If the trends from the first 9 hours continue in the future, determine which treatment will be better of the short-term, and which will be better over the long-term. Justify your answer.

Answers

7.05 Compare linear, quadratic, and exponential functions

What do you remember?

1. a Function 1
   b Function 3

2. a Quadratic
   b Linear

3. a $g(x)$

4. a Linear function: $f(x)$
      Exponential function: $g(x)$
      Quadratic function: $h(x)$
   b $f(2) = 8, g(2) = 4, h(2) = 8$
   c $g(x)$ because it is exponential it increases more quickly and will eventually surpass the linear and quadratic functions.
   d When $f(x) = 12, x = 3$.
      When $g(x) = 12, x \approx 3.5$.
      When $h(x) = 12, x \approx 2.5$.

5. a [Graph of $P(t)$]
   b [Graph of $Q(t)$]
   c The population of bacteria K is growing faster than the population of J.

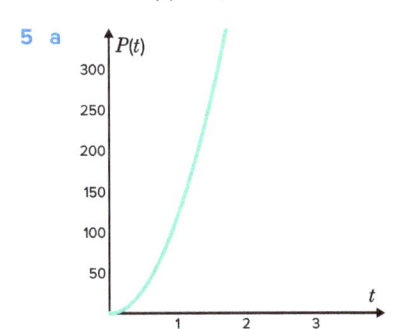

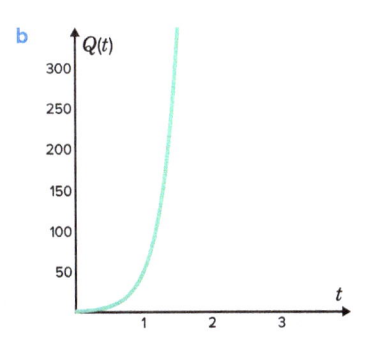

Let's practice

6. a Function 2
   b Function 4
   c Function 1
   d Function 3
   e Function 6

7. a 1
   b 0
   c Function A

8. a [Graph showing C and D]
   b Exponential function D.

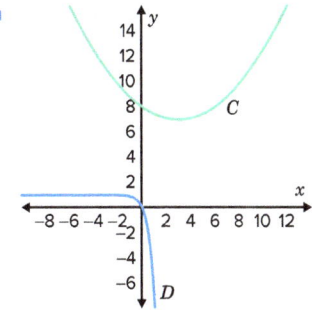

9. a [Graph showing E and F]
   b Function F.

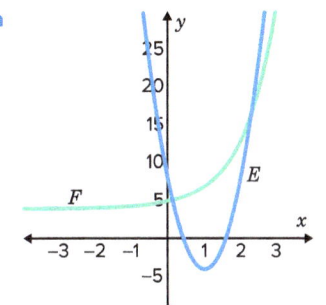

10. a Increasing
    b [Graph showing J and K]
    c Dilate $y = 3^x$ vertically by a factor of 5.
    d The exponention function K has the larger y-value of $y = 3645$.

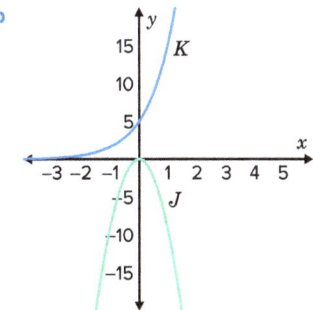

11. a [Graph showing P and Q]
    b Twice
    c They are equal at $x = 0$.

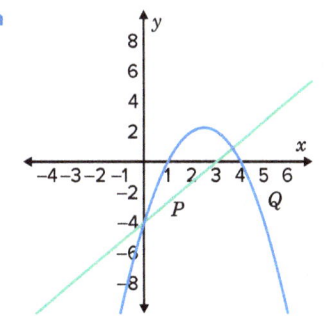

12 a Function P is a line and function Q is a parabola.

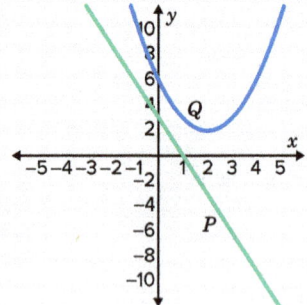

  b

  c Function Q

Let's extend our thinking

13 a 60 km/h   **b** 71 km/h
  c Bus

14 a We can fill out a table of values for each function and calculate how much they increase as x increases by 1.

x	$f(x)$	Increase in $f(x)$	$g(x)$	Increase in $g(x)$	$h(x)$	Increase in $h(x)$
0	0		0		1	
1	2	2	2	2	2	1
2	4	2	8	6	4	2
3	6	2	18	10	8	4
4	8	2	32	14	16	8
5	10	2	50	18	32	16
6	12	2	72	22	64	32
7	14	2	98	26	128	64

The linear function, $f(x)$, increases at a constant rate which is the slope of the line.

The quadratic function, $g(x)$, increases at a constantly increasing rate. The increase in $g(x)$ is increasing by 4 each time.

The exponential function, $h(x)$, is increasing at an exponentially increasing rate.

  b The graphs of $f(x)$ (green), $g(x)$ (blue) and $h(x)$ (purple) can help us to see how they increase comparatively.

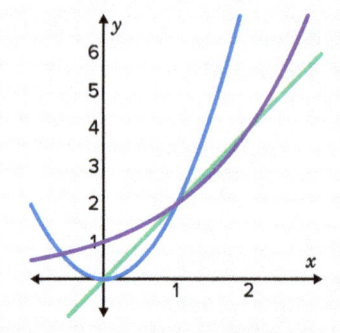

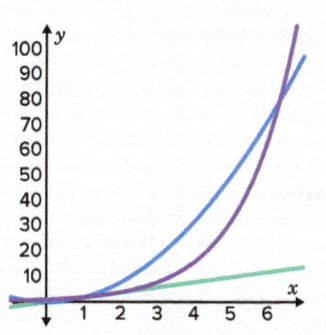

For very small values, $0 < x < 1$, linear function is generally increasing the most quickly and the exponential is increasing the slowest. For about $1 < x < 2.7$, the quadratic function increases more rapidly than the linear, and the exponential increases the slowest. For about $2.7 < x < 6.4$, the quadratic is increasing the most quickly, followed by exponential, and linear is the slowest. For large positive values of x, the exponential increases the most quickly, followed by quadratic, and linear is the slowest.

15 a Crest Corporation
  b Yes, they will.
  c Mint Corporation. The amount mined by Mint Corporation can be modeled by an exponential function, and that of Crest Corporation can be modeled by a quadratic function. Before the point of intersection the quadratic function was above the exponential function, but after the point of intersection the exponential function will increase much more rapidly than the quadratic function and so Mint Corporation will exhaust their mine first.

16 a Adravil, because the bacteria are only growing linearly, increasing at 12 per hour, while with Felicium they are growing exponentially, tripling every hour, which tends to infinity much quicker.
  b In the short-term, Tretonin is better than Adravil in the first 24 hours because it is growing by less than 12 microbes per hour, but the rate of growth is increase by 6 every three hours. In the long-term, Adravil is better than Tretonin because after 24 hours it will be increasing at a faster rate than Adravil as it is quadratic growth versus linear.

Topic 7 Assessment: Quadratic Functions

1 A function is represented by this rule.

> Three less than one-fourth the square of a number x is y.

Plot three points on the grid that are represented by this rule. Each point must have coordinates and integers.

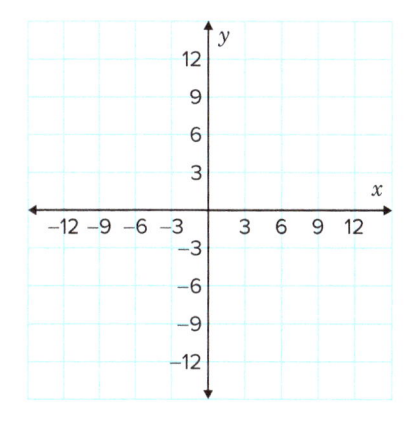

2 Which equation could represent a graph with x-intercepts of (8, 0) and (−3, 0)?

A $y = x^2 + 5x - 24$ B $y = x^2 - 5x + 24$ C $y = x^2 + 5x + 24$ D $y = x^2 - 5x - 24$

3 Select **every** function that has exactly one zero.

A $f(x) = 3(x - 4)$ B $f(x) = 4x^2 - 36$ C $f(x) = x^2 - 6x + 9$ D $f(x) = x^2 + 6x + 9$
E $f(x) = 2(x - 4)^2$ F $f(x) = x^2 - 2$

4 Select **every** function that has an x-intercept at 2.

A $f(x) = 3(x - 6)$ B $f(x) = x^2 - 36$ C $f(x) = x^2 - 6x + 8$ D $f(x) = x^2 + 8x + 16$
E $f(x) = 2(x + 2)^2$ F $f(x) = x^2 - 4$

5 A function f is described:
- $f(x) = (x - 4)^2 + 7$
- The domain of f is all real numbers greater than 2.

The range of f is all real numbers greater than or equal to

A 4   B 7   C 11   D 23

6 The graph of $h(x)$ shows the height of a bird diving to catch a fish, in meters, x seconds after beginning the dive.

a Find and interpret the y-intercept.
b Find and interpret $h(2)$.
c Find the coordinates of the vertex and describe what it means in context.
d State the domain of the function and describe what it represents in context.

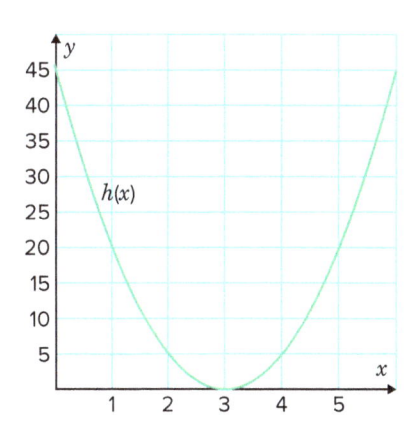

7 For each quadratic function:

i State the coordinates of the y-intercept.
ii Determine the axis of symmetry.
iii Determine the coordinates of the vertex.
iv State the domain and range.

a $y = -2(x - 1)(x - 5)$ b $y = (x - 2)^2 + 4$ c $y = -x^2 - 4x - 9$

8 For each of the following functions:
  i Graph the function.
  ii State the domain and range.
  a $f(x) = -(x + 3)(x - 5)$
  b $g(x) = 0.5(x + 3)^2 - 2$
  c $h(x) = 3x^2 - 12x + 12$
  d $p(x) = 12x^2 - 27$

9 For each function:
  i Describe the transformations from $y = x^2$.
  ii Sketch the graph.
  a $y = 3x^2 - 7$
  b $y = -\frac{1}{2}(x + 1)^2 + 4$

10 An object is thrown into the air. The height (in feet), h, reached by the object after t seconds is modeled by a quadratic function. The table of values shows some points on the function:

t	1	2	3	4	5	6	7	8
$h(t)$	7	12	15	16	15	12	7	0

  a Write the equation of the quadratic function in vertex form.
  b Determine and interpret $h(5.5)$.
  c Find the maximum height reached by the object.
  d Determine how long it will take the object to hit the ground.

11 Kyle throws a ball to his friend, Rick, from a height of 2.25 ft. The ball reach a maximum height of 18.25 ft, 1 second after being thrown.
  a Determine the equation in standard form that represents the situation.
  b Graph the corresponding parabola.
  c If Rick caught the ball after 2 seconds, determine the height of the catch.

12 For $f(x) = \dfrac{10(x + 7)^2}{49} - 3$ and $g(x) = 3(x - 5)(x - 4)$:
  a Determine which function has the lower minimum value.
  b Identify which parabola has the higher function value at $x = -2$.

13 Consider the following functions:

Function A:

x	−3	−2	−1	0	1	2	3
$a(x)$	−5	1	3	1	−5	−15	−29

Function B:

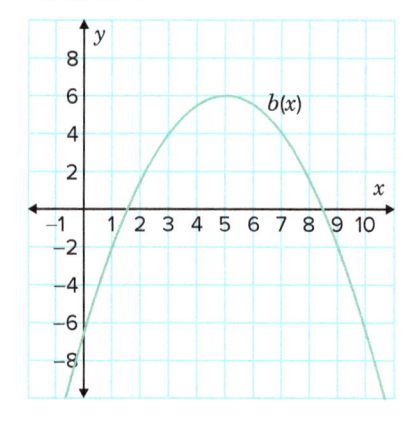

  a Determine which function has the higher maximum value.
  b Determine which function has a lower y-intercept.
  c Find $a(1)$.
  d Find x given that $b(x) = 4$.

14 Mary got a job offer from a company. The company offered her an income of $156 000 for the first year, and a projected income increase of $12 400 each year after that.

Alternatively, she can start her own business, where she estimates her initial annual income to be $52 000 for the first year, increasing by 38% each year after that.

  a Determine whether or not Mary's income for each situation could be modeled by a linear, quadratic, or exponential model.

  b Find her income after five years for both options.

15 The table shows the net profit (in thousands of dollars) over time of two restaurants where x is the time in weeks:

x	1	2	3	4	5	6	7
Restaurant A	2	4	8	16	32	64	128
Restaurant B	9	16	25	36	49	64	81

  a Determine the net profit for each restaurant in week 1.
  b Determine when the net profit of both restaurants will be equal.
  c Assuming both restaurants stay in business for a very long time, which restaurant would you expect to reach a profit of $1 million first? Explain your reasoning.

16 Prossy is starting a summer car wash business. Her revenue function represents the amount of money she makes in dollars for x car washes.

$$R(x) = -x^2 + 48x + 60$$

Prossy spent $68 on car wash supplies, and it costs her $7 per car for other related fees.

  a Write a function that represents Prossy's profit.
  b Prossy wants to make at least $400 this summer. Determine if she could make enough money based on her profit model. Explain your reasoning.
  c Draw a graph of $P(x)$.

Performance task

17 A diver dives off of a boat, following a parabolic path to her deepest point and returns to the surface. Let x represent her distance, in feet, from the boat and let y represent her depth, in feet. Each of the following quadratic equations represent the diver's path.

Standard form: $y = 0.15x^2 - 4.05x + 10.8$

Factored form: $y = 0.15(x - 3)(x - 24)$

Vertex form: $y = 0.15(x - 13.5)^2 - 16.537$

For each of the following, find the requested value and explain which form you used and why:

  a The deepest depth the diver reaches under the water.
  b The diver's depth when she is 10 ft away from the boat.
  c The height the diver jumped from.
  d The distance from the boat the diver was when she hit the water and when she came up for air.

18 A soccer ball is tossed into play by a player who is 6 ft tall. It has an initial upward velocity of 20 ft/s and the force of gravity causes the ball to change position by an additional -32 ft/s^2.

Description	Term in model
Starting height	
Travels upwards at 20 ft/s	
Pulled downward at 32 ft/s^2	$-16x^2$

Note: The standard model for projectile motion is given by $y = -\dfrac{gx^2}{2} + v_0 x + h$, where x is the time in seconds, v_0 is the initial upward velocity, h is the starting height, and g is 32 ft/s^2.

a   Complete the table above and write a quadratic equation to model this relationship.

b   What form of the quadratic equation will help you identify how long it takes the ball to reach its maximum height? Write the equation in that form and find the time.

c   What form of the quadratic equation will help you identify how long it takes the ball to hit the ground (assuming it doesn't come in contact with any players first)? Write the equation in that form and find the time.

d   What form of the quadratic equation will help you identify the height of the ball 0.5 seconds after it is thrown? Write the equation in that form and find the height.

e   Draw a graph of the function. What information from each form of the quadratic equation helped you to draw the graph?

Answers

Topic 7 Assessment: Quadratic Functions

1

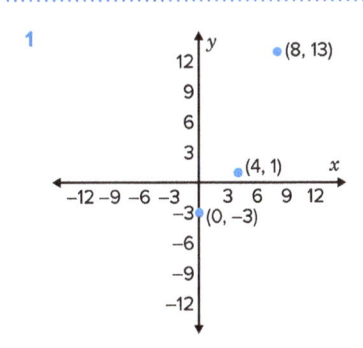

A.F.2c

2 D

A.F.2b

3 A, C, D, E

A.F.2b

4 A, C, F

A.F.2b

5 B

A.F.2b

6 a The y-intercept is $y = 45$. This means that initially the bird is 45 m above the water.

b $h(2) = 5$. This means that after 2 seconds the bird is 5 m above the water.

c $(3, 0)$

After 3 seconds, the bird has reached the water and caught the fish.

d Domain: $0 \leq x \leq 6$

The domain represents the seconds of the bird's dive. The dive lasted a total of 6 seconds.

A.F.2b, A.F.2g

7 a i $(0, 10)$ **ii** $x = 3$ **iii** $(3, 8)$

    iv Domain: All real values of x

    Range: $y \leq 8$

b i $(0, 8)$ **ii** $x = 2$ **iii** $(2, 4)$

    iv Domain: All real values of x

    Range: $y \geq 4$

c i $(0, -9)$ **ii** $x = -2$ **iii** $(-2, -5)$

    iv Domain: All real values of x

    Range: $y \leq -5$

A.F.2b

8 a i

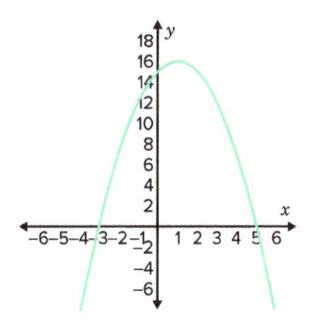

  ii Domain: All real values of x

  Range: $y \leq 16$

b i

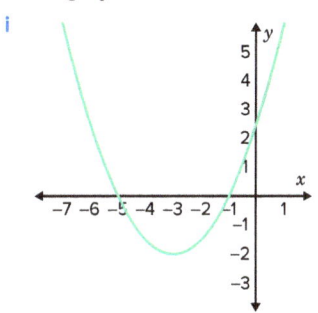

  ii Domain: All real values of x

  Range: $y \geq -2$

c i

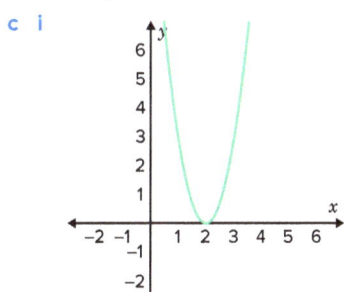

  ii Domain: All real values of x

  Range: $y \geq 0$

d i

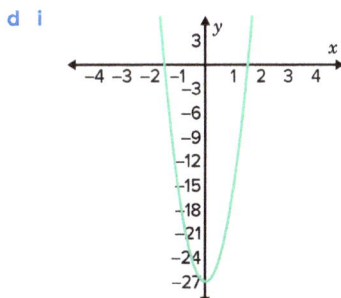

  ii Domain: All real values of x

  Range: $y \geq -27$

A.F.2b, A.F.2c, A.F.2d

9 a i Vertical dilation by a factor of 3 (stretch), vertical translation 7 units downwards

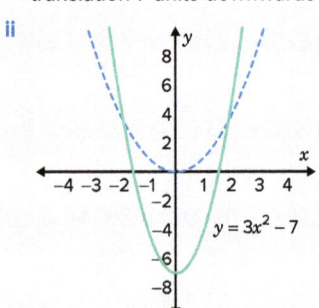

ii

$y = 3x^2 - 7$

b i Vertical dilation by a factor of $\frac{1}{2}$ (compression), reflection across the x-axis, vertical translation 4 units upwards, horizontal translation 1 unit to the left

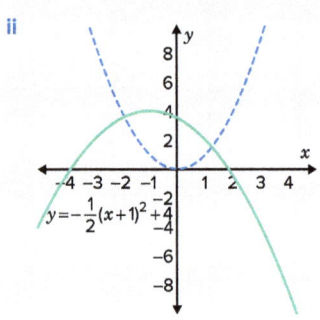

ii

$y = -\frac{1}{2}(x+1)^2 + 4$

A.F.2c

10 a $h(t) = -(t-4)^2 + 16$
   b $h(5.5) = 13.75$ ft. The height of the object after 5.5 seconds have elapsed is 13.75 ft.
   c 16 ft
   d 8 seconds

A.F.2b, A.F.2g

11 a $y = -16x^2 + 32x + 2.25$
   b

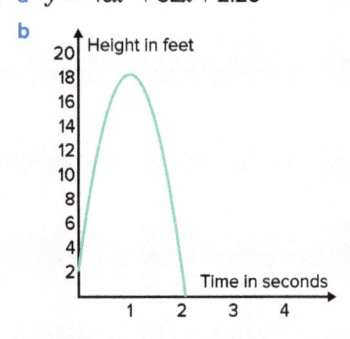

   c 2.25 ft

A.F.2c, A.F.2d, A.F.2g

12 a $f(x)$
   b $g(x)$

A.F.2b, A.F.2g, A.F.2h

13 a Function B
   b Function B
   c $a(1) = -5$
   d $b(3) - 4$ and $b(7) = 4$

A.F.2b, A.F.2g, A.F.2h

14 a Income in year n with the company is modeled by a linear function.

   Income in year n with her own business is modeled by an exponential function.

   b Company: Her income after five years would be $218 000.

   Business: Her income after five years would be $260 254.82.

A.F.1g, A.F.2g, A.F.2h

15 a Restaurant A: $2000, Restaurant B: $9000
   b The net profit of Restaurant A and Restaurant B will be equal after 6 weeks which is $64 000.
   c Restaurant A because the net profit is doubling each week while Restaurant B's net profit is increasing at a slower rate.

A.F.2g, A.F.2h

16 a $P(x) = R(x) - C(x)$
   $= (-x^2 + 48x - 60) - (7x + 68)$
   $= -x^2 + 41x - 8$

   b Prossy could make $400 because the maximum profit is $412.25 if she washes 20.5 cars.

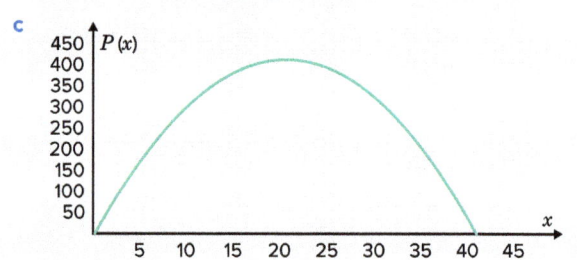

   c

A.F.2c, A.F.2g

Performance task

17 a −16.537 ft or 16.537 ft below the water. This is from the y-coordinate of the vertex and can be easily found from the vertex form.

   b −14.7 ft or 14.7 ft below the water. This can be found pretty easily from any of the forms by substituting 10 for x. Since we are substituting 10 the calculations from standard form are probably the simplest since the powers of 10 simplify the multiplication. Vertex form is the most complex to calculate mentally because of the squaring of a decimal.

   c 10.8 ft, this can be found from looking at the c value of the standard form equation since it is the y-intercept.

d   3 ft and 24 ft, these can be found from the factored form equation because each factor shows an x-intercept. In this case the x-intercepts are at $x = 3$ and $x = 24$. $x = 3$ is closer to the boat so that must be where she entered the water, making $x = 24$ the location where she came up for air.

A.F.2d, A.F.2g, A.EO.2e, MP2, MP5

18 a

Description	Term in model
Starting height	6
Travels upwards at 20 ft/s	$20t$
Pulled downward at 16 ft/s^2	$-16t^2$

Answers will vary. Forms can include:
$y = -16x^2 + 20x + 6$,
$y = -2(4x + 1)(2x - 3)$,
$y = -16(x - 0.625)^2 + 12.25$,
or another equivalent form of this same equation.

b   Vertex form: $y = -16(x - 0.625)^2 + 12.25$, 0.625 seconds.

c   Answers will vary. Any form is appropriate but standard form creates the most complex calculations while factored form is the least complex. 1.5 s.

d   Answers will vary. Any form is appropriate but vertex form creates the most complex calculations. 12 ft.

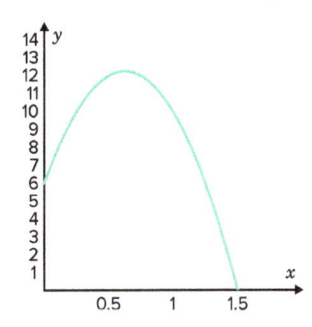

e

Standard form: y-intercept
Vertex form: coordinates of the vertex
Factored form: Positive x-intercept

A.F.2b, A.F.2d, A.F.2g, MP1, MP4, MP5

8 Quadratic Equations

> **Big ideas**
>
> A standard algorithm can be followed to solve a wide range of equations. This algorithm is reliable and useful in a variety of situations, but there is often a more efficient method that can be used based on the structure of the equation.

Chapter outline

8.01	Solve quadratics using graphs and tables (A.EI.3, A.F.2)	966
8.02	Solve quadratics by factoring (A.EI.3, A.F.2)	989
8.03	Solve quadratics using square roots (A.EI.3)	1006
8.04	Solve quadratics using the quadratic formula (A.EI.3)	1030
8.05	Solve quadratics using appropriate methods (A.EI.3)	1059

The arc that a whale makes when it leaps out of the water can be described by a quadratic equation. The highest point of the jump is the vertex of the parabola.

8. Quadratic Equations

Topic overview

Foundational knowledge

Evaluating standards proficiency

The skills book contains questions matched to individual standards. It can be used to measure proficiency for each.

Students should be proficient in these standards.

A.EI.1 — The student will represent, solve, explain, and interpret the solution to multistep linear equations and inequalities in one variable and literal equations for a specified variable.

A.EO.1 — The student will represent verbal quantitative situations algebraically and evaluate these expressions for given replacement values of the variables.

A.EO.2 — The student will perform operations on and factor polynomial expressions in one variable.

A.EO.4 — The student will simplify and determine equivalent radical expressions involving square roots of whole numbers and cube roots of integers.

A.F.1 — The student will investigate, analyze, and compare linear functions algebraically and graphically, and model linear relationships.

Big ideas and essential understanding

A standard algorithm can be followed to solve a wide range of equations. This algorithm is reliable and useful in a variety of situations, but there is often a more efficient method that can be used based on the structure of the equation.

8.01 — Quadratic equations can be solved using a variety of methods. Graphing or creating a table of values can be an efficient method when the equation has integer solutions.

8.02 — Quadratic equations can be solved using a variety of methods. Factoring can be an efficient method when the equation is factorable and is made up of constants and coefficients that are not large in value.

8.03 — Quadratic equations can be solved using a variety of methods. Using square roots can be an efficient method when the equation only has two terms and the constant term is a perfect square. Completing the square can be an efficient method for an equation that cannot be factored.

8.04 — Quadratic equations can be solved using a variety of methods. The quadratic formula can be used to solve any quadratic equation, but it is not always the most efficient method and is best used for equations that cannot be easily graphed or factored.

8.05 — There are many methods that can be used to solve a quadratic equation. The structure of the equation can give insight into which method might be the most efficient.

Standards

A.EI.3 — The student will represent, solve, and interpret the solution to a quadratic equation in one variable.

A.EI.3a — Solve a quadratic equation in one variable over the set of real numbers with rational or irrational solutions, including those that can be used to solve contextual problems.
8.01 Solve quadratics using graphs and tables
8.02 Solve quadratics by factoring
8.03 Solve quadratics using square roots
8.04 Solve quadratics using the quadratic formula
8.05 Solve quadratics using appropriate methods

A.EI.3b — Determine and justify if a quadratic equation in one variable has no real solutions, one real solution, or two real solutions.
8.01 Solve quadratics using graphs and tables
8.04 Solve quadratics using the quadratic formula

A.EI.3c — Verify possible solution(s) to a quadratic equation in one variable algebraically, graphically, and with technology to justify the reasonableness of answer(s). Explain the solution method and interpret solutions for problems given in context.
8.01 Solve quadratics using graphs and tables
8.02 Solve quadratics by factoring
8.03 Solve quadratics using square roots
8.04 Solve quadratics using the quadratic formula
8.05 Solve quadratics using appropriate methods

A.F.2 — The student will investigate, analyze, and compare characteristics of functions, including quadratic and exponential functions, and model quadratic and exponential relationships.

A.F.2c — Graph a quadratic function, $f(x)$, in two variables using a variety of strategies, including transformations $f(x) + k$ and $kf(x)$, where k is limited to rational values.
8.01 Solve quadratics using graphs and tables

A.F.2d — Make connections between the algebraic (standard and factored forms) and graphical representation of a quadratic function.
8.02 Solve quadratics by factoring

A.F.2g — For any value, x, in the domain of f, determine $f(x)$ of a quadratic or exponential function. Determine x given any value $f(x)$ in the range of f of a quadratic function. Explain the meaning of x and $f(x)$ in context.
8.01 Solve quadratics using graphs and tables
8.02 Solve quadratics by factoring

Future connections

A2.EI.2 — The student will represent, solve, and interpret the solution to quadratic equations in one variable over the set of complex numbers and solve quadratic inequalities in one variable.

A2.EI.5 — The student will represent, solve, and interpret the solution to an equation containing a radical expression.

A2.F.1 — The student will investigate, analyze, and compare square root, cube root, rational, exponential, and logarithmic function families, algebraically and graphically, using transformations.

A2.F.2 — The student will investigate and analyze characteristics of square root, cube root, rational, polynomial, exponential, logarithmic, and piecewise-defined functions algebraically and graphically.

Continuous Assessment

Measure standards proficiency with check-ins

Before starting a new topic, it's a great time to go online and have students complete a Skills Check-in to measure their readiness for the topic.

8.01 Solve quadratics using graphs and tables

Subtopic overview

Lesson narrative

In this lesson, students will explore the connections between the graphs and tables of equivalent equations. Students will analyze the structures of equivalent equations and the relationships between their graphs and tables in order to explain how equivalent equations can be used to solve quadratic equations of the form $f(x) = c$ for a real constant, c. By the end of the lesson, students will be able to interpret and represent contextual situations using quadratic equations, tables, or graphs and then, using the assistance of technology when necessary, solve them by finding intersections between linear constants and quadratic functions or by finding the zeros of equivalent expressions.

Learning objectives

Students: Page 450

> **After this lesson, you will be able to...**
> - use graphs and tables to solve quadratic equations.
> - graph quadratic equations using a table of values.
> - determine the number of solutions to a quadratic equation.

Key vocabulary

- equivalent equations
- solution (to an equation)
- zero (of a function)
- quadratic equation
- vertex
- root (of an equation)
- x-intercept

Essential understanding

Quadratic equations can be solved using a variety of methods. Graphing or creating a table of values can be an efficient method when the equation has integer solutions.

Standards

This subtopic addresses the following Virginia Standards of Learning for Mathematics standards.

Mathematical process goals

MPG1 — Mathematical Problem Solving

To integrate this goal, teachers can encourage students to approach the concept of quadratic functions as a problem-solving task. They can ask students to identify what they know about quadratic functions and what they need to know in order to graph them. When introducing the concept of solving a quadratic equation, teachers can present it as a problem to be solved and discuss various strategies for finding the solutions.

MPG4 — Mathematical Connections

To integrate this goal, teachers can help students make connections between their prior knowledge of quadratic functions and the new concept of solving quadratic equations. They can also help students see the connections between different methods of solving quadratic equations, such as using tables and using graphs. When presenting real-world problems, teachers can highlight the connections between the mathematical concepts and their practical applications.

MPG5 — Mathematical Representations

Teachers can integrate this goal by demonstrating how to represent quadratic functions and solutions to quadratic equations using tables and graphs. They can also encourage students to use these representations in their own problem-solving processes. When discussing the types of solutions to quadratic equations, teachers can guide students in representing these different possibilities visually on a graph. In solving contextual problems, teachers can help students represent the problem using a quadratic equation and then use graphs or tables to find the solutions.

Content standards

A.EI.3 — The student will represent, solve, and interpret the solution to a quadratic equation in one variable.

A.EI.3a — Solve a quadratic equation in one variable over the set of real numbers with rational or irrational solutions, including those that can be used to solve contextual problems.

A.EI.3b — Determine and justify if a quadratic equation in one variable has no real solutions, one real solution, or two real solutions.

A.EI.3c — Verify possible solution(s) to a quadratic equation in one variable algebraically, graphically, and with technology to justify the reasonableness of answer(s). Explain the solution method and interpret solutions for problems given in context.

A.F.2 — The student will investigate, analyze, and compare characteristics of functions, including quadratic and exponential functions, and model quadratic and exponential relationships.

A.F.2c — Graph a quadratic function, $f(x)$, in two variables using a variety of strategies, including transformations $f(x) + k$ and $kf(x)$, where k is limited to rational values.

A.F.2g — For any value, x, in the domain of f, determine $f(x)$ of a quadratic or exponential function. Determine x given any value $f(x)$ in the range of f of a quadratic function. Explain the meaning of x and $f(x)$ in context.

Prior connections

A.EI.1 — The student will represent, solve, explain, and interpret the solution to multistep linear equations and inequalities in one variable and literal equations for a specified variable.

A.EO.2 — The student will perform operations on and factor polynomial expressions in one variable.

A.EO.4 — The student will simplify and determine equivalent radical expressions involving square roots of whole numbers and cube roots of integers.

A.F.1 — The student will investigate, analyze, and compare linear functions algebraically and graphically, and model linear relationships.

Future connections

A2.EI.2 — The student will represent, solve, and interpret the solution to quadratic equations in one variable over the set of complex numbers and solve quadratic inequalities in one variable.

A2.F.1 — The student will investigate, analyze, and compare square root, cube root, rational, exponential, and logarithmic function families, algebraically and graphically, using transformations.

A2.F.2 — The student will investigate and analyze characteristics of square root, cube root, rational, polynomial, exponential, logarithmic, and piecewise-defined functions algebraically and graphically.

Continuous Assessment

🚩 Measure standards proficiency with check-ins

Once your students feel like they're proficient with a standard, it's a great time to go online and have them complete a Skills Check-in to measure their proficiency.

Lesson Preparation

Suggested review

Depending on your students' level of prior knowledge, consider revisiting the following lessons:

- **Algebra 1** — 7.01 Characteristics of quadratic functions
- **Algebra 1** — 7.03 Characteristics of quadratic functions

Tools

You may find these tools helpful:
- Graphing calculator
- Graph paper
- Spreadsheet application

Lesson supports

The following support may be useful for this lesson. More specific supports may appear throughout the lesson:

Concrete-Representational-Abstract (CRA) Approach
Targeted instructional strategies

Concrete: Engage students with physical manipulatives to model quadratic equations. Use a large floor grid or coordinate plane and have students physically place markers or sticky notes at points that satisfy a given quadratic equation. For example, provide students with numbered cards for x and have them calculate y using the equation $y = x^2$ or another simple quadratic. They can then place their markers at the corresponding points on the grid. This hands-on activity helps students see the shape of the parabola forming as they plot more points.

Representational: Transition to visual representations by guiding students to create tables of values for quadratic equations. Have them select values for x, calculate the corresponding y values, and record them in a table. Then, using graph paper, students can plot these points on a coordinate plane. Encourage them to connect the points smoothly to reveal the parabola's shape.

Abstract: Move to solving quadratic equations using algebraic symbols and methods. Teach students how to find the roots of the equation by setting $f(x) = c$ and solving for x. Introduce the quadratic formula and discuss how it can be used to find exact solutions. Encourage students to analyze the equation to determine the number of real solutions by calculating the discriminant. This abstract work connects to the graphs and tables they created, as the solutions correspond to the points where the graph intersects the x-axis.

Connecting the stages: Help students make connections between the physical activity, their graphs, and the algebraic equations. Discuss how the points they plotted with manipulatives match the points on their graphs and represent solutions to the equation.

Ask guiding questions like:
- "How does the shape we formed on the floor relate to the parabola on your graph?"
- "What do the points where the graph crosses the x-axis tell us about the solutions to the equation?"

By linking the concrete, representational, and abstract stages, students can better understand how each method represents the same mathematical concepts.

Student lesson & teacher guide

Solving quadratic equations using graphs and tables

Students explore solving quadratic equations using tables and graphs. The terms roots and zeros of the function are used to describe the x-intercepts. Students learn to solve quadratic equations by writing them in an equivalent form, where the y-value is set to zero, and then finding the roots.

Students: Pages 450–451

8.01 Solve quadratics using graphs and tables

After this lesson, you will be able to...
- use graphs and tables to solve quadratic equations.
- graph quadratic equations using a table of values.
- determine the number of solutions to a quadratic equation.

Solving quadratic equations using graphs and tables

A **quadratic equation** is a polynomial equation of degree 2. The solutions to a quadratic equation are the values that make the equation true. The solutions are also the ordered pairs that make up all of the points on the curve.

x	$x^2 = y$	Point
−2.8	$(-2.8)^2 = 7.84$	$(-2.8, 7.84)$
−2	$(-2)^2 = 4$	$(-2, 4)$
$-\frac{3}{2}$	$\left(-\frac{3}{2}\right)^2 = \frac{9}{4}$	$\left(-\frac{3}{2}, \frac{9}{4}\right)$
0	$(0)^2 = 0$	$(0, 0)$
$\frac{2}{3}$	$\left(\frac{2}{3}\right)^2 = \frac{4}{9}$	$\left(\frac{2}{3}, \frac{4}{9}\right)$
2.4	$(2.4)^2 = 5.76$	$(2.4, 5.76)$
3	$(3)^2 = 9$	$(3, 9)$

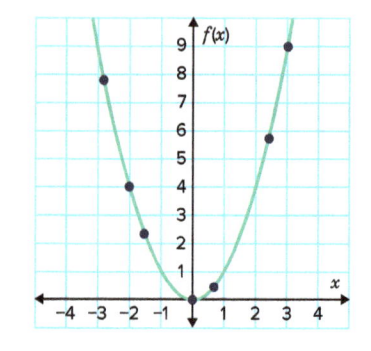

Some solutions to $f(x) = x^2$ are shown in the table

Solutions to $f(x) = x^2$ are any point on the curve

The solutions to a quadratic equation where y is equal to zero are the x-intercepts of the corresponding function. They are also known as the **roots of the equation** or the **zeros of the function**.

x	$f(x)$
−3	9
−2	4
−1	1
0	0
1	1
2	4
3	9

Solution to $x^2 = 0$ ⟶

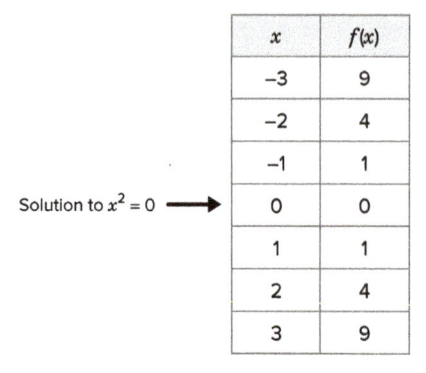

Table of $f(x) = x^2$

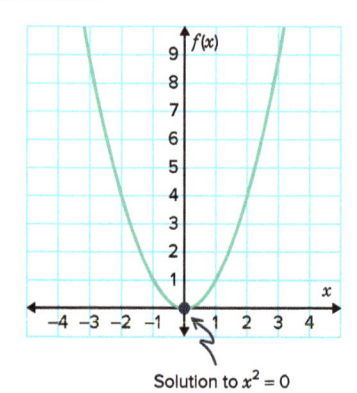

Solution to $x^2 = 0$

Graph of $f(x) = x^2$

---

970   Mathspace   Virginia SOL Algebra 1 Teacher Edition
mathspace.co

In the graph and table shown, we see $x = 0$ is the only solution. This is because $x = 0$ is the only value that makes $x^2 = 0$ true.

If we tried to find the solution to $x^2 = -2$ there would be no real solutions, because squaring any non-zero real number will give a positive result.

The **roots**, or **zeros**, in a quadratic function occur when $f(x) = 0$.

The method we will use to solve a problem such as $x^2 = 4$ is by creating an **equivalent equation** by rearranging it so it is equal to 0 and then identifying the x-intercepts.

$$x^2 = 4 \quad \text{Given equation}$$
$$x^2 - 4 = 0 \quad \text{Subtract 4 from both sides}$$

Next, we can replace the 0 in the equation with y to get $y = x^2 - 4$. The graph of this equation is the graph of $y = x^2$ shifted down 4 units so the graph of $y = x^2 - 4$ is:

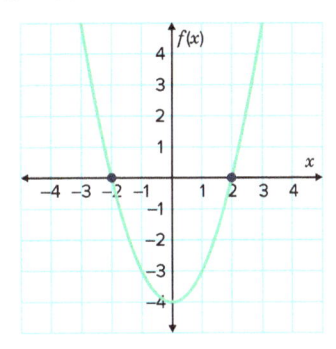

We can see that the graph crosses the x-axis at -2 and 2, so the solutions to $x^2 = 4$ are -2 and 2.

We can check this using substitution:

$$(-2)^2 = 4 \text{ and } (2)^2 = 4$$

We can follow this process to solve any quadratic equation graphically. In other words, for any function $f(x) = c$, for some real number constant, c, we can write the equivalent equation $f(x) - c = 0$, and find the x-intercepts of $g(x) = f(x) - c$ to solve for x.

A quadratic equation can have one, two or no real **solutions**.

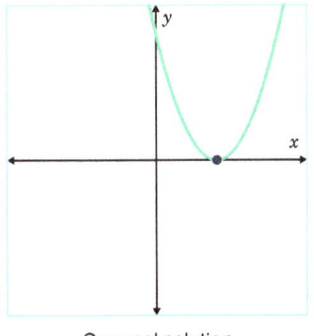

| One real solution | Two real solutions | No real solutions |

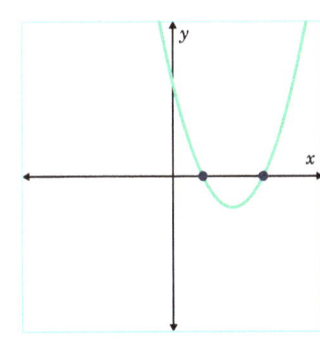

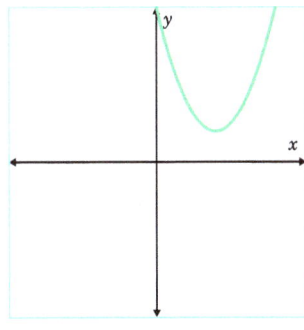

Think about the nature of the zeros
Targeted instructional strategies

Before attempting to find the zeros or roots of a quadratic equation, ask students whether they can determine if the equation has any x-intercepts or not.

Use a few examples to demonstrate to students that a quadratic equation will only have real zeros if:
- The parabola opens upwards and has a vertex below the x-axis, or
- The parabola opens downwards and has a vertex above the x-axis, or
- The vertex is on the x-axis

This can be checked by finding the coordinates of the vertex and comparing them to the sign of the leading coefficient.

Compare and connect
English language learner support

Students may struggle with the subtle differences between the vocabulary of "solutions", "x-intercepts", and "zeros". Use the two graphs and key features below to highlight the differences.

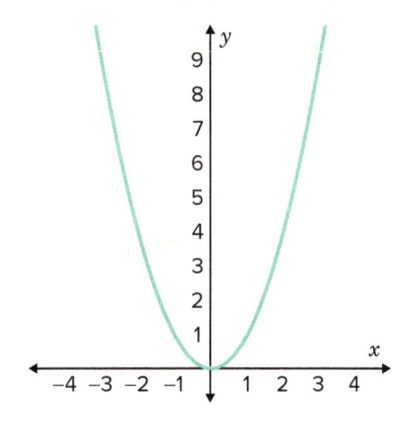

Equation: $x^2 = 9$

x	−3	−2	−1	0	1	2	3
y	9	4	1	0	1	4	9

- Solutions of $x = -3$ and $x = 3$
- x-intercept at $x = 0$
- Zero at $x = 0$

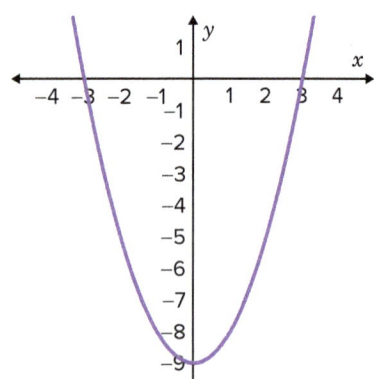

Equation: $x^2 - 9 = 0$

x	−3	−1	0	1	3
y	0	−8	−9	−8	0

- Solutions of $x = \pm 3$
- x-intercepts at $x = \pm 3$
- Zeros at $x = \pm 3$

Give students time in pairs to discuss comparisons between the two. Encourage students to connect the similiarities and differences between the vocabulary terms through conversation with their peers. Some guiding questions include:
- What differences do you notice between the graphs?
- What differences do you notice between the equations and the key features?
- Are the solutions always the zeros or x-intercepts?

Then as a class, discuss the connections between solutions, x-intercepts, and zeros. Summarize the findings of your discussion by highlighting thee differences between these terms.
- Solutions are any values that make an equation true.
- Zeros are solutions to the equation when it is set equal to zero.
- x-intercepts are the solution when $y = 0$.

Support perseverance - move through a frustrating point
Student with disabilities support

Since students do not know any algebraic methods for solving quadratic equations at this stage, it can be easy to get frustrated with methods that are imprecise or unreliable. For example, the table of values method may take a very long time or not work if there are no real solutions.

Give students guidance on where to start when solving problems in order to minimize frustration from a lack of direction, while also being sure to set problems which can be solved relatively efficiently.

Intercepts are not solutions to all quadratic equations
Address student misconceptions

It is important for students to recognize that "solutions" is not synonymous with "x-intercepts". Students should only look for the intercepts if the equation is set equal to zero. Rather than "x-intercepts", it would be better to only refer to them as "zeros" as this implies the equation must be set equal to zero first.

To reinforce this idea, teachers can provide a visual example of a graph that is not equal to zero and one that is. Use the two graphs to highlight the differences and make connections to the solutions.

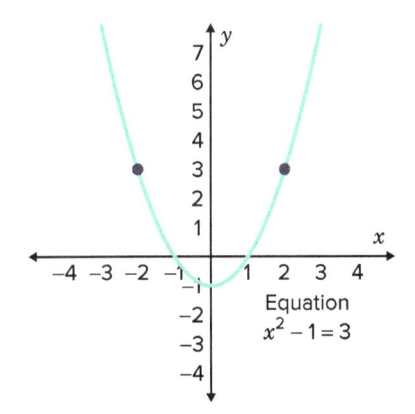

Equation
$x^2 - 1 = 3$

Solutions are $x = 2$ and $x = -2$

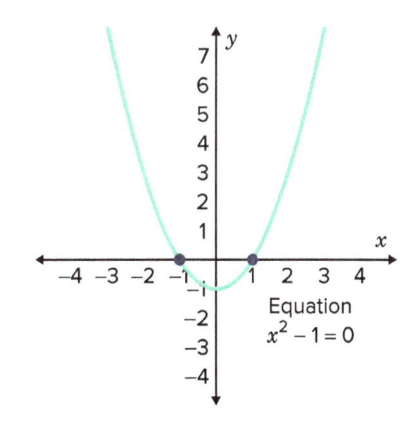

Equation
$x^2 - 1 = 0$

Solutions are $x = 1$ and $x = -1$

Examples
Students: Page 452

Example 1

Solve the equation $2x^2 = 18$.

Create a strategy

We can write an equivalent equation set equal to zero, and then use a table to find the zeros of the new function.

Apply the idea

If we set this equation equal to zero, we would get

$2x^2 = 18$ Given equation

$2x^2 - 18 = 0$ Subtraction property of equality

When building a table, we want to choose values within a suitable range so we don't have to do too many calculations. Start by finding the values in the domain $-4 \leq x \leq 4$. If the y-value (also called the function value) is zero for any of these x-values, then we have found a solution to the corresponding equation.

In the table, we are looking for the entries where $y = 0$.

x	-4	-3	-2	-1	0	1	2	3	4
y	14	0	-10	-16	-18	-16	-10	0	14

We can see the equation has solutions of $x = -3$, $x = 3$, which we can also write as $x = \pm 3$.

Reflect and check

We can see that the table of y-values has both positive and negative values. Whenever this is the case for a function of the form $f(x) = ax^2 + bx + c$, we know that the equation $0 = ax^2 + bx + c$ must have two real solutions, and the corresponding parabola will have two x-intercepts.

Purpose

Show students how to use an equivalent equation to solve a problem and demonstrate how a table can be used to find the zeros of a quadratic equation.

Expected mistakes

Students may substitute 0 in for x instead of finding the values that make y equal to 0. Or, students may only find one solution and not look for a second solution. Remind students to visualize the shape and orientation of the graph. Ask them to think about what it means to find $y = 0$ on the graph.

Reflecting with students

Ask students to describe other ways they could solve this problem. They could make a table for $y = 2x^2$ and then find where $y = 18$. They could divide both sides of the equivalent equation by 2 to get $x^2 - 9 = 0$ and recognize this as a difference of squares and factor the equation.

Visualizing quadratic equations   use with Example 1
Student with disabilities support

For students who struggle with abstract concepts, visualizing quadratic equations can be helpful. Start by setting the given equation equal to zero and creating a table of values. This table can then be used to plot the equation on a graph.

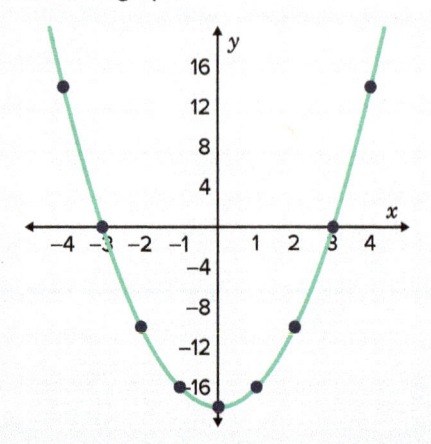

Discuss with students how the solutions of an equation that is equal to 0 correspond to the points where the parabola intersects the x-axis.

These points are also known as the zeros of the equation.

Encourage students to use this visual approach whenever they are solving quadratic equations. It can help them better understand the concept of solutions and how to find them.

Students: Pages 450–453

Example 2

Consider the function $y = (x - 2)^2 - 9$.

a Draw a graph of the function.

Create a strategy

The function is given in vertex form so we know the vertex is at $(2, -9)$. We can substitute $x = 0$ to find the y-intercept at $(0, -5)$. We can find other points on the curve by substituting in other values, and by filling a table of values.

Apply the idea

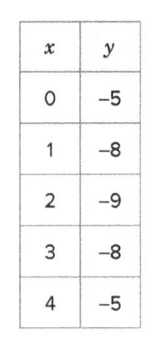

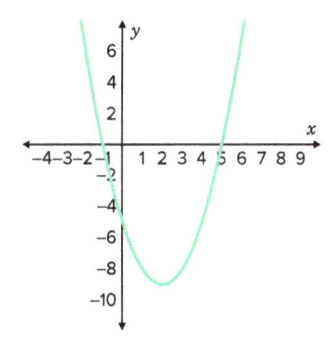

x	y
0	−5
1	−8
2	−9
3	−8
4	−5

Reflect and check

It is important when drawing graphs to clearly show the key features such as the **vertex** and the intercepts by choosing appropriate scales for the axes.

Purpose

Students demonstrate that they can use vertex form to create a graph and include all the key features of a quadratic function.

Reflecting with students

Ask students how they could draw the graph if they did not recognize the equation was in vertex form. Remind them that, for any function, we can always create a table of values to find points and plot the curve.

8.01 Solve quadratics using graphs and tables   975

mathspace.co

Students: Page 453

b Determine the solution(s) to the equation $0 = (x - 2)^2 - 9$.

Create a strategy
We can find the solution(s) by looking at the graph from part (a) and identifying where it crosses the x-axis.

Apply the idea
The solutions to the equation can be found at the x-intercepts of the graph we drew in part (a).

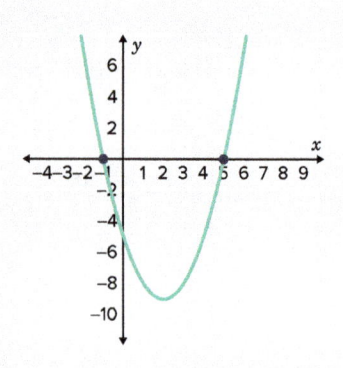

The solutions are $x = -1$ and $x = 5$.

Reflect and check
We can verify the solutions by substituting each one into the equation for x and substituting 0 for y. If the right side of the equation evaluates to 0 then it is a solution.

First, let's check the solution $x = -1$

$0 = (x - 2)^2 - 9$	Original equation
$0 = (-1 - 2)^2 - 9$	Substitute in $x = -1$
$0 = (-3)^2 - 9$	Simplify inside parenthesis
$0 = 9 - 9$	Evaluate the square
$0 = 0$	Subtract

$0 = 0$ is a true statement, so $x = -1$ is a solution to $0 = (x - 2)^2 - 9$.

Now, let's check our other solution, $x = 5$

$0 = (x - 2)^2 - 9$	Original equation
$0 = (5 - 2)^2 - 9$	Substitute in $x = 5$
$0 = (3)^2 - 9$	Simplify inside parenthesis
$0 = 9 - 9$	Evaluate the square
$0 = 0$	Subtract

$0 = 0$ is a true statement, so $x = 5$ is also a solution to $y = (x - 2)^2 - 9$.

Purpose
Show students that this is an equivalent expression to the previous equation, set equal to 0, and that they can find the roots to solve.

Expected mistakes
Students may give their answer in coordinates, $(-1, 0)$ and $(5, 0)$, which does not answer the question. Ask students what form the solutions to the equation should be in.

Finding non-integer solutions using technology
Targeted instructional strategies

use with Example 2

As an extension for advanced learners, ask them to find the solution(s) to the equation $5 = (x - 2)^2 - 9$. Encourage them to use computational thinking and consider tools like spreadsheets. Here is a possible solution:

1. Open a spreadsheet program, such as GeoGebra, GoogleSheets, Excel, Desmos, etc.

2. Fill in headings

	A	B	C
1	x	(x-2)^2-9	
2			

3. Use the graph from part (b), notice that $y = 5$ between $-2 < x < -1$ and $5 < x < 6$. Start by estimating the negative solution where $-2 < x < -1$.

   Fill in the cells using a formula and then dragging down. Emphasize that an equals sign must preceed the formula.

	A	B	C
1	x	(x-2)^2-9	
2	-2	=(A2-2)^2-9	
3	=A2+0.1		

4. Fill down

	A	B	C
1	x	(x-2)^2-9	
2	-2	7	
3	-1.9	6.21	
4	-1.8	5.44	
5	-1.7	4.69	

5. Refine to the interval of $-1.8 < x < -1.7$

	A	B	C
1	x	(x-2)^2-9	
2	-1.8	5.44	
3	=A2+0.01	5.3641	
4	-1.78	5.2884	
5	-1.77	5.2129	
6	-1.76	5.1376	
7	-1.75	5.0625	
8	-1.74	4.9876	

6. Refine to the interval of $-1.75 < x < -1.74$

	A	B	C
1	x	(x-2)^2-9	
2	-1.75	5.0625	
3	=A2+0.001	5.055001	
4	-1.748	5.047504	
5	-1.747	5.040009	
6	-1.746	5.032516	
7	-1.745	5.025025	
8	-1.744	5.017536	
9	-1.743	5.010049	
10	-1.742	5.002564	
11	-1.741	4.995081	

7. Estimate the solution to be in the interval $-1.742 < x < -1.741$.

8. Repeat for the positive solution. Or to be more efficient use symmetry.

Students: Page 454

Example 3

The graph shows the path of a rock after it has been thrown from a cliff where x represents the time in seconds and $f(x)$ represents the height of the rock in feet.

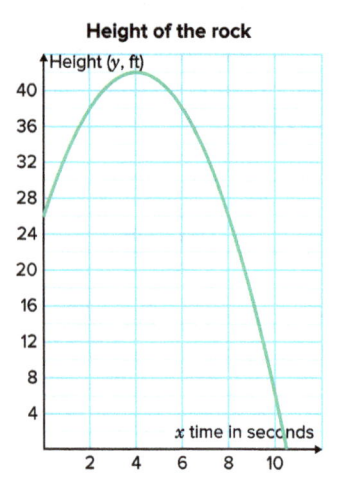

Height of the rock

a   Find and interpret $f(8)$.

Create a strategy

We are looking for the value of $f(x)$, the height of the rock, when the value of x is 8 seconds.

Apply the idea

Use the graph to identify the value of $f(x)$ when $x = 8$

Height of the rock

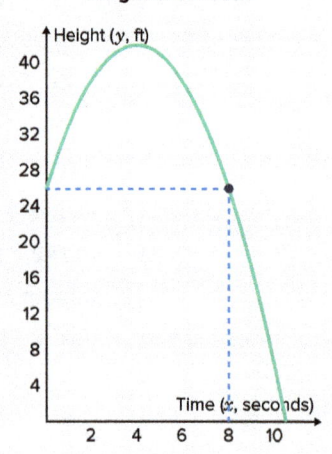

So, 8 seconds after being thrown the rock has reached a height of 26 feet.

Purpose

Show students how to interpret a point on a graph in a real-world context.

Reflecting with students

Remind students that $f(x) = y$. So, when we are given $f(8)$, we are really being given an x-value. When given notation like this, they must solve for y, by finding the value of y when $x = 8$.

Students: Page 455

    b Determine when the rock has a height of 38 feet.

Create a strategy
We are looking for when the rock reaches a height of 38 feet. In other words, we are given the height, the value of $f(x)$ and we are looking for the time, the x-values.

Apply the idea
Notice that there are 2 places where the graph has a y-value of 38. The solutions will be the x-values of those 2 points.

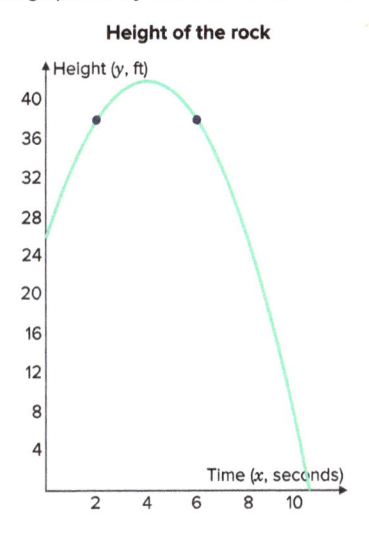

Height of the rock

[Graph showing a downward-opening parabola with Height (y, ft) on vertical axis and Time (x, seconds) on horizontal axis. Two points marked at y = 38, at x = 2 and x = 6.]

The rock reaches a height of 38 feet after 2 seconds and 6 seconds.

Reflect and check
We can use the vertex to determine the equation of this graph. The vertex is at (4, 42). The parabola is facing downward, so we know a will be negative. We can use the vertex form to write an equation:

$$y = a(x - 4)^2 + 42$$

We can plug in the coordinates for another known point, like the y-intercept, which is (0, 26) and then solve for a. In this case, the result will be $a = -1$. We just found the solutions to the corresponding equation $-(x - 4)^2 + 42 = 38$.

Purpose
Given the graph of a quadratic function in a context, show students how to use the mathematical model to find solutions to a contextual problem.

Reflecting with students
Ask students to consider why we look at $y = 38$ rather than looking at the x-intercepts. Students should be encouraged to consider the context of the problem and what the variables x and y represent. Relate the graph to the context and highlight that y represents height, and the known value in this part, which helps them to answer the given question.

Students: Page 455

c Estimate the viable solution. Explain why only one solution is viable.

Create a strategy

A viable solution is a solution that makes sense in the context of the problem. Keep in mind that time cannot be negative.

Apply the idea

There is a positive x-intercept at approximately (10.5, 0). This means the rock hits the ground after about (10.5, 0) seconds.

Looking at the graph we can see the other x-intercept is to the left of the origin which would represent a negative value for time which is not possible. This is why there is only one viable solution.

Purpose

To show students how to estimate a viable solution from a graph and determine the number of viable solutions based on the context of the problem.

Students: Page 456

Example 4

Identify the number of real solutions each quadratic function has.

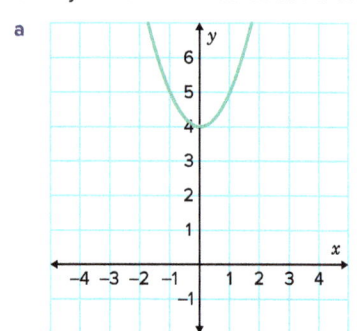

a

Create a strategy

Real solutions correspond with x-intercepts. How many x-intercepts does this function have?

Apply the idea

This quadratic never crosses the x-axis so there are no x-intercepts.

The function has 0 real solutions.

Purpose

To show students that a quadratic function has no real solutions if its graph does not intersect the x-axis.

Students: Page 456

b

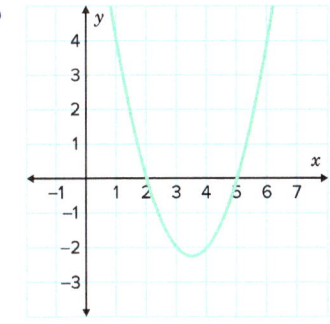

Create a strategy
Real solutions correspond with x-intercepts. How many x-intercepts does this function have?

Apply the idea
The quadratic crosses the x-axis in two different spots.

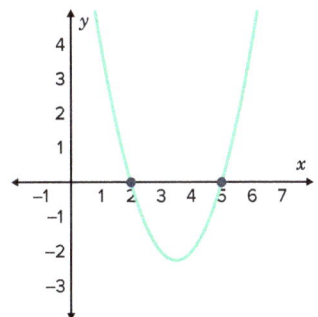

Reflect and check
We can determine from the graph the exact value of the two real solutions. The solutions are $x = 2$ and $x = 5$.

This quadratic has two real solutions.

Purpose
To show students that the number of real solutions corresponds to the number of x-intercepts shown on the graph of the function.

Students: Page 457

> **Idea summary**
>
> We solve a quadratic equation by creating an equivalent equation by making your equation set equal to 0.
>
> The solutions to a quadratic equation are any values that make the equation true.
>
> If the equation is equal to 0, the solutions are called **roots** of the equation or **zeros** of the function. These correspond to the x-intercepts of the graph.
>
> For any function $f(x) = c$, for some real number constant, c, we can write the equivalent equation $f(x) - c = 0$, and find the x-intercepts of $g(x) = f(x) - c$ to solve for x.

Practice

Students: Pages 457–460

What do you remember?

1 Using the given tables, find the solutions to the following equations:

a $x^2 + 7x + 12 = 0$

x	−6	−5	−4	−3	−2	−1
y	6	2	0	0	2	6

b $3x^2 − 27 = 0$

x	−4	−3	−2	−1	0	1	2	3	4
y	21	0	−15	−24	−27	−24	−15	0	21

2 Rewrite each equation so that it is equal to zero:

a $x^2 + 8x + 12 = 5$
b $4x^2 = 4$
c $(x − 3)^2 = 7$
d $6x^2 = 2x − 9$

3 Using the given graphs, find the solutions to the following equations:

a $x^2 + 2x − 8 = 0$

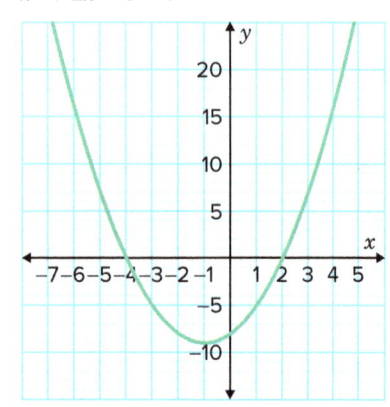

b $2x^2 − 12x + 16 = 0$

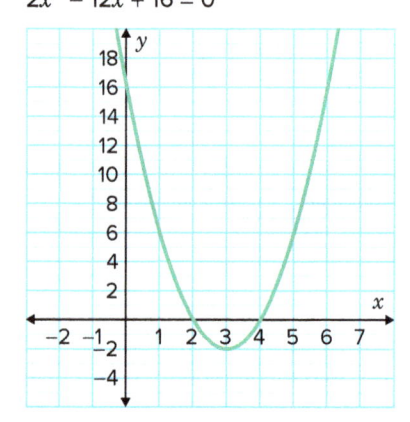

4 For the function $y = x^2 + 10x + 21$:

a Copy and complete the table of values.

x	−8	−7	−6	−5	−4	−3	−2
y							

b Draw the graph of the equation.

c Use the models from parts (a) and (b) to find:

i The value of x when $y = −4$.

ii The value of x when $y = 5$.

5 Determine the number of real solutions each quadratic function has:

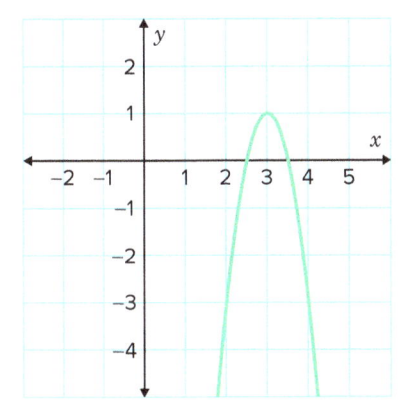

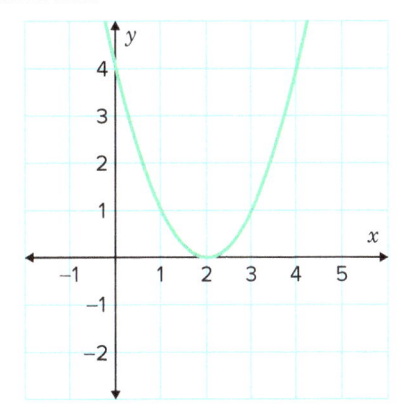

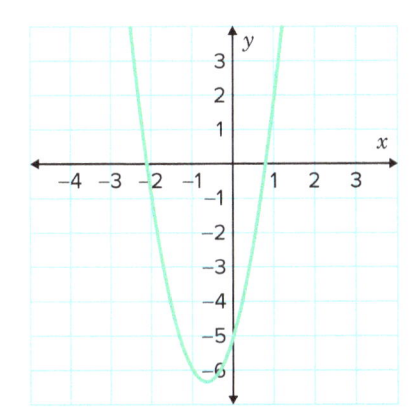

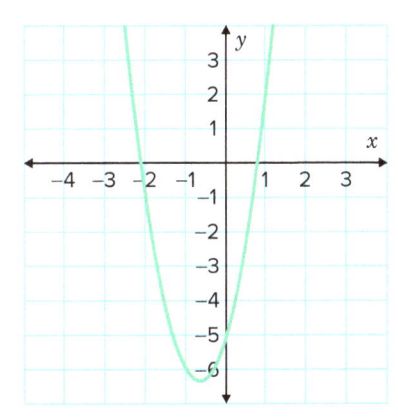

a

b

c

d

Let's practice

6 For each of the following quadratic functions:
  i Complete the table of values.
  ii Set each function equal to zero and use the table to determine the solution(s) to the equation.

a $y = -\dfrac{1}{2}x^2$

x	-2	-1	0	1	2
y					

b $y = -2x^2$

x	-1	0	1	2	3
y					

c $y = -2x^2 + 2$

x	-2	-1	0	1	2
y					

d $y = (x-2)^2 - 4$

x	0	1	2	3	4
y					

e $y = (x-5)(x-1)$

x	0	1	2	3	4	5	6
y							

f $y = x^2 - x - 2$

x	-2	-1	0	1	2	3
y						

7 Solve the following equations by drawing a graph of the corresponding function:
  a $x^2 - 15x + 54 = 0$
  b $-(x+5)^2 + 9 = 0$
  c $x^2 - 15x + 50 = 0$
  d $(x-5)^2 = 4$
  e $(x-3)(x+2) = 0$
  f $(x-1)^2 = 0$

8 For each of the following quadratic equations:
  i Draw the graph of the corresponding function.
  ii Use the graph to determine the solution(s) to the equation.

  a $0 = x^2$
  b $0 = -x^2 + 9$
  c $3x^2 = 3$
  d $0 = -(x-3)^2$
  e $x^2 + 12x = -32$
  f $(x-3)(x-2) = 0$
  g $2x^2 - 2x = 12$
  h $(x-5)^2 = 0$

9 A compass is accidentally thrown upward and out of an air balloon at a height of 100 feet. The height, y, of the compass at time x, in seconds, is given by the equation:

$$y = -20x^2 + 80x + 100$$

  a Graph the relationship $y = -20x^2 + 80x + 100$.
  b Find the time it takes for the compass to hit the ground.
  c When will the compass be 160 feet high?

10 A frisbee is thrown upward and away from the top of a hill that is 120 yards tall. The height, y, of the frisbee at time x in seconds is given by the equation $y = -10x^2 + 40x + 120$. This equation is graphed.

  a Determine when the frisbee reaches a height of 120 yards.
  b Determine how many seconds it takes for the frisbee to hit the ground.
  c Determine the height reached by the frisbee after 2 seconds.
  d Verify your answer to part (b) by substituting values into the equation.

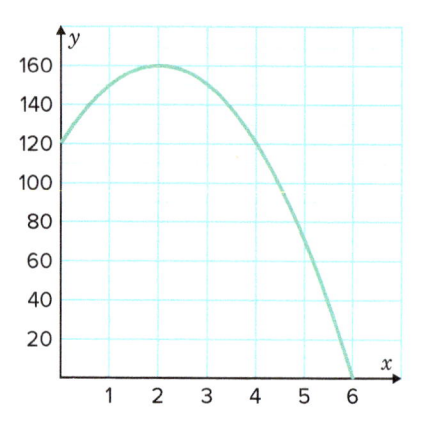

11 Beth throws a pebble vertically upwards. After t seconds, its height h feet above the ground is given by the formula $h = 18t - 2t^2$. This function has been graphed as shown.

  a Explain what the point at (4.5, 40.5) represents in context of the problem.
  b Find the values of t where the graph of h intercepts the horizontal axis.
  c Explain what the intercepts you found in part (b) represent in context of the problem.
  d Identify when the pebble is 36 feet above the ground.

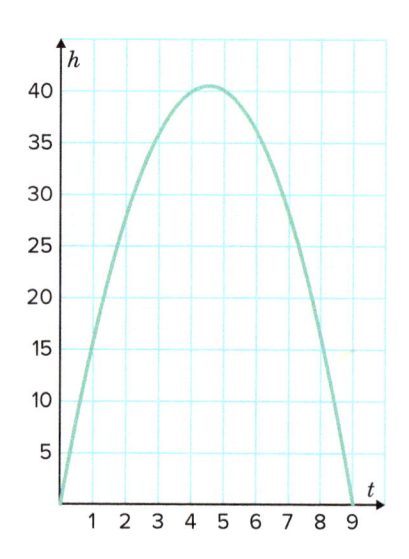

12 Use the given table to answer the following:

x	−3	−2	−1	0	1	2	3
y	9	4	1	0	1	4	9

  a Find $f(-2)$
  b Find x when $f(x) = 1$
  c Find the domain when the range is {9, 0}.
  d Find the range when the domain is {−2, 2, 3}.

984 Mathspace   Virginia SOL Algebra 1 Teacher Edition
mathspace.co

13 Use the graph below to answer the following.
   a   Find $f(-1)$
   b   Find x when $f(x) = 0$
   c   Find the domain when the range is $\{3, 4\}$.
   d   Find the range when the domain is $\{1, -1, -2\}$.

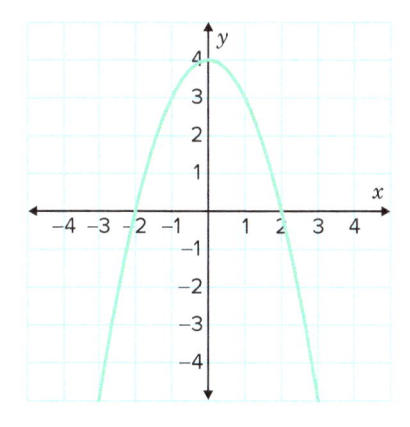

Let's extend our thinking

14 An object is released 900 meters above ground and falls freely. The distance the object is from the ground is modeled by the formula $d = 900 - 4.9t^2$, where d is the distance in meters that the object falls and t is the time elapsed in seconds.

Javier graphed the given equation, the line $d = 450$, and the point of intersection as shown below.

   a   Explain the point (9.583, 450) in context of the problem.
   b   Use the graph to estimate how many seconds it takes for the object to reach a height of 0.
   c   Explain how you could find a more precise answer to part (b). Find a more precise answer.

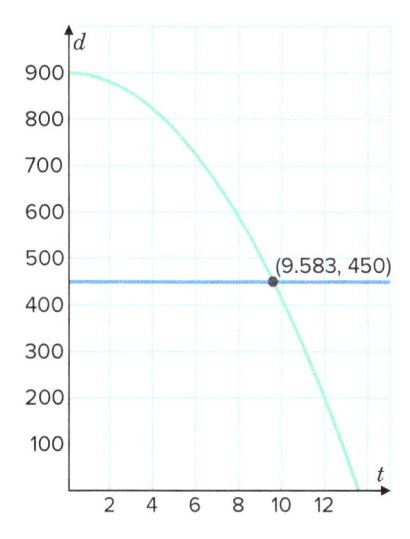

15 The kinetic energy E of a moving object is given by $E = \frac{1}{2}mv^2$, where m is its mass in kilograms and v is its speed in meters per second.
   a   Graph this equation for a vehicle with a mass of 1400 kg using a calculator or other technology.
   b   Use the graph to estimate the velocity when the kinetic energy is 137 200 J.

16 The formula for the surface area of a sphere is $S = 4\pi r^2$, where r is the radius in centimeters.
   a   Graph the relationship $S = 4\pi r^2$.
   b   Use your graph to estimate the surface area of a sphere with radius 5.5 cm.
   c   Use your graph to estimate the radius of a sphere with a surface area of 150 cm^2.

17 A rectangle has width a, height b, and area A. The graph shows the possible values of the area A (vertical axis) plotted against the width a (horizontal axis). The equation corresponding to the graph is $A = a(20 - a)$.
   a   List the values of a where the graph intercepts the horizontal axis.
   b   Explain why it is not possible to have a rectangle with a width of $a = 20$.
   c   Find the width and height of the rectangle corresponding with the largest possible value of A.

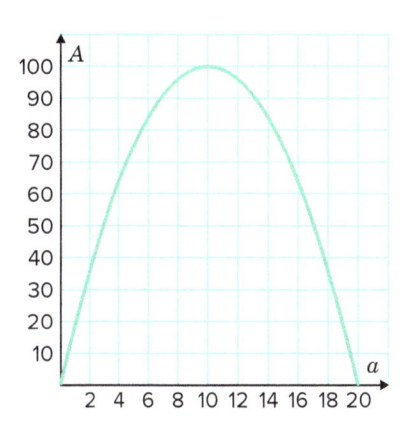

8.01 Solve quadratics using graphs and tables

Answers

8.01 Solve quadratics using graphs and tables

What do you remember?

1. a $x = -4, x = -3$
   b $x = -3, x = 3$

2. a $x^2 + 8x + 7 = 0$
   b $4x^2 - 4 = 0$
   c $(x - 3)^2 - 7 = 0$
   d $6x^2 - 2x + 9 = 0$

3. a $x = -4, x = 2$
   b $x = 2, x = 4$

4. a
x	-8	-7	-6	-5	-4	-3	-2
y	5	0	-3	-4	-3	0	5

   b

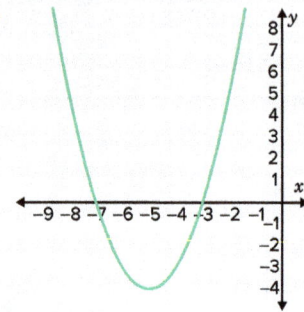

   c i $x = -5$ ii $x = -8$ and $x = -2$

5. a Two solutions
   b No solution
   c One solution
   d Two solutions

Let's practice

6. a i
x	-2	-1	0	1	2
y	-2	$-\frac{1}{2}$	0	$-\frac{1}{2}$	-2

   ii $x = 0$

   b i
x	-1	0	1	2	3
y	-2	0	-2	-8	-18

   ii $x = 0$

   c i
x	-2	-1	0	1	2
y	-6	0	2	0	6

   ii $x = -1, x = 1$

   d i
x	0	1	2	3	4
y	0	-3	-4	-3	0

   ii $x = 0, x = 4$

   e i
x	0	1	2	3	4	5	6
y	5	0	-3	-4	-3	0	5

   ii $x = 1, x = 5$

   f i
x	-2	-1	0	1	2	3
y	4	0	-2	-2	0	4

   ii $x = -1, x = 2$

7. a $x = 6, x = 9$

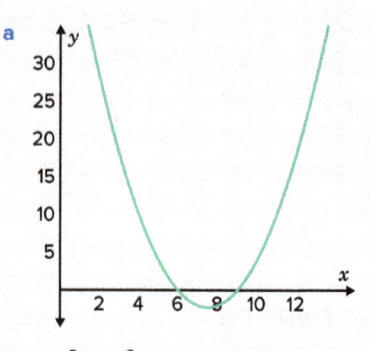

   b $x = -8, x = -2$

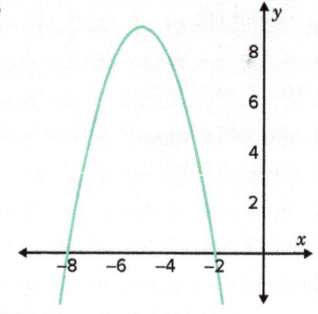

   c $x = 5, x = 10$

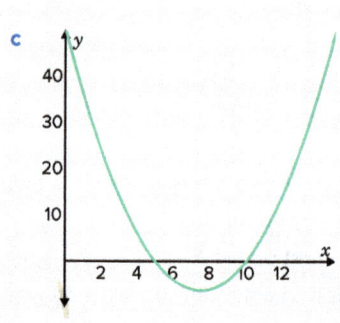

   d $x = 3, x = 7$

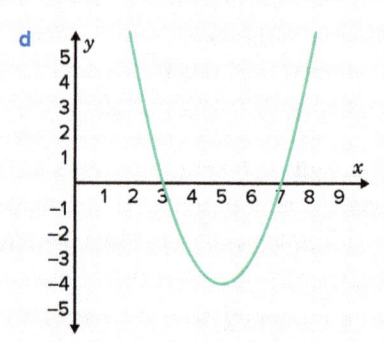

986 Mathspace Virginia SOL Algebra 1 Teacher Edition
mathspace.co

e

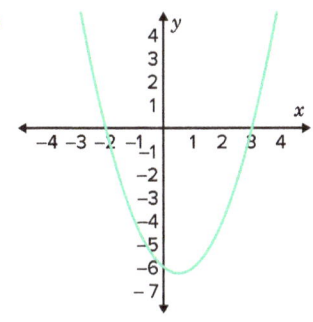

$x = -2, x = 3$

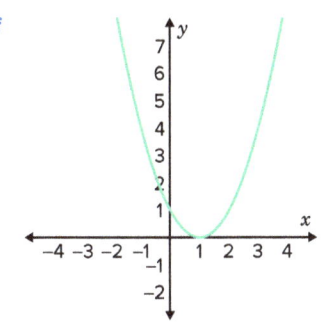

f

$x = 1$

8 a i

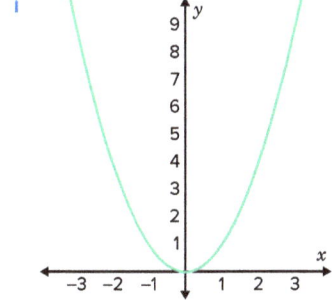

ii $x = 0$

b i

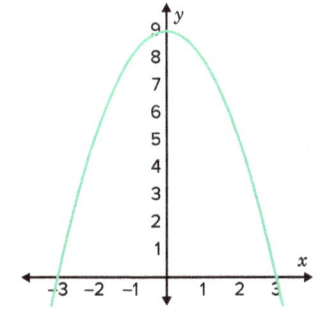

ii $x = 3, x = -3$

c i

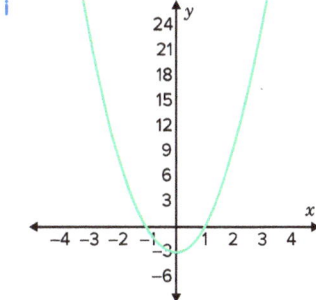

ii $x = 1, x = -1$

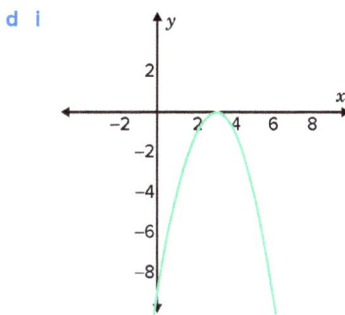

d i

ii $x = 3$

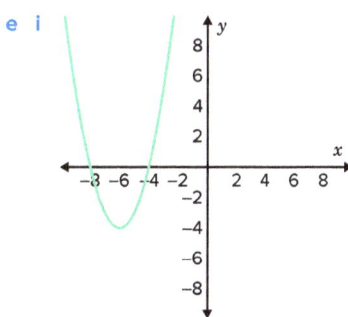

e i

ii $x = -4, x = -8$

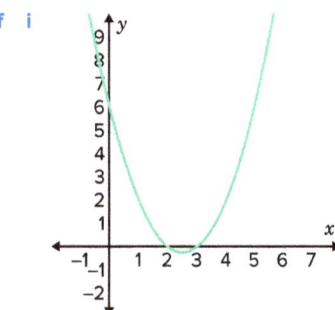

f i

ii $x = 2, x = 3$

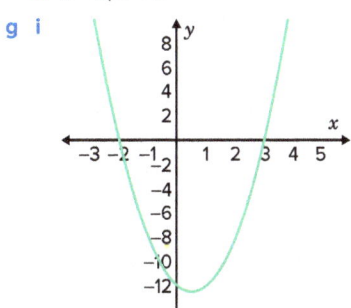

g i

ii $x = 3, x = -2$

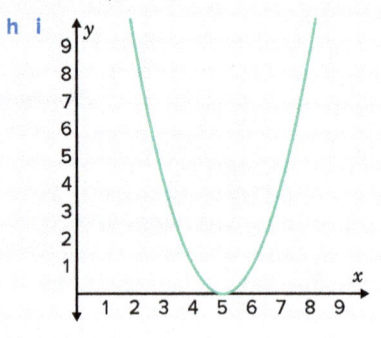

h i

ii $x = 5$

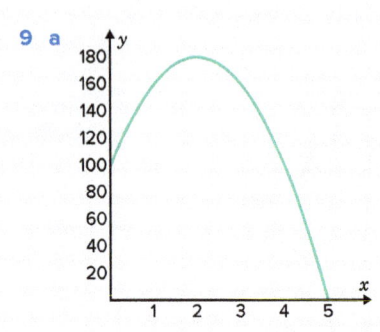

9 a

b 5 seconds
c At $x = 1$ second and $x = 3$ seconds

10 a Initially, at $t = 0$ and after 4 seconds.
b 6 seconds
c 160 yards
d $y = -10x^2 + 40x + 120$ Original equation
$0 = -10(6)^2 + 40(6) + 120$ Substitute $y = 0$ and $x = 6$
$0 = -360 + 240 + 120$ Evaluate the multiplication
$0 = 0$ Evaluate the addition

11 a After 4.5 seconds, the pebble is 40.5 feet above the ground.
The highest distance the pebble reaches above the ground is 40.5 feet.
b $t = 0, t = 9$
c The times when the pebble is on the ground.
d After 3 seconds and 6 seconds.

12 a $f(-2) = 4$ b $x = -1$
c Domain: {3, 0}   d Range : {4, 9}

13 a $f(-1) = 4$ b $x = 1$
c Domain: {-1, 0}   d Range : {0, 3, 4}

Let's extend our thinking

14 a After 9.583 seconds, the object will have a height of 450 meters.
b About 13.5 seconds
c Substitue $d = 0$ into the original equation and solve for t.
$0 = 900 - 4.9t^2$ Substitute $d = 0$
$4.9t^2 = 900$ Add $4.9t^2$ to both sides
$t^2 \approx 183.67$ Divide both sides by 4.9
$t \approx 13.55$ Take the square root of both sides
A more precise answer is 13.55 seconds.

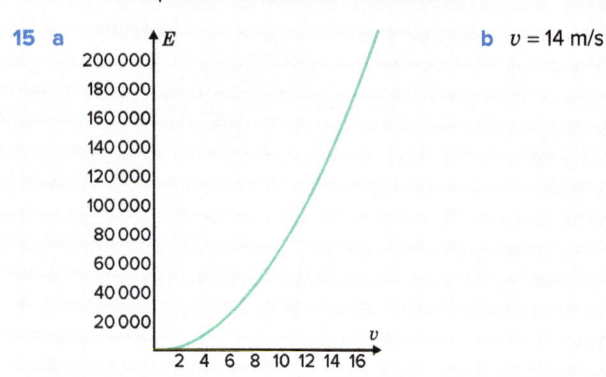

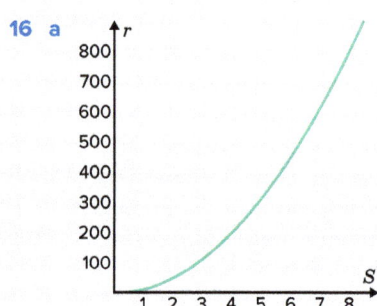

15 a   b $v = 14$ m/s

16 a

b The actual answer is about $S = 380$, so their answer should be close to this.
c The actual answer is about $r = 3.45$ cm, so their answer should be close to this.

17 a $a = 0, a = 20$
b There is no corresponding rectangle because its area would be 0 which is not possible.
c The largest area is 100. The width and height of the corresponding rectangle would both be 10.

8.02 Solve quadratics by factoring

Subtopic overview

Lesson narrative

In the lesson, students will discover how the zero product property can be used to solve quadratic equations in factored form. They will also connect the factors and x-intercepts to write the equation of a quadratic. By the end of the lesson, students will be able to examine the structure of quadratic equations to recognize when they can be solved using factoring and the zero product property.

Learning objectives

Students: Page 461

After this lesson, you will be able to...
- solve quadratic equations by factoring.
- create and solve quadratic equations in context.
- verify and justify solutions to quadratic equations in context.

Key vocabulary

- factored form
- x-intercept
- zero product property

Essential understanding

Quadratic equations can be solved using a variety of methods. Factoring can be an efficient method when the equation is factorable and is made up of constants and coefficients that are not large in value.

Standards

This subtopic addresses the following Virginia Standards of Learning for Mathematics standards.

Mathematical process goals

MPG2 — Mathematical Communication

This goal can be integrated by encouraging students to communicate their reasoning when solving problems. Teachers can ask students to explain the steps they used to solve a quadratic equation by factoring, and to justify their choice of factoring techniques. Student learning can be deepened by discussing, justifying, conjecturing, reading, writing, presenting, and listening to mathematical ideas during the lesson.

MPG3 — Mathematical Reasoning

Teachers can integrate this goal by encouraging students to use logical reasoning when solving problems. For instance, when teaching the Zero Product Property, teachers can ask students to justify why, if the product of two factors is zero, then at least one of the factors must be zero. Teachers can also encourage students to use reasoning to evaluate the validity of solutions to quadratic equations

MPG5 — Mathematical Representations

Teachers can integrate this goal by encouraging students to use different representations for solving quadratic equations by factoring. For example, teachers can demonstrate how to represent a quadratic equation in standard form and then factor the quadratic expression. Then, teachers can encourage students to use symbolic notation to apply the Zero Product Property and solve the resulting linear equations for the variable. Additionally, teachers can present real-world problems that can be modeled with quadratic equations, encouraging students to create and interpret mathematical representations in context.

Content standards

A.EI.3 — The student will represent, solve, and interpret the solution to a quadratic equation in one variable.

A.EI.3a — Solve a quadratic equation in one variable over the set of real numbers with rational or irrational solutions, including those that can be used to solve contextual problems.

A.EI.3c — Verify possible solution(s) to a quadratic equation in one variable algebraically, graphically, and with technology to justify the reasonableness of answer(s). Explain the solution method and interpret solutions for problems given in context.

A.F.2 — The student will investigate, analyze, and compare characteristics of functions, including quadratic and exponential functions, and model quadratic and exponential relationships.

A.F.2g — For any value, x, in the domain of f, determine $f(x)$ of a quadratic or exponential function. Determine x given any value $f(x)$ in the range of f of a quadratic function. Explain the meaning of x and $f(x)$ in context.

A.F.2d — Make connections between the algebraic (standard and factored forms) and graphical representation of a quadratic function.

Prior connections

A.EO.2 — The student will perform operations on and factor polynomial expressions in one variable.

Future connections

A2.EI.2 — The student will represent, solve, and interpret the solution to quadratic equations in one variable over the set of complex numbers and solve quadratic inequalities in one variable.

Engage Activity

A whale's jump   60 mins

Students will determine the key moments in a whale's jump and describe at least two methods that could be used to find when the whale reaches a height of 40 ft above the water.

Understanding and skills

> **Will use**
>
> Factoring quadratic expressions.
>
> Identifying solutions of equations from graphs and tables.

> **Will develop**
>
> Identifying appropriate solutions to quadratic equations in a real-world context.
>
> Connecting the factors of a quadratic equation with its solutions.
>
> Solving quadratic equations by factoring.

Preparation and materials
- Open and complete the student preview, anticipating classroom responses.
- **Materials:** Graphing technology, pencil, paper

Support students with disabilities
Support memory - use previously taught skills and concepts

Provide the formulas for the various forms of quadractic functions:

Vertex form: $f(x) = a(x - h)^2 + k$

Where:
- (h, k) are the coordinates of the vertex
- The sign of a indicates the direction of opening of the graph
- The value of a is the scale factor of the quadratic function

Factored form: $g(x) = a(x - x_1)(x - x_2)$

Where:
- x_1 and x_2 are the x-values of the x-intercepts
- The sign of a indicates the direction of opening of the graph
- The value of a is the scale factor of the quadratic function

Standard form: $h(x) = ax^2 + bx + c$

Where:
- The sign of a indicates the direction of opening of the graph
- The value of a is the scale factor of the quadratic function
- b helps us to find the axis of symmetry and vertex using the formula $x = -\dfrac{b}{2a}$
- c is the value of y-intercept

Support for English language learners
Collect and display

As pairs are working, listen for and collect vocabulary, phrases, and methods students use to find the coordinates for when the whale is at certain points along its jump. Consider grouping language for the various strategies. Continue to update collected student language throughout the entire activity. Remind students to borrow language from the display as needed.

Some terms and phrases may include: solutions, factors, quadratic equation, factoring, graphing, completing the square, maximum, vertex, x-intercepts, setting equation equal to 0, and solve.

Classroom guide

Hook
Open questions • 5 mins

Students compare the similarities and differences between substituting a zero into the standard form and factored form of a quadratic equation.

Implementation details
Highlight student responses that compare the forms of the quadratic expressions on the left hand side of the equation; the first equation is in standard form and the second equation is in factored form. Encourage students to explain what $x = 2$ represents in both equations, since it is a solution for each equation.

What are the similarities and differences between these equations?

Equation 1:
$$x^2 + 3x - 10 = 0$$
$$(2)^2 + 3(2) - 10 = 0$$

Equation 2:
$$(x + 5)(x - 2) = 0$$
$$(2 + 5)(2 - 2) = 0$$

Slide 1 from Student Engage Activity

Launch
5 mins

After students read the information, ask students what they think a 'key moment' means in terms of the whale's jump, and what the key moments might be. Ensure that students can articulate that the whale breaches the water's surface, reaches a maximum height before going back below the surface. It may be useful to show a quick video clip of breaching whales.

Important mathematical concepts: Quadratic, factors, maximum, minimum

Important contextual information: Breach, water surface

Suggested grouping: Form pairs

Jessie decides to join a whale-watching tour and manages to record a whale jumping out of the water.

Slide 2 from Student Engage Activity

Explore
Think-pair-share • 25 mins

Students who have successfully completed the activity will have times for the key moments in the whale's jump with justification and at least two different methods to determine when the whale reaches a height of 40 ft above the water. Encourage students to use multiple methods to solve for the times and note these different strategies for sequencing in the class discussion.

Anticipated strategies

Solve graphically
Students may solve graphically for the times when the whale is at key moments of its jump.

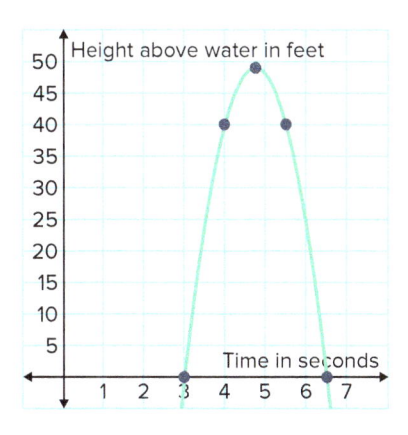

Solve using a table of values
Students may solve for the times when the whale is at key moments of its jump by using a table of values.

Solve by factoring
Students may solve for the times when the whale is at key moments of its jump by factoring and connecting the factors to its solutions.

One option for the factored form of the model of the whale jump:

$$f(x) = -(x - 3)(16x - 104)$$

Solve by completing the square
Students may solve for the times when the whale is at key moments of its jump by completing the square and converting to vertex form.

Vertex form of the model of the whale jump:

$$f(x) = -16(x - 4.75)^2 + 49$$

Key moments in the whale's jump modeled by $f(x) = -16x^2 + 152x - 312$:
- Leaves water at 3 seconds.
- Re-enters water at 6.5 seconds.
- When the times when the whale leaves and re-enters the water are inputed into the function and evaluated, the output of the function is 0 as these are the x-intercepts of the function.
- Highest peak of the jump is 49 ft above water at 4.75 seconds (a humpback whale jumps on average 45 – 50 ft above water!).
- Height of 40 ft at 4 and 5.5 seconds.

Misconceptions

Misinterpreting the x and y coordinates

What do the inputs of the function represent? What do the outputs represent? In your solution, which value is the height of the whale? Which is the amount of time elapsed? How do you know?

Purposeful questions

Use the following questions to check for understanding and encourage critical thinking:
- When does the whale leave and re-enter the water? How do you know?
- When does the whale reach its maximum height? What is the whale's maximum height during the jump? How do you know?
- How will you solve for when the whale reaches a height of 40 ft above the water? Can you solve the equation? Can a table be used to solve? A graph? Explain.
- Can you solve the quadratic equation using another method?

> **Continue when**
> Students have determined when the whale leaves the water, re-enters the water, and reaches the highest point in the jump, described what happens when they input the time when the whale leaves and re-enters the water in the function, and described at least two methods that could be used to find when the whale reaches a height of 40 ft above the water.

Discuss
25 mins

Begin with partner presentations. Consider sequencing the presentations by grouping different representations together and displaying at least one example of each strategy (graphing, table of values, algebraic methods) to compare.

Discussion guide

Start by inviting pairs to share the key features of the whale's jump that they found. Ask a few groups to explain their method for solving for the times of these key features and what happens when the times that the whale leave and re-enters the water are inputed into the function.

Next, ask how groups determined the time when the whale is 40 ft above the water. Start with groups that solved graphically or by using a table of values, then ask groups who solved algebraically by completing the square or factoring to share their work. If no groups solved by factoring, ask the class what other methods could be used to solve for the desired time.

Ask students to connect the algebraic solutions to the solutions in the graph. Specifically, what is known about the graph at its x-intercepts? How can this be related back to the equation? Must it be written in a specific form to reveal the intercepts? Similarly, ask how to connect the vertex of the graph to the equation. Is there a way to rewrite the equation to highlight the vertex?

It is possible that students may not know the connections yet between rewriting the equation and the solutions to the whale problem. You may wish to do a small example with students of an equation that can be easily rewritten, such as $y = x^2 + 4x + 4$ or even have students work backwards from an equation that is already factored such as $y = (x + 2)(x + 2)$ and try rewriting it in as many ways as possible. By using a small example, students may be able to understand that it is possible to do the same with the function of the whale's height, even if they don't yet have the procedural skills built for rewriting the function.

Lesson Preparation

Suggested review

Depending on your students' level of prior knowledge, consider revisiting the following lessons:

- **Algebra 1 —** 6.06 Factor trinomials
- **Algebra 1 —** 6.07 Factor using appropriate methods
- **Algebra 1 —** 7.02 Quadratic functions in factored form

Tools

You may find these tools helpful:
- Graphing calculator
- Graph paper

Student lesson & teacher guide

Solve quadratics by factoring

Students start by exploring the concept of the zero product property.

Concept development: the zero product property
Targeted instructional strategies

To help students better understand the zero product property, have them consider the equation
$$a(x - b)(x - c) = 0$$

Ask the question "What values of x make this equation true?" and ask students to justify their answer. Point out that the left-hand side of the equation is a product of three factors, and that any product including zero will be equal to zero. As such, if any of the factors are equal to zero then the equation is true.

Stronger and clearer each time
English language learner support

Ask students to write or otherwise communicate an explanation for the question: "Why are the factors of the factored form related to the solutions of the corresponding equation?"

Put students into pairs and instruct them to present their explanation to their partner. Give enough time for students to give feedback and discuss an explanation together.

A sample student response may be: "The factors of the factored form of the equation are related to the solutions of the corresponding equation because of the Zero Product Property. When we factor the equation, we can use the Zero Product Property to set each factor equal to zero. Solving each of these equations for x will give us the solutions to the original equation."

After their discussion, give students time to refine their explanation using the results of their discussion and any feedback they received.

Recall steps for factoring
Student with disabilities support

Review the different methods for factoring trinomials. Remind students of the steps for factoring:

1. Set the equation equal to zero
2. Factor out the GCF, if one exists
3. Factor by grouping, by using the box method, or by using any other appropriate strategy
4. Check that the answer will not factor further and verify the factored form by multiplication or the identities of special products:

- $(a + b)^2 = a^2 + 2ab + b^2$
- $(a - b)^2 = a^2 - 2ab + b^2$
- $(a + b)(a - b) = a^2 - b^2$

Focusing on process instead of concepts
Address student misconceptions

Students may incorrectly determine the solutions to an equation as the values they find during the solution process.

For example, they may identify the factors as the solutions, rather than solving to find the roots:

$$(x+3)(x+2)$$

Or, they may find the factors that sum to the coefficient of the linear term and state those values as their answer:

$$x = 3$$
$$x = 2$$

Refer students back to the question they are trying to answer. Ask them to explain what part of the process they are at, and explain the purpose of that step in the process.

Exploration

Students: Page 461

8.02 Solve quadratics by factoring

After this lesson, you will be able to...
- solve quadratic equations by factoring.
- create and solve quadratic equations in context.
- verify and justify solutions to quadratic equations in context.

Engage activity
Ask your teacher to get started

A whale's jump
Students will determine the key moments in a whale's jump and describe at least two methods that could be used to find when the whale reaches a height of 40 ft above the water.

Solve quadratics by factoring

Exploration

What values of the variables make each of the following equations true?

- $z - 7 = 0$
- $13a = 0$
- $3(d+4) = 0$
- $x \cdot y = 0$

Suggested student grouping: In pairs

Students explore the idea of inverse operations when solving equations set equal to zero. Students will rediscover the concept behind the zero product property.

Ideal student responses

These ideal responses may differ from other correct student responses. Less formal responses can be connected with the more precise mathematical language presented here.

1. What values of the variables make each of the following equations true?
   $z = 7$; $a = 0$; $d = -4$; either $x = 0$ or $y = 0$.

Purposeful questions

- When the operation between a constant and a variable is addition or subtraction, what property do you use to find the variable that makes the value zero? (additive inverse)
- When the operation between a constant and a variable is multiplication, what property do you use to find the variable that makes the value zero? (zero property of multiplication)
- When there is both multiplication and addition/subtraction in an equation, what properties allow you to isolate the variable? (multiplicative identity, additive identity)
- When there is a product of two unknowns set equal to zero, what must be true? Why? (at least one of the variables must be zero; zero property of multiplication.)

Possible misunderstandings

- Students may know how to solve the problems, but not be able to identify the arithmetic properties involved.
- For the last equation, students may think both x and y must be equal to zero at the same time. Help students articulate that either value being equal to zero (with any combination of real values for the other variable) will cause the entire product to equal zero.

Students will discover how the zero product property can be used to solve quadratic equations in factored form. They will also connect the factors and x-intercepts to write the equation of a quadratic.

Students: Page 461

The **zero product property** states that if a product of two or more factors is equal to 0, then at least one of the factors must be equal to 0. That is, if we know that $xy = 0$ then at least one of $x = 0$ or $y = 0$ must be true.

We can use this property to solve quadratic equations by first writing the equation in **factored form**:

$$a(x - x_1)(x - x_2) = 0$$

If we can write a quadratic equation in the **factored form**, then we know that either $x - x_1 = 0$ or $x - x_2 = 0$. This means that the solutions to the quadratic equation are $x = x_1$ and $x = x_2$. This approach can be useful if the equation has rational solutions.

Given a quadratic function $f(x)$, the following statements are equivalent for any real number, k, such that $f(k) = 0$:
- k is a zero of the function $f(x)$, located at $(k, 0)$
- $(x - k)$ is a factor of $f(x)$
- k is a solution or root of the equation $f(x) = 0$
- the point $(k, 0)$ is an **x-intercept** for the graph of $y = f(x)$

Let's take a look at this for a specific function:

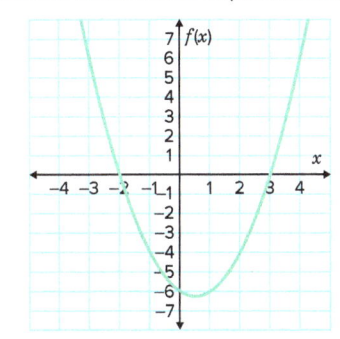

Here is the graph of $f(x) = (x - 3)(x + 2)$
- -2 and 3 are zeros of the function $f(x)$, located at $(-2, 0)$ and $(3, 0)$
- $(x + 2)$ and $(x - 3)$ are factors of $f(x)$
- -2 and 3 are solutions or roots of the equation $f(x) = 0$
- the points $(-2, 0)$ and $(3, 0)$ are x-intercepts for the graph of $y = f(x)$

Examples

Students: Page 462

> ### Example 1
>
> Solve the following equations by factoring:
>
> a $x^2 + 6x - 55 = 0$
>
> **Create a strategy**
>
> Since there are no common factors for all three terms, we proceed with finding the value of two integers that multiply to $ac = (1)(-55) = -55$ and add up to $b = 6$. After finding these integers, we use them to rewrite the middle term $6x$ as a sum of two terms, and then factor the trinomial by grouping.
>
> The factors of -55 are ± 1, ± 5, ± 11 and ± 55, and we want a factor pair whose sum is 6.
>
> **Apply the idea**
>
> The factor pair whose sum is 6 is -5 and 11.
>
> We can use this to rewrite the trinomial and factor by grouping as follows:
>
> $x^2 + 6x - 55 = x^2 + 11x - 5x - 55$ Rewrite polynomial with four terms
> $= x(x + 11) - 5(x + 11)$ Factor each pair
> $= (x + 11)(x - 5)$ Divide out common factor of $(x + 11)$
>
> There are no more common factors to be divided out, so the fully factored form of the polynomial is $(x + 11)(x - 5)$. This leads to the equation
>
> $$(x - 5)(x + 11) = 0$$
>
> We can then solve the equation by setting each factor equal to zero, giving us $x - 5 = 0$ and $x + 11 = 0$, which gives the solutions $x = 5$ and $x = -11$.
>
> **Reflect and check**
>
> The solutions of this equation are the x-intercepts because we solved the equation when it was equal to zero.

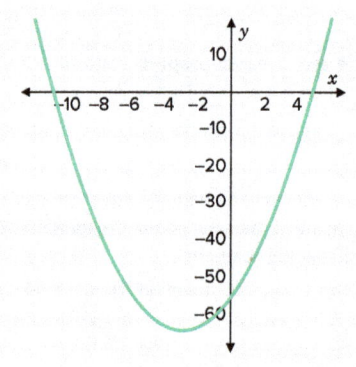

Purpose

Make students aware that with equations set equal to zero, after factoring by grouping, they can use the zero product property to find the solutions.

Expected mistakes

A student may not apply the zero product property, and instead determine that the solutions are $x = 11$ and $x = -5$, which are the constants of the factors. Remind students that after factoring the polynomial, we still need to set each factor equal to zero to solve for x.

Students: Pages 462–463

b $3x^2 + 3x - 10 = 8$

Create a strategy
To solve this equation by factoring, we need to create an equivalent equation first. We want the equation to be equal to zero so we can eventually use the zero product property.

Apply the idea

$3x^2 + 3x - 10 = 8$	Given equation
$3x^2 + 3x - 18 = 0$	Subtraction property of equality

Now, we can solve by factoring.

$3(x^2 + x - 6) = 0$	Factor out the GCF
$3(x^2 + 3x - 2x - 6) = 0$	Rewrite the trinomial as a polynomial with four terms
$3[x(x + 3) - 2(x + 3)] = 0$	Factor each pair of terms
$3(x + 3)(x - 2) = 0$	Divide out common factor of $(x + 3)$
$x + 3 = 0$ and $x - 2 = 0$	Zero product property
$x = -3$ and $x = 2$	Addition property of equality

Reflect and check
We can check our answers by substituting them back into the original equation to see if they make the equation true. We will check $x = -3$ first.

$3x^2 + 3x - 10 = 8$	Original equation
$3(-3)^2 + 3(-3) - 10 = 8$	Substitute $x = -3$
$27 - 9 - 10 = 8$	Evaluate the multiplication
$8 = 8$	Evaluate the subtraction

This is a solution to the equation. Now, we will check $x = 2$.

$3x^2 + 3x - 10 = 8$	Original equation
$3(2)^2 + 3(2) - 10 = 8$	Substitute $x = 2$
$12 + 6 - 10 = 8$	Evaluate the multiplication
$8 = 8$	Evaluate the subtraction

This also satisfies the equation, so it is a solution.

Purpose
Make students aware that an equation needs to be rewritten so that it is set equal to zero before factoring. Show students how to factor and solve a quadratic equation when the leading coefficient is not 1.

Expected mistakes
Students may try to factor the left side of the equation as written, without first setting the equation equal to zero. Remind students that factoring only helps us solve a problem if we can apply the zero product property, which requires an equation set equal to zero.

Memory support: use a multiplication chart
Student with disabilities support

use with Example 1

For students who are less confident in their mental factoring, offer an alternative method to factoring by grouping. The box method offers a visual approach to factoring that may be beneficial.

Students: Pages 463–464

Example 2

Luis throws a ball straight into the air. The path of the ball can be modeled by the equation $y = -5x^2 + 14x + 3$ where x represents the time the ball is in the air in seconds and y represents the height of the ball in meters. How long will it take the ball to hit the ground?

Create a strategy

The question is asking us to find the time (the x-value) it takes for the ball to hit the ground (the y-value). The ground represents a height of 0. In other words, the question is asking us to solve the equation $-5x^2 + 14x + 3 = 0$.

When we factor, we usually have a positive leading coefficient. To begin, we can factor out -1 which will give us a positive leading coefficient.

Apply the idea

$-(5x^2 - 14x - 3) = 0$	Factor out -1
$5x^2 - 14x - 3 = 0$	Divide both sides by -1

Next, we need to find two numbers that multiply to $ac = 5 \cdot -3 = -15$ and add to $b = -14$. The factor pair that satisfies these conditions is -15 and 1.

$5x^2 - 15x + x - 3 = 0$	Rewrite the polynomial with 4 terms
$5x(x - 3) + 1(x - 3) = 0$	Factor by grouping
$(5x + 1)(x - 3) = 0$	Factor out the GCF of $(x - 3)$
$5x + 1 = 0$ and $x - 3 = 0$	Zero product property
$5x = -1$ and $x = 3$	Addition property of equality
$x = -\dfrac{1}{5}$ and $x = 3$	Division property of equality

The x-values represent time, so a negative value does not make sense since we cannot go backward in time. This means $x = -\dfrac{1}{5}$ is a nonviable solution, and $x = 3$ is the only viable solution.
The ball hit the ground after 3 seconds.

Reflect and check

As we can see from the graph, $x = -\dfrac{1}{5}$ is an x-intercept.

But because it does not make sense in context, it is not a solution to the problem. We can picture Luis standing at the y-axis when he throws the ball since $x = 0$ would represent the present moment.

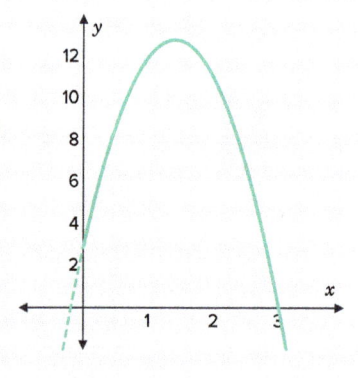

Purpose

Make students aware that various contextual situations may require finding the input values that cause the output values to be zero. Students will demonsrate using factoring by grouping to solve a contextual problem.

Expected mistakes

A student may not realize that "the ground" is represented by $y = 0$ as it represents a height of 0 m. Have students refer back to the independent and dependent variables in this context, then consider what information was given in the problem. Finally, have them relate that information to the given variables.

Reflecting with students

What if we wanted to find out what time the ball was at a particular height, rather than when it hit the ground? Ask students to describe how they could solve the problem. (They would need to rewrite the equation so it is equal to zero, then solve.)

Then, extend the problem by having students consider whether the factoring by grouping method work for any height chosen. Point out that not every equation will end up with values that can be factored. Challenge advanced learners to find a height other than 0 that would allow a factoring solution.

Three reads
English language learner support

use with Example 2

Advise students to read through the instructions multiple times, focusing on gathering different information each time in order to build up their understanding of what the question is asking.

On the first read, students should aim to identify the scenario represented in the equation. Ask students "What do you think is happening in this question?"

On the second read, students should aim to interpret the problem by answering questions like "What is the question asking you to find?" or "What information should be included in the answer?"

On the third read, students should look for important information in the instructions. In this question, important information includes:
- x represents the time the ball is in the air
- y represents the height of the ball in meters
- The ground represents a height of zero

Students can be prompted with questions like "What does each variable represent in this problem?"

Students: Page 464

Idea summary

We can use the zero product property to solve quadratic equations by first writing the equation in factored form:

$$a(x - x_1)(x - x_2) = 0$$

then setting each factor equal to zero and solving for x.

Practice

Students: Pages 465–466

What do you remember?

1 Solve the following equations by using the zero product property:
- a $x(x - 9) = 0$
- b $2m(m - 8) = 0$
- c $c(5c - 12) = 0$
- d $(k - 3)(k - 5) = 0$
- e $(y - 6)(y + 11) = 0$
- f $(3x - 9)(2x - 5) = 0$
- g $5(x + 5)(x - 5) = 0$
- h $(7a - 2)^2 = 0$

2 Consider the quadratic equation:
$$x^2 + 2x - 35 = 0$$
Select the solution of the quadratic equation.
- A $x = -5, x = 7$
- B $x = 5, x = -7$
- C $x = 5, x = 7$
- D $x = -5, x = -7$

3 Consider the quadratic equation:
$$x^2 - 4x - 12 = 0$$
Select the solution of the quadratic equation.
- A $x = -6, x = -2$
- B $x = -6, x = 2$
- C $x = 6, x = -2$
- D $x = 6, x = 2$

4 Determine the x-intercept(s) for each of the following quadratic function:
- a $y = (x + 8)(x + 4)$
- b $y = -(x - 10)^2$
- c $y = (x - 3)(x + 2)$
- d $y = (1 - x)(x + 5)$
- e $y = (x - 6)(x - 24)$
- f $y = -(x - 8)(x + 2)$
- g $y = -(x + 13)^2$
- h $y = x(x + 3)$

Let's practice

5 Solve the following equations by factoring:
- a $6x^2 + 54x = 0$
- b $4y - 8y^2 = 0$
- c $x^2 - 5x - 14 = 0$
- d $f^2 + 6f - 55 = 0$
- e $h^2 + 19h + 88 = 0$
- f $x^2 - 20x + 100 = 0$
- g $x^2 + 8x - 20 = 0$
- h $x^2 - 13x - 114 = 0$

6 Solve the following equations by first rearranging, and then factoring:
- a $x^2 - 14 = 5x$
- b $2y^2 = 9y + 5$
- c $3x^2 - 14x = -8$
- d $\dfrac{2g^2 - 16g}{3} = -8$

7 Solve the quadratic equations by factoring. Justify your work.
- a $x^2 - 3x - 10 = 0$
- b $x^2 + 7x + 12 = 0$
- c $x^2 + 3x = 28$
- d $x^2 - 11x + 19 = -5$

8 Solve:
- a $x(x + 18) + 80 = 0$
- b $x(x + 2) - 48 = 0$
- c $m^2 = 3m + 10$
- d $x^2 = 4 - 3x$
- e $x^2 - 12x = -20$
- f $m^2 + 5m = 14$
- g $-6y = y^2 + 8$
- h $10y = y^2 + 24$
- i $-m^2 - 7m = -18$
- j $-n^2 - 5n = -84$

9 Solve the quadratic equations and verify your solution(s) by graphing.
- a $x^2 + x - 42 = 0$
- b $x^2 - 9x = -20$
- c $x^2 - 35 = 2x$
- d $x^2 + 6x + 8 = 0$

10 Software engineers are designing a self-serve checkout system for a supermarket. They notice that the traffic through the store during the day is described by the function

$$C = -t(t - 12)$$

where C is the number of customers and t is the number of hours after the store opens.

To meet the peak demand, the engineers allow for an extra checkout machine to automatically turn on when the number of customers first reaches 32 people, and to automatically turn off when it next falls below 32 people.

a Find the times t when the number of customers is equal to 32 people.
b Determine how many hours it takes the extra checkout machine to turn on after opening.
c Determine how many hours the extra machine will be on for.

11 Delores needs a sheet of paper x in by 12 in for an origami alligator. The local art supply store only sells square sheets of paper.

The lower portion of the image shows the excess area A of paper that will be left after Delores cuts out the x in by 12 in piece. The excess area, in square inches, is given by the equation

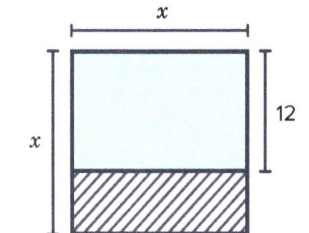

$$A = x(x - 12)$$

a Determine the lengths for which there will be no excess area.
b Determine the value of x that will allow Delores to make an origami alligator with the least amount of excess paper.

12 The area of a rectangle is 60 cm². If the area can be expressed as $A = 17x - x^2$, what are the dimensions of the rectangle?

13 For each of the following quadratic function:
  i Determine the solution(s).
  ii Write the equation in factored form.

  a $y = -x^2 + 5x + 6$
  b $y = x^2 - 8x + 12$
  c $y = -x^2 + 8x - 16$
  d $y = x^2 + 5x$

Let's extend our thinking

14 The school football field is in the shape of a rectangle and has stadium seating all the way around the field that is of a uniform width. If the total area of the field and the stadium is 8400 yd², determine the width of the stadium seating.

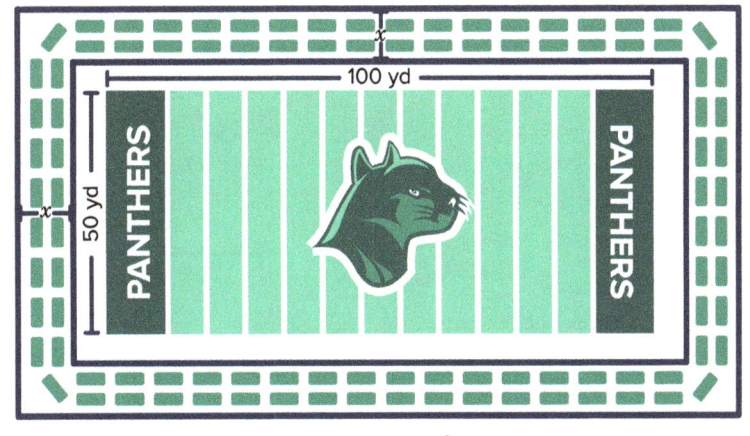

A = 8400 yd²

15 The sum of the series $1 + 2 + 3 + 4 + \ldots + n$ is given by $S = \dfrac{n(n+1)}{2}$. Determine a method to solve for n given any sum, and then find the number of integers required for a sum of 66.

Answers

8.02 Solve quadratics by factoring

What do you remember?

1. a $x = 0, x = 9$ b $m = 0, m = 8$
   c $c = 0, c = \frac{12}{5}$ d $k = 3, k = 5$
   e $y = 6, y = -11$ f $x = 3, x = \frac{5}{2}$
   g $x = 5, x = -5$ h $a = \frac{2}{7}$

2. B

3. C

4. a $(-8, 0), (-4, 0)$ b $(10, 0)$
   c $(3, 0), (-2, 0)$ d $(1, 0), (-5, 0)$
   e $(6, 0), (24, 0)$ f $(8, 0), (-2, 0)$
   g $(-13, 0)$ h $(0, 0), (-3, 0)$

Let's practice

5. a $x = 0, x = -9$ b $y = 0, y = \frac{1}{2}$
   c $x = 7, x = -2$ d $f = -11, f = 5$
   e $h = -8, h = -11$ f $x = 10$
   g $x = 2, -10$ h $x = 19, -6$

6. a $x = -2, x = 7$ b $y = 5, y = -\frac{1}{2}$
   c $x = \frac{2}{3}, x = 4$ d $g = 2, g = 6$

7. a
$x^2 - 3x - 10 = 0$	Given equation
$(x^2 - 5x + 2x - 10) = 0$	Rewrite the trinomial as a polynomial with four terms
$[x(x - 5) + 2(x - 5)] = 0$	Factor each pair of terms
$(x - 5)(x + 2) = 0$	Divide out common factor of $(x - 5)$
$x - 5 = 0$ and $x + 2 = 0$	Zero product property
$x = 5$ and $x = -2$	Addition property of equality

   b
$x^2 + 7x + 12 = 0$	Given equation
$(x^2 + 3x + 4x + 12) = 0$	Rewrite the trinomial as a polynomial with four terms
$[x(x + 3) + 4(x + 3)] = 0$	Factor each pair of terms
$(x + 3)(x + 4) = 0$	Divide out common factor of $(x + 3)$
$x + 3 = 0$ and $x + 4 = 0$	Zero product property
$x = -3$ and $x = -4$	Addition property of equality

   c
$x^2 + 3x = 28$	Given equation
$x^2 + 3x - 28 = 0$	Subtraction property of equality
$(x^2 + 7x - 4x - 28) = 0$	Rewrite the trinomial as a polynomial with four terms
$[x(x + 7) - 4(x + 7)] = 0$	Factor each pair of terms
$(x + 7)(x - 4) = 0$	Divide out common factor of $(x + 7)$
$x + 7 = 0$ and $x - 4 = 0$	Zero product property
$x = -7$ and $x = 4$	Addition property of equality

   d
$x^2 - 11x + 19 = -5$	Given equation
$x^2 - 11x + 24 = 0$	Given equation
$(x^2 - 8x - 3x + 24) = 0$	Rewrite the trinomial as a polynomial with four terms
$[x(x - 8) - 3(x - 8)] = 0$	Factor each pair of terms
$(x - 8)(x - 3) = 0$	Divide out common factor of $(x - 8)$
$x - 8 = 0$ and $x - 3 = 0$	Zero product property
$x = 8$ and $x = 3$	Addition property of equality

8. a $x = -8, -10$ b $x = 6, -8$
   c $m = 5, -2$ d $x = -4, 1$
   e $x = 2, 10$ f $m = -7, 2$
   g $y = -2, -4$ h $y = 4, 6$
   i $m = 2, -9$ j $n = -12, 7$

9. a $(x + 7)(x - 6) = 0$
     $x = -7, x = 6$

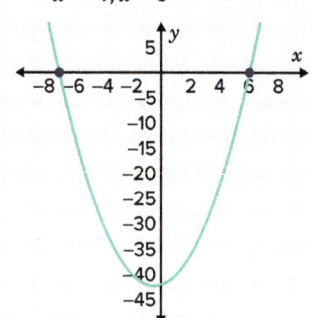

   b $x^2 - 9x + 20 = 0$
      $(x - 5)(x - 4) = 0$
      $x = 5, x = 4$

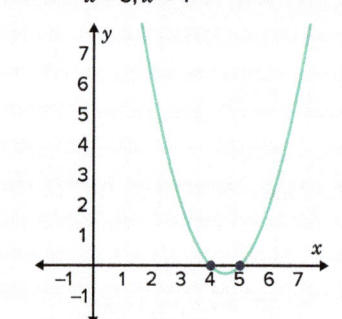

   c $x^2 - 2x + 35 = 0$
      $(x - 7)(x + 5) = 0$
      $x = 7, x = -5$

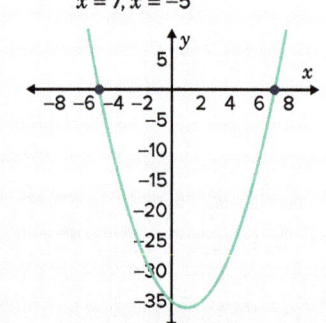

1004 Mathspace   Virginia SOL Algebra 1 Teacher Edition
mathspace.co

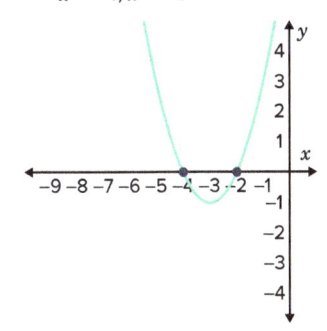

d $(x+4)(x+2) = 0$
$x = -4, x = -2$

Let's extend our thinking

14 10 yards

15 To find the number of integers we want to solve the quadratic equation $S = \frac{n(n+1)}{2}$. We can rearrange this equation into the form $n^2 + n - 2S = 0$. We can factor this and then use the zero product property to determine the two solutions. To find the number of integers required for a sum of 66 we substitute $S = 66$ giving the equation $n^2 + n - 132 = 0$. Factoring this gives $(n-11)(n+12) = 0$ which has solutions of $n = 11, n = -12$. We can exclude the solution of $n = -12$ as we are only considering the positive solution.

10 a $t = 4, t = 8$ **b** 4 hours
    c 4 hours

11 a $x = 0, x = 12$ **b** 12 in

12 5 cm × 12 cm

13 a i (−1, 0), (6, 0)   **ii** $y = -(x-6)(x+1)$
    b i (6, 0), (2, 0)   **ii** $y = (x-2)(x-6)$
    c i (4, 0)   **ii** $y = -(x-4)^2$
    d i (0, 0), (−5, 0)   **ii** $y = x(x+5)$

8.03 Solve quadratics using square roots

Subtopic overview

Lesson narrative

In this lesson, students will examine the structure of the equations and make generalizations leading to an understanding of using inverse operations to solve certain forms of quadratic equations using square roots. Students will also examine the completing the square method of solving quadratic equations. By the end of the lesson, students will be able to examine the structure of quadratic equations to complete the square and solve using the square root property.

Learning objectives

Students: Page 467

> **After this lesson, you will be able to...**
> - solve quadratic equations using inverse operations including square roots.
> - solve quadratic equations by completing the square.
> - create and solve quadratic equations for a real-world context.

Key vocabulary

- completing the square
- radicand
- perfect square
- simplified radical form
- perfect square trinomial
- square root

Essential understanding

Quadratic equations can be solved using a variety of methods. Using square roots can be an efficient method when the equation only has two terms and the constant term is a perfect square. Completing the square can be an efficient method for an equation that cannot be factored.

Standards

This subtopic addresses the following Virginia Standards of Learning for Mathematics standards.

Mathematical process goals

MPG1 — Mathematical Problem Solving

Teachers can integrate this goal in their instruction by providing students with a variety of practice problems that require solving quadratic equations using square roots and completing the square. They can encourage students to apply the steps outlined in the lesson and to connect their solution methods to their prior knowledge of simplifying radicals.

MPG3 — Mathematical Reasoning

Teachers can integrate this goal by asking students to justify their steps in solving the problems. They can also present situations where students have to decide whether a given solution to a quadratic equation is valid or not, thereby applying their reasoning skills.

Content standards

A.EI.3 — The student will represent, solve, and interpret the solution to a quadratic equation in one variable.

A.EI.3a — Solve a quadratic equation in one variable over the set of real numbers with rational or irrational solutions, including those that can be used to solve contextual problems.

A.EI.3c — Verify possible solution(s) to a quadratic equation in one variable algebraically, graphically, and with technology to justify the reasonableness of answer(s). Explain the solution method and interpret solutions for problems given in context.

Prior connections

A.EO.2 — The student will perform operations on and factor polynomial expressions in one variable.

A.EO.4 — The student will simplify and determine equivalent radical expressions involving square roots of whole numbers and cube roots of integers.

Future connections

A2.EI.2 — The student will represent, solve, and interpret the solution to quadratic equations in one variable over the set of complex numbers and solve quadratic inequalities in one variable.

A2.EI.5 — The student will represent, solve, and interpret the solution to an equation containing a radical expression.

Engage Activity

Designing tiles   60 mins

Students will design tiles and solve for exact measurments of tile pieces based on a range of area to introduce solving quadratic equations by completing the square.

Understanding and skills

> **Will use**
> Solving quadratic equations using square roots.

> **Will develop**
>
> Writing algebraic expressions for area of tiles.
>
> Solving quadratic equations to find exact measurements of tile pieces based on a range of areas.

> **Could extend**
>
> Solving quadratic equations by completing the square visually and algebraically.

Preparation and materials
- Open and complete the student preview, anticipating classroom responses.
- **Materials:** None.

Support students with disabilities
Support organization - solve multistep or complex problems

Chunk the task into smaller parts: for example, freely designing square tiles and designing square tiles using the applet.

Ask a group member to volunteer to be the time keeper for the activity or keep track of time for the whole class and remind them when they should be transition from one part of the work to the next. Use a visual display to show the chunked sections of time for students.

Support for English language learners
Three reads

Have students read the task aloud. On the first read, ask students to describe the situation.

Prompt: Students read the problem.

Students think/write: Answer the question "What is the problem about?"

Answers may look like:
- Leroy is designing floor tiles.
- Leroy is creating square tiles for a construction project.

Share: Students are called upon to discuss their answers with the class.

On the second read, ask students to interpret the question.

Prompt: Students read the problem.

Students think/write: Answer the question "What does an answer look like?"

Answers may look like:
- A design of square tiles.
- Combination of tiles that are in the shape of a square.

On the third read, have students identify important information.

Prompt: Students read the problem.

Students think/write: Answer the question "What are the important pieces of information given in the question?"

Answers may look like:
- The dimensions of each piece.
- The design must be in the shape of a square.
- Can only use one of piece 1 in the design.

Classroom guide

Hook

Open questions • 5 mins

Students compare the similarities and differences between a quadratic binominal set equal to a perfect square and a quadratic trinomial set equal to a perfect square.

What are the similarities and differences between these equations?

$$x^2 + 4x = 49 \qquad x^2 + 4x + 4 = 49$$

Slide 1 from Student Engage Activity

Implementation details

Students may start by describing similarities and differences about the structure of equation, such as the fact that both equations have a constant on the right hand side of the equation, but one equation has three terms while the other has two. Encourage students to think about how these quadratics might be solved using methods they currently know.

Launch

5 mins

Allow students to read the instructions individually before forming pairs. It may be helpful to ask students to think about the area of each piece before forming pairs.

Important mathematical concepts: Area model for quadratic expressions

Suggested grouping: Form pairs

Leroy has a summer job in construction and is helping to tile a floor. Leroy is designing different squares to be reviewed by his manager.

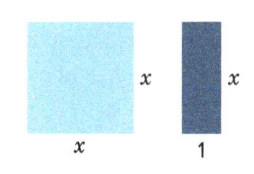

Slide 2 from Student Engage Activity

> **Continue when**
> Students have read the Launch and understand the context of the problem.

Explore

Think-pair-share • 25 mins

In the first stage of the Explore, students are designing square tiles using any combination of square and rectangular pieces so long as it contains exactly one $x \times x$ piece.

Anticipated strategies

Repeat a pattern

Students may design a single square, such as the design provided, then copy that design into larger and larger squares to meet the criteria of having five different designs.

Expand the design

Students may expand the given design by adding additional $x \times 1$ pieces and 1×1 pieces to fill in the space.

Answers will vary depending on the tile designed by each student.

Use the applet to design square tiles.

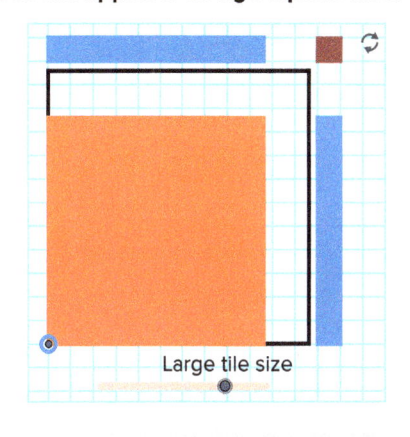

Large tile size

Slide 5 from Student Engage Activity

Utilize square pieces

Students may only use the square pieces to design their square tiles. Encourage these students to consider different designs that still incorporate the rectangular piece.

Misconceptions

Using the visual proportions to "match" dimensions

How many 1×1 pieces would you need to align to match a side length of x? How can we be sure two side lengths match up using these specific tiles?

In the second stage of the Explore, students are designing square tiles using the specific combination of $x \times x$ with an equal number of $x \times 1$ to the right and below it.

Anticipated strategies

Guess and check

Students may input different values of x into their expression until they reach a square area between 100 and 150 square units.

Solve algebraically

Students may write an expression for the area of the tile as $(x + b)^2$ or $x^2 + 2bx + b^2$ and set it equal to a value between 100 and 150 to solve.

Solve graphically

Students may write an equation for the area of the tile and use graphing technology to determine the inputs for when their quadratic function is between 100 and 150 square units.

Misconceptions

Miscalculating the area of the main tile pieces

What are the dimensions of each tile piece? What are the areas of each tile piece?

Check in with groups to make sure they understand the area of each piece:
- x^2 square units
- x square units
- 1 square unit

Combining non-like terms

What is the expression for the area of your tiles? What are like terms in the area expression and visually in your tile?

Expanding polynomial expressions incorrectly

What is the connection between your tile and the algebraic expression for area? How can the area expression be rwritten to represent the length and width of your tile?

Purposeful questions

Use the following questions to check for understanding and encourage critical thinking:
- What is the relationship between the number of rectangular pieces and 1×1 square pieces?
- What are the different ways you could write the expression for the area of the square design?
- Are there other ways to solve this problem?
- What restrictions does needing a square tile place on the problem?

> **Continue when**
>
> Students have five different tile designs and have solved for exact dimensions that meet the area criteria.

Discuss

25 mins

Have a whole class gallery walk. Consider making connections between knowing the number of 1×1 square pieces and the process of completing the square.

Discussion guide

Have groups share their tile designs and justifications, either through presentations or a gallery walk. This allows students to generalize and see multiple examples of the process of visually completing the square. Once designs are being displayed, ask groups to share their process and reasoning for finding the exact measurements of the large square and rectangular pieces.

Ask students if they can determine which method of solving quadratic equations were xplored through the task.

Lesson Preparation

Suggested review

Depending on your students' level of prior knowledge, consider revisiting the following lessons:

Algebra 1 — 5.06 Simplify radicals
Algebra 1 — 7.03 Quadratic functions in vertex form

Tools

You may find these tools helpful:
- Scientific calculator

Student lesson & teacher guide

The square root property

Students are guided through the steps for solving equations using square roots. They are introduced to the square root property, then they are shown how to simplify square roots by relating back to properties of exponents.

Students: Pages 467–468

8.03 Solve quadratics using square roots

After this lesson, you will be able to...
- solve quadratic equations using inverse operations including square roots.
- solve quadratic equations by completing the square.
- create and solve quadratic equations for a real-world context.

Engage activity
Ask your teacher to get started
Designing tiles
Students will design tiles and solve for exact measurments of tile pieces based on a range of area to introduce solving quadratic equations by completing the square.

The square root property

We can solve quadratic equations in the form $a(x - h)^2 = k$ by isolating the **perfect square**, then taking the **square root** of both sides of the equation.

1	$a(x-h)^2 = k$	Given equation
2	$(x-h)^2 = \dfrac{k}{a}$	Divide both side by a
3	$x - h = \pm\sqrt{\dfrac{k}{a}}$	Square root property
4	$x = h \pm \sqrt{\dfrac{k}{a}}$	Add h to both sides

Following these steps, we can see that if $\dfrac{k}{a}$ is not negative, then the equation will have real solutions.
Otherwise, the equation will have no real solutions.

Another thing to notice is that taking the square root of both sides introduces the $\pm$ symbol. This is because we have a positive and a negative root. These come from the fact that

$$x^2 = (-1)^2 \cdot x^2 = (-x)^2$$

so $\sqrt{x^2} = \pm x$.

When the **radicand** is not a perfect square, we need to simplify the expression. Radical expressions are written in **simplified radical form** if the **radicand** cannot be factored any further.

We can use the following facts to simplify radical expressions, for $a, b \geq 0$:

| $\sqrt{ab} = \sqrt{a}\sqrt{b}$ | Multiplication property of radicals |
| $\sqrt{\dfrac{a}{b}} = \dfrac{\sqrt{a}}{\sqrt{b}}$ | Division property of radicals |

We can simplify using properties of exponents, properties of radicals, or a perfect square factor:

Properties of exponents

$$\begin{aligned}\sqrt{24} &= (24)^{\frac{1}{2}} \\ &= (2 \cdot 2 \cdot 2 \cdot 3)^{\frac{1}{2}} \\ &= (2^2 \cdot 2 \cdot 3)^{\frac{1}{2}} \\ &= (2^2)^{\frac{1}{2}} \cdot (2)^{\frac{1}{2}}(3)^{\frac{1}{2}} \\ &= 2 \cdot (2 \cdot 3)^{\frac{1}{2}} \\ &= 2 \cdot (6)^{\frac{1}{2}} \\ &= 2\sqrt{6}\end{aligned}$$

When we simplified radicals using rational exponents we did the following. First, we converted the radical to a rational exponent. Then, we found the prime factors of 24 and applied properties of exponents to simplify.

Properties of radicals

$$\begin{aligned}\sqrt{24} &= \sqrt{2 \cdot 2 \cdot 2 \cdot 3} \\ &= \sqrt{2^2 \cdot 2 \cdot 3} \\ &= \sqrt{2^2} \cdot \sqrt{2} \cdot \sqrt{3} \\ &= 2 \cdot \sqrt{2 \cdot 3} \\ &= 2\sqrt{6}\end{aligned}$$

We can follow a similar process for this method, except we can leave the expression in radical form. First, we find the prime factors of 24, then we can use properties of radicals to simplify.

Perfect square method

$$\begin{aligned}\sqrt{24} &= \sqrt{4 \cdot 6} \\ &= \sqrt{4} \cdot \sqrt{6}\end{aligned}$$

This is the quickest method for simplifying a radical. Instead of finding all the prime factors of 24, we want to find the largest perfect square factor of 24. Then, we can use the multiplication

Scaffold by providing steps for solving equations using square roots
Student with disabilities support

For students who have difficulty remembering the procedure for solving using the square root method, provide the reasoning for each step of work as a scaffold. For example:

$2(x - 4)^2 + 11 = 29$

☐ = ☐	Subtract ☐ from both sides
☐ = ☐	Divide both sides by ☐
☐ = ☐	Evaluate the square root of both sides
☐ = ☐	Add ☐ to both sides

There are two solutions for square root equations
Address student misconceptions

Remind students not to forget the ± symbol when taking the square root of both sides of an equation. It can help to take some time at the start of the lesson to review why taking the square root gives both a positive and negative result.

Consider that $(-10)^2 = 100$ and $(10)^2 = 100$, so if $x^2 = 100$ then we have $x = \pm 10$.

Examples

Students: Page 468

> ### Example 1
>
> Solve the following equations by using square roots:
>
> a $x^2 = 9$
>
> **Create a strategy**
> In this equation we have 9 being equal to the square of x. This is equivalent to x being equal to the square root of 9.
>
> **Apply the idea**
> $$x = \pm 3$$
>
> **Reflect and check**
> Checking our answers:
> $$(-3)^2 = 9$$
> $$(3)^2 = 9$$
>
> Both answers satisfy the equation.

Purpose
Show students how to solve an equation by evaluating the square root of both sides.

Expected mistakes
Students may state that the solution is only positive 3. Students may be guided using questions such as "Is three the only number that when squared results in nine?" or "What is the sign of the product of two negative numbers?"

Students: Page 469

> b $4x^2 - 27 = 0$
>
> **Create a strategy**
> We can begin by isolating the variable, but we will need to simplify the radical since 27 is not a perfect square.
>
> **Apply the idea**
>
> | | |
> |---|---|
> | $4x^2 - 27 = 0$ | Given equation |
> | $4x^2 = 27$ | Addition property of equality |
> | $x^2 = \dfrac{27}{4}$ | Division property of equality |
> | $x = \pm\sqrt{\dfrac{27}{4}}$ | Square root property |
> | $x = \pm\dfrac{\sqrt{27}}{\sqrt{4}}$ | Division property of radicals |
>
> From here, we can factor 27. Our goal is to separate it into factors where one is a perfect square. $27 = 9 \cdot 3$ where 9 is a perfect square.
>
> | | |
> |---|---|
> | $x = \pm\dfrac{\sqrt{9}\sqrt{3}}{\sqrt{4}}$ | Multiplication property of radicals |
> | $x = \pm\dfrac{3\sqrt{3}}{2}$ | Evaluate the radicals |

Reflect and check

For nearly all of our work with solutions to functions and equations, it is standard practice to leave our final expression in exact form.

In questions involving applications of quadratics, we may be asked to evaluate the square root at the very end using a calculator, then approximate to a specific number of decimal places.

Purpose

Show students how to solve an equation that involves basic inverse operations for solving equations alongside evaluating and simplifying square roots.

Expected mistakes

Students may state that the solution is $\pm\frac{\sqrt{27}}{\sqrt{4}}$. Remind students to determine if the numbers inside of a radicand can continue to be simplified, either by checking their prime factorization or considering perfect square factors.

Reflecting with students

Ask students how they can check that their solution is correct. Students may substitute the final solutions into the original equation to check that the equation is valid.

Students: Pages 469–470

c $(x - 2)^2 - 100 = 0$

Create a strategy

In order to use square roots to solve, the squared expression must be isolated. In this example we want to isolate the term $(x - 2)^2$.

Apply the idea

$(x - 2)^2 - 100 = 0$	Given equation
$(x - 2)^2 = 100$	Add 100 to both sides
$x - 2 = \pm 10$	Take the square root of both sides

This leaves us with two equations $x - 2 = 10$ and $x - 2 = -10$. Add 2 to solve both equations and we find that the solutions are $x = -8, x = 12$.

Reflect and check

Looking at the structure of this equation, we see it is in the form $a(x - h)^2 + k = 0$ which is the vertex form of its equivalent function. The vertex of this related parabola is at $(2, -100)$, and we just found the zeros at $(-8, 0)$ and $(12, 0)$.

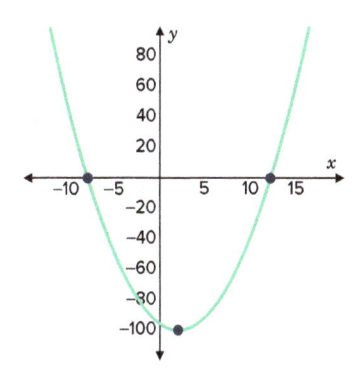

Purpose

Show students how to solve an equation in vertex form using square roots.

Expected mistakes

Students may state that the solutions of the equation are $x = \pm 12$, assuming that they do not need to separate the equation into two equations to see how the equations should be solved.

Students: Pages 470–471

d $(3x - 8)^2 = 25$

Create a strategy

Since the squared expression is already isolated, we are ready to solve by taking square roots.

Apply the idea

$(3x - 8)^2 = 25$	Given equation
$3x - 8 = \pm 5$	Take the square root of both sides
$3x = 8 \pm 5$	Add 8 to both sides
$x = \dfrac{8 \pm 5}{3}$	Divide both sides by 3

This leaves us with two equations:

$$x = \dfrac{8-5}{3} \text{ and } x = \dfrac{8+5}{3}$$

$$x = \dfrac{3}{3} \text{ and } x = \dfrac{13}{3}$$

The solutions are $x = 1$, $x = \dfrac{13}{3}$.

Reflect and check

We can check these answers by substituting them back into the original equation.

$(3x - 8)^2 = 25$	Original equation
$(3(1) - 8)^2 = 25$	Substitute $x = 1$
$(3 - 8)^2 = 25$	Evaluate the multiplication
$(-5)^2 = 25$	Evaluate the subtraction
$25 = 25$	Evaluate the exponent

Now checking the next solution:

$(3x - 8)^2 = 25$	Original equation
$\left(3\left(\dfrac{13}{3}\right) - 8\right)^2 = 25$	Substitute $x = \dfrac{13}{3}$
$(13 - 8)^2 = 25$	Evaluate the multiplication
$(5)^2 = 25$	Evaluate the subtraction
$25 = 25$	Evaluate the exponent

Both answers satisfy the original equation.

Purpose

Show students how to solve an equation using square roots where the coefficient of x is not 1.

Reflecting with students

The ± in the equation may confuse students and make them less confident in moving forward. Point out to students that this equation simplifies to two linear equations.

For students that are still unsure, separate into two linear equations sooner, like so:

$(3x-8)^2 = 25$	Given equation
$3x - 8 = \pm 5$	Square root property
$3x - 8 = -5$ and $3x - 8 = 5$	Separate into two equations
$3x = 3$ and $3x = 13$	Add 8 to both sides
$x = \dfrac{3}{3}$ and $x = \dfrac{13}{3}$	Divide both sides by 3

Students: Page 471

Example 2

State a quadratic equation that has the given solutions.

a $\quad x = -1 \pm \sqrt{7}$

Create a strategy

We can work backwards from solving to find the equation that had the given solutions.

Apply the idea

$x = -1 \pm \sqrt{7}$	Given solutions
$x + 1 = \pm \sqrt{7}$	Add 1 to both sides
$(x + 1)^2 = 7$	Square both sides

Reflect and check

This is one equation, but we could also subtract 7 from both sides to get an equivalent equation with the same solutions.

$(x + 1)^2 - 7 = 0$

Purpose

Show advanced learners how to work backwards to construct a quadratic equation from its solutions.

Reflecting with students

Ask students to walk through solving their final equation. Point out to students that the operations they use to solve the equation are simply the inverse operations they used to build it.

Students: Page 471

b $x = \dfrac{5 \pm \sqrt{10}}{3}$

Create a strategy
We can use a similar process as the previous problem, but this time we need to multiply both sides by 3 first.

Apply the idea

$x = \dfrac{5 \pm \sqrt{10}}{3}$ Given solutions

$3x = 5 \pm \sqrt{10}$ Multiply 3 to both sides

$3x - 5 = \pm\sqrt{10}$ Subtract 5 from both sides

$(3x - 5)^2 = 10$ Square both sides

Reflect and check
When completing the square, fractional solutions come from equations where $a \neq 1$. The 3 in the denominator came from the coefficient of x inside the parentheses.

Purpose
Provide an opportunity for advanced learners to deepen their understanding of solutions to quadratic equations by working backwards to construct a quadratic equation from its solutions.

Expected mistakes
Students may think they perform the multiplication by 3 on both sides last, since it appears in the denominator. Remind students that when solving an equation that has a number in the denominator as shown, we can only access the terms in the numerator by performing the multiplicaiton of the denominator term on both sides of the equation first.

Students: Page 472

Example 3

A square field has perpendicular lines drawn across it dividing it into 36 equal sized smaller squares. If the total area of the field is 225 square feet, determine the side length of one of the smaller squares.

Create a strategy
We know that there are 36 smaller squares in total on a larger square grid, so there must be 6 by 6 smaller squares on the grid. If we let the side of a smaller square be x, then the side of the larger square can be $6x$. This gives us the quadratic equation $(6x)^2 = 225$. We can then solve this equation by taking square roots.

Apply the idea

$(6x)^2 = 225$ Write the equation

$6x = \pm 15$ Take the square root of both sides

$x = \dfrac{\pm 15}{6}$ Divide both sides by 6

Simplifying the expression gives us the solutions $x = \pm 2.5$. We can exclude the negative solution as the length of the square must be positive. So, the smaller square has a side length of 2.5 feet.

Reflect and check
In most real-life applications, we will exclude the negative solution as it will be non-viable for the context.

Purpose
Show students how to write and solve an equation using square roots given a context, and determine extraneous solutions.

Expected mistakes
Students may state that the side length of each square is ±2.5 feet. Remind students to consider if their solutions make sense in the context of a problem. For this problem, students need to determine whether −2.5 feet makes sense as a distance.

Draw a visual representation of a problem in context — use with Example 3
Student with disabilities support

For students that cannot visualize the scenario in this problem, help them create a visual representation of what is happening. This shows the student that the square field is being subdivided into 36 equal parts, each part being a perfect square.

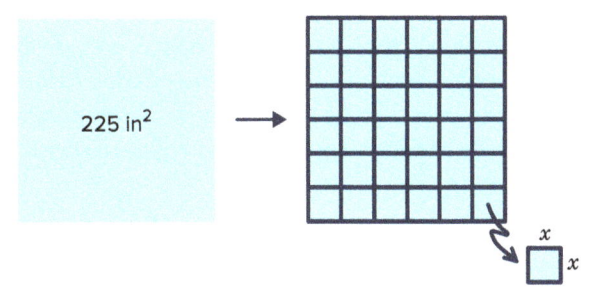

Show them how there are 6 of the smaller squares along the sides, where each square has a side length of x. This means the sides of the larger square have a length of $6x$, meaning the area of the large square is $(6x)^2$.

Students: Page 472

> **Idea summary**
> When we use the square root property, we always include the ± symbol to denote the positive and negative root.
> We can use the following facts to simplify radical expressions, for $a, b \geq 0$:
>
> $\sqrt{ab} = \sqrt{a}\sqrt{b}$ — Multiplication property of radicals
>
> $\sqrt{\dfrac{a}{b}} = \dfrac{\sqrt{a}}{\sqrt{b}}$ — Division property of radicals

Completing the square

Students recall that the process of completing the square leads to perfect square trinomials, and these equations can be solved using square roots. An exploration of an equation that may be solved by completing the square follows.

Students: Page 472

Completing the square

Completing the square is a method we use to rewrite a quadratic expression so that it contains a **perfect square trinomial** which can be factored as $A^2 + 2AB + B^2 = (A + B)^2$. We used this method in a previous lesson to convert a quadratic equation from standard form to vertex form. We will now learn to use the completing the square method combined with the square root property to solve quadratic equations.

Concrete-Representational-Abstract (CRA) Approach
Targeted instructional strategies

Concrete: Begin by engaging students with physical manipulatives to explore quadratic equations. Use algebra tiles to represent x^2, x, and constant terms on either side of the equation. Have students build squares using the tiles to visualize the process of completing the square. For example, provide tiles to model the equation $x^2 + 2x = 8$ and guide students to figure out how many unit tiles are needed to form a perfect square on the left side. Encourage them to rearrange the tiles to see how adding a certain number of unit tiles completes the square, but remind them that whatever is added to one side of an equation should also be added on the other side.

Finally, rearrange the tiles on the right side into a square and ask students how many unit tiles the x could be replaced with in order to make both squares the same size.

Representational: Transition to drawing representations of the algebra tiles. Have students sketch the shapes they used, with squares representing x^2, rectangles for x, and unit squares for constants. Use grid paper to help them keep proportions accurate. Guide them in illustrating the steps of completing the square, showing how they add squares to complete the larger square. Encourage them to label their drawings with the corresponding algebraic terms.

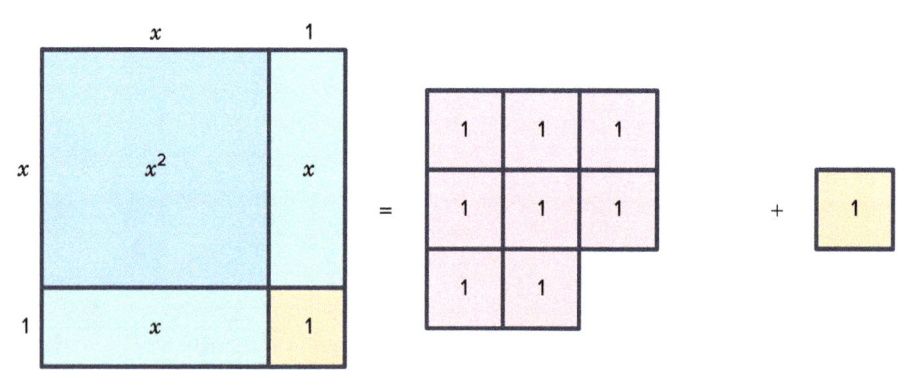

Abstract: Move on to solving quadratic equations using algebraic symbols and notation. Teach students how to use inverse operations and the square root property to solve equations. Show them how completing the square transforms an equation like $x^2 + 2x = 8$ into $(x + 1)^2 = 9$. Then, show how the sides of the squares on either side must then be equal, so $x + 1 = 3$. Provide practice problems where they apply these steps to solve different quadratics.

Encourage them to connect the algebraic steps back to the manipulatives and drawings they used earlier. This helps them see how the abstract equations relate to the concrete and representational stages. Include examples of solved equations, highlighting each step of the process.

Exploration

Students: Page 472

> ## Exploration
>
> Consider the equation $x^2 + 6x = 11$.
>
> 1. Try to develop a method for turning the left-hand side of the equation into a perfect square trinomial.
> 2. Remember that we need to keep both sides of the equation balanced. After making the perfect square trinomial, check that your equation is still balanced.
> 3. How could we solve the equation in this form?
> 4. How could you apply your method to $x^2 - 10x - 5 = 0$?

Suggested student grouping: In pairs

Students are presented with an equation. Students may use a previously-learned approach to attempt to answer the questions, leading them to eventually complete the square and solve the equation.

Ideal student responses

These ideal responses may differ from other correct student responses. Less formal responses can be connected with the more precise mathematical language presented here.

1. **Try to develop a method for turning the left-hand side of the equation into a perfect square trinomial.**
   In order to make $x^2 + 6x$ into a perfect square trinomial, we would need to add a constant term to it. The constant term that makes a perfect square trinomial is 9, so we could rewrite the left side as $x^2 + 6x + 9$ and then $(x + 3)^2$.

2. **Remember that we need to keep both sides of the equation balanced. After making the perfect square trinomial, check that your equation still balanced.**
   To keep the equation balanced, we should also add 9 to the right side of the equation, making the equation $(x + 3)^2 = 20$. This is a reasonable action to keep the equation balanced. Thinking back to completing the square with the vertex form of a quadratic function, adding values that keep the equation balanced should be a familiar part of completing the square.

3. **How could we solve the equation in this form?**
   This equation is now in a form that we can use square roots to solve. We start by evaluating the square root of both sides, then we add 3 to both sides.

4. **How could you apply your method to $x^2 - 10x - 5 = 0$?**
   Using the same method, we could move 5 to the right side of the equation, and then create a perfect square trinomial on the left side using $x^2 - 10x$. After keeping the equation balanced and factoring the trinomial, use square roots to solve for x.

Purposeful questions

- What does the expression $x^2 + 6x$ need in order to be classified as a perfect square trinomial?
- How do we keep equations balanced?
- How is this similar to completing the square for quadratic functions that we want to convert to vertex form?

Possible misunderstandings

- Students may forget that introducing terms to an equation is mathematically valid, as long as we perform the same operation on both sides of the equation.

After the exploration, students learn a step-by-step process for completing the square given a polynomial equation with a leading coefficient of 1. After completing the square, we can solve equations by using square roots, which students learned how to do earlier in the lesson.

Students: Pages 473

For quadratic equations where $a = 1$, we can write them in perfect square form by following these steps:

1	$x^2 + bx + c = 0$	
2	$x^2 + bx = -c$	Subtract c from both sides
3	$x^2 + 2\left(\dfrac{b}{2}\right)x = -c$	Rewrite the x term
4	$x^2 + 2\left(\dfrac{b}{2}\right)x + \left(\dfrac{b}{2}\right)^2 = -c + \left(\dfrac{b}{2}\right)^2$	Add $\left(\dfrac{b}{2}\right)^2$ to both sides
5	$\left(x + \dfrac{b}{2}\right)^2 = -c + \left(\dfrac{b}{2}\right)^2$	Factor the perfect square trinomial

If $a \neq 1$, we can first divide through by a to factor it out.

Note that when we were using completing the square to write an equation in vertex form, we keep the constant term on the same side of the equation as the variable terms. Then, to maintain equivalency and complete square, we add and subtract the same $\left(\dfrac{b}{2}\right)^2$ term. This results in all the terms being on the same side of the equation so we can identify the vertex of the parabola.

But, if we want to solve the equation, we keep the x terms together and move the constant term to the other side of the equation. Then the $\left(\dfrac{b}{2}\right)^2$ term is added to both sides of the equation to maintain equivalency and create a perfect trinomial. This gives us a squared factor on one side and a constant term on the other side of the equation, allowing us to use the square root property to solve for x. If we can rewrite an equation by completing the square, then we can solve it using square roots.

Examples

Students: Page 473

Example 4

Solve the following quadratic equations by completing the square.

a $x^2 + 18x + 32 = 0$

Create a strategy

To solve an equation by completing the square, start by moving the constant term to the other side of the equation. We will complete the square by finding half the coefficient of the x term, squaring it, and adding it to both sides of the equation. Once we've completed the square, we can solve.

Apply the idea

| $x^2 + 18x + 32 = 0$ | Given equation |
| $x^2 + 18x = -32$ | Subtract 32 from both sides |

Since the coefficient of the x-term is 18, we will need to add $\left(\dfrac{18}{2}\right)^2 = 81$ to both sides of our equation.

$x^2 + 18x + 81 = -32 + 81$	Complete the square
$(x + 9)^2 = 49$	Factor the perfect square trinomial
$x + 9 = \pm 7$	Take the square root of both sides

This leaves us with two equations $x + 9 = 7$ and $x + 9 = -7$. We can solve both equations by subtracting 9, so we get the solutions $x = -2$ and $x = -16$.

1022 Mathspace Virginia SOL Algebra 1 Teacher Edition
mathspace.co

Purpose
Show students how to solve a polynomial equation by completing the square and using square roots.

Reflecting with students
Ask students if they have a method to recall the $\left(\frac{b}{2}\right)^2$ step of completing the square. For instance, offer students the following fill-in-the-blanks:

$$x^2 + 18x + \square = -32 + \square$$
$$(x + \square)^2 = -32 + \square$$

Some students may point out that this is simply the algorithm for turning $x^2 + 18x$ into a perfect square trinomial and keeping the equation balanced. The term, in this case 81, is the value that makes $x^2 + 18x + 81$ a perfect square trinomial and therefore keeps the equation balanced.

Students: Page 474

b $\quad 2x^2 - 10x + 7 = 0$

Create a strategy
In this example, the coefficient of x^2 is 2, so we will need to divide this coefficient out before completing the square. We can then perform steps similar to the previous example.

Apply the idea

$2x^2 - 10x + 7 = 0$	Given equation
$x^2 - 5x + \frac{7}{2} = 0$	Divide both sides by 2
$x^2 - 5x = -\frac{7}{2}$	Subtract $\frac{7}{2}$ from both sides

The coefficient of x is $-\frac{10}{2} = -5$. Taking half of -5 and squaring it gives us $\left(\frac{-5}{2}\right)^2 = \frac{25}{4}$, so this is the value that completes the square.

$x^2 - 5x + \frac{25}{4} = -\frac{7}{2} + \frac{25}{4}$	Complete the square
$\left(x - \frac{5}{2}\right)^2 = \frac{18}{4}$	Factor the left side, evaluate the addition on the right side
$x - \frac{5}{2} = \pm\sqrt{\frac{18}{4}}$	Square root property
$x - \frac{5}{2} = \pm\frac{\sqrt{18}}{\sqrt{4}}$	Division property of radicals
$x - \frac{5}{2} = \pm\frac{\sqrt{9}\sqrt{2}}{\sqrt{4}}$	Multiplication property of radicals
$x - \frac{5}{2} = \pm\frac{3\sqrt{2}}{2}$	Evaluate the radicals

This leaves us with two equations: $x - \frac{5}{2} = \frac{3\sqrt{2}}{2}$ and $x - \frac{5}{2} = -\frac{3\sqrt{2}}{2}$.

Next, we add $\frac{5}{2}$ to solve both equations, and we find that the solutions are $x = \frac{5}{2} + \frac{3\sqrt{2}}{2}$ and $x = \frac{5}{2} - \frac{3\sqrt{2}}{2}$.

Reflect and check
These can also be combined into one fraction: $x = \frac{5 \pm 3\sqrt{2}}{2}$.

Purpose
Show students how to solve a polynomial equation with a leading coefficient $\neq 1$ by completing the square and using square roots.

Expected mistakes

Students may try to complete the square without factoring the leading coefficient from the equation. Remind students that we need to have a leading coefficient of one before trying to create a perfect square trinomial.

Reflecting with students

Ask students to explain why this example is more complex than the example in part (a). This example requires us to factor the leading coefficient, and the term that creates a perfect square trinomial is a fraction. We also need to simplify radicals in this example.

> **Provide a step-by-step procedure for when the leading coefficient is not 1**
> **Targeted instructional strategies**   use with Example 4

Students can complete the square for any quadratic equation in standard form with the steps:

1	$ax^2 + bx + c = 0$	
2	$x^2 + \dfrac{b}{a}x + \dfrac{c}{a} = 0$	Divide both sides by a
3	$x^2 + \dfrac{b}{a}x = -\dfrac{c}{a}$	Subtract $\dfrac{c}{a}$ from both sides
4	$x^2 + 2\left(\dfrac{b}{2a}\right)x = -\dfrac{c}{a}$	Rewrite the x-term
5	$x^2 + 2\left(\dfrac{b}{2a}\right)x + \left(\dfrac{b}{2a}\right)^2 = -\dfrac{c}{a} + \left(\dfrac{b}{2a}\right)^2$	Add $\left(\dfrac{b}{2a}\right)^2$ to both sides
6	$\left(x + \dfrac{b}{2a}\right)^2 = -\dfrac{c}{a} + \left(\dfrac{b}{2a}\right)^2$	Factor the trinomial

Notice that the constant term in the standard form does not affect the process of completing the square.

Since there are many algebraic manipulations in these steps, it can be very helpful for students to repeat the procedure using numerical examples. Seeing examples of algorithms in practice can model to students how to use it without being prompted.

> **Compare and connect**   use with Example 4
> **English language learner support**

Help students understand the similarities and differences between solving quadratic equations by factoring and solving by completing the square. Highlight the different approaches students take to arrive at the answer.

For example, ask students to compare the solutions of $x^2 + 18x + 32 = 0$ obtained by factoring and by completing the square. Then ask students to connect the steps in each method to the structure of the quadratic equation.

This routine will help students to see how both methods are based on the principle of balancing equations, but use different strategies to isolate the variable x.

Students: Page 474

> **Idea summary**
> Completing the square can be used to solve any quadratic in the form $ax^2 + bx + c = 0$, but it is easiest to use when $a = 1$ and b is even.

Practice

Students: Pages 475–477

What do you remember?

1 Fully simplify each square root.
   a $\sqrt{48}$
   b $\sqrt{75}$
   c $\sqrt{90}$
   d $\sqrt{180}$

2 Solve the following equations by using square roots:
   a $x^2 = 25$
   b $x^2 = 81$
   c $x^2 = 100$
   d $x^2 = 1$
   e $x^2 = 49$
   f $x^2 - 25 = 0$

3 State the quadratic equation that has the given solutions:
   a $x = \pm 5$
   b $x = \pm\sqrt{5}$

4 Complete the following expressions so they form a perfect square trinomial.
   a $x^2 - \square x + 16$
   b $x^2 - \square x + 1$
   c $x^2 - x + \square$
   d $x^2 + 5x + \square$

5 Complete the square by finding the missing values.
   a $x^2 - \dfrac{7}{4}x + \square = (x - \square)^2$
   b $x^2 - 5x + \square = (x - \square)^2$
   c $x^2 + 4x + \square = (x + \square)^2$

6 Solve the following quadratic equations by completing the square:
   a $x^2 + 18x + 32 = 0$
   b $x^2 - 6x + 8 = 0$
   c $x^2 - 9x + 8 = 0$
   d $x^2 - 2x - 32 = 0$

Let's practice

7 Solve the following equations by finding square roots:
   a $x^2 - 5 = 31$
   b $\dfrac{a^2}{25} - 3 = 6$
   c $25y^2 = 36$
   d $5x^2 - 45 = 0$
   e $(m - 7)^2 = 81$
   f $(4 - d)^2 = 9$
   g $(4x + 3)^2 = 64$
   h $5(p^2 - 3) = 705$
   i $(x - 10)^2 = 26$
   j $(x + 9)^2 = \dfrac{15}{2}$
   k $(x + 2)^2 = 20$
   l $2(x - 3)^2 = 8$

8 Solve the following equations by completing the square:
   a $x^2 + 2x - 8 = 0$
   b $x^2 - 6x + 5 = 0$
   c $x^2 - 8x - 9 = 0$
   d $x^2 + 14x - 51 = 0$
   e $2x^2 - 12x - 32 = 0$
   f $4x^2 + 11x + 7 = 0$

9 Solve the following quadratic equations by completing the square. Express your answers in simplest form.
   a $x^2 + 11x + 5 = 0$
   b $x^2 - 7x + 8 = 0$
   c $x^2 + 22x + 9 = 0$
   d $x^2 + 24x + 5 = 0$
   e $6x^2 + 48x + 24 = 0$
   f $x^2 + \dfrac{x}{3} - 3 = 0$
   g $5x^2 + 55x + 3 = 0$
   h $2x^2 + 5x + 1 = 0$

10 State the quadratic equation that has the given solutions:
   a $x = 2 \pm \sqrt{6}$
   b $x = \dfrac{-1 \pm \sqrt{3}}{2}$

11 Solve each quadratic equation below using either the square root property or by completing the square. Justify each step work.
   a $x^2 + 5 = 30$
   b $x^2 + 12x + 32 = 0$
   c $x^2 + 8x + 5 = 0$
   d $(8x + 9)^2 = 256$

12 Solve each quadratic equation below using either the square root property or by completing the square. Verify your work by graphing or with substitution.

    a $(x-5)^2 = 36$ b $x^2 + 13x + 36 = 0$ c $2x^2 - 12x - 54 = 0$ d $(5x-3)^2 = 49$

13 Harry is using a diving board to dive into a swimming pool. The distance from his head to the surface of the water can be represented as $(x-7)(x+7) = 147$. Find the viable solution to the quadratic equation.

14 Consider the equation $x^2 + 24x = 10$.

Janessa tried to solve the equation by completing the square.

1	$x^2 + 24x + 144 = 10$
2	$(x+12)^2 = 10$
3	$x + 12 = \sqrt{10}$
4	$x = -12 + \sqrt{10}$

    a   Identify the mistakes she made.   b   Solve the equation correctly.

15 On the graph of $y = x^2 - 4$, there are two points where $y = 12$. Without drawing the graph, find the x-coordinates of these two points.

16 On Earth, the equation $d = 4.9t^2$ is used to find the distance (in meters) an object has fallen through the air after t seconds.

Willow is sky diving and wants to release her parachute once she has fallen 400 m. Determine the time it will take her to fall 400 m, rounding your answer to the nearest second.

17 The kinetic energy E of a moving object is given by $E = \frac{1}{2}mv^2$, where m is its mass in kilograms and v is its speed in meters/second.

If a vehicle weighing 1600 kilograms has kinetic energy $E = 204\,800$, determine what speed it is moving.

18 Eduardo is trying to solve the equation $(x+9)^2 = 25$. He thinks that the equation is equivalent to $x + 9 = 5$. Nicolette, however, thinks he has performed the operations incorrectly, and that he should have subtracted 9 from both sides of the equation first giving an equivalent equation of $x^2 = 16$.

Describe any errors Eduardo and/or Nicolette have made, and find the correct solution to the equation.

Let's extend our thinking

19 The revenue y (in millions of dollars) of a company x years after it first started is modeled by

$$y = 12.5x^2 - 64x + 135$$

    a   Use this equation to predict the number of years it will take for the revenue to reach $1167 million.

    b   Describe another method you could use to calculate this.

20 Sauya's teacher gave her a square and a rectangle and asked her to use them to create a larger square.

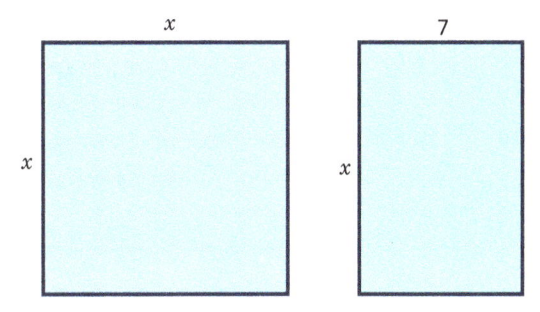

Sauya cut the rectangle in half, and placed the two pieces on either side of the square as shown below.

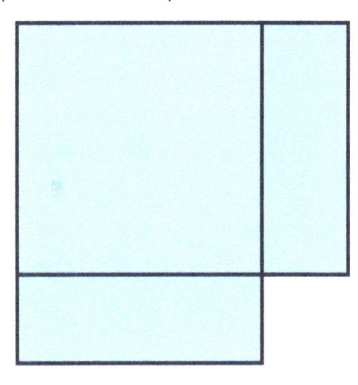

a   Determine the area of the smaller square that, when added, completes the larger square.

b   Find the total area of the larger square.

21 Complete the square of the quadratic equation, $ax^2 + bx + c = 0$, to fill in the blanks:
$$(x + \square)^2 = \square$$

Answers

8.03 Solve quadratics using square roots

What do you remember?

1 a $4\sqrt{3}$ b $5\sqrt{3}$ c $3\sqrt{10}$ d $6\sqrt{5}$

2 a $x = 5, x = -5$ b $x = 9, x = -9$
   c $x = 10, x = -10$ d $x = 1, x = -1$
   e $x = 7, x = -7$ f $x = 5, x = -5$

3 a $x^2 = 25$ b $x^2 = 5$

4 a 8 b 2 c $\dfrac{1}{4}$ d $\dfrac{25}{4}$

5 a $x^2 - \dfrac{7}{4}x + \dfrac{49}{64} = \left(x - \dfrac{7}{8}\right)^2$ b $x^2 - 5x + \dfrac{25}{4} = \left(x - \dfrac{5}{2}\right)^2$
   c $x^2 + 4x + 4 = (x + 2)^2$

6 a $x = -2, x = -16$ b $x = 4, x = 2$
   c $x = 8, x = 1$ d $x = 1 \pm \sqrt{33}$

Let's practice

7 a $x = 6, x = -6$ b $a = 15, a = -15$
   c $y = \dfrac{6}{5}, y = -\dfrac{6}{5}$ d $x = 3, x = -3$
   e $m = 16, m = -2$ f $d = 1, d = 7$
   g $x = \dfrac{5}{4}, x = -\dfrac{11}{4}$ h $p = -12, p = 12$
   i $x = 10 \pm \sqrt{26}$ j $x = -9 \pm \dfrac{\sqrt{30}}{2}$
   k $x = -2 \pm 2\sqrt{5}$ l $x = 5, 1$

8 a $x = 2, x = -4$ b $x = 5, x = 1$
   c $x = 9, x = -1$ d $x = 3, x = -17$
   e $x = 8, x = -2$ f $x = -1, x = -\dfrac{7}{4}$

9 a $x = \dfrac{-11 \pm \sqrt{101}}{2}$ b $x = \dfrac{7}{2} \pm \dfrac{\sqrt{17}}{2}$
   c $x = -11 \pm 4\sqrt{7}$ d $x = -12 \pm \sqrt{139}$
   e $x = -4 \pm 2\sqrt{3}$ f $x = -\dfrac{1}{6} \pm \dfrac{\sqrt{109}}{6}$
   g $x = \dfrac{-11}{2} \pm \dfrac{\sqrt{2965}}{10}$ h $x = \dfrac{-5 \pm \sqrt{17}}{4}$

10 a $(x - 2)^2 = 6$ or $x^2 - 4x + 4 = 6$
   b $(2x + 1)^2 = 3$ or $4x^2 + 4x + 1 = 3$

11 a

$x^2 + 5 = 30$	Given equation
$x^2 = 30 - 5$	Subtract 5 from both sides
$x^2 = 25$	Simplify the right side
$x = \pm\sqrt{25}$	Take the square root of both sides
$x = \pm 5$	Evaluate the square root

   b

$x^2 + 12x + 32 = 0$	Given equation
$x^2 + 12x = -32$	Subtract 32 from both sides
$x^2 + 12x + 36 = -32 + 36$	Complete the square
$(x + 6)^2 = 4$	Factor the perfect square trinomial
$x + 6 = \pm 2$	Take the square root of both sides
$x = -6 \pm 2$	Isolate x
$x = -4$ or $x = -8$	

   c

$x^2 + 8x + 5 = 0$	Given equation
$x^2 + 8x = -5$	Subtract 5 from both sides
$x^2 + 8x + 16 = -5 + 16$	Complete the square
$(x + 4)^2 = 11$	Factor the perfect square trinomial
$x + 4 = \pm\sqrt{11}$	Take the square root of both sides
$x = -4 \pm \sqrt{11}$	Subtract 4 from both sides

   d

$(8x + 9)^2 = 256$	Given equation
$8x + 9 = \pm\sqrt{256}$	Take the square root of both sides
$8x + 9 = \pm 16$	Evaluate the square root
$8x + 9 = 16$	Consider the positive case
$8x = 7$	Subtract 9 from both sides
$x = \dfrac{7}{8}$	Divide both sides by 8
$8x + 9 = -16$	Consider the negative case
$8x = -25$	Subtract 9 from both sides
$x = -\dfrac{25}{8}$	Divide both sides by 8

12 a $x = 11$ or $x = -1$

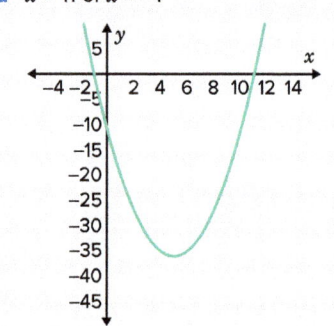

   b $x = -4$ or $x = -9$

$x^2 + 13x + 36 = 0$
$(-4)^2 + 13(-4) + 36 = 0$
$16 - 52 + 36 = 0$
$0 = 0$

$(-9)^2 + 13(-9) + 36 = 0$
$81 - 117 + 36 = 0$
$0 = 0$

c $x = 9$ or $x = -3$

$$2x^2 - 12x - 54 = 0$$
$$2(9)^2 - 12(9) - 54 = 0$$
$$2(81) - 108 - 54 = 0$$
$$162 - 108 - 54 = 0$$
$$0 = 0$$

$$2x^2 - 12x - 54 = 0$$
$$2(-3)^2 - 12(-3) - 54 = 0$$
$$2(9) + 36 - 54 = 0$$
$$18 + 36 - 54 = 0$$
$$0 = 0$$

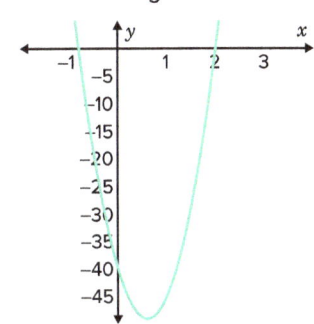

d $x = 2$ or $x = -\dfrac{4}{5}$

13 $x = 14$

14 a In step 1, she added 144 to the left-hand side, but did not add it to the right-hand side.

In step 3, she did not include a plus or minus sign in front of the radical.

b $x = -12 \pm \sqrt{154}$

15 $x = 4, x = -4$

16 $t = 9$ seconds

17 $v = 16$ meters/second

18 Eduardo has incorrectly taken the square root of both sides. When taking the square root of something, we need to consider both the positive and the negative case, so an equivalent equation would be $x + 9 = \pm 5$. Nicolette has incorrectly subtracted 9 from both sides before taking the square root. The correct equation to solve is $x + 9 = \pm 5$ giving an answer of $x = -9 \pm 5$.

Let's extend our thinking

19 a 12 years

b We could draw the graph of the quadratic function $y = 12.5x^2 - 64x + 135$ and also the line $y = 1167$ and find their points of intersection. The x-coordinates of the intercepts would be the required year. Discounting the negative value.

20 a $\left(\dfrac{7}{2}\right)^2 = \dfrac{49}{4}$

b Adding the areas of each rectangle, we get $A = x^2 + \dfrac{7}{2}x + \dfrac{7}{2}x + \dfrac{49}{4}$.

After simplifying, the equation becomes $A = x^2 + 7x + \dfrac{49}{4}$.

21 $\dfrac{b}{2a}, \dfrac{b^2 - 4ac}{4a^2}$

8.04 Solve quadratics using the quadratic formula

Subtopic overview

Lesson narrative

In this lesson, students will use completing the square from the previous lesson to derive the quadratic formula. Students will solve equations using the quadratic formula and they will explore how the discriminant of the quadratic equation determines the types of solutions. By the end of the lesson, students should be able to interpret quadratic models to solve problems in contextual situations to an appropriate degree of precision. Students will also be able to explain why the quadratic formula works as well as describe the relationships between the quadratic equation, the graph of the function, and the number and types of solutions.

Learning objectives

Students: Page 478

> **After this lesson, you will be able to...**
> - solve quadratic equations using the quadratic formula.
> - identify algebraically when a quadratic equation has zero, one, or two real solutions.
> - create and solve quadratic equations for a real-world context.

Key vocabulary

- discriminant
- quadratic formula

Essential understanding

Quadratic equations can be solved using a variety of methods. The quadratic formula can be used to solve any quadratic equation, but it is not always the most efficient method and is best used for equations that cannot be easily graphed or factored.

Standards

This subtopic addresses the following Virginia Standards of Learning for Mathematics standards.

Mathematical process goals

MPG1 — Mathematical Problem Solving

During the lesson, teachers can integrate problem-solving by providing students with a variety of practice problems that require solving quadratic equations using the quadratic formula. Teachers can encourage students to apply the steps outlined in the lesson and connect their solution methods to their prior knowledge of radicals. Teachers can also present real-world problems that can be modeled and solved using quadratic equations, allowing students to apply their mathematical skills in a practical context.

MPG2 — Mathematical Communication

Teachers can promote mathematical communication by encouraging students to explain their thought processes while solving problems. They can ask students to justify their choice of solution method and explain the reasoning behind their steps. Teachers can also ask students to explain the role of the discriminant within the quadratic formula and how it determines the type and number of real solutions.

MPG3 — Mathematical Reasoning

To enhance mathematical reasoning, teachers can ask students to use logical reasoning to determine the value of the discriminant and the number and type of real solutions. They can also encourage students to justify the steps in the quadratic formula and evaluate the validity of their solutions.

Content standards

A.EI.3 — The student will represent, solve, and interpret the solution to a quadratic equation in one variable.

A.EI.3a — Solve a quadratic equation in one variable over the set of real numbers with rational or irrational solutions, including those that can be used to solve contextual problems.

A.EI.3b — Determine and justify if a quadratic equation in one variable has no real solutions, one real solution, or two real solutions.

A.EI.3c — Verify possible solution(s) to a quadratic equation in one variable algebraically, graphically, and with technology to justify the reasonableness of answer(s). Explain the solution method and interpret solutions for problems given in context.

Prior connections

A.EO.1 — The student will represent verbal quantitative situations algebraically and evaluate these expressions for given replacement values of the variables.

A.EO.4 — The student will simplify and determine equivalent radical expressions involving square roots of whole numbers and cube roots of integers.

Future connections

A2.EI.2 — The student will represent, solve, and interpret the solution to quadratic equations in one variable over the set of complex numbers and solve quadratic inequalities in one variable.

Engage Activity

Conditions and roots   60 mins

Students will use various methods to solve quadratic equations to determine whether statements are always, sometimes, or never true. Students will determine the number and nature of solutions to a quadratic equation through investigating different conditions related to the discriminant.

Understanding and skills

> **Will use**
>
> Solving quadratic equations by completing the square.

> **Will develop**
>
> Determining the different types of roots visually (repeated real root, distinct real roots, no real roots).
>
> Determining the different types of roots algebraically.
>
> Connecting the value of $b^2 - 4ac$ to determining the different types of roots algebraically.

> **Could extend**
>
> Deriving the quadratic formula and explain how different values for the discriminant affects the solutions.

Preparation and materials
- Open and complete the student preview, anticipating classroom responses.
- **Materials:** Paper and pencil

> **Support students with disabilities**
>
> **Support conceptual processing** - self monitor understanding and ask clarifying questions

Have students reflect on their own learning using questions from KWL strategy: "What do I Know? What do I Want to learn? What have I Learned?"

Answers may look like:

Know - ask during the Launch
- I know what the variables a, b, and c stand for in a quadratic equation.
- I know how to solve quadratic equations.
- I know about the different types of solutions a quadratic equation can have.

Want to learn - ask during the second stage of the Explore
- I want to learn what roots each condition will result in.
- I want to learn how a graph can show me roots of a quadratic equation.
- I want to learn about the relationship between coefficients and the roots of a quadratic.

Learned - ask after the class discussion
- I have learned that when $b^2 - 4ac = 0$, the roots are always one repeated real root.
- I have learned that when $a > 0$, the roots sometimes are real roots.
- I have learned that when $b^2 - 4ac < 0$, the roots are never real roots.
- I have learned that when $\frac{b^2}{a} < 4c$, the roots are sometimes distinct, real roots.
- I have learned that when $c = 0$, the roots are always real roots.
- I have learned that when $b = 0$, the roots are sometimes one, repeated real roots.

> **Support for English language learners**
> **Collect and display**

As pairs are working, listen for and collect vocabulary, phrases, and methods students use for testing condition-result pairs. Consider grouping language for each part of the process (meeting the conditions, defining the number of roots). Continue to update collected student language throughout the entire activity. Remind students to borrow language from the display as needed.

Some terms and phrases may include: quadratic equation, solutions, roots, coefficients, repeated real roots, real roots, distinct roots.

Classroom guide

Hook

Open questions • 5 mins

Students write observations about the applet displaying a quadratic function and its type of roots.

Implementation details

Encourage students to connect what they have learned in the previous subtopic about solving quadratic equations by completing the square and the number and nature of solutions to a quadratic equation.

The applet does not have numbers, motivating students to find the solutions for their equation. Ask students to be precise when finding the solutions. If students are struggling to get started, encourage them to use the applet to visualize different types of roots before starting to solve algebraically.

Highlight different student responses that address the different types of roots seen visually in the applet as well as solutions students have found algebraically so far; no real roots, a repeated real root, two distinct real roots. If no one has one type of root, provide an example of a quadratic equation so students see all possibilities and have a chance to connect the graph to the quadratic equation and its solutions.

What do you notice? What do you wonder? Explore the applet.

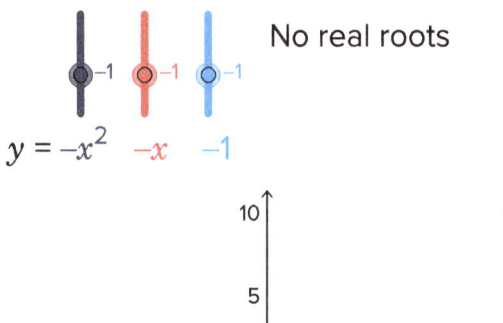

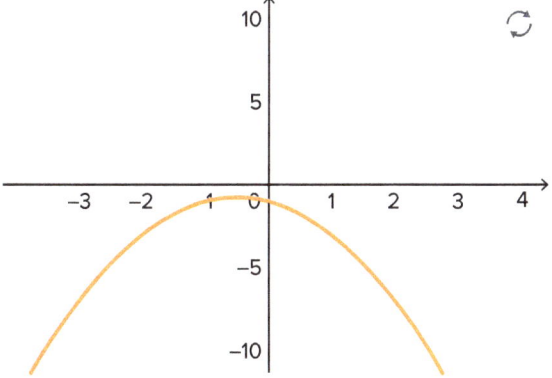

No real roots

$y = -x^2 \quad -x \quad -1$

Slide 1 from Student Engage Activity

8.04 Solve quadratics using the quadratic formula 1033
mathspace.co

Launch

5 mins

Students should read the instructions of the task individually before forming groups. This allows students an opportunity to read each condition and ask questions related to terminology or the goal of the task before moving into groups.

Important mathematical concepts: Coefficients of a quadratic function, standard form, roots, complete the square, discriminant

Suggested grouping: Form groups of 4 and assign roles

This activity relates to the quadratic equation

$$ax^2 + bx + c = 0$$

where a, b, and c are real numbers with $a \neq 0$.

Choose a condition from each column to investigate:

$b^2 - 4ac = 0$	A	$c = 0$	B
$b^2 - 4ac > 0$	C	$b = 0$	D
$b^2 < 4ac$	E	$a < 0$	F

Slide 2 from Student Engage Activity

> **Continue when**
> Students have read the Launch and understand the context of the problem.

Explore

Team roles • 25 mins

Anticipated strategies

Using graphs

Students sketch graphs or use the applet and determine validity of result based on the condition visually. Encourage students to come up with as many different examples as possible before deciding if something is "always" or "never" true. Once students have created multiple examples as justification, prompt them to generalize their observations about the graph, the equations that match the condition, and the number and nature of the roots.

Using algebra

Students complete the square for any quadratic equation that matches the condition (deriving the quadratic formula in some cases) and determine validity of result.

Use the applet to create quadratics that meet the conditions.

$y = -x^2 \quad -x \quad -1$

No real roots
$D = b^2 - 4ac$
$= (-1)^2 - 4(-1)(-1)$
$= -3$

Slide 4 from Student Engage Activity

Students will have a range of responses for their written and visual communication to explain their group's conclusions. Encourage multiple responses and forms for justification. Note the strategies each group is using to highlight in the class discussion.

Some example results:
- $b^2 - 4ac = 0$: Always has one repeated real root
- $b^2 < 4ac$: Always has no real roots
- $b^2 - 4ac > 0$: Always has two distinct real roots
- $a < 0$: Sometimes has distinct real roots, one repeated real root, no real roots
- $c = 0$: Sometimes has distinct real roots or one real root and never has no real roots
- $b = 0$: Sometimes has two distinct real roots, sometimes has repeated real roots, sometimes has no real roots

Misconceptions

Generalizing without testing all possible options
Are these all of the possible types of solutions based on this condition? How do you know?

Not including positive and negative values when multiplying inequality by unknown variable
What are the possible values for a? How could these possible values impact the inequality?

Purposeful questions

Use the following questions to check for understanding and encourage critical thinking:
- What does always, sometimes, or never true mean in this context?
- How can the graph of the quadratic equation be used to understand the statements?
- Can you show this algebraically as well as graphically (or vice versa)?
- Which statements so far are always, sometimes, or never true?
- Are there any patterns you are noticing about parts of the quadratic equation and the number and type of roots?

> **Continue when**
> Students have investigated the roots for two conditions.

Discuss 25 mins

Start with a group discussion. Consider sequencing the strategies presented from graphs, to using algebra.

Discussion guide

Ask groups to share their findings for their chosen statements. Start by asking a group to start the class discussion. Encourage groups to build on other classmate's ideas, such as if one group has a visual explanation for why a statement is always, sometimes, or never true ask if a group had a different way of justifying their group's decision.

If groups do not have an algebraic explanation, ask the class and return to the algebraic justification at the end of the discussion or during the start of the next class. Continue the class discussion to cover all six statements. If as a class some statements were not investigated, discuss them as a class now.

As an extension you may wish to give students the following prompt:

Return to the hook and derive the quadratic formula by completing the square. Ask the class what they notice about parts of the formula. You can introduce the discriminant ($b^2 - 4ac$, what is under the radical in the quadratic formula) and ask students to use their observations from class to try and generalize when the quadratic equation will have no real solutions, one real solution, and two real solutions. This is optional, as this will be discussed in more detail in the next lesson.
- $b^2 - 4ac < 0$: The equation has no real solutions, the graph does not cross the x-axis
- $b^2 - 4ac = 0$: The equation has one repeated real solution, the graph touches the x-axis at one point
- $b^2 - 4ac > 0$: The equation has two distinct real solutions, the graph crosses the x-axis at two points

Lesson Preparation

Suggested review

Depending on your students' level of prior knowledge, consider revisiting the following lessons:

Algebra 1 — 7.01 Characteristics of quadratic functions
Algebra 1 — 8.01 Solve quadratics using graphs and tables
Algebra 1 — 8.03 Solve quadratics using square roots

Tools

You may find these tools helpful:
- Graphing calculator
- Highlighter

Student lesson & teacher guide

The quadratic formula

Students begin with an exploration of solving quadratic equations using any method.

Check for reasonableness using a graph
Targeted instructional strategies

Encourage students to check the reasonableness of their answers by graphing the function. For example, graphing $f(x) = 16x^2 - 24x - 3$ can show that it has x-intercepts at the expected coordinates. This can lead into a discussion about why graphing is not always appropriate in the case of irrational solutions.

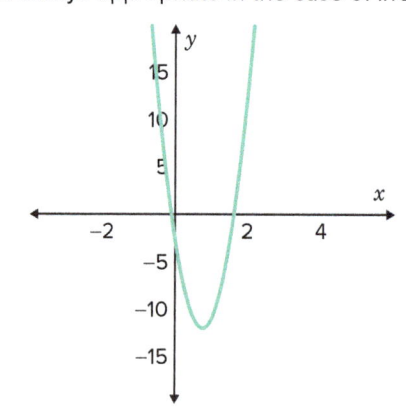

Compare and connect
English language learner support

The "Compare and Connect" strategy encourages students to identify, compare, and contrast different mathematical approaches, representations, concepts, and language, fostering their awareness and enhancing their understanding through reflective discussions.

Ask students to solve a quadratic equation using the square root method and compare their results to the quadratic formula.

Consider the equation $(3x + 5)^2 - 34 = 0$, which has the standard form $9x^2 + 30x - 9 = 0$.

Solving using the square root method gives the solutions:

$$(3x+5)^2 - 34 = 0$$
$$(3x+5)^2 = 34$$
$$3x+5 = \pm\sqrt{34}$$
$$3x = -5 \pm \sqrt{34}$$
$$x = \frac{-5 \pm \sqrt{34}}{3}$$

Solving using the quadratic formula gives the solutions:

$$x = \frac{-b \pm \sqrt{b^2 - 4ac}}{2a}$$
$$= \frac{-30 \pm \sqrt{30^2 - 4(9)(-9)}}{2(9)}$$
$$= \frac{-30 \pm \sqrt{1224}}{18}$$
$$= \frac{-30 \pm 6\sqrt{34}}{18}$$
$$= \frac{-5 \pm \sqrt{34}}{3}$$

Ask students which method they find more comfortable and why. Encourage students to use key vocabulary like "square roots," "substituting," "rearranging," etc. when explaining their reasons.

Double-check the signs in the quadratic formula
Address student misconceptions

When students first use the quadratic formula, forgetting the correct signs can be a common mistake, either with the leading negative sign or the ± sign before the square root.

Remind students to double-check their solutions by substituting them back into the starting equation. It can aso help to have the quadratic formula written out for students in a common place or resource from which they can copy or check.

Exploration

Students: Page 478

8.04 Solve quadratics using the quadratic formula

After this lesson, you will be able to...
- solve quadratic equations using the quadratic formula.
- identify algebraically when a quadratic equation has zero, one, or two real solutions.
- create and solve quadratic equations for a real-world context.

Engage activity
Ask your teacher to get started
Conditions and roots
Students will use various methods to solve quadratic equations to determine whether statements are always, sometimes, or never true. Students will determine the number and nature of solutions to a quadratic equation through investigating different conditions related to the discriminant.

The quadratic formula

Exploration

Solve each of the following quadratic equations:
- $x^2 + 0.5x - 3 = 0$
- $3x^2 + 5x - 11 = 0$

1. Which method did you choose and why?
2. Did you find it challenging to solve the problems? If so, why?

Suggested student grouping: In pairs
Students are given two quadratic equations to solve using any preferred method. A suggestion for implementation is to allow students to attempt the problems independently, then pairing up with a classmate who may have solved each equation using a different method.

Ideal student responses
These ideal responses may differ from other correct student responses. Less formal responses can be connected with the more precise mathematical language presented here.

1. **Which method did you choose and why?**
   Students may state that they solved equations by graphing, completing the square, or factoring.

2. **Did you find it challenging to solve the problems? If so, why?**
   When an equation is not factorable or is not written in a form that is set up to solve using square roots, it may be more challenging to solve or plan a strategy for solving. Graphing technology allows us to solve these equations easily, but we cannot always find the exact solution.

Purposeful questions
- Is it possible to factor the polynomial to solve the equation?
- If you could not graph the polynomial, how would you solve the equation?
- What methods for solving quadratic equations have we learned about in this course?

Possible misunderstandings
- Students may state methods that we can use to solve quadratic equations without actually solving the equations in the exploration. Encourage students to use those methods to solve the equations.

Students are presented with a new method for solving quadratic equations: the quadratic formula.

Students: Page 478

When given a quadratic equation, we can try to solve it by factoring, but not all equations are factorable. We can try to solve by graphing, but we would have to estimate the solutions if they are not integer values. We can try to solve using the square root property, but the equation needs to be in a specific form first. The only method we know so far that can solve any quadratic is completing the square.

The **quadratic formula** is another method that can be used to solve any quadratic equation.

Before we can use the quadratic formula, we have to rearrange the quadratic equation into the form $ax^2 + bx + c = 0$, where a, b, and c are any number and $a \neq 0$. Once the equation is in this form, the solutions are given by the quadratic formula:

$$x = \frac{-b \pm \sqrt{b^2 - 4ac}}{2a}$$

a The coefficent of x^2
b The coefficent of x
c The constant

We say that $a \neq 0$ because, if it were, we wouldn't have an x^2 term and the equation wouldn't be quadratic. However, the parameter a can be any other real number, and b or c can be any real number without restriction.

Examples

Students: Page 479

Example 1

The standard form of a quadratic equation is $ax^2 + bx + c = 0$.

a   Derive the quadratic formula by solving this equation for x.

Create a strategy
To solve for x, we can complete the square.

Apply the idea

$$ax^2 + bx + c = 0$$

$$x^2 + \frac{b}{a}x + \frac{c}{a} = 0 \qquad \text{Division property of equality}$$

$$x^2 + \frac{b}{a}x = -\frac{c}{a} \qquad \text{Subtraction property of equality}$$

$$x^2 + \frac{b}{a}x + \left(\frac{b}{2a}\right)^2 = \left(\frac{b}{2a}\right)^2 - \frac{c}{a} \qquad \text{Complete the square}$$

$$\left(x + \frac{b}{2a}\right)^2 = \left(\frac{b}{2a}\right)^2 - \frac{c}{a} \qquad \text{Factor the left side}$$

$$\left(x + \frac{b}{2a}\right)^2 = \frac{b^2}{4a^2} - \frac{c}{a} \qquad \text{Evaluate the exponent}$$

$$\left(x + \frac{b}{2a}\right)^2 = \frac{b^2 - 4ac}{4a^2} \qquad \text{Evaluate the subtraction}$$

$$x + \frac{b}{2a} = \pm\sqrt{\frac{b^2 - 4ac}{4a^2}} \qquad \text{Square root property}$$

$$x + \frac{b}{2a} = \pm\frac{\sqrt{b^2 - 4ac}}{2a} \qquad \text{Evaluate the square root}$$

$$x = -\frac{b}{2a} \pm \frac{\sqrt{b^2 - 4ac}}{2a} \qquad \text{Subtraction property of equality}$$

$$x = \frac{-b \pm \sqrt{b^2 - 4ac}}{2a} \qquad \text{Evaluate the addition}$$

Reflect and check

The standard form of a quadratic equation represents any quadratic equation. Since we solved this equation for x, this formula can be used to find the solution to any quadratic equation.

Purpose
Advanced learners show how to derive the quadratic formula from the standard form of a quadratic equation by completing the square.

Expected mistakes
Students may attempt to begin completing the square without factoring the coefficient of x^2 first. Point out to students that the coefficient of x^2 must be 1 when completing the square.

Reflecting with students
Remind students that if we know the formula we are attempting to derive, it may be helpful to look at the formula we are attempting to work toward as we work through the steps to derive it.

Students: Pages 479–480

b Use the quadratic formula to solve the equation $-x^2 + 6x - 8 = 0$

Create a strategy

First, we need to make sure the equation is in standard form and equal to zero. This one already is, so we can see that $a = -1$, $b = 6$, and $c = -8$. We can substitute these values into the quadratic formula to solve for x.

Apply the idea

$$x = \frac{-(6) \pm \sqrt{(6)^2 - 4(-1)(-8)}}{2(-1)}$$ Quadratic formula with $a = -1$, $b = 6$, and $c = -8$

$$= \frac{-6 \pm \sqrt{36 - 32}}{-2}$$ Evaluate the exponent and multiplication

$$= \frac{-6 \pm \sqrt{4}}{-2}$$ Evaluate the subtraction

$$= \frac{-6 \pm 2}{-2}$$ Evaluate the square root

Now, we can separate this into the two answers:

$$x = \frac{-6 + 2}{-2} \text{ and } x = \frac{-6 - 2}{-2}$$

When we simplify, we find the answers to be $x = 2$ and $x = 4$.

Reflect and check

Since the answers are rational, we could have solved the quadratic equation by factoring.

$-x^2 + 6x - 8 = 0$ Given equation
$-(x^2 - 6x + 8) = 0$ Factor out -1
$-(x - 4)(x - 2) = 0$ Factor the trinomial

Using the zero product property, we get the answers $x = 4$ and $x = 2$.

Purpose

Show students how to solve an equation using the quadratic formula.

Expected mistakes

Students may forget or skip using negative signs when initially working through the quadratic formula to solve a problem. Remind students that parentheses around values that we substituted for variables will help us keep track of the signage.

Reflecting with students

Ask students to check their answer using another method for solving a quadratic equation. Students may solve the equation by graphing, factoring, or completing the square.

Students: Pages 480–481

> c Use the quadratic formula to solve the equation $5x^2 = 8x + 1$.
>
> **Create a strategy**
> Before using the quadratic formula, we need to get the equation in the form $ax^2 + bx + c = 0$. Then, we can correctly identify the values of a, b, and c.
>
> **Apply the idea**
>
> $\quad\quad\quad\quad\quad 5x^2 = 8x + 1 \quad$ Given equation
>
> $\quad\quad\quad 5x^2 - 8x - 1 = 0 \quad$ Subtraction property of equality
>
> Now we can see $a = 5$, $b = -8$, $c = -1$.
>
> $x = \dfrac{-(-8) \pm \sqrt{(-8)^2 - 4(5)(-1)}}{2(5)} \quad$ Quadratic formula with $a = 5$, $b = -8$, and $c = -1$
>
> $\quad= \dfrac{8 \pm \sqrt{64 + 20}}{10} \quad$ Evaluate the exponent and multiplication
>
> $\quad= \dfrac{8 \pm \sqrt{84}}{10} \quad$ Evaluate the addition
>
> $\quad= \dfrac{8 \pm \sqrt{4}\sqrt{21}}{10} \quad$ Product of radicals
>
> $\quad= \dfrac{8 \pm 2\sqrt{21}}{10} \quad$ Evaluate the square root
>
> $\quad= \dfrac{4 \pm \sqrt{21}}{5} \quad$ Simplify by a factor of 2
>
> The answers are $x = \dfrac{4 + \sqrt{21}}{5}$ and $x = \dfrac{4 - \sqrt{21}}{5}$.
>
> **Reflect and check**
> When the answer is irrational, then the quadratic formula or completing the square are the only methods we could use to solve the quadratic equation.

Purpose
Show students how to solve a quadratic equation by first converting it to standard form and then using the quadratic formula.

Expected mistakes
Students may assume that $a = 5$, $b = 8$, and $c = 1$, without confirming that the equation is in the form $ax^2 + bx + c = 0$ first. Remind students that the equation must be set equal to zero to use the quadratic formula.

Reflecting with students
Ask students the number of x-intercepts the function $y = 5x^2 - 8x - 1$ would have if we graphed it on a coordinate plane. We know that when the equation is equal to zero, we have two solutions for x. This would mean that graphically when $y = 0$, there are two x-intercepts.

Students: Page 481

> **Example 2**

Solve:

a $5x^2 - 15x + 2 = 0$

Create a strategy

Rearrange the equation into the form $ax^2 + bx + c = 0$, then use the quadratic formula.

Apply the idea

The equation $5x^2 - 15x + 2 = 0$ is already in standard form so we can identify a, b, and c. We can see that $a = 5$, $b = -15$, and $c = 2$ and substitute them into the quadratic formula.

$x = \dfrac{-b \pm \sqrt{b^2 - 4ac}}{2a}$ Quadratic formula

$x = \dfrac{-(-15) \pm \sqrt{(-15)^2 - 4 \cdot 5 \cdot 2}}{2 \cdot 5}$ Substitute $a = 5$, $b = -15$, $c = 2$

$x = \dfrac{15 \pm \sqrt{(-15)^2 - 4 \cdot 5 \cdot 2}}{2 \cdot 5}$ Simplify the adjacent signs

$x = \dfrac{15 \pm \sqrt{(-15)^2 - 40}}{10}$ Evaluate the multiplication

$x = \dfrac{15 \pm \sqrt{225 - 40}}{10}$ Evaluate the exponent

$x = \dfrac{15 \pm \sqrt{185}}{10}$ Evaluate the subtraction

So the solutions are $x = \dfrac{15 + \sqrt{185}}{10}$ and $x = \dfrac{15 - \sqrt{185}}{10}$.

Purpose

Show students how to use the quadratic formula to find the roots of a quadratic equation.

Students: Pages 481–482

b $10 - 6m + 2m^2 = m^2 + 8m + 9$

Create a strategy

Rearrange the equation into the form $ax^2 + bx + c = 0$, and use the quadratic formula.

Apply the idea

$10 - 6m + 2m^2 = m^2 + 8m + 9$ Original equation

$10 - 6m + m^2 = 8m + 9$ Subtract m^2 from both sides

$10 - 14m + m^2 = 9$ Subtract $8m$ from both sides

$1 - 14m + m^2 = 0$ Subtract 9 from both sides

$m^2 - 14m + 1 = 0$ Write in descending order

Now we can see that $a = 1$, $b = -14$, and $c = 1$ so we can substitute these values into the quadratic formula.

$m = \dfrac{-b \pm \sqrt{b^2 - 4ac}}{2a}$ Quadratic formula

$m = \dfrac{-(-14) \pm \sqrt{(-14)^2 - 4 \cdot 1 \cdot 1}}{2 \cdot 1}$ Substitute $a = 1$, $b = -14$, $c = 1$

$m = \dfrac{14 \pm \sqrt{(-14)^2 - 4 \cdot 1 \cdot 1}}{2 \cdot 1}$ Simplify the adjacent signs

$m = \dfrac{14 \pm \sqrt{(-14)^2 - 4}}{2}$ Evaluate the multiplication

$m = \dfrac{14 \pm \sqrt{196 - 4}}{2}$ Evaluate the exponent

$m = \dfrac{14 \pm \sqrt{192}}{2}$ Simplify the expression inside the square root

$m = \dfrac{14 \pm 8\sqrt{3}}{2}$ Simplify the square root

$m = 7 \pm 4\sqrt{3}$ Divide out the common factor of 2

So the solutions are $m = 7 + 4\sqrt{3}$ and $m = 7 - 4\sqrt{3}$.

Purpose

Challenge students to rearrange a quadratic equation into standard form and solve it using the quadratic formula.

Students: Pages 482–483

Example 3

A ball is launched from a height of 80 ft with an initial velocity of 107 ft per second. Its height, h feet, after x seconds is given by

$$h = -16x^2 + 107x + 80$$

Determine the number of seconds it will take the ball to reach the ground. Explain your reasoning.

Create a strategy

On the ground the ball will have a height of 0 ft, so $h = 0$. This means we want to solve the equation $0 = -16x^2 + 107x + 80$. Since the numbers are large, the quadratic formula is an appropriate method for solving.

Apply the idea

For this equation, $a = -16$, $b = 107$, and $c = 80$. Substituting into the quadratic equation, we get

$x = \dfrac{-(107) \pm \sqrt{(107)^2 - 4(-16)(80)}}{2(-16)}$ Quadratic formula with $a = -16$, $b = 107$, and $c = 80$

$= \dfrac{-107 \pm \sqrt{11449 + 5120}}{-32}$ Evaluate the exponent and multiplication

$= \dfrac{-107 \pm \sqrt{16569}}{-32}$ Evaluate the addition

$= \dfrac{-107 \pm \sqrt{9}\sqrt{1841}}{-32}$ Product of radicals

$= \dfrac{-107 \pm 3\sqrt{1841}}{-32}$ Evaluate the square root

Therefore, $x = \dfrac{-107 + 3\sqrt{1841}}{-32}$ and $x = \dfrac{-107 - 3\sqrt{1841}}{-32}$.

The two solutions, rounded to two decimal places, are $x = -0.68$ and $x = 7.37$. Remember that x represents seconds. We can exclude the negative solution as it is outside the domain, which is $x \geq 0$, since time cannot be negative.

The ball will reach the ground after 7.37 seconds.

Reflect and check

In many real-world situations, negative numbers do not make sense. Always check that your answers satisfy the constraints of the variables.

Purpose
Students demonstrate how to solve an equation using the quadratic formula and determine an appropriate solution in context.

Expected mistakes
Students may leave their solution in exact form, rather than simplifying and using a decimal. Remind students that for problems that do not specify rounding or the form of the solution, particularly for contextual problems, students should use their judgment to make a decision about how to present a solution that is mathematically reasonable for the problem. In this case, writing the seconds in decimal form makes more sense than writing seconds in exact form.

Reflecting with students
Ask students why they can solve the equation for two solutions, but may only use one that is counted as valid. Point out the connection between the graph of the function having two x-intercepts, which occur when $h = 0$. Then refer to the context of the problem again.

Three reads
English language learner support

use with Example 3

Advise students to read through the instructions a few times, focusing on gathering different information each time in order to build up their understanding of what the question is asking.

On the first read, students should aim to identify the scenario presented in the question. Ask students "What do you think is happening in this question?" or "Can you explain what this question is about?"

On the second read, students should aim to interpret the problem by answering questions like "What is the question asking you to find?" and "What information should be included in the answer?"

On the third read, students should look for important information in the instructions. In this question, the important information includes: the equation for the height of the ball, h represents the height of the ball, and x is the number of seconds after the ball is thrown. Students can be prompted by framing these as questions like "What does each variable in the equation represent?"

Students: Page 483

> ### Example 4
>
> The amount of litter in a park at the end of the day can be modeled against the number of people who visited the park that day by the equation:
>
> $$L = -\frac{1}{50}(P^2 - 73P - 150)$$
>
> where L is the number of pieces of litter and P is the number of people.
>
> Determine the number of people who visited the park if there are 20 pieces of litter at the end of the day.
>
> **Create a strategy**
>
> We want to find the number of people, P, when there are 20 pieces of litter at the end of the day, $L = 20$.
>
> We can do this by substituting $L = 20$ into the equation, rearranging the equation into quadratic standard form, and then using the quadratic formula to solve for P.
>
> **Apply the idea**
>
> | | |
> |---|---|
> | $L = -\frac{1}{50}(P^2 - 73P - 150)$ | Model equation |
> | $20 = -\frac{1}{50}(P^2 - 73P - 150)$ | Substitute in $L = 20$ |
> | $-1000 = P^2 - 73P - 150$ | Multiply both sides by -50 |
> | $0 = P^2 - 73P + 850$ | Add 1000 to both sides |
> | $P = \frac{-(-73) \pm \sqrt{(-73)^2 - 4(1)(850)}}{2(1)}$ | Quadratic formula with $a = 1$, $b = -73$, and $c = 850$ |
> | $P = \frac{73 \pm \sqrt{1929}}{2}$ | Evaluate the operations |
>
> The two solutions (rounded to two decimal places) are $P = 58.46$ and $P = 14.54$. Since we are counting the number of people who visited the park, we want to round to the nearest whole number.
>
> If there are 20 pieces of litter in the park at the end of the day, then either 58 or 15 people visited the park that day.
>
> **Reflect and check**
>
> In real life applications where we are counting whole objects, we want to round to the nearest integer, so our solution makes sense in context.

Purpose

Students demonstrate how to substitute a value into an equation given with a context, and convert the equation to standard form in order to solve for the variable using the quadratic formula. Students interpret the solution to the equation in context.

Expected mistakes

Students may attempt to substitute the value of 20 as P and solve the equation for L. Point out to students that writing out or highlighting what variables in contextual problems represent is a skill for keeping track of whether the math we work through makes sense.

Students: Page 484

> 💡 **Idea summary**
> For any quadratic equation of the form $0 = ax^2 + bx + c$ where $a \neq 0$ and a, b, and c are real numbers, the quadratic formula can be used to solve for x.
> $$x = \frac{-b \pm \sqrt{b^2 - 4ac}}{2a}$$

The discriminant

Students learn that a specific expression within the quadratic formula is called the discriminant.

Students: Page 484

The discriminant

The radicand in the quadratic formula is called the **discriminant**.

$$x = \frac{-b \pm \sqrt{b^2 - 4ac}}{2a}$$

$b^2 - 4ac$ discriminant

The discriminant can be used to determine the number and type of solutions to any quadratic equation.

👥 Why the discriminant determines the number of real roots
Student with disabilities support

Some students may not immediately grasp why the discriminant can be used to determine the number and nature of the solutions to a quadratic equation.

Highlight the square root component of the quadratic formula and ask students what would happen to the solutions if the radicand was positive, negative, or zero.

$$x = \frac{-b}{2a} \pm \frac{\sqrt{b^2 - 4ac}}{2a}$$

If necessary, remind students that the square root of a negative number cannot be a real number, and the square root of zero is zero.

Point out that the radicand is the discriminant, so its value can be used to determine the number and nature of the roots.

Exploration

Students: Page 484

> **Interactive exploration**
> Explore online to answer the questions
>
> 🌐 mathspace.co

Use the interactive exploration in 8.04 to answer these questions.

1. What do each of the sliders represent?
2. How many types of roots can there be?
3. How do the types of roots relate to the value of the discriminant, D?
4. How do the x-intercepts relate to the value of the discriminant, D?

Suggested student grouping: In pairs

Students use a GeoGebra applet to manipulate a quadratic function. The applet substitutes the values from the function into the discriminant. Students discover that when the discriminant is positive there are two x-intcerepts, when the discriminant is zero there is one x-intercept, and when the discriminant is negative there are no x-intercepts.

Ideal student responses

These ideal responses may differ from other correct student responses. Less formal responses can be connected with the more precise mathematical language presented here.

1. **What do each of the sliders represent?**
   Each slider represents a coefficient or constant in the standard form of a quadratic function: $y = ax^2 + bx + c$. The gray slider represents the value of a, the red slider represents b, and the blue slider represents c.

2. **How many types of roots can there be?**
   There are three different types of solutions: one real root with one x-intercept, two real roots with two x-intercepts, and no real roots with no x-intercepts.

3. **How do the types of roots relate to the value of the discriminant, D?**
   When the discriminant is zero, there is one real root. When the discriminant is positive, there are two real roots. When the discriminant is negative, there are no real roots.

4. **How do the x-intercepts relate to the value of the discriminant, D?**
   When the discriminant is zero, there is one x-intercept. When the discriminant is positive, there are two x-intercepts. When the discriminant is negative, there are no x-intercepts.

Purposeful questions
- Where do the values in the discriminant, D, come from?
- What happens to the discriminant when the graph intersects the x-axis exactly once?

Possible misunderstandings
- Students may state that there are only two types of roots when moving the graph of the quadratic function. Use purposeful questions to guide students to graph a parabola that will intersect the graph exactly once as well.

Students compare the graphs of quadratic equations to the equations' real solutions when $y = 0$, the discriminant, and the x-intercepts.

Students: Pages 484–485

The values of a, b, and c affect the value of the discriminant. The type of number the discriminant is affects the number and type of x-intercepts on the graph.

Quadratic equations can have 3 types of solutions: 2 real solutions, 1 real solution, or no real solutions. The value of the discriminant quickly reveals which type of solution a quadratic equation has.

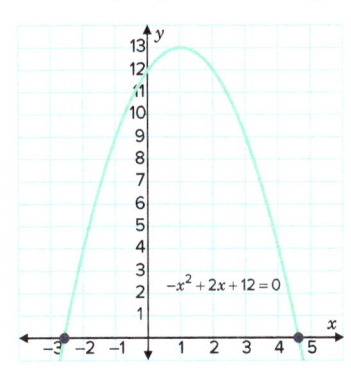

Discriminant (> 0):

$b^2 - 4ac = (2)^2 - 4(-1)(12) = 52$

Solutions:

$x = \dfrac{-2 \pm \sqrt{52}}{-2} = 1 \pm \sqrt{13}$

x-intercepts:

$\left(1 + \sqrt{13}, 0\right)$ and $\left(1 - \sqrt{13}, 0\right)$

The square root of a positive number is a real number, so the plus or minus sign ensures there will always be 2 real solutions when the discriminant is positive.

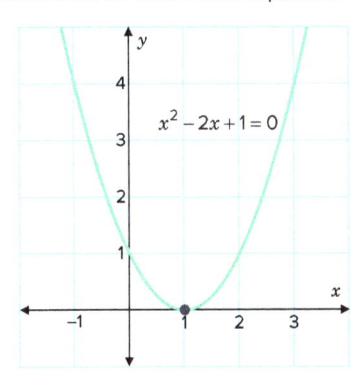

Discriminant ($= 0$):

$b^2 - 4ac = (-2)^2 - 4(1)(1) = 0$

Solution:

$x = \dfrac{2 \pm \sqrt{0}}{2} = 1$

x-intercept:

$(1, 0)$

The square root of zero is zero. This eliminates the radical part of the quadratic equation, leaving only $x = \dfrac{-b}{2a}$ which will result in a single value. So, when the discriminant is zero, there will be one real solution.

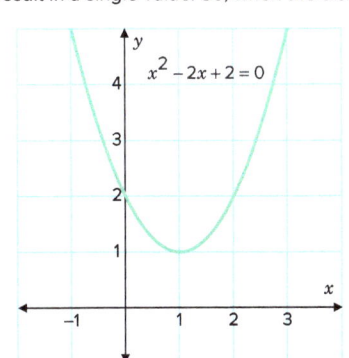

Discriminant (<0):

$b^2 - 4ac = (-2)^2 - 4(1)(2) = -4$

Solutions:

$x = \dfrac{2 \pm \sqrt{-4}}{2}$

x-intercepts:

None

No real number gives us a negative number when squared. Therefore, there are no real solutions when the discriminant is negative.

Examples

Students: Page 485

Example 4

Use the discriminant to determine the number and nature of the solutions of the following quadratic equations:

a $2x^2 - 8x + 3 = 0$

Create a strategy
For this equation, we have $a = 2, b = -8, c = 3$.

Apply the idea
The discriminant is $(-8)^2 - 4(2)(3) = 40$. Since it is positive, the equation has two real solutions.

Reflect and check
Two real solutions means the function has two x-intercepts.

Purpose
Make students aware that a positive discriminant will lead to an equation with two real solutions.

Reflecting with students
Students may be unsure how the discriminant for the problem indicates the number of real solutions when beginning to evaluate it. Help students visualize why this makes sense when the discriminant is positive, negative, or zero by graphing $y = 2x^2 - 8x + 3$ using technology and pointing out where $y = 0$ on the graph of the function. This is where the polynomial expression is equal to zero and we can visualize the number of x-intercepts.

Students: Page 486

b $-5x^2 + 6x - 2 = 0$

Create a strategy
For this equation, we have $a = -5, b = 6, c = -2$.

Apply the idea
The discriminant has a value of $(6)^2 - 4(-5)(-2) = -4$. Since it is negative, the equation has no real solutions.

Reflect and check
If the discriminant is negative, then the formula will involve taking the square root of a negative number which will result in no real solutions. This quadratic will not intercept the x-axis.

We can also see that if $4ac > b^2$ the discriminant will be negative, and the corresponding equation will have no real solutions.

Purpose
Make students aware that a negative discriminant will lead to an equation with no real solutions.

Reflecting with students
Ask students to write their own quadratic equations that will lead to a negative discriminant. Students may see a pattern in the equation itself as they proceed to attempt to write their own equations that lead to equations with no real solutions.

Students: Page 486

c $x^2 - 3x + 9 = 3x$

Create a strategy
Before identifying our variables, the equation must be in the form $ax^2 + bx + c = 0$, so we need to begin by subtracting $3x$ from both sides.
$$x^2 - 6x + 9 = 0$$
For this equation, we have $a = 1$, $b = -6$, $c = 9$.

Apply the idea
The discriminant has a value of $(-6)^2 - 4(1)(9) = 0$, so the equation has one real solution.

Reflect and check
When the discriminant is zero, the quadratic equation simplifies to be $x = -\dfrac{b}{2a}$, which is equal to the x-value of the vertex. This means the vertex lies on the x-axis and the x-coordinate of the vertex is the only solution to the quadratic equation.

Purpose
Make students aware that a discriminant of zero will lead to an equation with one real solution.

Expected mistakes
Students may forget we can only use the quadratic formula when equations are in the form $ax^2 + bx + c = 0$.

Help students see patterns in determining the sign of the discriminant use with Example 5
Targeted instructional strategies

Ask students if they can identify when the discriminant will always be positive. Draw their attention to the possible signs of the two terms, b^2 and $4ac$.

Remind students that the square of a real number must be positive, so if $4ac$ is negative then $-4ac$ will be positive. If this is the case, then the discriminant must also be positive. Ask students to consider when $4ac$ is negative. Direct students to the fact that the sign of a product is determined by the signs of the numbers being multiplied. In this case, $4ac$ will be negative when a and c have opposite signs.

This means that the discriminant of a quadratic equation in standard form with a and c having opposite signs will always have real solutions.

For further understanding, ask students if they can explain why this is the case (the explanation involves the direction in which the parabola opens and the y-intercept).

Students: Page 486

Idea summary
The discriminant, $b^2 - 4ac$, can help us determine the type and number of solutions to a quadratic equation without needing to solve the equation fully.

- $b^2 - 4ac > 0$ two real solutions
- $b^2 - 4ac = 0$ one real solution
- $b^2 - 4ac < 0$ no real solutions

Practice

Students: Pages 487–490

What do you remember?

1 Is each statement true or false?

a Any quadratic equation that can be solved by completing the square can also be solved by the quadratic formula.

b Any quadratic equation that can be solved by factoring can also be solved by the quadratic formula.

c The equation $3x^2 + 3x - 7 = 0$ can be solved using the quadratic formula.

d The quadratic formula will always give 2 unique solutions.

e For the equation $5x^2 - x - 2 = 0$, we would set $a = 5$, $b = 1$, and $c = -2$.

2 The standard form of a quadratic equation is $ax^2 + bx + c = 0$. Find the values of a, b and c in the following quadratic equations:

a $x^2 - 6x + 5 = 0$
b $-4x^2 + 15x - 8 = 0$
c $x^2 + 7x = 10$
d $\dfrac{x^2}{3} - 3x - 4 = 0$

e $2x^2 + 9x = 0$
f $-5(x - 3)^2 + 4 = 0$

3 Jeremy is using the quadratic formula for the equation $9y^2 = 8y$. He has correctly identified that $b = 8$, what are the values of a and c?

4 Given the quadratic equation $x^2 - 4x + k = 0$, where k is a constant, if one of the roots is $2 + \sqrt{3}$, what is the other root?

5 The solutions of a quadratic equation are 9 and –9. What can be said about the value of $b^2 - 4ac$?

6 Consider the quadratic equation:
$$x^2 + 3x - 5 = 0$$

Select the solution to the quadratic equation.

A $x = \dfrac{-3 + \sqrt{29}}{2}, x = \dfrac{-3 - \sqrt{29}}{2}$
B $x = \dfrac{-3 + \sqrt{14}}{2}, x = \dfrac{-3 - \sqrt{14}}{2}$

C $x = \dfrac{-3 + \sqrt{23}}{2}, x = \dfrac{-3 - \sqrt{23}}{2}$
D $x = \dfrac{-3 + \sqrt{8}}{2}, x = \dfrac{-3 - \sqrt{8}}{2}$

7 Consider the quadratic equation:
$$x^2 - 16x = 5x - 9$$

Select the solution to the quadratic equation.

A $x = \dfrac{21 + 3\sqrt{53}}{2}, x = \dfrac{21 - 3\sqrt{53}}{2}$
B $x = \dfrac{-21 + 3\sqrt{53}}{2}, x = \dfrac{-21 - 3\sqrt{53}}{2}$

C $x = \dfrac{21 + 9\sqrt{5}}{2}, x = \dfrac{21 - 9\sqrt{5}}{2}$
D $x = \dfrac{-21 + 9\sqrt{5}}{2}, x = \dfrac{-21 - 9\sqrt{5}}{2}$

Let's practice

8 For the following equations:

i Find the value of the discriminant.

ii State the number of real solutions for the equation.

a $3x^2 - 5x + 7 = 0$
b $x^2 - 4 = 0$
c $-x^2 - 8x - 16 = 0$
d $\dfrac{1}{2}x^2 + 3x + 9 = 0$

e $2x^2 - 2x = x - 1$
f $4x^2 - x = x^2 - 5$

9 For the following equations:
  i   Determine the number of real solutions. Explain your reasoning.
  ii Find the real solution(s) of the equation.

  a $x^2 - 8x - 48 = 0$
  b $4x^2 - 4x + 1 = 0$
  c $x^2 - 4x + 7 = 0$
  d $x^2 + 11x + 28 = 0$
  e $x^2 + 5x + \dfrac{9}{4} = 0$
  f $x^2 + 12x + 36 = 0$

10 For the following equations:
  i   Find the value of the discriminant.
  ii State the number and nature of the solutions to the equation.

  a $x^2 + 6x = -90$
  b $4x^2 = 6x - 7$
  c $2x^2 - 2x = x - 1$
  d $6 - 9x = -2x^2 - 4x$

11 Solve the following equations using the quadratic formula. Round your answers to two decimal places.

  a $13 + x^2 = -7x$
  b $-x^2 - 5x = 8$
  c $5x^2 + 13x + 10 = x^2 - 7x - 15$
  d $-7 + 3x = 2x^2 - 5$
  e $1.8x^2 + 5.2x - 2.3 = 0$
  f $3x(x + 4) = -3x + 4$

12 Solve each equation below using the quadratic formula. Justify your work. Leave your answer(s) in exact, simplified form.

  a $x^2 - 7x + 9 = 0$
  b $x^2 - 5x - 2 = 0$
  c $-2x^2 - 15x - 4 = 0$
  d $3x^2 + 9x - 4 = 0$
  e $-5x^2 - 15x + 3 = 0$
  f $5x = (x - 5)(3x + 3)$
  g $3n^2 = 2n^2 - 2n + 7$
  h $12 - 8m + 2m^2 = m^2 + 12m + 15$

13 Solve each equation below using the quadratic formula. Verify your solution(s) by graphing.

  a $x^2 + 5x + 6 = 0$
  b $x^2 - 5x + 6 = 0$
  c $2x^2 + 6x - 8 = 0$
  d $4x^2 - 10x + 4 = 0$
  e $2x^2 + 7x + 3 = 0$
  f $4x^2 - 17x - 15 = 0$

14 Yuri is playing baseball and hits a homerun with an initial velocity of 101 ft/s, from a height of 3 ft. After x seconds, its height (in feet) is given by
$$h = -16x^2 + 101x + 3$$
LaDeana is in the crowd and catches the homerun ball in the stands from a height of 15 ft above the ground.

Determine the number of seconds after Yuri hits the ball that LaDeana catches it. Round your answer to two decimal places.

15 The stopping distance of a car when the brakes are applied can be modeled by the equation $s = 2.2u + \dfrac{u^2}{20}$ where s is the stopping distance in feet and u is the initial speed in miles per hour.

  a Determine the speed the car was travelling if its stopping distance was 100 ft, rounding your answer to the nearest hundredth of a mile.
  b It takes 399 ft to stop when travelling at the speed limit of 70 mph. If it takes Ray 496 ft to stop, determine how fast over the speed limit Ray was driving.

16 The number of customers at a restaurant can be estimated by the equation
$$y = -x^2 + 28x - 159$$
where y is the number of people and x is the hour of the day (in 24-hour time).

Determine the opening hours of the restaurant. Explain your reasoning.

Let's extend our thinking

17 For each of the given solutions to a quadratic equation:
  i   Find the values of a, b and c.
  ii Write down the quadratic equation that has these solutions.

  a $x = \dfrac{-5 \pm \sqrt{5^2 - 4 \cdot (-7) \cdot 10}}{2 \cdot (-7)}$

  b $x = \dfrac{-22 \pm \sqrt{484 - 108}}{18}$

18 Use the discriminant to match each quadratic equation below with the correct graph. Explain your reasoning
  a $5x^2 - 10x - 35 = 0$ b $2x^2 + 8x + 8 = 0$ c $x^2 - x + 1 = 0$

A

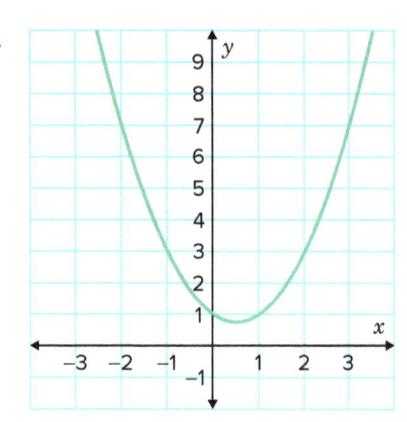

B

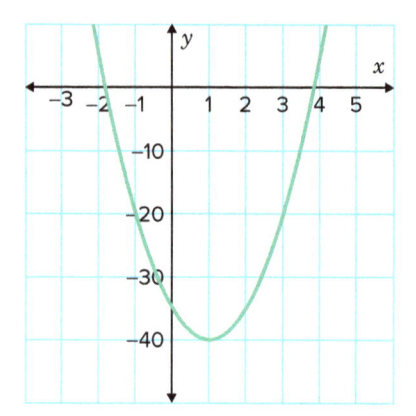

C

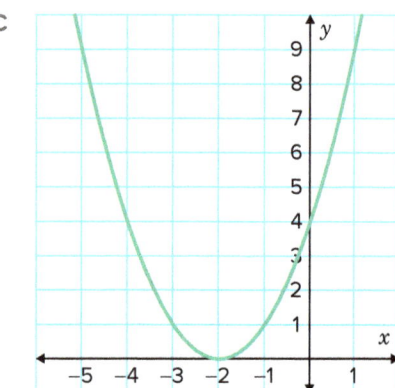

19 Consider the equation in terms of x:

$$mx^2 - 3x - 5 = 0$$

  a   Given that it has two unique solutions, determine the possible values of m.
  b   There is one value of m that must be eliminated from the range of solutions found in the previous part. Determine the solution and explain why it must be eliminated.

20 Find the values of n for which $x^2 - 8nx + 1296 = 0$ has one solution.

21 With reference to the discriminant, explain what determines the nature of the solutions to a quadratic equation.

22 Determine the range of values of the constant k such that the equation $3x^2 + kx + 12 = 0$ has no real solutions. Justify your answer.

23 Use an algebraic method to show that the graphs of the functions $f(x) = 3x^2 - x + 8$ and $g(x) = -x^2 + 2x - 4$ do not intersect.

24 A quadratic equation has two real solutions whose difference is k, for some positive value k. Determine algebraically a simplified expression for the discriminant of this equation.

25 Consider a right-angled triangle with side lengths x units, $x + p$ units and $x + q$ units, ordered from shortest to longest. No two sides of this triangle have the same length.

    a Complete the statement:

       p and q have lengths such that $0 < \square < \square$.

    b Write a quadratic equation in standard form that describes the relationship between the sides of the triangle in terms of x.

    c Find the discriminant of this quadratic equation.

    d Determine the number of real solutions.

    e Find the value of x when $q = 2p$. Give your answer in terms of p.

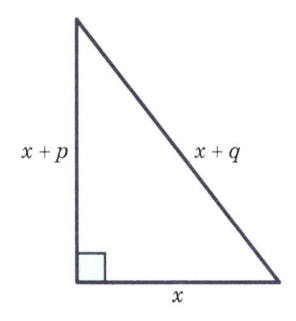

Answers

8.04 Solve quadratics using the quadratic formula

What do you remember?

1 a True b True c True d False
  e False

2 a $a=1, b=-6, c=5$ b $a=-4, b=15, c=-8$
  c $a=1, b=7, c=-10$ d $a=\frac{1}{3}, b=-3, c=-4$
  e $a=2, b=9, c=0$ f $a=-5, b=30, c=-41$

3 $a=-9, c=0$

4 $2-\sqrt{3}$

5 $b^2-4ac>0$

6 A

7 C

Let's practice

8 a i $\Delta=-59$ ii 0
  b i $\Delta=16$ ii 2
  c i $\Delta=0$ ii 1
  d i $\Delta=-9$ ii 0
  e i $\Delta=1$ ii 2
  f i $\Delta=-59$ ii 0

9 a i 2 real solutions because the discriminant is 256, greater than 0.
    ii $x=12, x=-4$
  b i 1 real solution because the discriminant is 0.
    ii $x=\frac{1}{2}$
  c i No real solutions because the discriminant is −12, less than 0.
    ii No real solutions
  d i 2 real solutions because the discriminant is 9, greater than 0.
    ii $x=-7, x=-4$
  e i 2 real solutions because the discriminant is 16, greater than 0.
    ii $x=-\frac{1}{2}, x=-\frac{9}{2}$
  f i 1 real solution because the discriminant is 0.
    ii $x=-6$

10 a i 0 ii The equation has 1 real solution.
   b i −76 ii The equation has 0 real solutions.
   c i 1 ii The equation has 2 real solutions.
   d i −23 ii The equation has 0 real solutions.

11 a No real solutions b No real solutions
   c $x=-\frac{5}{2}$ d No real solutions
   e $x=0.39, x=-3.28$ f $x=0.25, x=-5.25$

12 a $x^2-7x+9=0$ Given equation

  $x=\dfrac{-(-7)\pm\sqrt{(-7)^2-4(1)(9)}}{2(1)}$ Quadratic formula with $a=1, b=-7,$ and $c=9$

  $=\dfrac{7\pm\sqrt{49-36}}{2}$ Evaluate the exponent and multiplication

  $=\dfrac{7\pm\sqrt{13}}{2}$ Evaluate the subtraction

  $x=\dfrac{7\pm\sqrt{13}}{2}$

  b $x^2-5x-2=0$ Given equation

  $x=\dfrac{-(-5)\pm\sqrt{(-5)^2-4(1)(-2)}}{2(1)}$ Quadratic formula with $a=1, b=-5,$ and $c=-2$

  $=\dfrac{5\pm\sqrt{25+8}}{2}$ Evaluate the exponent and multiplication

  $=\dfrac{5\pm\sqrt{33}}{2}$ Evaluate the addition

  $x=\dfrac{5\pm\sqrt{33}}{2}$

  c $-2x^2-15x-4=0$ Given equation

  $x=\dfrac{-(-15)\pm\sqrt{(-15)^2-4(-2)(-4)}}{2(-2)}$ Quadratic formula with $a=-2, b=-15,$ and $c=-4$

  $=\dfrac{15\pm\sqrt{225-32}}{-4}$ Evaluate the exponent and multiplication

  $=\dfrac{15\pm\sqrt{193}}{-4}$ Evaluate the subtraction

  $=\dfrac{-15\pm\sqrt{193}}{4}$ Distribute the negative sign

  $x=\dfrac{-15\pm\sqrt{193}}{4}$

  d $3x^2+9x-4=0$ Given equation

  $x=\dfrac{-(9)\pm\sqrt{(9)^2-4(3)(-4)}}{2(3)}$ Quadratic formula with $a=3, b=9,$ and $c=-4$

  $=\dfrac{-9\pm\sqrt{81+48}}{6}$ Evaluate the exponent and multiplication

  $=\dfrac{-9\pm\sqrt{129}}{6}$ Evaluate the addition

  $x=\dfrac{-9\pm\sqrt{129}}{6}$

  e $-5x^2-15x+3=0$ Given equation

  $x=\dfrac{-(-15)\pm\sqrt{(-15)^2-4(-5)(3)}}{2(-5)}$ Quadratic formula with $a=-5, b=-15,$ and $c=3$

  $=\dfrac{15\pm\sqrt{225+60}}{-10}$ Evaluate the exponent and multiplication

  $=\dfrac{15\pm\sqrt{285}}{-10}$ Evaluate the addition

  $=-\dfrac{15\pm\sqrt{285}}{10}$ Distribute the negative sign

$$x = \frac{-15 \pm \sqrt{285}}{10}$$

f $5x = (x-5)(3x+3)$ Given equation

$5x = 3x^2 - 12x - 15$ Expand the right-hand side

$0 = 3x^2 - 12x - 15 - 5x$ Subtract 5x from both sides to set the equation to zero

$0 = 3x^2 - 17x - 15$ Combine like terms

$x = \frac{-(-17) \pm \sqrt{(-17)^2 - 4(3)(-15)}}{2(3)}$ Quadratic formula with $a = 3$, $b = -17$, and $c = -15$

$= \frac{17 \pm \sqrt{289 + 180}}{6}$ Evaluate the exponent and multiplication

$= \frac{17 \pm \sqrt{469}}{6}$ Evaluate the addition

$x = \frac{17 \pm \sqrt{469}}{6}$

g $3n^2 = 2n^2 - 2n + 7$ Given equation

$n^2 + 2n - 7 = 0$ Subtraction property of equality

$n = \frac{-(2) \pm \sqrt{(2)^2 - 4(1)(-7)}}{2(1)}$ Quadratic formula with $a = 1$, $b = 2$, and $c = -7$

$= \frac{-2 \pm \sqrt{4 + 28}}{2}$ Evaluate the exponent and multiplication

$= \frac{-2 \pm \sqrt{32}}{2}$ Evaluate the addition

$= \frac{-2 \pm 4\sqrt{2}}{2}$ Evaluate the square root

$= -1 \pm 2\sqrt{2}$ Simplify by a factor of 2

$n = -1 \pm 2\sqrt{2}$

h $12 - 8m + 2m^2 = m^2 + 12m + 15$ Given equation

$2m^2 - 8m + 12 - m^2 - 12m - 15 = 0$ Subtraction property of equality

$m^2 - 20m - 3 = 0$ Combine like terms

$m = \frac{-(-20) \pm \sqrt{(-20)^2 - 4(1)(-3)}}{2(1)}$ Quadratic formula with $a = 1$, $b = -20$, and $c = -3$

$= \frac{20 \pm \sqrt{400 + 12}}{2}$ Evaluate the exponent and multiplication

$= \frac{20 \pm \sqrt{412}}{2}$ Evaluate the addition

$= \frac{20 \pm \sqrt{4}\sqrt{103}}{2}$ Product of radicals

$= \frac{20 \pm 2\sqrt{103}}{2}$ Evaluate the square root

$= 10 \pm \sqrt{103}$ Simplify by a factor of 2

$m = 10 \pm \sqrt{103}$

13 a $x = -2, -3$

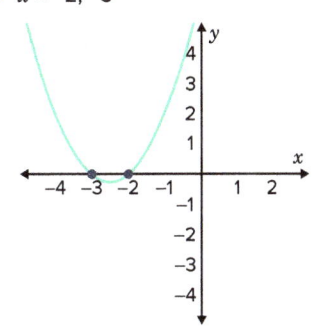

b $x = 2, 3$

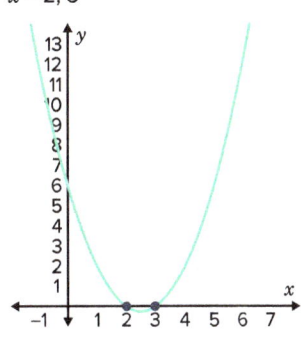

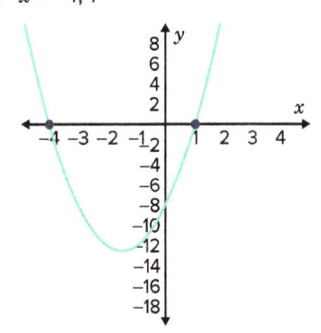

c $x = -4, 1$

d $x = \frac{1}{2}, 2$

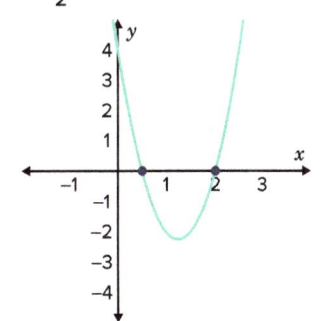

e $x = -\frac{1}{2}, -3$

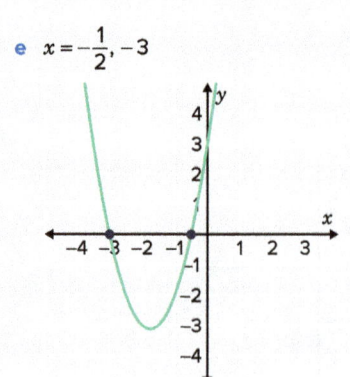

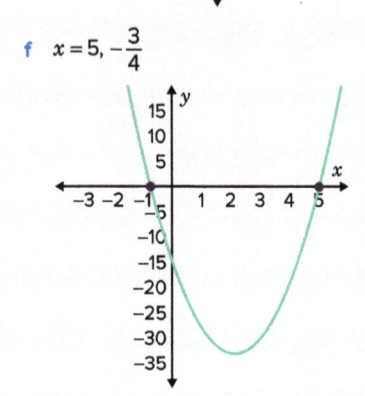

f $x = 5, -\frac{3}{4}$

14 6.19 seconds

15 a 27.84 mph

b Ray was driving 10 mph over the speed limit.

16 If we let $y = 0$, we can solve the equation $-x^2 + 28x - 159 = 0$ using the quadratic formula to get:

$$x = \frac{-28 \pm \sqrt{(-28)^2 - 4(-1)(-159)}}{2(-1)}$$

Evaluating this gives us the approximate solutions $x = 7.92$ and $x = 20.08$.

Since it makes more sense for a restaurant to open and close on the hour, we can round to the nearest hour to determine that the restaurant has opening hours from 8 am to 8 pm (converting to 12-hour time).

Let's extend our thinking

17 a i $a = -7, b = 5, c = 10$ **ii** $-7x^2 + 5x + 10 = 0$
b i $a = 9, b = 22, c = 3$ **ii** $9x^2 + 22x + 3 = 0$

18 a B **b** C **c** A

19 a $m > -\frac{9}{20}$

b The solution of $m = 0$ must be excluded. The denominator in the quadratic formula is equal to $2a$ and if $m = 0$ then $2a = 0$ but we cannot divide by zero.

20 $n = \pm 9$

21 When the discriminant is positive there are two distinct real solutions. If the discriminant is of the form n^2 for some integer n, then it will have integer solutions.

If the discriminant is equal to zero there will be one real solution. This is because the ± sign applies only to the square root of the discriminant. Consider that plus zero and minus zero give the same result.

A negative discriminant means that there will be no real solutions, because the square root of a negative number is not a real number.

22 The quadratic will have no real solutions when the discriminant is less than zero. This will occur when $b^2 < 4ac$. This gives us $k^2 < 144$. Taking the square root of both sides gives us $-12 < k < 12$.

23 The two graphs will intersect when $f(x) = g(x)$, so we can equate the two equations and solve.

1    $3x^2 - x + 8 = -x^2 + 2x - 4$ Equating the two functions
2    $4x^2 - 3x + 12 = 0$ Rearranging to set equation equal to zero

We can determine the number of real solutions by finding the discriminant.

1    $b^2 - 4ac = (-3)^2 - 4 \cdot 4 \cdot 12$ Substituting in values for a, b and c
2    $b^2 - 4ac = -183$ Evaluating the numerical expression
3    $0 > -183$ Comparing to zero
4    $0 > b^2 - 4ac$ Substitution property of equality

As the determinant is less than zero there are no real number solutions and therefore the two functions do not intersect at all.

24 Assume the roots are α and $\alpha + k$, then expand the factored form into the standard form.

1    $(x - \alpha)(x - (\alpha + k)) = 0$ Writing quadratic equation in factored form using the known roots
2    $x^2 - (\alpha + k)x - \alpha x + \alpha(\alpha + k) = 0$ Expand using the distributive property
3    $x^2 - (2\alpha + k)x + (\alpha^2 + \alpha k) = 0$ Combine like terms

This gives us $b = -(2\alpha + k)$ and $c = \alpha^2 + \alpha k$
Substituting into $b^2 - 4ac$

1    $b^2 - 4ac = (-(2\alpha + k))^2 - 4 \cdot 1 \cdot (\alpha^2 + \alpha k)$
     Substituting in values for a, b and c
2    $b^2 - 4ac = 4\alpha^2 + 4\alpha k + k^2 - 4\alpha^2 - 4\alpha k$
     Expand using the distributive property
3    $b^2 - 4ac = k^2$ Combining like terms

25 a $0 < p < q$
b $x^2 + 2(p - q)x + p^2 - q^2 = 0$
c $8q(q - p)$
d Two real solutions
e $x = 3p$

8.05 Solve quadratics using appropriate methods

Subtopic overview

Lesson narrative

In this lesson, students will summarize the different methods they have learned for solving quadratics. They will analyze quadratic equations in different forms to discuss which method is most ideal for solving each form and why. By the end of the lesson, students should be able to create and interpret quadratic models to solve problems in contextual situations, choosing their tools and using appropriate degree of precision.

Learning objectives

Students: Page 491

After this lesson, you will be able to...
- use the structure of a quadratic expression to identify ways to rewrite it.
- choose appropriate methods for solving quadratic equations based on the structure of the quadratic expression.
- create and solve quadratic equations for real-world contexts.

Key vocabulary

- quadratic equation

Essential understanding

There are many methods that can be used to solve a quadratic equation. The structure of the equation can give insight into which method might be the most efficient.

Standards

This subtopic addresses the following Virginia Standards of Learning for Mathematics standards.

Mathematical process goals

MPG1 — Mathematical Problem Solving

Teachers can integrate this goal by asking students to apply different methods to solve quadratic equations. They can provide a variety of problem situations that require the use of different solution methods such as graphing, factoring, square roots, and the quadratic formula. Teachers can also encourage students to develop their own problem-solving strategies and to articulate their reasoning.

MPG2 — Mathematical Communication

Teachers can encourage students to communicate their mathematical thinking by explaining their process in solving quadratic equations, discussing their choice of methods, and justifying their solutions. They can also ask students to articulate the reasoning behind their choice of methods, and to share their strategies and reasoning with their peers.

MPG3 — Mathematical Reasoning

Teachers can integrate this goal by asking students to analyze the given quadratic equation, determine the most efficient method for solving it, and justify their choice. They can also ask students to evaluate their solutions and verify the correctness of their reasoning.

Content standards

A.EI.3 — The student will represent, solve, and interpret the solution to a quadratic equation in one variable.

A.EI.3a — Solve a quadratic equation in one variable over the set of real numbers with rational or irrational solutions, including those that can be used to solve contextual problems.

A.EI.3c — Verify possible solution(s) to a quadratic equation in one variable algebraically, graphically, and with technology to justify the reasonableness of answer(s). Explain the solution method and interpret solutions for problems given in context.

Prior connections

A.EO.2 — The student will perform operations on and factor polynomial expressions in one variable.

A.EO.4 — The student will simplify and determine equivalent radical expressions involving square roots of whole numbers and cube roots of integers.

A.F.2 — The student will investigate, analyze, and compare characteristics of functions, including quadratic and exponential functions, and model quadratic and exponential relationships.

Future connections

A2.EI.2 — The student will represent, solve, and interpret the solution to quadratic equations in one variable over the set of complex numbers and solve quadratic inequalities in one variable.

Lesson Preparation

Suggested review

Depending on your students' level of prior knowledge, consider revisiting the following lessons:

Algebra 1 — 8.01 Solve quadratics using graphs and tables
Algebra 1 — 8.02 Solve quadratics by factoring
Algebra 1 — 8.03 Solve quadratics using square roots
Algebra 1 — 8.04 Solve quadratics using the quadratic formula

Tools

You may find these tools helpful:
- Scientific calculator
- Graphing calculator
- Strategy comparison graphic organizer

Student lesson & teacher guide

Solving quadratic equations using appropriate methods

Students review the various methods for solving quadratic equations that they learned about through the chapter. Some of these methods may have advantages and disadvantages, but students are reminded that no single method is the only way to solve quadratic equations.

Students: Pages 491–492

8.05 Solve quadratics using appropriate methods

After this lesson, you will be able to...
- use the structure of a quadratic expression to identify ways to rewrite it.
- choose appropriate methods for solving quadratic equations based on the structure of the quadratic expression.
- create and solve quadratic equations for real-world contexts.

Solving quadratic equations using appropriate methods

We have several methods we can use to solve **quadratic equations**. To determine which method is the most suitable we need to look at the form of the quadratic equation.

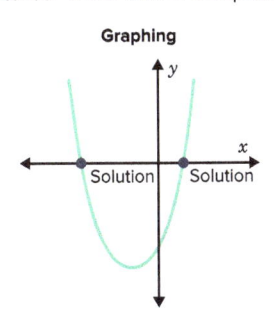

Graphing

Advantages: Helps us visualize the quadratic and its key features

Disadvantages: Only best when intercepts are integers, in which case it could have been factored instead

Equation form: Any form is fine if using technology, otherwise it is best in a form that is equal to 0

Factoring $a(x-b)(x-c) = 0$ $x = b, x = c$	Advantages: This is usually the fastest method Disadvantages: Not all polynomials are factorable, some factorable polynomials are difficult to factor Equation form: $ax^2 + bx + c = 0$ where a, b, c are small
Square root property $x^2 = k$ $x = \pm\sqrt{k}$	Advantages: Simplest method for solving equations in vertex form or equations missing an x-term Disadvantages: Few equations are given in this form Equation form: $x^2 = k$ or $a(x-h)^2 = k$
Completing the square $x^2 + bx + c = 0$ $x^2 + bx = -c$ $x^2 + 2\left(\frac{b}{2}\right)x = -c$ $x^2 + 2\left(\frac{b}{2}\right)x + \left(\frac{b}{2}\right)^2 = -c + \left(\frac{b}{2}\right)^2$ $\left(x + \frac{b}{2}\right)^2 = -c + \left(\frac{b}{2}\right)^2$	Advantages: Can be used to solve any quadratic equation Disadvantages: Requires more steps than other methods, fractions make it difficult Equation form: $x^2 + bx + c = 0$ where b is even
Quadratic formula $x = \dfrac{-b \pm \sqrt{b^2 - 4ac}}{2a}$	Advantages: Can be used to solve any quadratic equation Disadvantages: Can be time-consuming, many opportunities to make miscalculations, although calculators simplify its use Equation form: $ax^2 + bx + c = 0$ where a, b, c are large

There is not one correct method for solving a quadratic equation. You would not be wrong by using one method over another; it is just easier, sometimes more practical, to use some methods over others.

Provide a graphic organizer for comparing solving methods
Targeted instructional strategies

We can solve a quadratic equation in a variety of ways. Have students consider which thinking strategy or concept they can use. In particular, students can compare and contrast strategies using a graphic organizer like the Strategy comparison graphic organizer found in our lesson support templates.

Support the comparison by asking questions like:
- What possible strategies could I use to solve this problem?
  - Of the strategies I know, which seem to best fit this particular problem? Why?
- Will the strategy I chose always work? Why? How can you change the given problem so that this strategy does not work?
- Could the equation have been solved with fewer steps or in a simpler way?

Stronger and clearer each time
English language learner support

Present an equation for all the students to try and solve. Then, ask students to explain their approach to solving the equation to a partner. Encourage students to communicate their reasoning with reference to "key features" of the equation and "operations" of particular methods. After giving the students some time to discuss with their partner, present a similar equation to the students and ask them to try and solve it.

Support organization - provide a flowchart for decision-making
Student with disabilities support

Encourage all students to use Algorithmic Thinking to develop a flowchart that shows how to identify an appropriate strategy.

Some students may require additional support to make flowcharts. This could include indicating what features they should look for or providing them with all of the possible strategies and questions written on paper for them to move around and draw the arrows between.

While some students may benefit from being given a flowchart along with explicit instruction of how to use it.

For example:

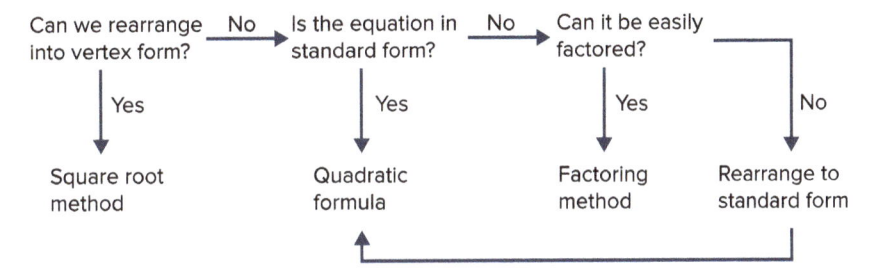

```
Can we rearrange    No    Is the equation in    No    Can it be easily
into vertex form?  ───▶   standard form?       ───▶   factored?        ─────┐
        │                        │                          │                │
       Yes                      Yes                        Yes              No
        ▼                        ▼                          ▼                ▼
   Square root              Quadratic                   Factoring       Rearrange to
     method                  formula                    method          standard form
                                ▲                                             │
                                └─────────────────────────────────────────────┘
```

Note that different students may require different flowcharts to reflect their personal strengths and weaknesses with each method. For example, a student who is comfortable with square roots, but has difficulty finding factor pairs may prioritize the factoring method last.

Allow students to solve quadratics using their preferred method
Address student misconceptions

Students may have the misconception that there is a "correct" method for solving a quadratic equation, and that they may be marked incorrectly for using a "less efficient" or "less appropriate" method.

Make sure to avoid phrasing which positions one method as being better than another and communicate to students that the most appropriate method is the one which they find most comfortable.

If a student prefers to always use the same method for every problem, ask them why they find it most comfortable. Take this as an opportunity to identify potential gaps or weaknesses in a student's knowledge and review concepts with them if appropriate. After they have gained some confidence in the prerequisite skills, encourage the student to try using the other methods.

Examples

Students: Page 492

Example 1

For the following quadratic equations, find the solution using an efficient method. Justify which method you used.

a $x^2 - 7x + 12 = 0$

Create a strategy

The leading coefficient of x^2 is 1, so we can check if this can be easily factored. The factors of 12 are $\pm 1, \pm 2, \pm 3, \pm 4, \pm 6, \pm 12$, and we want to find two factors that have a product of 12 and sum to -7. As the product is positive but the sum is negative, we know both factors must be negative.

Apply the idea

Since the equation can be factored by grouping, we will factor the equation and solve it.

The two factors that have a product of 12 and a sum of –7 are –3 and –4. We can write the equation in factored form as $(x - 4)(x - 3) = 0$, which gives us two solutions $x = 3$ and $x = 4$.

Reflect and check

In general, if the coefficients are small, and especially if $a = 1$, it is worth checking to see if we can easily factor the equation to solve.

Purpose

Show students how to use factoring to solve a quadratic equation when an expression can be factored.

Expected mistakes

Students may solve the equation using a different method, and assume they are wrong because the method used in the problem is factoring. Remind students to use whichever method of solving equations is preferred and that their solutions should match the solutions given for x.

Students: Pages 492–493

b $x^2 - 11 = 21$

Create a strategy

Here we have $b = 0$, and can easily isolate the x^2, which means we can solve this by using square roots.

Apply the idea

Since we can easily isolate x^2, we will solve the equation using square roots as follows:

$x^2 - 11 = 21$	Given equation
$x^2 = 32$	Add 11 to both sides
$x = \pm\sqrt{32}$	Evaluate the square root of both sides
$x = \pm\sqrt{16 \cdot 2}$	Factor 32
$x = \pm\sqrt{16}\sqrt{2}$	Multiplication property of radicals
$x = \pm 4\sqrt{2}$	Evaluate the radical

$x = \pm 4\sqrt{2}$, giving us two solutions: $x = 4\sqrt{2}$ and $x = -4\sqrt{2}$

Reflect and check

In general, if we can easily rearrange the equation into the form $(x - h)^2 = k$ for some positive value of k then solving using square roots is a suitable method.

Purpose

Show students how to use square roots to solve a quadratic equation.

Reflecting with students

Ask students whether a solution in decimal form would be acceptable. Discuss with students the appropriate and expected times to offer exact versus decimal solutions if neither is specified in the problem. This is at the discretion of the teacher.

Students: Page 493

c $3x^2 - 24x + 20 = 5$

Create a strategy

For most of the methods we know, the quadratic needs to be equal to zero first. We can subtract 5 from both sides, then check see if factoring can be used.

Apply the idea

Since the trinomial is equal to a constant, we will first set the equation equal to zero and attempt to factor the trinomial. Then, we can determine an approach that is appropriate for solving this equation.

$3x^2 - 24x + 20 = 5$	Given equation
$3x^2 - 24x + 15 = 0$	Subtract 5 from both sides
$3(x^2 - 8x + 5) = 0$	Factor the GCF of 3
$x^2 - 8x + 5 = 0$	Divide by 3 on both sides

From here, we can see that the equation cannot be factored further. Since $a = 1$ and b is even, we can use completing the square to solve.

$x^2 - 8x = -5$	Subtraction property of equality
$x^2 - 8x + 16 = -5 + 16$	Complete the square
$(x - 4)^2 = 11$	Factor the left side, evaluate the right side
$x - 4 = \pm\sqrt{11}$	Evaluate the square root of both sides
$x = 4 \pm \sqrt{11}$	Add 4 to both sides

Reflect and check

The quadratic formula could have been used, but it may have been more time-consuming, especially if we didn't factor out the GCF first.

$3x^2 - 24x + 15 = 0$	Original equation set equal to 0
$x = \dfrac{-(-24) \pm \sqrt{(-24)^2 - 4(3)(15)}}{2(3)}$	Substitute a, b, c into quadratic formula
$= \dfrac{24 \pm \sqrt{396}}{6}$	Evaluate the division
$= \dfrac{24 \pm \sqrt{36}\sqrt{11}}{6}$	Multiplication property of radicals
$= \dfrac{24 \pm 6\sqrt{11}}{6}$	Evaluate the radical
$= 4 \pm \sqrt{11}$	Evaluate the division

Purpose

Show students how to solve a quadratic equation by completing the square.

Reflecting with students

Ask students what their preferred method for solving this equation is and why. Point out to students that they may even choose to graph the function $y = x^2 - 8x + 5$ and determine the x-intercepts to solve the equation for when $y = 0$.

> **Support explanations - use sentence stems to help students justify their reasoning**
> **Student with disabilities support**   use with Example 1

Help students justify why they chose a particular method by providing them with the sentence frames:
- I can see that a key feature of the equation is...
- I know that the ... method is appropriate when the equation is...
- I find it most comfortable to use the ... method when...

Students: Page 494

> **Example 2**

A rectangular enclosure is to be constructed from 100 meters of wooden fencing. The area of the enclosure is given by $A = 50x - x^2$, where x is the length of one side of the rectangle. If the area is 525 m^2, determine the side lengths.

Create a strategy

We can set up and solve a quadratic equation, $50x - x^2 = 525$. Since the values are large we will try solving this problem with the quadratic formula. The two solutions will be the side lengths of the enclosure.

Apply the idea

Rearranging the equation into standard form we get $x^2 - 50x + 525 = 0$.

We can solve this using the quadratic equation:

$x = \dfrac{-b \pm \sqrt{b^2 - 4ac}}{2a}$ Quadratic formula

$x = \dfrac{-(-50) \pm \sqrt{(-50)^2 - 4(1)(525)}}{2(1)}$ Substitute $a = 1, b = -50, c = 525$

$x = \dfrac{50 \pm \sqrt{400}}{2}$ Evaluate the operations

$x = \dfrac{50 \pm 20}{2}$ Evaluate the square root

This leaves us with two values, $x = \dfrac{50 + 20}{2}$ and $x = \dfrac{50 - 20}{2}$. Evaluating each expression for x we get $x = 35$ and $x = 15$ as the side lengths of the rectangular enclosure.

Reflect and check

We can confirm our answer is correct by checking the conditions of the problem. We had 100 meters of fencing and $2(35 + 15) = 100$. We needed the area to be 525 m^2 and $35(15) = 525$ as required.

Since there are two rational solutions, the quadratic equation was also factorable: $x^2 - 50x + 525 = (x - 35)(x - 15)$, but these factors are not immediately obvious.

Purpose

Show students how to use a context to write and solve an equation with the quadratic formula.

Expected mistakes

Students may struggle to write an equation that represents the context. Writing expressions as words may help students translate from the words to mathematics.

Reflecting with students

Ask students to check if the solutions they find are correct by checking the conditions of the problem. We had 100 meters of wooden fencing and an area of 525 m^2, so the sum and product of the two solutions should match these values.

Since $2(35 + 15) = 100$ and $35 \cdot 15 = 525$, we can confirm that this solution is correct.

Advanced learners: Exploring optimization   use with Example 2
Targeted instructional strategies

Extend the problem for advanced students by asking them to find the maximum possible area for the enclosure with the given perimeter. Students should recognize that the area function is a downward facing quadratic function, so the y-value of its vertex represents the maximum area.

Prompt students to calculate the value of x at the vertex and interpret its meaning in the context of the problem. This exploration allows students to connect quadratic equations to real-world optimization and deepen their understanding of solving quadratics for values other than the x-intercepts.

Students: Page 494

> 💡 **Idea summary**
> Below is a list of the easiest method to use and the form of the quadratic equation for which we should use it:

	Easiest equation form
Graphing	Any form is fine when using technology
Factoring	$ax^2 + bx + c = 0$ where a, b, c are small
Square root property	$x^2 = k$ or $a(x - h)^2 = k$
Completing the square	$x^2 + bx + c = 0$ where b is even
Quadratic formula	$ax^2 + bx + c = 0$ where a, b, c are large

Practice

Students: Pages 495–497

What do you remember?

1 Solve the following equations:
  a $(x - 3)^2 = 64$
  b $(2 - x)^2 = 81$
  c $x(x + 7) = 0$
  d $(10x - 9)^2 = 0$
  e $(x - 6)(x + 7) = 0$
  f $\frac{m}{2}(m + 5) = 0$
  g $x^2 - 8x + 15 = 0$
  h $x^2 - 4x - 22 = 0$

2 The formula for the surface area of a sphere is $S = 4\pi r^2$, where r is the radius.

Determine the radius of a sphere that has a surface area of 804 in^2, rounding your answer to two decimal places.

3 Consider the quadratic equation:

$$x^2 - 3x - 108 = 0$$

Select the solution to the quadratic equation.

  A $x = 9, x = -12$
  B $x = -9, x = 12$
  C $x = -9, x = -12$
  D $x = 9, x = 12$

4 Consider the quadratic equation:

$$x^2 - 200 = -79$$

Select the solution to the quadratic equation.

  A $x = 10\sqrt{2}, x = -10\sqrt{2}$
  B $x = 3\sqrt{31}, x = -3\sqrt{31}$
  C $x = 200, x = -79$
  D $x = 11, x = -11$

5 A square lot has an area of 289 m^2. Find the length of one side of the square lot if $A = s^2$.

  A $s = 144.5$ m
  B $s = 72.25$ m
  C $s = \sqrt{17}$ m
  D $s = 17$ m

Let's practice

6 For the following quadratic equations, find the solution using an efficient method. Justify which method you used.

  a $x^2 - 10 = 15$
  b $x^2 - 7x + 6 = 0$
  c $25y^2 = 36$
  d $4x^2 + 5x + 1 = 0$
  e $x^2 + 24x + 63 = 0$
  f $x^2 - 7x = 0$
  g $5k^2 - 17k + 13 = 0$
  h $x^2 + 9x + 20 = 0$

7 Solve the following equations:

  a $(x - 6)^2 - 2 = 0$
  b $24x^2 = 71x - 35$
  c $x^2 + 27x + 23 = 3x - 40$
  d $3x^2 - 36x + 33 = 0$
  e $3x^2 - 12x - 36 = 0$
  f $4x^2 - 13x + 2 = 0$
  g $x^2 + 18x + 32 = 0$
  h $(x + 5)^2 - 2 = 15$
  i $11x + x^2 + 5 = 0$
  j $-4 + 2x^2 - 5x = 0$

8 Solve the following equations. Justify your work.

  a $4x^2 = 2 + 8x$
  b $x^2 - 18x = -6$
  c $x^2 - 2x - 15 = 0$
  d $x^2 - 4x = -1$

9 Solve the following equations. Verify your solution(s) by graphing or substitution.

  a $x^2 - 4x = 32$
  b $2x^2 + 3x - 5 = 0$
  c $x^2 = -2x + 24$
  d $3x^2 - 2x + 5 = 10x + 1$

10 The following rectangle has a length of $L = 56y + 11$ and a width of $W = 5y^2$:

  a Write the perimeter of the figure in terms of y.
  b If the perimeter is equal to 630, find y.

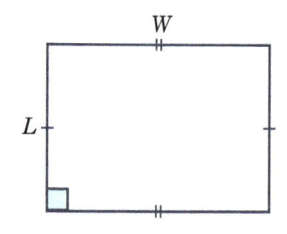

11 At time t seconds, the distance, s, traveled by an object moving in a straight line is given by

$$s = ut + \frac{1}{2}at^2$$

where u is its starting speed and a is its acceleration.

When $u = 16$ and $a = 8$, find how long it would take for the object to travel 128 m.

12 The base of a triangle is 3 m more than twice its height. The area of the triangle is 115 m². Let x be the height of the triangle.

  a Find the height by solving for x.
  b Find the length of the base.

13 A rectangular swimming pool is 16 m long and 6 m wide. It is surrounded by a pebble path of uniform width x m. The area of the path is 104 m².

  a Find an expression for the area of the path in terms of x.
  b Write an equation and solve for x, the width of the path.

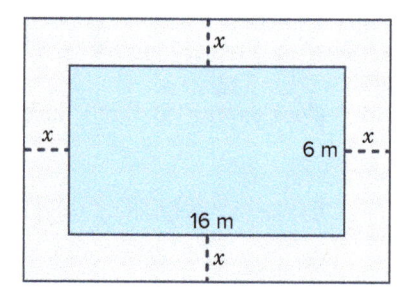

14 14 Harry is using a diving board to dive into a swimming pool. The distance from his head to the surface of the water can be represented as $(x - 7)(x + 7) = 147$. Select the viable x-value to the quadratic equation.

  A $x = 14$
  B $x = -14$
  C $x = 49$
  D $x = 7$

Let's extend our thinking

15 For each of the following equations determine, without solving them, the most efficient method for solving them. Explain your thinking.

a $x^2 - 3x + 2 = 0$

b $8x = x^2$

c $16x^2 - 81 = 0$

d $\frac{3}{2}x^2 + \frac{13}{19}x - \frac{23}{15} = 0$

16 Executives at the Widget Emporium are discussing whether to merge their company with the Trinket Bazaar, a large competitor.

Market analysis shows that the extra revenue the company will receive can be modelled by the equation $R = 0.25t^2$, and the extra costs by the equation $C = 3.5t$. R and C are measured in thousands of dollars and t is measured in months after the merger.

a Find the times at which the extra revenue R will match the extra cost C.

b The executives decide that they can only afford to operate at a loss for one year. Based on this requirement, state whether you would advise that the Widget Emporium merge with the Trinket Bazaar.

17 An interplanetary freight transport company has won a contract to supply the space station orbiting Mars. They will be shipping stackable containers, each carrying a fuel module and a water module, that must meet certain dimension restrictions.

The design engineers have produced a sketch for the modules and container, shown below. The sum of the heights of both modules equal to the height of the container.

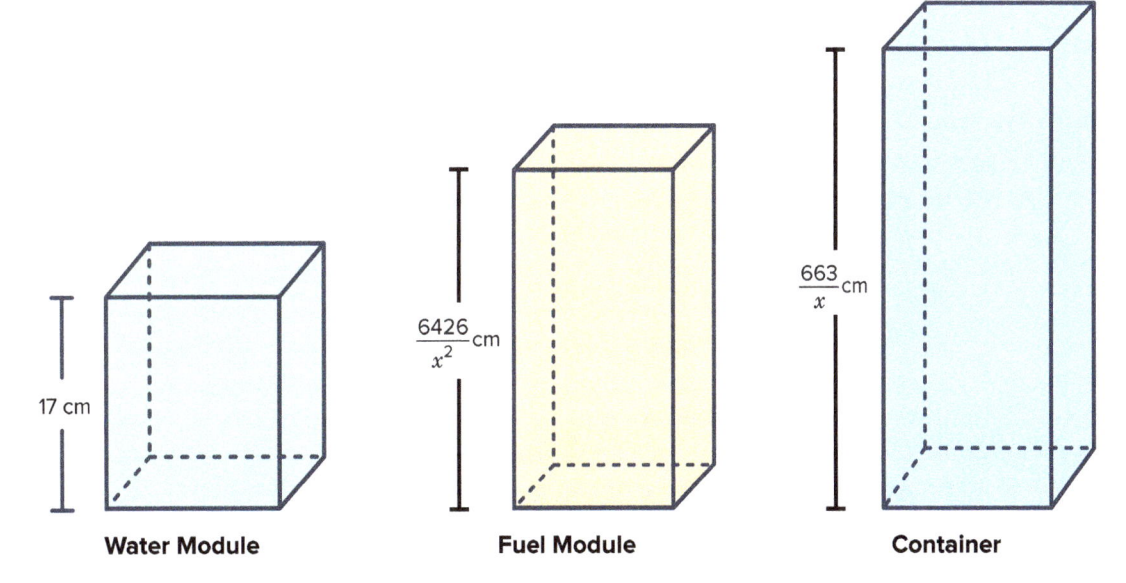

Water Module: 17 cm

Fuel Module: $\frac{6426}{x^2}$ cm

Container: $\frac{663}{x}$ cm

a Write an equation that equates the height of the container and the sum of the heights of the modules.

b Find the tallest possible height of the container, rounding your answer to two decimal places. Explain your method.

18 The shaded area in the rectangle has a uniform width and an area of 11 ft²:

a Determine a quadratic equation to represent this situation.

b Find the value of x, rounding your answer to two decimal places.

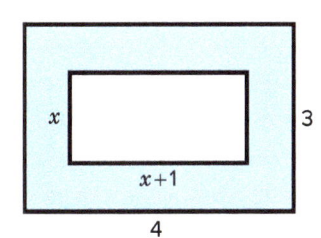

(Rectangle dimensions: outer x by $x+1$, inner 3 by 4)

Answers

8.05 Solve quadratics using appropriate methods

What do you remember?

1. a. $x = 11, x = -5$
   b. $x = 11, x = -7$
   c. $x = 0, x = -7$
   d. $x = \dfrac{9}{10}$
   e. $x = 6, x = -7$
   f. $m = 0, m = -5$
   g. $x = 5, x = 3$
   h. $x = 2 + \sqrt{26}, x = 2 - \sqrt{26}$

2. $r = 8.00$ in

3. B

4. D

5. D

Let's practice

6. a. $x = 5, x = -5$
   Using the method of taking square roots. We can add 10 to both sides to get $x^2 = 25$.

   b. $x = 6, x = 1$
   Using the method of factoring. Using the fact $-6 - 1 = -7$ and $-6 \cdot -1 = 6$, we can rewrite as $(x - 6)(x - 1)$.

   c. $y = \dfrac{6}{5}, y = -\dfrac{6}{5}$
   Using the method of taking square roots. We can divide both sides by 25 to get $x^2 = \dfrac{36}{25}$.

   d. $x = -\dfrac{1}{4}, x = -1$
   Using the quadratic formula as $a \neq 1$ and it is not easily factorable.

   e. $x = -3, x = -21$
   Using completing the square, we can add subtract 63 from both sides and then add $\left(\dfrac{24}{2}\right)^2 = 144$ to both sides of the equation giving $x^2 + 24x + 144 = 81$ which can be rewritten in the form $(x + 12)^2 = 81$ which can then be solved by taking square roots.

   f. $x = 0, x = 7$
   We can easily factor this quadratic $x(x - 7)$.

   g. $k = \dfrac{17 + \sqrt{29}}{10}, k = \dfrac{17 - \sqrt{29}}{10}$
   Using the quadratic formula as $a \neq 1$ and it is not easily factorable.

   h. $x = -5, x = -4$
   Using the method of factoring. Using the fact $4 + 5 = 9$ and $4 \cdot 5 = 20$, we can rewrite as $(x + 4)(x + 5)$.

7. a. $x = 6 + \sqrt{2}, x = 6 - \sqrt{2}$
   b. $x = \dfrac{5}{8}, x = \dfrac{7}{3}$
   c. $x = -3, x = -21$
   d. $x = 11, x = 1$
   e. $x = 6, x = -2$
   f. $x = \dfrac{13 \pm \sqrt{137}}{8}$
   g. $x = -2, x = -16$
   h. $x = -5 \pm \sqrt{17}$
   i. $x = \dfrac{-11 \pm \sqrt{101}}{2}$
   j. $x = \dfrac{5}{4} \pm \dfrac{\sqrt{57}}{4}$

8. a. Rearrange the equation
   $4x^2 - 8x - 2 = 0$ Move $8x$ and 2 to the left side
   Use the quadratic formula: $x = \dfrac{-b \pm \sqrt{b^2 - 4ac}}{2a}$
   $x = \dfrac{-(-8) \pm \sqrt{(-8)^2 - 4 \cdot -4 \cdot -2}}{2 \cdot 4}$ Substitute $b = -8, a = 4, c = -2$
   $= \dfrac{-(-8) \pm 4\sqrt{6}}{2 \cdot 4}$ Evaluate the multiplication inside the square root
   $= \dfrac{2 \pm \sqrt{6}}{2}$ Simplify

   b. Rearrange the equation
   $x^2 - 18x + 6 = 0$ Move 6 to the left side
   Use the quadratic formula: $x = \dfrac{-b \pm \sqrt{b^2 - 4ac}}{2a}$
   $x = \dfrac{-(-18) \pm \sqrt{(-18)^2 - 4 \cdot 1 \cdot 6}}{2 \cdot 1}$ Substitute $b = -18, a = 1, c = 6$
   $= \dfrac{-(-18) \pm 10\sqrt{3}}{2 \cdot 1}$ Evaluate the multiplication inside the square root
   $= 9 \pm 5\sqrt{3}$ Simplify

   c. Use the quadratic formula: $x = \dfrac{-b \pm \sqrt{b^2 - 4ac}}{2a}$
   $x = \dfrac{-(-2) \pm \sqrt{(-2)^2 - 4 \cdot 1 \cdot -15}}{2 \cdot 1}$ Substitute $b = -2, a = 1, c = -15$
   $= \dfrac{-(-2) \pm 8}{2 \cdot 1}$ Evaluate the multiplication inside the square root
   $= 5, -3$ Simplify

   d. Rearrange the equation
   $x^2 - 4x + 1 = 0$ Move 1 to the left side
   Use the quadratic formula: $x = \dfrac{-b \pm \sqrt{b^2 - 4ac}}{2a}$
   $x = \dfrac{-(-4) \pm \sqrt{(-4)^2 - 4 \cdot 1 \cdot 1}}{2 \cdot 1}$ Substitute $b = -4, a = 1, c = 1$
   $= \dfrac{-(-4) \pm 2\sqrt{3}}{2 \cdot 1}$ Evaluate the multiplication inside the square root
   $= 2 \pm \sqrt{3}$ Simplify

9. a. $x = 8, -4$
   $8^2 - 4 \cdot 8 = 32$ Substitute $x = 8$
   $32 = 32$ Evaluate
   $-4^2 - 4 \cdot -4 = 32$ Substitute $x = -4$
   $32 = 32$ Evaluate

b $x = 1, -\dfrac{5}{2}$

$2 \cdot (1)^2 + (3 \cdot 1) - 5 = 0$ Evaluate $x = 1$

$0 = 0$ Evaluate

$2 \cdot \left(-\dfrac{5}{2}\right)^2 + \left(3 \cdot -\dfrac{5}{2}\right) - 5 = 0$ Substitute $x = -\dfrac{5}{2}$

$0 = 0$ Evaluate

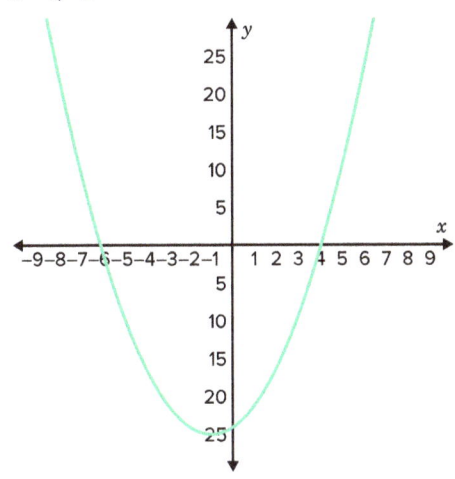

c $x = 4, -6$

d $x = \dfrac{2(3 \pm \sqrt{6})}{3}$

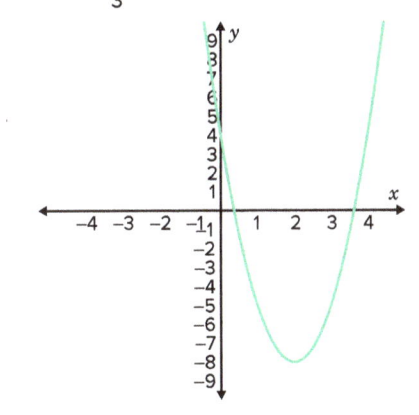

10 a $10y^2 + 112y + 22$ b $y = 4$

11 $t = 4$

12 a $x = 10$ b 23 m

13 a $4x^2 + 44x$ m^2 b $x = 2$

14 A

Let's extend our thinking

15 a Using the method of factoring. The factors of this quadratic are whole numbers and can be found by considering the factors of the constant.

b Using the method of factoring. We can see that there is a factor of x on both sides of the equation.

c Using the method of taking square roots. We can isolate x^2 on one side of the equation and everything else on the other.

d Using the quadratic formula. The coefficients are not easily factored.

16 a 0 and 14 months

b No, after one year the company will still be spending more money than it is making.

17 a $17 + \dfrac{6426}{x^2} = \dfrac{663}{x}$

b Solving the equation found in part (a) for x and multiplying entire equation by x^2 gives $17x^2 - 663x + 6426 = 0$. We can factor this as $17(x - 18)(x - 21)$. Solving the quadratic gives two solutions $x = 18$ and $x = 21$. Now, the height of the container $\dfrac{663}{x}$ is inversely proportional to x so we want to choose the least solution of x, that is $x = 18$. Substituting $x = 18$ into $\dfrac{663}{x}$ gives us a height of 36.83 cm

18 a $(4 + x)(3 - x) = 11$ b $x = 0.61$

Topic 8 Assessment: Quadratic Equations

1 Using the given table, find the solutions to the equation $x^2 - 2x - 8 = 0$:

x	−4	−3	−2	−1	0	1	2	3	4
y	16	7	0	−5	−8	−9	−8	−5	0

2 Find the solutions to $f(x) = 3x^2 + 21x + 30$, using the graph provided.

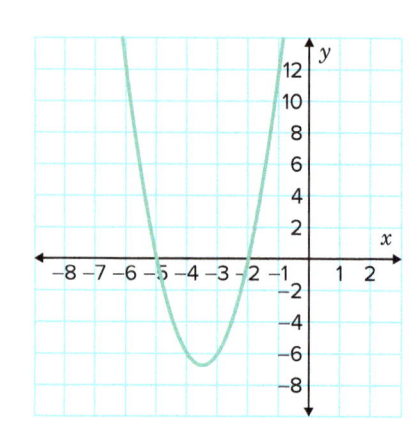

3 Solve the following equations:
  a $x^2 + 6x - 27 = 0$
  b $4x^2 - 29x = -30$
  c $x^2 - 81 = 0$
  d $(x + 4)^2 = 121$
  e $x^2 - \frac{3}{4}x - 2 = 0$
  f $5 + 6x = 2x^2$

4 The area of a rectangle is 32 cm². If the dimensions can be expressed as $12 - x$ and x, find the dimensions of the rectangle.

5 On Earth, the equation $d = 4.9t^2$ is used to find the distance, in meters, an object has fallen through the air after t seconds. Kevin is sky diving and wants to release his parachute once he has fallen 510 m.

Determine the time it will take him to fall 510 m, rounding your answer to the nearest second.

6 The revenue of a toy manufacturing company is modeled by the function

$$r(t) = -4t^2 + 450t$$

where t is time in days and $r(t)$ is the revenue in dollars. A company's break-even is obtained when the revenue first reaches $7500.

Find the time it takes the company to reach break-even. Round your answer to the nearest hundredth.

7 Find the discriminant of the equation $5x^2 - 4x + 2 = 0$ and state what it reveals about the solutions.

SOL 8 Fill in the blanks with your answers.

The solutions to $2x^2 - 8x + 6 = 0$ are: ☐ and ☐

9 Determine whether or not the following equations have real solutions:
  a $x^2 + 5x - 14 = 0$
  b $4x^2 - 8x + 12 = 0$

10 Identify if each function has exactly one zero. Justify your reasoning.
  a $f(x) = 7x^2 - 3$
  b $f(x) = 9(x - 6)$
  c $f(x) = x^2 + 6x + 8$
  d $f(x) = x^2 - 4x + 16$
  e $f(x) = -2(x + 5)(x + 2)$

SOL 11 What are the real roots of $x^2 - 8x + 12 = 0$?
  A 2 and 6
  B 1 and 12
  C −1 and −12
  D −2 and −6

12 What values of x are solutions of $3x^2 + 7x = 10$?

A 1 and $-\frac{10}{3}$
B 10 and $-\frac{1}{3}$
C $\frac{10}{3}$ and -1
D $\frac{1}{3}$ and -10

13 The graph of $y = x^2 - 4x - 12$ is shown.

What are the solutions to $x^2 - 4x - 12 = 0$?

A $x = 2$ and $x = -16$
B $x = 0$ and $x = -12$
C $x = 6$ and $x = 2$
D $x = -2$ and $x = 0$

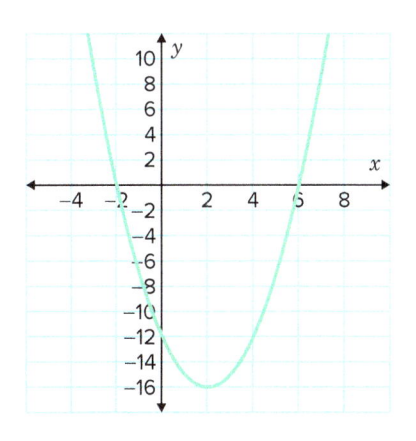

14 Look at function g:

$$g(x) = 8x^2 - 18$$

Which set contains only the zeros of function g?

A $\{-18, 8\}$
B $\{-18, 0, 8\}$
C $\left\{\frac{3}{2}, -\frac{3}{2}\right\}$
D $\left\{\frac{3}{2}, 0, -\frac{3}{2}\right\}$

15 The graph of $y = -x^2 - 2x + 24$ is shown.

On the grid, identify each solution to $-x^2 - 2x + 24 = 0$.

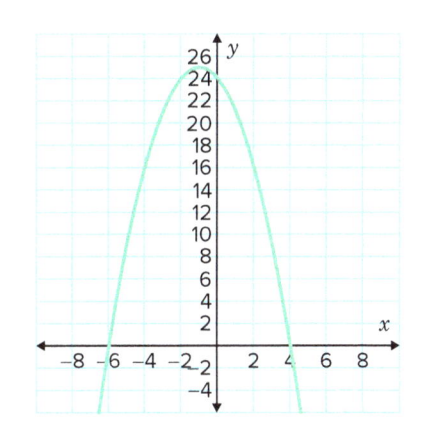

16 Consider the function h:

$$h(x) = x^2 + 9x - 36$$

a State a number that is a zero of the function h?
b Explain at least two different ways to verify that the solution from part (a) is a zero of the function.

17 Let $h(x) = -4x^2 + kx + 16$.

a If $h(1) = -3$, what is the value of $h(-3)$?
b How many zeros does the function have?

18 A scientist dropped an object from a height of 350 feet. She recorded the height of the object in 0.5-second intervals. Her data is shown.

a Find the value of $f(x)$ when $x = 3$.
b Explain the meaning of the answer from part (a) and what $x = 3$ represents in context.

x	$f(x)$
0.0	350
0.5	345
1.0	335
1.5	315
2.0	285
2.5	245

SOL **19** Which of these functions has exactly two different zeros?

A $f(x) = \frac{1}{5}x + 3$
B $g(x) = \frac{2x-8}{4}$
C $h(x) = x^2 - 6x + 9$
D $k(x) = x^2 + 9x + 20$

Performance task

20 Ursula is launching a pumpkin off the edge of the physics building at her school with a small catapult.

a Determine an equation, defining any variables, that models the path of the pumpkin given the following information:
- The physics building is 24 m high.
- When the pumpkin is 2 m from the building, it is 44 m high.
- When the pumpkin is 3 m from the building, it is 30 m high.

b Use an efficient method to find how far from the building the pumpkin hits the ground.

Explain your method.

c Ursula wants to do a demonstration where she launches the pumpkin into a target. If the target is 2 m high, how far from the building does she need to place it so it gets hit by the pumpkin? Explain.

Answers

Topic 8 Assessment: Quadratic Equations

1. $x = -2, x = 4$
   A.EI.3a

2. $x = -2, x = -5$
   A.EI.3a

3. a $x = 3, x = -9$ b $x = \frac{5}{4}, x = 6$
   c $x = 9, x = -9$ d $x = 7, x = -15$
   e $x = \frac{3}{8} \pm \frac{\sqrt{137}}{8}$ f $x = \frac{3}{2} \pm \frac{\sqrt{19}}{2}$
   A.EI.3a

4. 8 cm · 4 cm
   A.EI.3a

5. $t = 10$ seconds
   A.EI.3a

6. 20.35 days
   A.EI.3a

7. The discriminant is –24 which means that the solutions to the equation are non-real solutions.
   A.EI.3b

8. 1 and 3
   A.EI.3a

9. a Real solutions
   b No real solutions
   A.EI.3b

10. a No, it has two zeros. The function is a quadratic with zeroes at $x = \frac{\sqrt{21}}{7}$ and $x = -\frac{\sqrt{21}}{7}$.
    b Yes, it has exactly one zero. The function is a linear function, and all linear functions have exactly one zero. In this case, the zero is at $x = 6$.
    c No, it has two zeros. The function is a quadratic with a positive leading coefficient (1), so it opens upwards. The discriminant ($b^2 - 4ac$) is positive, indicating that there are two distinct real zeros.
    d No, it has no zeros. The function is a quadratic with a positive leading coefficient (1), so it opens upwards. The vertex is above the x-axis, so it never crosses the x-axis.
    e No, it has two zeros. The function is a quadratic with a negative leading coefficient (–2), so it opens downwards. There are two distinct zeros at $x = -5$ and $x = -2$.
    A.EI.3b

11. A
    A.EI.3a

12. A
    A.EI.3a

13. C
    A.EI.3a

14. C
    A.EI.3a

15. $x = -6, 4$
    A.EI.3a

16. a $x = -12$, or 3
    b Answers may vary. One possible solution:
       1. Substitute the values of x into the equation $h(x) = x^2 + 9x - 36$ and check if the result is 0.
       2. Factor the equation $h(x) = x^2 + 9x - 36$ into $(x + 12)(x - 3)$ and check if the values of x make either factor equal to 0.
    A.EI.3a, A.EI.3c

17. a $h(-3) = 25$ b 2 zeros
    A.F.2g, A.EI.3b

18. a $f(3) = 195$
    b The object is 195 feet above the ground at 3 seconds after it was dropped. The $x = 3$ represents the time in seconds.
    A.F.2g

19. D
    A.EI.3b

Performance task

20. a $y = -8x^2 + 26x + 24$ where x represents the horizontal distance from the edge of the building and y represents the vertical height above the ground.
    b Substitute 0 for y to represent a height of 0 m when the pumpkin is on the ground. The right hand side of the equation is factorable which gives the equation $0 = -2(4x + 3)(x - 4)$. Solving gives $x = -\frac{3}{4}$ and $x = 4$. The negative solution does not make sense in terms of this context so the pumpkin must hit the ground 4 m from the building.
    c Substituting 2 for y in the original equation gives the equation $2 = -8x^2 + 26x + 24$.
    Putting the equation in standard form gives $0 = -8x^2 + 26x + 22$. It can then be solved using the quadratic formula. She needs to place the target about 3.95 m from the building.
    A.EI.3, A.F.2g, MP1, MP3, MP4, MP5

9 Data Analysis

Big ideas

- Collecting and analyzing data can inform predictions and decisions, as long as the data is based on a valid sample.
- Different representations of data highlight different characteristics of the data.
- Many sets of bivariate data can be modeled using familiar functions.

Chapter outline

9.01	Data and sampling (A.ST.1)	1080
9.02	Scatterplots (A.ST.1)	1109
9.03	Linear regression (A.ST.1)	1139
9.04	Quadratic regression (A.ST.1)	1170
9.05	Analyze bivariate data (A.ST.1)	1196

Data analysis helps experts track and study wildlife patterns to protect endangered species.

9. Data Analysis

Topic overview

Foundational knowledge

Evaluating standards proficiency

The skills book contains questions matched to individual standards. It can be used to measure proficiency for each.

Students should be proficient in these standards.

8.PS.3 — The student will apply the data cycle (formulate questions; collect or acquire data; organize and represent data; and analyze data and communicate results) with a focus on scatterplots.

A.F.1 — The student will investigate, analyze, and compare linear functions algebraically and graphically, and model linear relationships.

A.F.2 — The student will investigate, analyze, and compare characteristics of functions, including quadratic and exponential functions, and model quadratic and exponential relationships.

Big ideas and essential understanding

Collecting and analyzing data can inform predictions and decisions, as long as the data is based on a valid sample.
9.01 — Representative samples are crucial if a data set will be used to make predictions and decisions.

Different representations of data highlight different characteristics of the data.
9.02 — Correlation does not imply causation.

Many sets of bivariate data can be modeled using familiar functions.
9.03, 9.04, 9.05 — The relationship between the variables in a set of bivariate data reveals the type of function that best models the data.

Standards

A.ST.1 — The student will apply the data cycle (formulate questions; collect or acquire data; organize and represent data; and analyze data and communicate results) with a focus on representing bivariate data in scatterplots and determining the curve of best fit using linear and quadratic functions.

A.ST.1a — Formulate investigative questions that require the collection or acquisition of bivariate data.
9.01 Data and sampling
9.02 Scatterplots
9.03 Linear regression
9.04 Quadratic regression
9.05 Analyze bivariate data

A.ST.1b — Determine what variables could be used to explain a given contextual problem or situation or answer investigative questions.
9.01 Data and sampling
9.02 Scatterplots
9.03 Linear regression
9.04 Quadratic regression
9.05 Analyze bivariate data

A.ST.1c — Determine an appropriate method to collect a representative sample, which could include a simple random sample, to answer an investigative question.
9.01 Data and sampling
9.02 Scatterplots
9.03 Linear regression
9.04 Quadratic regression
9.05 Analyze bivariate data

A.ST.1d — Given a table of ordered pairs or a scatterplot representing no more than 30 data points, use available technology to determine whether a linear or quadratic function would represent the relationship, and if so, determine the equation of the curve of best fit.
9.02 Scatterplots
9.03 Linear regression
9.04 Quadratic regression
9.05 Analyze bivariate data

A.ST.1e — Use linear and quadratic regression methods available through technology to write a linear or quadratic function that represents the data where appropriate and describe the strengths and weaknesses of the model.
9.03 Linear regression
9.04 Quadratic regression
9.05 Analyze bivariate data

A.ST.1f — Use a linear model to predict outcomes and evaluate the strength and validity of these predictions, including through the use of technology.
9.03 Linear regression
9.05 Analyze bivariate data

A.ST.1g — Investigate and explain the meaning of the rate of change (slope) and y-intercept (constant term) of a linear model in context.
9.03 Linear regression
9.05 Analyze bivariate data

A.ST.1h — Analyze relationships between two quantitative variables revealed in a scatterplot.
9.02 Scatterplots
9.03 Linear regression
9.04 Quadratic regression
9.05 Analyze bivariate data

A.ST.1i — Make conclusions based on the analysis of a set of bivariate data and communicate the results.
9.02 Scatterplots
9.03 Linear regression
9.04 Quadratic regression
9.05 Analyze bivariate data

Future connections

A2.ST.1 — The student will apply the data cycle (formulate questions; collect or acquire data; organize and represent data; and analyze data and communicate results) with a focus on univariate quantitative data represented by a smooth curve, including a normal curve.

A2.ST.2 — The student will apply the data cycle (formulate questions; collect or acquire data; organize and represent data; and analyze data and communicate results) with a focus on representing bivariate data in scatterplots and determining the curve of best fit using linear, quadratic, exponential, or a combination of these functions.

Continuous Assessment

🚩 Measure standards proficiency with check-ins

Before starting a new topic, it's a great time to go online and have students complete a Skills Check-in to measure their readiness for the topic.

9.01 Data and sampling

Subtopic overview

Lesson narrative

In this lesson, students will learn about the data cycle, forming an investigative question, and analyze various methods of data collection and their impact on data quality. It expands upon previous knowledge of univariate data to create a definition of bivariate data and how it can be collected. The lesson distinguishes between populations and samples, and reviews different sampling methods for gathering responses to investigative questions. By the end of the lesson, students will understand the data cycle and various sampling methods, exploring the advantages and disadvantages of each method, considering factors like cost, time, and accuracy.

Learning objectives

Students: Page 500

After this lesson, you will be able to...
- form questions that collect responses that can be represented by bivariate data.
- determine the appropriate sampling method for collecting a representative sample.

Key vocabulary

- bias
- convenience sampling
- independent variable
- observation
- sample survey
- statistical variable
- systematic sampling
- bivariate data
- data cycle
- investigative question
- population
- simple random sampling
- stratified sampling
- univariate data
- cluster sampling
- dependent variable
- measurement
- sample
- statistical question
- survey

Essential understanding

Representative samples are crucial if a data set will be used to make predictions and decisions.

Standards

This subtopic addresses the following Virginia Standards of Learning for Mathematics standards.

Mathematical process goals

MPG1 — Mathematical Problem Solving

Teachers can integrate this goal by posing real-world problems that require the application of bivariate data analysis. For example, presenting a situation where students need to collect and analyze data on two different variables, such as height and weight, to identify any existing relationship.

MPG2 — Mathematical Communication

This goal can be integrated by having students explain their thought process when formulating investigative questions or choosing appropriate sampling methods. Teachers can encourage students to use mathematical language and notation in their explanations. Students can also be asked to present their findings to the class, effectively communicating their mathematical reasoning.

MPG3 — Mathematical Reasoning

Teachers can facilitate this goal by asking students to justify their choice of variables and sampling methods in the given context. They should reason why their chosen methods are appropriate for the investigative question at hand. This encourages the use of logical reasoning and critical thinking.

MPG5 — Mathematical Representations

Teachers can integrate this goal by asking students to visually represent the bivariate data they collect, such as using scatterplots. They should make connections between the visual representation and the mathematical concepts it represents. For instance, students can be asked to represent the relationship between two variables in a graph, and interpret its meaning in the context of the problem.

Content standards

A.ST.1 — The student will apply the data cycle (formulate questions; collect or acquire data; organize and represent data; and analyze data and communicate results) with a focus on representing bivariate data in scatterplots and determining the curve of best fit using linear and quadratic functions.

A.ST.1c — Determine an appropriate method to collect a representative sample, which could include a simple random sample, to answer an investigative question.

A.ST.1a — Formulate investigative questions that require the collection or acquisition of bivariate data.

A.ST.1b — Determine what variables could be used to explain a given contextual problem or situation or answer investigative questions.

Prior connections

8.PS.3 — The student will apply the data cycle (formulate questions; collect or acquire data; organize and represent data; and analyze data and communicate results) with a focus on scatterplots.

Future connections

A2.ST.1 — The student will apply the data cycle (formulate questions; collect or acquire data; organize and represent data; and analyze data and communicate results) with a focus on univariate quantitative data represented by a smooth curve, including a normal curve.

A2.ST.2 — The student will apply the data cycle (formulate questions; collect or acquire data; organize and represent data; and analyze data and communicate results) with a focus on representing bivariate data in scatterplots and determining the curve of best fit using linear, quadratic, exponential, or a combination of these functions.

Engage Activity

Populations and samples

60 mins

Students will look at a conclusion made from a sample and identify points of bias. They will simulate a survey of a population and make conclusions based on the results.

Understanding and skills

Will use
Using data from a random sample to make predictions about a population.

Will develop
Estimating a population total or percentage using data from a sample survey.
Analyzing a sample for bias.

Could extend
Determining a way to sample without bias.

Preparation and materials
- Open and complete the student preview, anticipating classroom responses.
- **Materials:** None.

Support students with disabilities
Support memory - use math vocabulary

This task will include vocabulary such as: survey, data, simulate, poll, bias, population, percentage, conclusion, random sample, and analyze. Preview vocabulary terms prior to the lesson and have students define the vocabulary words on a resource sheet, or provide resource sheets for the vocabulary terms.

Support for English language learners
Discussion supports

Provide the following sentence frames for students to use precise language when discussing the validity of Javier's survey:
- "I noticed ☐, so I ☐."
- "I know ☐ because ☐."
- "If ☐ then ☐ because ☐."
- "☐ reminds me of ☐ because ☐."

Classroom guide

Hook
Co-craft questions • 5 mins

Students create questions about a poster created for a student body election.

Implementation details
We want students to consider where the statistics on the poster came from and question their validity.

Some possible questions include:
- How many students were surveyed?
- How was the survey conducted?
- Which students were surveyed?
- How did Javier find or select these students?
- Is this sample representative of all students at Javier's school?

What mathematical questions could we ask about this situation?

9/10 students want pizza for lunch everyday!
I CAN MAKE IT HAPPEN.
VOTE FOR **JAVIER!**

Slide 1 from Student Engage Activity

Launch
5 mins

When Javier ran for student council Vice President, he wanted to research topics that his fellow students care about. To find this information, he conducted a survey of his friends.
Javier stated that: "I asked 20 students and 18 of them said they want pizza for lunch everyday. I decided to say '9 out of 10' on the poster because it was catchy, but it means the same thing."

Slide 4 from Student Engage Activity

Before starting the task, ask students to define the terms sample and population. Ask students to share what they think makes a "good" sample for conducting a survey.

Important mathematical concepts: Sample, population, survey, simulate

Suggested grouping: Form pairs

> **Continue when**
> Students have read the Launch and understand the context of the problem.

Explore
Think-pair-share • 25 mins

In this task, students will be asked a number of open-ended questions. Students will be asked to articulate whether or not they think Javier's survey was large enough to represent the school's population and whether there was any bias introduced by only polling his friends.

Use the applet to investigate the problem.

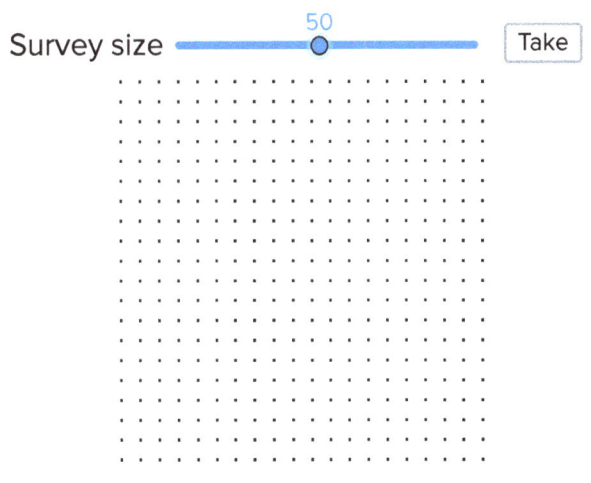

Survey size — 50 — Take

Anticipated strategies

Estimate a population total

Students will use a sample percentage to work out a population total. Based on the given information about $\frac{9}{10}$ students stating they want pizza for lunch every day, students may calculate

$$\frac{9}{10} \cdot 2342 = 2107.8$$

to estimate the proportion of the whole student population who wants pizza for lunch each day.

Slide 5 from Student Engage Activity

Students may choose to round this value to 2107 or 2108 as you cannot have a fraction of a student, or they may keep the exact value of 2107.8 since it is an estimate and not an actual quantity of students.

Analyze a sample

Students will consider a sample and the corresponding statistics to draw conclusions about the validity of the conclusions made.

Some observations students might make are:

- Javier only polled his friends so the statistic $\frac{9}{10}$ might not be representative of the whole population.
- If Javier polled a different group of 20 students he might see different results.
- Javier polled 20 people total and this could be too few (or too many) people to poll.

Simulate a sample

Students will simulate sampling of a population using the applet. During the simulation, students may observe:
- The proportion of the sample that prefers pizza for lunch everyday can vary from one simulation to the next.
- In many simulations, the proportion of students who want pizza for lunch every day is less than $\frac{9}{10}$, which was Javier's claim.
- For small simulations (about $n < 20$), there is much more variability in the results of the simulation.

Misconceptions

Conflating survey bias with sample size issues

What does it mean for survey to have bias? Can you think of any examples? How does the sample size affect the validity of a survey? Is it possible to survey too many or too few people? Is this the same idea as bias? What issues might there be Javier only surveying his friends? Do you think this contributes to any bias? What percent of the school did Javier survey? Do you think this enough to accurately represent the views of the entire school? Why or why not? If not, how many would you poll to feel comfortable representing the views of the school?

Purposeful questions

Use the following questions to check for understanding and encourage critical thinking:
- What sample size do you think is 'big enough'? Is there is sample size that is too big or too small?
- Is there bias in Javier's original survey? What evidence supports/refutes this?
- Did the simulation(s) change your opinion on how big of a sample should be surveyed? Explain.

> **Continue when**
>
> Students have determined how big of a sample is 'big enough' for Javier's survey, and whether they would do anything differently if they were to replicate the poll.

Discuss   25 mins

Pairs will begin by filling in a class data chart, then having a whole class discussion of each pair's results. Consider sequencing the strategies presented from estimating a population total, to analyzing a sample, to stimulating a sample, to a discussion on bias.

Discussion guide

Create a class chart where pairs will fill in how big of a sample they would poll if they were to recreate Javier's survey.

Begin by calling on several pairs to explain how they determined how many is 'enough' to survey. Allow students to critique one another's answers, and if any groups have significantly higher or lower sample sizes than the others, spend some time discussing. Some questions you can ask to promote discussion:
- For small samples, say less than 10% of the school population: Consider the simulations you did in the activity. How many of them with a sample size of (insert student answer of 10% or less) were representative of Javier's survey? Was there more variability in the outcomes of the small samples? How do you know?
- For large samples, say 1000 or more: What logistical issues arise from having a very large sample? Does it take longer to survey? Do the pros outweigh the cons?

Next, ask students to share if there were any other issues with the survey besides the sample size. Ask for examples of what kind of bias occurs when you only ask your friends for their opinion and not other groups of people. Some questions you can ask to promote discussion:
- Does it result in many of the same opinions being overrepresented?
- What happens when other voices aren't included?

Students may wish to share other examples of bias they have heard about in real world situations, such as advertisements, politics, or articles making health and medical claims.

As an extension, you may provide students with the prompt:
- Design a method of population sampling which results in a representative data set and reduces the amount of bias in the survey.

Lesson Preparation

Suggested review

Depending on your students' level of prior knowledge, consider revisiting the following lessons:

Grade 8 — 3.04 Independent and dependent variables
Grade 8 — 4.01 Data collection and sampling

Lesson supports

The following supports may be useful for this lesson. More specific supports may appear throughout the lesson:

Understanding the data cycle
Targeted instructional strategies

Start with a brief discussion about the data cycle, which includes planning, collecting, processing, and interpreting data. Ask students to list each part of the data cycle and describe in their own words what each part entails. This image could be posted publicly as a reminder.

Possible responses could be:
- Formulate questions
  - Finding a context we want to investigate
  - Write a statistical question for the investigation
- Collect or acquire data
  - Deciding whether we need univariate or bivariate data
  - Write survey questions and give it to a random sample of people
  - Measure objects or quantities
  - Plan an observation strategy
  - Design a scientific experiment
  - Research online
- Organize and represent data
  - Draw a graph or diagram
- Analyze and communicate results
  - Summarize findings
  - Answer the statistical question

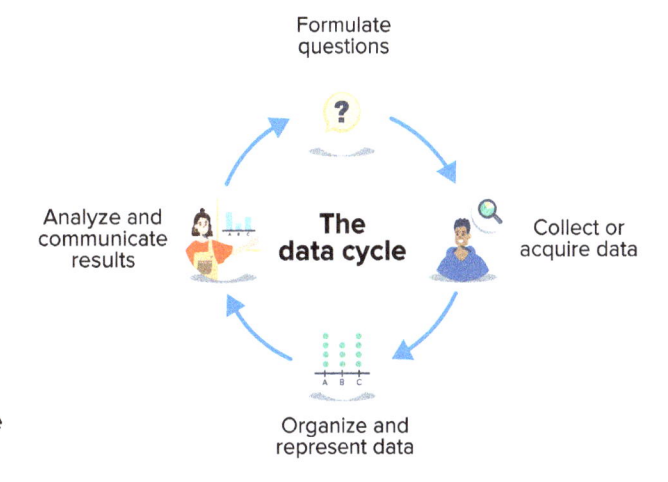

The data cycle is cyclical
Address student misconceptions

Students may mistakenly believe that the data cycle is a linear process. It's crucial to correct this misconception by explaining that the data cycle is a circular process, with each step feeding into the next. This is also called an iterative process. If data is interpreted and new questions arise, the cycle begins again with new planning.

Emphasize that iterative processes that refine the product or conclusion are widely applicable. For example, in coding, code can often be improved to be more efficient, or a bakery can make micro-adjustments to their recipes.

Student lesson & teacher guide

Formulate questions for bivariate data

Students will learn about bivariate data, its importance, and how it allows for the exploration of relationships between two variables. They will learn how to formulate an statistical question that focuses on the relationship between these variables, and understand the importance of identifying the correct variables for accurate data analysis.

Students: Pages 500–501

9.01 Data and sampling

After this lesson, you will be able to...
- form questions that collect responses that can be represented by bivariate data.
- determine the appropriate sampling method for collecting a representative sample.

Engage activity
Ask your teacher to get started

Populations and samples
Students will look at a conclusion made from a sample and identify points of bias. They will simulate a survey of a population and make conclusions based on the results.

Formulate questions for bivariate data

Data is a crucial aspect of our day to day lives. It helps us to understand the world around us and make informed decisions. The process of working with data involves a series of steps commonly referred to as the **data cycle**. This cycle includes formulating questions, collecting or acquiring data, organizing and representing data, analyzing data, and communicating results.

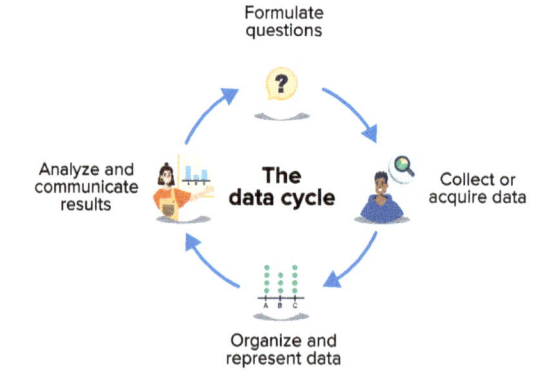

To help us formulate appropriate questions, it is helpful to know what type of data we want to explore.

> **Univariate data**
> Information gathered around a single characteristic. This data can be numerical or categorical.
> Displays include: bar graphs, line plots/dot plots, stem-and-leaf plots, circle graphs, histograms, and boxplots.
> Example: Grades in a course, time spent outside, preferred type of fruit

---

1086 Mathspace   Virginia SOL Algebra 1 Teacher Edition
mathspace.co

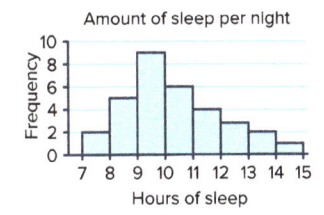

This histogram displays numerical data of the length of time people slept per night.

Notice that there is only one characteristic (or attribute), time, that is being explored. The axes are the attribute and the frequencies. We can only compare the amount of sleep in different groups/bins within the data set.

> **Variables**
>
> Variables are quantities or qualities that can be measured or classified.
>
> **Independent variable**
>
> The variable that is varied or controlled to explore the effect it has on the dependent variable.
>
> **Dependent variable**
>
> The variable that depends on the independent variable.
>
> We typically want to explore the effect that the independent variable has on the dependent variable.
>
> **Bivariate data**
>
> Bivariate data is data that is collected from two different variables and compared against each other. This data is typically numerical.
>
> Example: Age versus height, or 1-mile time versus 5-mile time

Person	Age (years)	Systolic blood pressure (mmHg)
Art	30	121
Kumi	40	140
Isla	50	134
Daria	60	154
Xia	70	146

For a study about heart health, a person's systolic blood pressure is measured against their age.

Their age is the independent variable and can be any value. Their systolic blood pressure is the dependent variable that is recorded against their age.

Notice that each person's age and systolic blood pressure make a pair of values in the bivariate data set.

To start working with bivariate data, we need to formulate a statistical question.

> **Statistical question**
>
> A statistical question that can be answered by collecting data and whose answer may vary depending on the sample the data is collected from.
>
> Also called an **investigative question**.

Statistical question	Not statistical question
Is there a relationship between age and systolic blood pressure?	What is your blood pressure?
Do test scores increase as the amount of time studying increases?	How long did you study and what was your grade?
Does how long a pen lasts impact the cost of the pen?	Are there pens under five dollars that will last all year?

A statistical question is different from a **survey question** that is asked to those in the people in a study.

We need to make sure that questions are not leading people to answer a particular way. This means not using emotive language or suggesting a particular answer.

Good survey question	Leading question
Do you watch soccer?	Do you watch the most popular sport in the world, soccer?
How would you rate your meal?	What did you think of the meal from the outstanding chef?
What was your average speed driving here?	Did you do the wrong thing and go over the speed limit to get here?

Notice how the good questions are very neutral and the leading questions may encourage people to respond in a particular way.

Examples and non-examples of statistical questions
Targeted instructional strategies

To formulate effective statistical questions, students may benefit from a discussion of what makes a statistical question "good" or "bad."

Using the examples and non-examples from the lesson:

Statistical question	Not statistical question
Is there a relationship between age and systolic blood pressure?	What is your blood pressure?
Do test scores increase as the amount of time studying increases?	How long did you study and what was your grade?
Does how long a pen lasts impact the cost of the pen?	Are there pens under five dollars that will last all year?

Discuss with students why these are good or bad examples. Some discussion points might be:
- The second statistical question makes the intent of the investigation clear; we want to determine if there is an increasing trend between test scores and study time. To answer the question, we will need to collect bivariate data from various people, represent the data, and analzye the trend in the data.
- "What is your blood pressure?" is not a statistical question because there is a single response to this question. This is actually a survey question because it would help us collect data, but it does not lead us to investigate the data.

After the discussion, encourage students to create their own examples and non-examples of statistical questions.

Critique, correct, and clarify
English language learner support

Display the leading survey question, "Did you love the movie *The Boys in the Boat*?"

In pairs, students can discuss why the question is leading how they could rewrite the question to be a better survey question. Prompt student discussion with questions such as, "Which part of the question makes it leading?" or "When you read the question, does it make you feel a certain way about the movie?"

After discussing with their partners, allow students to write an argument for why they think the question is leading and write a better survey question. After a few minutes, invite students to share their arguments and survey questions with the class.

Better survey questions might be:
- What did you think to the movie *The Boys in the Boat*?
- What did you like or dislike about the movie *The Boys in the Boat*?
- Would you recommend watching the movie *The Boys in the Boat*?

Examples

Students: Page 502

Example 1

Select the question(s) which could be answered by collecting bivariate data. Select all that apply.

A How much does it typically cost to own a horse?
B Does the amount of fertilizer used impact the number of tomatoes a plant produces?
C What is the relationship between reaction time and age?
D What interest rate can I expect on a car loan?

Create a strategy

For bivariate data each member of the sample or population would have two characteristics recorded.

Apply the idea

Let's go through each of the options:

Option A: The characteristic that would be collected for each horse would be the cost of owning. This is a single characteristic and would be different for different horses. This could be answered by collecting univariate data, not bivariate.

Option B: For each tomato plant we would record how much fertilizer was used and the number of tomatoes produced. These are two numerical characteristics, so this could be answered with bivariate data.

Option C: The characteristics being collected from each member of the sample would be reaction time and age. There are two characteristics being compared, so this is bivariate data.

Option D: There is no characteristic being collected here. This is a fact with a single answer, so would not have bivariate data collected to answer it.

The correct answers are B and C.

Reflect and check

For option B, we can't collect.

Purpose

Determine if students can identify questions that require bivariate data to answer.

Students: Pages 502–503

Example 2

The local ice cream shop has noticed that their sales seem to be related to the temperature outside. They want to investigate this relationship more closely.

Write a statistical question related to this scenario.

Create a strategy

When creating a statistical question, it's important that data can be collected to answer the question. For bivariate data, the question should focus on the relationship between the two variables involved, which in this case are temperature and ice cream sales.

Apply the idea

Some possible statistical questions might be:

1. Does an increase in temperature lead to an increase in ice cream sales?
2. Is there a relationship between temperature and the number of ice creams sold?
3. Is there a specific temperature range that results in the most ice cream sales?

Each of these questions is clear and concise, focusing specifically on the relationship between temperature and ice cream sales. They each propose a different aspect of the relationship to investigate, making them effective statistical questions.

Reflect and check

After one round of the data cycle we may formulate a new question to further explore the topic.

Purpose

This example checks whether students can formulate clear and relevant statistical questions to explore a relationship between two variables, in this case, temperature and ice cream sales.

Expected mistakes

Students may write questions that are vague or not directly related to the relationship between temperature and ice cream sales. For instance, a question like "Does weather affect ice cream sales?" is too broad as it doesn't specify the aspect of weather (in this case temperature) being considered.

Reflecting with students

After formulating the statistical question, it would be interesting to discuss with students the kind of data that could be collected to answer these questions and how they might go about analyzing it. This could lead to a deeper understanding of the investigative process.

Students: Page 503

Example 3

In a study conducted at a high school, students' study times (in hours) and their corresponding test scores (out of 100) were recorded for one particular examination. The data is to be analyzed to understand the relationship between study time and test scores.

a   Identify the variables involved in this scenario.

Create a strategy

A variable is any characteristic, number, or quantity that can be measured or counted.

There are two types of variables: dependent and independent. The dependent variable is what is being measured or observed (the outcome), while the independent variable is what is being manipulated or changed (the likely cause).

Apply the idea

In this case, the two variables are study time and test scores.

The independent variable is the study time. This is because it is the variable that we think will cause changes in the test scores.

The dependent variable is the test score. This is because it may change in response to changes in the study time. Test scores are what we are interested in predicting or explaining.

Reflect and check

It's important to consider potential confounding variables in any study. A confounding variable is an outside influence that may impact one or both of the variables. These may lead to a false conclusion. For example, the difficulty of the test, the student's previous knowledge, and other external factors (like health, sleep, etc.) could all potentially impact a student's test score.

Purpose

Check students can identify independent and dependent variables in a real-world scenario.

Students: Page 503

b Rewrite this question so it is not leading and it could be used to accurately collect data.

"We believe students who study more do better on tests. How much time did you spend studying last night? Did you do well on the test?"

Create a strategy

We need to make sure that the question is not leading people to answer a particular way. This means not using emotive language or suggesting a particular answer.

Apply the idea

"How much time did you spend studying last night? Did you do well on the test?"

Purpose

Check if students can rewrite a question to make it non-leading.

Students: Page 504

> **Idea summary**
> - **Data Cycle**: A process for working with data, which includes formulating questions, collecting data, organizing and representing data, analyzing data, and communicating results.
> - **Bivariate Data**: A type of data that involves two variables, allowing us to explore potential relationships between them.
> - **Statistical question**: A clear, concise question that can be answered by collecting and analyzing data.
> - **Variables**: Quantities or qualities that can be measured or classified, which help explain a given situation or answer statistical questions
>
> Examples of bivariate data analysis include studying the relationship between a person's study time and their test scores, or a city's population density and its air quality.

Collect data using samples

Students will learn about the concept of sampling in data collection and its various methods including simple random, systematic, stratified, and cluster sampling. They will understand the strengths and weaknesses of each method and how to choose the appropriate method for their data collection. The lesson also explains how to maintain the representativeness of the sample.

Students: Pages 504–506

Collect data using samples

Once we have formulated our statistical question and identified our variables, we are now ready to collect the necessary data.

There are several main methods for data collection:
- Observation: Watching and noting things as they happen
- Measurement: Using tools to find out how much, how long, or how heavy something is
- Survey: Asking people questions to get information
- Experiment: Doing tests in a controlled way to get data
- Acquire existing data: Using a secondary source, usually an online database, to get raw or summarized data.

This is where sampling may come into play. Sampling methods are techniques used to select a representative subset of the population, known as a sample. A **population** refers to every member of a group. A **sample** is a subset (or a smaller group) of the population. The type of sampling method we choose can greatly influence the quality of our data and, therefore, the conclusions we draw from it.

Collecting data from every member of a population is the most accurate way of gathering information, but it is not always the most practical and can be very expensive or time consuming. Typically, a **sample survey** is instead done on a sample from the population to make it quicker and less expensive.

There are several types of sampling methods, each with its own strengths and weaknesses. The goal is to have a sample that is representative, so has the same characteristics as the population.

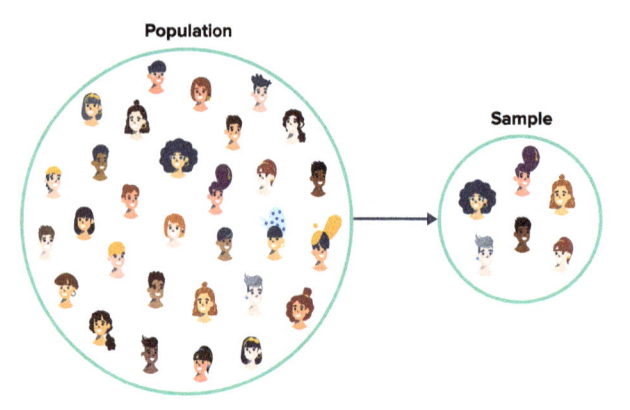

Simple Random Sampling
A sampling method where every member of the population has an equal chance of being selected.

In this method, a sample is formed by selecting members from the population at random, where each member of the population has an equally likely chance of being selected. In simple cases, a sample could be created by drawing names from a hat. For most samples though, it is more common to use a random number generator.

While simple random sampling can be one of the cheapest and least time-consuming methods, it may not be representative every sub-group within larger populations.

If a sample is not representative, we may say it is **biased**.

One particular type of biased or non-random sample is a convenience sample.

Convenience sample
A sample of people who are convenient, easy to ask, or close by. For example, your class or people in your building.

They typically aren't representative of the population.

There are other sampling techniques that can lead to more representative samples. These include:
- **Systematic Sampling**: A sampling technique where a starting point is chosen at random, and then items are chosen at regular intervals. This method is often used by manufacturers for sampling products on a production line. For example, we may call every tenth business in the phone book or select every fifth bottle from a production line.

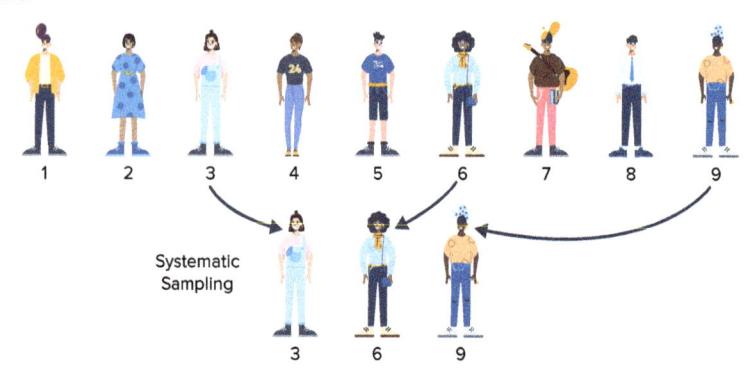

- **Stratified Sampling**: A sampling method that involves dividing the population into subgroups, or strata, and then selecting a separate random sample from each stratum. If one subgroup is larger than another then, we should proportionally select more people from that strata. For example, dividing a group into children, adults, and seniors and then selecting a proportional number of people from each group.

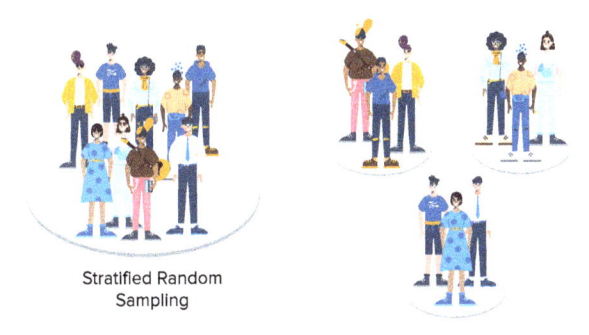

Stratified Random Sampling

- **Cluster sampling**: A sampling method where the population is divided into groups, or clusters. Then, a random sample of clusters is selected, and all members within selected clusters are included in the sample. It is like taking a sample of small samples.

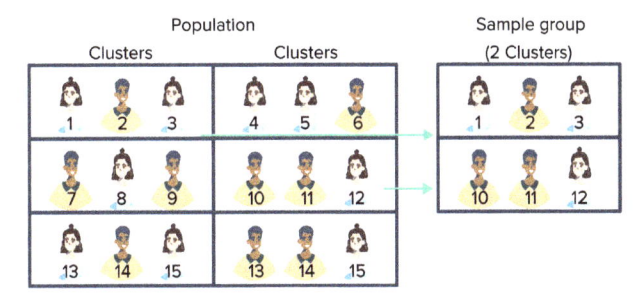

It's important to select an appropriate method to collect a representative sample. This will help to accurately analyze the relationship between our two variables. For example, if we wanted to investigate the relationship between exercise frequency and overall health across different age groups, we might choose a stratified sample to ensure we collect data from all age groups.

Concrete-Representational-Abstract (CRA) Approach
Targeted instructional strategies

Concrete: Engage students with hands-on activities to explore different sampling methods. Begin by creating a physical representation of a population. For example, fill a large container with a variety of colored beads or marbles, where each color represents a different characteristic within the population. Introduce various sampling methods:
- Simple Random Sampling: Have students close their eyes and randomly select a specific number of beads from the container, ensuring each bead has an equal chance of being chosen.
- Systematic Sampling: Line up the beads and instruct students to select every nth bead (e.g., every 5th bead) from the sequence.
- Stratified Sampling: Divide the beads into groups based on color (strata). Then, have students randomly select a proportional number of beads from each group to represent the entire population.
- Cluster Sampling: Group the beads into clusters (e.g., small bags or sections) and randomly select entire clusters to include in the sample.

Encourage students to physically perform each sampling method, allowing them to experience how samples are collected and how different methods can yield different results.

Representational: Transition to visual representations of the sampling methods. Guide students to create diagrams, charts, or graphs that illustrate each method:
- Simple Random Sampling: Draw the entire population and use random dots or highlights to indicate the randomly selected samples.
- Systematic Sampling: Depict the population in a line or grid format and mark every n^{th} item that is selected.
- Stratified Sampling: Illustrate the population divided into distinct strata based on characteristics, showing the proportional samples taken from each group with colored sections.
- Cluster Sampling: Represent the population divided into clusters, highlighting the entire clusters that are selected for the sample.

These visual tools help students understand the process and rationale behind each sampling method. Encourage them to label their diagrams clearly and use different colors or symbols to distinguish between groups and samples.

Abstract: Move on to discussing the sampling methods using formal definitions and statistical concepts:
- Simple Random Sampling: Explain that every member of the population has an equal chance of being selected. Discuss its benefits in reducing bias and how randomness is achieved.
- Systematic Sampling: Describe how selecting every nth member can simplify the sampling process but may introduce bias if there is a hidden pattern in the population.
- Stratified Sampling: Emphasize how dividing the population into strata ensures representation from all subgroups, improving the accuracy of the sample in reflecting the population's diversity.
- Cluster Sampling: Explain that selecting entire clusters can be more practical and cost-effective, especially with large populations spread over wide areas, but may increase sampling error if clusters are not representative.

Introduce terms like "population," "sample," "bias," and "representativeness." Encourage students to compare the advantages and disadvantages of each method, considering factors such as ease of use, cost, time efficiency, and accuracy

Connecting the stages: Help students make connections between the concrete activities, their visual representations, and the abstract concepts. Ask guiding questions such as:
- "How did physically selecting beads help you understand the concept of randomness in sampling?"
- "What did you notice when comparing the different sampling methods during the activity?"

Encourage students to relate their diagrams to the hands-on activities by explaining how each visual representation maps onto the steps they performed. Facilitate discussions on how the sampling method chosen can impact the data collected and the conclusions drawn from it. By connecting all three stages, students can better monitor their thinking and make informed decisions about which sampling method to use in different investigative scenarios. This holistic understanding reinforces the importance of choosing appropriate sampling methods to collect representative data for predictions and decisions.

Collect and display
English language learner support

As students are working, note how students describe the concepts of "sample," "population," "sampling methods" and how they relate this to "representative sample" and "potential biases". Collect the different ways that students find to understand these concepts and display them in a common place for the students to access.

If students do not come up with alternative ways to word these concepts and are confused by them, suggest some of your own. For example:

Population:
- Everyone we wish we could survey
- Who or what the survey is about
- Can be people, animals, objects, or cases

Sample:
- Some people or objects from the population
- Subset of the population
- Represents the population
- Who we can actually access to survey

Sampling methods
- Strategies for selecting a subset of individuals from a population
- Ways to collect data from a group

Representative sample
- A subset of a statistical population that accurately reflects the members of the entire population
- A small quantity that accurately reflects the larger entity

Potential biases
- Factors that may skew the sampling process, leading to unrepresentative results
- Unfair influence that may affect the outcome of the study

Provide visuals and specific examples for each sampling method
Student with disabilities support

For each type of sampling method, include an explanation of the definition, a real-world example and an illustration to support student understanding.

Here are some examples that could be used for each sampling method:
- Simple random sampling
  - Definition: Explain that in random sampling, each member of the population has an equal chance of being selected for the sample.
  - Real-world example: Describe how names might be drawn from a hat to decide who will serve on a committee.
  - Illustration:

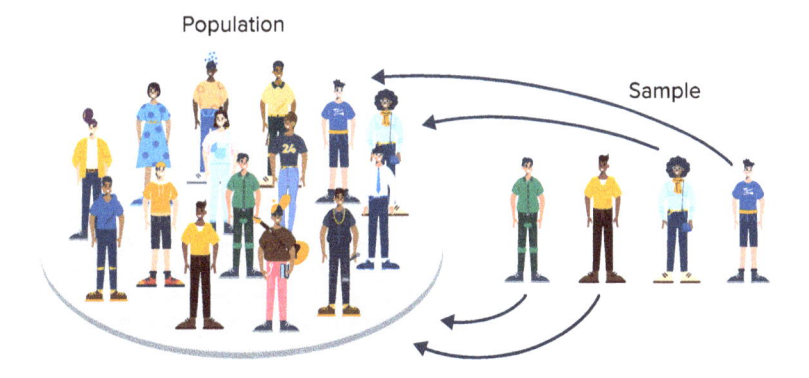

- Convenience sampling
  - Definition: Explain that a convenience sample involves only collecting data from people who are easy to reach or within your group of acquaintances.
  - Real-world example: A student might only survey students in their class.
  - Illustration:

- Systematic sampling
  - Definition: Describe how in systematic sampling, a starting point is randomly chosen, and then every nth member of the population is selected for the sample.
  - Real-world example: A factory might inspect every 10th item coming off the assembly line to check for defects.
  - Illustration:

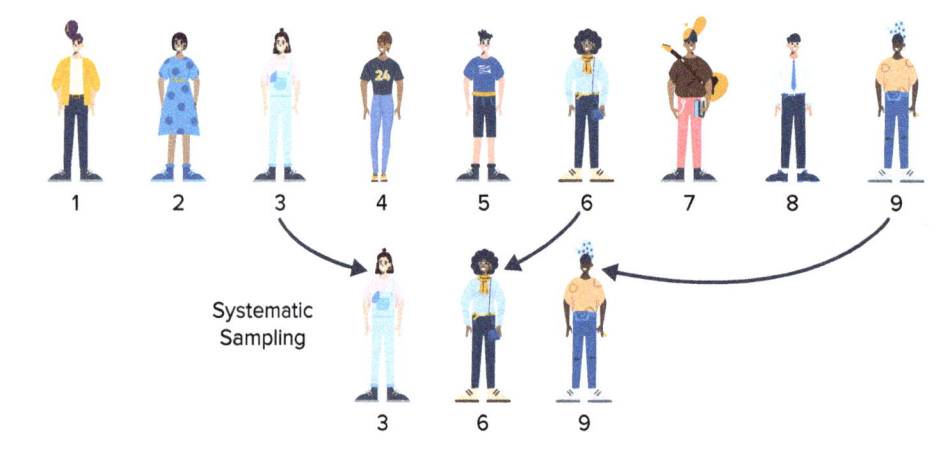

- Stratified sampling
  - Definition: Explain how stratified sampling involves dividing the population into homogeneous subgroups and then taking a random sample from each subgroup.
  - Real-world example: A television network wanting to get a balanced view of people's opinions on a new TV show might take a sample that includes a set number of viewers from different age groups.
  - Illustration:

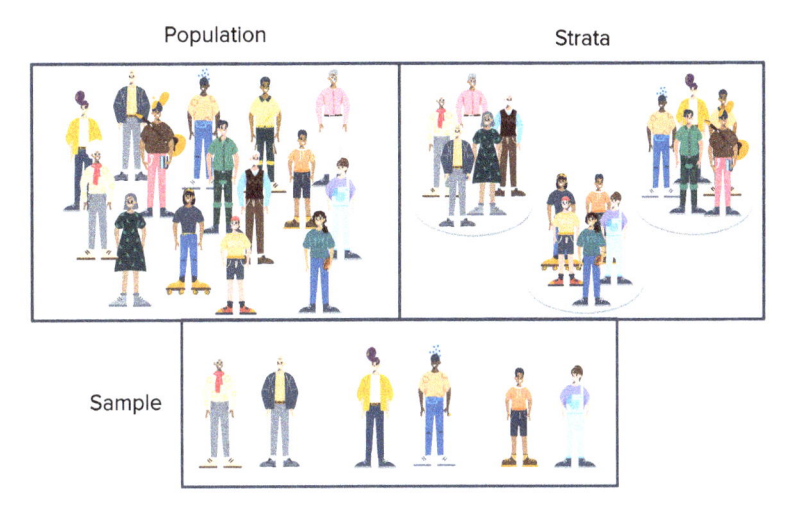

- Cluster sampling
  - Definition: Explain how cluster sampling involves dividing the population into groups. Then, entire groups are randomly selected.
  - Real-world example: At a conference, attendees are seated at tables with 10 people each. The person leading the conference randomly invites 3 tables of people to help with a demonstration.
  - Illustration:

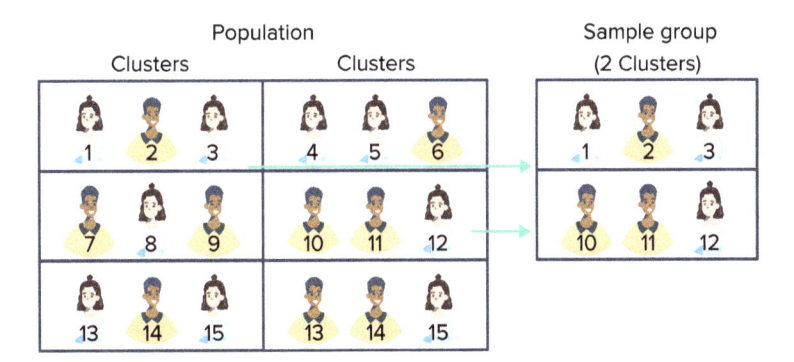

Best sampling method
Address student misconceptions

Students may believe that there is a "best" sampling method. Correct this misconception by explaining that the method will depend on the specific situation and research question. Discuss the advantages and disadvantages of each method in different scenarios to reinforce this point.

Examples

Students: Page 506

Example 4

Determine whether each situation demonstrates a sample survey, an experiment, or an observational study.

a A hospital wants to compare the recovery rates of patients using a new dosage versus those using a standard treatment.

Create a strategy

A sample survey would not make sense in this situation. An observational study determines correlation, but it cannot determine if the dosage was the cause of specific growth differences. An experiment can determine cause and effect relationships.

Apply the idea

Since the hospital wants to know if different dosages were the cause of the recovery rates, the hospital should design an experiment.

Reflect and check

Although an observational study could have identified a correlation between dosage and recovery, other factors (like the family support or prior health levels) may have also caused a difference in recovery.

If they use an experiment, the hospital can control the other factors. This will help them determine if the dosage was truly the cause of the recovery rate.

Purpose

Evaluate students' ability to choose an optimal sampling method given the specific scenario.

Reflecting with students

Help students better understand experiments by describing that there are typically two groups in an experiment: the control group and the experimental group.
- The control group is the "normal" group. In this example, "those using a standard treatment" would be considered the control group.
- The experimental group are the ones with the "new" routine or the ones "testing" a theory. In this example, "patients using a new dosage" are in the experimental group.

By having a control group and an experimental group, we can determine that any changes observed in the experimental group are caused by the "new routine" or the thing being tested.

Students: Pages 506–507

b A new book has been released. A library wants to know if their patrons prefer e-books or physical books to determine how many of each to get.

Create a strategy

To determine which type of design is best for this situation, we need to determine how the data can be collected.

Apply the idea

Because the library wants to know their patrons' opinions, they will need to ask them about their preference on book type. A sample survey is the best design for gathering this information.

Reflect and check

If the library got an equal number of each and wanted to know which was getting more use, an observational study would be a suitable design.

Purpose

Evaluate students' ability to choose an optimal sampling method given the specific scenario.

Students: Page 507

c A gym wants to know if there is a relationship between the number of visits someone had in the their first month and the length of time they will be at the gym.

Create a strategy
We can first think about if the data already exists or if the gym would need to create it.

Apply the idea
Since we are looking for data on something that has already happened, acquiring existing data would be the best choice.

Reflect and check
It is unlikely that if people were surveyed they would remember how many times they went in the first month, so a survey would not be a good choice.

Purpose
Evaluate students' ability to choose an optimal sampling method given the specific scenario.

Expected mistakes
Students might say an observational study would be best for collecting data. While an observation is valid, it would be difficult to collect this data by observing people. For example, how would they know which people had been visiting for a month or less? And how could they get a random sample of those people?

Students: Page 507

Example 5

A social worker notices that many of the children he helps say they want to go to the playground during their sessions. He is curious if there is a relationship between age of children and time spent at playgrounds each week in his town.

a Identify the target population.

Apply the idea
The target population would be children in the social worker's town.

Reflect and check
He could look at all children, but playground usage would likely vary significantly based on population density, country, and number of playgrounds.

Purpose
Determine if students' are able to identify the target population in a given scenario.

Students: Page 507

b Which method would be best to collect the relevant data?

- **A** Observation
- **B** Measurement
- **C** Survey
- **D** Acquire secondary data

Create a strategy

We want to know somewhat personal information like age and habits.

Apply the idea

Let's look at each option:

Option A: Can we watch the children and determine their age and how much time they spend at the playground each week? No, it would be difficult to just watch and get this information.

Option B: Can we measure the children and determine their age and how much time they spend at the playground each week? No, their age and habits are not able to be measured using measurement tools.

Option C: Can we ask the children (or their guardian) their age and how much time they spend at the playground each week? Yes, by asking them a specific question about their age and playground habits we can get the data we need.

Option D: Would there be existing data to answer this question? No, it is unlikely that this question has already been asked to a sample which represents the current population.

The answer is C: Survey.

Purpose

Evaluate students' ability to choose the best collection method for a given scenario.

Students: Page 508

c Explain why doing a sample of the children at a park one Monday morning would not be a good sample.

Create a strategy

For the sample to be representative of the population, different children of varying ages with various playground habits should be included.

Apply the idea

This sample would be convenient, so is a convenience sample which is not representative.

This sample likely wouldn't include school age children who would be at school, not at the playground on a Monday morning. It also wouldn't include children who don't regularly get to go to the playground.

Finally, there may not be many children at the park, but the population of children might be large in comparison.

Purpose

Check students' understanding of a good sample.

Students: Page 508

> **Example 6**

Dr. Jane is a health researcher and she formulated the question "Is there a relationship between the frequency of exercise and overall health among working adults in Washington, DC?" She wants to collect data for her research. Choose an appropriate sampling method.

Create a strategy

When selecting a sampling method, Dr. Jane needs to consider several factors such as the size of her target population, the resources she has available, and potential biases that could influence the results.

Apply the idea

An appropriate sampling method for this study could be stratified sampling.

Considering Washington, DC's large and diverse population, stratified sampling would ensure that all segments of the population are represented in the sample. Dr. Jane could divide the population into different strata based on factors like age, occupation, or zipcode, and then randomly select participants from each stratum.

Reflect and check

While stratified sampling can provide a representative sample, it can be more complex and time-consuming to implement, and it might not be feasible if information about the different strata is not readily available.

An alternative method might be simple random sampling, where every individual in the population has an equal chance of being selected. However, this method might not guarantee that all segments of the population are adequately represented, especially for a diverse population.

Purpose

To assess students' understanding of how to select an appropriate sampling method based on the characteristics of the population and the statistical question.

Reflecting with students

Remind students that the goal of stratified sampling is to ensure that all segments of the population are represented. While a simple random sample is a valid sampling method, it could lead to certain subgroups being under represented in the sample.

Ask students what examples of subgroups of the population might look like and why it is important to consider the diversity of the population. For example, subgroups might be adults above 50, immigrants or refugees, or students between the ages of 16 and 24. It is important to consider different subgroups as frequency of exercise affect people's bodies in different ways.

Advanced learners: Discussion of various sampling methods use with Example 6
Targeted instructional strategies

Invite students to consider multiple sampling methods that Dr. Jane could use for her research beyond stratified sampling. Encourage them to think about the methods not mentioned in the lesson (cluster sampling, systematic sampling, and convenience sampling) and discuss how each could be implemented in the context of Washington, DC's working adults.

Ask open-ended questions such as, "How might using cluster sampling affect the representativeness of Dr. Jane's data?" or "What are the potential benefits and drawbacks of using systematic sampling in this scenario?" By exploring various methods and their implications, students can develop a more comprehensive understanding of how sampling choices impact the validity and reliability of research findings.

Collect and display
English language learner support

use with Example 6

As students are working, note how students describe the various sampling methods. Collect the different ways that students find to understand these concepts and display them in a common place for the students to access.

If students do not come up with alternative ways to word these concepts and are confused by them, suggest some of your own. For example:

- Random sampling
  - Picking members of a population by chance
  - Every member has an equal chance to be selected
  - No system for how the sample is chosen
- Systematic sampling
  - Using a consistent pattern for choosing the sample
  - Count the number of people/objects, then choose the multiples of a number for the sample
- Stratified sampling
  - Dividing a population into categories, then randomly picking members from each category
  - Ensuring all segments of the population are represented
- Cluster sampling
  - Dividing a population into groups, then randomly picking entire groups
  - All members of the selected groups are included in the sample

Encourage students to use these alternative ways of understanding and expressing these concepts as they discuss the problem and work towards a solution.

Students: Page 509

> ### Idea summary
>
> After we formulate a clear statistical question, we use the data cycle to collect, show, and explain information. To get data, we can use methods like:
>
> - Watching **(Observation)**
> - **Measuring**
> - Asking questions **(Survey)**
> - Doing **experiments**
> - Acquiring existing **secondary data**
>
> Sampling methods are techniques to collect data from a representative subset of the population, known as a sample.
>
> - **Population**: every member of a group.
> - **Sample**: a subset of the population.
>
> Types of sampling methods include:
>
> - **Simple Random Sampling**: every member of the population has an equal chance of being selected.
> - **Systematic Sampling**: involves selecting every nth member of the population.
> - **Stratified Sampling**: dividing the population into subgroups, and then selecting a separate random sample from each subgroup.
> - **Cluster Sampling**: the population is divided into groups, or clusters. Then, a random sample of clusters is selected, and all members within selected clusters are included in the sample.
>
> The type of sampling method chosen can greatly influence the quality of data collected and the conclusions drawn from it.

Practice

Students: Pages 509–513

What do you remember?

1 What is the difference between bivariate data and univariate data?

2 Give an example of a real-world situation where the relationship between two variables can be investigated using bivariate data.

3 State whether each statistical question could be answered by collecting univariate data or bivariate data:
- a How are the weights of students on the wrestling team distributed?
- b Is there a relationships between iron levels in soil and weed growth?
- c What shoe sizes are the most common at each of my local schools?
- d Is taxable income related to latitude of home address?
- e Does the number of days children spend in daycare affect the number of days spent home sick?
- f Is there a relationship between the amount of natural sunlight in a classroom and students' exam results?
- g Typically how old are people when they learn to skate on ice? Does it vary by country?

4 State whether each statement about statistical questions is true or false.
- a The question must have a yes or no answer.
- b The question allows for surveys to be conducted.
- c The answers to question may vary from one person to another.
- d The answers to question requires only numerical values.
- e They are only used for bivariate data
- f They should include your hypothesis for what you think the answer will be.

5 State whether each of the following questions are statistical questions:
- a Which city is the capital of France?
- b How far away is the moon from the Earth, right now?
- c Which is a typical maximum temperature during the summer in Chesterfield, VA?
- d How much do kittens weigh?
- e How far do you have to travel from home to school each day?
- f How old are Olympic gold medal winners when they win their medal?
- g How far do students have to travel to get from their home to school each day?
- h How far do you have to travel from home to school each day?
- i How many calories do people burn per day?

6 Determine which data collection method best describes each of these scenarios.
- a Asking people on the street about the age of their oldest living relative and recording their answers.
- b Using a batter bowl and a scale to determine the density of dough before and after it rises to see if there is a relationship.
- c A long term study that provides different levels of subsidies for childcare and looks to see if this affects the income and mental well-being of those children when they reach adulthood.
- d Watching a variety of gardens to see how many pollinators visit per hour.

7 Is each question leading or not?
   a   Do you take a multi-vitamin?
   b   How much time do you waste on social media per day?
   c   How much time do you spend reading every week?
   d   Do you think the government should be allowed to cut down some of the oldest trees in the area to construct a metro railway line in the city?
   e   Do you think bike helmets should be mandatory for all bike riders?
   f   Do you eat at least the recommended number of servings of fruits and vegetables to ensure a healthy and long life?
   g   How much time do you spend sitting every day?

8 Determine whether the scenario represents collecting data from a population or sample:
   a   Oscar has determined the cost of 5% of houses from each suburb in Richmond.
   b   Ainsley tests every lamp that the factory produces.
   c   Habib scans every carry-on bag for a flight Roanoke.
   d   Drake does a checkup on all children brought to his doctor's office to assess the health of all children in the city.

9 In which type of sampling does every individual in the population have an equal chance of being selected?
   A   Random sampling
   B   Stratified sampling
   C   Systematic sampling

10 What is the main difference between random and systematic sampling?
   A   Random sampling involves selecting individuals at regular intervals, while systematic sampling involves selecting individuals randomly.
   B   Random sampling involves selecting individuals randomly, while systematic sampling involves selecting individuals at regular intervals.
   C   There is no difference between random and systematic sampling.

11 John is conducting a research study on the satisfaction levels of employees in a company. He decides to use random sampling.
   a   Which option best describes the process of random sampling?
      A   Random sampling involves dividing the population into distinct subgroups based on specific characteristics and then randomly selecting participants from each subgroup.
      B   Random sampling involves selecting participants from a population in a completely random manner, ensuring each individual has an equal chance of being chosen.
      C   Random sampling involves selecting participants from a population at regular intervals, using a predetermined starting point.
   b   Which option best describes one advantage of using this random sampling?
      A   One advantage of using this method is that it reduces the chances of bias and provides a representative sample of the population.
      B   One advantage of using this method is that it ensures representation from each subgroup, allowing for more accurate estimates for each group.

12 A school principal wants to estimate the number of students who ride a bicycle to school. Is each sample biased?
   a   All students who are in the school band.
   b   Eight students in the hallway after school.
   c   Ten students from each grade, chosen at random.
   d   130 randomly selected students during the lunch periods.

13 For each statistical question, identify the independent and dependent variables.
  a   Is there a relationship between the number of website visitors and the percentage of visitors who make a purchase?
  b   Is there a relationship between the number of words in a child's vocabulary and the number of books that are read to them per week?"

14 Is there likely to be a relationship between each pair of variables?
  a   Time spent on phone per day and number of apps on phone
  b   Amount spent on pet food and amount spent on candy
  c   Price of lemons and average SAT scores
  d   Car speed and gas mileage

Let's practice

15 For each scenario:
  i   Identify possible independent and dependent variables.
  ii Write a statistical question related to the scenario.

  a   Gertrude notices the eggs with more Omega-3 tend to cost more and wonders if these are related.
  b   Latisha has started baking bread from scratch. As she gets more experienced she finds it takes less time. She wonders if there is a link between experience and time it takes to bake bread.
  c   Theo likes running and is working on his hill sprints on different hills. He is curious about his maximum speed on different slopes.

16 Change the following questions to make them statistical questions.
  a   How many books does your teacher have?
  b   How many points did the grade school basketball team score in its last game?
  c   What is your grade in Algebra 1 during the first term?

17 Jeremiah formulated the statistical question "Is there a relationship between spending on advertisement and business revenue?"
  Design a simple study that could be used to collect data to answer her question.

18 Natalie notices that finding coats that are long enough for her is difficult. She is curious what other body measurements are the best predictor of torso length.
  She formulates the question "Is there a relationship between arm length and torso length in teenagers?"
  a   Should she use measurement, observation, or acquire data to collect the data?
  b   What type of data would she be collecting?
  c   What type of sample should she use to ensure it is representative of the population?

19 Rewrite each question so it is not leading and it could be used to accurately collect data using a sample survey.
  a   A new study said that using more than two bottles of shampoo per year is wasteful. How many bottles of shampoo do you use per year?
  b   Most people with nice hair use some kind of oil product, what is your favorite hair product?
  c   Would you describe your hair as beautiful?
  d   How strong is the relationship between hair length and intelligence?

20 The owner of a movie theater wants to use stratified sampling in their survey of people who come to their theater. Are these methods considered to be stratified sampling?
   a   Interview 10% of the people who used the concessions and 10% of people who didn't.
   b   Interview every person that sees a romantic movie.
   c   Interview 10% of the people from each movie.
   d   Interview every 10th person that purchases a ticket.

21 For each scenario, determine the type of sampling method used:
   a   Drawing out the winning ticket in a lottery
   b   Choosing every 50th person on the class roll to take part in a survey
   c   Choosing 5% of the of the students in each grade for grades 7–12

22 David is conducting a research study to investigate the eating habits of people in a particular city. He opts for stratified sampling. What is an advantage of using this method?

23 Sarah is conducting a survey to gather data about the shopping preferences of customers in a large retail store. She chooses to use systematic sampling. What is a disadvantage of using this method?

24 Explain why the following samples are biased:
   a   Hannah is surveying customers at a shopping mall. She wants to know which stores customers shop at the most. She walks around an entertainment store and chooses 30 customers from the store for the survey.
   b   A TV station wants to know what the most popular type of music is, so they ask listeners to contact them and vote for their favorite type of music.
   c   The community health nurse wants to survey the students in a school about their eating habits. At lunchtime, she stands by a vending machine and surveys every student who purchases something from the machine.

Let's extend our thinking

25 Imagine you are investigating the relationship between a student's SAT score and their college GPA. Identify potential confounding variables that could influence this relationship and how you might account for them in your investigation.

26 Patricia surveys her class about their favorite music. Her results are shown in the table:

Genre	Country	Pop
No. students	15	2

   a   According to the survey, which genre is most popular among her class?
   b   This was her survey question:
       "The coolest kids like country music, and nobody likes pop. Do you like country music or pop music?"
       Do you trust the results of Patricia's survey? Explain your answer.

27 You want to survey a group of n students about their favorite sports, but you only have time to survey 20 students. How would you use systematic sampling to select the 20 students for the survey?

28 You want to conduct a survey of the reading habits of students at your school. How would you use stratified sampling to ensure a representative sample?

29 Discuss the importance of formulating appropriate statistical questions in the data cycle. How does this impact the subsequent steps in the cycle such as data collection, analysis, and interpretation?

30 For a topic that interests you, consider a relationship that might exist.
   a   Formulate a statistical question that could be used to explore the relationship.
   b   Describe a sampling and data collection method that could be used.

Answers

9.01 Data and sampling

What do you remember?

1. Univariate data involves a single variable while bivariate data involves two variables. Bivariate data is used to find the relationship or association between the two variables.

2. An example could be investigating the relationship between a baby's age and weight.

3. a Univariate data b Bivariate data
   c Univariate data d Bivariate data
   e Bivariate data   f Bivariate data
   g Univariate data

4. a No   b Yes   c Yes   d No
   e No   f No

5. a No   b No   c Yes   d Yes
   e No   f Yes   g Yes   h No
   i Yes

6. a Survey   b Measurement
   c Experiment d Observation

7. a Not leading b Leading
   c Not leading d Leading
   e Not leading f Leading
   g Not leading

8. a Sample   b Population
   c Population d Sample

9. Option A

10. Option B

11. a Option B b Option A

12. a Biased   b Biased
    c Not biased d Not biased

13. a Independent variable: Number of website visitors
       Dependent variable: Percentage of visitors who make a purchase
    b Independent variable: Number of books read to the child per week
       Dependent variable: Number of words in the child's vocabulary

14. a Yes b No c No d Yes

Let's practice

15. a i Independent variable: Amount of Omega-3
         Dependent variable: Cost of eggs
       ii Is there a relationships between the amount of Omega-3 in eggs and their cost per dozen?
    b i Independent variable: Month or years of experience baking
         Dependent variable: Time to bake bread
       ii Is there a relationship between the experience of a baker and the time it takes them to bake bread?
    c i Independent variable: Steepness of the hill
         Dependent variable: Maximum sprinting speed
       ii Is there a relationship between the steepness of a hill and maximum sprinting speed on the hill?

16. a Answers will vary. A possible answer is: How many nooks do teachers in our school have?
    b Answers will varry. A possible answer is What is a typical number of points scored by the grade school basketball team in its games this season?
    c Answers will vary. A possible answer is: What are the grades Algebra 1 students during the first term?

17. Many possible designs. For example:
    1. Determine the population:
       - Target Population: All businesses in Jeremiahs's town
    2. Develop a sampling strategy:
       - Sampling Method: Use stratified sampling to ensure diverse representation from various types of businesses like photographers, manufacturers, publishers, cleaners, transportation, etc.
       - Sample Size: Depending on the resources available, he should choose the largest number of possible businesses
    3. Collect the data:
       He would probably need to do a survey or acquire data from a secondary source.
       - Distribution method: He could distribute the survey electronically through school email or giving a link to an online form to make data collection easy and efficient. Alternatively, he could provide paper surveys with pre-paid return envelopes for those who don't like using the internet.

18. a Measurement
    b We would be collecting two lengths which are measureable numerical data.
    c Using a stratified sample would be appropriate in this case, because it would ensure that people with a wide variety of body types, ages, and backgrounds would be included.
    She should make the survey anonymous to ensure that people will feel comfortable to respond honestly.

19. a How many bottles of shampoo do you use per year?
    b What is your favorite hair product?
    c How would you describe your hair in one word?
    d Is there a relationship between hair length and intelligence?

20   a Yes   b No   c Yes   d No
21   a Random sampling   b Systematic sampling
     c Stratified sampling

22   Stratified sampling ensures representation from different segments or groups within the population, allowing for more accurate analysis and conclusions about specific subgroups.

23   One disadvantage of using systematic sampling is that it may introduce a potential bias if there is a systematic pattern or periodicity in the population's characteristics, leading to an underrepresentation or overrepresentation of certain individuals or groups in the sample.

24   a The sample is not representative of the target population.
     b The sample is from self-selecting participants, i.e. only those that made an effort to respond.
     c The sample is not representative of the target population.

Let's extend our thinking

25   Several variables could influence the relationship between a student's SAT score and their college GPA, including the student's study habits, course load, major, and involvement in extracurricular activities. To account for these variables, we could collect data on these additional factors and include them in our analysis as control variables. Alternatively, we could focus our investigation on a more specific population (e.g., students within the same major) to reduce the impact of these variables.

26   a Country
     b No, because the question uses emotive or leading language and suggests that country music is cool. It also asks two questions rather than one, as it's possible to like both types of music (or neither).

27   Example answer: You would first create a list of all the students, and then choose every nth student on the list, where n is the total number of students divided by 20.

28   Example answer: You would first divide the students into different groups based on reading level, grade level, or other relevant factors. Then, you would randomly select students from each group to ensure representation from each subgroup.

29   Formulating appropriate statistical questions is a critical first step in the data cycle because it guides the subsequent steps. The question determines what kind of data needs to be collected, how it should be collected, and what kind of analysis methods are appropriate. A poorly formulated question can lead to irrelevant or inaccurate data, inappropriate analysis methods, and misleading or invalid interpretations. Conversely, a well-formulated question can help ensure that the data collected is relevant and accurate, that the analysis is appropriate and meaningful, and that the interpretations and conclusions are valid and useful.

30   a Answers vary. Sample answer: In Ultimate Frisbee, is there a relationship between the height of a player and number of goals they score in the season? Does it vary by league?
     b For teams in the UFA, we could use secondary data and use the website to acquire the data for each player. This might be time consuming without writing a script or program to source all the data. We could do a stratified sample and select 5 players from each team with a mix of positions if we were short on time.
     For local teams, we could do a survey and ask 10 players from each team that were selected using a systematic sample two questions: How tall are you? and How many goals have you scored this season?

9.02 Scatterplots

Subtopic overview

Lesson narrative

In this lesson, students will be representing the relationship between two variables on a scatterplot. Students will be analyzing the relationship between bivariate data using concepts such as correlation and causation, as well as determining best-fit models for the data. Students should be able to justify whether or not two variables are correlated, as well as identify the strength of the correlation. By the end of the lesson, students should be comfortable plotting data with a linear pattern on a scatterplot and estimating a best-fit line. This is essential as in future lessons students will be required to fit functions to data.

Learning objectives

Students: Page 514

After this lesson, you will be able to...
- determine variables needed to represent a given contextual situation.
- create a scatterplot given a set of data.
- describe the relationship shown in a scatterplot.
- analyze relationships of variables represented in scatterplots.

Key vocabulary

- bivariate data
- dependent variable
- negative linear relationship
- quantitative variable
- correlation
- independent variable
- positive linear relationship
- scatterplot

Essential understanding

Correlation does not imply causation.

Standards

This subtopic addresses the following Virginia Standards of Learning for Mathematics standards.

Mathematical process goals

MPG1 — Mathematical Problem Solving

Teachers can encourage mathematical problem solving by guiding students to apply the concepts of bivariate data and scatterplots to solve real-world problems. For example, students can be asked to create their own scatterplots from real-world data, such as tracking the relationship between temperature and ice cream sales over a certain period. Teachers can also engage students in identifying potential problems in scatterplot representations, like outliers or unaccounted variables, thereby promoting critical thinking.

MPG2 — Mathematical Communication

Teachers can foster mathematical communication by having students explain their reasoning when identifying the type of relationship in a scatterplot. For instance, students can be asked to justify their reasoning when classifying scatterplots as having positive linear relationships, negative linear relationships, or no relationship. Additionally, students can share their observations and interpretations of scatterplots in group discussions or in written form.

MPG5 — Mathematical Representations

Teachers can integrate the goal of mathematical representations by having students represent bivariate data using scatterplots, both manually and using technology. Students can be taught to understand that each point on the scatterplot represents a pair of values for the two variables. Teachers can also encourage students to use different representations, such as tables or graphs, to further reinforce the concept of scatterplots. They can also have students explain the meaning of the scatterplots they've created in their own words, reinforcing the concept that representation is both a process and a product.

Content standards

A.ST.1 — The student will apply the data cycle (formulate questions; collect or acquire data; organize and represent data; and analyze data and communicate results) with a focus on representing bivariate data in scatterplots and determining the curve of best fit using linear and quadratic functions.

A.ST.1a — Formulate investigative questions that require the collection or acquisition of bivariate data.

A.ST.1b — Determine what variables could be used to explain a given contextual problem or situation or answer investigative questions.

A.ST.1c — Determine an appropriate method to collect a representative sample, which could include a simple random sample, to answer an investigative question.

A.ST.1h — Analyze relationships between two quantitative variables revealed in a scatterplot.

A.ST.1i — Make conclusions based on the analysis of a set of bivariate data and communicate the results.

A.ST.1d — Given a table of ordered pairs or a scatterplot representing no more than 30 data points, use available technology to determine whether a linear or quadratic function would represent the relationship, and if so, determine the equation of the curve of best fit.

Prior connections

8.PS.3 — The student will apply the data cycle (formulate questions; collect or acquire data; organize and represent data; and analyze data and communicate results) with a focus on scatterplots.

Future connections

A2.ST.1 — The student will apply the data cycle (formulate questions; collect or acquire data; organize and represent data; and analyze data and communicate results) with a focus on univariate quantitative data represented by a smooth curve, including a normal curve.

A2.ST.2 — The student will apply the data cycle (formulate questions; collect or acquire data; organize and represent data; and analyze data and communicate results) with a focus on representing bivariate data in scatterplots and determining the curve of best fit using linear, quadratic, exponential, or a combination of these functions.

Engage Activity

Happiness scores   60 mins

Students will investigate a sample of bivariate data and determine possible reasons as to why the two variables have an association.

Understanding and skills

Will use	**Will develop**
Creating scatterplots.	Understanding correlation.

Preparation and materials
- Open and complete the student preview, anticipating classroom responses.
- **Materials:** None.

Support students with disabilities
Support language - write explanations of mathematical thinking

When students are describing possible reasons for association in the data, use sentence starters such as:
- I think there is an association between ☐ and ☐ because…
- Countries with high sugar consumption have ☐ happiness ratings.
- Countries with sugar consumption have ☐ happiness ratings.
- I think the relationship between sugar consumption and happiness is ☐ because…

Support for English language learners
Three reads

Have students read the titles on the graph aloud. On the first read, ask students to describe the graph.

Prompt: Students read the problem.

Students think/write: Answer the question "What is the problem about?"

Answers may look like:
- Sugar consumption vs. happiness
- Different countries sugar consumption and happiness
- Investigating data and making inferences

Share: Students are called upon to discuss their answers with the class.

On the second read, ask students to interpret the question.

Prompt: Students read the problem.

Students think/write: Answer the question "What does an answer look like?"

Answers may look like:
- A claim and evidence to support or refute the claim
- An explanation of whether the two variables in the problem have any causation

On the third read, have students identify important information.

Prompt: Students read the problem.

Students think/write: Answer the question "What are the important pieces of information given in the question?"

Answers may look like:
- The individual data points
- The units and labels on the axes of the graph

Classroom guide

Hook

Notice and wonder • 5 mins

Students write observations about bivariate data presented as a scatterplot. Students look for conclusions that can be made from the data, or questions they have about the data that would require further research or information provided.

What do you notice? What do you wonder?

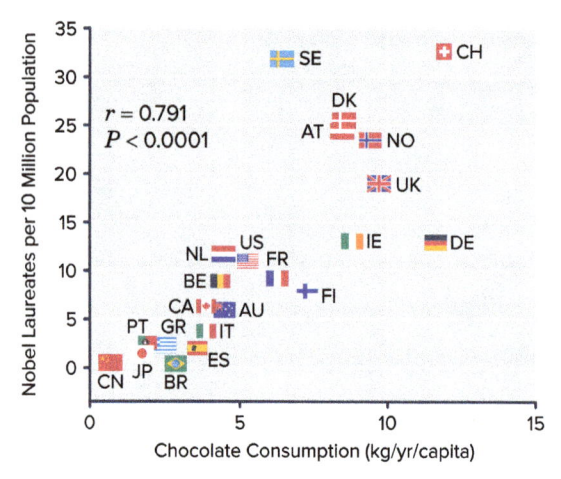

Implementation details

Ask students to look at individual flags and the data as a whole, and encourage them to notice and wonder about individual data points as well as the data set as a whole. Since correlation and causation are often conflated with one another, it may be challenging for students to articulate why one statement is a notice while the other must be a wonder. For example, a student might wonder, "Does more chocolate consumption produce more Nobel laureates?" while another student might think they can say "chocolate consumption influences the number of Nobel laureates" which is not necessarily true.

Slide 1 from Student Engage Activity

Launch

5 mins

Ask students if they have ever heard of the happiness score. You may wish to share a summary of what the score and how it is reported, which can be found here: https://worldhappiness.report/faq/. You may also allow students to quickly research the score and summarize it in with their partner before having a brief share-out to the class.

Important mathematical concepts: Scatterplot, two-way frequency table, relative frequency table, bivariate data

Important contextual information: Happiness score

Suggested grouping: Form pairs

The following graph shows data for various country's sugar consumption compared to their national happiness score ranking:

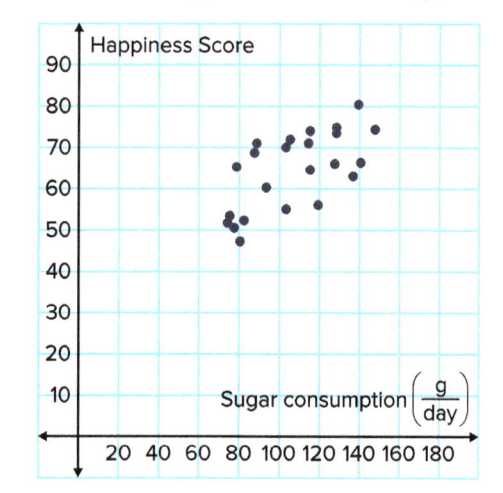

Slide 2 from Student Engage Activity

Continue when

Students have read the Launch and understand the context of the problem.

1112 Mathspace   Virginia SOL Algebra 1 Teacher Edition
mathspace.co

Explore

Think-pair-share • 35 mins

Anticipated strategies

Interpret data to make claim

Students may wish to interpret the given data to make a claim.

Students will produce their own claim based on the data. One such claim that students might make would be, "The higher a country's sugar consumption, the higher their happiness score."

After researching their claim, they may be able to recognize that both sugar consumption and happiness scores are typically higher in countries with higher GDPs and thus a causal relationship is unlikely.

During the second stage of the Explore, the goal is to have students recognize that there is a positive association between sugar consumption and happiness scores, but that there are likely other variables influencing both happiness and sugar consumption simultaneously, namely the wealth of the nation and its level of development. Whether or not they are actually valid claims, it is theoretically possible for the two variables to have an association for other reasons as well, such as a coincidence or perhaps sugar consumption is just one of many factors influencing happiness and not the sole factor.

Misconceptions

Correlation is the same as causation

Does it mean that simply owning books leads to better grades? What about income levels or parent's education level? Might those be influencing both the number of books and the students' grades?

Purposeful questions

Use the following questions to check for understanding and encourage critical thinking:
- Is there any information in the graph to imply that sugar consumption causes happiness?
- Is it possible for two variables to have an association without causation? How might that be possible?
- What are some reasons that two variables may have an association?

> **Continue when**
>
> Students have written a claim about the data and justified whether or not their claim is supported by any reputable sources they found during their investigation.

Discuss

15 mins

Start with a class discussion. Consider making connections from the discussion to how to determine if a source is credible or not.

Discussion guide

Ask several pairs to share their claim with the class. Allow the class to decide whether they think each claim is true before asking the pair whether or not they found evidence to support their claim. The discussion is a great opportunity to have students practice determining whether a source is credible evidence of a particular claim. Feel free to allow groups to determine which sources used are credible or not credible.

After several pairs have presented, ask several other pairs to share the possible factors for why the two variables have an association. As pairs are sharing their answers with the class there may be themes in what kinds of answers are being shared. Use this as an opportunity to have students generalize the types of claims into different categories such as "A is just one cause of B" or "C causes both A and B." If the claims produced in class seem to fall heavily into one or two categories, you may wish to provide additional examples of claims for students to try and generalize.

Lesson Preparation

Suggested review

Depending on your students' level of prior knowledge, consider revisiting the following lessons:

Grade 8 — 3.04 Independent and dependent variables
Grade 8 — 4.05 Scatterplots and lines of best fit
Algebra 1 — 9.01 Data and sampling

Tools

You may find these tools helpful:
- Statistics calculator
- Graph paper

Lesson supports

The following support may be useful for this lesson. More specific supports may appear throughout the lesson:

Concrete-Representational-Abstract (CRA) Approach
Targeted instructional strategies

Concrete: Begin by engaging students in a hands-on activity to explore the relationship between two variables. Have them collect real-world data, such as measuring each other's heights and arm spans, or recording the time spent walking and the distance covered. Provide tools like measuring tapes or stopwatches for data collection. This physical activity helps students understand how variables can be related and gives them concrete data to work with.

Representational: Guide students to organize the collected data into a table. Then, teach them how to create a scatterplot using graph paper or a digital graphing tool. Show them how to plot each data pair accurately, with one variable on the x-axis and the other on the y-axis. Encourage them to observe any patterns or trends in the plotted data, such as clusters or a general direction.

Abstract: Introduce the concepts of correlation and causation using mathematical terminology. Explain how to describe the relationship shown in the scatterplot as positive correlation, negative correlation, or no correlation. Teach students how to estimate and draw a line of best fit through the data points. Discuss how this line can be represented with an equation and how the slope relates to the strength of the correlation. Emphasize that correlation does not imply causation, and provide examples to illustrate this concept

Connecting the stages: Help students connect their hands-on data collection with the scatterplots and abstract concepts.

Ask guiding questions like:
- "How does the pattern in our scatterplot relate to the measurements we took?"
- "What does the line of best fit tell us about the relationship between these variables?"

Encourage them to consider whether one variable causes the other or if they are simply correlated. By linking the concrete activity, visual representation, and abstract ideas, students will develop a deeper understanding of analyzing relationships in scatterplots.

Student lesson & teacher guide

Scatterplots

Students are guided through key features of the analysis of bivariate data. These features include the form, strength, and direction of the relationship. Additionally, the inclusion of categorical variables in scatterplots is discussed to enhance understanding

Examples of data sets with different strength and direction are given.

Students: Pages 514–515

9.02 Scatterplots

After this lesson, you will be able to...
- determine variables needed to represent a given contextual situation.
- create a scatterplot given a set of data.
- describe the relationship shown in a scatterplot.
- analyze relationships of variables represented in scatterplots.

Engage activity
Ask your teacher to get started

Happiness scores
Students will investigate a sample of bivariate data and determine possible reasons as to why the two variables have an association.

Scatterplots

We often analyze **bivariate data** to determine whether a relationship between the two variables exists. A **scatterplot** can be used to display bivariate, numerical data once the **independent and dependent variables** are defined.

The analysis of bivariate data should include:
- Form, usually described as a **linear relationship** or a **nonlinear relationship**
- Strength, describing how closely the data points match the model line or curve

If the relationship between the variables is linear, the direction of the relationship can be described as positive or negative.
- Positive relationship: as the independent variable increases, the dependent variable increases
- Negative relationship: as the independent variable increases, the dependent variable decreases

The dashed lines in the scatterplots will help us visualize possible trends in the data.

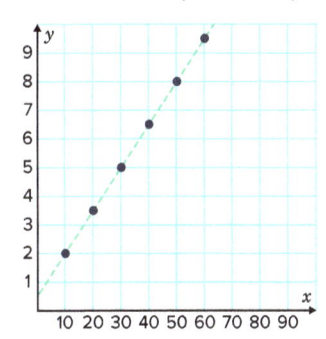

Perfect positive relationship since points are exactly along the model with a positive slope

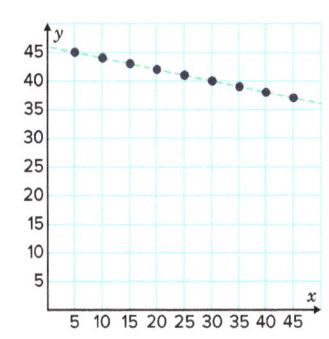

Perfect negative relationship since points are exactly along the model with a negative slope

9.02 Scatterplots 1115
mathspace.co

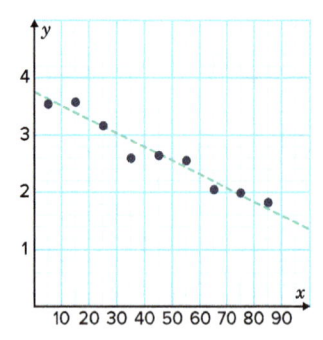

Strong negative relationship since points are tightly clustered along the model

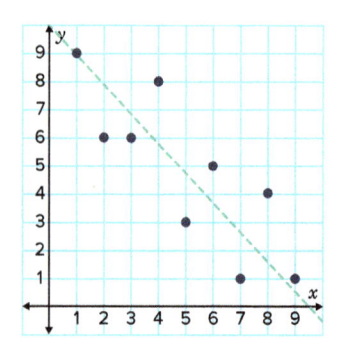

Moderate negative relationship since points are relatively clustered along the model

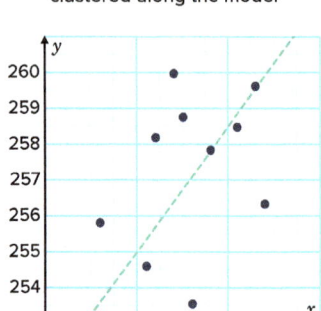

Weak positive relationship since points are loosely clustered along the model

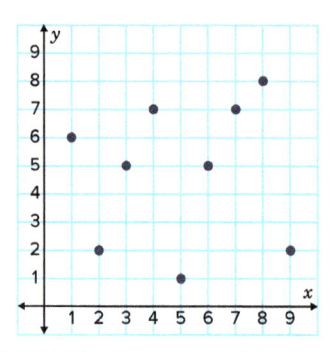

No relationship since there is no evident clustering of the data

When comparing bivariate data, it may be necessary to separate the data into categories. For example, when comparing the weights of dogs during their first year after birth, the data might not show a relationship because large dogs (like Boxers) will grow much more than small dogs (like Yorkies).

We can compare categorical variables in scatterplots by using different colors or symbols.

The weights of small, medium, and large dogs over time are shown in the scatterplot.

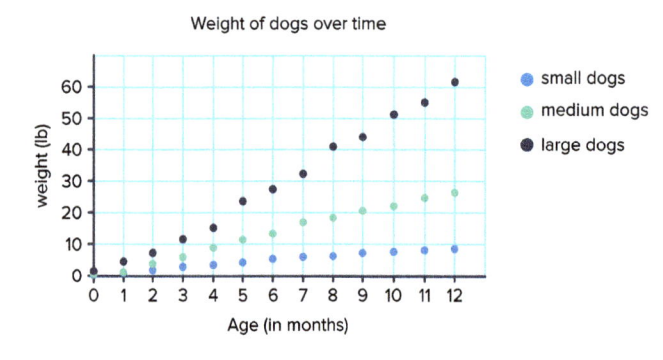

Weight of dogs over time

- small dogs
- medium dogs
- large dogs

Different colored dots represent the different categories or sizes of dogs.

For each category, there is a strong, positive linear relationship between the dogs' age and weight.

It is important to note that the existence of a relationship between two variables in a scatterplot, regardless of strength, does not necessarily imply that one causes the other. Causation can only be determined from an appropriately designed statistical experiment.

Provide a list of guiding questions for student analysis
Targeted instructional strategies

When asked to describe the relationship between variables represented in a scatterplot, there are several factors that students need to consider. For example, the variables, form, direction, and strength of the relationship between those variables.

Provide this list of guiding questions for students to ask themselves during their analysis:

1. What are the independent and dependent variables?
2. Is there a relationship between the variables? If so, it is linear or nonlinear?
3. If the relationship is linear, is it positive or negative?
4. How strong is the relationship?

After answering these questions, students must describe the relationship in context. Provide the following sentence frame:

The relationship between (independent variable) and (dependent variable) is (strength), (direction if linear), and (form). This means that as (independent variable) increases, (dependent variable) tends to (describe the behavior of the y-values).

Consider providing various examples to help students feel comfortable describing various types of relationships in context.
- The relationship between age and height is strong, positive, and linear. This means that as age increases, height tends to increase.
- The relationship between the number of items produced and the cost of producing those items is moderate and nonlinear. This means that as the number of items produced increases, the cost of production tends to increase at first, then decrease.
- The relationship between time and savings is strong and nonlinear. This means that as time increases, savings tends to increase at an increasing rate.

Information gap
English language learner support

Prepare a set of cards where half contain various scatterplots, and the other half have descriptions of the form, strength, and direction of relationships in scatterplots. Half of the class will be given a scatterplot card, and the other half will be give a description card.

Inform students that they are not allowed to show each other their cards or use the words found on their cards. The students with the description cards must ask questions to the students with the graph cards and find the person that has the graph that matches their description.

To support the discussions, provide example questions like the following:
- How tighly clustered are the points in your graph?
- Do the points in your graph roughly follow a straight line or a curve?
- As the x-values of the points in your graph increase, do the y-values also increase?

🔍 Relationship of data forming vertical and horizontal lines
Address student misconceptions

Students might think that data forming vertical or horizontal lines have a strong, linear relationship since it forms a line.

The strength of the relationship measures how well we can predict the value of one variable given the other. With a vertical line, knowing the value of x does not give a good indication for what the value of y should be since there are y-values along the entire range. Similarly, with horizontal lines, knowing the value of y does not help predict the value of x.

We can conclude that there is no relationship between the quantities.

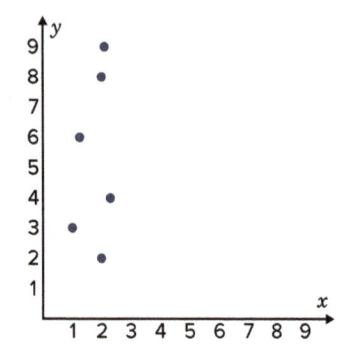

Horizontal trend, no relationship

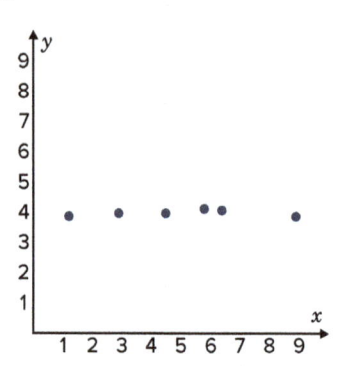

Vertical trend, no relationship

Examples

Students: Page 516

Example 1

For each scatterplot, determine whether the variables have a linear relationship, a nonlinear relationship, or no relationship. If there is a relationship, describe its strength.

If the relationship is linear, describe the direction as positive or negative.

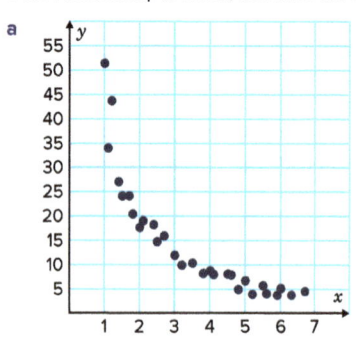

a

Create a strategy

A relationship between two variables exists if the points follow a similar trend. The points will roughly form a line (linear) or a curve (nonlinear) if there is a relationship.

To describe the strength of the relationship, we can analyze how tightly the data points are clustered or grouped together.

Reflect and check

The y-values are decreasing at a slower and slower rate, causing the point to form a curve. This shows there is a nonlinear relationship between the variables.

Because the points are tightly clustered, the relationship is strong.

Purpose

Check if students can visually determine whether variables have a relationship, estimate the strength, and identify the direction of the relationship.

Students: Pages 516–517

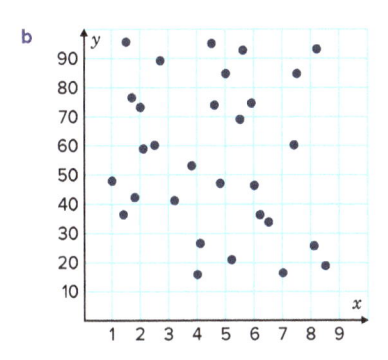

b

Create a strategy

A relationship between two variables exists if the points follow a similar trend. If there is no trend or no shape to the data, then there is no relationship between the variables.

Apply the idea

There is no trend in this data, meaning there is no relationship between the variables.

Reflect and check

We could try to sketch a line of fit for the data, like the one shown, but the points are far from the line. A negative, linear trend would suggest that y decreases as x increases, which we cannot conclude for this data set.

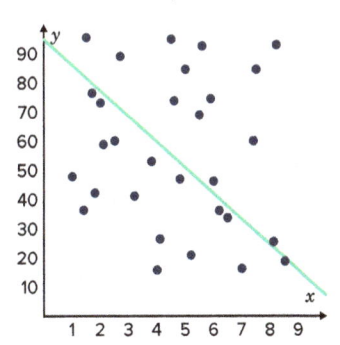

Purpose

Check if students can visually determine whether variables have a relationship, estimate the strength, and identify the direction of the relationship.

Expected mistakes
Students might try to draw a line from the top left corner of the scatterplot to the bottom right side of the scatterplot to indicate a weak, negative linear relationship. Remind them that a weak, negative linear relationship implies that the y-values *decrease* as the x-values increase.

Then, ask them if they think the previous statement is valid. Highlight some of the points on the graph, such as (8.2, 92). Help them see that x is relatively large, but y is also large, meaning that the relationship is not necessarily negative.

Students: Page 517

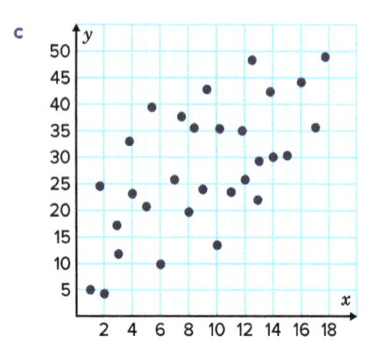

Create a strategy
First, we must determine if a relationship between the variables exists. If a relationship exists, we can describe the strength by analyzing how tightly the data points are clustered.

If the relationship between the variables is linear, the direction of the relationship can be described as positive or negative.
- Positive relationship: as the independent variable increases, the dependent variable increases
- Negative relationship: as the independent variable increases, the dependent variable decreases

Apply the idea
As the x-values increase, the y-values also increase. This indicates there is a positive, linear relationship between the variables.

However, the points are not tightly clustered, so the relationship between the variables is moderate.

Purpose
Check if students can visually determine whether variables have a relationship, estimate the strength, and identify the direction of the relationship.

Outline the points to visualize the relationship
Student with disabilities support

use with Example 1

If students struggle to visualize whether there is a linear relationship, nonlinear relationship, or no relationship in the scatterplot, encourage them to outline the points. Then, have them draw a path down the middle of the outline, from one end to the other.

- If the outline has an oval shape, draw a path that connects the two ends of the oval, dividing the length of the oval in half. This indicates a linear relationship.
  - The thinner the oval, the stronger the relationship.
- If the outline looks like a worm or snake, draw a path through the middle, connecting the two ends of the outline. This indicates a nonlinear relationship.
  - The thinner the worm, the stronger the relationship.
- If the outline is a square or circle, there is no relationship.

For the scatterplots in this example, the drawing may look like the ones shown.

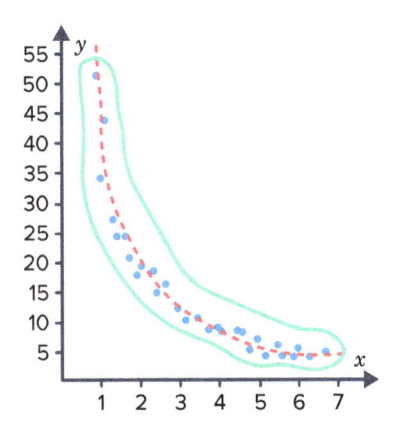

The outline looks like a worm, so the path connecting the ends is a curve.

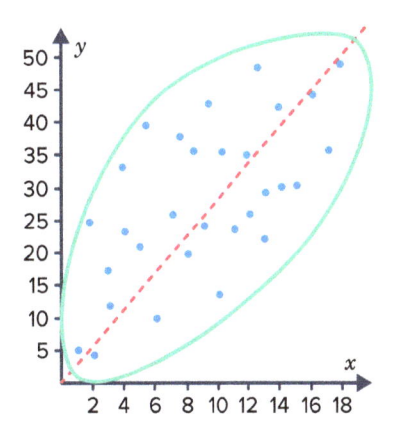

The outline is an oval, so the path connecting the ends is a straight line.

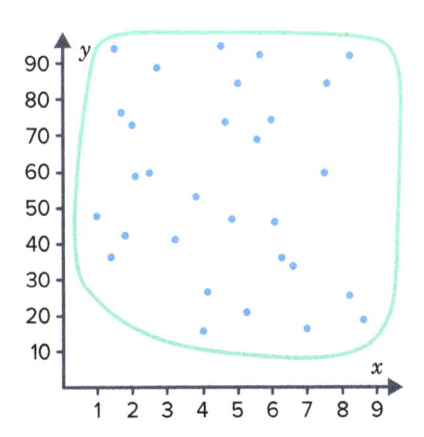

For the scatterplot in part (b), the outline would form a rough square shape.

Students might want to connect the corners of the square. If they do, point out that there are multiple lines we could draw (such as a vertical line down the middle or a horizontal line across the middle).

Show them that the points are far from each of the lines, so no line is better than the other. This indicates that there is no relationship between the variables.

9.02 Scatterplots 1121
mathspace.co

Students: Page 518

Example 2

Justin recently had surgery for a torn muscle in his leg. He is taking medication for the pain as well as attending regular physical therapy sessions. He learns that not everyone's insurance plan covers physical therapy.

a Justin wants to investigate whether the post-surgery pain from a torn muscle lasts longer for patients who only take medication compared to those who can attend physical therapy sessions. Which question should he use for his investigation?

   A What are the pain levels of patients that have had surgery for torn muscles?
   B What type of medication do doctors prescribe for pain management in surgery patients?
   C How does the pain level change over time in patients using physical therapy and medication compared to those using medication only?
   D What percentage of people have insurance plans that cover physical therapy costs?

Create a strategy

Consider the factors that Justin is interested in investigating and whether the questions would lead to data that addresses each of the factors.

Apply the idea

Option A: The answer to this question would only focus on the pain levels of the patient. Since Justin wants to know how long the pain lasts as well, this question would not be suitable for his investigation.

Option B: The answer to this question would lead to categorical data (types of medication), which Justin is not interested in. This question would not be suitable for his investigation.

Option C: This question considers multiple factors: the pain level of patients, the length of time that they feel pain, whether patients take medication only, or whether they take medication and attend physical therapy sessions. This accounts for all the factors that Justin is interested in for his investigation.

Option D: Similar to Option A, this question focuses on how many people have insurance plans that cover physical therapy, rather than considering how long pain lasts or how much pain the patient is in. This question would not be suitable for her investigation.

Justin should use the question in Option C.

Reflect and check

Remember that Justin's statistical question is different from the survey questions that he would use to collect the data. Possible survey questions might be:
- Do you take medication for your pain?
- Do you attend physical therapy sessions?
- On a scale of 1–10, how painful is it to move your repaired muscle?

Purpose

Assess whether students can identify questions that explore the relationship between two variables.

Students: Pages 518–519

b Describe the data that would need to be collected to answer Justin's statistical question.

Create a strategy

Use the statistical question from part (a) to identify the variables and/or categories of interest.

Apply the idea

The bivariate, numerical data that needs to be collected is:
- The pain levels in patients that had surgery for a torn muscle (measured on a numerical scale like 1–10)
- The time (measured in days or weeks) since the surgery

The data should be separated into two categories:
- Patients that take medication only
- Patients that take medication and attend physical therapy sessions

Reflect and check

Since the data is bivariate and numerical, it can be represented by a scatterplot. The independent variable is time, and the dependent variable is the patients' pain level. An example scatterplot is shown:

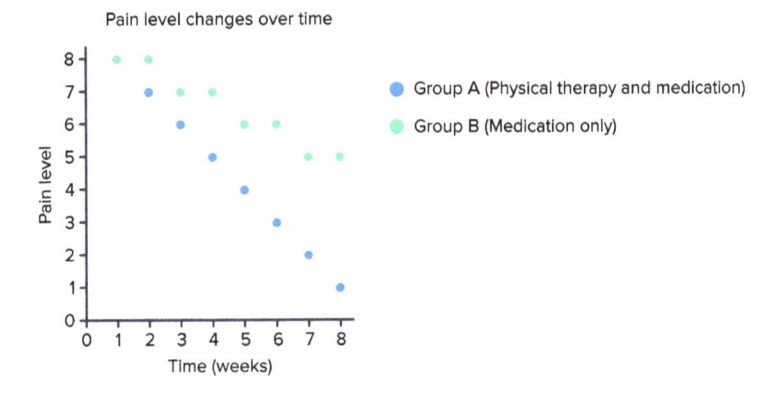

Pain level changes over time

- Group A (Physical therapy and medication)
- Group B (Medication only)

Purpose

Check if students can identify the bivariate data needed to answer a statistical question.

Students: Pages 519–520

Example 3

A surfing company is located in various coastal states across the U.S. When analyzing their data, they separate the store locations into two regions: the Western region and the Eastern region. The scatterplot shows data collected to answer the question, "How have the sales of our product changed over time in each of the sales regions?"

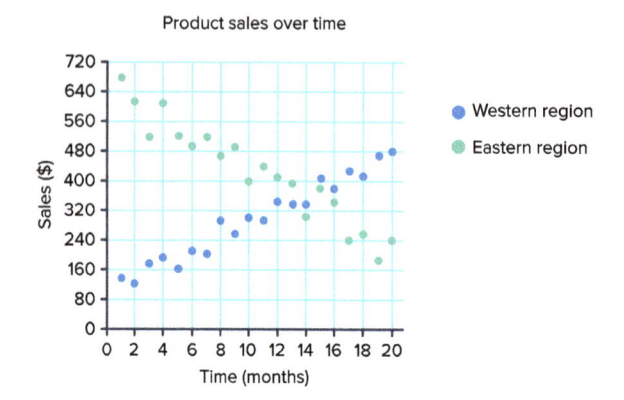

a Identify the independent and dependent variables in this context.

Create a strategy

Recall that the independent variable is not affected by the other variable, while the dependent variable may be affected or changed by the other variable.

On a scatterplot, the independent variable is placed on the horizontal axis, and the dependent variable is placed on the vertical axis.

Apply the idea

The independent variable is time (measured in months), and the dependent variable is the amount of sales (measured in dollars).

Purpose

Check if students can identify the independent and dependent variables in a given context.

Students: Page 520

b The owner of the company makes this conclusion: "The sales of the product are improving with time." Which sales region was the owner analyzing?

Create a strategy

In part (a), we found that the amount of sales is the dependent variable, and time is the independent variable. This means the owner concluded that the dependent variable increases as the independent variable increases.

Apply the idea

According to the owner's statement, both variables are increasing which indicates a positive relationship. Both sets of data values show a linear relationship, but only the blue dots show a positive relationship. According to the key (or legend), the blue points represent data from the Western region.

Reflect and check

If the owner was analyzing the Eastern region (the black points), the conclusion would have been, "The sales of the product are decreasing over time."

Purpose
Check if students can connect conclusions and plotted data.

Reflecting with students
Extend this problem by prompting advanced learners to consider other factors that might explain the different sales patterns in each region, such as marketing efforts, weather patterns, or cultural trends. This investigation will also remind them that while the scatterplot shows a correlation between time and sales, it does not necessarily imply that time is the cause of the change in sales.

Students: Page 520

Example 4

Adria heard that children who learn to speak at a young age are more likely to be gifted and talented in later stages of life. She decides to investigate this using the data cycle.

a Formulate a statistical question for Adria that would lead to the collection of data that can be represented in a scatterplot.

Create a strategy

First, we need to identify the variables of interest. Then, we need to write a question such that the answer to the question addresses both variables.

Apply the idea

From the given information, we gather that Adria is interested in two variables:

1. The age when a child first spoke
2. Their intelligence level later in life

The information is not specific about the later stages of life. We can choose any stage of life after birth, such as the teenage years.

One possible statistical question is, "What is the relationship between the age at which a child first spoke and their level of intelligence as teenagers?"

Reflect and check

Other possible questions are:
- How does the age at which a child first spoke influence their level of intelligence as adults?
- If a child first spoke at 6 months old, what level of intelligence are they expected to have as a teenager?
- Which range of ages for when a child first spoke correspond to the highest levels of intelligence?

This could also be separated into multiple categories: age when a child first spoke versus intelligence level after middle school, after high school, and after university.

Purpose
Check if students can formulate statistical questions that would lead to the collection of data that can be represented in a scatterplot.

Students: Page 521

b The table shows the ages of some teenagers when they first spoke and their results in an aptitude test:

Age when first spoke (months)	14	27	9	16	21	17	10	7	19	24
Aptitude test results	96	69	93	101	87	92	99	104	93	97

Create a scatterplot to model the data.

Create a strategy

Let x represent the age when the child first spoke and y represent the aptitude test results as a teenager.

The minimum value for x is 7 and the maximum is 27, so we can use a scale of 5 to label the x-axis. The minimum value for y is 69 and the maximum is 104, so we can use a scale of 20 to label the x-axis.

Apply the idea

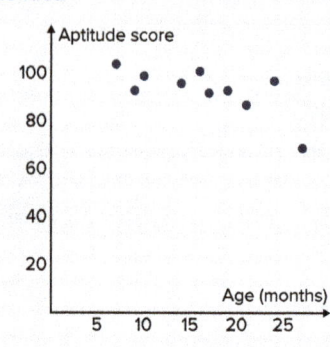

Purpose
Check if students can recognize the independent and dependent variables and create a scatterplot with appropriate scale and labels.

Reflecting with students
Ask students whether they think the relationship is affected by the scale of the graph. The choice of scale may affect how strong the relationship appears, but it does not affect the actual relationship. The following graphs show the same data as the example, but by eye, a different interpretation of the strength of the relationship may be given.

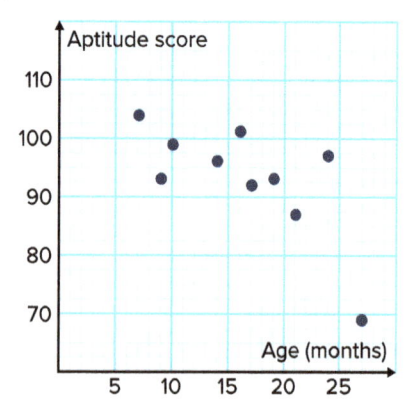

Points appear more widely spread 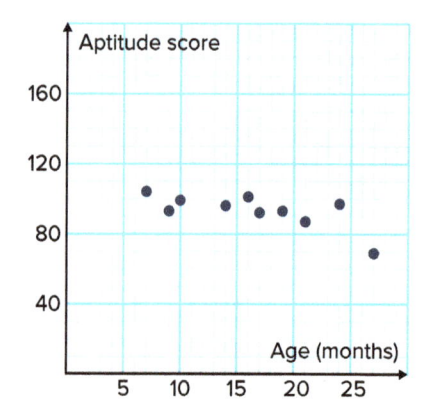   Points appear more closely clustered

To remove subjectivity, it is important to consider the best scale for the data set. For this lesson, students should be aware that an inappropriately chosen scale may distort the strength of the relationship.

Students: Page 521

c Draw a conclusion about the data by answering the statistical question from part (a).

Create a strategy

To describe the relationship between the age at which a child first spoke and their level of intelligence as teenagers, we can analyze the following features of the data:
- Form: linear or nonlinear
- Strength: strong or weak

If the data follows a linear trend, we can describe the direction as positive or negative.

Apply the idea

The points are relatively close together, indicating a strong relationship. As the age increases, the aptitude score decreases slightly, indicating a negative, linear relationship.

The relationship between the age when a child first spoke and their aptitude test score as a teenager has a strong, negative, linear relationship.

This suggests that as the age at which a child first spoke increases, their intelligence level as a teenager tends to decrease.

Reflect and check

The closer the points are to forming a line or curve, the stronger their relationship will be. A strong relationship between two quantities suggests that the value of one quantity can be predicted with some accuracy given the other quantity, but is not enough evidence to suggest that changes in one quantity directly cause changes in the other.

Purpose

Check if students can derive a conclusion from a scatterplot to answer a statistical question.

Reflecting with students

Encourage students to use an iterative approach and consider what another cycle of the data cycle could look like to further refine the question and conclusion.

Creating scatterplots with technology
Student with disabilities support

use with Example 4

For students who struggle to draw scatterplots by hand, allow them to create scatterplots with technology.

The steps for creating a scatterplot using the GeoGebra Statistics calculator are shown:

1. Enter the x-values into the first column and enter the y-values in the second column.

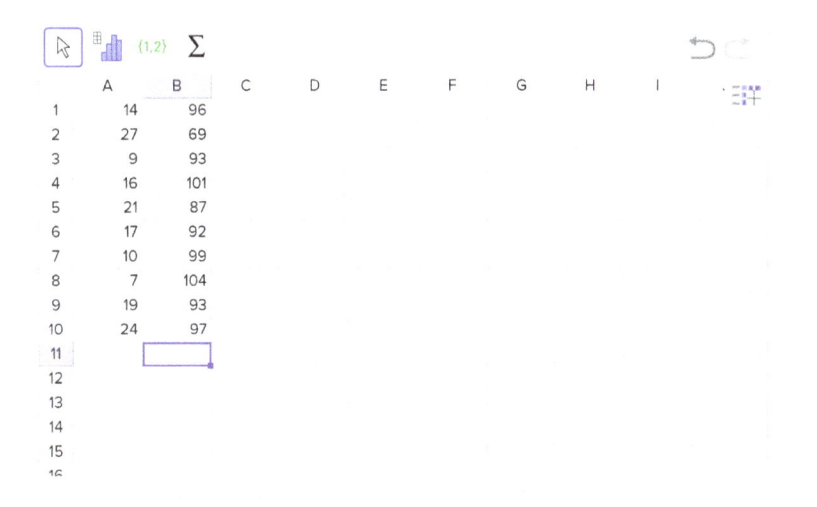

	A	B
1	14	96
2	27	69
3	9	93
4	16	101
5	21	87
6	17	92
7	10	99
8	7	104
9	19	93
10	24	97

2. Highlight all the data, and click the icon with a histogram. Select Two Variable Regression Analysis.

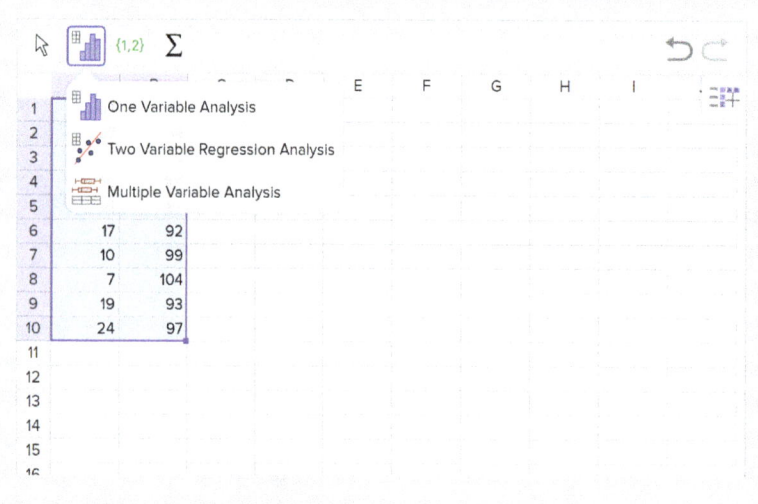

3. A scatterplot will automatically populate on the right side of the screen.

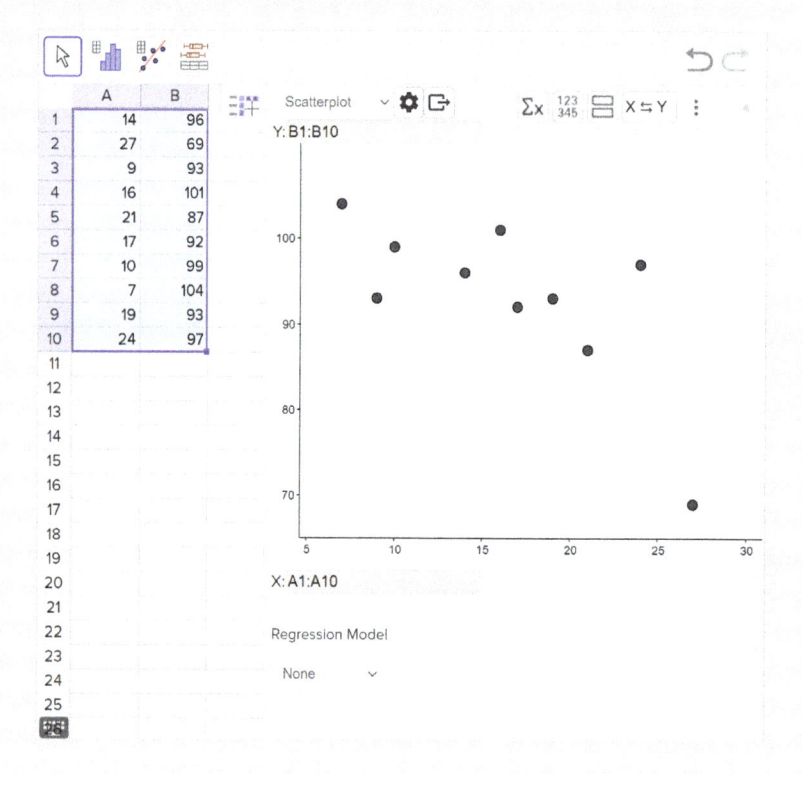

Students: Page 522

> **Idea summary**
>
> The analysis of bivariate data should include:
> - Form, usually described as a **linear relationship** or a **nonlinear relationship**
> - Strength, describing how closely the data points match the model line or curve
>
> If the relationship between the variables is linear, the direction of the relationship can be described as positive or negative.
> - Positive relationship: as the independent variable increases, the dependent variable increases
> - Negative relationship: as the independent variable increases, the dependent variable decreases

Practice

Students: Pages 522–528

What do you remember?

1 Create a scatterplot that models each set of data. Include labels and scales on each axis.

   a The heights and weights of the female Olympic "All around champions" in gymnastics.

	Height (inches)	Weight (lbs)
Suni Lee	60	112
Simone Biles	57	104
Gabby Douglas	59	90
Nastia Liukin	62	99
Carly Patterson	59	97
Simona Amanar	62	97

   b The test scores on the midterm and final exam for a sample of students.

Midterm Exam	95	90	88	84	75	77	65	70	99	85
Final Exam	90	92	83	80	62	80	60	74	100	85

2 Scientists conducted a study where each person was asked to read a paragraph then recount as much information as they could remember. They found that the longer the paragraph, the less information each person could retain.

If the length of the paragraph were plotted (on the horizontal axis) against the amount of information retained (on the vertical axis), would the relationship be positive or negative?

3 For each pair, identify the independent and dependent variable:
   a Amount of fertilizer and plant height
   b Length of stride and height
   c Number of family members and time (in hours) spent cooking
   d Time spent traveling and distance to destination
   e Time spent practicing and performance in piano lessons

4 Which question would lead to data that could be represented by a scatterplot?
  A On which days of the week do most teenagers play videos?
  B How many hours does an average teenager spend playing video games each day?
  C What is the difference in the number of hours teenagers play video games?
  D How does the amount of time spent outside impact the amount of time spent playing video games?

5 Does each scatterplot show a linear or nonlinear relationship?

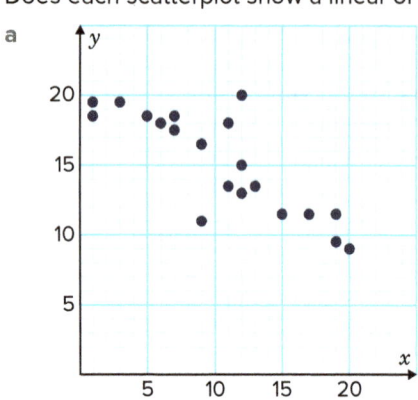

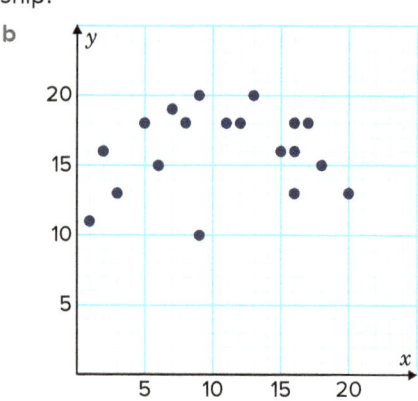

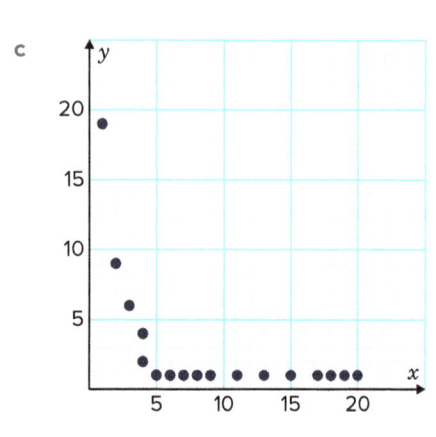

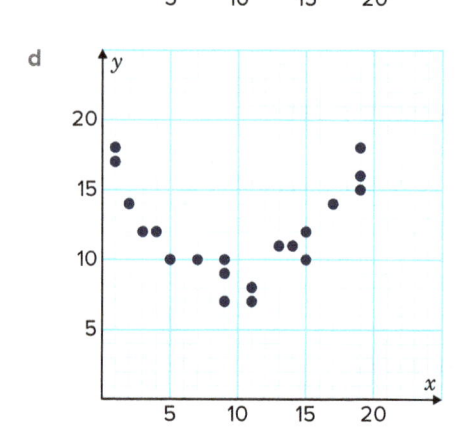

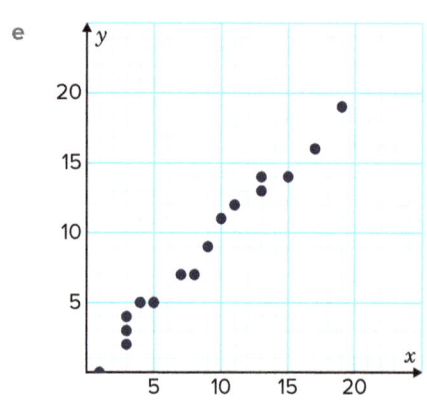

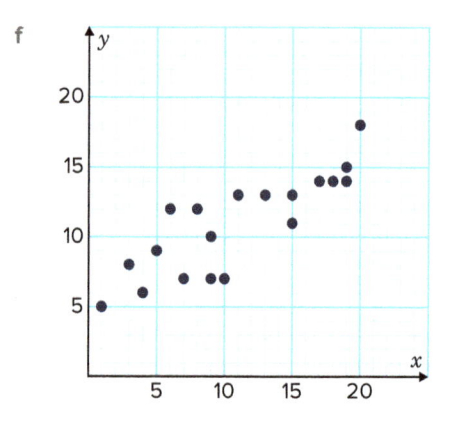

a

b

c

d

e

f

Let's practice

6 Describe the strength and direction for each linear association.

a

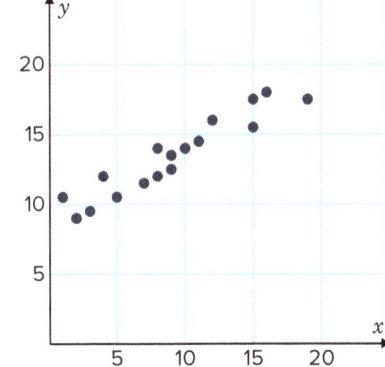

b

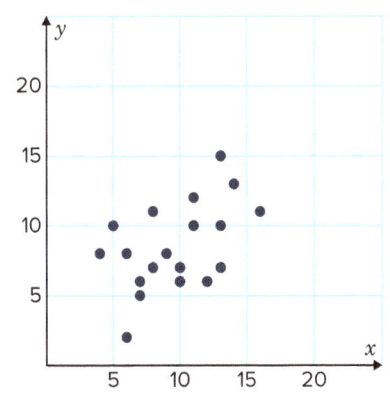

c

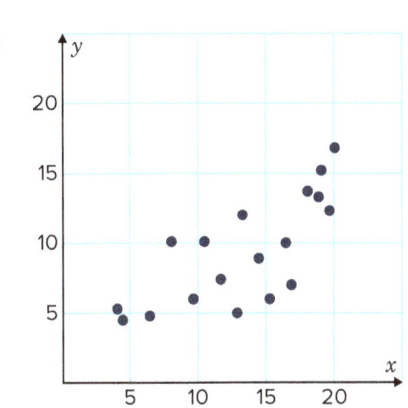

d

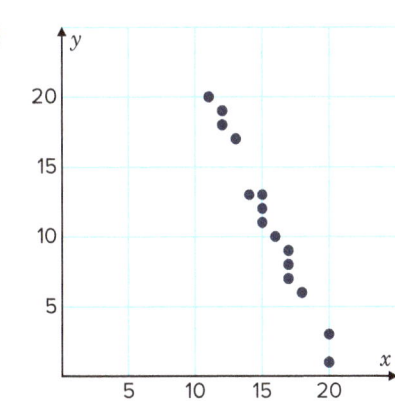

7 Four different classes with four different professors had the same final exam. The exam results and number of classes attended by each student is displayed for each class.

Does each graph suggest that there is an association between number of classes attended and final exam grade?

a

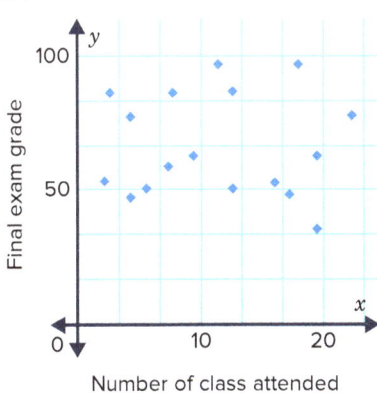

b

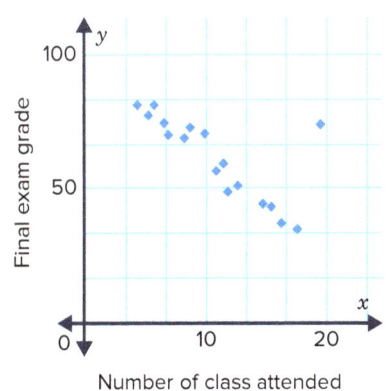

c

Final exam grade vs Number of class attended

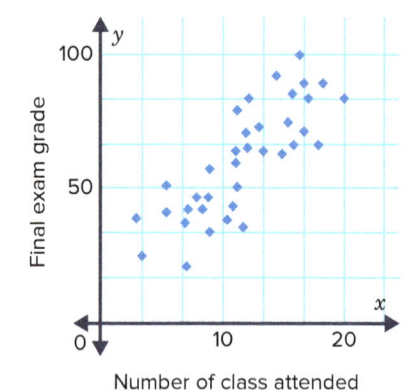

d

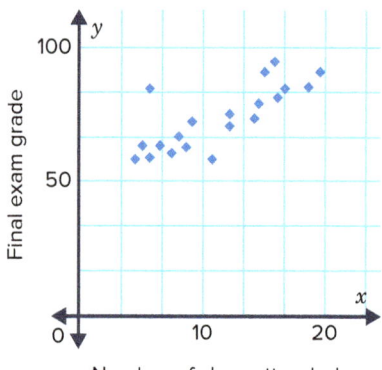

Final exam grade vs Number of class attended

8 This scatterplot shows the relationship between air and sea temperature.

   a Which is the best description of the relationship between the variables?

     A Strong, positive, linear

     B Moderate, negative, linear

     C Weak, nonlinear

   b Describe the relationship between the variables in context.

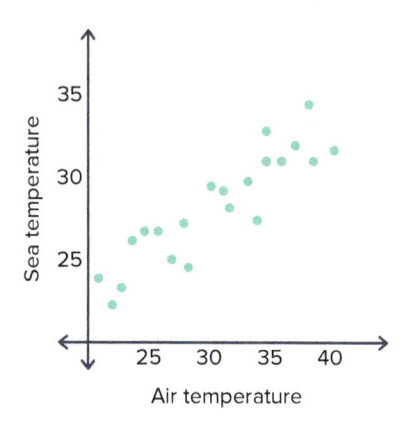

9 This table shows the scores of 12 students in math and P.E. class.

   a Select the question that could be answered by the data.

     A Do students prefer Math or P.E.?

     B If a student does well in Math, do they also do well in P.E.?

     C Does a student's Math grade impact their P.E. grade?

     D How many students are enrolled in Math and P.E.?

   b Construct a scatterplot for the students' scores in math versus their scores in P.E. class.

   c Is the relationship between students' grades in math and P.E. linear or nonlinear? If it is linear, describe the direction as positive or negative.

   d Describe the strength of the relationship between students' grades in math and P.E.

Student	Maths	P.E.
1	63	44
2	82	94
3	60	52
4	79	70
5	88	67
6	81	60
7	61	73
8	91	86
9	72	84
10	62	93
11	66	57
12	92	92

10 A shop owner in Morocco collected data to answer the statistical question, "How does the temperature outside impact the number of fans sold?" The data is shown in the table:

Temperature (°C)	6	8	10	12	14	16	18	20
Number of fans sold	12	13	14	17	18	19	21	23

   a Identify the independent and dependent variables.

   b Which method was most likely used to collect the data?

     A Measurement   **B** Observation   **C** Survey   **D** Experiment

   c Construct a scatterplot using the data from the table.

   d Describe the relationship between the temperature and the number of fans sold.

11 Data was collected to answer the statistical question, "What is the relationship between the age at which a child first walked and the age at which they first spoke?" The data collected is shown in the table:

Age first walked	12	18	10	15	13	17	9	16	14	11	20
Age first spoke	12	21	12	16	20	19	13	22	17	15	20

    a   Construct a scatterplot for the data.

    b   What is the relationship between the age at which a child first walked and the age at which they first spoke?

12 A researcher is studying the relationship between the number of passers-by in an emergency, and the time taken (in seconds) before a passer-by helps a stranger during an emergency. The data is recorded in this table.

Number of passers-by (n)	1	2	3	4	5	6
Time until help is offered (t)	8	19	26	37	51	65

    a   Was the data most likely collected through measurement, observation, a survey or an experiment?

    b   Construct a scatterplot using the data from the table.

    c   Describe the relationship between the number of passers-by and the time until assistance is offered.

    d   As more passers-by are present, what happens to the time taken until help is offered?

13 Each point on the scatterplot shows the time (in weeks) Sumon spent training for a half marathon and the corresponding miles they were able to run.

Using the scatterplot, are these statements true or false?

    a   The number of weeks that Sumon trained for the half marathon is the independent variable.

    b   The y-coordinates of the points represent the time spent by Sumon training.

    c   There is evidence to suggest that the longer Sumon trains, the further they can run.

    d   The relationship between the number of weeks training and the number of miles Sumon is able to run is positive.

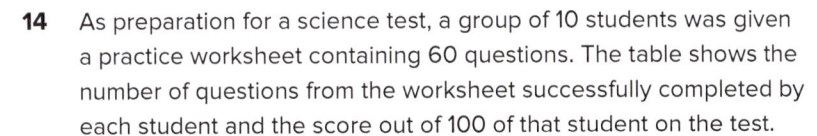

14 As preparation for a science test, a group of 10 students was given a practice worksheet containing 60 questions. The table shows the number of questions from the worksheet successfully completed by each student and the score out of 100 of that student on the test.

Number of questions	Test result
11	20
14	23
36	62
60	97
57	100
42	66
20	35
27	52
50	87
59	99

    a   Formulate a question that could be answered by the data.

    b   Was the data most likely collected through measurement, observation, a survey or an experiment?

    c   Which variable is independent and which variable is dependent?

    d   Construct a scatterplot of the data.

    e   Draw a conclusion about the data by answering the statistical question from part (a).

15. A chemical company is testing the effect of different chemicals on slowing the melting of snow. They are currently testing four different chemicals with the results showing how much ice is remaining after 3 hours at a certain temperature.

A

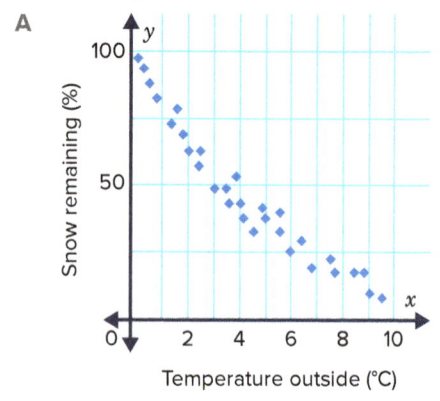

B

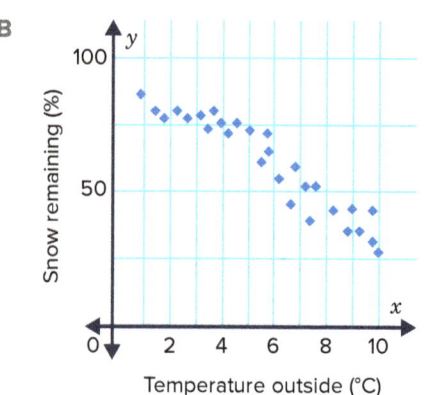

C

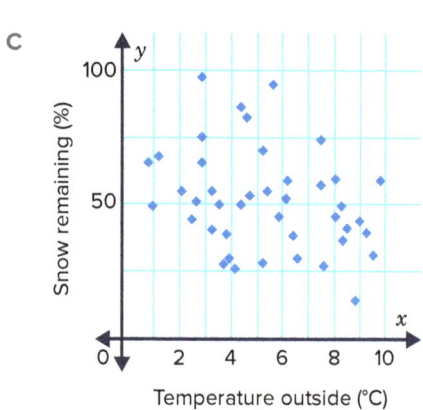

D

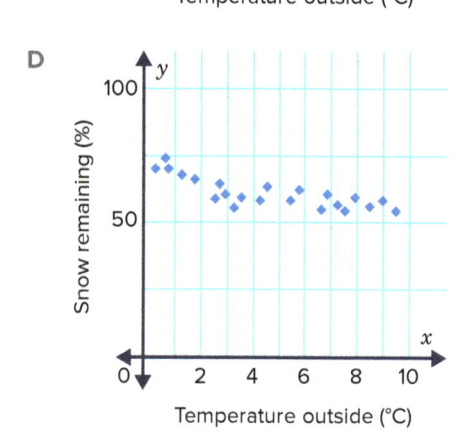

A snow sculpture company wants a chemical that will keep snow from melting.

a Which chemical should they choose to ensure that at least half of the snow is still there after 3 hours?

b If the company operates at a temperature of 3 °C to 4 °C, which chemical should they choose?

16. Mona has a checking account and a savings account with her bank. Her savings accout accrues interest from the bank, and she tries to deposit and withdraw from both accounts equally. She has been tracking the balance of each account over the past year.

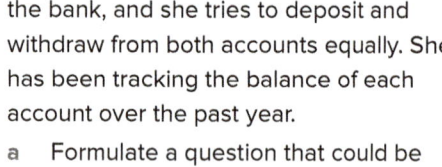

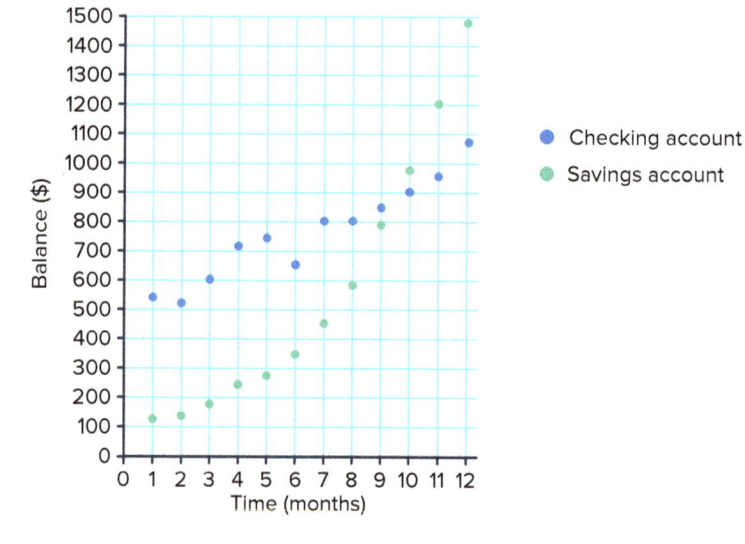

a Formulate a question that could be answered by the scatterplot.

b Describe a method that Mona could have used to collect the data.

c Identify the independent and dependent variables.

d Which account had a higher balance at the beginning of the year?

e Which account had a higher balance at the end of the year?

f Draw a conclusion about the data by answering the statistical question from part (a).

Let's extend our thinking

17 Determine whether each statement is true or false. Provide an example to support your claim.
  a If the value of variable A increases as the value of variable B increases, there is a relationship between variable A and variable B.
  b If there is a relationship between variable A and variable B, then changes in variable A directly cause changes in variable B.
  c If variable A and variable B move in opposite directions (as one increases, the other decreases), then they have a negative relationship.

18 Consider the scatterplot:
  a Explain why the relationship between the variables is weak.
  b Determine whether the following pairs of variables could be represented by the data set:
      i   Scores in an English test and distance traveled from home to school.
      ii   Cost of cars and cost of gasoline.
      iii Distance traveled in a car and the cost of a driver's license.

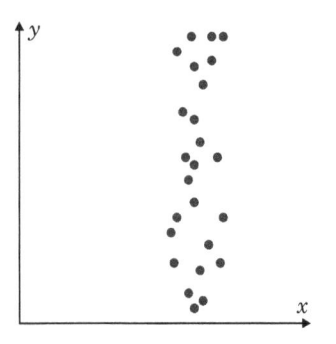

19 Brody wants to take his dog on a hike, then stop to pick up groceries on the way home from the hike. However, he is worried about leaving his dog in the car for half an hour while he is inside the store because he has heard it is unsafe.

Brody wants to use the data cycle to investigate the temperature inside the car over time
  a Formulate a question which could be investigated using a scatterplot.
  b Determine what variables could be used to answer your investigative question.
  c The current temperatures where Brody lives are between 70–80 °F. He acquired data on the temperature inside a car on a 70 °F day and an 80 °F day, shown in the table. Plot each set of data on the same scatterplot.
  d Draw a conclusion about the data by answering the statistical question from part (a).
  e Brody learns that at 103 °F, dogs lose their ability to regulate their body temperature. Determine an approximate range of time that it takes for the inside of a car to reach 103°F when outside temperatures are between 70°F and 80°F.

Temperature over time in a closed car

Time in minutes	Temperature in car on 70°F day	Temperature in car on 80°F day
0	70°F	80°F
5	83°F	94°F
10	89°F	99°F
15	94°F	105°F
20	99°F	109°F
25	102°F	111°F
30	104°F	114°F
35	106°F	117°F
40	108°F	118°F
45	110°F	119°F
50	111°F	121°F
55	112°F	122°F
60	113°F	123°F

20 When Sherrie was trying on shoes, the sales attendant told her to always try on both shoes because, for most people, one foot is longer than the other. Go through the whole data cycle at least once to investigate tge relationship between the lengths of a person's feet.

Answers

9.02 Scatterplots

What do you remember?

1 a The scale on the axes should count by equal amounts. The values on the x-axis must begin at or below the minimum value of 57 and end at or above the maximum value of 62. The values on the y-axis must begin at or below the minimum of 90 and end at or above the maximum of 112. The chosen scale should display the data clearly.

For example:

[Scatterplot: Weight (lbs) vs Height (inches), y-axis 80-120, x-axis 50-65]

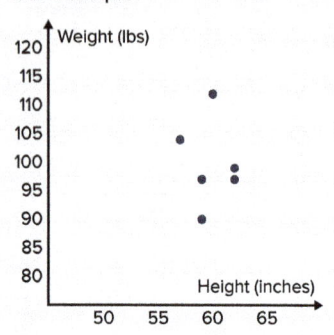

   b The scale on the axes should count by equal amounts. The values on the x-axis must begin at or below the minimum value of 65 and end at or above the maximum value of 99. The values on the y-axis must begin at or below the minimum of 60 and end at or above the maximum of 100. The chosen scale should display the data clearly.

For example:

[Scatterplot: Final Exam vs Midterm Exam, y-axis 55-95, x-axis 55-95]

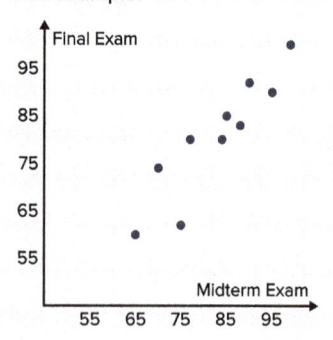

2 Negative

3 a Independent variable: amount of fertilizer
      Dependent variable: plant height
   b Independent variable: height
      Dependent variable: length of stride
   c Independent variable: number of family members
      Dependent variable: time (in hours) spent cooking
   d Independent variable: distance to destination
      Dependent variable: time spent traveling
   e Independent variable: time spent practicing
      Dependent variable: performance in piano lessons

4 a D

5 a Linear relationship   b Nonlinear relationship
   c Nonlinear relationship   d Nonlinear relationship
   e Linear relationship   f Linear relationship

Let's practice

6 a Positive and strong
   b Positive and weak
   c Positive and moderate-weak
   d Negative and strong

7 a No   b Yes   c Yes   d Yes

8 a A
   b As air temperature increases, sea temperature increases.

9 a C
   b [Scatterplot: P.E. vs Math, y-axis 40-90, x-axis 40-90]
   c Positive, linear   d Weak

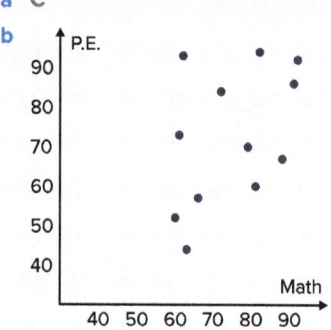

10 a The independent variable is the temperature, and the dependent variable is the number of fans sold.
   b B
   c [Scatterplot: Number of fans sold vs Temperature (°C), y-axis 2-24, x-axis 2-24]
   d Strong, positive, linear. As the temperature increased, the number of fans sold increased.

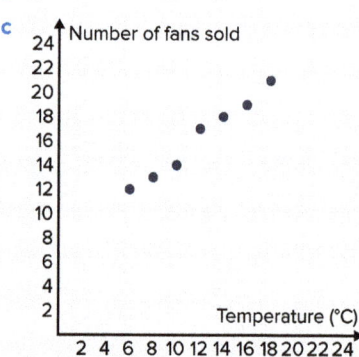

1136 Mathspace Virginia SOL Algebra 1 Teacher Edition
mathspace.co

11 **a**

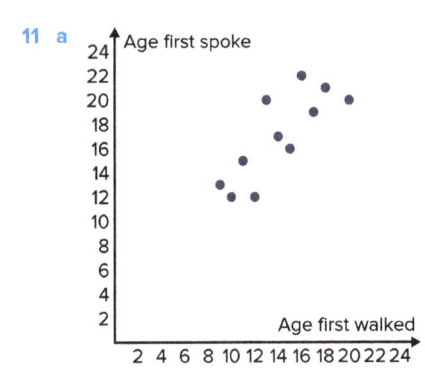

Scatterplot: Age first spoke (y-axis, 2–24) vs Age first walked (x-axis, 2–24).

b There is a moderate, positive, linear relationship between the age at which a child first walked and the age at which they first spoke. This means that as the age a child first walked increased, the age at which they first spoke also increased.

12 **a** Observation

b

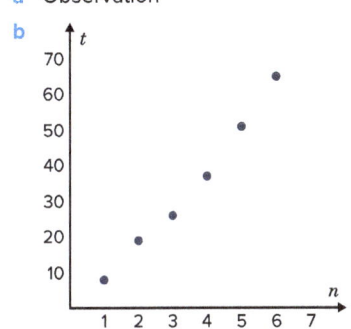

Scatterplot: t (y-axis, 10–70) vs n (x-axis, 1–7).

c Strong, positive, linear   **d** Increases

13 **a** True   **b** False   **c** True   **d** True

14 **a** Many possible answers, for example, "As the number of questions completed increases, how does a students' test result change?"

b Survey

c The independent variable is the number of questions and the dependent variable is the test result.

d

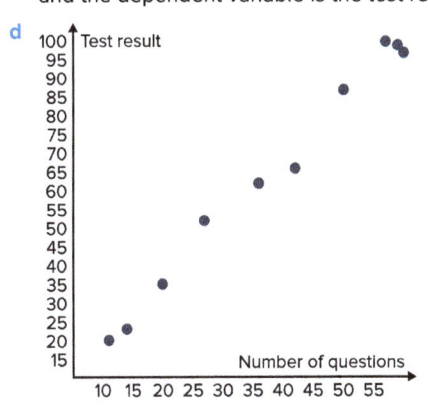

Scatterplot: Test result (y-axis, 15–100) vs Number of questions (x-axis, 10–55).

e There is a strong, positive, linear relationship between the variables which shows that as the number of completed questions increases, the students' test score also increased.

15 **a** D   **b** B

16 **a** Many possible answers, for example, "How does the balance of each account change over time?"

b A bank issues a statement each month that provides the transactions and ending balance of the account. Mona could have acquired this data from those statements.

c The independent variable is time in months, and the dependent variable is the balance of each account in dollars.

d Checking

e Savings

f Both accounts are growing over time. The checking account increases at a linear rate, while the savings account increases at a nonlinear rate. The savings account is growing faster than the checking account over time.

Let's extend our thinking

17 **a** True. For example, if as the temperature increases, the sale of ice cream also increases, then there is a positive relationship between temperature and ice cream sales. This does not imply causation but indicates a relationship where both variables move in the same direction.

b False. For example, if there is a relationship between the number of ice cream sales and the number of sunglasses sold, that does not mean increasing ice cream sales directly cause an increase in sunglasses sales. There could be a third factor, such as warm weather, influencing both.

c True. For example, as the amount of rainfall increases, the amount of time spent outdoors may decrease, indicating a negative relationship between rainfall and time spent outdoors. This shows an inverse relationship but does not imply one causes the other.

18 **a** It appears that y can change significantly without much corresponding change in x.

b **i** Yes   **ii** Yes   **iii** Yes

19 **a** Many possible answers, for example, "How does the temperature inside a car change over time?"

b Answers will vary based on the question in part (a). Using the example question, "How does the temperature inside a car change over time?":

The independent variable could be time in minutes, and the dependent variable could be the temperature (in degrees Fahrenheit) inside a closed car.

There could be categorical variables, such as the specific temperature outside of the car.

c Temperature in a closed car over time

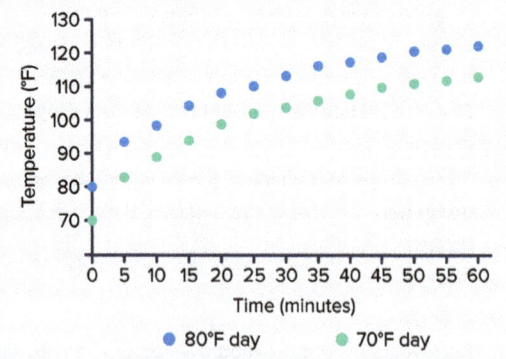

● 80°F day   ● 70°F day

d There is a strong, nonlinear relationship between the time and the temperature of a closed car. The temperature increases fastest during the first 10 minutes, then the temperature increases at a slower rate.

The temperature increases in the same pattern regardless of the temperature outside. The warmer it is outside, the warmer it is inside the car, and the temperature inside the car is always hotter than the temperature outside the car.

e It would take about 13–27 minutes for the car to reach 103 °F when outside temperatures are between 70 °F and 80°F.

20 1. **Formulate questions**

   Possible questions:
   - What is the relationship between the length of a person's left and right feet?
   - How does the length of the right foot differ from the length of the left foot?
   - Which foot tends to be longer?

2. **Collect data using the questions above.**

   We can collect data by measuring a person's left foot and right foot in centimeters. The table shows an example sample of 30 students.

| Right foot (cm) | 22.9 | 23.1 | 23.2 | 23.8 | 23.9 | 24.3 | 24.5 | 24.6 | 25.1 | 25.2 |
| Left foot (cm) | 23.4 | 24.4 | 23.9 | 24.3 | 24.3 | 25.3 | 24.5 | 25.2 | 25.1 | 25.7 |

| Right foot (cm) | 25.3 | 25.3 | 25.4 | 25.2 | 25.6 | 25.6 | 25.9 | 25.9 | 26 | 26.1 |
| Left foot (cm) | 25.2 | 25.6 | 25.3 | 25.5 | 25.8 | 26.6 | 25.6 | 26.9 | 26.7 | 26.8 |

| Right foot (cm) | 26.2 | 26.3 | 26.4 | 26.8 | 26.8 | 27.2 | 27.8 | 28 | 28.4 | 28.6 |
| Left foot (cm) | 27.3 | 26.6 | 26.4 | 26.8 | 27 | 27.2 | 28.2 | 28.2 | 29.3 | 28.4 |

3. **Create a data display using a scatterplot.**

   This scatterplot represents the sample data from the previous part.

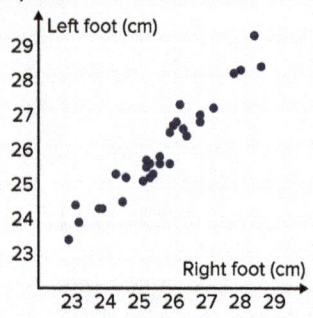

4. **Analyze and explain the results.**

   From the scatterplot, we can observe that there is a strong, positive linear relationship between the length of a person's left and right feet. The relationship shows that as the length of one foot increases, the length of the other foot also increases.

   However, the relationship between the lengths of each foot is not 1 : 1. Instead, the scatterplot shows that the left foot tends to be slightly longer than the right foot.

   This could lead us to formulate a new question like "How does the relationship between a person's foot length compare between people who are right-hand dominant versus left hand dominant?" or "How does the difference in people's feet lengths affect how shoes are made?"

9.03 Linear regression

Subtopic overview

Lesson narrative

In this lesson, students will develop their knowledge of fitted functions from the previous lesson as they learn how to fit functions to data using technology, and use the correlation coefficient to assess the strength of the model's fit to the data. By the end of the lesson, students will be able to find linear regression models for a set of data, interpret the coefficient of determination to determine the strength of the fit, interpret how the model relates to the context, and use the model to make predictions.

Learning objectives

Students: Page 529

After this lesson, you will be able to...
- determine if a table of values represents a linear model.
- determine the equation of the line of best fit given a table of values.
- interpret key characteristics of a linear model in context.
- predict values using a linear model.

Key vocabulary

- extrapolation
- interpolation
- line of best fit

Essential understanding

The relationship between the variables in a set of bivariate data reveals the type of function that best models the data.

Standards

This subtopic addresses the following Virginia Standards of Learning for Mathematics standards.

Mathematical process goals

MPG1 — Mathematical Problem Solving

Teachers can challenge students to solve real-world problems using scatterplots and linear regression. For example, they can provide a dataset related to a real-world scenario and ask students to use their knowledge of scatterplots, line of best fit, and linear regression to analyze the data and solve the problem.

MPG4 — Mathematical Connections

Teachers can help students make mathematical connections by relating the concept of scatterplots and linear regression to other mathematical topics they have learned. For example, they can discuss how the slope and y-intercept in the linear regression model relate to the concepts they learned in the linear functions unit.

MPG5 — Mathematical Representations

Teachers can encourage students to use various representations to express their understanding of linear regression. For instance, they can ask students to represent the relationship between two variables in a scatterplot visually, then use a line of best fit to model this relationship. They can also ask students to express this relationship algebraically by writing the equation of the line of best fit. It's also important to show how these representations relate to real-world contexts, such as predicting outcomes based on the linear model.

Content standards

A.ST.1 — The student will apply the data cycle (formulate questions; collect or acquire data; organize and represent data; and analyze data and communicate results) with a focus on representing bivariate data in scatterplots and determining the curve of best fit using linear and quadratic functions.

A.ST.1a — Formulate investigative questions that require the collection or acquisition of bivariate data.

A.ST.1b — Determine what variables could be used to explain a given contextual problem or situation or answer investigative questions.

A.ST.1c — Determine an appropriate method to collect a representative sample, which could include a simple random sample, to answer an investigative question.

A.ST.1d — Given a table of ordered pairs or a scatterplot representing no more than 30 data points, use available technology to determine whether a linear or quadratic function would represent the relationship, and if so, determine the equation of the curve of best fit.

A.ST.1e — Use linear and quadratic regression methods available through technology to write a linear or quadratic function that represents the data where appropriate and describe the strengths and weaknesses of the model.

A.ST.1f — Use a linear model to predict outcomes and evaluate the strength and validity of these predictions, including through the use of technology.

A.ST.1g — Investigate and explain the meaning of the rate of change (slope) and y-intercept (constant term) of a linear model in context.

A.ST.1h — Analyze relationships between two quantitative variables revealed in a scatterplot.

A.ST.1i — Make conclusions based on the analysis of a set of bivariate data and communicate the results.

Prior connections

8.PS.3 — The student will apply the data cycle (formulate questions; collect or acquire data; organize and represent data; and analyze data and communicate results) with a focus on scatterplots.

A.F.1 — The student will investigate, analyze, and compare linear functions algebraically and graphically, and model linear relationships.

Future connections

A2.ST.2 — The student will apply the data cycle (formulate questions; collect or acquire data; organize and represent data; and analyze data and communicate results) with a focus on representing bivariate data in scatterplots and determining the curve of best fit using linear, quadratic, exponential, or a combination of these functions.

Engage Activity

Nutrition facts   60 mins

Students will create a nutrition fact label by using the line of fit and the context of the data for calories and macronutrients.

Understanding and skills

> **Will use**
>
> Writing and interpreting linear functions from a graph.

> **Will develop**
>
> Solving real-world problems using the line of fit and the context of the data.
>
> Fitting a linear function to a data set displayed in a scatterplot that suggests a linear association with and without technology.
>
> Interpreting key features of the line of fit in context, such as slope and y-intercept.

Preparation and materials
- Open and complete the student preview, anticipating classroom responses.
- **Materials:** Paper, pencil
- Download and print copies of the students graphic organizer from the student Launch slide.

Support students with disabilities
Support conceptual processing - make generalizations

Provide students a list of potential macronutrient values to test against the scatterplot.

Choose the most reasonable value for carbohydrates (carbs), fats, and proteins from the table provided. Choices do not need to come from the same row.

For the 600 calorie item:

Carbs	Fats	Protein
10	40	30
20	50	35
30	60	40
40	70	45

For the 1000 calorie item:

Carbs	Fats	Protein
55	100	40
65	125	60
75	150	80
85	175	100

Once students have chosen their values, encourage them to justify mathematically and refine their estimations.

Support for English language learners
Compare and connect

Invite students to share their representations for estimating the protein content in both the 600 calorie menu item and the 1000 calorie item. With their partners, ask students to find the similarities and differences in the strategies used to estimate the macronutrient contents of each item. Consider asking:

"For which item does the strategy appear to be more accurate? What other strategies might help with the other menu item?"

Listen for and amplify observations which include the advantages and disadvantages to different approaches, such as drawing an extending a line for the 1000 calorie item.

Classroom guide

Hook

Co-craft questions • 5 mins

Students create questions about a nutrition facts label.

Implementation details

The objective of the Explore is to create a nutrition fact label. The Hook allows students to interact with a label and ask questions related to the categories and specific values displayed. Some questions may include:

- What is the ratio of fat to protein in the chicken nuggets?
- What is the conversion factor between kJ and calories?
- What is a healthy ratio of saturated fat to calories?
- Are the chicken nuggets a nutrient dense food? How can we interpret the given nutritional values to determine that?

What mathematical questions could we ask about this?

Nutrition Facts		
Calories 275		(1149 kJ)
Chicken Nuggets (6 piece)		
		% Daily Value[1]
Total Fat	17.3 g	27%
Sat. Fat	3 g	15%
Cholesterol	42 mg	14%
Sodium	597 mg	25%
Total Carbs.	16.1 g	5%
Dietary Fiber	0 g	0%
Sugar	0 g	
Protein	14.3 g	
Calcium	11.9 mg	
Potassium	0 mg	

Slide 1 from Student Engage Activity

Launch

5 mins

Give students time to explore the scatterplots in the applet and familiarize themselves with the context terms unique to this problem. Engage students in a discussion on macronutrients and calories as needed.

Important mathematical concepts: Line of fit, estimate, linear function, scatterplot, slope, intercepts

Important contextual information: Macronutrient, carbohydrates, fats, proteins, calories

Suggested grouping: Form pairs

Consider the following applet:

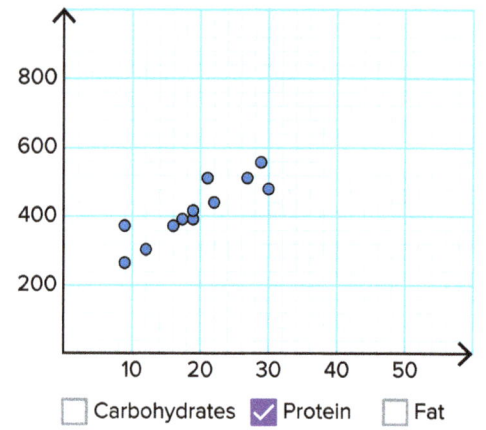

☐ Carbohydrates ☑ Protein ☐ Fat

Slide 2 from Student Engage Activity

> **Continue when**
> Students have read the Launch and understand the context of the problem.

1142 Mathspace Virginia SOL Algebra 1 Teacher Edition
mathspace.co

Explore

Think-pair-share • 35 mins

Anticipated strategies

Draw a line of fit on the graph

Students may draw a line on the graph and estimate the values for carbohydrates, protein, and fat for a 600 and 1000 calorie item.

Use prompts to encourage students to recognize informally strong correlation and weak correlation:
- Which macronutrient was easiest to work with? Why?
- Which macronutrient do you think might have the most error in the estimation? Why?
- Do you think other pairs could have different answers?

Then, push students to formalize their process and use mathematics as a tool to explain their reasoning:
- How did you come up with this value? How would you convince someone else your solution is valid?
- How can you use mathematics to support your reasoning and solution?

Write an equation for line on graph

Students may write equation for line drawn on graph or line that best models data and use equation to find the values for carbohydrates, protein, and fat for a 600 and 1000 calorie item.

Visually estimate

Students may visually estimate the values for carbohydrates, protein, and fat for a 600 and 1000 calorie item.

Students who have successfully completed this activity will submit a nutrition facts label representing the carbohydrates, protein, and fat in the 600 calorie and 1000 calorie menu item.

Answers will vary significantly. The values below are from the line of best fit for each.

600 calorie item:
- Carbohydrates: 38g
- Protein: 36g
- Fat: 71g

1000 calorie item:
- Carbohydrates: 84g
- Protein: 73g
- Fat: 143g

The accompanying descriptions will include an analysis of the meaning for both the slope and y-interecept for each macronutrient.

Misconceptions

Thinking the y-intercept needs to pass through the origin for line of best fit

What is the y-intercept of the line you drew on the graph? What does this mean in context? How do you know?

Purposeful questions

Use the following questions to check for understanding and encourage critical thinking:
- What are the macronutrient values for your 600 calorie/1000 item?
- Can you use the points on the graph to make a prediction about the macronutrients in your 600 calorie/1000 item?
- How is a line of best fit useful for determining each of the macronutrient values in your item?

> **Continue when**
> Students have created and submitted two nutrition facts labels.

Discuss
15 mins

Pairs of students will present to the whole class before facilitating a class discussion. Consider sequencing the strategies presented from visually estimating, to drawing a line of best fit, to writing an equation for the line.

Discussion guide

Select several pairs to present their nutrition facts labels. You should choose groups who made a wide range of predictions on the macronutrient values for each menu item, including one group who underestimated, one group who overestimated, and 2 – 3 groups who had estimates around the same values as one another. As each pair shares their nutrition label, focus the discussion around how each scatterplot was used to inform their estimation. If any pairs used a line of best fit, have them present last.

Questions to ask pairs as they present:
- What strategy did you use to estimate the macronutrients for the 600 calorie menu item? Did you use the same strategy for the 1000 calorie menu item?
- What do the scatterplots tell us about the nutrition of the menu overall? Were there any trends in the data that you noticed?

After having pairs present you may provide the whole class an opportunity to revisit their work and make a revised estimation for each of the macronutrient values after seeing presentations on how different groups produced their estimates. You may have students reflect on the following prompt:

If you were to estimate the macronutrient values for a 100 calorie menu item, what method would you use to determine the macronutrient values? Is this the same method you used in the Explore? Why or why not?

If time permits students can apply their method to solve for the macronutrients in the 100 calorie item.

Lesson Preparation

Suggested review

Depending on your students' level of prior knowledge, consider revisiting the following lessons:

Grade 8 — 4.05 Scatterplots and lines of best fit
Algebra 1 — 3.01 Slope
Algebra 1 — 3.03 Slope-intercept form
Algebra 1 — 9.02 Scatterplots

Tools

You may find these tools helpful:
- Statistics calculator
- Graph paper

Student lesson & teacher guide

Linear regression

Collect and display
English language learner support

As students are working, note how students describe the concepts of "regression", "interpolation" and "extrapolation". Collect the different ways that students find to understand these concepts and display them in a common place for the students to access.

If students do not come up with alternative ways to describe these concepts and are confused by them, suggest some of your own. For example:
- Regression
  - Creating a model to estimate the relationship between variables
  - Finding the line of best fit for data points
  - Predicting future values based on past data
- Interpolation
  - Predicting points between other known points
  - A way of using the trend of the actual data to make a reliable prediction
  - Using an x-value that is between the other x-values to make a prediction for y
- Extrapolation
  - Predicting a point that is to the left or right of all other data points
  - A less reliable form of prediction because we do not know if the trend of the actual data continues
  - Using an x-value that is outside the domain of the other x-values to make a prediction for y

Take care to address any rewordings that contradict or are too similar to other concepts that the student will learn in the future, such as ensuring students know that it is not limited to linear relationships.

Interpreting mathematics in context
Student with disabilities support

Provide some tips and sentence frames to support with interpreting the meaning of the slope and y-intercept.

Slope: (y is the dependent variable, x is the independent variable)
- The slope is the $\frac{\text{Change in } y}{\text{Change in } x}$
- Use the units to help, they will be "unit of y" per "unit of x"
- Sentence frame: The slope means that for each increase by 1 in (insert independent variable), the (insert dependent variable) (increases/decreases) by (insert rate of change).

y-intercept: (y is the dependent variable)
- y-intercept occurs when $x = 0$
- Use the units of y to help
- Sentence frame: The y-intercept means that the initial value is (insert y-intercept)
- Sentence frame: The y-intercept means that when (insert independent variable) is 0, the (insert dependent variable) is (insert y-intercept).

Reliability of predictions
Address student misconceptions

Students might assume that any prediction made with the line of best fit is reliable. Remind them that the reliability of the predictions decrease if:
- The relationship between the variables is not strong (the points are not tightly clustered around the line), or
- The prediction was made using extrapolation.

To help students understand why these two factors decrease the reliability of the predictions, use specific examples that show the difference between actual data values and predicted data values.

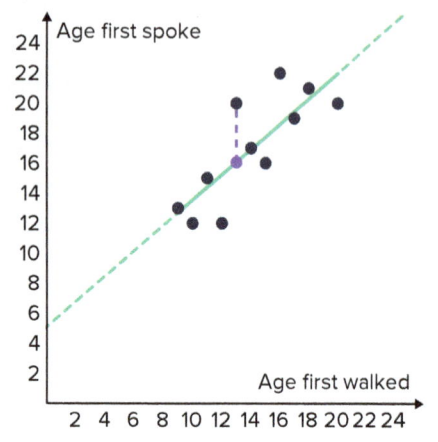

For example, this graph shows data collected on the age (in months) a child first walked and the age they first spoke (in months).

If we use the line of best fit to predict the age a child will speak if they start walking at 13 months, we might expect them to start talking at 16 months old.

However, according to the actual data value, a child that talked at 13 months started talking at 20 months. There is a 4 month difference between the predicted age and the actual age.

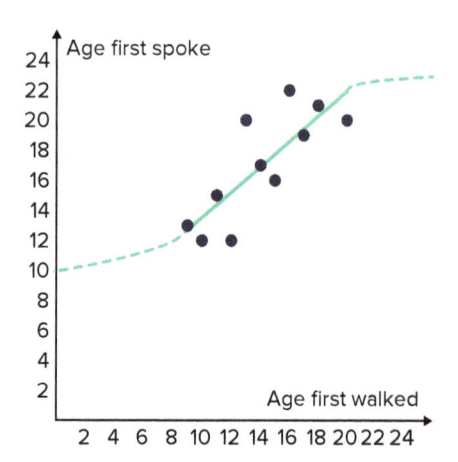

In addition, explain to students that when we make predictions outside the range of known data values, we are assuming that the trend of the data will continue.

However, the trend may not necessarily continue in the same way, as shown in this example.

Exploration

Students: Page 529

9.03 Linear regression

After this lesson, you will be able to...
- determine if a table of values represents a linear model.
- determine the equation of the line of best fit given a table of values.
- interpret key characteristics of a linear model in context.
- predict values using a linear model.

Engage activity
Ask your teacher to get started
Nutrition facts
Students will create a nutrition fact label by using the line of fit and the context of the data for calories and macronutrients.

Linear regression

Exploration

Consider the graph shown:

Car value over time

1. Is there a relationship between the years since purchased and the value in thousands of dollars? Explain.
2. Which of the lines on the graph is the line of best fit?

Suggested student grouping: In pairs

Students are asked to determine if there is a relationship between the variables shown in a scatterplot and to select the line of best fit. The aim is to connect the concept of correlation from the previous lesson with identifying a line that appears to best fit the trend of the data.

Ideal student responses

These ideal responses may differ from other correct student responses. Less formal responses can be connected with the more precise mathematical language presented here.

1. **Is there a relationship between the years since purchased and the value in thousands of dollars? Explain.**
   Yes, there is a strong, negative linear trend between the value of the car and the time since the car was purchased. That is, as the time since purchase increases, the value of the car decreases.

2. **Which of the lines on the graph is the line of best fit?**
   The dashed blue line better represents the line of best fit. The blue line has a balance in the number of points above and below the line.

Purposeful questions

- How do we know when there is a relationship between two variables in a scatterplot?
- Can you relate the relationship observed to the context in real-life?
- Which line would generally give closer predictions for the value of a car given its age?
- Would you consider predictions made from the line reliable?

Possible misunderstandings

- Students may come up with different criteria for what determines the line of best fit, such as passing through the most data points or joining the first and last data points. Remind them that in 8th grade, the goal was to draw a line with a similar number of points above and below the line.

Following the exploration, students are shown that the line of best fit is best approximated by technology. They will learn how to interpret the key features of a line of best fit, including the slope and y-intercept, and use it to predict values not represented in the data.

Students are also introduced to the terms interploation and extrapolation to help them evaluate the validity and strength of their predictions.

Students: Pages 529–531

A **line of best fit** (or trend line) is a straight line that best represents the data on a scatterplot. We can use lines of best fit to help us make predictions or conclusions about the data.

We previously approximated a line of best fit by trying to balance the number of points above the line with the number of points below the line. This can result in multiple different models.

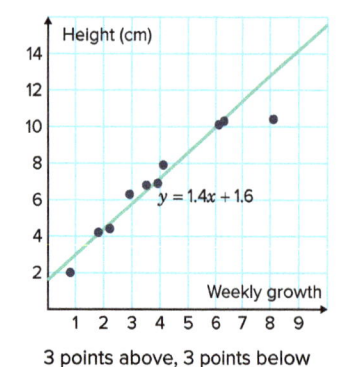

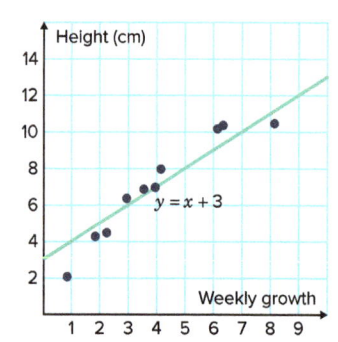

$y = 1.4x + 1.6$
3 points above, 3 points below

$y = x + 3$
5 points above, 4 points below

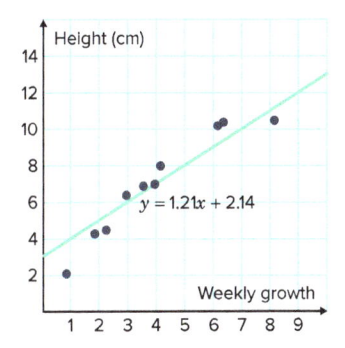

We get a more accurate line of best fit when we use technology, referred to as linear regression analysis.

Once we have found the line of best fit for a scatterplot, we can interpret the key features and use the line to predict values that don't appear in the data set.

In the context of a line of best fit, the slope-intercept form represents

$$y = mx + b$$

- m the rate of change for y with respect to x
- b the starting value of y when x is 0

For example, this graph models a plant's growth over several weeks.

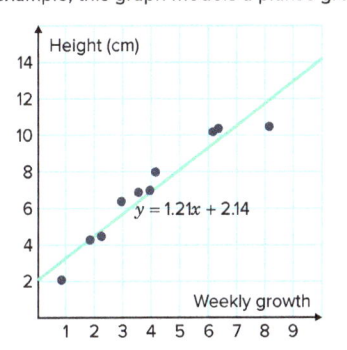

The slope of the line $y = 1.21x + 2.14$ means that the plant is growing at a rate of 1.21 centimeters per week.

The y-intercept of 2.14 means the plant was 2.14 centimeters tall at week 0. This is feasible if the plant was not a seed when measurements began.

These terms describe the range in which we make predictions:
- **Interpolation**: Prediction within the range of x-values in the data
- **Extrapolation**: Prediction outside the range of x-values in the data

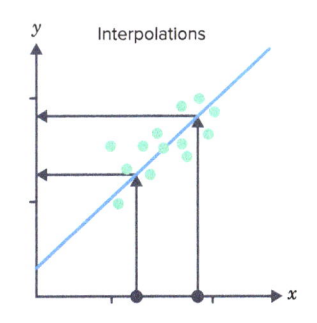

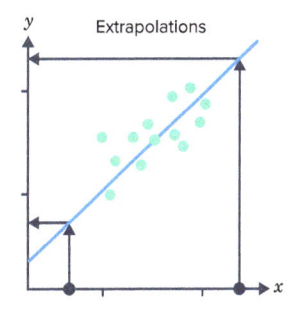

Using the previous example of the plant height over time:

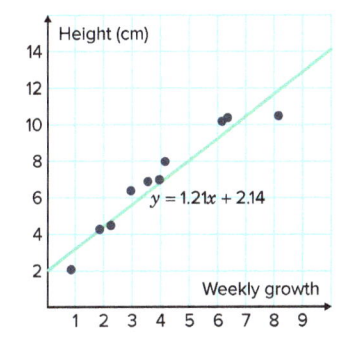

Interpolating which week the plant was 9 centimeters tall, we will solve $9 = 1.21x + 2.14$. The plant was 9 centimeters tall at 5.67 weeks.

Extrapolating the plant's height at 10 weeks, we will evaluate $y = 1.21(10) + 2.14$. The plant will be 14.24 centimeters tall at 10 weeks.

9.03 Linear regression

The reliability of predictions depends on the strength of the relationship, whether the data is interpolated or extrapolated, and the number of points in the data set.
- A larger sample size increases reliability.
- Interpolation with a strong correlation implies a reliable prediction.
- Interpolation with a moderate or weak correlation leads to a less reliable prediction.
- Extrapolation generally leads to an unreliable prediction. The further outside the range of known values, the less reliable it is.

Examples

The following support may be useful for the examples in this section.

Calculator steps for Desmos and TI graphing calculators
Targeted instructional strategies

The examples provide students with the steps to finding the line of best fit using the GeoGebra Statistics calculator. Steps for finding the line of best fit on a TI-84 or with Desmos are shown.

TI-83 or TI-84:

1. Select the STAT button.
2. Select EDIT.
3. Enter the x-values under L_1 in the table.
4. Enter the y-values under L_2 in the table.
5. Press the STAT button again.
6. Press the right arrow to select CALC at the top of the screen.
7. Select LinReg(ax+b).
8. Press these buttons in this order:
   - 2ND (blue button in the top left)
   - 1 (has L_1 in blue above it)
   - , (the comma above 7)
   - 2ND
   - 2 (has L_2 in blue above it)

   Your screen should show LinReg(ax+b)(L_1,L_2)
9. Select ENTER.

Desmos:

1. Click the + in the top left and select the table.
2. Enter the x-values under x_1 in the table.
3. Enter the y-values under y_1 in the table.
4. If you do not see the points on the graph, click the magnifying glass with the plus sign at the bottom left of the table.
5. In row 2 below the table, enter the following formula: $y_1 \sim ax_1 + b$

These steps will produce the values of a and b. The value of a is the slope of the line, and the value of b is the y-intercept.

Students: Pages 531–533

Example 1

Natalia collected data to answer the question, "What is the relationship between the years since purchasing a car and its value?" Her data is shown in the table.

Time since purchase (years)	0.5	0.8	1.2	1.3	1.5	1.7	1.8	2.1	2	2.5
Value (thousands of dollars)	29	28.5	28.5	27.4	28.5	27	25.9	25.9	24.7	26.4

Time since purchase (years)	2.6	2.8	3.1	3.4	3.6	3.9	4.05	4.6	4.8
Value (thousands of dollars)	24.6	23.5	24.6	23.3	21	21	22	21	20.1

a Find the equation of the line of best fit.

Create a strategy

To find the equation using technology, we can follow these steps:

1. Enter the x-values and y-values in two separate columns.
2. Highlight the data and select Two Variable Regression Analysis.
3. Under the Regression Model drop down menu, choose Linear.

Apply the idea

Enter the x-values and y-values in two separate columns.

1. Enter the x-values and y-values in two separate columns.

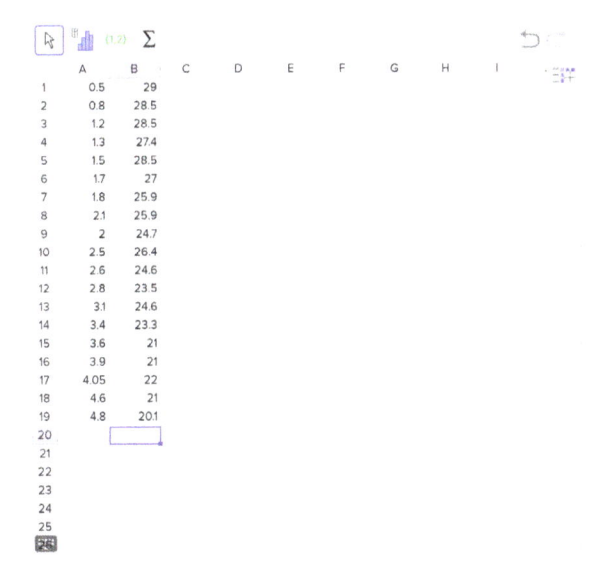

	A	B
1	0.5	29
2	0.8	28.5
3	1.2	28.5
4	1.3	27.4
5	1.5	28.5
6	1.7	27
7	1.8	25.9
8	2.1	25.9
9	2	24.7
10	2.5	26.4
11	2.6	24.6
12	2.8	23.5
13	3.1	24.6
14	3.4	23.3
15	3.6	21
16	3.9	21
17	4.05	22
18	4.6	21
19	4.8	20.1

2. Highlight the data and select Two Variable Regression Analysis.

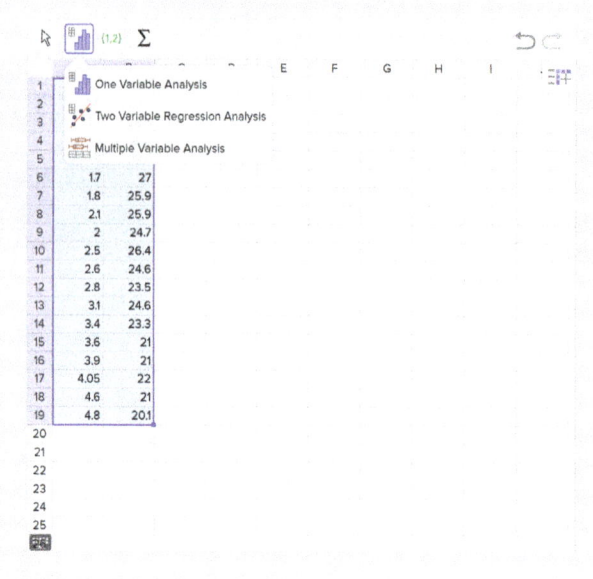

3. Under the Regression Model drop down menu, choose Linear.

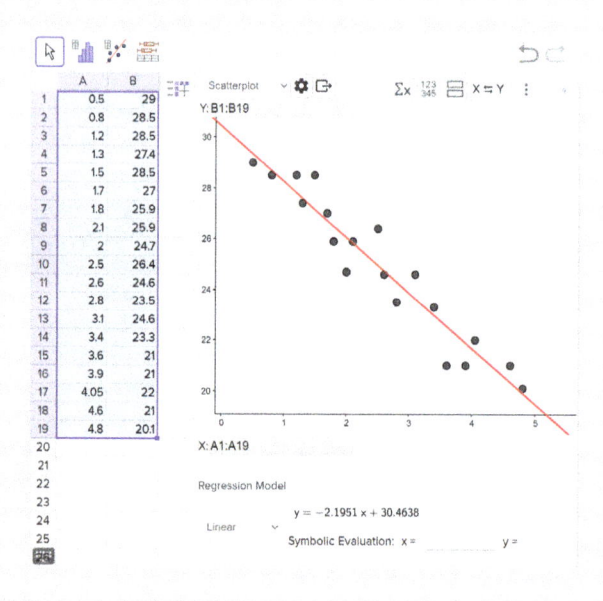

If we round the coefficients to two decimal places, the equation of the line of best fit is $y = -2.2x + 30.46$.

Reflect and check

The points are tightly clustered around the line, indicating that the relationship between the years since the car was purchased and the value of the car is strong. This means the line of best fit can be used to make relatively reliable predictions.

Remember, a strong relationship does not imply that one variable causes changes in the other. We cannot say that the year since the car was purchased causes the value of the car to decrease, as there may be other factors that affect the value of the car.

Purpose

Demonstrate how to find the line of best fit for a set of data using technology.

Students: Pages 533–534

b Interpret the slope and y-intercept of the line.

Create a strategy

Use the independent and dependent variables to determine the units of the slope and y-intercept.

Car value over time

[Scatterplot showing Value (thousands of dollars) on y-axis from 0 to 30, and Time since purchase (years) on x-axis from 1 to 5, with a decreasing line of best fit.]

To help us visualize the relationship better, we can sketch the scatterplot and line of best fit, and add labels on the axes of the graph.

Remember that the y-values are in thousands of dollars. This means we will need to multiply the y-value of the slope and y-intercept by 1000 when interpreting them in context.

Apply the idea

The y-intercept of (0, 30.46) means that at the time of purchasing the car, it would have a value of $30460.

The slope of −2.2 means that each year, the car's value would decrease by $2200.

Purpose

Check if students can interpet the slope and y-intercept in context.

Expected mistakes

Students might not consider the units of the dependent variable, causing them to state the y-values as is rather than converting them to thousands. Remind them that the y-values are in thousands of dollars, which means each value should be multiplied by 1000.

For example, $y = 30.46$ in context is "30.46 thousand" which is

$$30.46 \cdot 1000 = 30\,460$$

Reflecting with students

Encourage students to evaluate the reasonableness of these values. Is it realistic for a car to initally be worth $30 460? Is it reasonable to assume the car's value drops by $2200 each year? If students are not familiar with the cost of cars or how they depreciate, encourage them to research the current prices and average depreciation of cars.

Students: Page 534

c Make a prediction about the value of a car after 3 years.

Create a strategy

We are given the years since the car was purchased, which is the indpendent variable (x), and we are looking for the value of the car, which is the dependent variable (y).

We can use the graph to estimate the y-value at $x = 3$ or use the line of best fit to get a more accurate prediction.

Apply the idea

When we substitute $x = 3$ into the equation, we get

$$y = -2.2(3) + 30.46$$
$$= 23.86$$

Based on the equation of the line of best fit, a car that is initially valued at $30460 will be worth $23860 three years after it was purchased.

Reflect and check

When using technology to evaluate $x = 3$, we will get a slightly different answer. This is because the coefficients were rounded in our line of best fit. The calculator does not round the coefficients, making its result more accurate.

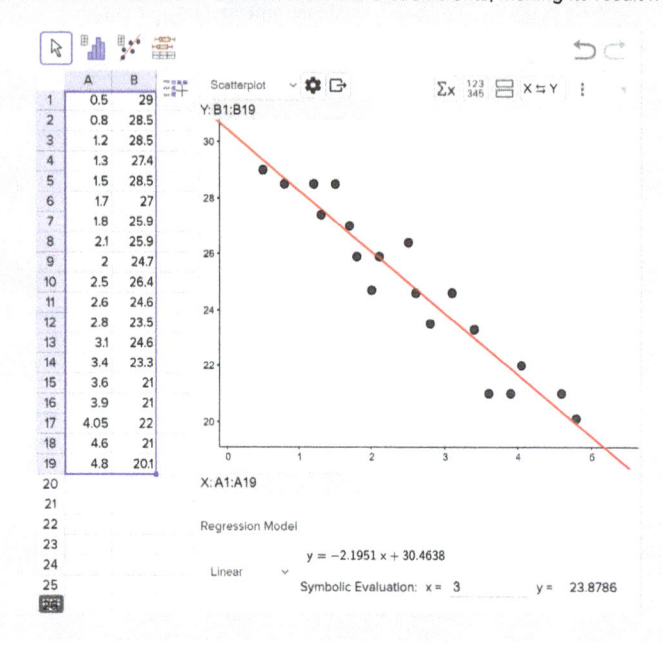

Purpose

Check students' ability to use the equation of a line to make predictions.

Students: Page 535

d Make a prediction about the value of a car after 10 years.

Create a strategy

Since 10 years after purchase is not shown on the graph, we can use the equation of the line of best fit to determine the value of a car at that time.

Apply the idea
We can use technology to find the value of y when $x = 10$.

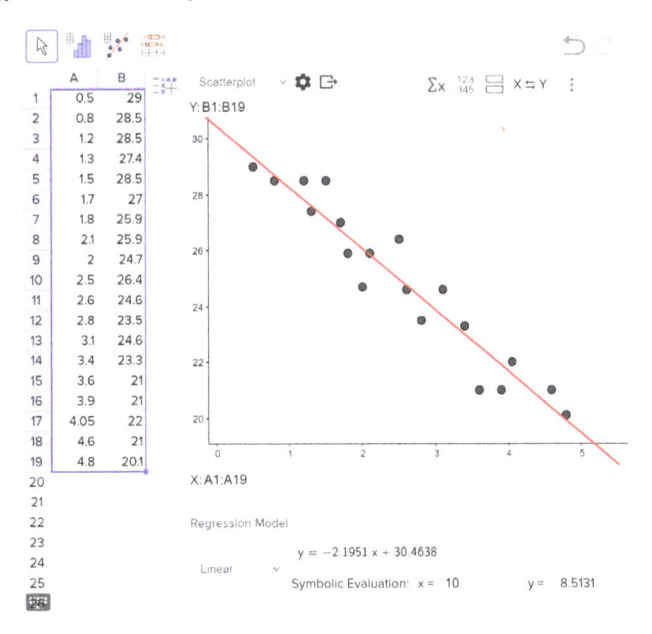

[Scatterplot showing data from columns A (x-values 0.5 to 4.8) and B (y-values), with regression line. Regression Model: $y = -2.1951x + 30.4638$ (Linear). Symbolic Evaluation: $x = 10$, $y = 8.5131$]

A car that is initially valued at \$30 460 will be worth \$8513 ten years after it was purchased.

Purpose
Check students' ability to use the equation of a line to make predictions outside the range of the given data.

Students: Page 535

e Is the prediction for the car's value after 3 years or after 10 years more reliable?

Create a strategy
To determine the reliability of the predictions, consider whether interpolation or extrapolation was used to make the prediction. Interpolation leads to a more reliable outcome than extrapolation.

Apply the idea
The given data ranges between $x = 0.5$ and $x = 4.8$. This means the prediction of the car's value after 3 years falls within the range of known data, while the prediction after 10 years falls outside of that range. The prediction of the car's value after 3 years is more reliable.

Reflect and check
Interpolation is more reliable than extrapolation because the predictions follows the same pattern as the known data values. With extrapolation, we assume that the trend continues beyond the known data values. Realistically, the trend may not continue which makes extrapolation less reliable.

Purpose
To assess students' understanding of interpolation and extrapolation.

Reflecting with students
Prompt advanced learners or all students to determine an appropriate domain for the linear model and to defend their choices. Students should consider when the model is most reliable. Then, have them find the corresponding range for their domain choice.

Students: Page 536

Example 2

A teacher recorded the number of days since a student last studied for an exam and their score out of a possible 80 points on the exam.

Days since studying	3	2	6	4	4	1	6	3	4	2
Exam score	64	59	42	57	58	72	33	63	55	62

a   Formulate an investigative question that can be answered by the data.

Create a strategy

The question should be focused on the relationship between the variables represented by the data. The independent variable is the number of days since studying, and the dependent variable is the score on the exam.

Apply the idea

One possible question is, "How does the number of days since a student last studied impact their exam score?"

Reflect and check

Other possible questions are:
- What is the relationship between the number of days since a student last and their exam score?
- How many days prior to the exam should a student study to increase their exam score?
- If a student studies on the same day as the exam, what is their expected score on the exam?

Purpose

Check students' ability to formulate investigative questions given a data set.

Students: Page 536

b   Was the data most likely collected through measurement, observation, a survey or an experiment?

Apply the idea

The teacher did not measure, observe, or control the time since a student studied. Instead, it is more likely that the teacher asked the students how many days it has been since they last studied.
The data was most likely collected through a survey.

Reflect and check

Although the teacher may have had access to the students' exam scores (assuming the teacher was the one that assigned the exam), they could have still included a survey question about the exam score to keep the data organized.

For example, their survey questions could have been, "How many days has it been since you last studied for this subject?" and "What was your score on the exam?"

Purpose

Assess the students' understanding of different data collection methods and their ability to determine which method is applicable in a given scenario.

Students: Pages 536–537

c   Describe the relationship between the number of days since studying and the exam score.

Create a strategy

To describe the relationship, we should construct a scatterplot to get a visual of the data. Then, we will consider the form (linear or nonlinear), strength (strong, moderate or weak), and direction (positive or negative).

Apply the idea

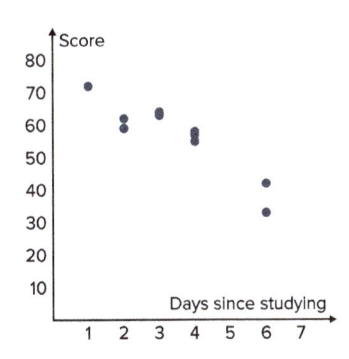

The data appears to have a strong, negative, linear relationship.

Relating this back to the context, we can say that as the number of days since a student last studied increases, and their score on the exam tends to decrease.

Purpose

Check the students' ability to create and analyze a scatterplot.

Students: Pages 537–538

d   Calculate the line of best fit using technology.

Create a strategy

To find the equation using technology, we can follow these steps:

1. Enter the x-values and y-values in two separate columns.
2. Hightlight the data and select Two Variable Regression Analysis.
3. Under the Regression Model drop down menu, choose Linear

Apply the idea

1. Enter the x- and y-values in two separate columns:

	A	B
1	3	64
2	2	59
3	6	42
4	4	57
5	4	58
6	1	72
7	6	33
8	3	63
9	4	55
10	2	62

9.03 Linear regression

2. Highlight the data and select Two Variable Regression Analysis:

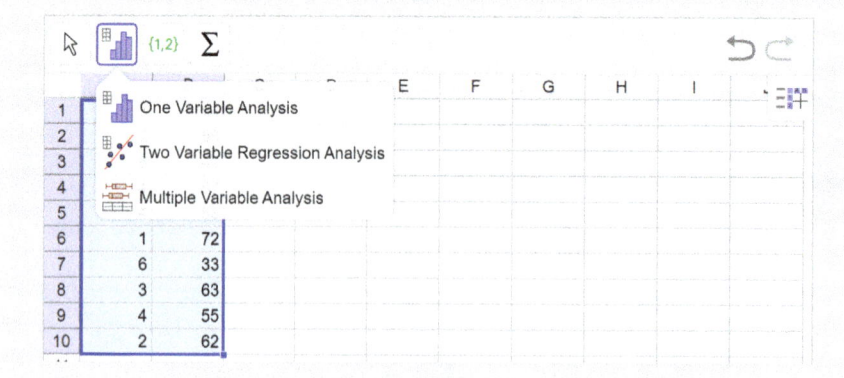

3. Choose Linear under the Regression Model drop down menu to find the line of best fit:

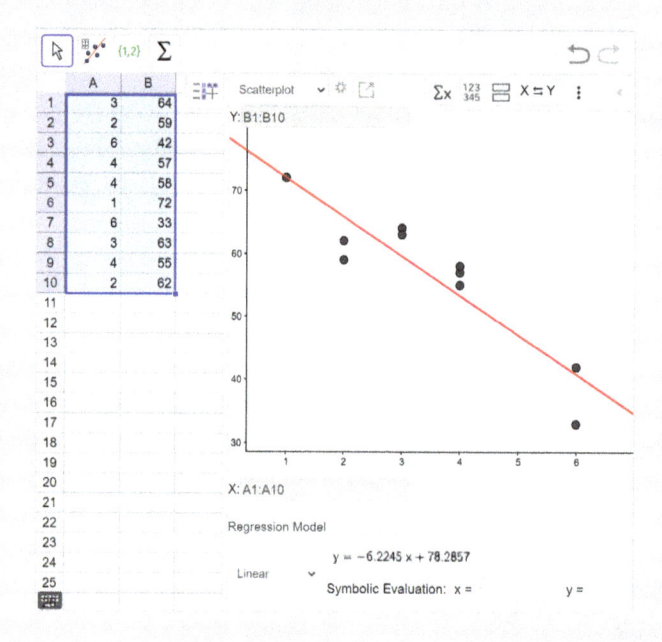

Apply the idea

The equation of the line of best fit is

$$y = -6.22x + 78$$

Reflect and check

If the instructions do not specify to round the coefficients, it is best to include all the digits given by the calculator. This increases the accuracy of the model and the predictions.

Purpose

Check that students can find the line of best fit for a set of data using technology.

Students: Page 539

e Answer the question formulated in part (a).

Create a strategy

To answer the question, "How does the number of days since a student last studied impact their exam score?", we can describe the direction of the linear relationship. To be more specific, we can interpret the slope of the line in context.

In the previous part, we found the equation of the line of best fit to be $y = -6.2245x + 78.2857$, which tells us the slope is -6.2245.

Apply the idea

As the number of days since a student last studied increases, their exam score decreases. More specifically, for each additional day since a student last studied, their exam score is expected to decrease by about 6 points.

Reflect and check

Matching the rise and run of the slope to their respective units can help us interpret its meaning in context.

$$\text{slope} = \frac{\text{rise}}{\text{run}} = \frac{\text{change in } y}{\text{change in } x} = \frac{-6.2245}{1}$$

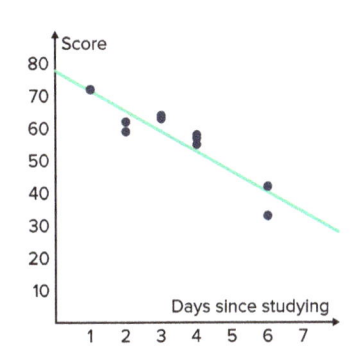

The y-values represent the exam score, which is the "rise" of the slope. The x-values represent the number of days since studying, which is the "run" of the slope.

Since the slope is negative, it represents a decrease of 6.2245 in the exam score for every 1 day since studying.

Purpose

Determine if students can interpret the slope of the line in context.

Reflecting with students

Discuss with students whether or not the number of days since studying causes test scores to decrease. Remind students that a strong relationship does not imply that one variable causes a change in the other variable.

Ask students to list other factors that might have an impact on test grades. Examples may include the number of absences from school recently, hours of sleep the night before the test, average class participation amount, etc. In other words, we cannot say the number of days since stuydying causes the test scores to decrease as there may be other factors at play. If an experiment was conducted to control the outside factors and the test scores still decreased, then we can say there is a causal relationship there.

Students: Page 539

> **f** If a student studied the same day as the exam, what would we expect their score to be?
>
> **Create a strategy**
> If the number of days since a student last studied is 0, then their exam score is the y-value of the y-intercept.
>
> **Apply the idea**
> The y-intercept tells us that a student who has studied on the day of the exam has a predicted score of 78.2857, according to the linear model.
>
> **Reflect and check**
> Although this value was found through extrapolation, $x = 0$ is not very far outside of the range of known values. Since the relationship is strong, this prediction is relatively reliable.

Purpose
Check the students' ability to interpret the y-intercept of a linear regression model.

Students: Page 540

> ### Idea summary
>
> A **line of best fit** for a set of data can be used to interpret a given situation and make predictions about values not represented by the data.
>
> A line of best fit has an equation of the form $y = mx + b$. We can use technology to perform the linear regression analysis.
>
> In the context of a line of best fit, the slope-intercept form represents
>
> $$y = mx + b$$
>
> - m the rate of change for y with respect to x
> - b The starting value of y when x is 0
>
> These terms describe the range in which we make predictions:
>
> - **Interpolation**: Prediction within the range of x-values in the data
> - **Extrapolation**: Prediction outside the range of x-values in the data
>
> The reliability of predictions depends on the strength of the relationship, whether the data is interpolated or extrapolated, and the number of points in the data set. In general, interpolation is more reliable than extrapolation.

Practice

Students: Pages 540–545

What do you remember?

1. Choose the line of best fit for this scatterplot.

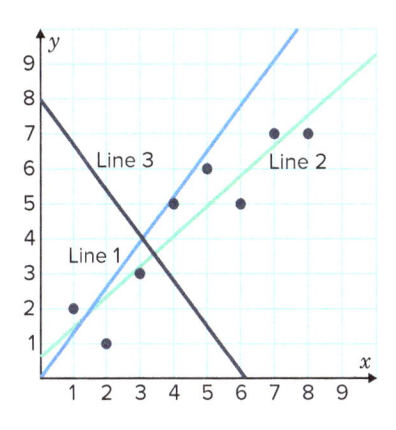

2. Sketch the line of best fit for each scatterplot:

    a.

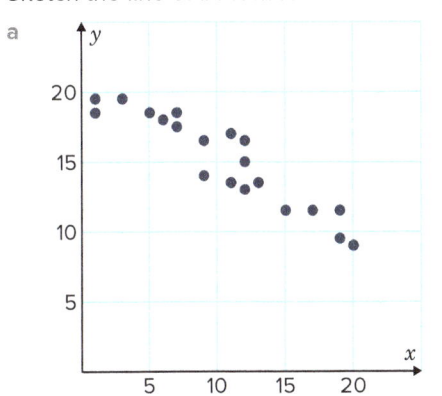

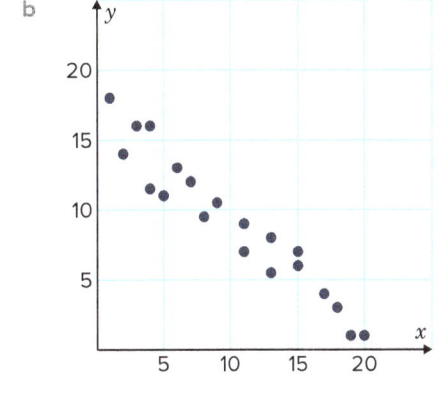

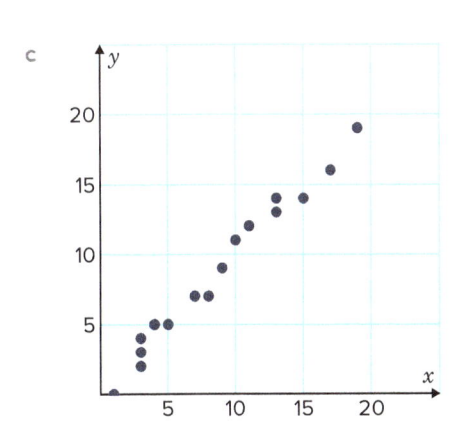

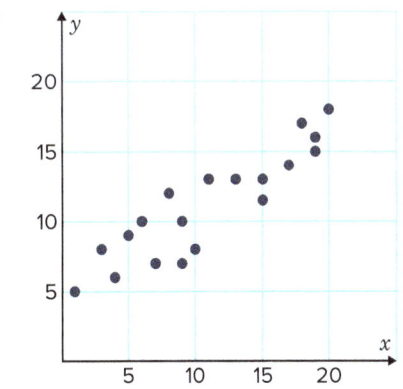

    b.

    c.

    d.

3 The scatterplot represents the given data set:

$$\{(36, 114), (20, 164), (22, 154), (24, 150), (26, 140), (28, 138), (30, 134), (32, 122), (34, 118)\}$$

a Create a table of values for the data set.
b Find the equation of the line of best fit.

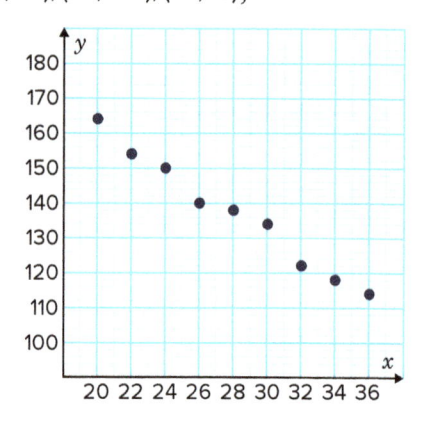

4 Does each graph show interpolation or extrapolation?

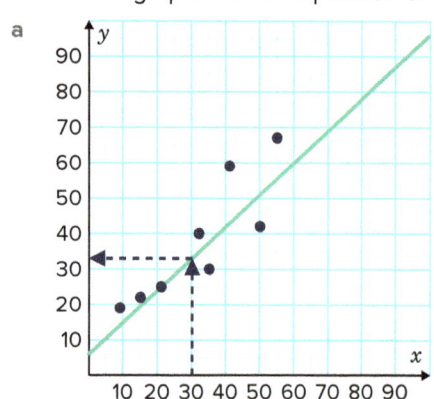

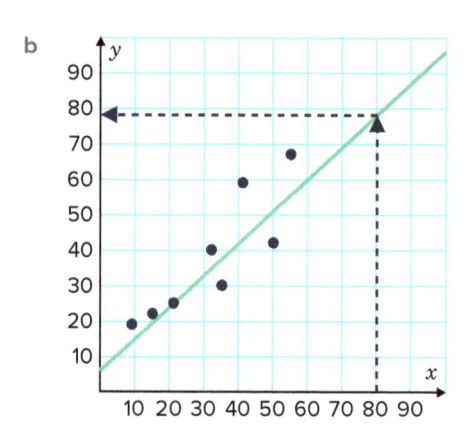

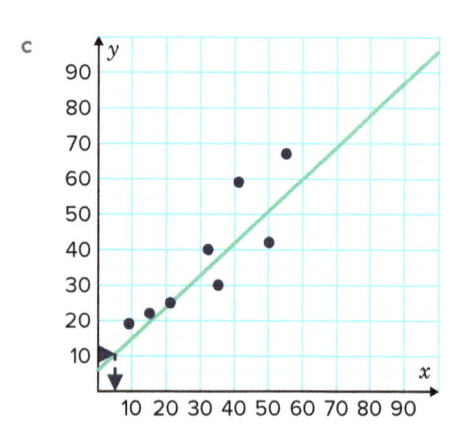

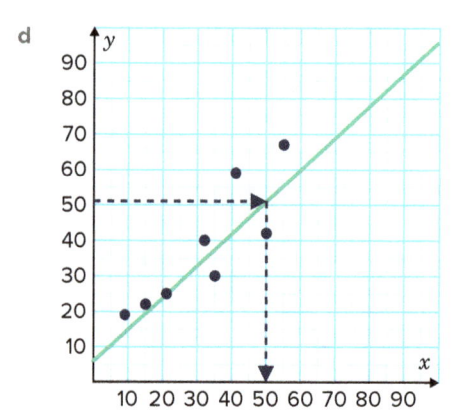

a

b

c

d

5 Is each statement true or false?

a The line of best fit can only be used for interpolation, not extrapolation.
b Using the line of best fit for extrapolation is generally more reliable than interpolation.
c Interpolation is more accurate when the data points are tightly clustered around the line of best fit.
d A line of best fit may not accurately represent the relationship between variables if the relationship is non-linear.
e It is not important to consider the validity of predictions when using interpolation or extrapolation.
f Considering the strengths and weaknesses of a regression model helps ensure that the conclusions are accurate and reliable.

Let's practice

6 Find the equation of the line of best fit for each data set.

a
x	28	30	32	34	36	38
y	3926	6482	10 589	17 098	28 236	46 985

b
x	17	19	21	23	25	27	29
y	16	19	21	16	17	27	19

c
Speed	20	25	30	35	40	45	50	55	60	65
Time	85	87	75	82	69	73	60	57	45	49

d
Age	20	25	30	35	40	45	50	55	60	65
Accidents	41	44	39	34	30	25	22	18	19	17

7 For the data set shown:

$$\{(93, 51.2), (57, 25.4), (86, 38.9), (97, 58.6), (78, 38.2), (96, 60.8),$$
$$(68, 26.3), (69, 28.5), (54, 5.4), (92, 92)\}$$

a Find the equation of the line of best fit.
b Predict the value of y when $x = 3.49$. Round your answer to two decimal places.
c Is the prediction in part (b) an example of interpolation or extrapolation?

8 A cafe manager collected data about sales of hot cocoa during a winter weekend. The data included the outside temperature and the number of hot cocoa sold every two hours.

Outside temperature in °F, t	0	2	5	2	1	3	6	4
Number of hot cocoas sold, n	20	16	3	16	18	17	8	12

a Is the relationship between the outside temperature and the number of hot cocoa sold linear or nonlinear?
b Calculate the regression model for this data set. Round all values to the nearest tenth.

9 The amount of money households spend on dining out each week, D, is measured against their weekly income, I.

This linear model $D = 0.3I + 27$ is fit to the data.

a Explain the meaning of the y-intercept.
b State the slope of the line.
c If the weekly income of a family increases by $200, by how much can we expect their spending on dining out to increase?

10 The life expectancy (E), in years, of individuals at different annual incomes (I), per $1000, is shown:

The equation of the line of best fit is $E = 0.09I + 72.55$.

a By how much does average life expectancy change for each $1000 of annual income?
b Find the average life expectancy of someone who earns no income.

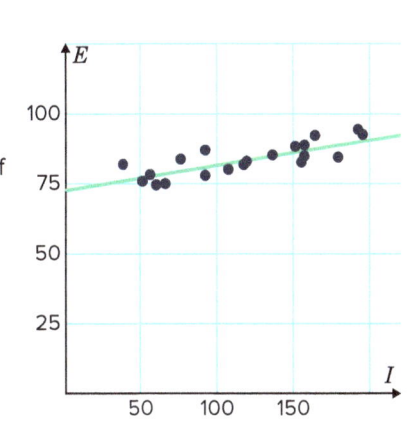

11 Scientists collect data to answer the statistical question, "What is the relationship between the number of aphids and the number of ladybugs in various areas?" The data is shown in the scatterplot.

$A = -3.82L + 3865.21$ represents the line of best fit.

   a Describe the variables the scientists used to answer their statistical question.
   b How much does the average aphid population change by with each extra ladybug? Round your answer to the nearest aphid.
   c Find the average aphid population of a region with no ladybugs. Round your answer to the nearest aphid.

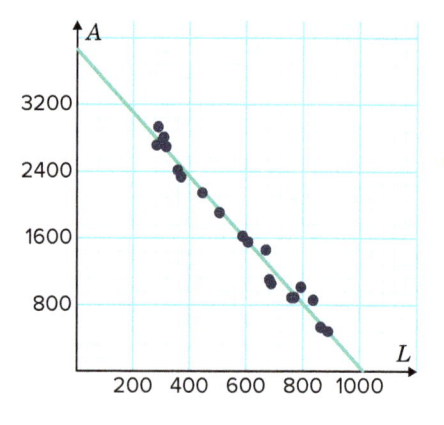

12 The average monthly temperature and the average wind speed in a particular location was plotted over several months. The graph shows the points for each month's data and their line of best fit.

   a Identify the independent and dependent variables used in this study.
   b Use the line of best fit to approximate the wind speed on a day when the temperature is 41 °F.
   c How reliable is this prediction? Explain your answer.

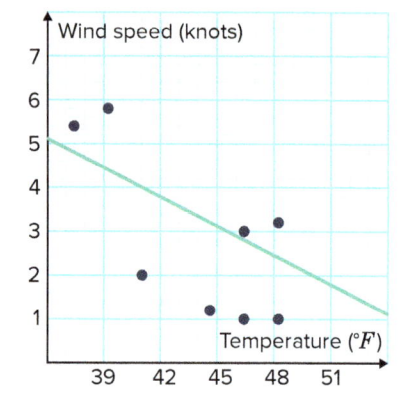

13 The scatterplot shows data collected on the amount of caffeine consumed, in milligrams, in a day and the number of hours of sleep for 30 adults.

   a Formulate a question that can be answered by the scatterplot.
   b Which equation is most likely the line of best fit?
      A $y = 0.015x + 9.58$
      B $y = 0.015x - 9.58$
      C $y = -0.015x + 9.58$
      D $y = -0.015x - 9.58$
   c Describe the strength of the relationship. Explain what this relationship implies in context.

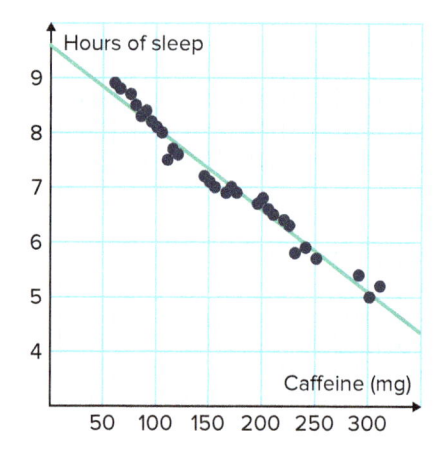

14 Scientists conducted a study to analyze the time it took people to perform a simple matching activity after they've had different amounts of sleep. The participants were placed in similar rooms under the same conditions, and they were all given the same matching activity. The data is shown in the table and scatterplot, along with the line of best fit.

Number of hours sleep (x)	1.1	1.5	2.1	2.5	3.5	4
Completion time in seconds (y)	4.66	4.1	4.66	3.7	3.6	3.4

   a Formulate a question that could be answered by the data.
   b Which data collection method was used?
      A Measurement   B Observation   C Survey   D Experiment
   c Use technology to find the equation for the line of best fit.
   d Use the line of best fit to predict the task completion time for someone who has slept 5 hours.
   e Predict the number of hours someone has slept if they complete the matching task in 4 seconds.

1164 Mathspace Virginia SOL Algebra 1 Teacher Edition
mathspace.co

15 A student collected data to answer the statistical question, "How does the temperature outside impact the number of people at the beach?" Their data is shown in the table.

Temperature (°F)	69	72	74	77	79	80	82	83	85	87
Number of people	80	88	120	134	162	177	180	188	220	230

a Did the student collect the data through measurement, observation, a survey or an experiment?
b About how many people might be at the beach when the temperature is 80°F?
c What is the temperature when there are 81 people at the beach?
d About how many people might be at the beach when the temperature is 90°F?
e Is the prediction for 80°F or 90°F more reliable?

16 One liter of gas is raised to various temperatures, and its pressure is measured. The results are shown in the table.

Temperature (K)	300	302	304	308	310	312	314	316	318
Pressure (Pa)	2400	2416	2434	2462	2478	2496	2512	2526	2546

a Use technology to calculate the equation for the line of best fit.
b Use the line of best fit to predict the pressure when the temperature is 306 K.
c Is the prediction in part (a) an example of interpolation or extrapolation?
d Is the prediction in part (a) reliable?
e Will using the line of best fit to predict pressure within each of these ranges of temperatures result in a reliable prediction?
  i $300 \leq$ Temp ≤ 320
  ii $300 \leq$ Temp ≤ 600
  iii $0 \leq$ Temp ≤ 320
  iv $280 \leq$ Temp ≤ 340

17 Concern over student use of the social media app SnappyChatty leads to a study of student grades in Mathematics versus minutes spent using the app. The results are shown in the table.

Minutes, M	292	153	354	253	11	42	195	7	162	254
Grade, P %	26	63	13	37	97	89	51	98	59	36

a Predict the grade of a student who spends no time on the SnappyChatty app. Use a model to justify your response.
b Use your model to explain and interpret the relationship between minutes spent on the SnappyChatty app and mathematics grades.

Let's extend our thinking

18 Based on the given scatterplot and line of best fit, could the model be used to make reliable predictions? Explain.

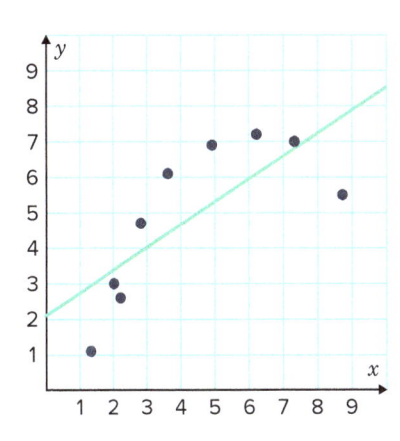

19 Lorena and Frasier each draw a possible line of best fit.

  a Frasier said he noticed that there was a point that was far away, so he moved his line closer to it. Does Frasier's line represent a line of best fit? Explain.

  b Lorena said she noticed that there was a point that was far away, but decided to ignore it. Would Lorena's line better represent a line of best fit? Explain.

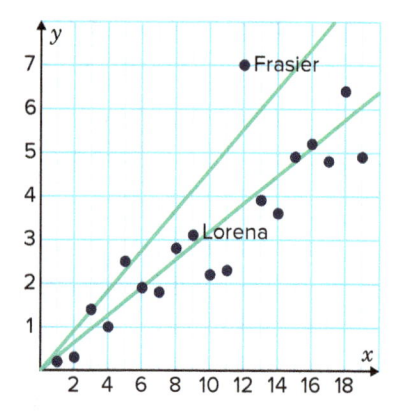

20 Each week, a school counselor helps students who are struggling in Math and English organize tutoring sessions. He hopes that the tutoring sessions will have a positive effect on students' grades.

  a Formulate a question which could be investigated using a scatterplot.
  b Determine what variables could be used to answer the statistical question from part (a).
  c Describe a method the school counselor could use to collect the data.
  d The data the school counselor collected on the students who receive Math and English tutoring is shown in the tables. Create a scatterplot of the data.

Math students

Hours of tutoring per week	1.5	3.5	1	4	2	2.5	3
Math grade	63	75	60	79	68	69	71

Hours of tutoring per week	3.25	1.75	2.25	3.75	1.25	2.75	4.5
Math grade	72	66	68	74	62	70	79

English students

Hours of tutoring per week	1	2.5	0.75	1.5	4	1.25	2
English grade	69	80	64	72	91	71	77

Hours of tutoring per week	3.5	1.25	2.75	1.75	3	2.25	3.75
English grade	89	67	83	73	85	79	87

  e Find the regression model for each set of data.
  f Draw a conclusion about the data by answering the statistical question from part (a).
  g Use the regression models to predict the grades of a math student and an English student who each receive 3 hours and 15 minutes of tutoring each week. Explain whether these predictions are reliable.

21 Go through the whole data cycle at least once to investigate whether a relationship between a person's height and the length of their stride exists.

Answers

9.03 Linear regression

What do you remember?

1. Line 2

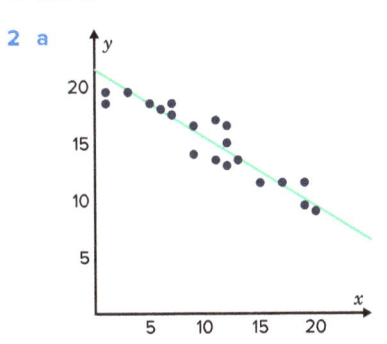

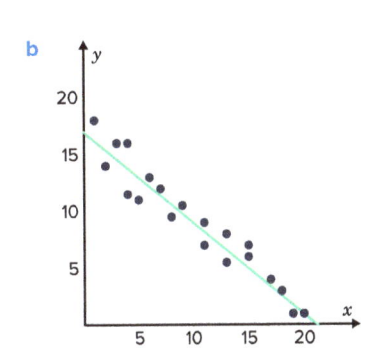

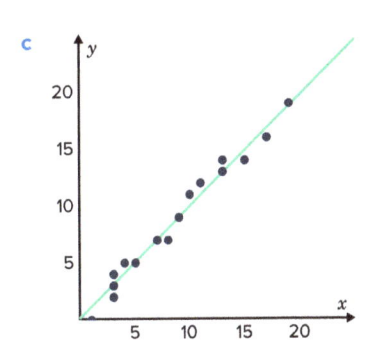

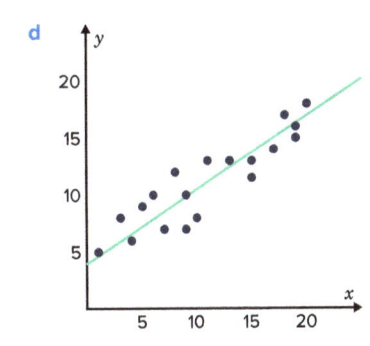

2. a. [scatter plot with decreasing trend line]
   b. [scatter plot with decreasing trend line]
   c. [scatter plot with increasing trend line]
   d. [scatter plot with increasing trend line]

3. a.
x	36	20	22	24	26	28	30	32	34
y	114	164	154	150	140	138	134	122	118

   b. $y = -3.08x + 223.44$

4. a. Interpolation b. Extrapolation
   c. Extrapolation d. Interpolation

5. a. False b. False c. True d. True
   e. False f. True

Let's practice

6. a. $y = 4100.9x - 116\,445$ b. $y = 0.375x + 10.661$
   c. $y = -0.93x + 107.87$ d. $y = -0.65x + 56.56$

7. a. $y = 1.26x - 57.01$ b. $y = -52.61$
   c. Extrapolation

8. a. Linear b. $n = -2.5t + 20.9$

9. a. When a family has no income, their average spending on dining out is $27.
   b. 0.3 c. $60

10. a. 0.09 years per $1000 b. 72.55 years

11. a. The independent variable is the number of ladybugs, and the dependent variable is the number of aphids.
    b. −4 b. 3865

12. a. The independent variable is the average monthly temperature, and the dependent variable is the average wind speed. Each point represents one month, so data was collected over 8 months.
    b. 4 knots
    c. This prediction is not very reliable because the sample size is small and the relationship between the variables is weak.

13. a. Many possible questions, for example, "Does higher caffeine consumption correlate with fewer hours of sleep among adults?"
    b. C
    c. There is a strong relationship between the variables. We expect adults who consume more caffeine to sleep less.

14. a. Many possible questions, for example, "What is the relationship between the hours of sleep someone gets and their reaction time?"
    b. D
    c. $y = -0.406294x + 5.01542$
    d. 3.8 seconds
    e. 2.5 hours

15. a. Observation b. 168 people
    c. 70°F d. 256 people
    e. 80°F

16. a. $y = 7.98333x + 4.93333$
    b. 2448 Pa
    c. Interpolation
    d. Yes

e i Yes   ii No   iii No   iv No

17 a A scatterplot can help visualize the relationship between the quantities, but is not necessary for a complete response:

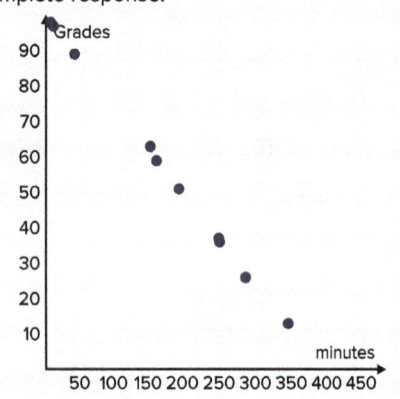

[Scatterplot: Grades vs minutes, showing negative linear trend. Y-axis "Grades" 10–90, X-axis "minutes" 50–450.]

There is a strong, negative, linear relationship between minutes spent on SnappyChatty and math grades. The linear regression model is $y = -0.25x + 99.6$
A student who spends 0 minutes on SnappyChatty is predicted to have a 99.6% grade in mathematics.

b According to the linear model, for every additional minute spent on SnappyChatty, a student's math grade is expected to drop 0.25%. Or, for every additional 100 minutes spent on SnappyChatty, a student's grade is predicted to drop 25%

Let's extend our thinking

18 No, the line does not follow the pattern in the data. A nonlinear model would be more appropriate for making predictions.

19 a There are only 2 points above the line and 18 points below it, so this line does not go through the middle of the data. It is too heavily impacted by the outlier, so is not a line of best fit.

b An outlier should not be completely ignored, but the line should go through the majority of the data. Lorena's line has 9 points above it and 10 points below it, and goes through the middle of the data, so it is a line of best fit.

20 a Many possible questions, for example, "How have the weekly tutoring hours impacted grades for math and English students?"

b Answers will vary based on question from part (a). Using the example, "How have the weekly tutoring hours impacted grades for math and English students?":

The independent variable is the hours of tutoring per week, and the dependent variable is the students' class grades. The cateogrical variables are students who receive tutoring for Math and students who receive tutoring for English.

c If there is a relatively small number of students receiving tutoring, the school counselor could collect data on all students receiving tutoring. Since he is already tracking the tutoring hours each student receives, he only needs to collect data on the students' grades. He could acquire this data from the school's online system or from the students' Math and English teachers.

d [Scatterplot: Grade vs Weekly tutoring hours (1–4), with two series: English (light) and Math (dark), both showing positive linear trends. Y-axis "Grade" 60–90.]
● English ● Math

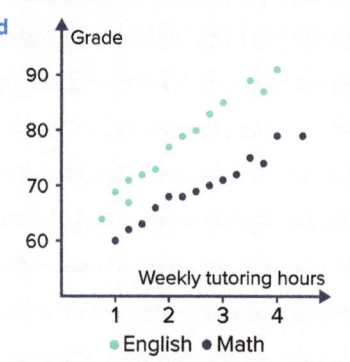

e Math students: $y = 5.3396x + 55.6024$
English students: $y = 8.0136x + 59.7553$

f Answers will vary based on question from part (a). Using the example, "How have the weekly tutoring hours impacted grades for math and English students?":

There is a strong, positive, linear relationship between the weekly tutoring hours and grades of both math and English students. This implies that the weekly tutoring sessions have had a positive impact on students' grades.

As the weekly tutoring hours increase, the students' grades also increase. More specifically, an increase in 1 hour of tutoring each week can increase a math student's grade by about 5% and an English student's grade by about 8%.

g 3 hours and 15 minutes corresponds to $x = 3.25$.
For math students: $y \approx 73\%$
For English students: $y \approx 86\%$
Since there is a strong relationship between the variables and both predictions are interpolations, these predictions are reliable.

21 1. **Formulate questions**
Possible questions:
- What is the relationship between a person's height and their stride length?
- How does a person's stride length change with their height?
- What are the stride lengths of people between 5 and 6 feet tall?

2. **Collect data using the questions above.**

   We can collect data by measuring a person's height in inches and the length of their stride in inches. The table shows an example sample of 30 students.

Height	64	59	65	70	66	63	68	60	62	65
Stride	29.4	28.1	28.2	32.1	29.4	28.2	29.1	28.5	27.9	29.6

Height	58	62	66	66	63	60	59	63	64	58
Stride	26.5	28.7	29.4	29.7	28.4	27.7	26.4	28.3	27.6	25.3

Height	61	60	57	63	67	69	61	57	67	60
Stride	28.4	28.6	25.3	28.7	29	30.6	27	27.2	30.5	25.6

3. **Create a data display using a scatterplot.**

   This scatterplot represents the sample data from the previous part. Since it shows an approximate linear relationship, a line of best fit has been drawn.

   The equation of the line of best fit is $y = 0.364x + 5.44$.

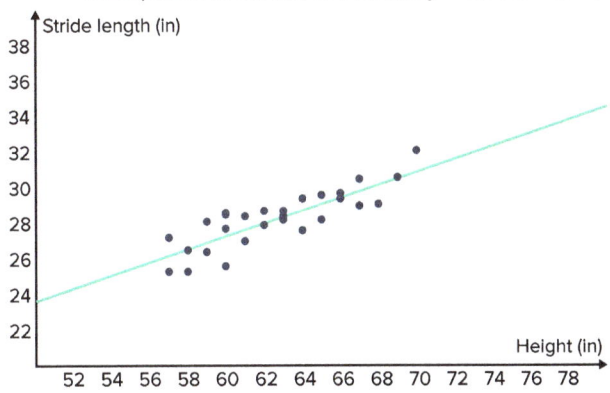

4. **Analyze and explain the results.**

   From the scatterplot, we can observe that there is a moderate, positive linear relationship between a person's height and their stride length. The relationship shows that as height increases, stride length tends to increase.

   This could lead us to formulate a new question like "How does the relationship between height and stride length compare between boys and girls?" or "What is the expected stride length of someone who is 6 feet tall?"

9.04 Quadratic regression

Subtopic overview

Lesson narrative

In this lesson, students will use their knowledge of graphs to determine if a graph is quadratic. Given a set of data points, students will graph the points to determine the type of equation needed. Students will find the quadratic regression equation when the graph is quadratic. This equation will be used to make predictions about other values not in the problem. By the end of this lesson, students will be able to find the quadratic regression and apply it to find additional values.

Learning objectives

Students: Page 546

> **After this lesson, you will be able to...**
> - determine if a table of values represents a quadratic model.
> - determine the equation of the curve of best fit given a table of values.
> - predict values using a quadratic model.

Key vocabulary

- bivariate data
- scatterplot
- domain constraint
- standard form (of a quadratic function)

Essential understanding

The relationship between the variables in a set of bivariate data reveals the type of function that best models the data.

Standards

This subtopic addresses the following Virginia Standards of Learning for Mathematics standards.

Mathematical process goals

MPG2 — Mathematical Communication

Teachers can foster mathematical communication by encouraging students to explain their reasoning when deciding the type of relationship between variables, calculating the curve of best fit, or evaluating the strength and weaknesses of a quadratic model. Students should be encouraged to articulate their understanding of the coefficients in a quadratic equation, the meaning of R^{2}, and the limitations of their models.

MPG4 — Mathematical Connections

Teachers can make mathematical connections by linking the concepts of scatterplots, linear regression, and quadratic regression with previous lessons, thereby helping students see the relevance and applicability of their prior knowledge. For instance, connecting the concept of quadratic regression to lessons on the standard form of a quadratic equation or the meaning of coefficients in this context.

MPG5 — Mathematical Representations

Teachers can incorporate mathematical representations into their lessons by having students use technology to create scatterplots and perform quadratic regression. Students can then write the equation of their quadratic function and use it to predict outcomes. They can also visually represent the curve of best fit and interpret the meaning of the coefficients in this context. Teachers should encourage students to make connections among different representations — such as the scatterplot (visual), the equation (symbolic), and the real-world context (contextual).

Content standards

A.ST.1 — The student will apply the data cycle (formulate questions; collect or acquire data; organize and represent data; and analyze data and communicate results) with a focus on representing bivariate data in scatterplots and determining the curve of best fit using linear and quadratic functions.

A.ST.1b — Determine what variables could be used to explain a given contextual problem or situation or answer investigative questions.

A.ST.1c — Determine an appropriate method to collect a representative sample, which could include a simple random sample, to answer an investigative question.

A.ST.1d — Given a table of ordered pairs or a scatterplot representing no more than 30 data points, use available technology to determine whether a linear or quadratic function would represent the relationship, and if so, determine the equation of the curve of best fit.

A.ST.1e — Use linear and quadratic regression methods available through technology to write a linear or quadratic function that represents the data where appropriate and describe the strengths and weaknesses of the model.

A.ST.1h — Analyze relationships between two quantitative variables revealed in a scatterplot.

A.ST.1i — Make conclusions based on the analysis of a set of bivariate data and communicate the results.

A.ST.1a — Formulate investigative questions that require the collection or acquisition of bivariate data.

Prior connections

8.PS.3 — The student will apply the data cycle (formulate questions; collect or acquire data; organize and represent data; and analyze data and communicate results) with a focus on scatterplots.

A.F.2 — The student will investigate, analyze, and compare characteristics of functions, including quadratic and exponential functions, and model quadratic and exponential relationships.

Future connections

A2.ST.2 — The student will apply the data cycle (formulate questions; collect or acquire data; organize and represent data; and analyze data and communicate results) with a focus on representing bivariate data in scatterplots and determining the curve of best fit using linear, quadratic, exponential, or a combination of these functions.

Lesson Preparation

Suggested review

Depending on your students' level of prior knowledge, consider revisiting the following lessons:

Algebra 1 — 7.03 Quadratic functions in vertex form
Algebra 1 — 7.04 Quadratic functions in standard form

Tools

You may find these tools helpful:
- Statistics calculator

Student lesson & teacher guide

Quadratic regression

Students are introduced to the idea of using quadratic models to represent nonlinear data. The lesson describes situations in which the different forms of a quadratic equation could be most efficient, based on the information given.

Students: Page 546

9.04 Quadratic regression

After this lesson, you will be able to...
- determine if a table of values represents a quadratic model.
- determine the equation of the curve of best fit given a table of values.
- predict values using a quadratic model.

Quadratic regression

Functions can be used to model real-world events and interpret data from those events. Data that measures or compares two characteristics of a population is known as **bivariate data**.

When analyzing data, we previously described the relationship between two variables as linear or nonlinear. In this lesson, we will focus on nonlinear relationships that can be modeled by a quadratic function.

Stronger and clearer each time
English language learner support

Provide students with the following scatterplot and quadratic model and ask, "What is the relationship between days and profit?" Have students individually write an explanation of the quadratic relationship shown.

After a few minutes, pair students to share their explanations and receive feedback. In these pairs, encourage students to ask their partners for further clarification of their response. They can ask questions such as:
- Why did/didn't you include an explanation of the strength of the relationship?
- Should the relationship be described as nonlinear or quadratic?
- Do we need to describe what happens to the y-values?

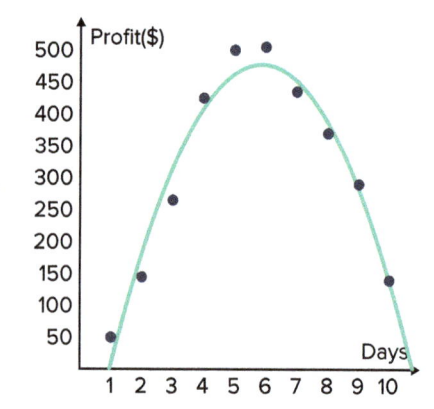

Then, mix pairs for further refinement of their explanations. Finally, students should be given time to individually refine their original explanations, incorporating feedback and new ideas. Encourage students to share their final explanations with the class.

Highlight good explanations or provide students with an example of a good explanation, such as, "There is a strong, quadratic relationship between days and profit. Between 1 and 6 days, the profit increases. After 6 days, the profit decreases."

1172 Mathspace   Virginia SOL Algebra 1 Teacher Edition
mathspace.co

🔍 Quadratic relationships are not the only type of nonlinear relationship
Address student misconceptions

In Algebra 1, students only focus on linear and quadratic relationships. However, this might create the misconception that quadratic relationships are the only type of nonlinear relationship between two variables.

Students may benefit from seeing examples of data that have other types of nonlinear relationships, like the ones shown:

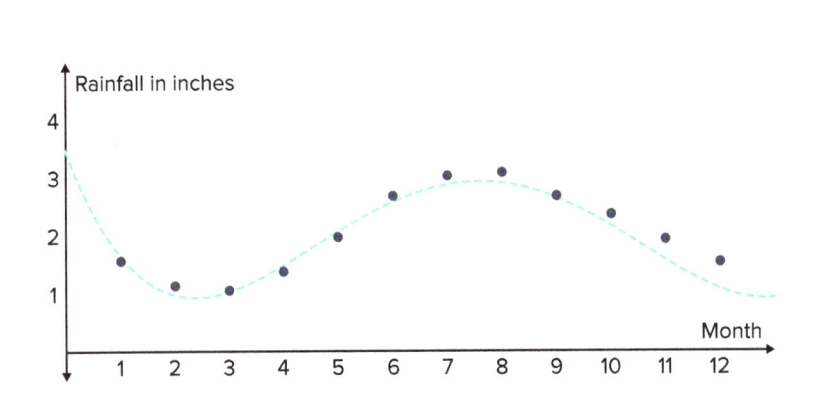

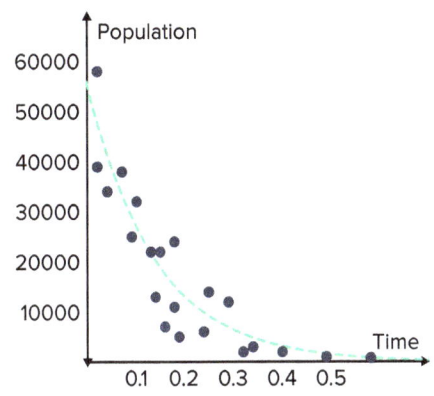

Exploration

Students: Page 546

Exploration

Each table shown represents a different set of data.

Table 1

x	0	0.2	0.4	0.6	0.8	1	1.2	1.4	1.6	1.8
y	13	7	4	3	1	0	2	3	6	9

Table 2

x	3	3.5	4	4.5	5	5.5	6	6.5	7	7.5	8
y	63	68	77	90	104	100	112	120	114	127	127

Table 3

x	0	1	2	3	4	5	6	7	8	9	10
y	63	65	61	59	58	59	54	55	53	52	50

Table 4

x	1	2	2.5	3	4	5	6.3	6.8	7.2	7.4	8
y	1.5	3	4.8	5	7.4	8	7	6	5.5	4	2

Without creating a scatterplot:

1. Does the data in Table 1 have a linear or quadratic relationship? Explain your answer.
2. Does the data in Table 2 have a linear or quadratic relationship? Explain your answer.
3. Does the data in Table 3 have a linear or quadratic relationship? Explain your answer.
4. Does the data in Table 4 have a linear or quadratic relationship? Explain your answer.

Suggested student grouping: small groups

In this exploration, students are examining four tables of data and looking at the relationship between x and y in each. Without creating a scatterplot, students will determine if the data represents a linear or quadratic relationship, explaining their reasoning.

Ideal student responses

These ideal responses may differ from other correct student responses. Less formal responses can be connected with the more precise mathematical language presented here.

1. **Does the data in Table 1 have a linear or quadratic relationship? Explain your answer.**
   The data in Table 1 seems to have a quadratic relationship. The y-values decrease, reach a minimum value, then increase, which is typical of a quadratic function.

2. **Does the data in Table 2 have a linear or quadratic relationship? Explain your answer.**
   The data in Table 2 seems to have a linear relationship because the y-values are only increasing for each half unit increase in x.

3. **Does the data in Table 3 have a linear or quadratic relationship? Explain your answer.**
   The data in Table 3 seems to have a linear relationship. The y-values are only decreasing for each unit increase in x.

4. **Does the data in Table 4 have a linear or quadratic relationship? Explain your answer.**
   The data in Table 4 seems to have a quadratic relationship. The y-values increase, reach a maximum value, then decrease, which is typical of a quadratic function.

Purposeful questions

- As the x-values increase, what happens to the y-values?
- Choose a y-value in the center of the table and compare it to the first and last y-values in the table. Does it appear that the values have only increased, only decreased, or have increased and decreased?

Possible misunderstandings

- Students might think that the y-values should change by the same amount for linear functions, or that the values should only increase/decrease. Remind them that real data is messy, and encourage them to instead consider the overall trend of the data.
- Students might not consider the entire domain of the data, instead only looking for what happens to the first few outputs. Emphasize the importance of considering the entire domain, as the y-values of quadratic functions will change direction at some point in the domain.

Students: Page 547

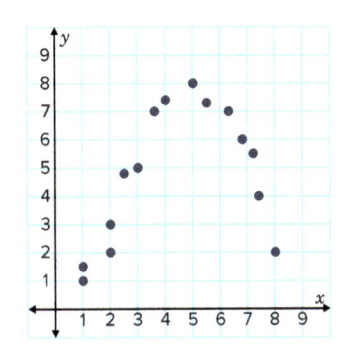

To more easily analyze a set of data and determine if there is a quadratic relationship between the variables, we often construct a **scatterplot**.

Data presents a quadratic relationship if it forms a symmetric curve or parabolic shape.

The quadratic curve of best fit that approximately models the data can be calculated using technology. Most calculators will write the model in **standard form (of a quadratic function)**, $y = ax^2 + bx + c$.

If points are more tightly clustered along the model, it represents a stronger relationship between the variables.

The curve of best fit can help us make predictions or conclusions about the data. If we are given an x-value, we can predict the y-value by substituting x into the equation and solving for y.

We can also use the graph of the model to approximate x and y-values.

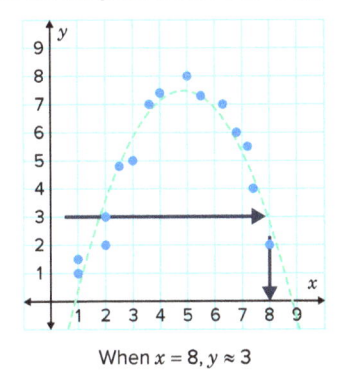

When $x = 8$, $y \approx 3$

When $y = 7$, $x \approx 4$ and 6

When anayzing the data, it is often helpful to interpret the x-intercepts or the vertex in context. For example, if the equation models a company's sales over time, the x-intercepts represent the times the company made no sales, and the vertex represents the time the highest amount of sales were made.

It is important to consider the context of the data when communicating results as the model may only be appropriate over a part of the domain.

> **Domain constraint**
>
> A limitation or restriction of the possible x-values, usually written as an equation, inequality, or in set-builder notation

Examples

The following support may be useful for the examples in this section.

> **Calculator steps for Desmos, TI graphing calculators, and Google Sheets**
> **Targeted instructional strategies**

The examples provide students with the steps to finding the line of best fit using the GeoGebra Statistics calculator. Steps for finding the line of best fit with other technologies are shown.

TI-83 or TI-84:

1. Select the STAT button.
2. Select EDIT.
3. Enter the x-values under L_1 in the table.
4. Enter the y-values under L_2 in the table.
5. Press the STAT button again.
6. Press the right arrow to select CALC at the top of the screen.
7. Select QuadReg.
8. Press these buttons in this order:
   - 2ND (blue button in the top left)
   - 1 (has L1 in blue above it)
   - , (the comma above 7)
   - 2ND
   - 2 (has L2 in blue above it)

   Your screen should show QuadReg(L₁, L₂)
9. Select ENTER.

Desmos:

1. Click the + in the top left and select the table.
2. Enter the x-values under x_1 in the table.
3. Enter the y-values under y_1 in the table.
4. If you do not see the points on the graph, click the magnifying glass with the plus sign at the bottom left of the table.
5. In row 2 below the table, enter the following formula: $y_1 \sim ax_1^2 + bx_1 + c$

These steps will produce the values of a, b and c. The value of a is the leading coefficient, the value of b is the coefficient of the middle term, and the value of c is the y-intercept.

Google Sheets:

1. Enter the data from the table into two rows or columns with labels
2. Highlight the data and navigate to "Insert" and click "Chart"
3. By default it should insert a scatterplot, but if not change the "Chart type" to "Scatter chart"
4. Under the Chart editor click on "Customize" and under "Horizontal axis" and "Vertical axis" set an appropriate view
5. Under the Chart editor click on "Customize" and under "Series" tick the box for "Trendline" and change the "Type" to "Polynomial" and "Label" to "Use Equation"

Notice that the equation is displayed by default to 3 significant figures, so the rounding may vary from a given solution.

Students: Page 548

Example 1

For each scatterplot, determine whether the variables have a linear relationship or a quadratic relationship. If there is a relationship, describe its strength.

a

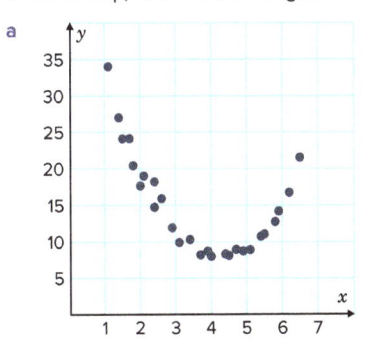

Create a strategy

A relationship between two variables exists if the points follow a similar trend. The points will roughly form a line if there is a linear relationship or a parabola if there is a quadratic relationship. To describe the strength of the relationship, we can analyze how tightly the data points are clustered or grouped together.

Apply the idea

As the x-values increase, the y-values decrease then increase, causing the points to form a U-shaped curve. This shows there is a quadratic relationship between the variables. Because the points are tightly clustered, the relationship is strong.

Purpose

Show students how to determine the type and strength of a relationship between variables from a scatterplot.

Students: Page 548

b

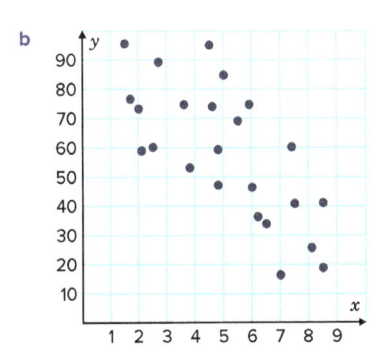

Apply the idea

As the x-values increase, the y-values decrease. This indicates there is a linear relationship between the variables. However, the points are not tightly clustered, so the relationship between the variables is moderate.

Reflect and check

Recall that we can describe a linear relationship as positive or negative. For this data set, the relationship is negative since one variable increases and the other decreases. This implies that the equation of the line of best fit would have a negative slope.

Purpose
Test students' understanding of how scatterplots can be used to identify and describe the strength of a relationship between variables.

Students: Page 549

c

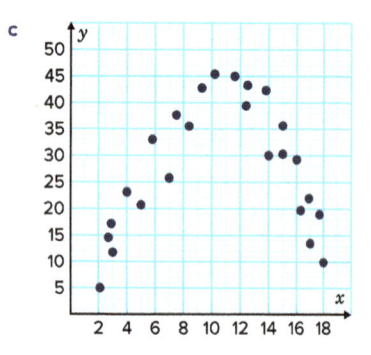

Apply the idea
A relationship between two variables exists if the points follow a similar trend. If the y-values increase and decrease over the domain, the relationship can be modeled by a quadratic function.

Reflect and check
As the x-values increase, the y-values increase then decrease, causing the points to form an upside down, U-shaped curve. This shows there is a quadratic relationship between the variables.

Because the points are not tightly clustered, the relationship is moderate.

Purpose
Test students' ability to identify quadratic relationships from scatterplots and assess the strength of the relationship.

Students: Page 549

Example 2

A conservationist tracks the population, y, of manatees that regularly visit a river over a number of years, x, (starting at zero). The data is displayed in the table:

x	0	1	2	3	4	5	6
y	65	61	58	60	66	74	90

a   Was the data most likely collected through measurement, observation, a survey or an experiment?

Create a strategy
Consider whether the population was measured (with a measurement tool such as a rule or protractor) or observed. Also consider whether anyone was surveyed or whether any variables were controlled.

Apply the idea
The population of manatees was not measured, and the conservationist did not survey anyone to collect the data. The information does not specify whether any other variables were controlled, so we can assume that an experiment was not used.

The data was most likely collected by observation.

Reflect and check
Many times, populations of species are tracked using tracking devices. It is possible that the manatees each have a tracking device, and a conservationist collects data from those devices each year.

Purpose
Show students how to deduce the method used to collect data based on the nature of the data and context given.

Students: Page 550

  b Determine if the manatee population over time has a quadratic relationship.

  Create a strategy
  Construct a scatterplot to visually determine if a linear or quadratic model is a better fit.

  Apply the idea
  After plotting the data on a graph, we get the following scatterplot:

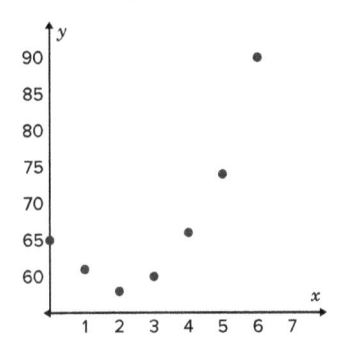

  There is a clear curve in the pattern of the data, so a quadratic function would better fit the data.

Purpose
Show students how to use graphical analysis to determine whether the relationship between two variables is quadratic.

Reflecting with students
Ask students to describe the strength of the quadratic relationship between the variables. Point out that although the relationship is strong, it is not perfectly quadratic. While it is possible for relationships to be perfectly quadratic, it is rare to see that in real-world data.

Students: Pages 550–551

  c Using technology, determine an appropriate equation to model the data set. Round all values to two decimal places.

  Create a strategy
  We can use technology to calculate the quadratic regression equation. Remember that a quadratic function is a polynomial of degree 2.
  To find the equation using technology, we can follow these steps:
  1. Enter the x-values and y-values in two separate columns.
  2. Highlight the data and select Two Variable Regression Analysis.
  3. Under the Regression Model drop down menu, choose Polynomial. The degree drop down menu defaults to 2, which is a quadratic function.

Apply the idea

1. Enter the x-values and y-values in two separate columns.

	A	B
1	0	65
2	1	61
3	2	58
4	3	60
5	4	66
6	5	74
7	6	90

2. Highlight the data and select Two Variable Regression Analysis.

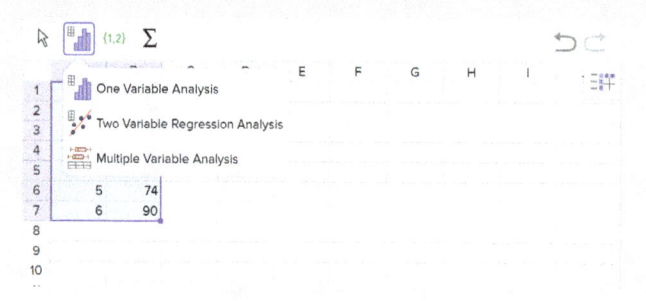

   - One Variable Analysis
   - Two Variable Regression Analysis
   - Multiple Variable Analysis

3. Under the Regression Model drop down menu, choose Polynomial. The degree drop down menu defaults to 2, which is a quadratic function.

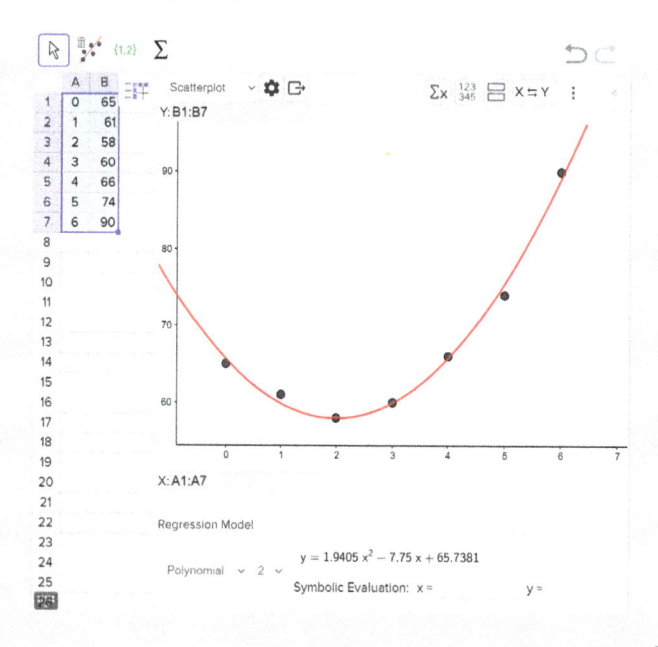

   Scatterplot
   Y: B1:B7
   X: A1:A7

   Regression Model
   Polynomial 2
   $y = 1.9405\,x^2 - 7.75\,x + 65.7381$
   Symbolic Evaluation: x =   y =

Rounding the values to two decimal places, we find the approximate curve of best fit is $y = 1.94x^2 - 7.75x + 65.74$.

Purpose

Show students how to use Algorithmic thinking to follow a set of step to perform regression analysis with technology to find an equation that best fits a set of data.

Students: Page 552

d Using the model in part (b), determine the population 10 years afer the numbers were first recorded.

Create a strategy

We can find the population, y, after 10 years by substituing $x = 10$ into the equation of the curve of best fit.

Apply the idea

$y = 1.94x^2 - 7.74x + 65.74$ State the equation

$y = 1.94(10)^2 - 7.74(10) + 65.74$ Substitute $x = 10$

$y = 182.34$ Evaluate

We can see that after 10 years, the population will have grown to about 182 manatees.

Reflect and check

Remember that the coefficients in the equation for the curve of best fit have been rounded. Rounding values reduces the accuracy of the prediction. If we had used technology to make this prediction, we would have gotten a slightly different answer.

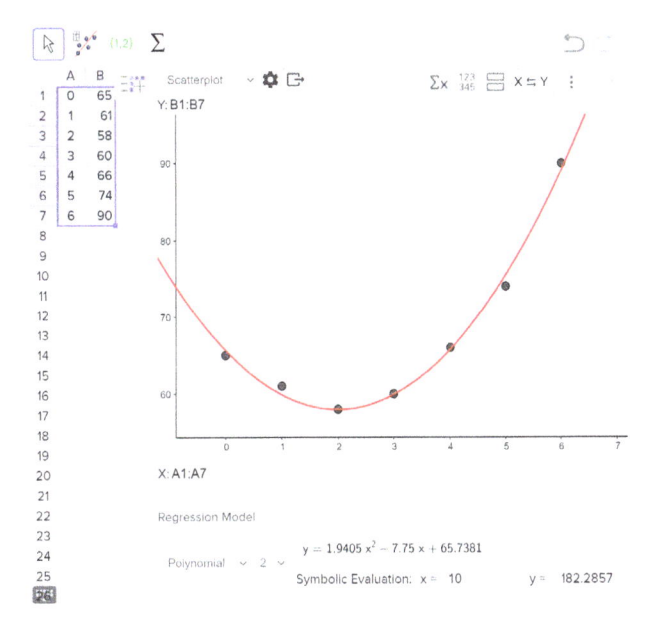

The calculator's answer is more accurate because it includes more decimal values in the coefficients and does not round them to only four place values. However, the differences between these values is small and does not change our final, rounded answer.

Purpose

Show students how to use a quadratic model to predict future values of a variable.

Expected mistakes

Students might not consider the context of the problem and state the population as a decimal value. Remind students that we cannot have part of a manatee, so we need to round to the nearest whole manatee.

Converting data to vertical tables
Student with disabilities support

use with Example 2

When working with regressions and curves of best fit, students may benefit from additional practice converting from ordered pairs to tabular data. Since most technology requires entering the data into columns, creating a vertical table can help them avoid entry mistakes.

For example, data sets given as a set of coordinate pairs or a horizontal table:
- $\{(-7.5, 82.1), (-6.9, 60.4), (-5.8, 45.2), (3.12, 21.5), (5.38, 53.7), (7.1, 99.4)\}$
-

x	−7.5	−6.9	−5.8	3.12	5.38	7.1
y	82.1	60.4	45.2	21.5	53.7	99.4

can be written as a table with columns instead:

x	y
−7.5	82.1
−6.9	60.4
−5.8	45.2
3.12	21.5
5.38	53.7
7.1	99.4

This allows students to enter the data into their calculators exactly as shown on their paper.

Students: Page 553

Example 3

Carlos is a goalie on the school soccer team. When he kicks a soccer ball dropped from his hands, he notices that the angle of trajectory for each kick is different. He also notices that there are times when the ball does not travel as far as other times. He wants to investigate this further using the data cycle.

a Formulate a statistical question that Carlos can use for his investigation.

Create a strategy

We can assume that Carlos is interested in determining the optimum angle at which he should kick a soccer ball dropped from his hands to achieve the maximum distance. There are many statistical questions we can ask, but we should focus the question around the purpose of the investigation.

Apply the idea

One possible statistical question is, "At what angle should Carlos kick the soccer ball for it to travel farthest?"

Reflect and check

Other possible questions are:
- How does the distance the ball travels change with the angle of trajectory?
- If Carlos kicked the ball and it traveled 130 feet, what was the ball's angle of trajectory?
- If the ball is kicked at the optimum angle, what is the farthest distance the ball will travel?

Purpose

Make students aware that they can formulate a statistical question based on a given scenario.

Students: Page 553

b Determine what variables could be used to answer the statistical question formulated in part (a).

Apply the idea

The two things that Carlos would need to collect data on to answer the question are the angle of trajectory for each kick and the distance the ball travels.

Reflect and check

The angle of trajectory can impact the distance the ball travels, but the distance the ball travels cannot impact the angle of trajectory. This means the angle of trajectory is the independent variable, and the distance the ball travels is the dependent variable.

Purpose

Show students how to identify the independent and dependent variables in a statistical investigation.

Students: Page 553

c Carlos records 10 kicks and analyzes them to determine the angle of trajectory and also the distance traveled. His results are recorded in the table:

Angle (degrees)	24	30	33	37	43	48	51	56	60	64
Distance (feet)	112	129	138	155	161	164	158	148	134	124

Determine if the data suggests a linear or quadratic relationship. Explain your answer.

Create a strategy

We can determine if the data suggests a linear or quadratic relationship by plotting the points on a coordinate plane and determining if the data resembles a line or a parabola.

To do this using technology, we can follow these steps:

1. Enter the x-values and y-values in two separate columns.
2. Highlight the data and select Two Variable Regression Analysis.

Apply the idea

1. Enter the x-values and y-values in two separate columns.

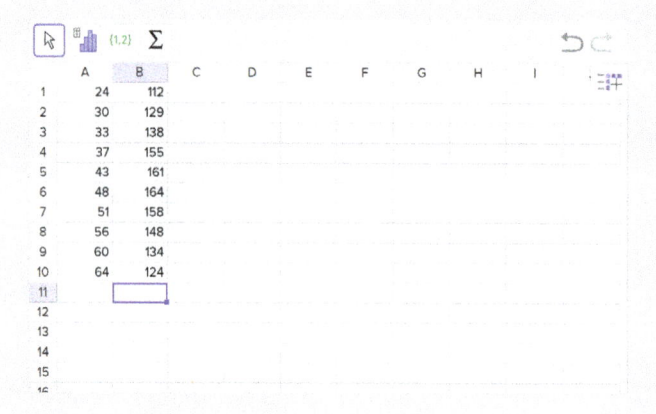

	A	B
1	24	112
2	30	129
3	33	138
4	37	155
5	43	161
6	48	164
7	51	158
8	56	148
9	60	134
10	64	124

2. Highlight the data and select Two Variable Regression Analysis.

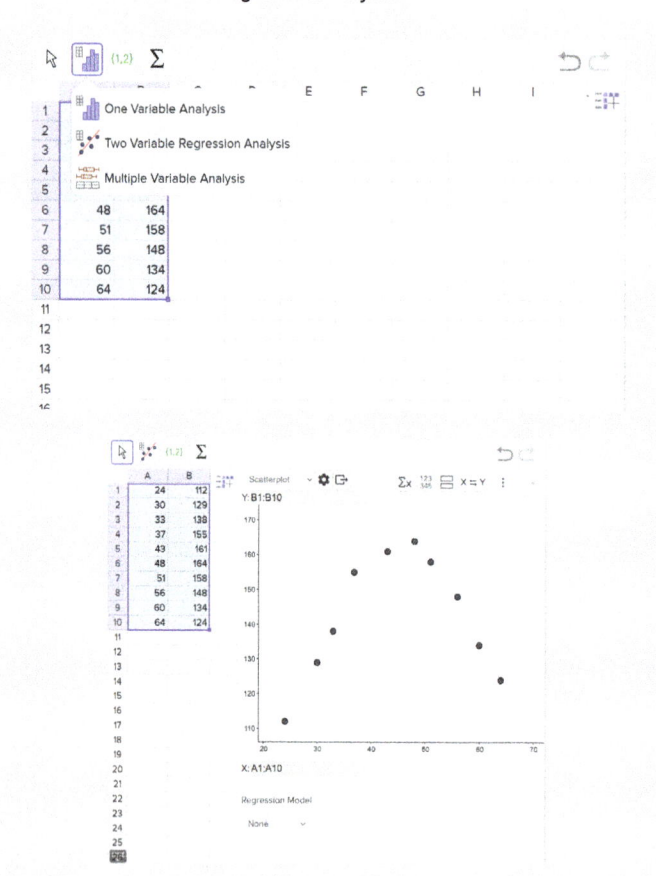

The data has a parabolic shape which is symmetric. The y-values begin increasing, then reach a maximum value, then decrease after. This means the data has a quadratic relationship.

Purpose

Challenge students to identify the type of relationship between two variables by examining a scatterplot.

Students: Page 555

d Using technology, determine an appropriate equation to model the data set.

Create a strategy

We can use technology to calculate the quadratic regression equation. Remember that a quadratic function is a polynomial of degree 2.

Apply the idea

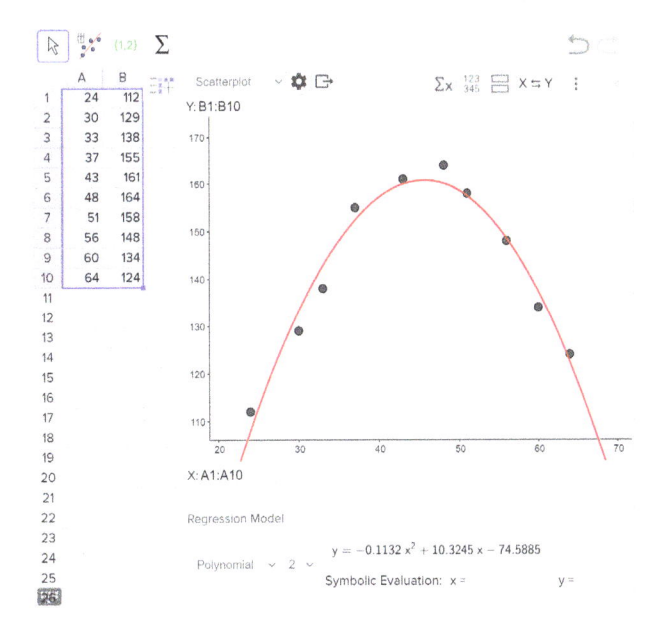

	A	B
1	24	112
2	30	129
3	33	138
4	37	155
5	43	161
6	48	164
7	51	158
8	56	148
9	60	134
10	64	124

Regression Model: Polynomial, 2

$y = -0.1132x^2 + 10.3245x - 74.5885$

$y = -0.1132x^2 + 10.3245x - 74.5885$, where x is the angle of trajectory (in degrees) and y is the distance traveled (in feet).

Reflect and check

If the instructions do not specify to round the coefficients, it is best to include all the digits given by the calculator. This increases the accuracy of the model and the predictions.

Purpose

Show students how to use technology to find a quadratic regression equation for a given set of data.

Reflecting with students

If students state the equation without describing what the variables in the equation represent, encourage them to describe what x and y represent. If they struggle to do this, ask them which variabls is the independent variable and which is the dependent variable. Then, they can connect the variables in the equation back to the contextual variables they identified in part (b).

Students: Pages 555–556

e   Draw a conclusion about the data by answering the statistical question from part (a).

Create a strategy

The statistical question from part (a) is, "At what angle should Carlos kick the soccer ball for it to travel farthest?" When considering the quadratic regression model, the largest y-value represents the farthest distance traveled by the ball.

The vertex is the maximum point of the parabola and represents the angle of trajectory (x) that Carlos should kick the ball for it to travel farthest (y). We can find this angle (x-value) using the equation $x = -\frac{b}{2a}$.

Apply the idea

The vertex represents the optimum angle to kick the ball to achieve the maximum distance traveled.

The equation of the curve of best fit is $y = -0.1132x^2 + 10.3245x - 74.5885$, where $a = -0.1132$ and $b = 10.3245$.

$x = -\dfrac{b}{2a}$ Equation of the x-value of the vertex

$x = -\dfrac{10.3245}{2(-0.1132)}$ Substitute $a = -0.1132$, $b = 10.3245$

$x \approx 45.6$ Simplify

For the ball to travel farthest, Carlos would need to kick the ball at an angle of about 45.6°.

Reflect and check

To find the farthest distance the ball is expected to travel, we can substitute $x = 45.6$ into the equation and solve for y.

$y = -0.1132x^2 + 10.3245x - 74.5885$ State the equation

$y = -0.1132(45.6)^2 + 10.3245(45.6) - 74.5885$ Substitute $x = 45.6$

$y \approx 160.8$ Simplify

The vertex occurs at about (45.6, 160.8) which means that the maximum distance of 160.8 feet is achieved by kicking the ball at an angle of 45.6°.

When looking at the raw data, we see that Carlos actually kicked the ball farther than this. One of his kicks traveled 164 feet when it was kicked at an angle of 48°. This implies that there are other factors that affect the distance the ball travels, such as the force Carlos uses to kick the ball.

Purpose

Challenge students to draw conclusions from a statistical investigation by using the results of a quadratic regression analysis.

Expected mistakes

If students do not consider the independent and dependent variables in this problem, they might think the x-values represent the distance the ball travels horizontally, and therefore think the rightmost x-intercept represents the farthest distance.

To help students understand the problem, draw a few examples of Carlos' kicks using the angle of trajectory and the distance the ball travels.

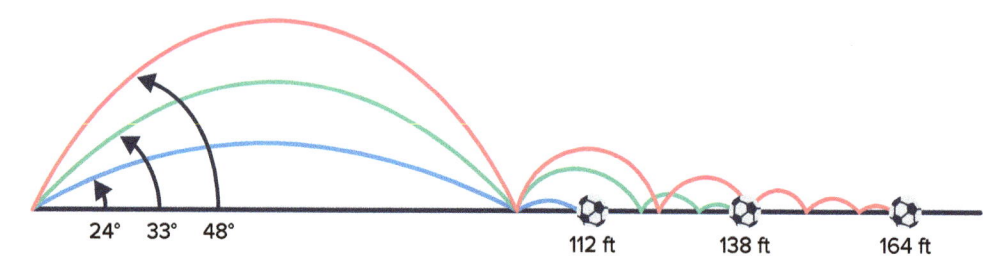

Then, help students see that the angles are the x-values of the points, and the distances are the y-values of the points. Then, point out that the balls that travel farther are the ones with higher y-values.

Scaffold the data cycle
Student with disabilities support

use with Example 3

To help students with disabilities navigate the data cycle in Carlos's soccer kick investigation, provide explicit support at each stage of the cycle. Start by introducing the data cycle visually—display the diagram of the data cycle in the classroom and refer to it frequently. Break down each step:

1. *Formulate questions*: Guide students in crafting the statistical question by providing sentence starters or question templates. For example, "What is the relationship between ☐ and ☐?" Encourage them to identify what Carlos wants to find out about his kicks.

2. *Collect or acquire data*: Model how data can be collected in this context. Use a sample data table similar to Carlos's and demonstrate how to record angles and distances. Provide students with a blank data table template to fill in.

3. *Organize and represent data*: Assist students in organizing the data by creating graphs or charts. Offer graph paper with labeled axes or use graphing software with preset parameters. Walk them through plotting the data points step-by-step.

4. *Analyze and communicate results*: Teach students how to interpret the graphs by identifying patterns or trends. Use guiding questions like, "What do you notice about the shape of the data?" Provide sentence frames to help them articulate their conclusions, such as "The data suggests a ☐ relationship because ☐."

By scaffolding each phase of the data cycle, you enable students to focus on one component at a time, reducing cognitive load. Incorporate periodic check-ins after each step to ensure understanding before moving on. This structured approach makes the statistical investigation more accessible and helps students build confidence in working with data.

Students: Page 556

> **Idea summary**
>
> Data presents a *quadratic relationship* if it forms a symmetric curve or parabolic shape.
>
> If points are more tightly clustered along the model, it represents a stronger relationship between the variables.

Practice

Students: Pages 556–561

What do you remember?

1 Masturah is using an app on her phone to learn French. She uses the app to learn and practice her French each day, and the following day, the app quizzes her on how much she remembered from the previous day.

    a Which statistical question would lead to data that can be represented by a scatterplot?

        A What is the average amount of time Masturah spends learning French each day?

        B What day of the week does Masturah practice French the longest?

        C How many times does Masturah practice French in a week?

        D What amount of time should Masturah practice French each day to maximize the amount she remembers for the following day?

    b Determine the variables that could be used to answer the statistical question.

2 Determine whether or not the following are quadratic functions:

    a $y = 4x^2 + 5$ **b** $y^2 = x^2 - 5x + 6$ **c** $y = x + 2$ **d** $y = (x - 5)(x - 8)$

    e $y = 10x + 9$ **f** $y = 4(x - 7)^2 + 8$

3 Determine whether or not the following graphs could represent a quadratic relation:

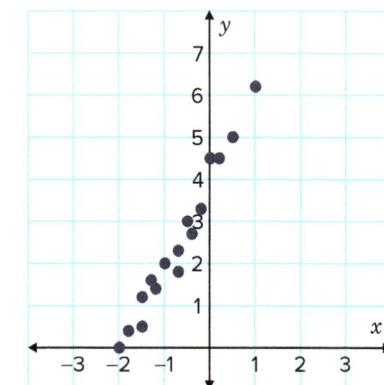

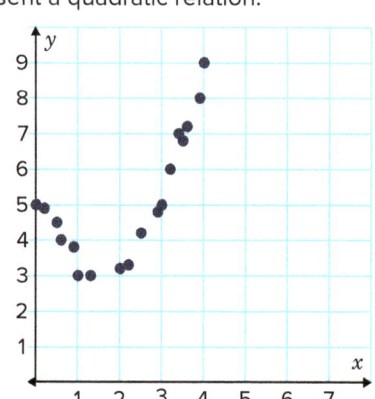

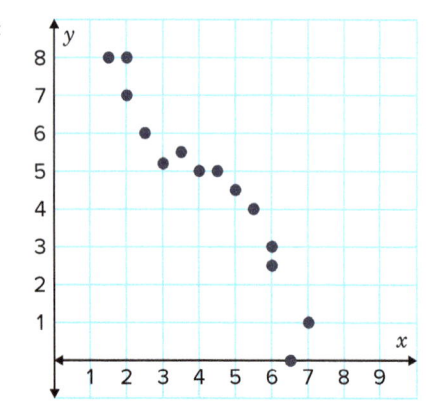

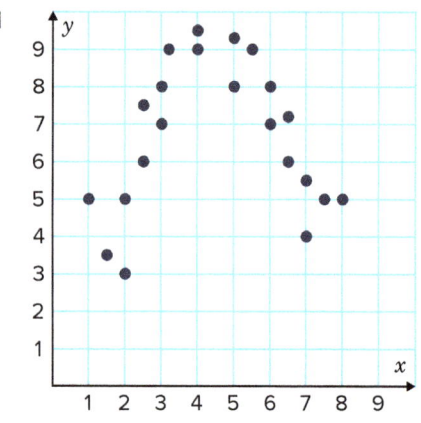

4 Determine whether or not the following tables could represent a quadratic function:

a
x	−2	−1	0	1	2
y	40	24	10	8	18

b
x	1	2	3	4	5
y	−6	−16	−24	−29	−26

c
x	12	13	14	15	16
y	6	2	1	0	−6

d
x	0	1	2	3	4
y	9	9	9	9	9

5 Consider the scatterplot:

Select a quadratic function that fits the data the best.

A $y = 0.3(x - 9)^2 + 1.2$
B $y = -0.03(x - 20)^2$
C $y = -0.003(x - 19)^2 + 1$
D $y = 3(x - 25)^2 + 0.8$

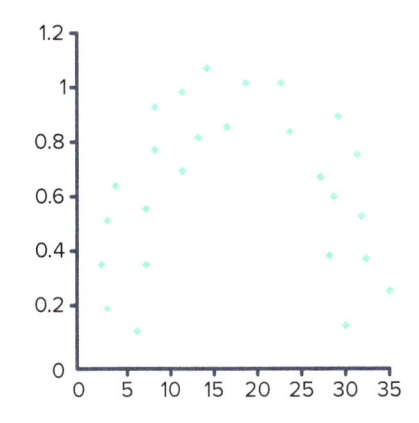

Let's practice

6 Consider the data set shown:

$\{(-8, 15.3), (-6, 25.1), (-4, 31.5), (-2, 35.2), (0, 37.8), (2, 35.6), (4, 30.1), (6, 21.7), (8, 10.4)\}$

Select the equation of the curve of best fit.

A $y = 0.38x^2 - 0.3x + 37$
B $y = 1.3x^2 + 0.27x + 37$
C $y = -1.3x^2 - 0.3 + 37.1$
D $y = -0.38x^2 - 0.27x + 37.1$

7 Calculate the quadratic curve of best fit for each data set:

a
x	−3	−2	−1	0	1	2	3
y	−18	−20	−26	−23	−24	−19	−14

b
x	0	1	2	3	4	5	6
y	17	10	3.5	2	0	2	5.5

c
x	−3	−2	−1	0	1	2	3
y	3.1	8.8	15.9	19.5	17.2	10.7	5.1

d
x	−7	−6	−5	−4	−3	−2	−1
y	−12	−4	1	6	5	−2	−9

8 Match each regression model to the set of data it fits best.

i $y = 0.4x^2 - 5.67x + 41$

ii $y = -0.22x^2 + 2.72x + 8.52$

iii $y = -0.32x^2 + 0.48x + 19.7$

iv $y = 0.22x^2 - 1.6x + 2.27$

a

x	0.9	1.8	6.2	7.3	8.5	7.6
y	1	0.1	1	2	4.7	2.9

b

x	13	7	2.8	16	0	19
y	35	20	27	52	42	75

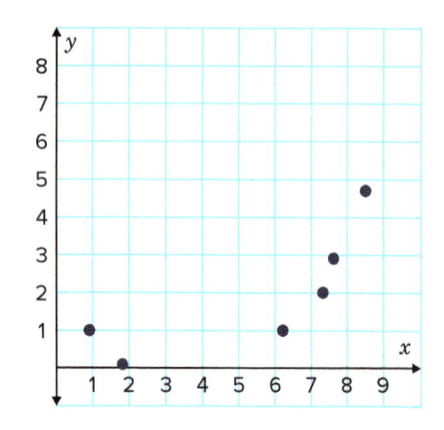

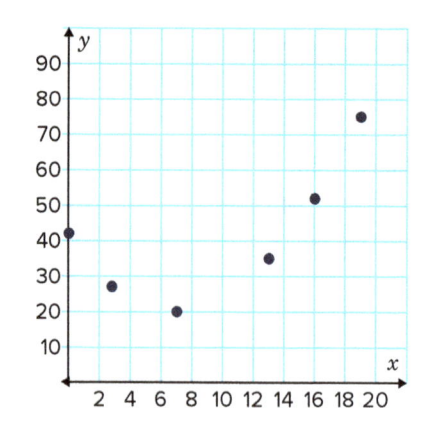

c

x	3.7	8.3	0.5	2.8	6.1	9
y	15	6	19	18	12	3

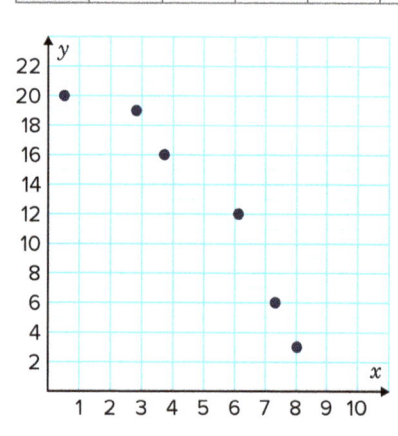

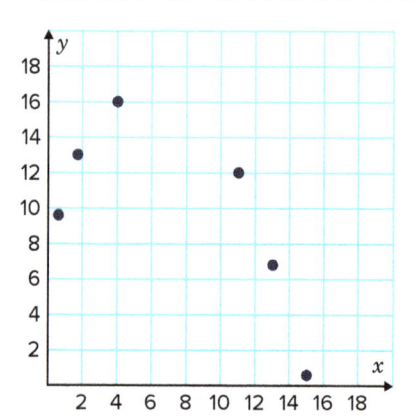

d

x	4	11	0.6	1.7	13	15
y	16	12	9.6	13	6.8	0.6

9 The creators of the online game Nomad's Horizon formulated the statistical question, "How has the number of people playing our game changed over time?" They collected data on the number of people, y, playing the game in the years after its release, x.

x	0	1	2	3	4	5	6
y	419	112	13	148	397	855	1602

a Describe the independent and dependent variables.

b Is the relationship between the variables linear or quadratic?

c Find the equation of the curve of best fit. Round all values to two decimal places.

10 The population, y, of a particular species of bird is tracked over a number of years, x, (starting at zero), with the data displayed in the table:

x	0	1	2	3	4	5	6	7	8	9	10	11	12
y	64	63	65	75	82	86	96	113	127	149	161	180	208

    a   Formulate a question that could be answered by the data.
    b   Which data collection method was most likely used?
          A   Measurement   B   Observation   C   Survey   D   Experiment
    c   Determine an appropriate equation to model the data. Round all values to two decimal places.
    d   Using the model in part (c), predict what the population will be 20 years after the species was first recorded.

11 Ten pregnant women at various weeks of pregnancy were asked at their medical appointments to rate their level of discomfort on a scale of 0 to 10 where 0 is completely comfortable and 10 is in severe discomfort or pain. The results are displayed in the given graph table.

Week	8	12	16	20	22	24	28	32	36	40
Discomfort Level	5	3	2	1	1	2	3	6	7	10

    a   Was the data collected through measurement, observation, a survey or an experiment?
    b   Determine if the data suggests a quadratic relationship. Explain your answer.
    c   Determine an appropriate equation to model the data set. Round all values to four decimal places.
    d   Interpret the meaning of the vertex of the model.
    e   Explain the significance of there being no x-intercepts.

12 Jiang is helping his mom to determine the best price for a dozen eggs for new contracts.
Some experimentation and research provided the results shown for different expected profits based on the price.

Price per dozen	1.3	1.35	1.4	1.45	1.5	1.55	1.6
Profit per month($)	3200	3230	3250	3210	3100	3000	2800

    a   Formulate a question that could be answered by the data.
    b   Determine if the data suggests a quadratic relationship. Explain your answer.
    c   Determine an appropriate equation to model the data set with integer coefficients.
    d   Determine the price which the model predicts would result in the highest profit.
    e   Interpret the y-intercept.
    f   Interpret the x-intercepts.

13 Researchers collected data to answer the statistical question, "How does the electricity consumption (in kilowatt-hours) of households change throughout the afternoon and evening hours?"

    a   Describe the variables that could be used to answer the statistical question.

    b   The data the researchers collected is shown in the table. Describe the relationship between the variables.

Hours after noon	0.5	2.5	3.5	4.5	5	6.5	7.5	1	8.5
Usage (kWh)	1.2	2.3	2.7	3	3.4	3	3.2	1.5	2.6

Hours after noon	2	9.5	10.5	0	11.5	1.5	3	4	12
Usage	1.9	2.3	2	1	1.4	1.7	2	2.2	0.9

Hours after noon	5	6	7	8	9	10	11	12
Usage (kWh)	2.8	3.5	3.8	3.6	3	2.5	1.8	1.2

    c   Calculate the regression model for this data.

    d   Answer the researchers' statstical question.

    e   Use the curve of best fit to predict a household's electricity consumption at 5 p.m.

    f   What time(s) of the day is the model's predictions most reliable?

       A   From noon to 2:30 p.m. and from 10:30 p.m. to midnight

       B   From 2:30 p.m. to 10:30 p.m.

       C   From noon to 7 p.m.

       D   From 7 p.m. to midnight

Let's extend our thinking

14 At the beginning of the school year, Shirah and her friends decided that they want to take a trip during spring break in March. They researched average prices of flights and found the following data.

Months until trip	7	6	5	4	3	2	1	0
Average price	$547	$540	$503	$461	$432	$450	$520	$637

    a   Formulate a question Shirah and her friends can use for their investigation.

    b   Calculate the regression model for this data.

    c   Determine when Shirah should purchase her flight and accommodation. Explain your reasoning.

15 The table shows the average weekly wage (in dollars) of an American resident from 1996 to 2006, where x is the number of years since 1996.

Year	1996	2000	2003	2006
x	0	4	7	10
$f(x)$	800	961.76	1065.86	1155.20

    a   Determine whether a linear or quadratic function would accurately model this situation. Explain your reasoning.

    b   Predict the average weekly wage of an American in 2010.

    c   Would the model from part (a) make sense for long term analysis? Explain your answer.

    d   Write a report about the changes in the average weekly wage of an American resident from 1996–2016.

16 The populations of U.S. cities are constantly changing. Some cities see large increases in population, while others face large decreases in population size.

- a Formulate a question about the population of Pittsburgh, Pennsylvania that would require the collection of bivariate data.
- b Describe the variables that could be used to answer the question from part (a).
- c Collect the census data on the population of Pittsburgh, Pennsylvania from 1870 to 2000.
- d Use technology to create a scatterplot and describe the form or shape of the data.
- e Use technology to find an appropriate equation to model the data set.
- f Draw a conclusion about the data by answering the question formulated in part (a).
- g Could the model from part (e) be used to make reasonable predictions after 2000? Explain your answer.

Answers

9.04 Quadratic regression

What do you remember?

1. a D
   b The independent variable is the amount of time Masturah practices French daily, and the dependent variable is the amount she remembers the following day.

2. a Yes b No c No d Yes
   e No   f Yes

3. a No   b Yes c No d Yes

4. a Yes b Yes c No d No

5. C

Let's practice

6. C

7. a $y = 0.976x^2 + 0.571x - 24.5$
   b $y = 1.12x^2 - 8.64x + 17.1$
   c $y = -1.62x^2 + 0.396x + 18$
   d $y = -1.75x^2 - 13.4x - 20.7$

8. a iv: $y = 0.22x^2 - 1.6x + 2.27$
   b i: $y = 0.4x^2 - 5.67x + 41$
   c iii: $y = -0.32x^2 + 0.48x + 19.7$
   d ii: $y = -0.22x^2 + 2.72x + 8.52$

9. a The independent variable is the years after the game's release, and the dependent variable is the number of people playing the game.
   b Quadratic
   c $y = 98.61^2 - 398.12x + 419$

10. a Many possible questions, for example, "How has the population of this species of bird changed over time?"
    b B
    c $y = 0.98x^2 + 0.14x + 63.02$
    d 458 birds

11. a Survey
    b Yes, a quadratic model is appropriate because when drawn on a graph it has a parabolic shape which is symmetric.
    c $y = 0.0223x^2 - 0.8950x + 10.5078$, where x is the number of weeks and y is level of discomfort
    d The vertex is a minimum and occurs at about (20.07, 1.53) which means that women are generally the most comfortable around 20 weeks and are fairly comfortable then.
    e This means that there is no point in pregnancy where these women felt completely comfortable.

12. a Many possible questions, for example, "What price of eggs will yield the highest profit?"
    b Yes, a quadratic model is appropriate because when drawn on a graph, it has a parabolic shape which is symmetric.
    c $y = -9000x^2 + 24807x - 13845$, where x is the price of eggs and y is the profit.

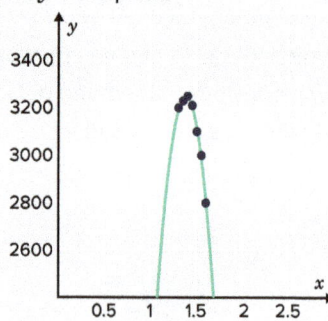

    d The vertex is a maximum and occurs at about (1.378, 3249) which means that the model predicts $1.38 to be the price that would result in the highest profit.
    e If they were to give their eggs away for free (a price of $0, then they would lose $13 845 per month with the cost of the hens.
    f The x-intercepts are the two prices that will result in breaking even, so the cost of the hens is equal to the amount of money earned by selling the eggs. This will occur at the prices of $0.78 and $1.98.

13. a The independent variable is the time of day between noon and midnight, and the dependent variable is the electricity consumption in kilowatt-hours.
    b By creating a scatterplot, we can see that their is a quadratic relationship between the variables.

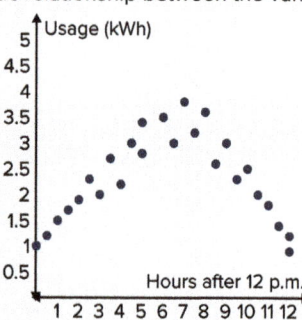

    c $y = -0.064x^2 + 0.8072x + 0.6719$ where x is the hours after 12 p.m. and y is the electricity consumption in kilowatt-hours
    d The electricity consumption of households increases from noon to about 7 p.m., then it decreases from 7 p.m. to midnight.
    e The approximate electricty consumption of a household at 5 p.m. ($x = 5$) is 3.1 kWh.
    f A

Let's extend our thinking

14 a Many possible answers, for example, "In what month will the price of flights be lowest?"

b If x is defined as the number of the month with the current month being $x = 0$, next month is $x = 1$, etc., then the month of the trip is month 7. An example of a scatterplot using this definition is shown:

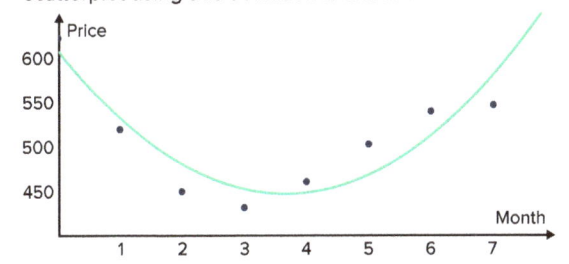

A quadratic model can be used to analyze the data. Using technology to find the quadratic regression function for the data gives $f(x) = 12.05x^2 - 88.40x + 609.83$ where $f(x)$ represents the price of the flight.

b Example answer: Shirah should purchase her flight between the middle of November and beginning of December. According to the model, flights are cheapest in the middle of November. Based on past data, flights are cheapest at the beginning of Decemeber. Regardless, flights are the cheapest within that range of dates compared to the rest of the year.

15 a When graphed, the data values appear as shown:

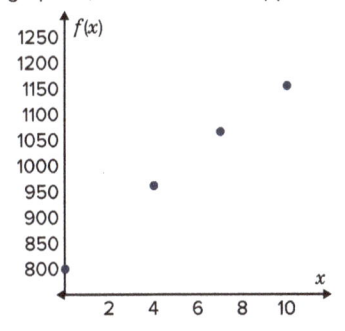

A quadratic model fits the data best because the increase in average weekly wage is decreasing over time, and the curve slopes upward more steeply for smaller values of x. Using technology to determine a regression model, a quadratic function would model the data perfectly.

b Example of a quadratic regression model:
$f(x) = -0.82x^2 + 43.72x + 800$
Using the quadratic model: $1 251.36

c If the long term implications are assessed, a linear model would be more accurate because wages will only increase. It would not make sense for wages to eventually decrease, as a quadratic model suggests. Using technology to determine a regression model, a linear function could model relatively well.
Example of a linear regression model: $f(x) = 36x + 809$

d From 1996–2016, weekly wages of an American resident have increased by almost $546.40
Weekly wages increased by an average of $35.52 each year from 1996–2006, but only increased by an average of $19.12 each year from 2006–2016.
This study only analyzed how weekly wages increased from 1996–2016. No research was conducted on why the weekly wages were increasing more each year before 2006.

16 a Many possible questions, for example, "How has Pittsburgh's population changed over time?"

b Answers will vary based on question from part (a). Using the example, "How has Pittsburgh's population changed over time?":
The independent variable is the time in years, and the dependent variable is the population.

c

Census	1	2	3	4	5	6	7
Year	1870	1880	1890	1900	1910	1920	1930
Population (in thousands)	86.1	156.4	238.6	321.6	533.9	588.3	669.8

Census	8	9	10	11	12	13	14
Year	1940	1950	1960	1970	1980	1990	2000
Population (in thousands)	671.7	676.8	604.3	520.1	424	369.9	334.6

d Let x represent the census row of the table, where the 1870 census is represented by $x = 1$, the 1880 census is $x = 2$, etc. Let y represent the population in thousands.

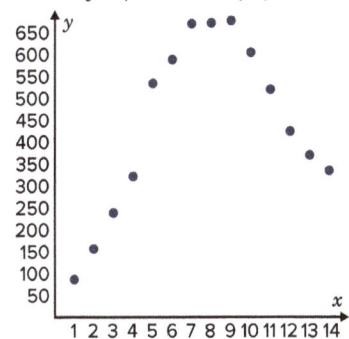

The data has a quadratic relationship because it has a parabolic shape.

e $y = -11.3212x^2 + 190.162x - 162.85$

f Answers will vary based on question from part (a). Using the example, "How has Pittsburgh's population changed over time?":
Pittsburgh's population increased at a slower and slower rate from 1870 (when $x = 1$) to 1950 (when $x = 9$), then decreased at an increasing rate from 1950 to 2000 (when $x = 14$).

g No, it cannot be used to make reasonable predictions after 2000. According to the model, Pittsburgh's population will continue decreasing, and there will be no one living there by 2020. According the actual data, Pittsburgh's population was about 305 400 in 2010 and about 302 800 in 2020. This shows that the model does not follow the trend in the actual data after 2020.

9.05 Analyze bivariate data

Subtopic overview

Lesson narrative

In this lesson, students will use their knowledge of regression to determine the model needed given a set of data. Given a set of data points, students will graph the points to determine the type of equation needed. Students will find the appropriate regression model depending if it is linear or quadratic. Students will interpret the correlation coefficient or coefficient of determination to determine if the model represents a good fit of the data. By the end of the lesson, students will be able to determine the appropriate regression model, calculate the regression model for the data set, draw conclusions about the bivariate data, and use the correlation coefficient or coefficient of determination to evaluate if the model is a good fit.

Learning objectives

Students: Page 562

After this lesson, you will be able to...
- analyze relationships of variables given a set of bivariate data.
- make conclusions given a set of bivariate data.

Key vocabulary

- bivariate data
- regression equation
- linear model
- scatterplot
- quadratic model

Essential understanding

The relationship between the variables in a set of bivariate data reveals the type of function that best models the data.

Standards

This subtopic addresses the following Virginia Standards of Learning for Mathematics standards.

Mathematical process goals

MPG1 — Mathematical Problem Solving

Teachers can integrate this goal into their instruction by having students solve real-world problems where they determine which model, linear or quadratic, best represents the relationship between two variables. Through these problems, students can apply mathematical concepts and skills and the relationships among them to solve problem situations of varying complexities. This can be especially effective with the use of technology, such as graphing calculators or software, to perform both linear and quadratic regression on the same set of data and compare the results.

MPG2 — Mathematical Communication

To incorporate this goal, teachers can emphasize the importance of communicating the results of the analysis, including a clear explanation of the chosen model and the reasoning behind the choice. Teachers can encourage students to use the language of mathematics, including graphs, equations, and descriptive language, to effectively communicate their results.

MPG4 — Mathematical Connections

To incorporate this goal, teachers can build on students' prior knowledge of scatterplots, linear regression, and quadratic regression from previous lessons. By making connections between these previous concepts and the current lesson on analyzing bivariate data, students can see mathematics as an integrated field of study. Real-world examples can be used to reinforce the relevance of these mathematical connections.

MPG5 — Mathematical Representations

Teachers can integrate this goal into their instruction by encouraging students to represent and describe mathematical ideas, generalizations, and relationships using a variety of methods in the context of analyzing bivariate data. This can include physical, visual, symbolic, verbal, and contextual representations. For example, students could use scatterplots to visually represent data, equations for symbolic representation, and written explanations for verbal representation.

Content standards

A.ST.1 — The student will apply the data cycle (formulate questions; collect or acquire data; organize and represent data; and analyze data and communicate results) with a focus on representing bivariate data in scatterplots and determining the curve of best fit using linear and quadratic functions.

A.ST.1a — Formulate investigative questions that require the collection or acquisition of bivariate data.

A.ST.1b — Determine what variables could be used to explain a given contextual problem or situation or answer investigative questions.

A.ST.1c — Determine an appropriate method to collect a representative sample, which could include a simple random sample, to answer an investigative question.

A.ST.1d — Given a table of ordered pairs or a scatterplot representing no more than 30 data points, use available technology to determine whether a linear or quadratic function would represent the relationship, and if so, determine the equation of the curve of best fit.

A.ST.1e — Use linear and quadratic regression methods available through technology to write a linear or quadratic function that represents the data where appropriate and describe the strengths and weaknesses of the model.

A.ST.1f — Use a linear model to predict outcomes and evaluate the strength and validity of these predictions, including through the use of technology.

A.ST.1g — Investigate and explain the meaning of the rate of change (slope) and y-intercept (constant term) of a linear model in context.

A.ST.1h — Analyze relationships between two quantitative variables revealed in a scatterplot.

A.ST.1i — Make conclusions based on the analysis of a set of bivariate data and communicate the results.

Prior connections

8.PS.3 — The student will apply the data cycle (formulate questions; collect or acquire data; organize and represent data; and analyze data and communicate results) with a focus on scatterplots.

A.F.1 — The student will investigate, analyze, and compare linear functions algebraically and graphically, and model linear relationships.

A.F.2 — The student will investigate, analyze, and compare characteristics of functions, including quadratic and exponential functions, and model quadratic and exponential relationships.

Future connections

A2.ST.2 — The student will apply the data cycle (formulate questions; collect or acquire data; organize and represent data; and analyze data and communicate results) with a focus on representing bivariate data in scatterplots and determining the curve of best fit using linear, quadratic, exponential, or a combination of these functions.

Lesson Preparation

Suggested review

Depending on your students' level of prior knowledge, consider revisiting the following lessons:

> **Algebra 1** — 9.03 Linear regression
> **Algebra 1** — 9.04 Quadratic regression

Tools

You may find these tools helpful:
- Graphing calculator
- Statistics calculator

Student lesson & teacher guide

Analyze bivariate data

Students will learn about analyzing bivariate data using scatterplots and mathematical models. They will use technology to perform linear and quadratic regression on data sets, comparing linear and quadratic models to determine the best fit. They will also learn the importance of visual inspection and context in determining the best model.

Students start with an exploration in which they determine the appropriate function for the given data.

Students: Page 562

9.05 Analyze bivariate data

After this lesson, you will be able to...
- analyze relationships of variables given a set of bivariate data.
- make conclusions given a set of bivariate data.

Analyze bivariate data

The process of analyzing **bivariate data** involves a two-step process. First, we plot the data on a **scatterplot**. This allows us to visually inspect the relationship between the two variables. Then, we use mathematical models to describe this relationship. Two common models that we have used are the **linear regression model** and the **quadratic regression model**.

Reflection questions for the data cycle
Targeted instructional strategies

Provide students with the following reflection prompts to use as they work through the full data cycle:
- Is my goal to determine the potential relationship between these two variables?
- Does my statistical question require the collection of data?
- What is the context of the data to be collected?
- What variables could represent the context?
- What is an appropriate amount of data?
- Will this data answer my statstical question?
- Is there a relationship between the variables? If so, what type of relationship?
- Is my goal to make predictions about these variables?
- Does a line (or curve) of best fit help me make predictions about this data?
- What behavior should the data have to be consistent with this model?
- What conclusions can and cannot be drawn from the data?

These questions can act as a guide as students formulate questions, collect or acquire data, organize and represent data, analyze data and communicate results of statistical investigations.

Discussion supports
English language learner support

The following sentence frames can provide support for students who need help describing relationships between variables:
- The relationship is (positive/negative) and linear because (dependent variable) (increases/decreases) as (independent variable) increases.
- The relationship is quadratic because (dependent variable) (increases then decreases/decreases then increases) as (independent variable) increases.
- The relationship is nonlinear because (dependent variable) (increases at an increasing rate/decreases at a descreasing rate/increases and decreases more than once/etc.) as (independent variable) increases.
- The relationship is (strong/moderate/weak) because the points (are/are somewhat/are not) tightly clustered around the (line/curve).

Provide examples of scatterplots for comparison
Student with disabilities support

Provide students with several examples of various scatterplots to help them distinguish between situations where a linear, quadratic, or nonlinear regression model should be used. Discuss how they can use the shape of the data to identify the function that best models the relationship.

Students can compare these examples to the scatterplots they create throughout the topic. Examples of scatterplots with varying form and strength are shown:

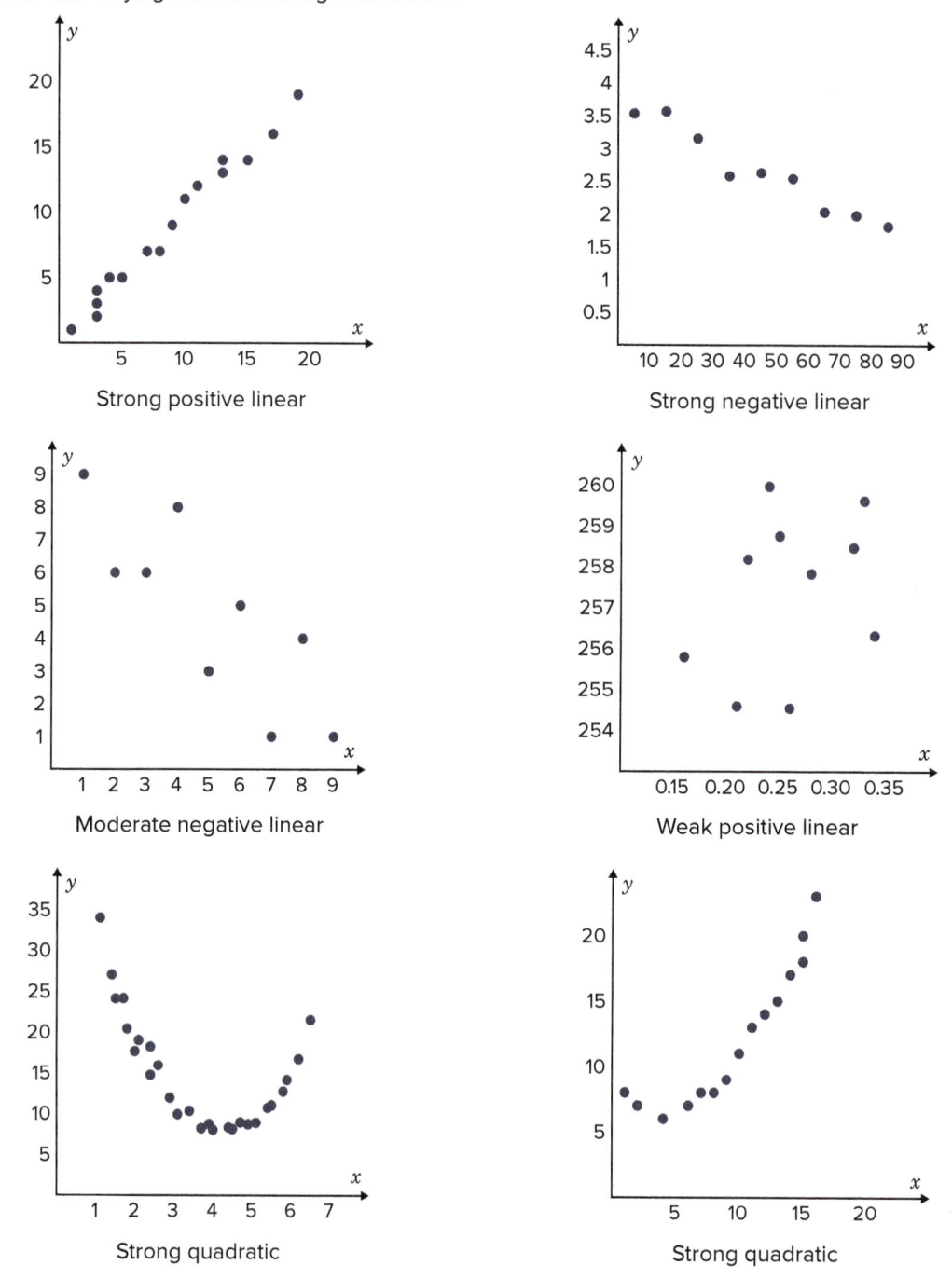

Strong positive linear

Strong negative linear

Moderate negative linear

Weak positive linear

Strong quadratic

Strong quadratic

Moderate quadratic

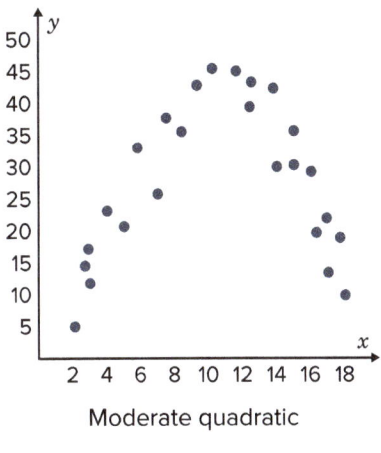

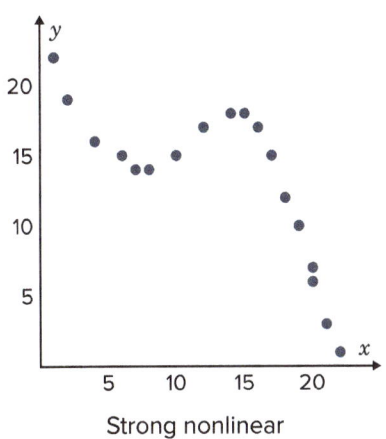

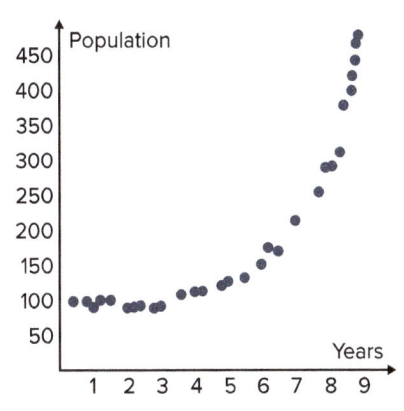

Strong nonlinear relationship

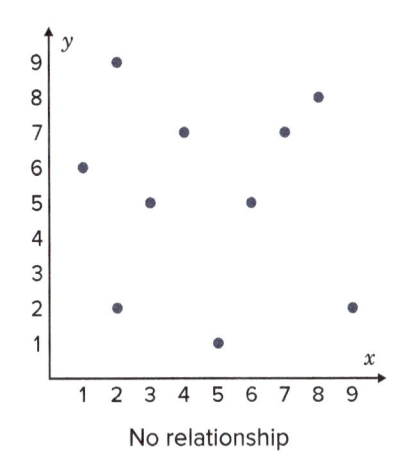

Strong nonlinear

No relationship

Exploration

Students: Page 562

> **Interactive exploration**
> Explore online to answer the question
> mathspace.co

Use the interactive exploration in 9.05 to answer this question.

1. Which function fits the data better? How do you know?

Suggested student grouping: In pairs
Students manipulate a line and a curve to identify which model best fits a given set of data. The purpose of the exploration is to provide students with an opportunity to describe the trend of quadratic data and to justify why a quadratic model is better than a linear model.

Ideal student responses

These ideal responses may differ from other correct student responses. Less formal responses can be connected with the more precise mathematical language presented here.

1. **Which function fits the data better? How do you know?**
   The quadratic function fits the data better because the curved line closely follows the trend, with more points clustered near the curve compared to a straight line.

Purposeful questions

- Which model best represents all the data values?
- What model would make the most reliable predictions?
- Why do you think your curve fits the data best?

Possible misunderstandings

- Students might not realize that they can drag the curves to fit them to the data. Encourage them to move the points with the blue circles to model the curves to the data.
- Students might struggle to explain why the function they chose best fits the data. Remind them to consider things like the trend or clustering of the data.

Following the exploration, students are shown a set of data with a line and a curve of best fit. The lesson explains that the quadratic curve is a better fit because it better models the trend of all the data values in the set.

Students: Pages 562–563

To determine the curve of best fit for a set of bivariate data, we can use technology such as graphing calculators or software. These tools allow us to perform both linear and quadratic regression on the same set of data and compare the results.

To decide which curve best models the data, we can visually assess whether the curves follow the trend in the data and how close the points are to each curve. We can also use the context to determine if a model is a good fit.

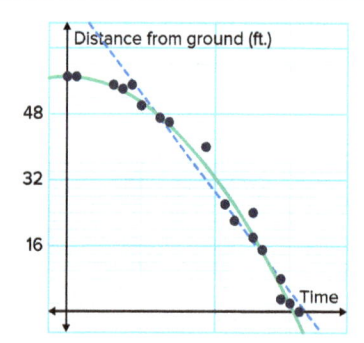

In the models shown, we can see the data points more closely follow the quadratic curve. Especially upon inspection of x-values closer to 0, the quadratic model more closely aligns with the data in the scatterplot. A better model will have data that is more tightly clustered along the curve.

Linear model	Quadratic model
A type of relationship between two variables that can be expressed as a straight line on a graph. It is described by the equation $y = mx + b$, where m is the slope and b is the y-intercept.	A type of relationship between two variables that can be expressed as a curve on a graph. It is described by the equation $y = ax^2 + bx + c$, where a, b, and c are constants.

Examples

Students: Page 563

Example 1

A ball is dropped off of a building that is 25 feet high. The table below shows its distance from the ground over time.

Time since being thrown (seconds)	0	1	2	3	4	5	5.5	6
Distance from ground (feet)	25	24.5	23	20.4	17.1	11.5	6.5	1

a Describe the relationship between the time since the ball was dropped and its distance from the ground. Is it quadratic or linear?

Create a strategy

Construct a scatterplot to get a visual of the data.

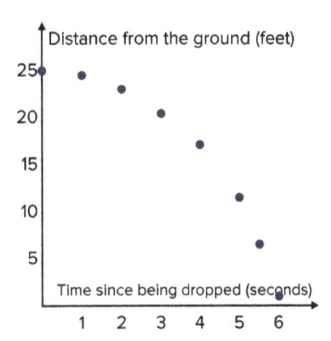

Then consider the form, strength, and direction.

Apply the idea

The data appears to fit a strong quadratic model.

Purpose

Check students' understanding of scatterplot models and how they can be used to describe the relationship between two variables. This question also tests their understanding of the difference between linear and quadratic associations.

Expected mistakes

Students may misinterpret the scatterplot and assume the association is linear. Inspecting behavior near the endpoints of the graph can help them identify patterns that may indicate a quadratic association.

Students: Pages 563–564

b Use technology to create a model and graph the model alongside a scatterplot of the data.

Create a strategy

We can use technology to calculate the quadratic regression equation. Remember that a quadratic function is a polynomial of degree 2.

To find the equation using technology, we can follow these steps:

1. Enter the x-values and y-values in two separate columns.
2. Highlight the data and select Two Variable Regression Analysis.
3. Under the Regression Model drop down menu, choose Polynomial. The degree drop down menu defaults to 2, which is a quadratic function.

Apply the idea

1. Enter the x-values and y-values in two separate columns.

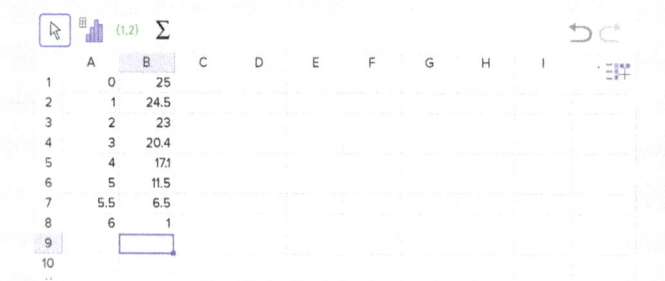

	A	B
1	0	25
2	1	24.5
3	2	23
4	3	20.4
5	4	17.1
6	5	11.5
7	5.5	6.5
8	6	1

2. Highlight the data and select Two Variable Regression Analysis.

   - One Variable Analysis
   - Two Variable Regression Analysis
   - Multiple Variable Analysis

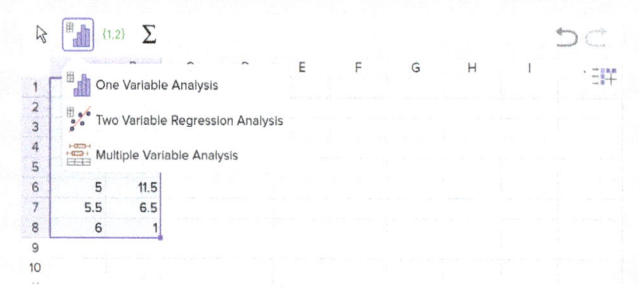

3. Under the Regression Model drop down menu, choose Polynomial. The degree drop down menu defaults to 2, which is a quadratic function.

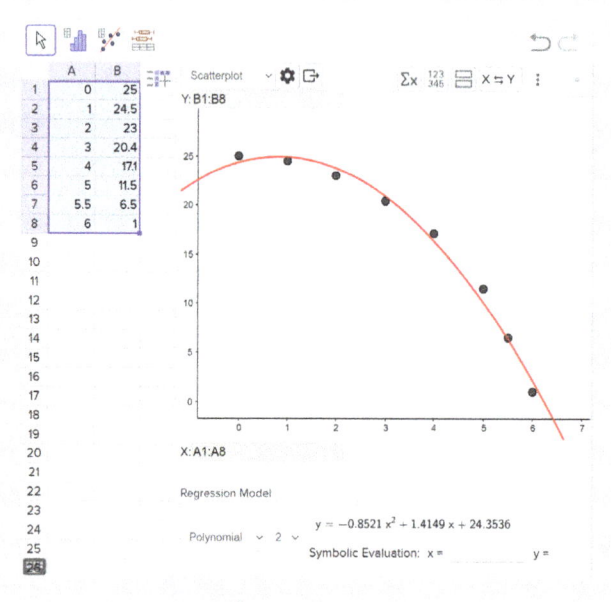

   Regression Model: Polynomial, 2

   $y = -0.8521x^2 + 1.4149x + 24.3536$

The equation of the curve of best fit is $y = -0.8521x^2 + 1.4149x + 24.3536$.

Purpose

Check if students can create and graph a regression model.

Reflecting with students

Encourage advanced learners or all students to analyze the differences between the quadratic model they've created and the actual data points. Specifically, prompt them to investigate why the model predicts a maximum height of approximately 24.94 feet at around 0.83 seconds, even though the ball was dropped from 25 feet at 0 seconds.

Engage them in a discussion about the limitations of regression models and how the method of least squares aims to minimize the overall error but might not perfectly fit critical points in the data, such as the initial conditions.

Students: Page 565

c Based off your model, when would you predict the ball would hit the ground?

Create a strategy

Looking at the graph, the ball would hit the ground when the distance from the groud is zero feet. Follow the pattern of the scatterplot or look at the model created using technology and predict when that would be. Alternatively, we can verify our solution by finding the x-intercept for our regression model.

Apply the idea

Looking at the model made with technology, the ball would hit the ground after approximately 6.25 seconds, which is the x-intercept when the distance from the ground is 0 feet.

Reflect and check

Remember, that this prediction is just an educated guess based on our model, and your answer may differ slightly based on the model you chose. According to this one, a more precise answer is about 6.24 seconds.

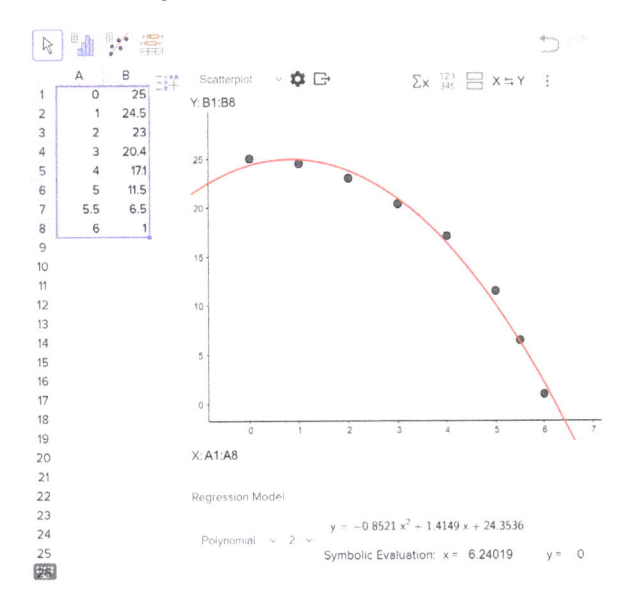

	A	B
1	0	25
2	1	24.5
3	2	23
4	3	20.4
5	4	17.1
6	5	11.5
7	5.5	6.5
8	6	1

Regression Model

$y = -0.8521\,x^2 + 1.4149\,x + 24.3536$

Polynomial 2

Symbolic Evaluation: $x = 6.24019$ $y = 0$

Purpose

Ensure students can use their model to make predictions about the data.

Reflecting with students

Encourage students to think of alternate ways to solve this problem. Students also could have found the x-intercepts directly from the regression equation which would result in an answer of 6.24 seconds which is very close to our visual estimate.

Students: Pages 565–566

> **Example 2**
>
> Ronaldo is looking to rent a two-bedroom apartment. He wants something that is spacious, but affordable. He decides to use the data cycle to explore rental options in his area.
>
> a. Identify the two variables that Ronaldo should collect data for in his investigation of potential apartments and then formulate a statistical question to investigate them.
>
> **Create a strategy**
>
> Consider the factors that Ronaldo is interested in:
> - A two-bedroom apartment
> - A spacious apartment
> - An affordable rental price
>
> Then, determine which factors would require the collection of data.
>
> **Apply the idea**
>
> Ronaldo should collect data that describes the size of the apartment, usually measured by square footage, and the rental price, usually given as a monthly rate. The apartments should all have two bedrooms, since that is the type (category) of apartment he is interested in.
>
> One possible question is, "What is the price range of two-bedroom apartments with 1000–1200 square feet?"
>
> **Reflect and check**
>
> In this context, the size of the apartment (in square feet) is the independent variable, and the monthly rental price (in dollars) is the dependent variable.
>
> Other possible questions are:
> - How does the monthly rental price of a two-bedroom apartment change with the size of the apartment?
> - What size apartments are typically $1500–$1700 per month?
> - How do the prices and sizes of two-bedroom apartments compare to those of two-bedroom houses?

Purpose

Check if students can identify the relevant variables and formulate a statistical question for a given scenario.

Expected mistakes

Students might struggle to identify the two variables of interest, especially if they are unsure of how to quantify "spacious" and "affordable." Begin by asking students what Ronaldo wants in an apartment. If they say he wants a two-bedroom apartment, ask if this is a characteristic that can take on different values or if this is a category. If they correctly identify that he wants something spacious and affordable, ask students how we might measure spaciousness and affordability. This discussion should help them realize that the apartment size and rental price are the two variables.

Students: Page 566

b Collect data that could be used to answer the statistical question you formulated.

Create a strategy

Previously, we determined that data should be collected on the size of the apartment, usually measured by square footage, and the rental price, usually given as a monthly rate.

This information can be acquired online. Typically, rental properties in an area are advertised on websites such as Zillow.com or Apartments.com.

Apply the idea

This is an example data set of current rental properties around Norfolk, VA:

Square footage	1000	1400	755	1172	1200	1050	1166	1195	900	900
Rental price	2049	2179	1324	1881	1775	1500	1870	2075	1425	1700

Square footage	822	1383	1183	1113	850	783	884	750	1000	1224
Rental price	1909	2150	1500	1969	1600	1350	1500	1400	1299	1695

Square footage	980	866	802	904	1250	850	750	1025	1117	1027
Rental price	1200	1495	1260	1750	1700	1350	1600	1550	2300	1800

Reflect and check

Remember that the sample should be collected randomly, and there should be a decent amount of two-bedroom apartments in the sample to be representative of the population.

Purpose

Ensure that students are capable of collecting necessary data.

Reflecting with students

Ask students to explain which variable is the independent variable and which is the dependent variable. They should explain that the square footage affects the rental price; the rental price does not affect an apartment's size. Hence, the apartment size is the independent variable.

Students: Pages 566–568

c Determine whether a linear or quadratic function would represent the relationship best. Calculate the equation of the curve of best fit.

Create a strategy

First, we can use technology to create a scatterplot and examine the shape of the data. After determining which function models the data best, we can find the equation of the curve of best fit with technology.

To find the equation using technology, we can follow these steps:

1. Enter the x-values and y-values in two separate columns.
2. Highlight the data and select Two Variable Regression Analysis. This will generate the scatterplot.
3. Under the Regression Model drop down menu, choose Linear or Polynomial, depending on the shape of the data.

Apply the idea

Enter the data into the GeoGebra statistics calculator, and perform the Two Variable Regression Analysis.

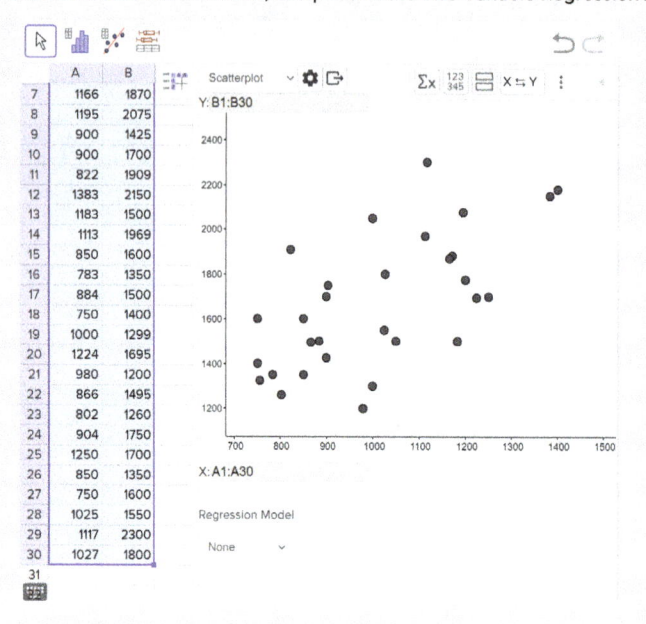

The relationship between the variables is not strong, but the y-values tend to increase as the x-values increase. This indicates there is a moderate, linear relationship between the variables.

Now, we can find the equation of the line of best fit by choosing Linear under the Regression Model drop down menu.

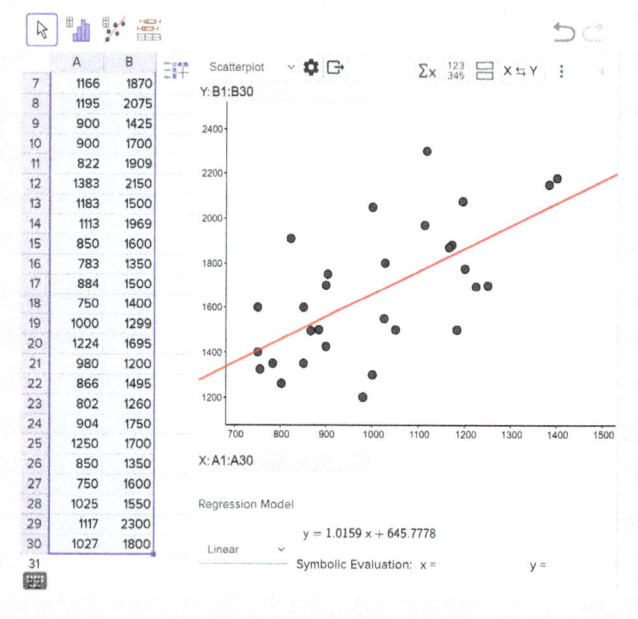

The equation of the line of best fit is $y = 1.0159x + 645.7778$.

Reflect and check

When analyzing the quadratic curve of best fit, we can see that the curve does not model the data better than the linear model. In fact, the section of the parabola shown does not have much curve to it. This means that prediction made with either model would be similar.

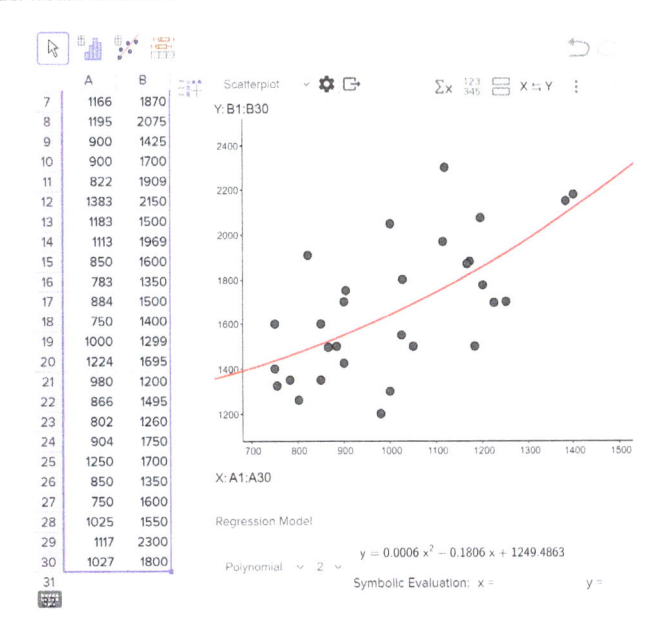

Purpose

Check if students can create scatterplots, draw the line or curve of best fit, and calculate the equation of the line or curve of best fit using technology. Afterward, they should identify which function best fits the data.

Reflecting with students

If students collected their own data individually or in groups, encourage them to share their results with the class and compare the models they found. Highlight that, because the data is different, each person or group will have different models.

Students: Page 568

d Ideally, Ronaldo would like an apartment that is 1100 ft². Predict the monthly rental price of an apartment of this size.

Create a strategy

In the previous part, we found the equation of the line of best fit to be $y = 1.01586x + 645.7778$, where x represents the size of an apartment in square feet and y represents the monthly rental price in dollars. We can substitute $x = 1100$ into the equation to find the monthly rental price.

Apply the idea

$y = 1.0159x + 645.7778$ Line of best fit

$= 1.0159 (1100) + 645.7778$ Substitute $x = 1100$

$= 1763.2678$ Evaluate

An 1100 ft² apartment will cost about $1763 per month.

Reflect and check

This prediction was made with interpolation because it falls within the range of the known data values. However, the prediction is not very strong because the points are not tightly clustered around the line.

Purpose
Check if students can make predictions using the equation of the line.

Reflecting with students
Ask students to discuss whether they think this result is reasonable or if they think it is unrealistic. If students are unaware of rental prices in their area, discuss whether they think the prediction is reliable based on the strength of the relationship shown in the scatterplot.

Students: Page 569

> e Ronaldo's budget is $1650. Predict the size of the apartment he can afford.
>
> **Create a strategy**
> The monthly rental price is the dependent variable (y), and the size of the apartment is the independent variable (x). We must substitute $y = 1650$ into the equation of the line of best fit, and solve for the x-value.
>
> **Apply the idea**
>
> | | |
> |---|---|
> | $y = 1.0159x + 645.7778$ | Line of best fit |
> | $1650 = 1.0159x + 645.7778$ | Substitute $y = 1650$ |
> | $1004.2222 = 1.0159x$ | Subtract 645.7778 from both sides |
> | $988.505 = x$ | Divide both sides by 1.0159 |
>
> $1650 a month can get Ronaldo an apartment with about 988.5 square feet of space.

Purpose
Check if students can make predictions using the equation of the line.

Expected mistakes
Students might try to estimate the apartment size from the scatterplot, leading to a less accurate result. Point out that the equation is linear, and they have skills they can use to solve linear equations in one variable.

Students: Page 569

> f Draw a conclusion by answering the statistical question from part (b) and summarize the results of the investigation.
>
> **Create a strategy**
> The statistical question from part (b) was, "What is the price range of two-bedroom apartments with 1000–1200 square feet?"
>
> **Apply the idea**
> If Ronaldo wants a two-bedroom apartment that is 1100 ft², he should expect to pay about $1763 per month. This is outside of his budget, so he should look for apartments that are around 988 ft² to stay within his desired price range.
>
> However, according to the raw data, the montly rental price of an apartment with 1000–1200 square feet ranges from $1300–$2300. This shows that it is possible to find an 1100 ft² apartment within the $1650 price range.
>
> There are most likely other factors, such as the neighborhood or distance from downtown Norfolk, that affect the price of the property that Ronaldo should take into consideration when making his final decision.
>
> **Reflect and check**
> These results could help Ronaldo make a decision about the apartment he would like to rent, or it could lead him to ask another question. For example, Ronaldo might ask the question, "How does the size of an apartment impact the monthly rental price of a one-bedroom or two-bedroom apartment?" He could use the slope of the line of best fit to conclude that for each 1 square foot increase in apartment size he can expect to pay around $1.02 more per month.
>
> This might lead Ronolado to explore one-bedroom apartments instead. He could repeat the data cycle, collecting data on one-bedroom apartment sizes and prices. Then, he can plot the data on the same scatterplot in part (d), but use a different color for the points representing one-bedroom apartments.

Purpose

Verify that students can drawn conclusions and answer statistical questions from investigation results.

Making predictions with technology
Student with disabilities support

use with Example 2

For the prediction in part (e), students may benefit from instruction on how to identify the x-value when given a y-value using technology, rather than estimating from the graph. Show students that, rather than tracing a horizontal line from the y-axis to the line, they can graph the horizontal line $y = 1650$. This highlights the point on the line they are looking for.

Next, they can use technology to find the x-value of the point where their horizontal line intersects their linear regression model. It's the same process as they would use when estimating, but this method is more accurate.

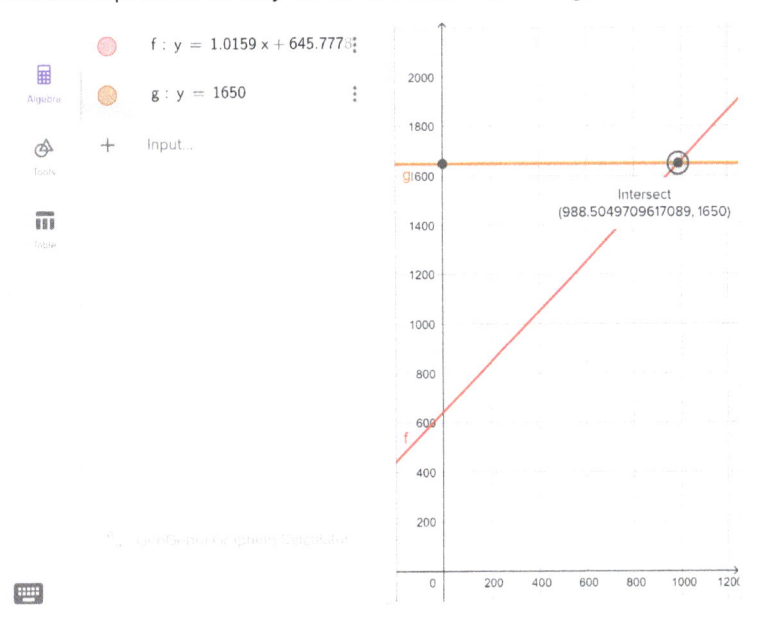

Students: Page 569

> ### Idea summary
> We can use technology to analyze bivariate data by creating and comparing regression models. To choose the model with the best fit, we analyze the visual fit on the scatterplot and the context of the problem. If the points are clustered more closely, the model is the better fit.

Practice

Students: Pages 570–575

What do you remember?

1 For each of the following scatterplots:
   i State the type of function that best models the data.
   ii State whether the slope of the line (for a linear model) or coefficient of x^2 (for a quadratic model) is positive or negative.

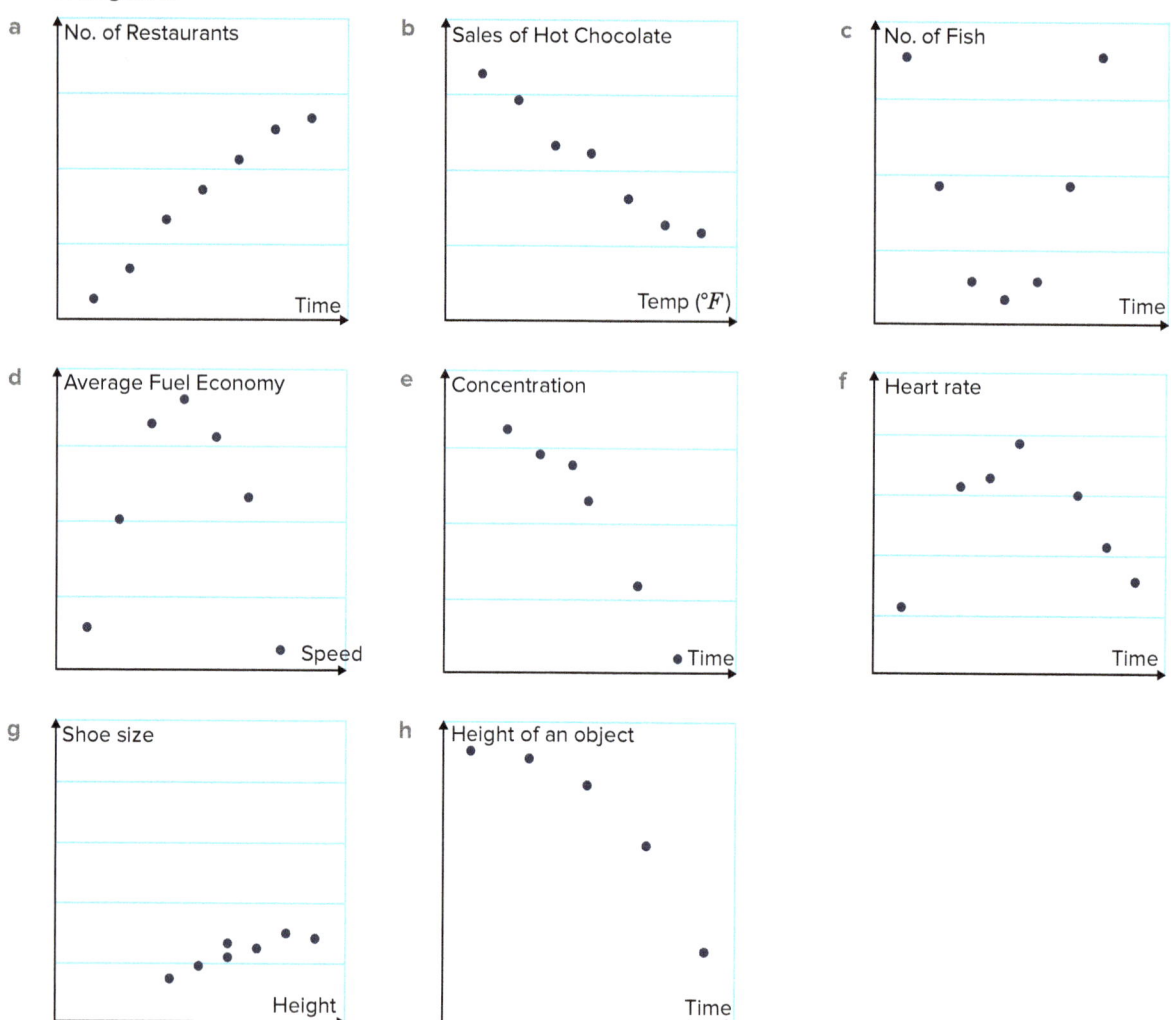

a No. of Restaurants vs Time

b Sales of Hot Chocolate vs Temp (°F)

c No. of Fish vs Time

d Average Fuel Economy vs Speed

e Concentration vs Time

f Heart rate vs Time

g Shoe size vs Height

h Height of an object vs Time

2 Which one of the following types of functions is an appropriate model for the data shown on each graph?
- Linear, $f(x) = mx + b$
- Quadratic, $f(x) = ax^2 + bx + c$, $a > 0$
- Quadratic, $f(x) = ax^2 + bx + c$, $a < 0$

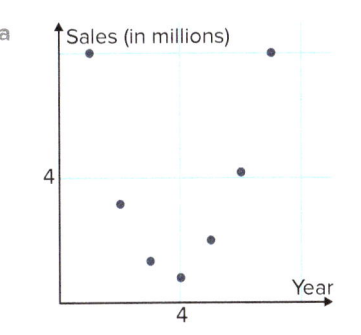

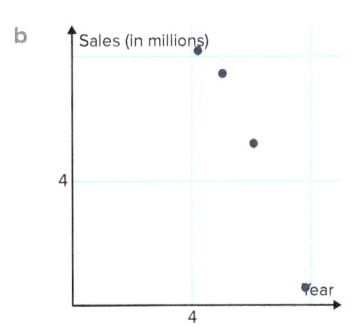

a Sales (in millions) vs Year

b Sales (in millions) vs Year

3 Hermione has just purchased a new car and wants to know how the speed at which she drives changes the gas consumption of her car. With the help of a friend, she records the gas consumption at several different speeds.

Speed, x km/hr	Fuel consumption, y L/100 km
30	13
40	7
50	5
60	6
70	14
80	23

QuadReg
$y = Ax^2 + Bx + C$
$A = 0.02053571$
$B = -2.053214$
$C = 56.15$

a Plot the data points from the table.
b Using the data from your plotted graph, what type of model would be most appropriate?
c A graphing utility has fitted the data from the table to a quadratic model. The calculator's output is shown. Use these results to build a quadratic model from the data, giving each of the constants correct to two decimal places.

Let's practice

4 Nine data points have been plotted with a quadratic curve of best fit:

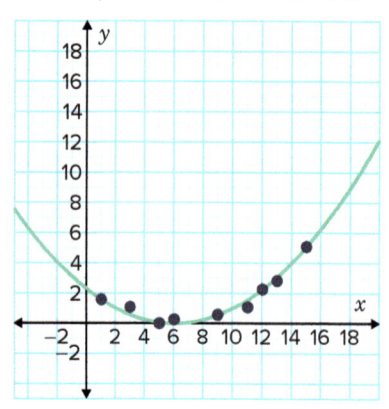

    a Predict the y-value of a point with an x-value of 2.
    b Determine whether the following points would be predicted by the quadratic curve of best fit:
        i (9, 3)   **ii** (3, 4)   **iii** (12, 0)   **iv** (14, 4)

5 Answer the following questions using the scatterplot.

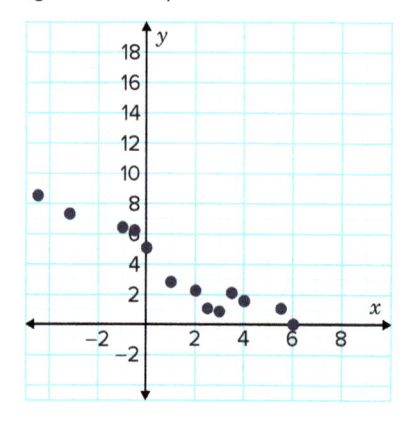

    a Using only the scatterplot, decide whether a linear of quadratic regression model would be a better fit. Justify your answer.
    b Predict the y-value of a point with an x-value of –2. Justify your answer.

6 Nine data points have been plotted with a quadratic curve of best fit:

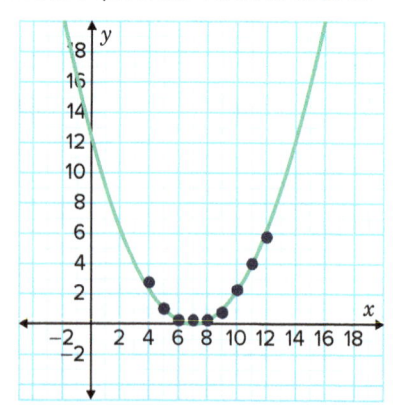

    a Predict the y-value of a point with an x-value of 13.
    b Determine whether the following points would be predicted by the quadratic curve of best fit:
        i (3, 4)   **ii** (14, 10)   **iii** (2, 9)   **iv** (15, 15)

7 A scatterplot has been created from a set of data:

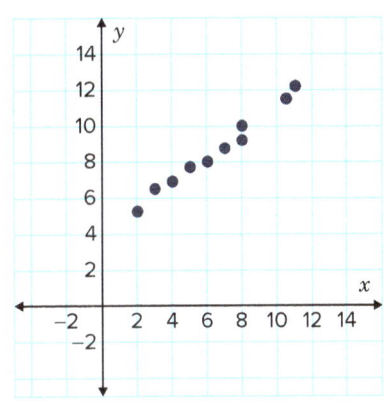

    a How would you describe the strength and form of the relationship? Justify your answer.

    b Determine which of the following is the best estimate of y-intercept for the regression model:

        A 0   B 4   C 6   D −4

8 The distance d in kilometers that Emma runs was measured at different times t minutes after she started. The following quadratic curve of best fit was graphed:

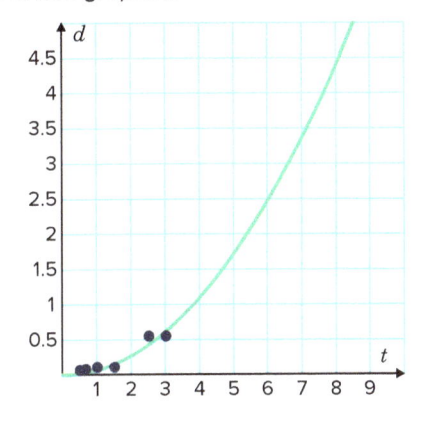

    a Identify the independent and dependent variables.

    b Formulate a question that could be answered by the scatterplot.

    c Using the curve of best fit, find the predicted distance Emma runs after:

        i 2 minutes   **ii** 8 minutes

    d Which of the predictions in part (c) is less reliable? Explain your answer."

9 A computer program compares and orders the scores of all students who sit an exam. The time taken (T, in milliseconds) for the program to completely order all students is shown in the table for different numbers of students, n:

Number of students (n)	2	4	6	8	10	12	14	16	18	20
Time (T)	10	60	150	280	450	660	910	1200	1530	1900

Write an equation to model the data.

10 The table shows data collected to answer the question, "What is the relationship between a location's altitude and its average annual temperature?" The data represents ten randomly selected locations on Earth.

Altitude (yd)	2600	2400	1000	200	600	1600	2200	2800	1200
Temperature °F	−9	−2	28	50	37	21	7	−13	21

a Describe a method that may have been used to collect the data.
b What type of function best models the relationship between the altitude of a location and its average annual temperature?
c Write and graph a function to model the relationship.
d Complete the table by using the model to approximate the average annual temperature of locations at the given altitudes.

Altitude (x)	Average Annual Temperature (y)
500	
1000	
2000	

e Dylan starts a mountain hike at an altitude of 940 yd and plans to reach the summit at an elevation of 1850 yd. According to the model, by how much will the temperature decrease?

11 A sample of 20 cars were weighed and their average fuel consumption (measured in gallons per mile) measured. The data is shown in the table.

a Formulate a question that can be answered by the data.
b What type of function best models the relationship between the weight of a car and its average fuel consumption?
c Write and graph a function to model the relationship.
d Identify the slope and y-intercept of the function and explain what they mean in terms of the context.
e Complete the table by using the model to approximate the average fuel consumption of cars with the given weights.

Weight (x)	Average Fuel Consumption (y)
3200	
3100	
1500	

f Bob lives in the city, so he wants to purchase a car that is relatively fuel efficient. Two cars that he is considering weigh 1600 lb and 2900 lb respectively. According to the model, which car should he choose if fuel consumption is the only consideration?

Weight (lb)	Fuel consumption
3400	120
3100	125
3000	110
2500	112
2900	111
2400	93
2000	105
2600	103
3300	128
3200	110
2700	108
2600	110
3900	138
2200	94
3700	131
3600	129
2900	117
2700	115
2300	103
3000	124

12 A social researcher claims that the longer people stay in their job, the less satisfaction they gain from their work. She asked a sample of people how many years they had been employed in their current job and to rate their level of satisfaction out of 10. The results are presented in the table.

Number of years employed	Satisfaction Rating
2	9
3	5
5	4
6	2
8	5
10	7
12	8
13	7
15	9

a Was the data collected through measurement, observation, a survey or an experiment?

b Create a scatterplot for the data collected.

c Does the scatterplot support the social worker's claims?

d Write the equation that would be best suited to model the relationship between the number of years employed and satisfaction with the job.

e The social researcher herself has been employed in her current job for 4 years and rates her satisfaction with her work a 10 out of 10.
Find the difference between the satisfaction rating approximated by the model and her actual rating.

Let's extend our thinking

13 Every year, a popular movie trailer is released and people anticipated the day it will arrive in theaters. It is common for people to try to see the movie soon after it comes out. Typically, the movie's highest daily box offices sales is the day the movie hits theaters.

a Formulate a question related to this context which could be investigated using a scatterplot.

b Describe the variables that could be used to answer the question from part (a).

c Collect data on a recent, popular movie that could be used to answer the statistical question from part (a).

d Use technology to create a scatterplot and describe the form and strength of the relationship.

e Use technology to find an appropriate equation to model the data set.

f Draw a conclusion about the data by answering the question formulated in part (a).

g Describe the domain over which the curve of best fit found in part (e) could be used to make reasonable predictions. Explain your answer.

14 People use social media as a way to connect with friends, a way to discover new places to travel, or as a platform for their business, to name a few. In some cases, it is important to track things such as the number of followers you have or the amount of engagement your content receives.

Go through the whole data cycle at least once to investigate whether a relationship exists between the amount of time spent on social media and the number of followers someone has.

Answers

9.05 Analyze bivariate data

What do you remember?

1. a i Linear   ii Positive
   b i Linear   ii Negative
   c i Quadratic   ii Positive
   d i Quadratic   ii Negative
   e i Linear   ii Negative
   f i Quadratic   ii Negative
   g i Linear   ii Positive
   h i Quadratic   ii Negative

2. a Quadratic, $f(x) = ax^2 + bx + c, a > 0$
   b Linear, $f(x) = mx + b$

3. a 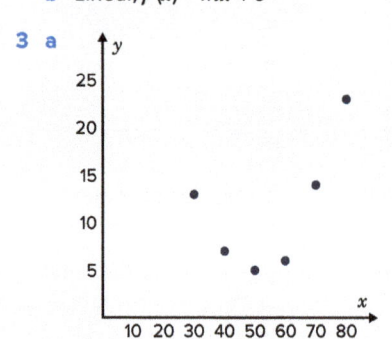

   (scatter plot with points from x = 10 to 80, y values ranging up to about 23)

   b Quadratic
   c $y = 0.02x^2 - 2.05x + 56.15$

Let's practice

4. a 1
   b i No   ii No   iii No   iv Yes

5. a A linear model would be a better fit. There is no discernible curve in the trend of the data to suggest a quadratic relationship.
   b 6

   If we follow the trend of the graph and visualize a line of best fit, it would approximately go through the point (−2, 6).

6. a 9
   b i Yes   ii No   iii No   iv No

7. a The points are very tightly clustered along a linear pattern. This implies a strong, linear correlation.
   b B

8. a The independent variable is the time in minutes, and the dependent variable is the distance in kilometers.
   b Many possible questions, for example, "How does the distance Emma runs change with the time she runs?"
   c i 0.25 km   ii 4.375 km

   d The extrapolation at $t = 8$ minutes is less reliable since the model predicts that Emma continues to increase her speed for the entire duration of her run.

9. $y = 5x^2 - 5x$

10. a One possible method is by acquiring data on the altitude and average annual temperatures of each location from a reliable, online source.
    b Linear function
    c $y = -0.022747x + 52.4569$ 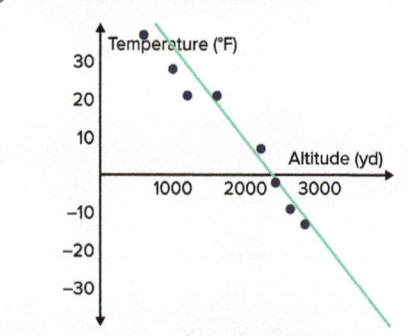

    (graph of Temperature (°F) vs Altitude (yd) with linear fit)

    d

Altitude (x)	Average Annual Temperature (y)
500	41.08
1000	29.71
2000	6.96

    e 20.7°F

11. a Many possible questions, for example, "How does a car's fuel consumption change with its weight?"
    b Linear function
    c $y = 0.020677x + 54.3359$ 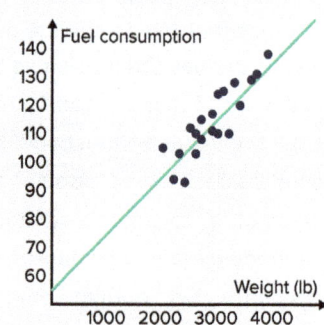

    (graph of Fuel consumption vs Weight (lb) with linear fit)

    d The slope is 0.020677 and means the fuel consumption increases by 0.020677 gallons per mile for each 1 pound increase in the weight of the car.

    The y-intercept: is 54.3359 and means that a 0 pound car would have a fuel consumption of 54.3359 gallons per mile. This doesn't really make sense because it is not possible to have a 0 pound car, but it does tell us that no car will have a fuel consumption this low or lower than this.

e

Weight (x)	Average Fuel Consumption (y)
3200	120.5
3100	118.43
1500	85.35

f The 1600 lb car

12 a Survey

b

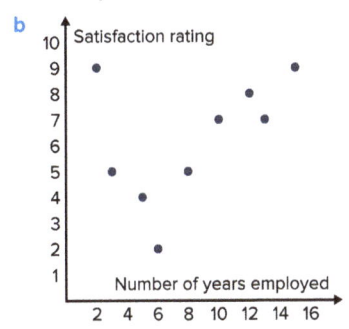

Satisfaction rating scatter plot with Number of years employed on x-axis (2-16) and Satisfaction rating on y-axis (1-10).

c No

d $y = 0.5x^2 - 6x + 20$

e 6

Let's extend our thinking

13 a Many possible questions, for example, "What is the relationship between the number of weekend days (Friday, Saturday, and Sunday) since the movie was released and the day's box office sales?"

b Answers will vary based on question formulated in part (a). Using the example, "What is the relationship between the number of weekend days since the movie was released and the day's box office sales?":

The independent variable is the number of weekend days since the movie was released. The weekend days are Friday Saturday, and Sunday. If the movie was released on a Saturday, for example, that would be day 0, Sunday would be day 1, and the next Friday would be day 3.

The dependent variable is the box office sales corresponding to each weekend day.

c An example data set collected on the Barbie movie during the first 5 weekends it was in theaters is shown:

Weekend day	x	Box office sales	y
Friday	0	70 503 178	70.5
Saturday	1	47 812 356	47.8
Sunday	2	43 706 510	43.7
Friday	3	29 032 661	29.0
Saturday	4	34 586 429	34.6
Sunday	5	29 392 512	29.4
Friday	6	16 543 731	16.5
Saturday	7	19 476 666	19.5
Sunday	8	16 988 250	17.0
Friday	9	10 016 672	10.0
Saturday	10	13 178 714	13.2

Weekend day	x	Box office sales	y
Sunday	11	10 637 908	10.6
Friday	12	6 358 617	6.4
Saturday	13	8 378 293	8.4
Sunday	14	6 293 418	6.3

d Scatter plot of Box office sales (in millions) vs Weekend days since release.

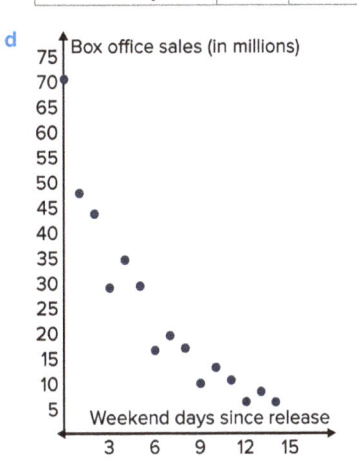

There is a strong, quadratic relationship between the weekend days since the movie's release and the box office sales.

e $y = 0.368x^2 - 8.901x + 61.586$ where x is the number of weekend days since the movie's release and y is the box office sales in millions of dollars.

f Answers will vary based on question formulated in part (a). Using the example, "What is the relationship between the number of weekend days since the movie was released and the day's box office sales?":

When the Barbie movie was initially released, it had a very high number of box office sales. Each weekend day following opening day, the box office sales decreased at a decreasing rate.

g Analyzing the graph of the quadratic regression model, it can only be used to make reasonable predictions over the domain of known data values. In this case, the domain is the first 5 weekends since the movie was released. After this time, the curve of best fit would curve upwards, which would not make sense in context. Typically, most people would have seen the movie within the first month, so the sales will continue to decrease after this domain.

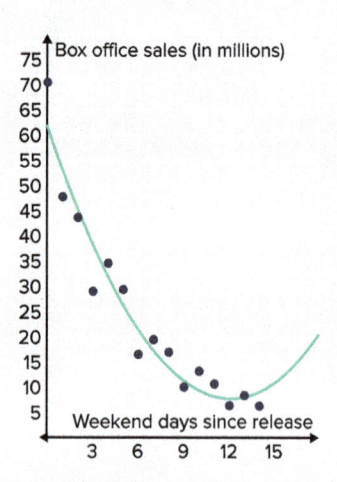

[Graph: Box office sales (in millions) vs Weekend days since release, showing a curve decreasing from ~70 at day 0 to a minimum around day 12, then slightly increasing]

14 1. **Formulate questions**

   Possible questions:
   - What is the relationship between the amount of time spent on social media and the number of followers someone has?
   - How does the number of followers someone has change with the time they spend on social media daily?
   - If I want to reach 2000 followers, how much time should I spend on the social media platform daily?

2. **Collect data using the questions above.**

   The time spend on social media is generally tracked on a person's phone, so we can collect data through a survey. The table shows an example sample of 30 students.

Hours	3.2	4	0.8	2	1.5	1.5	3.8	2.2
Followers	2317	2698	905	1299	997	1205	2498	1302

Hours	0.6	3	2.7	4	1.2	2.8	2.4	0.5
Followers	502	1754	1879	1956	1232	1984	1867	1022

Hours	2.5	1	1.75	2.5	2.1	1.2	3.6	1.8
Followers	1503	798	1088	1722	1154	935	2250	1023

3. **Create a data display using a scatterplot.**

   This scatterplot represents the sample data from the previous part. Since it shows an approximate linear relationship, the line of best fit has been drawn. The equation of the line of best fit is $y = 513.065x + 369.879$.

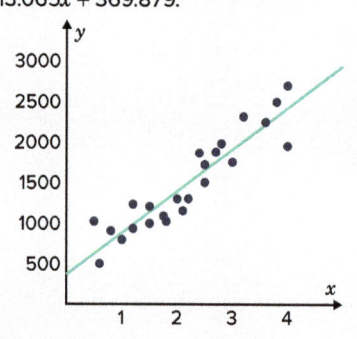

   [Scatterplot showing positive linear relationship between x (1 to 4) and y (500 to 3000) with line of best fit]

4. **Analyze and explain the results.**

   From the scatterplot, we can observe that there is a strong, positive linear relationship between the average amount of time someone spends on social media daily and the number of followers they have. The relationship shows that as the time spent on social media increases, the number of their followers also tends to increase.

   More specifically, for each additional hour spend on social media, the number of followers is expected to increase by about 513 people. According to the model, a person who spends an average of about 3.2 hours on social media daily has about 2000 followers. Because the correlation is strong, these conclusions are fairly reliable.

   This could lead us to formulate a new question like "How many days of consistent social media use does it take to reach 10 000 followers?" or "What other factors have an impact on the number of followers someone has?"

Topic 9 Assessment: Data Analysis

1. A science class is conducting a study on the relationship between physical activity and academic performance among students. They write the question "Do students who engage in regular physical activity have higher science test scores than those who do not?"

   a. Is this a statistical question?

   b. Which of the following variables are needed to answer the question?
   - Frequency of physical activity
   - Science test scores
   - Grade level
   - Study habits

   c. Identify the independent and dependent variable.

   d. Which of the following units could be used to measure academic performance?
   - Test scores as percentages
   - Letter grades
   - GPA (Grade Point Average)
   - Standardized test percentiles

2. For each scenario, match it with the type of sampling method used:

   i. Simple random sampling   ii. Systematic sampling
   iii. Clustered sampling   iv. Stratified sampling

   a. A market researcher randomly selects 10 representative cities across the country and then surveys every household within the chosen cities.

   b. A health official generates a list of all the patients registered at a clinic and uses a computer program to randomly select 200 of them for a study.

   c. To understand company morale, a manager divides the organization into departments and randomly selects employees from each department.

   d. A scientist numbers every fifth plant in a row in a large field to collect samples for genetic testing.

3. A gym manager wants to estimate the number of members who would attend yoga classes if they were added to the schedule.

   a. Which method would be appropriate to collect data? Explain your answer.

   A Experiment   B Survey/poll   C Observation   D Acquire data

   b. Is each sample representative of the population or biased?
   i. All members who participate in the morning spin class.
   ii. Every 10th member that enters the gym over two days.
   iii. Twelve members near the water refill station.

4. For each question, state if the question is leading or not. If it is leading, rewrite it so that it is not biased.

   a. A new study said that the amount people compost was related to their score on aptitude tests. How much do you compost each month?

   b. Most people with nice skin use at least one product with hylauronic acid in it, what is your favorite skin product?

   c. How are height and shoe size related?

   d. How weak is the relationship between age and income?

   e. How tall are you? What is your take-home annual income?

5 The table shows the scores of 10 students for their mathematics and geography tests:

Mathematics	89	88	85	86	93	92	83	89	77	90
Geography	85	92	77	88	87	93	85	92	82	91

a Create a scatterplot for the set of data.

b Determine whether the data show a positive or a negative linear relationship and interpret what this means within the context.

6 In recent years, beekeepers and scientists have become concerned over a phenomenon known as colony collapse disorder (CCD), where the majority of worker bees in a hive disappear, leaving behind the queen and immature bees. The percentage of beehive losses that can be attributed to CCD each year, since 2006, is shown in the table:

Year	Y	Hives lost to CCD, (H)%
2006	0	22
2007	1	17
2008	2	27
2009	3	30
2010	4	32
2011	5	34

a Identify the independent and dependent variables.

b Construct a scatterplot and find an approximate line of best fit for this data. State the equation of the approximate line of best fit.

c Interpret the meaning of the y-intercept.

d Describe the relationship between the number of years passed and the number of hives lost to CCD.

e Interpret the slope of the line.

7 Determine whether the most appropriate model would be linear, quadratic, or neither.

a

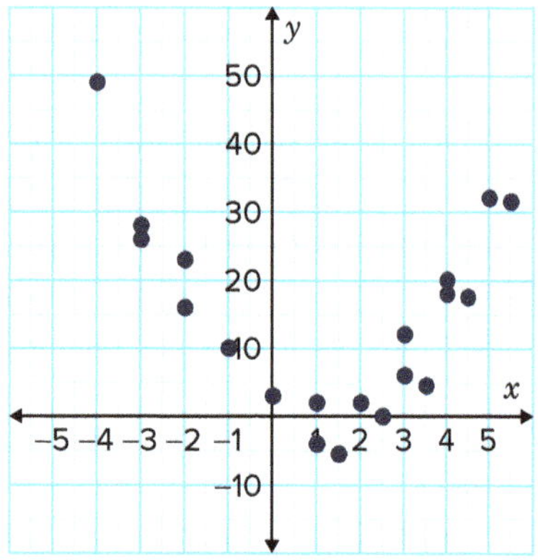

b

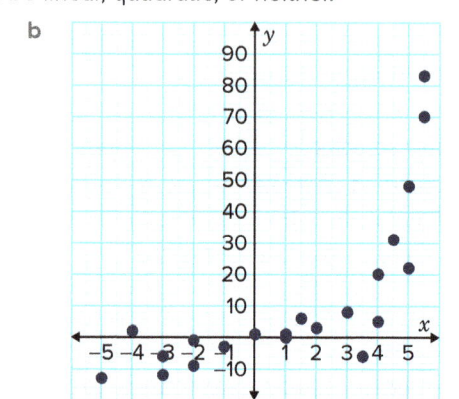

c

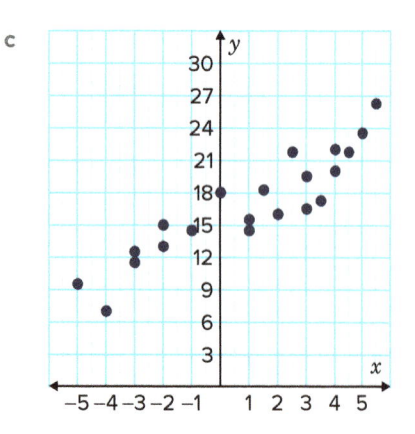

d

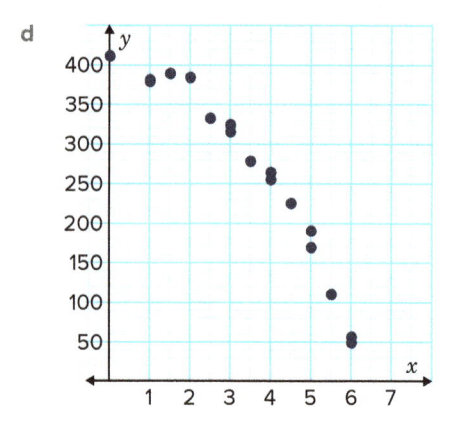

8 Maria operates a small bakery and is experimenting with the pricing of her signature chocolate cake. She conducted a study to determine the relationship between the price of the cake and the monthly profit. The table below shows the data she collected.

Price per cake ($)	10	10.5	11	11.5	12	12.5	13
Profit per month ($)	2000	2150	2250	2300	2260	2100	1950

  a Analyze whether the data indicates a quadratic relationship. Justify your reasoning.
  b Graph the data and find a quadratic equation with whole number coefficients to model it.
  c Calculate the price that the model suggests would maximize the profit.
  d Explain the meaning of the y-intercept.
  e Interpret the x-intercept.

9 For each data set:
  i Determine whether the most appropriate model would be linear, quadratic, or neither.
  ii If a linear or quadratic model is appropriate, find a function that models the data.

  a
x	−4	−3	−2	−1	0	1	2	3	4
y	40	27	12	3	0	3	11	28	38

  b
x	−4	−3	−2	−1	0	1	2	3	4
y	−11	−9	−7	−3	0	2	6	8	13

  c
x	−4	−3	−2	−1	0	1	2	3	4
y	6	8	−1	−4	1	−1	−3	5	0

  d
x	−4	−3	−2	−1	0	1	2	3	4
y	11	16	19	20	18	16	10	6	−13

10 Using the quadratic curve of best fit, which equation most closely represents the set of data?

$$\{(-9, 102.1), (-8, 82.4), (-4, 16.8), (2, -15.2), (4, 19.2), (6, 60.4), (8, 128.8)\}$$

  A $y = 2.2x^2 - 4.5x + 2$
  B $y = 2.2x^2 - 4.9x - 5.6$
  C $y = 2x^2 + 2.5x - 18$
  D $y = x^2 - 5x + 3.2$

11 The table shows a jogger's distance from home, y (in miles), after x minutes.
  a Determine whether a linear or quadratic function would model this situation more accurately.
  b Create a model and use it to predict the jogger's distance from home after 33 minutes.
  c Could your model be used to predict the jogger's distance from home after 90 minutes? Explain your reasoning.
  d Describe the strengths or weaknesses of the model.

Time (min), x	Distance (mi), y
5	0.3
10	0.7
15	1.1
20	1.4
25	1.6
30	1.9
35	2.3
40	2.6
45	2.8
50	3.2
55	3.5
60	3.9
65	4.1
70	4.4
75	5.0

12 Using the equation of the line of best fit, which number is the best prediction of the output when the input is 8?

$$\{(-4, 12), (1, 25), (6, 54), (7, 60), (10, 85), (12, 105)\}$$

A 72   B 77   C 81   D 86

13 This table shows the number of months used and the approximate distances driven, in miles, for seven trucks in a logistics company.

Using the line of best fit for these data, which value is the best prediction of the distance driven, in miles, by a truck that has been used for 30 months?

A 60 200
B 62 100
C 65 300
D 67 500

Truck	Months Used	Distances Driven (miles)
Truck A	5	8200
Truck B	8	15 500
Truck C	10	20 300
Truck D	14	28 700
Truck E	18	36 400
Truck F	22	44 800
Truck G	24	49 600

14 The table shows the age, x, in years and the price, y, in dollars of various second-hand Mitsubishi Lancers.

Age (x)	2	4	3	1	5	1	3	7
Price (y)	12 000	11 100	11 700	17 750	9500	17 900	12 000	4800

a Calculate the regression model for this data set. Round all values to three decimal places.
b Interpret the slope and y-intercept of the line of fit.
c Predict the price of a second-hand Mitsubishi Lancer if its age is 8 years.
d Predict the price of a second-hand Mitsubishi Lancer if its age is 30 years. Evaluate the validity of using the equation of best fit for this prediction.

15 The height above the ground (in centimeters) of a radish sprout over time is shown on the scatterplot:

a Describe the meaning of the y-intercept in context.
b Does the interpretation in the previous part make sense in this context? Explain your answer.
c After how many days will the sprout be 16 cm tall?

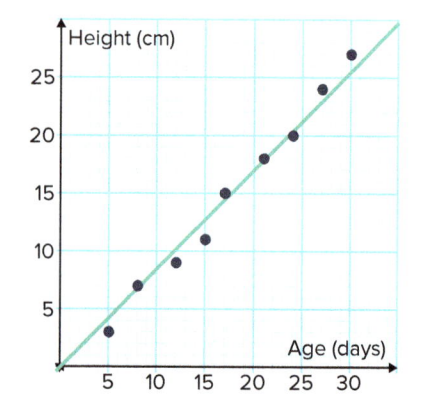

16 The table shows the average number of days of exercise and the average number of sick days of students over a six month period:

	Number of days of exercise	Number of sick days
Month 1	2	7
Month 2	7	5
Month 3	12	4
Month 4	15	3
Month 5	20	1
Month 6	24	0

a Create a scatterplot for the set of data.
b A statement is made: "As the number of days a student exercises increases, the number of days they are sick decreases." Is this claim correct? Explain your answer.

17 A survey was conducted to explore the relationship between the number of hours students spend studying per week and their self-reported satisfaction with their academic performance.

The data collected is presented in the table.

a   Create a scatterplot for the given data.

b   Examine the scatterplot. What trend do you observe between study hours and satisfaction rating?

c   Write an equation to model the relationship between study hours (H) and satisfaction rating (S). Round all values to four decimal places.

d   If a student studies for 15 hours per week, predict their satisfaction rating using the model from part (b). Round your answer to the nearest whole number.

Study hours per week	Satisfaction rating
1	0
3	0
4	0
6	1
7	1
8	1
9	2
10	2
12	2
13	3
14	3
14	4
15	4
15	5
16	5
17	6
18	7
18	8
19	9
20	10

18 The table represents the monthly sales figures of a new software product in its first year in the market.

a   Formulate a statistical question that could be answered with this data.

b   Construct a scatterplot for this data.

c   Describe the relationship between the month and the sales figures.

Month	Sales (in thousands)
Jan	15
Feb	18
Mar	20
Apr	21
May	22
Jun	22
Jul	23
Aug	22
Sep	23
Oct	24
Nov	24
Dec	26

Performance task

19 Jeremiah's parents have just purchased a newer truck that is much more heavy-duty that their previous one. The truck weighs a lot more and also has much lower fuel economy (miles per gallon) than their old truck.

Go through the whole data cycle at least once to explore vehicle weight and mileage (fuel economy).

Answers

Topic 9 Assessment: Data Analysis

1 **a** Yes
  b Frequency of physical activity and science test scores
  c Independent variable: Frequency of physical activity
     Dependent variable: Science test scores
  d Test scores as percentages or GPA
  A.ST.1a, A.ST.1b

2 **a** iii: Clustered sampling
  b i: Simple random sampling
  c iv: Stratified sampling
  d ii: Systematic sampling
  A.ST.1c

3 **a** B: Survey/poll would be an appropriate method as the question is looking for people's opinions/preferences. We can go through each option. An experiment is usually used to explore cause and effect or relationships, but there is only one variable here, so it is not appropriate. Observation would not work as they can't see if people like the class if it isn't on the schedule. We cannot acquire data because this is for this particular gym which may have customers that vary from other gyms.
  b i Biased
     ii Representative of the population
     iii Biased
  A.ST.1c

4 **a** Leading. How much do you compost each month?
  b Leading. What is your favorite skin product?
  c Not leading
  d Leading. Is there a relationship between age and income?
  e Not leading
  A.ST.1a

5 **a** [Scatter plot: Geography vs Mathematics]
  b Positive relationship. This means that when a student has a high score in one subject, they are likely to have a high score in the other subject as well.
  A.ST.1d, A.ST.1h, A.ST1i

6 **a** Independent variable: Years since 2006
     Dependent variable: Hives lost to colony collapse disorder
  b An approximate line of best fit: $y = 3x + 19$

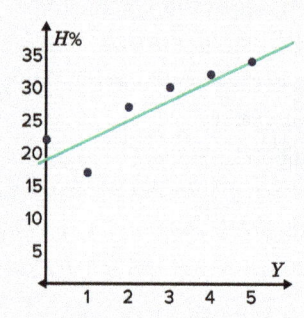

  [Scatter plot with line of best fit: H% vs Y]

  c The y-intercept indicates the number of hives lost to CCD in 2006.
  d The number of years passed has a strong positive relationship with the number of hives lost to CCD. As the number of years passed increases, the number of hives lost to CCD also increases.
  e For every year that passes, the percentage of hives lost to CCD increases by 3%.
  A.ST.1b, A.ST.1d, A.ST.1e, A.ST.1g, A.ST.1h

7 **a** Quadratic relationship   **b** Neither
  c Linear relationship   **d** Quadratic relationship
  A.ST.1d

8 **a** Yes, a quadratic model is suitable because a graph of the data shows a parabolic trend.
  b [Scatter plot with parabolic curve: Profit per month vs Price per cake]

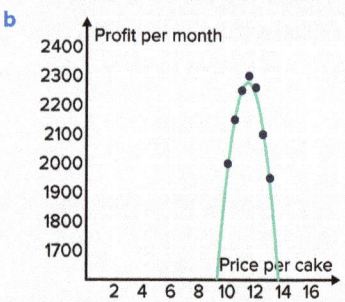

  $y = -142x^2 + 3247x - 16\,284$, where x is the price per cake and y is the profit per month.
  c The model's vertex indicates a maximum at approximately (11.43, 2277.64), suggesting that a price of $11.43 per cake would yield the highest profit.
  d At a price of $0, the bakery would incur a loss of $16\,284 per month, considering the costs of ingredients and operation.
  e The x-intercepts represent the prices at which the bakery breaks even. These occur at prices of $7.43 and $15.44, where the costs balance the revenue from cake sales.
  A.ST.1d, A.ST.1e, A.ST.1h, A.ST.1i

1226 Mathspace   Virginia SOL Algebra 1 Teacher Edition
mathspace.co

9 a i Quadratic ii $y = 2.4x^2 - 0.12x + 1.5$
   b i Linear   ii $y = 3x - 0.11$
   c i Neither   ii No equation
   d i Quadratic ii $y = -1.2x^2 - 2.5x + 19$
   A.ST.1d, A.ST.1e

10 C
   A.ST.1e

11 a Linear
   b $y = 0.064x + 0.047$
      2.2 miles
   c Assuming the jogger continues running away from home at the same rate, it could be used to predict their distance from home. It could not be used if the jogger stops, changes pace, or starts running toward home.
   d For times between 0–75, the model is strong because the data points are tightly clustered around the line. Times within this domain or shortly after that time can provide a good prediciton for the jogger's distance from home.
      A weakness is that the model cannot make predictions for longer run times. This is because other factors will influence the model, such as the jogger's stamina or whether they want to run in a different direction. It is not reasonable to assume the jogger will continue to run further from home at the same rate forever.
   A.ST.1d, A.ST.1e, A.ST.1f, A.ST.1h, A.ST.1i

12 A
   A.ST.1e, A.ST.1f

13 B
   A.ST.1e A.ST.1f

14 a $y = -1972.458x + 18\,504.237$
   b The slope is −1972.458. This means that the price of Mitsubishi Lancer decreases by $1972.46 per year.
      The y-intercept is 18 504.237. This means that price of a Mitsubishi Lancer when it is brand new is $18 504.24.
   c $2724.57
   d −$40 669.50
      It is not valid to use the model for this prediction because the results don't make sense contextually and there is no data on longer lifespans of the cars.
   A.ST.1d, A.ST.1e, A.ST.1f, A.ST.1g

15 a The y-intercept suggests that when the radish is 0 days old, it has no height above the ground.
   b Yes, it is plausible that a seed will not sprout above the ground on the same day it is planted.
   c 19 days
   A.ST.1f, A.ST.1g

16 a [scatterplot: Days of exercise vs Sick days, showing decreasing trend]
   b Yes, the statement is correct. The scatterplot shows that the data forms a decreasing, linear relationship, meaning that as a student exercises more, they get sick less.
   A.ST.1h

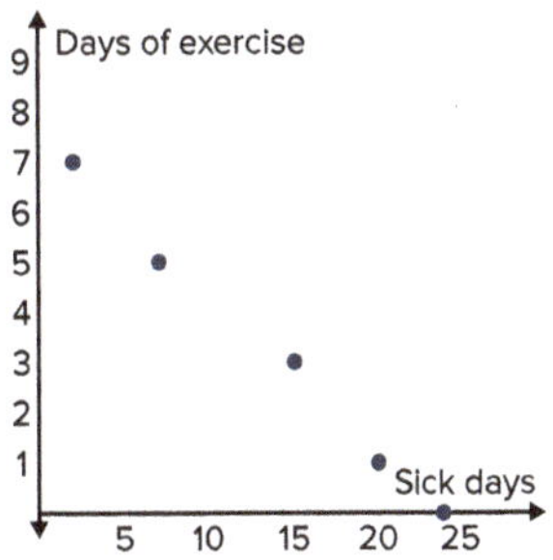

17 a [scatterplot: Satisfaction rating vs Study hours per week, showing increasing curved trend]
   b There seems to be a positive, quadratic correlation between study hours and satisfaction rating, suggesting that as study hours increase, satisfaction tends to increase at an increasing rate.
   c $S = 0.0356H^2 - 0.2689H + 0.6934$
   d 5
   A.ST.1d, A.ST.1e, A.ST.1h, A.ST.1i

18 a For example: Is there a relationship between time of year and sales for this new software product?
   b [scatterplot: Sales (in thousand) vs Month 1-12, showing increasing trend]
   c Moderate, positive, linear. As the year progresses, the sales figures tend to increase.
   A.ST.1a, A.ST.1d, A.ST.1h

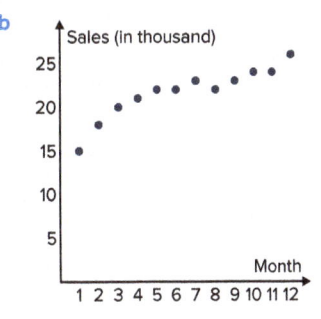

Performance task

1. **Formulate a statistical question to explore a relationship:**

   Many possible questions, for example, let look at: "Is there a relationship between vehicle weight and fuel economy?"

2. **Collect or acquire data:**

   Data on vehicle specifications including weight, fuel economy (miles per gallon), and type (trucks, SUVs, cars, hybrids, diesels) should be collected. This can be sourced from comprehensive databases like the U.S. Department of Energy's Fuel Economy website or the EPA's Automotive Trends Report.

   For reference:
   - https://www.fueleconomy.gov/
   - https://www.epa.gov/automotive-trends/download-automotive-trends-report

   This is a possible data set:

Vehicle Make and Model	Vehicle Type	Fuel type	Weight (lbs)	Fuel Economy (mpg)
VW Golf TDI	Compact car	Diesel	3020	26
Land Rover Range Rover Sport	SUV	Diesel	5119	17
Toyota Corolla	Compact car	Gas	2910	36
BMW 3 Series	Compact car	Gas	3583	30
Honda Accord	Mid-sized car	Gas	3131	33
Mercedes C-Class	Sedan	Gas	3417	28
Nissan Altima	Sedan	Gas	3212	35
Kia Soul	CUV	Gas	3289	30
Kia Sorento	SUV	Gas	3794	27
Subaru Outback	SUV	Gas	3634	23
Ford Explorer	SUV	Gas	4345	25
Honda Pilot	SUV	Gas	4036	25
Toyota Highlander	SUV	Gas	4145	27
Jeep Wrangler	SUV	Gas	4449	19
Mazda CX-5	SUV	Gas	3541	28
Nissan Titan	Truck	Gas	5588	15
Ford F-150	Truck	Gas	4729	22
Ford Ranger	Truck	Gas	4380	21
Toyota Prius	Compact car	Hybrid	3075	57
Hyundai Sonata	Mid-sized car	Hybrid	3325	47

3. **Organize and represent data:**

   We can represent this data into a scatterplot.

   From the scatterplot, we can see that the relationship could be linear with two outliers, or quadratic. We can create both models and see which fits better.

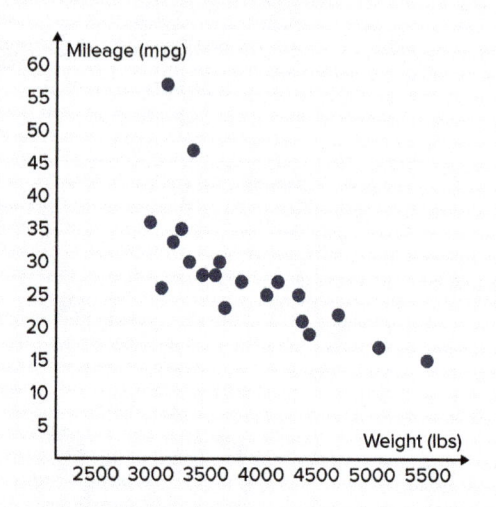

Linear model

Has equation $M = -0.0095W + 65.0939$, where M is mileage and W is weight. There are two clear outliers for the hybrids.

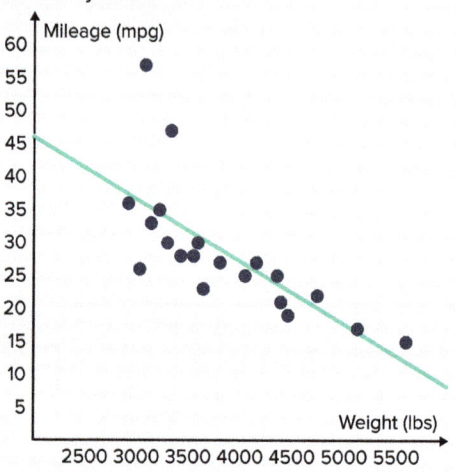

If we remove the hybrids:

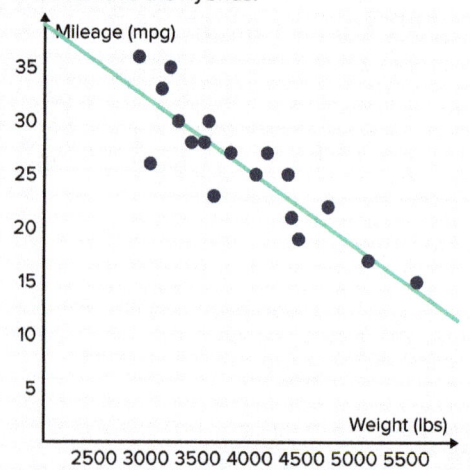

Quadratic model

Has equation $M = 0.000\,002W^2 - 0.03W + 103.8$, where M is mileage in mpg and W is weight in lbs. A more appropriate equation might be to use W in thousands

of pounds: $M = 2.36542W^2 - 29.0185W + 103.8183$.
There are still two clear outliers for the hybrids.

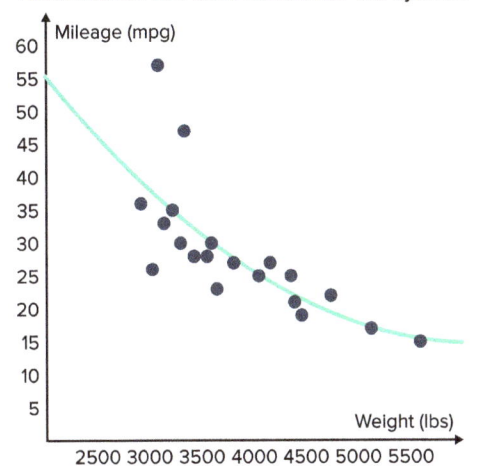

[Scatterplot: Mileage (mpg) vs Weight (lbs), showing data points with a fitted decreasing curve from about (2500, 55) down to (5500, 15).]

If we remove the hybrids:

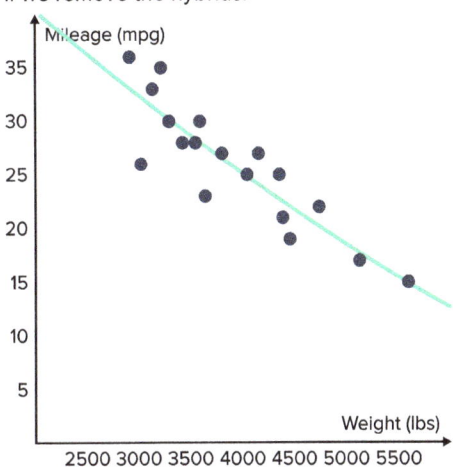

[Scatterplot: Mileage (mpg) vs Weight (lbs), showing data points with a fitted decreasing curve after hybrids removed.]

4. **Analyze data and communicate results:**

   The data shows a trend where heavier vehicles generally have lower fuel economy. The scatterplot shows the negative relationship between weight and fuel efficiency. A linear or quadratic model could be appropriate, but hybrids are outliers, so with more gas and diesel vehicles it might be clearer which model is more suitable.

5. **Another cycle:**

   As we can see from this table showing the average mileage for different types of vehicles, it may be worth further exploring the relationship within different categories.

	Average mileage (mpg)
Car	36.5
SUV	23.88
Truck	19.33

A.ST.1a, A.ST.1b, A.ST.1c, A.ST.1d, A.ST.1e, A.ST.1h, A.ST.1i

www.ingramcontent.com/pod-product-compliance
Lightning Source LLC
Jackson TN
JSHW050030070225
78283JS00010B/5